Re-imagining Ukrainian Canadians
History, Politics, and Identity

Ukrainian immigrants to Canada have often been portrayed in history as sturdy pioneer farmers cultivating the virgin land of the Canadian west. The essays in this collection challenge this stereotype by examining the varied experiences of Ukrainian Canadians in their day-to-day roles as writers, intellectuals, national organizers, working-class wage earners, and inhabitants of cities and towns. Throughout, the contributors remain dedicated to promoting the study of ethnic, hyphenated histories as major currents in mainstream Canadian history.

Topics explored include Ukrainian-Canadian radicalism, the consequences of the Cold War for Ukrainians both at home and abroad, the creation and maintenance of ethnic memories, and community discord embodied by pro-Nazis, Communists, and criminals. *Re-Imagining Ukrainian Canadians* uses new sources and non-traditional methods of analysis to answer unstudied and often controversial questions within the field. Collectively, the essays challenge the older, essentialist definition of what it means to be Ukrainian Canadian.

RHONDA L. HINTHER is the Western Canadian History curator at the Canadian Museum of Civilization.

JIM MOCHORUK is a professor in the Department of History at the University of North Dakota.

Re-imagining Ukrainian Canadians

History, Politics, and Identity

Edited by
Rhonda L. Hinther and Jim Mochoruk

UNIVERSITY OF TORONTO PRESS
Toronto   Buffalo   London

ISBN 978-1-4426-4134-1 (cloth)
ISBN 978-1-4426-1062-0 (paper)

Printed on acid-free and 100% post-consumer recycled paper
with vegetable-based inks

Library and Archives Canada Cataloguing in Publication

Re-imagining Ukrainian Canadians : history, politics, and identity /
edited by Rhonda L. Hinther and Jim Mochoruk.

(Canadian social history series)
Includes bibliographical references and index.
ISBN 978-1-4426-4134-1 (bound)
ISBN 978-1-4426-1062-0 (pbk.)

1. Ukrainian Canadians – History – 20th century.   2. Ukrainian Canadians
– Politics and government – 20th century.   3. Ukrainian Canadians – Social
conditions – 20th century.   I. Hinther, Rhonda L., 1974–   II. Mochoruk,
James David, 1957–   III. Series: Canadian social history series

FC106.U5R44 2011   971'.00491791   C2010-905890-9

University of Toronto Press acknowledges the financial assistance to its publishing program of the Canada Council for the Arts and the Ontario Arts
Council.

 Canada Council   Conseil des Arts   ONTARIO ARTS COUNCIL
for the Arts   du Canada   CONSEIL DES ARTS DE L'ONTARIO

University of Toronto Press acknowledges the financial support of the
Government of Canada through the Canada Book Fund for its publishing
activities.

This book has been published with the help of a grant from the Canadian Federation for the Humanities and Social Sciences, through the Aid to Scholarly
Publications Program, using funds provided by the Social Sciences and Humanities Research Council of Canada.

This volume is dedicated to one of the great unsung heroes of Ukrainian-Canadian scholarship: Myron Momryk. In a career spanning four decades, Myron has been a tireless advocate for multicultural history, an archivist and scholar of Ukrainian and Canadian history, and perhaps most important, a mentor to entire generations of scholars of ethnicity in Canada. Without his efforts in acquiring, accessing, and disseminating many new and important archival collections, many of the articles in this book might never have been written.

Contents

Acknowledgments / ix

Introduction / 3
Jim Mochoruk and Rhonda L. Hinther

Part One: New Approaches to Old Questions

1 Generation Gap: Canada's Postwar Ukrainian Left / 23
  Rhonda L. Hinther

2 Locating Identity: The Ukrainian Cultural Heritage Village as a
  Public History Text / 54
  Karen Gabert

3 'A Vaguely Divided Guilt': The Aboriginal Ukrainian / 85
  Lindy Ledohowski

Part Two: Leaders and Intellectuals

4 'Great Tasks and a Great Future': Paul Rudyk, Pioneer
  Ukrainian-Canadian Entrepreneur and Philanthropist / 107
  Peter Melnycky

5 The Populist Patriot: The Life and Literary Legacy of
  Illia Kiriak / 129
  Jars Balan

6 Sympathy for the Devil: The Attitude of Ukrainian War
  Veterans in Canada to Nazi Germany and the Jews,
  1933–1939 / 173
  Orest T. Martynowych

Part Three: Diplomacy and International Concerns

7 The 'Ethnic Question' Personified: Ukrainian Canadians and
   Canadian–Soviet Relations 1917–1991 / 223
   Jaroslav Petryshyn

8 Monitoring the 'Return to the Homeland' Campaign:
   Canadian Reports on Resettlement in the USSR from South
   America, 1955–1957 / 257
   Serge Cipko

9 Polishing the Soviet Image: The Canadian–Soviet Friendship
   Society and the 'Progressive Ethnic Groups,' 1949–1957 / 279
   Jennifer Anderson

Part Four: Internal Strife on the Left

10 'Pop & Co' versus Buck and the 'Lenin School Boys':
   Ukrainian Canadians and the Communist Party of Canada,
   1921–1931 / 331
   Jim Mochoruk

11 Fighting for the Soul of the Ukrainian Progressive Movement
   in Canada: The Lobayites and the Ukrainian Labour-Farmer
   Temple Association / 376
   Andrij Makuch

Part Five: Everyday People

12 'Of course it was a Communist Hall': A Spatial, Social,
   and Political History of the Ukrainian Labour Temples in
   Ottawa, 1912–1965 / 403
   S. Holyck Hunchuck

13 'I'll Fix You!': Domestic Violence and Murder in a
   Ukrainian Working-Class Immigrant Community in
   Northern Ontario / 436
   Stacey Zembrzycki

   Conclusion / 465
   Jim Mochoruk and Rhonda L. Hinther

Contributors List / 469
Index / 473

Acknowledgments

This volume is the result of what we have come to view as an excellent example of scholarly collaboration and hard work on the part of many individuals. We would especially like to thank our contributors first for providing such excellent pieces of work and second, for consistently responding to our requests for revisions in a timely and enthusiastic manner. Two of Canada's foremost scholars of ethnicity, Franca Iacovetta and Frances Swyripa, must also be singled out for praise. Despite incredibly busy work schedules they both took the time to offer careful and thoughtful feedback that helped to strengthen the book's introduction. The constructive and insightful commentaries offered by the manuscript's two anonymous reviewers were also of enormous help. And, as is always the case, the authors and editors owe an immense debt of gratitude to the librarians and archivists who aided the research process in a host of locations across Canada – and beyond.

We also cannot say enough about Len Husband at the University of Toronto Press (UTP) for his constant encouragement and assistance throughout this book's various stages of development. His willingness to assist with all issues, be they great or small, was much appreciated. Others at UTP, especially Frances Mundy, also offered wise counsel that helped to smooth the later stages of the publication process. The Social Science and Humanities Research Council's Aid-to-Publication provided the all important financial aid that has made publication of this volume possible.

We would also like to thank our families for their support of this project, which demanded long working hours and, in Rhonda's case, travel and much time away from home. Rhonda would especially like to thank Aaron Floresco, Evelyn Hinther, Lynne Onofreychuk, Keegan Onofreychuk, and Sophie Skolny for their support and assistance. She would also like to acknowledge the support of the History and Archeology Department at the Canadian Museum of Civilization for helping to make this project possible. As for Jim, it is the forbearance, love, and support of Mary, Kaitlin, Brendan, and Colleen Mochoruk that has made his involvement in this project possible. He would also like to thank his colleagues in the History Department at the University of North Dakota for offering critical insights and more importantly, for consistently providing an atmosphere of intellectual challenge and collegiality.

Finally, we would also like to thank Myron Momryk. His role – as an archivist, scholar, mentor, friend, and colleague – was the inspiration for this volume. Thank you, Myron, for all your work in bringing so much Ukrainian Canadian history to light.

Re-imagining Ukrainian Canadians
History, Politics, and Identity

Introduction

Jim Mochoruk and Rhonda L. Hinther

Perhaps this book should start with a confession. Despite the title and
the overwhelmingly Ukrainian-Canadian content of the essays in this
collection, this work is more about Canadian history – writ large – than
it is a basic study of Ukrainians in Canada. Indeed, it is not even purely
historical in nature, as the contributors come from a broad range of academic, professional, and disciplinary traditions and as such are concerned with questions that go well beyond the typical scope of the
historian. This is only fitting, though, as the field of Ukrainian-Canadian studies has long benefited from the contributions of curators,
archivists, public historians, education specialists, geographers, literary
critics, art and architectural historians, government officials, and independent scholars. This collection continues that tradition of cross- and
interdisciplinary work even as it suggests that Ukrainian-Canadian history should not – or at least should no longer – be deemed a distinct
field of inquiry. Rather, this work is dedicated to the proposition that
ethnic, hyphenated histories should be viewed as major currents in what
collectively constitutes the mainstream of Canadian history.

While this proposition will not shock anyone who is already engaged
in ethnic studies, it may sound counter-intuitive to those entering this
area of study for the first time. Indeed, it may sound particularly strange
given the iconic status of Ukrainians in Canadian immigration and ethnic history. Even those who have little or no expertise in Ukrainian
studies have some image in their minds of the first Ukrainian settlers
and how these 'Galacians,' 'Bukovinians,' or 'Ruthenians' came to
Canada in the 1890s and early years of the twentieth century as part of

the Laurier government's attempt to fill the Canadian West with settlers. Clifford Sifton, the Minister of the Interior who devised the immigration policy that brought tens of thousands of Ukrainian speakers (and other eastern and central Europeans) to Canada between 1897 and 1913, is best remembered for this policy – and for his defence of it when these immigrants were accorded what can only be described as a 'negative' reception by the host society. Though he himself was every bit as racist as most members of the dominant society, Sifton rather famously defended these 'stalwart' peasants – these 'men in sheepskin coats,' their 'stout wives,' and their myriad children – as exceptionally good value for the government's immigration and settlement dollar.

This description has had real staying power. The narrative accounts and visual images of Ukrainian families stopping in Winnipeg and other western railway centres before heading out to the western lands have made their way into the national consciousness and have long shaped portrayals of Ukrainian Canadians among both scholars and the public. Seen in this light, the new arrivals were a stolid peasantry, inured to suffering by generations of privation, but they were also a somewhat exotic, non-Western people whose Canadian experience would be determined by their pre-existing culture, by the landscape they were to settle and 'tame' (and that might also 'tame' them), and finally by what most Canadians hoped would be the inexorable process of adaptation and assimilation to the 'Canadian' way of life.

Given the staying power of these images and their ubiquity in Canadian historical discourse, it is understandable that most non-specialists see Ukrainians as a monolithic group whose experience in Canada has been a singular 'shared reality' of either hardship or triumph on the virgin lands of the West – or a mixture of both. This is precisely the sort of simplistic image that Ukrainian-Canadian scholars have been challenging for quite some time. Subsequent waves of Ukrainian immigration during the interwar period (under the Railways Agreement Act) and then after the Second World War (when 'displaced persons' began arriving in Canada), as well as dramatic internal migrations from country to city and from West to East, changed the basic demographics of the Ukrainian-Canadian community in the years following the first major wave of Ukrainian immigration. Yet these changes have had little impact on public perceptions of Ukrainians in Canada: to a very large extent, despite the arrival of large numbers of labourers in the

1920s and later of intellectuals and professionals, the vast majority of whom were urban dwellers, the popular image of Ukrainian Canadians has remained that of farm-dwelling Westerners.

Of course, there is at least one other set of images concerning Ukrainian Canadians: that they were 'dangerous foreigners' – a term that could be used in a broad variety of ways. For example, they were dangerous because they didn't assimilate quickly enough to mainstream society and therefore threatened the Canadian social fabric. *Or,* they were dangerous because they supposedly drank too much and were prone to violence and criminality. *Or* – even worse – they were dangerous because they were either Bolsheviks or potential followers of clever and manipulative Bolshevik leaders. For many years these various perceptions of Ukrainians as 'dangerous foreigners' inspired many Ukrainian-Canadian leaders and writers to present their communities' best possible faces to the dominant society, sometimes even whitewashing the experiences of those communities in order to demonstrate Ukrainian 'respectability.'

Because of these perceptions, and the role that scholars have played in shaping or debunking them, it is particularly important for student and non-specialist readers of this collection to have a basic appreciation of the work that has already been done in the field. To begin with, very soon after Ukrainian speakers began arriving in Canada in large numbers, a lively literature on them arose. Written largely by non-Ukrainian 'experts' on the 'Ukrainian question,' these works focused mainly on this question: 'Now that we have let these people into the country, how can we best Canadianize them?' Even the kindest of these 'experts' – including the director of Winnipeg's All Peoples' Mission, the Reverend J.S. Woodsworth – despaired of assimilating the older immigrants and placed most of their hopes in the children. Far less positive – and more widely read – were the assessments of Woodsworth's fellow Social Gospel minister, the Reverend Charles Gordon (writing as Ralph Connor), whose novel *The Foreigner* (1909) was a brutal indictment of the Ukrainian-Canadian way of life.[1]

These deeply unflattering portrayals aside, many of the early contributors to Ukrainian-Canadian studies shared traits with other early interpreters of the 'ethnic experience' in Canada. As a group, they were an interesting mix of popular and scholarly authors, who quite understandably focused on 'firsts': the first settlers, the first manifestations of organizational life, the first religious and lay leaders, and the first great accomplishments of Ukrainians in Canada. As Frances Swyripa noted back in 1982, many of these works endeavoured to make Ukrainians and Ukrainian-Canadian history 'respectable' to the dominant society.[2] Thus they often emphasized the rural and Western Canadian 'origins' of the Ukrainian-Canadian community, focusing on the idea that Ukrainians had played a key role in 'taming' and settling the western frontier. They also tended to downplay community divisions. The so-called nationalist/progressive divide in the Ukrainian-Canadian community (essentially a political division between those who supported pro-communist organizations on one side, and almost all other Ukrainian groups on the other) was ignored whenever possible, and the histories of competing groups within the community – the Orthodox, the Roman Catholic, the Ukrainian Catholic, the Presbyterian, and myriad secular groupings – were marginalized in the histories written by those associated with one particular group or another. The usual end result was a somewhat monolithic and triumphalist version of Ukrainian-Canadian history[3] – a version, moreover, that was dominated strongly by men. As Swyripa would later argue, in these early works 'both settlement and community development were typically explained through the male members of a family and the group, with their activities the focus.'[4]

But eventually, as both the community and the scholarship matured, the narrative and positivist approach inherent in these works – the 'look at the accomplishments of our people' story – began giving way to increasingly sophisticated and nuanced analyses of the many different Ukrainian-Canadian experiences. This was of a piece with the sophisticated work being done in other fields of Canadian ethnic history, most notably in Italian-, Irish-, and Jewish-Canadian studies.[5] There was obvious value to the pioneering work of scholars such as Vladimir Kaye, Michael Marunchak, Ol'ha Woycenko, and Paul Yuzyk, who had provided much useful statistical and political information on Ukrainians and in so doing had outlined a positivist account of the 'onwards and upwards' history of the Ukrainian-Canadian experience in Canada. However, by the late 1970s and early 1980s their work was being superseded – or at least built on in unexpected ways – by a generation of scholars whose concerns focused variously on social history, local history, labour history, the urban experience, the role of women in the community, and several other subgenres of what was by then being styled as 'the new history.' As it turned out, these new intellectual inspirations were well timed, for they coincided with renewed public interest in the white ethnic groups that constituted what was by then being referred to as the 'Canadian mosaic.' As a result, these scholars were able to benefit from the same sources of institutional and academic support as were being made available through the Canadian government's Multiculturalism Directorate, the Canadian Institute of Ukrainian Studies (CIUS) at the University of Alberta, the Chair of Ukrainian Studies at the University of Toronto, and the Centre for Ukrainian Studies at St Andrew's College at the University of Manitoba. Given this intellectual and institutional synergy, it is not surprising that scholarship in Ukrainian and Ukrainian-Canadian history expanded exponentially. New scholarship related to Ukrainians filled the pages of *Journal of Ukrainian Studies, Canadian Ethnic Studies, Canadian Slavonic Papers, Prairie Forum,* and several other journals of Western Canadian history. It also resulted in the numerous book-length publications of the CIUS, including several important collections of essays.[6]

Of the works produced during this period, none was more important than the collection of essays titled *A Heritage in Transition: Essays in the History of Ukrainians in Canada.* Part of the 'Generations' series, which was supported in part by the federal Multiculturalism Directorate, *A Heritage in Transition* was a breakthrough work in many regards. It brought together the work of several of the older, established members of the Ukrainian scholarly community (Kaye – posthumously – as well as Yuzyk and Woycenko) with that of a well-established, often university-based intermediate generation (Robert Klymasz, Manoly Lupul, and Oleh Gerus) and combined it with the research interests of an up-and-coming generation of researchers represented by Frances Swyripa and Orest Martynowych.[7] As a result, *A Heritage in Transition* was extremely well-balanced: it documented an already rich historiographical tradition of Ukrainian-Canadian studies, branched out in some new directions, and was able to proudly declare that students of Ukrainian-Canadian history need no longer prove Ukrainian 'respectability' and need 'no longer [be] obsessed with demonstrating that Ukrainians have managed to adapt to the Canadian way of life.'[8]

Another notable historiographical development of the 1970s and 1980s was the role played by scholars who had no personal ties to the

Ukrainian community. John Lehr, a historical geographer originally from Britain, began his work on patterns and styles of Ukrainian settlement in Western Canada during this period – work that would eventually make him one of the most influential Canadian scholars of the settler experience. Donald Avery, a historian of immigration and worker radicalism at the University of Western Ontario, paid particular attention to Ukrainians and other eastern and central European immigrants in his important 1979 study *'Dangerous Foreigners.'* Six years later an influential Canadian Historical Association pamphlet, *The Ukrainians in Canada* (influential because these pamphlets were so useful to non-specialist professors, who increasingly were being expected to comment intelligently on the 'ethnic experience' in their classes on Canadian social history), was co-authored by the decidedly Anglo-Celtic J.E. Rea and one of the recognized leaders in the field of Ukrainian-Canadian studies, Oleh Gerus. John Herd Thompson, yet another well-known Anglo-Canadian historian, also entered the field of Ukrainian-Canadian history at this time, co-editing *Loyalties in Conflict: Ukrainians in Canada during the Great War* with Frances Swyripa.[9] Meanwhile, non-Ukrainian scholars of Canadian labour history and the history of Canadian radicalism found themselves paying far more attention to Ukrainians, as witnessed by the work of Greg Kealey on the state's repression of the ethnic left, Joan Sangster's study of women on the Canadian left, and Ivan Avakumovic, Norman Penner, and Ian Angus's work on the history of the Communist Party of Canada.[10] On at least one level, this particular trend – and the success of *A Heritage in Transition* – indicated that Ukrainian-Canadian history was breaking into the mainstream of Canadian historical discourse. Indeed, even a quick perusal of reading lists for students enrolled during the 1980s in ethnic studies, labour history, social history, educational history, and human geography – and even basic Canadian history and Canadian studies courses – proves this was the case.

   Most notable about the work coming from younger scholars such as Swyripa and Martynowych was that much harder questions were being asked, and answered, regarding Ukrainians in Canada. The largely celebratory and uncritical tone of earlier works (at least, uncritical when it came to most members of the Ukrainian community) was abandoned once these people began publishing their major works early in the 1990s. Martynowych's *Ukrainians in Canada* and Swyripa's *Wedded to the Cause* took an unflinching look at the dynamics of various Ukrainian-Canadian communities and helped to move the discourse of Ukrainian studies away from an almost exclusively rural focus. Martynowych's concentration on Winnipeg as an organizational centre of Ukrainian life and his even-handed treatment of the several religious, ideological, and spatial divides in the earliest phase of Ukrainian-Canadian history made it a breakthrough work. Meanwhile, Swyripa's work, with its powerful feminist analysis of the roles assigned, taken, and shaped by women in the organized life of various Ukrainian-Canadian communities and institutions, represented a major break from the existing historiography which had focused upon the elite, male leadership of these communities.[11] It is worth noting that the publication of these works coincided with the production of a number of other landmark studies about other ethnic groups. Royden Loewen's work on Mennonites, Franca Iacovetta's on Italian working-class women and men, and Ruth Frager's study of Jewish labour activists and workers examined many parallel social and cultural dynamics.[12] Indeed, it is of some importance that all three of these works, as well as Varpu Lindstrom's ground-breaking study of radicalized Finnish-Canadian women,[13] paid serious attention to women and gender issues in their ethnic communities (as Swyripa's work had done for the Ukrainians). This would be a hallmark of many of the new community studies, which would dominate the field of ethnic and immigration history for the foreseeable future.

Though not planned to coincide with any particular event, it is significant that the seminal works by Swyripa and Martynowych appeared at roughly the same time that Canada's Ukrainian community was celebrating the hundredth anniversary of the arrival of the first Ukrainian immigrants to Canada. This, of course, had generated a great deal of popular interest in Ukrainian-Canadian history. Many works celebrating Ukrainian history, and acknowledging the pioneer legacy of that first generation of 'heroic' settlers and their role as nation builders, were published in the years surrounding this anniversary. And there was always a strong market for such works, as witnessed by the success of the many titles on the Ukrainian pioneers that were self-published by Michael Ewanchuk from the 1970s through to the turn of the present century.[14] These works had their own intrinsic value; that said, the work of Swyripa and Martynowych was a much needed counterbalance to the overtly filiopietistic tone of such endeavours. On another positive historiographical note, this anniversary provided the occasion for the publication of two more important scholarly collections, which also sought to push the field of Ukrainian studies in new directions.

Lubomyr Luciuk and Stella Hryniuk's co-edited *Canada's Ukrainians: Negotiating an Identity* (1991) was – as the subtitle indicated – a deliberate attempt to understand 'how Ukrainians came to think of themselves as a people within Canada.'[15] Many of the essays critically examined the Ukrainian community's – or rather communities' – connection to and engagement with the Canadian state and other social institutions of the majority culture, the implication being that such engagement played a key role in shaping the ethnic identity of Ukrainian Canadians. 'Ukrainian-ness' was no longer an 'essentialist' category; rather, it was something shaped and constructed and that had constantly been evolving in the course of these interactions, from the immigration and settlement period up to the present. Just as important, one part of the collection consisted of essays devoted to exploring the de facto dividing lines in the Ukrainian community, be they religious, ideological, spatial, class, or gender related.

The other major collection planned for the centennial year (though not published until 1993) was a special edition of *Journal of Ukrainian Studies*. Again, Ukrainians were being considered in new ways. The chronological focus was on the vastly understudied interwar period, and several of the articles signalled the development of new scholarly interests. To begin with, the arts and popular culture were examined in a new context. Instead of the well-established trope of peasant 'folklore studies,' seminal articles were produced on the Ukrainian-Canadian stage, on film production, and on organized Ukrainian teams in Canadian sports. Also included were a careful examination of Ukrainian criminality in Alberta, a sympathetic re-examination of Vera Lysenko's controversial 1947 study of Ukrainian-Canadian history, *Men in Sheepskin Coats;* and a carefully crafted piece by Myron Momryk on the Ukrainian-Canadian volunteers who had served in the International Brigades during the Spanish Civil War. These were hardly the sorts of topics that an earlier generation – seeking 'respectability' and acceptance – would have chosen to explore or, in some cases, expose in a public forum.[16]

Of course, it almost goes without saying that since the publication of these important works of the early 1990s, our understanding of Ukrainians has continued to grow and move in new directions. Scholars have been turning their attention to the post–Second World War era and to the impact of the 'displaced person' (DP) migration of the late 1940s and 1950s.[17] Sensitive topics (and therefore almost forbidden), such as the internment of Ukrainians, the history of the Ukrainian-Canadian pro-communist left, and the struggle for power within various secular and religious organizations, have become 'growth industries.'[18] Meanwhile, works that place the Ukrainian experience in a broadly defined context of Canadian multiculturalism – in contrast to the exceptionalist, singular interpretations of an earlier period – are growing in importance. In this regard a series of broad-ranging and innovative research programs carried out at the Peter and Doris Kule Centre for Ukrainian and Canadian Folklore at the University of Alberta warrant particular attention. The centre's recently completed 'Local Culture and Diversity on the Prairies Project' – a multicultural and interdisciplinary study launched by the centre but completed with the involvement of a series of partner institutions – has brought scholars from many disciplines and 'ethnic' specialties together to interview people from various ethnic communities in the prairie West and to compile new archival sources for a wide array of researchers. This is an excellent example of how folklore, ethnography, cultural anthropology, history, women's studies, and several other disciplines are being brought together for the sake of better understanding Canada's multicultural past.[19] Indeed, the case can be made that Canada's official policy of multiculturalism may well be the result of work by leading scholars in the field of Ukrainian-Canadian studies such as Manoly Lupul.[20] The past fifteen to twenty years have witnessed an immense expansion of the field, which has continued to attract ever more practitioners, with or without Ukrainian roots. Especially striking is that not all of those who are currently interested in this field would actually define themselves as specialists within Ukrainian-Canadian studies.

What does this mean? Well, in a sense, it means we have arrived at a fascinating juncture, a historiographical turning point of sorts. Established Ukrainian-Canadian scholars have attracted a whole new generation to the study of matters that, one way or another, involve Ukrainian Canadians. But because of their training, their language skills (or lack thereof), their particular scholarly interests, and their distance from the organized Ukrainian-Canadian community, some members of this 'new generation' are helping reorient the entire field. More often than not, their degrees were earned in Canadian history, geography, literature, and museology. And while some have Ukrainian roots, they tend not to be tied to any of the established parts of the organized Ukrainian community. Thus they might best be described as 'inside–outsiders': sometimes they conduct their research by consciously 'sharing authority' through active collaboration with the communities and individuals who are the subjects of their studies, in effect democratizing the process of historical inquiry. Translators are often employed, newer methodological approaches such as oral history are being utilized, and vastly different theoretical paradigms are being applied. Influenced by trends in contemporary scholarship outside the field of Ukrainian studies, and by notions of 'intersectionality' (i.e., of gender, class, ethnicity, and age), of transnationalism, and of new forms of feminist and literary analyses, these scholars are bound to move down some new paths. This current collection features some of the work of the best and brightest of this cohort.

Having said all that, this collection does not pretend to break completely from past treatments of Ukrainian-Canadian history. Rather, it seeks to extend the work of the 'second wave' scholarship. Seen in this light, these essays constitute some of the logical next steps in attempting to understand the multifaceted experiences of Ukrainian-Canadians in all their complexity. We also hope these essays will bring these experiences more fully into the contemporary discourse of Canadian history.

Readers may well be struck by how wide an academic net the co-editors have cast in recruiting contributors. Essays derived from just completed or still-in-process dissertations feature prominently in this collection. And this is an unmitigated good, for it is often the newest scholars who bring fresh perspectives – and new questions – to a topic. But note as well that some of the most important names in Ukrainian-Canadian studies over the past thirty years have also made major contributions.

This book has five parts – 'New Approaches to Old Questions,' 'Leaders and Intellectuals,' 'Diplomacy and International Concerns,' 'Internal Strife on the Left,' and 'Everyday People' – and follows up on the work of the scholars who dominated the field in the 1980s and 1990s. Utilizing a variety of analytical tools – some derived from postmodernism, feminist and gender theory, and literary criticism – as well as empirical analyses applied to new questions, it seeks to provoke thought and stimulate new research almost as much as it seeks to answer concrete questions, though it does that as well. For example, several of the essays challenge common notions about the monolithic nature of the Ukrainian-Canadian left; others re-examine at considerable depth various assumptions concerning an important portion of the Ukrainian nationalist community. Note also that several of these contributions are rooted in the urban, non-agricultural experience, bringing parts of the Ukrainian community to light in such vastly understudied areas as Ottawa and Sudbury; as well, urban centres such as Winnipeg, Edmonton, and Toronto are given more exposure than has long been the norm. And a number of these essays are explicitly interethnic and transnational rather than solely concerned with Ukrainians in Canada. Many of the pieces consider how a sense of ethnicity among Ukrainians has been constructed and maintained. Most notable of all is that all of these essays, to varying degrees, have moved away from the idea that the Ukrainian-Canadian experience can be understood as a singular phenomenon.

In part 1, 'New Approaches to Old Questions,' Rhonda L. Hinther examines the generational and gender issues that framed the postwar progressive Association of United Ukrainian Canadians. It provides a unique contribution to the literature partly through its use of oral history but also through its new interpretation of the reasons why the Ukrainian left declined. Karen Gabert's essay provides a provocative interpretation of the representation and construction of an 'ethnic' past for public consumption at the Ukrainian Cultural Heritage Village. Located at the intersection of public and academic history, this work delves into questions of memory and commemoration, identity construction, and the myriad uses of material culture and folklore to represent a people to themselves and to the world at large. Lindy Ledohowski offers a completely new understanding of the Ukrainian-Canadian relationship to the land. Rooted in an interethnic examination of literature, identity construction, and alienation from traditional models of ethnicity, this essay interrogates the entire category of 'Ukrainian-ness.'

In part 2, 'Leaders and Intellectuals,' Peter Melnycky offers a fascinating analysis of the transformation of one radical 'village intellectual' – Paul Rudyk – into a 'respectable' Canadian businessman. This is important since the 'village intellectual' is an often cited but seldom

studied archetype in the literature on the founding generation of
Ukrainian Canadians. In Jars Balan's reconsideration of an important
literary figure, Illia Kiriak, one will find a Ukrainian working-class hero
among the literati. A careful reading of this piece will yield a new understanding of what some scholars might term the homosociality that
nurtured the development of the first generation of male Ukrainian-
Canadian leadership. Meanwhile, Orest T. Martynowych's contribution
confronts an extremely sensitive topic within the Ukrainian-Canadian
community. Nuanced yet bold, this essay highlights the intellectual discourse of a small, but active and vocal, group of Ukrainian-Canadian
supporters of fascism and Nazism in the United Hetman Organization
and the Ukrainian National Federation.

Part 3, 'Diplomacy and International Concerns,' begins with Jaroslav
Petryshyn's careful consideration of the intellectual space occupied by
a variety of Ukrainian Canadians in the debates surrounding Canadian–
Soviet diplomacy. A broad overview of twentieth-century discourse,
this essay firmly locates Ukrainian Canadians at the heart of the 'ethnic question' in Canadian–Soviet relations. Serge Cipko offers a highly
unusual perspective on an aspect of transnational history. He explores
how, at the height of the Cold War, the Canadian government closely
monitored the responses of South American governments to the Soviet
recruitment of 'homeland returnees' among their Ukrainian communities – largely in an effort to shape the Canadian state's responses to its
own potential wave of Ukrainian out-migration. Jennifer Anderson then
deals with transnational issues through her nuanced examination of the
interethnic relationships within the Canadian Soviet Friendship Society.
While not exclusively concerned with Ukrainians, her work illustrates
the importance of understanding how cross-ethnic alliances affected
Ukrainian-Canadian activism. Utilizing oral histories and previously
unexamined Soviet and Canadian sources, her study hints at the ongoing assimilationist pressures arising from the left, offers insights into
the use of visual imagery as propaganda, and has much to say about
the construction of a view of the postwar Soviet Union in Canada and
abroad.

Part 4, 'Internal Strife on the Left,' deals with the always controversial topic of the pro-communist left. Jim Mochoruk provides a careful
analysis of the connection and separation between English and
Ukrainian radicals in the 1920s and early 1930s. Using recently re-

leased Comintern documents, he provides a detailed rendering of the complex and tension-fraught relationship between the Ukrainian Labour-Farmer Temple Association leaders and the Anglo-Celtic leaders of the Communist Party of Canada (CPC). Andrij Makuch provides the first detailed analysis of the fight that almost destroyed the supposedly monolithic Ukrainian-Canadian left in 1935. Among other things, his analysis of the 'Lobay Crisis' demonstrates the impact that 'Old Country' events and ideological differences had on the Ukrainian progressive community in Canada.

Part 5, 'Everyday People,' offers two microstudies of Ukrainians outside the usual geographic parameters of academic examination. S. Holyck Hunchuck looks at how one small group of radicalized working-class Ukrainians built and maintained a sense of community in the hostile environment of Ottawa. In doing so, she considers the importance of small local institutions as critical spaces for ethnic expression. Stacey Zembrzycki's contribution focuses on crime, gender, the state, and ethnicity along the resource frontier of northwestern Ontario. Her study examines the construction and use of ethnicity by the state and analyses the changing perceptions of 'Ukrainian-ness' in the community of Sudbury in the first three decades of the twentieth century.

As editors and contributing authors, we are confident that this collection of essays will help advance the discourse on Canadian immigration and ethnic history. The wide-ranging theoretical character of these pieces and the variety of topics they cover should help foster considerable discussion among experts and – indeed, particularly – among students. It is our profound hope that these essays will be of use in many different classrooms and courses. Students grappling with social history, community studies, public history, family history, and the history of Canadian radicalism will all benefit from reading and discussing the essays in this volume. But having said that, we also feel quite certain that these essays will help stimulate not just discussion but new research as well. And those who read to the end of this work will find that we even suggest some of the directions that future research might take. We look forward to the new conversations and critiques that will undoubtedly arise, generating new insights into not only the Ukrainian-Canadian experience, but also the collective Canadian experience.

Notes

1   Chief among the works in this genre are books, sociological treatises,
    novels, articles in various church publications, and reports produced by
    Protestant ministers, educators, and immigration agents who had various
    reasons for being in contact with Ukrainian communities. Between 1897
    and the First World War, publications such as *Christian Guardian, Mis-
    sionary Outlook*, and *Epworth Era* and the widely distributed annual re-
    ports of institutions such as the All Peoples' Mission in Winnipeg – as
    well as pieces written by many of the same authors in mainstream West-
    ern Canadian newspapers – were filled with stories about the problems
    associated with Ukrainian immigration. One of the best-known deroga-
    tory depictions of Ukrainians, however, was to be found in a novel by
    Canada's most popular author of that era, the Reverend Charles Gordon.
    Writing as Ralph Connor, he published *The Foreigner: A Tale of
    Saskatchewan* in 1909 to critical and popular acclaim. That same year,
    one of Western Canada's leading emissaries of the Social Gospel move-
    ment, and the future founder of the Co-operative Commonwealth Federa-
    tion, the Reverend J.S. Woodsworth, published his famous *Strangers
    Within Our Gates: Or Coming Canadians*. This offered a somewhat
    more sympathetic treatment of Eastern European immigrants than Con-
    nor had written; even so, it was an overtly assimilationist tract in which
    the author often despaired of assimilating adult immigrants from Eastern
    Europe to the Canadian way of life. In 1918, in a similar vein, J.T.M.
    Anderson, the future Conservative premier of Saskatchewan (elected to
    that post with the overt aid of the Saskatchewan branch of the Ku Klux
    Klan in 1929), published *The Education of New Canadians: A Treatise
    on Canada's Greatest Educational Problem*. The title of his work says it
    all – 'new Canadians' in general and Ukrainians in particular were
    Canada's greatest educational problem – and, reading between the lines,
    its greatest social one as well.
      These works are but the tip of the iceberg; that said, they provide a
    fairly accurate sampling of the concerns and interpretations of Canada's
    leading English-speaking 'experts' on Ukrainian Canadians.
2   Frances Swyripa, 'A Survey of Ukrainian-Canadian Historiography,' in *A
    Heritage in Transition: Essays in the History of Ukrainians in Canada*,
    ed. Manoly R. Lupul (Toronto: McClelland and Stewart, 1982), 318.
3   See, for example, Vladimir J. Kaye, *Early Ukrainian Settlements in
    Canada, 1895–1900: Dr Josef Oleskow's Role in the Settlement of the
    Canadian Northwest* (Toronto: University of Toronto Press, 1964);
    Michael H. Marunchak, *The Ukrainian Canadians: A History* (Win-
    nipeg: Ukrainian Free Academy of Sciences, 1970); Ol'ha Woycenko,

The Ukrainians in Canada (Winnipeg: Canada Ethnica, 1967); and Paul Yuzyk, *The Ukrainians in Manitoba: A Social History* (Toronto: University of Toronto Press, 1953).

4 Frances Swyripa, *Wedded to the Cause: Ukrainian-Canadian Women and Ethnic Identity, 1891–1991* (Toronto: University of Toronto Press, 1993), 221.

5 Robert Harney, 'Montreal's King of Italian Labour: A Case Study of Padronism,' in *Labour/Le travail* 4 (1979): 57–84; Irving M. Abella and Harold Martin Troper, *None Is Too Many: Canada and the Jews of Europe, 1933–1948* (Toronto: Lester and Orpen Dennys, 1982); Donald H. Akenson, *The Irish in Ontario: A Study in Rural History* (Kingston: McGill-Queen's University Press, 1984).

6 For more detail on how the Canadian Institute for Ukrainian Studies (hereafter CIUS) was founded in 1976, see Manoly R. Lupul, 'The Establishment of the Canadian Institute of Ukrainian Studies at the University of Alberta: A Personal Memoir,' *Canadian Ethnic Studies* 26, no. 2 (1994): 88–111. *Journal of Ukrainian Studies* was launched in the 1970s as *Journal of Ukrainian Graduate Studies;* a number of those who would become influential in the field were first published in the latter. *Canadian Ethnic Studies* was an early and important venue for Ukrainian-related topics, as were *Prairie Forum, Manitoba History, Saskatchewan History,* and *Alberta History.* Regarding the books published by the CIUS in the late 1970s and early 1980s, see for example Manoly R. Lupul, ed., *Ukrainian Canadians, Multiculturalism, and Separatism: An Assessment* (Edmonton: University of Alberta Press for CIUS, 1978); W. Roman Petryshyn, ed., *Changing Realities: Social Trends among Ukrainian Canadians* (Edmonton: CIUS, 1980); Manoly R. Lupul, *Visible Symbols: Cultural Expression among Canada's Ukrainians* (Edmonton: CIUS, 1984); and Frances Swyripa and John Herd Thompson, eds., *Loyalties in Conflict: Ukrainians in Canada during the Great War* (Edmonton: CIUS, 1983).

7 Lupul, *A Heritage in Transition.*

8 Frances Swyripa, 'A Survey of Ukrainian-Canadian Historiography,' in ibid., 344.

9 Some examples of Lehr's early work: 'Ukrainian Houses in Alberta,' *Alberta Historical Review* 21, no. 4 (1973): 9–15; 'The Ukrainian Presence on the Prairies,' *Canadian Geographic* 97, no. 2 (1978): 28–33; 'The Landscape of Ukrainian Settlement in the Canadian West,' *Great Plains Quarterly* 2, no. 2 (1982): 94–105; 'Government Perceptions of Ukrainian Immigrants to Western Canada, 1896–1902,' *Canadian Ethnic Studies* 19, no. 2 (1987): 1-12. See also Donald Avery, *'Dangerous Foreigners': European Immigrant Workers and Labour Radicalism in*

Canada, 1896–1932 (Toronto: McClelland and Stewart, 1979); Oleh
W. Gerus and J.E. Rea, *The Ukrainians in Canada*, vol. 10 (Ottawa:
Canadian Historical Association, 1985); and Swyripa and Thompson,
Loyalties in Conflict.

10 See, for example, Greg Kealey, 'State Repression of Labour and the Left
in Canada, 1914–20: The Impact of the First World War,' *Canadian His-
torical Review* 73, no. 3 (1992): 281–314; idem, 'The Surveillance State:
The Origins of Domestic Intelligence and Countersubversion in Canada,
1914–21,' *Intelligence and National Security* 7, no. 3 (1992): 179–210;
idem, 'The Early Years of State Surveillance of Labour and the Left in
Canada: The Institutional Framework of the Royal Canadian Mounted
Police Security and Intelligence Apparatus, 1918–26,' *Intelligence and
National Security* 8, no. 3 (1993): 129–48; Joan Sangster, *Dreams of
Equality: Women on the Canadian Left, 1920–1950* (Toronto: McClel-
land and Stewart, 1989); Ivan Avakumovic, *The Communist Party in
Canada* (Toronto: McClelland and Stewart, 1975); Norman Penner,
Canadian Communism: The Stalin Years and Beyond (Toronto: Methuen,
1988); and Ian Angus, *Canadian Bolsheviks: The Early Years of the
Communist Party of Canada* (Montreal: Vanguard, 1981).

11 Orest Martynowych, *Ukrainians in Canada: The Formative Years, 1891–
1924* (Edmonton: CIUS, 1991); Swyripa, *Wedded to the Cause.*

12 Royden Loewen, *Family, Church, and Market: A Mennonite Community
in the Old and the New Worlds, 1850–1930* (Toronto: University of
Toronto Press, 1993); Franca Iacovetta, *Such Hardworking People: Italian Immigrants in Postwar Toronto* (Montreal: McGill-Queen's University Press, 1992); Ruth A. Frager, *Sweatshop Strife: Class, Ethnicity, and
Gender in the Jewish Labour Movement of Toronto, 1900–1939*
(Toronto: University of Toronto Press, 1992).

13 Varpu Lindstrom, *Defiant Sisters: A Social History of Finnish Immigrant
Women in Canada* (Toronto: Multicultural History Society of Ontario,
1988).

14 Michael Ewanchuk's best-known works include *Spruce, Swamp, and
Stone: A History of the Pioneer Ukrainian Settlements in the Gimli Area*
(Winnipeg: M. Ewanchuk, 1977); *Pioneer Settlers: Ukrainians in the
Dauphin Area, 1896–1926* (Winnipeg: M. Ewanchuk, 1988); *Reflections
and Reminiscences: Ukrainians in Canada, 1892–1992* (Winnipeg: M.
Ewanchuk, 1995); *East of the Red* (Winnipeg: M. Ewanchuk, 1998); and
*Growing Up on a Bush Homestead: Pioneer Life as Seen through the
Eyes of the Children* (Winnipeg: M. Ewanchuk, 2003).

15 Lubomyr Luciuk and Stella M. Hryniuk, eds., *Canada's Ukrainians: Negotiating an Identity* (Toronto: Ukrainian Canadian Centennial Committee in association with University of Toronto Press, 1991).

16 See Jars Balan, 'Backdrop to an Era: The Ukrainian-Canadian Stage in the Interwar Years'; Bohdan Nebesio, '*Zaporozhets za Dunaiem* (1938): The Production of the First Ukrainian-Language Film in Canada'; K.W. Sokolyk, 'The Role of Ukrainian Sports Teams, Clubs, and Leagues, 1924–1952'; Gregory Robinson, 'Rougher Than Any Other Nationality? Ukrainian Canadians and Crime in Alberta, 1915–1929'; Myron Momryk, 'Ukrainian Volunteers from Canada in the International Brigades, Spain, 1936–39'; and A.K. Glynn, 'Vera Lysenko, *Men in Sheepskin Coats* (1947): The Untold Story,' all in *Journal of Ukrainian Studies* 16, nos. 1–2 (1991). As noted in the text, while the date of this special edition was 1991, it did not actually appear until 1993, owing to a publication backlog.

17 Lubomyr Y. Luciuk, *Searching for Place: Ukrainian Displaced Persons, Canada, and the Migration of Memory* (Toronto: University of Toronto Press, 2000).

18 For recent examples of the literature on internment, see Lubomyr Luciuk, *Without Just Cause: Canada's First National Internment Operations and the Ukrainian Canadians, 1914–1920* (Kingston: Kashtan, 2006); idem, *In Fear of the Barbed Wire Fence: Canada's First National Internment Operations and the Ukrainian Canadians, 1914–1920* (Kingston: Kashtan, 2001); and Bohdan S. Kordan and Craig Mahovsky, *A Bare and Impolitic Right: Internment and Ukrainian-Canadian Redress* (Montreal: McGill-Queen's University Press, 2004). Examples of literature on the Ukrainian left include Rhonda L. Hinther's '"They Said the Course Would Be Wasted on Me because I Was a Girl": Mothers, Daughters, and Shifting Forms of Female Activism in the Ukrainian Left in Twentieth-Century Canada,' *Atlantis* 32, no.1 (2006): 100–10; idem, 'Raised in the Spirit of the Class Struggle: Children, Youth, and the Interwar Ukrainian Left in Canada,' *Labour/Le travail* 60 (2007): 43–76; diem, '"Sincerest Revolutionary Greetings": Progressive Ukrainians in Twentieth-Century Canada' (PhD diss., McMaster University, 2005); Joan Sangster, 'Robitnytsia, Ukrainian Communists, and the "Porcupinism" Debate: Reassessing Ethnicity, Gender, and Class in Early Canadian Communism, 1922–1930,' *Labour* 56 (2005): 51–89; and Jim Mochoruk, *The People's Co-op: The Life and Times of a North End Institution* (Halifax: Fernwood, 2000). Franca Iacovetta's *Gatekeepers: Reshaping Immigrant Lives in Cold War Canada* (Toronto: Between the Lines, 2006) stands as one of the most thorough and critical analyses of Vladimir Kaye to date. On matters of religious dispute and differentiation, see John C. Lehr, '"Shattered Fragments": Community Formation on the Ukrainian Frontier of Settlement, Stuartburn, Manitoba, 1896–1921,' *Prairie Forum* 28, no. 2 (2003): 219–34; Myroslaw Tataryn, 'Fa-

ther Nicholas Shumsky and the Struggle for a Ukrainian Catholic Identity,' *Journal of Ukrainian Studies* 28, no. 2 (2003): 69–87; and Oleh W. Gerus, 'The Ukrainian Orthodox Church of Canada: The Formative Period,' *Ukrainian Quarterly* 57, nos. 1–2 (2001): 65–90.

19   For more information on this project, visit 'Local Culture and Diversity on the Prairies Project,' http://www.arts.ualberta.ca/~ukrfolk/Local_Cultureweb/Participants.htm.

20   Recently, Lupul was rewarded for his role in creating Canada's official multiculturalism policy by being named to the Order of Canada. A detailed understanding of his struggle for multiculturalism can be found in his autobiography, *The Politics of Multiculturalism: A Ukrainian-Canadian Memoir* (Edmonton: CIUS Press, 2005).

PART ONE

New Approaches to Old Questions

What it *means* to be Ukrainian has been, and remains, a complicated question, and the essays in this part highlight this complexity. The three contributors take a new and theoretically sophisticated approach to examining community hall life, museums, and literature, respectively. In so doing they interrogate various manifestations of Ukrainian and Ukrainian-Canadian identity and challenge essentialist notions that there is a common and uncontested 'Ukrainian-ness' – notions that were all too apparent in the work of so many early scholars of the Ukrainian-Canadian experience. The essays here raise important questions regarding conflicting identities, divided loyalties, and various Ukrainians' relationships with other Ukrainians, the Canadian state, and other ethnicities and cultural groups. Collectively they underline one absolutely crucial point: being Ukrainian has meant profoundly different things to different people in different times and places.

Using oral history and a range of hitherto underexplored documentary sources, Rhonda L. Hinther exposes the gender and generational disparities – rooted in divergent and conflicting notions of 'Ukrainian-ness' (and Canadian-ness) – that contoured and challenged the Association of United Ukrainian Canadians (AUUC) and that ultimately contributed to its postwar decline. Joining other contributors to this collection (Mochoruk, Makuch, and Hunchuck) in challenging the prevalent historiography of the Ukrainian-Canadian left, Hinther also makes a novel contribution to questions of assimilation and generational conflict in the Cold War era. By doing so, she charts much new territory.

Karen Gabert's contribution examines Alberta's Ukrainian Cultural Heritage Village, exploring how both the Alberta government and individuals of Ukrainian descent have constructed and maintained a particular type of Ukrainian identity and past. Central to the essay is the 'repackaging' process through which provincial officials transformed – one might say rebranded – the Village and the Ukrainian pioneers' experience to make it universally representative of Alberta's rural past. In the process, Gabert underscores the hegemony of public history and commemorative processes in influencing public and personal perceptions of the past. When we read this essay in light of those by Lindy Ledohowski and Stacey Zembrzycki, we see emerging a vastly different way of viewing the 'construction' of Ukrainian-Canadian identity.

Finally, Lindy Ledohowski's piece offers a careful deconstruction of the work of poet Andrew Suknaski and novelist and literary critic Lisa Grekul, both of Ukrainian descent. Ledohowski examines the tensions evident among later generations of Ukrainian Canadians as they attempted to understand their ancestors' – and their own – relationship with the Canadian Prairies and its multiracial/multiethnic past. Utilizing a far different set of methodologies than Jars Balan's contribution to this volume on Illia Kiriak, Ledohowski explores subsequent generations' struggles to negotiate personal and collective notions of 'Ukrainian-ness' within the colonial legacy of prairie settlement and the broader Canadian discourse of multiculturalism.

1

Generation Gap:
Canada's Postwar Ukrainian Left

Rhonda L. Hinther

Zenovy Nykolyshyn was born in 1935. He grew up in the West Toronto Ukrainian Labour Temple. His mother was an active member of 'the hall,' and his father, when he was not busy running the family's store, helped at plays by volunteering as a prompter. They enrolled young Zeny in Ukrainian school at the labour temple. There he also took violin and Ukrainian dance lessons and served a term as president of the Junior Section. As a teenager he was an active member of the hall's Youth Club and, through the Labour Temple, the peace movement – a risky pursuit at times. 'In the early 1950s I was delivering peace pamphlets to neighbourhood homes,' he recalled. 'A Catholic priest saw what I was distributing and came chasing after me and tried to give me a kick. Fortunately I managed to run away.'[1]

Nykolyshyn, like many of his Canadian-born cohort, had been raised to take over the reins of the Association of United Ukrainian Canadians (AUUC). Unfortunately, as they came of age, many – the younger men especially – encountered few opportunities to exercise meaningful leadership. Instead they found themselves constantly stymied by the immigrant-generation men, who were unwilling to relinquish their hold on the institutions of the Ukrainian left. According to Nykolyshyn, many members of the immigrant generation 'felt that before they could pass the torch to the Canadian born, they would have to teach them for at least two to three years' – which, he asserted, was unnecessary, because the younger men had already acquired these skills through their past organizational involvement. Those younger men who did achieve

leadership positions or other employment with the movement found
that they had to tread softly. When he questioned the organizational
methods of the immigrant generation, this 'caused problems, and I was
given less and less responsibility.' Things could get so difficult at times
that 'if there had been a Siberia for the older members to send the
younger members, many would have been sent there.' Frustrated,
Nykolyshyn abandoned his career with the movement. He and his wife
Lucy, who also grew up in the movement, for many years remained active only in the AUUC bowling league. He returned to organizational
work in 1977 around the time that the aging immigrant generation
began to 'realize they needed the young people.' But the intergenerational conflict persisted for another twenty years, until the early 1990s,
when 'the old-timers [many of whom were by then in their eighties]
left the leadership.'[2] By then the AUUC was a shell of its former vibrant
self.

As Nykolyshyn's story illustrates, the children of the founders of the
Ukrainian Labour Farmer Temple Association (ULFTA) often when
they reached adulthood had a difficult time finding a place for themselves in the movement. Their efforts to do so created a distinct
Ukrainian-Canadian leftist experience. The Canadian born were het-
erogeneous – the women and the men of this group, though sharing
certain disadvantages in relation to the established leadership, enjoyed
distinct albeit uneven advantages within certain sectors of the movement. For their part, the immigrant-generation women, who had long
exercised authority over their own activities in their Women's Branch;
and immigrant-generation men, both the leaders and the rank and file,
also experienced the Ukrainian left differently. Well into the Cold War
era, their roles, which remained rigidly sex-specific, exhibited a clear
continuity with those of the interwar period. Among adults, then, four
divergent but occasionally overlapping experiences emerged after the
war.

Certainly, there was unity among all generations with regard to some
causes supported and activities embraced. At times the immigrant-generation women and the Canadian-born women banded together. In other
instances, the Canadian-born women worked with their male counterparts, expressing their identities and political activism as Ukrainian
Canadians while the immigrant-generation women and men united
around causes that spoke to their experiences as radical immigrants –

and, for some, as non-citizens. Sometimes all the adult constituencies joined together to support a single cause, though gender and generation nearly always interacted to shape the nature of that involvement. As time wore on, however, gendered and generational division – and decline – came to characterize the movement. This essay examines the broader currents that contoured the postwar Ukrainian left by considering the specific experiences of these adult supporters, interrogating how women's and men's positions at particular intersections of gender, generation, and ethnicity shaped their opportunities and activism, as well as the movement as a whole.[3]

It is clear that internal dynamics were not solely responsible for the AUUC's decline. External factors – including assimilation, the influence of North American popular culture, and expanded opportunities for education, jobs, and political activism elsewhere – also helped bring this result. Nor can the impact of the Cold War be ignored. In Canada and abroad, the Cold War generated a chilly social and political climate for leftists, especially for those who (like many AUUC leaders) continued to maintain open ties to the Labour Progressive Party / Communist Party of Canada (LPP/CPC) and who openly supported and travelled to the Soviet states. All of this exacerbated the Ukrainian left's often negative public image and ongoing difficult relationship with the state and with other Canadians. We shall see that AUUC members and supporters, like other leftists, were subject to frequent and vitriolic state surveillance and 'Cold Warrior' harassment, which led many supporters to reconsider their connection to the movement. This study, then, besides expanding our relatively limited understanding of postwar Ukrainians and Ukrainian Canadians (and the left in particular), also engages with the dynamic and recently growing body of literature on the Cold War, especially those works focusing on state and community repression of dissent and the responses of dissidents to this harassment.[4]

This paper also builds on existing studies of the Ukrainian left in Canada. Most such studies have focused on the interwar years, especially on the ULFTA leaders' relations with the Communist Party of Canada (CPC). The essays in this volume by Jim Mochoruk and Andrij Makuch are important and innovative additions to this historiography.[5] While the CPC connection was certainly critical, radical politics were but one component of the Ukrainian community's activities. This essay, with its postwar focus and top-down, bottom-up approach, seeks to expand our understanding of (a) the connection between the priorities and activities of the AUUC leaders and those of the rank and file, and (b) the variety of ways each expressed their political, cultural, and social interests. It takes particular care to consider how postwar constructions of gender identity intersected with understandings of Ukrainian-ness – especially radical Ukrainian-ness – to shape opportunities and activities in the movement. Scholars in Canada examining Ukrainians and other ethnic and racialized groups have demonstrated the methodological effectiveness of an intersectional approach. By considering class, ethnicity, and gender, Frances Swyripa has fruitfully interrogated the similarities and differences that emerged among nationalist and progressive Ukrainian women.[6] Ruth Frager has demonstrated how the uneven convergence of ethnicity, gender, and class with external social, economic, and political forces eventually undermined the efforts of Jewish garment workers to 'bring about a fundamental socialist transformation' in the early half of the twentieth century in Toronto.[7] The collected articles in *Sisters or Strangers: Immigrant, Ethnic, and Racialized Women in Canadian History* (2004), with their attention to categories such as race, ethnicity, and class, challenge and enrich our understanding of women's experiences of immigration, community and nation building, and citizenship.[8] This article contributes to this canon and that of Ukrainian-Canadian history generally by expanding our understanding of the Ukrainian left in several new directions using an intergenerational approach, with particular attention to gender roles and ethnic identity. It focuses on the postwar era of ULFTA/AUUC history.

The ULFTA and the AUUC

Over the course of the twentieth century, Ukrainian leftists created one of the most dynamic working-class movements in Canadian history. Members and supporters were drawn from the first (1891–1914, 170,000 immigrants) and second (1925–1930, 70,000 immigrants) waves of peasant Ukrainian emigration from Bukovina and Galicia. Nationally and locally, the Ukrainian left attracted supporters through cultural and social activities, pro-labour newspapers, links with the CPC, and ties to the fight for peace, social justice, and workers' rights. In the course of these activities, over several generations, meanings of 'Ukrainian-ness' were reinforced, shaped, and changed. Through the

Ukrainian Labour-Farmer Temple Association, members and supporters across Canada focused their energies on two key priorities – improving the circumstances of workers and farmers in Canada and around the world, and preserving and expressing Ukrainian cultural traditions in their adopted Canadian homeland. At various times, certain constituencies of the community valued and supported these priorities differently. Nonetheless, however or whenever they arose, these concerns reflected both the adaptation and the resistance the immigrants and their children employed in adjusting to and improving their personal and community circumstances. The Ukrainians were not unusual in this: similar patterns existed among other 'ethnics' during the same era. Studies of leftist Jews, Finns, Hungarians, and others have noted the rich tapestry of social and cultural activities that were so central to defining these groups' leftist politics and 'ethnic hall' socialism.[9]

The Ukrainian left enjoyed relative stability and prosperity during Canada's interwar years, attracting more and more members and supporters, both women and men, children and adults. By the end of the interwar period, it counted some 15,000 members in 87 Ukrainian Labour Temples. Its two Ukrainian-language newspapers reached more than 20,000 subscribers, and in halls across the country, Ukrainian-language plays and concerts routinely played to full houses.[10] The interwar years were a golden age for Ukrainian cultural and political radicalism in Canada. The movement suffered a great setback during the Second World War when the King government banned the ULFTA, interned many of its male leaders, and expropriated many Ukrainian Labour Temples because of the organization's communist sympathies. Often led by their female supporters, the former ULFTAers successfully confronted these charges and formed a new group, the AUUC, through which to conduct their activities. By 1944, 10,000 members had regrouped. That same year, the AUUC newspapers' circulation rose back to 'well over 20,000' subscriptions.[11] The movement was able to enter the postwar era with high hopes. Those hopes soon waned, however; within a decade or two, the AUUC was slowly but clearly declining.

Like other contemporary radical groups, Ukrainian leftists developed a gendered discourse predicated on male domination and female subordination. Peasant village values brought from the 'old country' influenced these models. Evident in a system of unequal power relations, these values were further reinforced by Canadian manifestations of male gender privilege and female subordination, especially within the CPC and other leftist organizations such as unions, which were also deeply sexist and patriarchal. From this grew a structured hierarchy that privileged men and their experiences and that defined class and activism through a male lens of experience and opportunity. During the interwar years, men held virtually all leadership positions in the ULFTA and were among its most visible supporters. Meanwhile, Ukrainian radical women performed invisible yet critical roles that ensured the movement's financial, organizational, cultural, and political survival. Despite these contributions, women endured frequent criticism for being 'backward' or for failing to pursue male-defined methods of activism. At the same time, those who did wish to move beyond women's traditional sphere in the movement encountered hostility or contempt.[12] Similar patterns continued in the postwar era, though not without challenge (in some cases, *significant* challenge). The complex intersection of gender with generation and ethnicity meant that some of the movement's members found themselves privileged by gender in traditional ways in some capacities even while their authority was diminished in other respects. As we shall see, gendered advantage and status played out in some curious ways within the AUUC.

Running the Ukrainian Left

Within the Ukrainian left, roles were readily available for all members. However, the degree of power, status, and influence those in each position enjoyed could vary quite considerably. A complex interaction of generation and gender shaped these opportunities. Nykolyshyn's experiences highlight some of the problems younger men had finding a place with the movement. Their female Canadian-born counterparts had a somewhat different experience. Some found positions in the national leadership, though nearly all such positions involved working with children or women's groups and were framed as extensions of women's traditional domestic duties.[13] Since very few immigrant-generation women had come remotely near the national or local leadership, the Canadian-born women did not find themselves in the same position to compete for leadership roles as the Canadian-born men were. The younger women also took on paid employment with the movement. During the interwar years a handful of women had done so as cultural teachers and itinerant organizers and occasionally as support staff with enterprises such as the Workers Benevolent Organization (WBA), the People's Co-op Dairy, and Ukrainian Labour Temple cultural and language schools. After the war, when the AUUC expanded its business and publishing interests – for example, by opening Globe Tours and the Ukrainska Knyha, an international book and parcel service – women's roles as (inexpensive) workers took on new importance. The Canadian-born women's bilingualism was essential to businesses that needed to function in both English and Ukrainian. Their apparent willingness to work for low wages increased the profit margins and thereby helped build these businesses in ways that men's higher-paid labour could not.

Canadian-born men seeking some measure of authority for themselves often had to turn to other facets of organizational life. Some found this authority within the unisex English-Speaking Branch, an entity created after the war to serve the needs of those Canadian born who, unlike their parents and grandparents, preferred to conduct their activism in English rather than Ukrainian. Working together, younger men and women used the English-Speaking Branch to define their own sense of Ukrainian-ness and to shape their organizational life according to their own interests – which, as the postwar period wore on, came to focus less on political work and more on social and cultural activities. For example, in Winnipeg the men of the English-Speaking Branch organized a fishing club in 1962.[14] Two years later, female and male members of the same branch were running a bowling league in which they competed against other Ukrainian leftists from across Canada.[15] In 1968 their Toronto counterparts took part in weightlifting classes at the local Ukrainian Labour Temple.[16]

At the same time, the Canadian-born women were using the English-Speaking Branch to carve out a space of their own, separate from those of the Canadian-born men and their mothers and grandmothers. During the war they had established English-language Young Women's Victory Clubs to aid the war effort, separate from the immigrant-generation's Women's Branch (established in 1922). At war's end, they continued under the auspices of the Young Women's Club, which became a subsection of the English-Speaking Branch. Despite the separation, the activities of the Young Women's Clubs and the Women's Branch were often parallel. At the grassroots level both groups carried on with activism framed as support work. Their volunteer labour remained the mainstay of funding and guaranteed the existence of many activities at the halls. In 1947, for example, the Young Women's Club at Winnipeg's Ukrainian Labour Temple took care of outfitting club rooms for meetings and other activities; and in 1953 the Edmonton group made jackets for the Labour Temple's Christmas production of *Hryts*. Young Women's Clubs took part in AUUC bake sales, bazaars, teas, and handicraft activities, organizing these events both on their own and in tandem with the Women's Branch.[17]

The Women's Branch also raised money and organized events.[18] These older women tended to dominate kitchen work and hall maintenance (labour they had also done before the war). In many locations after the war – especially in larger urban centres, and thanks to the introduction of properly outfitted kitchens in many halls – these women's kitchen work expanded to catering to outside groups renting hall space, and to selling foodstuffs to a broader public that was discovering Ukrainian cooking. For example, throughout the 1950s the Calgary Women's Branch catered weddings and parties at their Ukrainian Labour Temple; and during the early 1970s the Regina group sold perogies out of the hall on Sundays.[19]

Though vital as fund-raisers and 'financial managers,' these women did not enjoy high status within the movement. Indeed, kitchen work often precluded involvement in influential activities of higher status. This 'upstairs–downstairs' status was evident in a description of the AUUC National Convention, held in Toronto in 1948. An AUUC newspaper reported that there, 'Toronto women who had put in so much work to feed the delegates (oh, those *vareniki* and *holubtsi*!) were given a surprise. They were called up to the stage amid ringing cheers of the delegates and had corsages pinned on them … Then they went downstairs to prepare supper.'[20] Thus, while they kept the movement running, helped fund newspapers and pay (mainly male) organizers' salaries, and allowed conventions to be run on a shoestring, these women had little access to formal decision-making power within the Progressive Ukrainian community.

According to Nykolyshyn, most of the decisions were made by the immigrant-generation men who ran the AUUC and its related organizations. At the local level, these men controlled the halls. After the war, what had been the ULFTA branch came to be known as the AUUC

Branch – and, more often, the Men's Branch, since in most communities the AUUC was made up entirely of men (as had been the case in the interwar years). And despite the name's inclusive sound, the Men's Branch did not include (or welcome) all men to its ranks. Generally, those immigrant-generation men who had belonged to the ULFTA before the war remained active in the Men's Branch. Since its meetings and other activities were conducted mainly in Ukrainian, Canadian-born men uncomfortable working entirely in Ukrainian were left in the cold. Even those who did speak Ukrainian well may have wanted to work separately from the older generation (as the Young Women's Club members did), engaging themselves in activities that spoke to their Canadian *and* their Ukrainian interests. In doing so, they became isolated from significant power at all levels. Locally and nationally, then, the immigrant-generation men tended to hold most editorial, managerial, and executive-committee positions. Certainly not *all* immigrant-generation men reached such heights – many, in fact, took part in activities similar to those of the women and the younger men, raising funds and attending meetings and performances. That said, as older men, by virtue of their gender and generation, they had access to this power within the AUUC even if they chose not to pursue it.

Cultural Work

Younger men often found it easier to carve out a leadship niche in the field of cultural activism and expression. In fact, this was often at the expense of men of the immigrant generation, especially in the field of drama. The ULFTA's Ukrainian-language drama productions had been wildly popular before the war and had offered many immigrant-generation men (and some women) the opportunity to shine on the stage. After the war few younger members – whom the movement was keen to retain – spoke Ukrainian well enough to participate in or enjoy watching Ukrainian-language plays. Plays also waned in popularity because of the competition in the postwar era from professional theatre companies and other public leisure activities. The odd play continued to be produced, but often these were in English, and overall, theatrical productions never recovered their prewar scale and frequency. The status of immigrant-generation men as cultural participants was further eroded as a result of the emphasis that came to be placed on forms of

Ukrainian cultural expression for which no language skills were necessary. Certainly many of these men remained culturally active, singing in AUUC choirs and other musical ensembles. But in culture generally, it was the younger men – the ones who had been educated both in the Canadian school system *and* on the Ukrainian left – who rose to take the lead; in this regard, their position was enhanced by their understanding of the cultural interests of the immigrant *and* Canadian-born generations. They were able to apply this understanding to cultural activities in the movement, and those who were willing to endure the difficult working conditions and poor pay did much to shape new forms of cultural work and expression in the postwar period.

The importance of Canadian-born men to cultural activities was felt at both the local level and nationally, and some younger men emerged as important cultural leaders. Two of these men were Myron Shatulsky and Eugene Dolny. Both possessed talents they had honed while participating in cultural activities as children and youth growing up in the Ukrainian left. As well, like many other Progressive Ukrainian young men of their generation, they benefited from the opportunity to study abroad in the Soviet Union once travel opened up after the war. After the two finished an AUUC leadership-development course in 1951, the AUUC sent Dolny and Shatulsky to Soviet Ukraine. According to Shatulsky, during his three-year stay he studied 'choral and orchestral conducting and dance.'[21] He then returned to Canada, where he was assigned to Winnipeg. There he 'organized choirs, a school of folk-dancing, and conducted orchestra.'[22] He combined his experiences as a Canadian-born man with his Ukrainian cultural traditions, increasingly shaping cultural activities not only in Ukrainian folk culture but also in mainstream contemporary folk music and traditional music from other national groups. Nationally, these younger men did much to further one of the most significant new forms of cultural expression to emerge in the postwar period for the Ukrainian left: the national festival. In 1961 the two coordinated the cultural component of one of the most important AUUC national celebrations, the Shevchenko Year, held in 1961 to commemorate the centenary of the death of Taras Shevchenko. Across the country that spring, local and provincial celebrations took place, culminating in July in a National Festival of Ukrainian Song, Music, and Dance and a Festival Picnic at the AUUC's Camp Palermo.[23] Dolny served as coordinator and conductor of the main concert; Shatulsky choreographed a 'Canadian Suite.'[24] According to a description of the presentation, the 'original and unique work' featured more than two hundred dancers performing 'fragments from a number of national dances – Ukrainian, Russian, Scottish, Indian, French, Slovak.'[25]

Like the Canadian-born men, women – especially those of the immigrant generation – found their status raised where cultural work was concerned. This was largely because no Ukrainian-language skills were needed to appreciate the forms of cultural expression with which they most obviously engaged – Ukrainian embroidery and handicrafts. As noted earlier, women's preparation of traditional Ukrainian food had long been crucial to the survival of the Ukrainian left. Ukrainian embroidery and other traditional handicrafts now rose in significance, for these were readily associated with the Ukrainian community, accessible to Ukrainian and non-Ukrainian Canadians alike, generally well received, and important for raising much needed money. As an act of diversity in citizenship, the embroidery of women was crucial to creating a positive community image.

Like other forms of cultural and political expression, Ukrainian embroidery had taken on new forms by the Cold War era. In the past, handicrafts been been displayed mainly within the walls of the Labour Temples or other movement-related venues, and exhibits of Ukrainian handiwork had often featured Progressive and Communist symbols. Now, displays at the halls continued but gone were the hammers and sickles. Moreover, as part of the effort to exhibit loyalty to Canada and a commitment to Canadian citizenship, such displays were just as likely to take place in more mainstream venues, with the Ukrainian left using women's handiwork to celebrate events with a broader Canadian purpose. As early as June 1947, for example, Toronto women took part in an Exhibit of Ukrainian Embroidery and Handicrafts held at the Toronto Art Gallery.[26] Such displays were important, especially given the often negative reputation the movement suffered because of Cold War politics and rivalry with other Ukrainian groups. The leadership was well aware of the importance of these women's cultural contributions. As a National Executive Committee memo suggested in 1965, their handicrafts 'not only beautify our exhibitions, but also bring financial help as well as extend our influence among our co-citizens of other nationalities who buy them.'[27] In the postwar era, then, the immigrant-generation women's cultural skills and participation assumed new levels of national importance.

At the local level, embroidery was key to attracting Canadian-born women and girls to the movement and to bringing them together with immigrant-generation women. In many Labour Temples across the country, older women taught younger women and girls how to embroider traditional Ukrainian patterns and designs.[28] By then, fewer young women were fluent in Ukrainian; thus embroidery – for which no language proficiency was required – was one of the more accessible forms of Ukrainian artistic expression. It was also easily adaptable, in that it offered the younger women an outlet for expressing their Canadian *and* Ukrainian identities. 'Ukrainian Cross-stitch Goes Mod' read an October 1969 headline in the English-language paper *Ukrainian Canadian*. According to the article, the Toronto Ukrainian Labour Temple was holding classes in embroidery, and for a fashion show, young women were making clothes that integrated traditional Ukrainian embroidery patterns with contemporary styles.[29] Thanks to its adaptability and accessibility, Ukrainian embroidery was an attractive form of cultural expression for women of all ages; in that way, it helped the movement remain relevant and responsive to younger women's interests.

Besides taking part in embroidery classes, the Canadian-born women contributed to Ukrainian cultural expression by acting as cultural teachers. They had always done such work in the past to a limited degree; now, as jobs outside the movement became both more available and better paying for men, the movement increasingly turned to women to fill these vacated positions after the war. In the early 1950s, for example, women in Regina were holding important positions in the local Labour Temple's cultural groups. Josie Hawenka and her sister Dolly led the dance group there, while Anne Lapchuk directed the choir in the early 1950s.[30] Thus in terms of cultural work, the Ukrainian left was welcoming more women to positions of authority. Their presence, and the cultural contributions of immigrant-generation women and Canadian-born men, were crucial to the movement. Their interest in cultural work eventually pushed the AUUC to emphasize it as a principal form of activism. Indeed, it remains to this day one of the few effective ways through which the AUUC retains its members and supporters.[31]

Political Activism

While their influence lessened when it came to the AUUC's cultural agenda, the older men's interests continued to dominate its political agenda. For them, the CPC remained important, and – as during the interwar period – their complicated and often turbulent relationship with it endured.[32] Because of what many AUUC members had experienced during the war, in terms of rhetoric it seems that the organization maintained a more subdued postwar connection with the Party.[33] Still, members openly supported the CPC and its platform in many ways. For example, they persisted in presenting the Soviet Union in a positive light, despite strong evidence that such praise was sometimes unwarranted. Writing to *Ukrainski zhyttia*, an AUUC Ukrainian-language newspaper, from the Soviet Union in 1947, John Weir described the communist nation's successes, which he attributed to its leader: 'Everywhere we observe intense love for the leader of the Soviet people, Stalin, and at every step we feel the certainty of the fact that it is precisely the party line, Stalin's line, which is achieving these miracles which can be vouched for by everyone who first arrives in the Soviet land. Such a passionate, warm, filial love for one's leader I have seen nowhere on the face of this earth.'[34]

This political agenda drew passionate challenges that intensified as the Cold War heated up. Some of the most vocal and visible Cold War opposition to it came from other organized Ukrainians. The Ukrainian nationalists and their supporters, individually and under the auspices of their political, cultural, and religious organizations – such as the Ukrainian Canadian Committee (UCC), the Ukrainian National Federation (UNF), and various churches – continued to condemn leaders like Weir and Korol (and the AUUC generally) for their positive characterization of communism in the Soviet Union. Some of the most vehement critics emerged from the postwar wave of Ukrainian immigrants, the displaced persons (DPs), who had experienced the Soviet experiment first-hand. Fuelling their ire was the fact that many AUUC leaders had actively opposed their admittance to Canada, arguing in some instances that, as a mainly educated and professional class, they had a responsibility to remain in Soviet Ukraine to help rebuild it after the war. At a meeting at the Toronto Ukrainian Labour Temple in December 1949, John Naviziwsky warned the audience 'against listening to Displaced Persons who condemned the Ukrainian government.' So noted an RCMP informant, who added: 'He said that even if they were relatives, even so they should receive no help at all from any member of the AUUC.'[35] The AUUC leaders were especially vigorous in their condemnation of the eight thousand Ukrainian men captured in Italy in Nazi uniform serving in the Ukrainian SS Division Halychyna, whose applications for admission to Canada immigration agents had consistently refused. In press releases, newspaper articles, speeches, and letters to the federal government, Matthew Shatulsky, Naviziwsky, William Teresio, and others called these men fascists, war criminals, and voluntary collaborators. The UCC campaigned on the soldiers' behalf, arguing, as Donald Avery explains, that this group had only fought with the Germans to liberate Western Ukraine from Russian communism. As a result of this pressure, by 1950 the immigration policy had changed, and officials began granting these men admission to Canada.[36]

This war of words translated into physical confrontation and violence on many occasions. Typical were the circumstances Peter Krawchuk encountered as he toured Canada in 1948 reporting on his recent trip to the Soviet Union. On 10 October, at an unnamed town hall somewhere in Saskatchewan, Krawchuk addressed a crowd 'which consisted of a few Displaced Persons, recent arrivals from Europe, and district residents.' According to an RCMP informant present at the event, the DPs heckled and challenged Krawchuk's praise of the Soviet Union, suggesting he 'was painting the wrong picture of the whole situation ... and that conditions are not as [Krawchuk described them].' The situation escalated and a fight broke out among audience members. Among other acts of violence, the informant observed, 'one woman slapped another man's face.' The gathering broke up when 'one Displaced Person [having] no handy weapon at his disposal, took off one of his shoes and threw it at [Krawchuk].' Shortly afterwards, Krawchuk and his supporters retired to a nearby farm to finish the meeting. Krawchuk had met with similar opposition earlier that month at a gathering at the Winnipeg Ukrainian Labour Temple. 'The meeting was turned into a riot,' an RCMP informant reported, 'when some of the attending displaced persons raised objections to the manner Kravchuk [sic] answered their pertinent questions.' The trend continued into December, when Krawchuk spoke at a gathering in Timmins, Ontario. *Ukrainske zhyttia* reported a 'bloody clash ... resulting in the injuries of several persons,' including Stanley Kremyr and Nick Hubaly, both prominent local AUUC leaders.[37]

The Ukrainian left and its members and supporters were also targets of various levels of the Cold War state. In the 1950s, when she was liv-ing in St Catharines and working as a cultural teacher at the AUUC hall, Canadian-born Olga Shatulsky found herself summoned to the local post office. 'I liked to read *Soviet Literature Magazine* and *Soviet Woman* because I liked the articles and used them in my teaching [at the hall],' she explained. 'When I got to the post office, the postal worker started to question me about why I subscribed and asked if I was sure I wanted them.'[38] On behalf of the Timmins AUUC branches, Nick Hubaly attempted to rent the local high school auditorium to hold a Golden Jubilee Summer Festival in 1962. School trustee Joe Behie at-tacked him and the group in the local press. Behie dismissed the AUUC as 'a Communist organization ... to hell with that sort of thing.' Call-ing Hubaly 'one of the top Commies in town,' Behie insisted that the board not rent the hall to the AUUC.[39] In Quebec, Maurice Duplessis's Padlock Law, introduced in 1937, created an especially dire situation. The statute allowed authorities to padlock any building where com-munist activities were believed to have been taking place and to con-fiscate any related materials. Police raided the Montreal-area hall searching raffle tickets, books, and other materials in an effort to link the AUUC to the LPP. In the end, the hall stayed open; however, these items were confiscated and local members could not afford to pursue their return through the courts. Many were afraid to go to the Labour Temple themselves or to send their children to its activities. The Supreme Court of Canada struck down the Padlock Law in 1957, but by then the damage had been done. By 1966, the Montreal branch was all but dead and the hall was physically falling apart. 'We have no place to hold meetings,' a Montreal member reported to the AUUC National Convention that year, 'and as a result of this are unable to carry out any organizational work.'[40]

The federal government was especially active, using the RCMP to watch the Ukrainian left for evidence of subversion. The Mounties clipped and translated newspaper articles, paid informants to report on AUUC meetings, classes, and concerts, maintained detailed dossiers, and confronted individual members about their activities. Though they were unaware of the extent of this surveillance, many of those associated with the AUUC knew they were being watched. Some had noticed officers following them; some had been stopped on the street by Mounties, who even visited homes to question AUUC members and their families. Those who were being spied on applied a number of strategies to deal with this RCMP red baiting. In this vein, Gary Kinsmen has demonstrated how members of Ottawa's gay and lesbian community employed individual and collective responses to Cold War RCMP surveillance – for example, they were cautious about revealing their own or other people's identities to the police. They also used 'humour and camp' when an officer confronted them directly or was present in their social spaces[41] – a method favoured in certain circumstances by some AUUC members. Surveillance vehicles were often sighted outside Labour Temples. During an AUUC convention at the hall in Toronto in the 1960s, Nykolyshyn noticed one across the street: 'I went over to their car and invited them into the hall for a coffee … The agents got very angry and left.' Within half an hour, two new agents in another car had taken their place.[42]

Over the course of the Cold War, the AUUC leaders and their pro-communist activities faced challenges from other quarters (and circumstances) as well. Some of the most damaging came from within the left itself. Stalin's death in March 1953 shifted the political climate in the Soviet Union. Ukrainian leftists were shocked, and many leaders discredited, when Khrushchev at the Twentieth All-Union Congress in February 1956 confirmed the long-suspected atrocities carried out under Stalin, which the leadership of the CPC and ULFTA had in earlier decades downplayed or denied. Then came the violent suppression of the Hungarian Revolution in 1956, Khrushchev's fall from power in 1964, and the invasion of Czechoslovakia in 1968. These events cast the Cold War Soviet Union in a negative light and caused many supporters – Ukrainian or not – to turn away from domestic communist organizations in the West. The response among AUUC members of the Party was mixed, often falling along generational lines. Most younger members voted against the Party with their feet. When Khrushchev was deposed, Nykolyshyn left the Party for more than a decade. Betsey Bilecki was among the many who left the Party over Czechoslovakia. Others, like Myron Shatulsky, lingered but eventually departed (in 1970) because of the way the Party was run in Canada. Shatulsky cited the anti-Semitism he had witnessed among the Ukrainian leaders in the Winnipeg Maple

Leaf Club as the final straw for him. Nykolyshyn, who had rejoined the Party in 1977 when he was hired to work for the WBA, left it again in 1990, frustrated by what he characterized as a lack of respect on the part of the Anglo-Celtic Party leadership towards the Ukrainian leaders. The immigrant generation and many of the older Canadian-born men – especially those with leadership positions in the Party and/or the AUUC – remained more consistently loyal to the Party than other Canadian-born supporters from the AUUC and Party members of other ethnicities. In the wake of so many mass resignations, these Ukrainians found that their proportion and influence increased in Party circles.[43]

They remained loyal, but this is not to suggest that these Ukrainian male leaders lent unquestioning support to the CPC, the Soviet Union, and Soviet Ukraine. As they had in the interwar period, they were especially willing to reject or challenge Party policy and perspectives where issues of Ukrainian culture and language were concerned. The most serious shake-up between the AUUC leaders and the CPC came in 1967 over the issue of Russification in Soviet Ukraine. After the war, charges made by DPs, concerns brought back by tourists (many of whom had associations with the AUUC) who had visited Soviet Ukraine, and accusations made by former CPC and AUUC member John Kolasky brought to the surface the Russification controversy. Many of the male leaders of the Ukrainian Left mounted pressure on the Party, and in 1967 the Party convened a delegation made up of AUUC leaders and Party officials to investigate. After a three-week tour of Soviet Ukraine, the men returned and submitted an explosive report. There were many problems with Russian being the official language in Ukraine, they asserted. They felt that while there had been some improvements over the previous years, there was still much work to do to ensure the presence and use of Ukrainian in Ukraine. Implying that the Ukrainian language had been marginalized, they insisted that 'the Ukrainian language has to be encouraged, promoted, and developed in all areas of life in Ukraine. It is not to be forced upon the people, whether of Ukrainian, Russian, or other origins, but the climate has to be created for its freest flourishing and interdevelopment with other languages and cultures.'[44] Despite strong arm-twisting by both the CPC and the Communist Party of the Soviet Union, both of which were extremely displeased with the report, the Ukrainian leaders refused to back down or retract their findings.

Few women ever joined the CPC, and those who did were more likely to be drawn from the Canadian born. For example, Mary Prokop got her start as a teenager working on Party election campaigns in Alberta during the Great Depression.[45] When it came to traditional models of political activism, Canadian-born and the immigrant-generation AUUC women tended strongly to embrace the peace and feminist movements (with the former often strongly linked to the Party). The AUUC officially supported the peace movement, but women were the most engaged members by far. Often the Canadian-born women coordinated these efforts – their language skills enabled them to liaise more easily between the Ukrainian-speaking immigrant-generation women and mainstream activism organizations. The AUUC was affiliated with the Canadian Peace Congress, an organization founded in 1948 and headed by James Endicott. It conducted its work in a vein that endorsed the Soviet Union – a view that the Ukrainian left could easily support. Like the AUUC, its opponents attempted to discredit its efforts by labelling it a communist front organization.[46] During the 1950s the AUUC supported the congress's petition to ban the bomb. The AUUC women carried out most of the resulting work, canvassing door to door for signatures. This was not always easy. In Timmins, for example, the immigrant-generation women found 'that it was very difficult for them to explain what was going on and what the petition was about because they did not speak English well.'[47] Notwithstanding such problems, the national campaign succeeded. The Vancouver Women's Branch, for example, succeeded in gathering 1,450 signatures.[48]

A casualty of the Cold War and red baiting, the Canadian Peace Congress declined in the early 1950s.[49] This did not mark the end of these women's peace activism, however. They actively pursued peace in a variety of ways. In 1955, for example, *Ukrainske zhyttia* reported that members of the Edmonton Women's Branch were 'taking an active part in a campaign against the rearming of West Germany [by] collecting signatures to cards and petitions, and circulating leaflets, against "remilitarization," thus to "influence the government not to vote for the ratification of the London and Paris agreements."'[50] As the threat of nuclear war intensified in the 1960s, underscored by events like the Cuban Missile Crisis (1962) and the Vietnam War (1954–75), so too did women's peace work intensify within the AUUC. They knitted and sewed for Vietnamese women and children, and they raised money to aid people in other war-torn areas.[51] Often, like other women, they framed their activism through their roles as mothers. Leader Hannah Polowy emphasized this in a 1963 report to the AUUC Women's Conference in British Columbia: 'If we are to guarantee life to our children, then we as women and mothers must exert every ounce of energy and support to the peace movement in Canada which is demanding that we not become a nuclear power.'[52]

As with so many other postwar feminists, the AUUC women's interest in feminism often developed from or overlapped with their work in the peace movement. Increasingly, it drew their energies outside the AUUC. For example, they were active in the Congress of Canadian Women (CCW), which had been formed on International Women's Day, 8 March 1950, as an umbrella group to encompass women's groups affiliated with or sympathetic to the LPP. As AUUC member Mary Kardash explained in 1952, the CCW at its founding 'adopted a program of working and fighting for women's rights and the well-being of our children. As a section of the Women's International Democratic Federation (WIDF), it also has as its aim the mobilization of women for the cause of peace.'[53] Throughout the 1950s and beyond, AUUC women participated in local chapters of the CCW and joined CCW international delegations meant to foster peace and international understanding. Katherine Stefanitsky of the Toronto AUUC Women's Branch, for example, was a member of the CCW's five-member delegation to China during the 1950s.[54]

From this activism, a unique brand of feminism emerged influenced by these women's class and gender positions, one that reflected the AUUC's working-class political legacy. In 1965, for example, the women collected some three thousand signatures on a petition calling on the government to lower to sixty women's qualifying age for Old Age Security.[55] The AUUC, represented by four of its leading female members, was also among those groups in 1968 that presented a brief to the Royal Commission on the Status of Women in Canada. Improved working conditions and educational opportunities – issues that touched the lives of most leftist Ukrainian women – were central to the construction of their socialist feminist analysis of Canadian society. In their brief they complained that women were being socialized into secondary roles from a young age and were being pushed into educational opportunities that funnelled them towards homemaking occupations. Fur-

thermore, they argued, because the cost of higher education was pro-
hibitive for many families, boys, who were perceived as future bread-
winners, were often chosen over girls in a family to attend university.
The AUUC brief called for guarantees for higher education for girls. It
went on to analyse women's experiences as workers, arguing that day-
care should be available for children of all women. They also advocated for equal pay for work of equal value and declared that maternity
leave should be available to all women. Moreover, they asserted, birth
control and abortion should be readily accessible and paid for by Medi-
care. Whether to have children and when, they argued, should be a
woman's choice and no one else's. The brief concluded by advocating
for income tax deductions for child care and household help, and continued to press for Old Age Security for women at age sixty.[56]

Despite their keen interest in feminism and peace work, most women
found that these causes remained peripheral to the AUUC's male-defined political agenda. This was especially evident where women's
rights were concerned. Winnipeg Young Women's Club members Beth
Krall and Mary Kardash often attended women's conferences and related events as AUUC representatives. Back at the hall, Krall found the
cause marginalized: 'Women's issues weren't the main concern of the
Ukrainian Labour Temple. Nobody cared that Mary and I went to
women's meetings.'[57] Consequently, many women, especially the
Canadian born, shifted their energies outside the AUUC. So did many
of the politically active Canadian-born men. As they increasingly came
to identify more with the Canadian side of their ethnocultural heritage,
they found that the New Left, rather than the old Ukrainian left, held
more appeal. It was the New Left that offered a venue for leadership
opportunities and a chance for them to shape more actively their own
activism.

Outside the Party and the peace and feminist movements, many immigrant-generation women and men united around causes that reflected
their (sometimes negative) shared experiences as radical immigrants. In
the 1960s, for example, these older AUUC members lobbied with other
leftist immigrants to challenge the red baiting they faced when applying for Canadian citizenship under the 1946 Canadian Citizenship
Act.[58] A good number had found their earlier naturalization applications denied because of their connections with the ULFTA – a trend
that continued under the new act. It took very little to be blacklisted. To

read ULFTA/AUUC newspapers, to give money to ULFTA/AUUC-supported causes, to attend events at a Labour Temple, or to take part in worker demonstrations was often sufficient to warrant denial. By 1961 the AUUC had helped organize a national campaign to fight this political discrimination, a campaign coordinated by the interethnic Canadian Slav Committee (an organization founded and headed by several key AUUC members).[59] Their efforts highlighted the profound and dire financial and personal consequences faced by those denied citizenship. Barbara Mashtalar, for example, welcomed the campaign after her application had been rejected numerous times. This rejection had prevented her from visiting her dying mother in Ukraine whom she had not seen since she herself left Galicia many years before. Devastated, Mashtalar told the AUUC's *Ukrainian Canadian* newspaper: 'I cried with the pain of knowing that Canada had prevented me from seeing my mother once again before she died ... I had given many hard years of labor to Canada. I had never once committed a criminal act and never harmed anyone consciously. Why does Canada treat me like a cruel stepmother?'[60] It is not known whether Mashtalar's subsequent applications were successful, but accounts of the campaign suggest that it 'gained citizenship for hundreds of immigrants who had been this status for many decades.'[61]

Decline of the Ukrainian Left

By the time the citizenship campaign was in full swing in the 1960s, the AUUC was noticeably in decline. Besides those factors already outlined, a host of others were drawing the Canadian born away from the organizations of the Ukrainian left. Their (and in some cases their parents') move to the cities in search of work and other opportunities had decimated many of the rural halls. In the cities, many women found themselves needing to balance marriage with motherhood (with baby-boom numbers of children) and with paid work outside the home (often outside the movement). Thus they were too busy to be active in the AUUC. At the same time, Canadian-born men were finding more lucrative job opportunities outside the organization, in positions that paid better and that offered benefits and promotions. The impact of red baiting on both membership numbers and the level of involvement by the Canadian born cannot be overemphasized. In 1966 an Alberta father wrote to the AUUC National Executive Committee about his daughter, a former Youth Section member, in response to a survey of Canadian-born members they had sent her. After completing Grade Twelve she had moved to Edmonton to take a Medical Filing course, and her studies allowed her no time for AUUC activities. More than that, he explained, she worried that continued membership might negatively affect her job prospects. She had reason to be nervous: her brother Donald, the father asserted, 'went through a lot' because of his AUUC ties.[62]

With the better wages they often earned, many Canadian-born women and men bought cars and suburban homes, moving away from the working-class neighbourhoods surrounding the Labour Temples. More and more of them were spending their disposable income on leisure activities at venues other than the Labour Temple, or they were simply staying at home to watch TV. Some still sent their children to Ukrainian school, dance lessons, and Junior or Youth Section activities. Organizers at some halls attempted to increase adult membership numbers through these children's activities – unsuccessfully, as it turned out. For example, in 1960 the Edmonton Young Women's Club courted the Junior Section members' mothers. 'We have been talking individually with some of the Mothers,' organizer Hazel Strashok wrote to the AUUC National Executive Committee, 'but soon we will hold a tea or some other affair inviting all our members and prospective members, and then maybe we will be able to have some of them join our club.'[63]

Among the immigrant generation the factors contributing to the movement's decline were somewhat different. Mainly, the movement was unable to attract new members from the postwar wave of Ukrainian-speaking immigrants, who weren't interested in buttressing the communism they had fled. Besides, the AUUC membership base was aging. After the war the numbers of new members of the Women's and Men's Branches were never high enough to ensure sustained growth. As the original members aged, declined in health, and passed away, the immigrant-generation branches rapidly diminished in size.[64] Some of these branches attempted to stave off the problem through mergers, often forming Senior Citizens' Clubs. It is noteworthy that many Women's Branch members, concerned about the possibility of male dominance, resisted such mergers as long as possible. In any case, this battle could not be won. By the 1970s, RCMP surveillance officers were characterizing the AUUC as 'primarily ... made up of old timers.'[65] By 1975 the AUUC's total membership – including adults and youth – was a mere 1,995.[66] As the immigrant-generation members and their supporters aged and died, and the Canadian born turned elsewhere for political, social, cultural, and economic engagement, the Ukrainian left dwindled in both numbers and influence.

There exists today in the AUUC an active and extremely dedicated core of Canadian-born members, who still run Ukrainian folk dance classes, hold special events to commemorate Ukrainian holidays, and engage in political activism. Halls remain in larger centres – in Winnipeg, Edmonton, Calgary, Regina, and Toronto, to name a few. However, many AUUC branches have downsized from their original Labour Temples to smaller facilities. The AUUC continues to publish a bilingual (Ukrainian and English) newspaper, *Ukrainian Canadian Herald,* the product of a 1991 merger of the two postwar papers, *Ukrainian Canadian* and *Zhittia i slovo* (*Life and Word* – itself the product of a merger of two papers: *Ukrainske zhyttia* and *Ukrainske slovo* [*Ukrainian Life* and *Ukrainian Word*]). Both had been suffering from falling circulation and rising publication costs. Yet support for the AUUC, though tenacious, continues to decline; new members are difficult to attract, and the remaining postwar Canadian-born supporters are growing older and passing away.

Conclusion

The Ukrainian left's postwar history was marked by deeply gendered intergenerational divisions that shaped identity and thereby often promoted conflict and disunity (sometimes subtle, sometimes overt) among the movement's supporters. Always apparent was a gendered discourse that privileged and valued the immigrant-generation men's priorities as activists. After the war, this discourse effectively marginalized immigrant-generation women's contributions and perspectives, with serious consequences for how Canadian-born women and men engaged with the Ukrainian left. Comparing and contrasting the women and men of the two generations is a valuable approach by which to understand the challenges the Ukrainian left faced after the Second World War.

During this period, men's roles in the movement could be characterized by both continuity and change, though as we have seen, this was not experienced evenly across the board. During the interwar years an individual man's experience depended greatly on whether he was a leader or an ordinary member or supporter. After the war, generation usurped class as the principal determinant of male opportunity and activity. The degree to which an individual man encountered change and continuity thus depended largely on the generation to which he belonged. Older men of the immigrant generation who had come of age during the interwar years resisted change and continued to hold most of the power in the Ukrainian left, just as they had before the war. As a consequence, younger men often found such power inaccessible, and their leadership opportunities limited, and found themselves marginalized as a result. In some parts of the movement, Canadian-born men remained active and carved out a niche for themselves. Most younger men, however, found themselves excluded. Thus many turned away from the AUUC, seeking jobs and political outlets through other means. In this way a stark generational divide developed between the immigrant and Canadian-born generations of men. While other factors contributed to this pattern, and to the decline of the Ukrainian left, it was this sharp generational division that did the most to shape experiences and opportunities as well as the overall form the movement would assume after the Second World War.

Women's experiences, too, possessed elements of continuity and change. Immigrant-generation women maintained the cultural and political activism they had developed in the interwar era. Culturally speaking, however, they gained influence as traditional Ukrainian cooking and embroidery gained status as activities, both in the movement and later in Canadian society. Even so, their opportunities were limited, just as in the past, for their male counterparts continued to control the movement. Increasingly, these women looked for leadership not to their men but to their Canadian-born counterparts. Unlike the men of their generation, some Canadian-born women were advantaged in the movement, though often this advantage came because of the gendered discourse that existed in the movement – a discourse that privileged immigrant-generation men over all other members and supporters. Even while their male counterparts found themselves unable to access power, Canadian-born women were able to move into new positions, largely because they were willing (at least initially) to put up with the wages and power inequities that the men of their generation rejected.

Eventually, though, this generated strong dissatisfaction among the Canadian-born women, leading many to challenge the movement's attitudes towards gender roles, often by taking their talents and activism elsewhere.

Gender, generation, ethnicity, and class in this way contoured the postwar Ukrainian left along with its adult members and supporters, thereby defining power and opportunity. Older members (especially the male leaders) sought to engage the younger generation, but their reluctance to relinquish power and authority and to address significant generational and gender-related issues ultimately rendered ineffective their efforts to attract and retain younger Ukrainian Canadians. There were better economic conditions and stronger opportunities for activism in other areas of Canadian society, so Canadian-born women and men moved on. The movement's failure to address this gendered generation gap in a meaningful way, combined with the historical context of Cold War Canada, the international communist situation, postwar upward mobility, and assimilation, hastened the Ukrainian left's decline.

Notes

1 Zenovy Nykolyshyn, interviewed by Rhonda L. Hinther [hereafter RLH], August 1998.

2 Nykolyshyn interview.

3 Children and youth, because of the Cold War context, assimilation, and the influence of North American popular and youth culture, also had distinct experiences as members or children of members of the AUUC and its associated organizations. For additional commentary on AUUC children's and youth's activities and experiences and the difficulties associated with being a 'Red' during the Cold War in Canada, consult my doctoral thesis, '"Sincerest Revolutionary Greetings": Progressive Ukrainians in Twentieth-Century Canada,' McMaster University, 2005.

4 Some key monographs include Reg Whitaker and Steve Hewitt, *Canada and the Cold War* (Toronto: Lorimer, 2003); Steve Hewitt, *Spying 101: The RCMP's Secret Activities at Canadian Universities, 1917–1997* (Toronto: University of Toronto Press, 2002); and Franca Iacovetta, *Gatekeepers: Reshaping Immigrant Lives in Cold War Canada* (Toronto: Between the Lines, 2006). Iacovetta's detailed examination of the activities of 'gatekeeper' Vladimir Kaye stands as one of the best examples of postwar Ukrainian-Canadian history to date. Two notable collections of articles featuring the work of some of the best Cold War scholars are

Richard Cavell, ed., *Love, Hate, and Fear in Canada's Cold War* (Toronto: University of Toronto Press, 2004); and Dieter K. Buse, Mercedes Steedman, and Gary William Kinsman, *Whose National Security? Canadian State Surveillance and the Creation of Enemies* (Toronto: Between the Lines, 2000).

5 The Communist question is evident in Jaroslav Petryshyn, *Peasants in the Promised Land: Canada and the Ukrainians, 1891–1914* (Toronto: Lorimer, 1985); John Kolasky, *The Shattered Illusion: The History of Ukrainian Pro-Communist Organizations in Canada* (Toronto: PMA, 1979); idem, *Prophets and Proletarians: Documents on the History of the Rise and Decline of Ukrainian Communism in Canada* (Edmonton: Canadian Institute of Ukrainian Studies, 1990); Marco Carynnyk, 'Swallowing Stalinism: Pro-Communist Ukrainian Canadians and Soviet Ukraine in the 1930s,' in *Canada's Ukrainians: Negotiating an Identity*, ed. Lubomyr Luciuk and Stella Hruniuk (Toronto: University of Toronto Press, 1991), 187–205; Orest Martynowych, *The Ukrainians in Canada: The Formative Years, 1891–1924* (Edmonton: CIUS, 1991); Donald Avery, 'Divided Loyalties: The Ukrainian Left and the Canadian State,' in Canada's Ukrainians, ed. Luciuk et al. 271–87; and Paul Yuzuk, 'The Ukrainian Communist Delusion,' in *The Ukrainians in Manitoba: A Social History* (Toronto: University of Toronto Press, 1953), 96–112.

6 Frances Swyripa, *Wedded to the Cause: Ukrainian-Canadian Women and Ethnic Identity, 1891-1991* (Toronto: University of Toronto Press, 1993).

7 Ruth Frager, *Sweatshop Strife: Class, Ethnicity, and Gender in the Jewish Labour Movement of Toronto, 1900–1939* (Toronto: University of Toronto Press, 1992), 216.

8 Marlene Epp, Franca Iacovetta, and Frances Swirypa, eds., *Sisters Or Strangers? Immigrant, Ethnic, and Racialized Women in Canadian History* (Toronto: University of Toronto Press, 2004).

9 For some examples, see Carmela Patrias, *Patriots and Proletarians: Politicizing Hungarian Immigrants in Interwar Canada* (Montreal and Kingston: McGill-Queen's University Press, 1994); and idem, 'Relief Strike: Immigrant Workers and the Great Depression in Crowland, Ontario, 1930–35,' in *A Nation of Immigrants: Women, Workers, and Communities in Canadian History*, ed. Franca Iacovetta, Paula Draper, and Robert Ventressa (Toronto: University of Toronto Press, 1998), 322–58. See also Paul C. Mishler, *Raising Reds: The Young Pioneers, Radical Summer Camps, and Communist Political Culture in the United States* (New York: Columbia University Press, 1999); Ester Reiter, 'Secular "Yiddishkait": Left Culture, Politics, and Community,' *Labour/ Le travail* 49 (2002): 121–46; and idem, 'Camp Navelt and the Daughters of the Jewish Left,' in *Sister or Strangers?* ed. Epp, Iacovetta, and Swirypa.

10 For more information on the ULFTA's general history, see Peter
    Krawchuk, *Our History: The Ukrainian Labour-Farmer Movement in
    Canada, 1907–1991* (Toronto: Lugus, 1996); and my doctoral thesis,
    '"Sincerest Revolutionary Greetings."'
11 LAC, RG146, vol. 3793, AUUC: Winnipeg, Manitoba, pt 13, report
    dated 26 December 1944 re [UCA] Meeting held at Winnipeg, 21 De-
    cember 1944.
12 For a more detailed description of women's experiences with the
    ULFTA, see Joan Sangster, '*Robitnytsia*, Ukrainian Communists, and the
    "Porcupinism" Debate: Reassessing Ethnicity, Gender, and Class in
    Early Canadian Communism, 1922–1930,' *Labour/Le travail* 56 (Fall
    2005): 51–89; my doctoral thesis, '"Sincerest Revolutionary Greetings"';
    and my article '"They Said the Course Would Be Wasted on Me because
    I Was a Girl": Mothers, Daughters, and Shifting Forms of Female Ac-
    tivism in the Ukrainian Left in Twentieth-Century Canada,' *Atlantis* 32,
    no. 1 (2007): 100–10.
13 'Alberta School Principal Heads Ukrainian Canadians,' *Winnipeg Free
    Press*, 1 January 1946; and LAC, RG146, vol. 4677, Matthew Shatulsky,
    file pt 2, report dated 15 February 1946 re Ukrainian-Canadian Associa-
    tion – National Convention – Winnipeg, Man., January 11th to 16th,
    1945.
14 Annual Membership Meeting of English-Speaking Branch, 11 February
    1962, and Executive Meeting, 13 February 1962, in AUUC English-
    Speaking Branch [Winnipeg] Minutes, circa 1960s, WBA Archives, Win-
    nipeg.
15 Ibid.
16 LAC, MG28, vol. 154, file 3, AUUC Fonds, Club 326 Calendar of Activ-
    ities for 1968.
17 Executive Meeting, 30 November 1947, minutes, 1947–8, English-
    Speaking Branch 324, Winnipeg, found at WBA; 'AUUC Doings by
    Rose Mickoluk,' *UC*, 15 December 1953. For examples of activities, see
    letters from Mrs Victoria Kassian and Emma Shewchuk in LAC, MG28,
    vol. 154, file 7, AUUC fonds, AUUC – English-Speaking Branches, Ed-
    monton, 1956; LAC, MG28, vol. 154, AUUC fonds, container 2, report
    from delegate from Winnipeg English-Speaking Branch in file 20,
    AUUC – 8th National Convention [1958]; LAC, MG28, vol. 154, file 4,
    AUUC fonds, Conventions; letter from Hazel Strashok, Young Women's
    Club, Edmonton, in Correspondence: AUUC – English-Speaking
    Branches, 1961–2.
18 See, for example, LAC, RG146, vol. 128, records of CSIS, report re Os-
    hawa, Ontario, in *Ukainske Zhyttia*, 17 December 1958, AUUC Oshawa.
19 LAC, RG146, vol. 3818, pt 1, in records of CSIS, AUUC – Women's
    Branch, Calgary, Alta., 'On Organizational Activity of the Women's

Branch of the AUUC in Calgary in 1954,' in *Ukrainske Slovo,* 16 February 1955, translated by RCMP; *UC*, December 1971.

20 Mary Skrypnyk, 'Highlights of the Convention,' *UC*, 1 March 1948.

21 Myron Shatulsky, interviewed by RLH, 1998.

22 Ibid.

23 Peter Krawchuk, *Our Stage: The Amateur Performing Arts of the Ukrainian Settlers in Canada* (Toronto: Kobzar, 1984), 278.

24 Ibid., 280.

25 Steve Macievich as quoted in ibid., 280.

26 Mary Prokopchak in *Reminiscences of Courage and Hope: Stories of Ukrainian-Canadian Women Pioneers*, ed. Petro Kravchuk (Toronto: Kobzar, 1991), 468–82. See also Mike Mokry, 'Manitoba AUUC Plans Geared to Centennial,' *UC*, 1 April 1967; and LAC, MG28, vol. 154, AUUC fonds, letter dated 2 December 1965 from Mary Prokop, Secretary of National Women's Committee, and Minutes of National Women's Committee Meeting, 12 June 1967, 'AUUC – National Women's Committee, 1963–9.'

27 NAC, RG146, vol. 128, records of CSIS, memo from National Executive Committee to Women's Branch and Clubs dated 19 October 1965, translated by RCMP.

28 See, for example, LAC, RG146, vol. 3818, pt 3, records of CSIS, 'AUUC – Women's Branch, Calgary, Alta,' 2 March 1970, translated by RCMP.

29 'Ukrainian Cross-Stitch Goes Mod,' *UC,* October 1969.

30 LAC, MG28, vol. 154, AUUC fonds; vol. 12, file 28, letter from Regina English-Speaking Branch dated 8 February 1951, 'AUUC – English-Speaking Branches, 1951.' See also Mary Skrypnyk, 'Windsor Festival – a Triumph,' *UC*, 1 April 1961.

31 For some examples of the ways some branches and their members responded to non-cultural work, see LAC, MG28, vol. 11, file 24, AUUC fonds, letter from Vancouver Women's Branch dated 1 December 1956, 'Branches,' translated by Myron Momyruk; see also letter from Timmins Women's Branch dated 12 September 1954, translated by Myron Momyruk.

32 For more information on the Ukrainian left's complicated relationship with the party, see the pieces by Jim Mochoruk and Andrij Makuch in this volume, as well as '"Sincerest Revolutionary Greetings."'

33 See for example, John Weir, 'About the AUUC: What are our Politics?' *UC*, 1 November 1948.

34 LAC, RG146, vol. 4677, pt 4, records of CSIS, Matthew Shatulsky, *UZ*, 20 March 1947.

35 LAC, RG146, vol. 'John Navis,' records of CSIS, report re AUUC,

GENERATION GAP: CANADA'S POSTWAR UKRAINIAN LEFT 51

Toronto, Ontario dated 20-12-49, meeting held at 300 Bathurst, Sunday 11 December, 'John Navis.'

36 LAC, RG146, vol. 4678, pt 5(2), records of CSIS, *UC*, 15-12-48: 'Inner Politics of the DP's' by Matthew Shatulsky; LAC, MG28, vol. 154, file 26, AUUC fonds, 'Correspondence – Individuals' in Teresio, William, 1948–9, press release, 4 May 1949, from Teresio, president, and Prokop, secretary, to Prime Minister Louis St Laurent;; Donald Avery, *Reluctant Host: Canada's Response to Immigrant Workers, 1896–1994* (Toronto: McClelland and Stewart, 1995), 157., 157.

37 LAC, RG28, vol. 3742, pt 4 [AH-2000/00233], report re Association of United Ukrainian Canadians, Saskatchewan, 28 October 1948, in RCMP Files: AUUC: Saskatchewan, Correspondence; LAC, RG146, vol. 4678, pt 5(3), records of CSIS, 'Matthew Shatulsky,' *US*, 26 October 1949, 'Concerning the Visit of Peter Kravchuk in Winnipeg,'; LAC, RG146, vol. 'John Navis,' records of CSIS, 'Put an End to Gangsterism of DP's: Canada Is Not Hitlerite Germany,' in 'John Navis.'

38 Interview with Olga Shatulsky.

39 Joe Behie quoted in 'Timmins AUUC Battles for a Concert Hall,' *UC*, 15 April 1962. See also the experiences of Mitch Sago, who was attacked while on tour in Vancouver, *UC*, 15 February 1962.

40 LAC, MG28, vol. 154, file 29, AUUC fonds, 'National Executive Committee – Circulars and Newsletters,' Letter to the Editor (no newspaper listed), 1949; interview with Z. Nykolyshyn; LAC, RG150, vol. 128, records of CSIS, '2nd Session on 21 March 1966,' in RCMP report re AUUC, 12th National Convention, 1966.

41 Gary Kinsmen, 'The Canadian Cold War on Queers,' in *Love, Hate, and Fear in Canada's Cold War* (Toronto: University of Toronto Press, 2004), 121.

42 Interview with Nykolyshyn.

43 Ivan Avakumovic, *The Communist Party in Canada: A History* (Toronto: McClelland and Stewart, 1975); LAC, RG146, vol. 3792, pt 4, records of CSIS, 'AUUC: Saskatchewan, Correspondence'; vol. 4678, report re Association of United Ukrainian Canadians, Saskatchewan, 28 October 1948, 'Concerning the Visit of Peter Kravchuk in Winnipeg'; 'Matthew Shatulsky,' pt 5(3); interviews with Bilecki, Shatulsky, and Nykolyshyn. For a detailed discussion of Party relations during this period, see Kolasky, *The Shattered Illusion*, 140–54.

44 'Report of the Delegation to Ukraine: Central Committee Meeting –16, 17, and 18 September 1967, in *Viewpoint* (Discussion Bulletin issued by the Central Executive Committee, Communist Party of Canada), January 1968.

45 Mary Prokopchak, in *Reminiscences of Courage and Hope: Stories of Ukrainian Women Pioneers,* ed. Peter Krawchuk (Toronto: Kobzar, 1991), 468–82.

46 For an extensive discussion of the policies of the Canadian Peace Congress and the views and work of Endicott, see Victor Huard, 'The Canadian Peace Congress and the Challenge to Postwar Consensus, 1948–53,' *Peace and Change* 19, no. 1 (1994): 25-49.

47 LAC, MG28, vol. 154, AUUC fonds, letter from Timmins Women's Branch dated 24 May 1955, to National Women's Committee, AUUC, translated by Myron Momyruk, in 'Branches,' vol. 11: 'Correspondence - Women's Branches.'

48 LAC, MG28, vol. 154, file 24, AUUC fonds, letter from Vancouver Women's Branch dated 18 May 1955 to National Women's Committee, AUUC, translated by Myron Momyruk.

49 Huard, 'The Canadian Peace Congress,' 46.

50 *UZ*, 20 January 1955, RCMP translation, in LAC, RG146, vol. 3814, records of CSIS, 'AUUC Women's Branch, Edmonton, Alta. corresp. to 11.6.58 incl.' For an additional example, see letter from Young Women's Club dated 8 March 1959 to Duff Roblin and Mayor of Winnipeg in envelope labelled 'AUUC Women's Committee, Handicraft Display and Baking Sale,' in envelopes labelled 'Provcom Women's Committee' at WBA, Winnipeg.

51 Mary Prokop, in LAC, MG28, vol. 154, file 29, AUUC fonds, container 2, Introduction and Discussion of Resolution on Work in the Women's Field, in AUUC – 13th National Convention, 1968; see also letter from Beth Krall and Mary Kardash, Provincial Women's Committee, Manitoba, dated 18 December 1968 to National Women's Committee, AUUC, Toronto, in envelope marked 'Correspondence: Provincial Women's Committee, AUUC, 1969-70' in collection of envelopes marked 'Provcom Women's Committee' found at WBA, Winnipeg.

52 Hannah Polowy's Report to the Women's Conference, AUUC BC, 1963, in 'AUUC Women's Committee Correspondence, Mailing List,' at WBA, Winnipeg.

53 Mary Kardash, 'March 8–Women's Day,' *UC*, 1 March 1952.

54 Katherine Stefanitsky, in Prokopchak, *Reminiscences of Courage and Hope*, 489–96.

55 LAC, RG146, vol. 128, records of CSIS, Memo from National Women's Committee, NEC, AUUC, dated 10 November 1965, to Women's Branches and Club re: Upcoming Campaign.

56 'Free Education Important Point in AUUC Brief on Status of Women,' *UC*, 15 June 1968.

57 Beth Krall, interviewed by RLH, 1998.
58 For some of the problems these Ukrainians and other radical immigrants encountered when applying for citizenship, see 'RCMP Violates Rights, New Democrat Says,' *Globe and Mail*, 1 April 1963.
59 The *UC* throughout 1962 carried articles and features on the campaign. For examples, see *UC*, 15 November, 1 June, and 1 March 1962.
60 Barbara Mashtalar, 'Story of a Second Class Citizen,' *Ukrainian Canadian*, 15 June 1962.
61 Joseph Zuken, 'Memorandum to Minister Bell and MPs' in *UC*, 15 November 1962; Obituary of Mitch Sago, *UC*, September 1989.
62 LAC, MG28, vol. 154, files 17–18, AUUC fonds, response to AUUC Membership Questionnaire (Canadian-born), 1965–6.
63 LAC, MG28, vol. 154, file 4, AUUC fonds, letter from Hazel Strashok, Young Women's Club, Edmonton, dated 23 January 1960, in 'Correspondence: AUUC - English-speaking Branches, 1961–2.'
64 For examples, see LAC, MG28, vol. 154, AUUC fonds, 'Organization/Fund-Raising Campaigns'; RG146, vol 128, records of CSIS, letter from NEC, AUUC, Toronto, dated 19 September 1963, to all provincial and district committees and branches, AUUC, RCMP translation; 'AUUC Organizational Campaign in 1963,' RCMP translation, *UZ*, 24 April 1963, in LAC, RG146, vol. 128, records of CSIS; 'New Membership Report for Period Between X and XI Conventions' in LAC, MG28, vol. 154, AUUC fonds; 'National Membership Totals since 33rd and 32nd and 33rd Conventions,' in LAC, MG28, vol. 154, AUUC fonds, National Executive Committee – Minutes.'
65 RCMP Annual Report for Ontario Concerning the AUUC in 1974 re AUUC – Canada, in LAC, RG 146, Vol 3756, records of CSIS, 'Association of United Ukrainian Canadians – National Executive Committee Canada,' pt 21, 103.
66 LAC, MG28, vol. 154, AUUC fonds, 'Membership in All Branches Including Youth Clubs (but not Children), 33rd National Convention,'.

2

Locating Identity:
The Ukrainian Cultural Heritage
Village as a Public History Text

Karen Gabert

On the long section of the Yellowhead Highway between Saskatoon and Edmonton, one of the most memorable landmarks is the Ukrainian Cultural Heritage Village. As one cruises past at highway speed, it is difficult to miss the towering grain elevator, onion-domed Orthodox church, and thatch-roofed barn, all in remarkable proximity. This is the largest open-air museum in Alberta and one of the most visited historic sites in the province. Situated in the Ukrainian bloc settlement of east-central Alberta, it showcases the period of Ukrainian settlement in the area (from 1892 to 1930). Historic buildings have been moved to this site from across the region, then restored and interpreted to present a typical Ukrainian-Canadian community. The buildings are situated in a careful reconstruction of a historical prairie landscape, one that is both accessible and novel. The buildings and landscape at the Ukrainian Village provide a visual record of the pioneer history of the region. They reflect Old World building traditions and New World adaptations, and they provide an interesting diversion for tourists both local and non-local.

Open-air museums are an enduring attraction as much for the responses these sites invoke in visitors as for the commemorative messages they convey. The idea of re-creating a historical environment for contemporary consumption reminds us of the unyielding linearity of time, and also of the possibility of challenging time: if we must accept that time travel is impossible, this is the next-best thing. Tied up with such ahistorical imaginings is a faith in the ability of historical experts to accurately construct such sites through scientific inquiry. Museum curators are able to win over the most sceptical of visitors at open-air sites, in part because they stay invisible. Traditional museum exhibits bear the clear marks of their creators; open-air exhibits can erase or at least ignore all such evidence and encourage the fantasy of having happened upon an in situ historic wonderland.

This essay explores the interface of perception and reality at the Ukrainian Village, examining the methods by which the site's creators have sought to gain the visitors' trust and approval. As a public institution, the Ukrainian Village is a vehicle through which the state imparts messages about the past to the citizenry. It is also a venue for negotiating those messages, and as evidenced in the following pages, the Ukrainian community played an active role in determining the site's commemorative intent. Meanwhile, the general public has been encouraged to see the universality of the pioneer settlement story and thereby consider the collectivity that binds them as Albertans. The overarching theme of progress communicated by the historic site invites visitors to place themselves on a continuum of material wealth and social development and to feel proud of their forebears' achievements. This essay examines how these messages have been refined over the course of the site's development; it also considers the public's response to those messages.

Community Origins

It seems that Ukrainian Canadians are fascinated by origin myths. Commemorations of Ukrainians in Canada generally highlight their agricultural, rural, and prairie-based origins. Though some Ukrainians settled in cities and worked at industrial jobs, most took advantage of Canada's western settlement policy and claimed homesteads in a series of bloc settlements stretching southeast from Edmonton to southeastern Manitoba. It is this aspect of the Ukrainian immigrant experience that is most recognized both by the general public and by the community itself. Immigration happened in a series of waves: the first, from 1891 until 1914, drew 170,000 Ukrainians to Canada; the second, from 1918 to 1939, brought 68,000;[1] and the third and smallest, from 1945 to 1954, attracted around 35,000 more. Each group was the product of unique historical experiences and thus contributed distinct aspects to the group's identity. However, in commemorations of Ukrainian-Canadian history, the first wave, the pioneer generation, is the most visible. The mythology of the stalwart peasant family in sheepskin coats, bravely clearing its quarter-section of wilderness for future prosperity, occupies much space in official histories of the Canadian Prairies as well as in the collective memory of the group. In Western Canada, where agriculture has long been the primary industry, Ukrainians are ascribed a special founding status for their role in bringing millions of acres of land into productive use. Similarly, local histories produced by the communities themselves stress the homesteading era over later ones. The image of the Ukrainian pioneer, then, is both a projection from outside and an acknowledged reality from within Ukrainian-Canadian society.

The mythology of the pioneer is the product of a series of social constructions based on historical imaginings. These constructions include ideas about independence, strength, bravery, perseverance, morality, health, and wilderness. David Lowenthal suggests that such romantic constructions are poignant precisely *because* of the remoteness of the reality. Nostalgia – the longing for a distant time – requires a sense of estrangement, and the brevity of the pioneer era ensured such estrangement from an early date.[2] Within collective ethnic memories, the pioneer generation is often endowed with a sense of authenticity that is perceived as lacking in present-day experience. The sense that direct interactions with nature allowed the pioneers to live fuller, healthier lives, and the historical fact of their primacy in place, offer the pioneer experience a position of authority and reverence. The era is easy to revere precisely *because* it is gone: 'We increasingly hark back to a past we ourselves have never known, one more imagined than real. The romance of pioneering suits our wistful longing for ways of life so briefly and variously experienced that we invest them with whatever forms we choose.'[3]

In Alberta, monuments to the pioneers began to be raised in the 1950s, just as the pioneer generation was dying out. Before that time, Ukrainian-Canadian commemorations – consisting of temporary exhibitions of Ukrainian culture – focused on the present, active material culture of the group rather than on that of past generations. A turning point in Ukrainian-Canadian commemoration was reached in the 1950s, when interest in the pioneers began to bring about a shift from a 'this is us' approach to one of 'this *was* us.' As farms became increasingly mechanized and Ukrainians integrated with the Canadian mainstream, community members recognized the ephemerality of the traditional homestead and worked to preserve it. In 1959 a group of local farmers at Shandro, northeast of Edmonton, established the Historical Village and Pioneer Museum. A rather haphazard collection of early-twentieth-century buildings was maintained by a small group of dedicated volunteers, but it failed to achieve a high profile outside the local area. This grassroots project to commemorate pioneer life lacked the focused commemorative intent encountered at later, more successful sites. Yet it shared the same impulse to venerate an era that no longer existed except in memories and stories, at a time when the community found itself being transformed by a rapidly industrializing commercial economy.

Drawing greater attention was the Ukrainian Pioneer Home, a turn-of-the-century-style house built in Elk Island National Park east of Edmonton. This building, officially opened by Prime Minister Louis St Laurent in August 1951, was the first purpose-built Ukrainian museum in Canada. It housed a collection of pioneer artefacts and traditional folk handicrafts. It was the site of regular community gatherings throughout the 1950s and 1960s, making it perhaps the most recognized memory site for the local Ukrainian-Canadian community. During this period, the Ukrainian Pioneers' Association held its annual Ukrainian Day outside the house; various other celebrations, picnics, and family reunions were also often held there. The Ukrainian Pioneers' Association involved itself mainly in the publication of books and pamphlets on the early history of Ukrainians in Canada, but it was also interested in promoting and celebrating Ukrainian-Canadian ethnic identity. The commemorative activities based around the Pioneer Home provided the nucleus around which the Ukrainian Village was formed in the 1970s.

Frank Lakusta and the Ukrainian Cultural Heritage Village Society

The seventy-fifth anniversary of Ukrainian settlement in Canada fell in 1966, and the Ukrainian Pioneers' Association planned a special Ukrainian Day celebration to mark the occasion. They invited Prime

Minister Lester Pearson to join the festivities, and his arrival at the site in a helicopter caused much excitement. In his address to the assembled crowd, Pearson promised federal funding for private community-development initiatives designed to have wide public benefit.[4] This was consistent with his government's commitment to promoting Canadian nationalism within the various ethnic communities across the country; at the time, many such projects revolved around celebrating Canada's Centennial Year.[5] The federal government believed that ethnic communities had a central role to play in national life and in the largest commemorative project in the country's history. The Ukrainian community in Alberta was eager to participate, and Pearson's announcement at Elk Island Park was received warmly.

That announcement was especially welcome to Frank Lakusta, a local farmer and businessman who was working on an idea to create an open-air museum commemorating the settlement experience of Ukrainians in east-central Alberta. Lakusta had been assembling an extensive collection of pioneer artefacts from the Ukrainian bloc settlement of east-central Alberta and beyond, and he wanted to display it in an environment of restored farm and village buildings. He had purchased two quarters of farmland adjacent to Elk Island National Park with the intention of locating his museum there. Now he was looking for funding to get the project moving. For him, Pearson's speech could not have come at a better time.

The initiative to create the Ukrainian Cultural Heritage Village was part of the great museological trend of the 1960s: the open-air pioneer museum. In Canada, these collections of historic buildings – arranged within an enclosed space, and furnished and interpreted to provide an entertaining and educational message about the pioneer history of the region – first appeared in Ontario and the Maritimes. Their predecessors included trading posts and military forts operated by the Parks Branch of the Department of the Interior in the first half of the twentieth century; but they were also heavily influenced by trends in the United States and northern Europe. There had been outdoor folk museums in Scandinavia since the late nineteenth century; however, interest in folk culture did not catch on in North America until after the Second World War. At that time, open-air sites such as Colonial Williamsburg and Greenfield Village – both of which opened in the United States in the interwar years – were less interested in folk culture than in elite and industrial culture. In Canada at the time, the only open-air museums were restored military sites such as Fort Anne, Port Royal, and the Prince of Wales Martello Tower in Nova Scotia, and fur trading posts such as Fort William in Ontario and Fort Langley in British Columbia.[6] Not until the 1960s did 'regular folks' – especially pioneers – appear as subject matter for museum curators. The most influential open-air pioneer museum was Upper Canada Village near Morrisburg, Ontario. Morrisburg was only one of more than a dozen pioneer villages that opened in Ontario alone between 1957 and 1975.[7] This movement paralleled the academic trend towards social history and the interest in writing history from the bottom up. It was also a product of the postwar antimodernism mentioned earlier, out of which communities launched projects to commemorate a way of life as it disappeared.

Ukrainians were playing a leading role in the development of federal multiculturalism policy,[8] and at the community level they were eager to support a project that highlighted their contribution to the nation-building project being celebrated in the 1960s. Lakusta was aware of the opportunities for his project within the multiculturalism framework, and he hoped to take advantage of the federal Liberals' program of cultural grants.[9]

In the late 1960s, Lakusta assembled a small group of supporters, who included William Hawrelak, former mayor of Edmonton, the Reverends Myroslaw Kryschuk and M. Sopulak, Ukrainian Orthodox and Ukrainian Catholic priests respectively, and Dr M. Snihurowych, a local physician.[10] Not all of these community leaders would sign the application to form the Ukrainian Cultural Heritage Village Society in November 1971; even so, their early involvement lent credibility to the project and helped encourage others to join. The society was formed on the advice of federal officials after Lakusta and Hawrelak travelled to Ottawa in April 1971 to lobby for federal funding through the Privy Council Office. They were directed to Robert Klymasz of the Canadian Centre for Folk Culture at the National Museum of Man, and to Roman Fodchuk at the National Capital Commission.[11] Klymasz and Fodchuk were enthusiastic about the project, and both would become further involved with the Village in later years. Fodchuk provided advisory and planning services and encouraged the society to develop a living history museum. On Fodchuk's advice, Lakusta revised his original plan – which had consisted of a row of restored buildings, a restaurant, and a motel with a commercial theme – to reflect a more historically appropriate arrangement.[12] Fodchuk helped the group present a revised program proposal which succeeded – in 1972 the society received a federal grant of $177,000.[13]

The expressed purposes of the society were outlined in 1971 as follows:

(i) to sustain, develop and promote the cultural heritage of Canadians of Ukrainian descent;

(ii) to establish and maintain museums, archives, libraries, display facilities and the like calculated to reflect the Ukrainian culture in Canada and elsewhere;

(iii) to acquire by way of gift, donation, bequest, subscription, purchase, or otherwise howsoever, property, both real and personal, artifacts and things whatsoever, with a view to reflect the lives and environment of Canadian people of Ukrainian descent;

(iv) to conduct research and other programs calculated to enhance the cultural, educational, religious and moral values of people of Ukrainian background.[14]

A noteworthy omission from this statement is reference to the past. The word 'heritage' in the first point provides the only clue that the Ukrainian Cultural Heritage Village Society had taken on the responsibility of commemorating more than contemporary culture. The expressed purpose to gather artefacts 'with a view to reflect the lives and environment of Canadian people of Ukrainian descent' was belied by the actual practice of gathering mainly agricultural artefacts. In this way the society was blurring the distinction between contemporary and historical culture; in the process, it was denying any deviations from the rural settlement norm. Though the society claimed that it was 'promot[ing] the cultural heritage of Canadians of Ukrainian descent,' first-generation immigrant mechanics in nearby Vegreville and Ukrainian-Canadian lawyers in Edmonton might not have found much of their own cultural heritage among the wooden ploughs and grain flails on display. They would, however, feel that they *should* identify with such items, as they absorbed the message that Ukrainian-Canadian identity was tied to the pioneer experience. In this way, a collective memory was being constructed and a consensus established as to the nature of Ukrainian-Canadian culture. In the process, the community was being mobilized to claim ownership in the national past, as settlers of the Canadian frontier.

Though support for the project was widespread, some of the more politicized community members were reluctant, for Lakusta and some of the board members were associated with the pro-communist faction.[15] Ukrainians in Canada had been split between the majority nationalists and the minority progressives (i.e., communists) since the interwar years, and this divide only widened during the Cold War era.[16] Support for the project from the organized community in Edmonton would have been stronger had it not been for this association, which was perhaps more perceived than real. It seems that Lakusta had rather inconsistent political leanings, joining and leaving organizations with some regularity.[17] In any case, the association of the Ukrainian Village with communism existed, which prevented some people from supporting what they otherwise would have viewed as a worthy project.[18] At least one person declined Lakusta's invitation to sit on the board for this reason.[19]

The ambitious activities under way at the Ukrainian Village reflected the wider 'heritage boom' in Alberta and in Canada more generally. The time was ripe to establish museums of all sizes: third-generation Albertans were reacting to the passing of the pioneer generation; postwar construction activity was threatening Canada's built and natural heritage; and politicians and business people were beginning to appreciate the economic benefits of heritage tourism.[20] Increased leisure time, private and public wealth, and improved educational facilities also contributed to a heightened interest in the past. This generalized nostalgia was reflected in the original plan for the site, which amounted to an unfocused scattering of buildings around a central 'Main Street.' That a Main Street was part of the site layout from the beginning reflects the popular appeal of small towns during the late 1960s and 1970s.[21] As symbols of constancy and conservatism, small towns were invested with the feelings of reminiscence that many open-air museums were trying to exploit during this era. The most famous example was Disneyland's Main Street USA, created in 1955. Main Street was the central feature of many open-air museums, regardless of their theme. The use of the word 'village' in the names of so many sites reflects the centrality of the role of Main Street to their interpretive programs. Like the pioneer homestead, the small-town main street was a victim of postwar urbanization and suburbanization; as a result, it had earned itself a leading role in the open-air museum movement and the conservation field in general.

Sale of the Site

By 1975 the financial realities of operating the site were apparent to Lakusta and the board. To obtain, move, restore, and furnish all the buildings they wanted, and to develop the site for visitors, would cost millions of dollars, and the grant money they had so far received did not come close to covering those costs. Lakusta again used his political connections to secure patronage for the site. He approached Peter Savaryn, president of the province's Progressive Conservatives, to ask for his support for the idea of selling the site to the province. The board supported this decision, and Savaryn recognized the site's potential as a means to recognize the role that Ukrainians had played in Alberta's early development.[22] Savaryn approached Horst Schmidt, Minister of Culture, and Bill Yurko, Minister of Housing and Public Works, asking them how much they would be able to contribute. He then sold the idea to Premier Peter Lougheed, who authorized Yurko to purchase the site. The province purchased 23 acres from the society for $150,000; the society donated the remaining 297 acres.

In terms of commemorative impulse, the Ukrainian Albertan example is exceptional: compared to other ethnic groups in the province, they were well organized. Also, the high density of settlement within a defined region allowed for a high degree of linguistic retention and cultural identification. The Ukrainians' common collective identity, however fractured and dynamic it was, worked to unite the group around the desire to commemorate the activities of earlier generations in response to rapid cultural change.

With public ownership, much changed at the Ukrainian Village. Key was the involvement of heritage professionals and academics, who contributed a high level of expertise to the planning of the Village as a Provincial Historic Site. This project was conducted with the intention of creating a state-of-the-art facility based on extensive local and professional knowledge. This was part of a broader effort to develop a for-

mal museum community in the province, along the lines of similar efforts in other provinces, notably Ontario.[23] To counter Alberta's relatively slow progress on this front, the provincial government contracted
out research and later hired professional staff with degrees from the
University of Toronto and Queen's University. This policy was most
ambitiously tested at the Ukrainian Village, the flagship of the
province's expanding network of Provincial Historic Sites.

Professionalization under Provincial Governance

The purchase of the Ukrainian Village in 1975 marked an important
turning point for the Department of Culture. Even in its relatively undeveloped state, the Village was the largest site in the provincial network and offered an important opportunity to develop the heritage
profession from within the public service. The earliest actions taken by
the department after the sale involved external contracts to non-gov-
ernment employees, which soon led to the hiring of permanent staff. In
1975 the province retained a private landscape-architecture firm,
Roman Fodchuk and Associates, to draft a master development plan
for the site. Fodchuk had been advising the Ukrainian Village Society
on behalf of the federal government since 1971 and by now had established his own practice with offices in Edmonton and Calgary. The most
significant component of his Site Development Master Plan was the
site plan, which provided the thematic framework around which future
plans would be structured. The plan is still in evidence today. Fodchuk
divided the site into zones: town site, rural community, and farmsteads.
This tripartite layout was designed to reflect the historical arrangement
of the early bloc settlement: homesteaders travelled to town for their
commercial activities, while their recreational, religious, and political
lives centred on rural institutions such as the school, the church, and the
community hall. Within this spatial structure, a chronological progression was demonstrated: the earliest homesteads were set in the bush,
while the rural school and churches were located on cleared land, off-
set by enough distance to suggest the spatial isolation of these communities. Developed from the existing Main Street, the town site was
expanded along the grid pattern that typified prairie rail towns.
    Fodchuk's statement of intent – the first to be articulated under
provincial administration – was ambitious.[24] It contained the first def-

inition of an interpretive period and a clear expression of the intention to create living history. Its emphasis on historical accuracy and authenticity demonstrated the province's commitment to devote significant resources to professional research and development. At this point, provincial officials recognized the Village as a community project and acted to maintain its Ukrainian character. One of the conditions of the sale of the site had been that its name not be changed; this was a way of guaranteeing that the Ukrainian pioneer experience would be recognized. The society's board members had been adamant that the site not be interpreted as an ethnically generic pioneer village, and the province concurred. This was likely a gesture of recompense to the Ukrainian community for its support of the Conservative party in its rise to power. There was certainly an expectation of payback among some community leaders in this regard.[25] During the 1970s, in a similar gesture to engage the community and to reward them for their support, Premier Lougheed had appointed Alberta's first cabinet ministers of Ukrainian heritage. It should also be noted that the provincewide emphasis on commemorative heritage projects in general during this time placed the Ukrainian Village in the right place at the right time. The Master Plan was presented to a Select Ministers' Committee that included Bill Yurko, Horst Schmid, and three Ukrainian ministers: John Batiuk, Bert Hohol, and George Topolnisky.[26] It was unanimously approved.

A comparison of the statements of intent of the society in 1971 and of the province in 1977 points to both a narrowing of focus and a broadening in the conceptions of the site's audience and commemorative purpose. An inward perspective is assumed in the earlier document, which emphasizes the enhancement of various values 'of people of Ukrainian background.' The latter document is broader in outlook, defining its audience as 'Albertans and visitors' and 'the general public.' Such an attempt to give the site wider relevance to non-Ukrainians is also evident in the expressed goal of presenting intra- and intercultural relationships at the site. At the same time, the focus has narrowed: the document drops the intention to create 'museums, archives, libraries, display facilities and the like,' instead focusing on the development of a singular 'living museum.' To supplement the living-history style of interpretation – still a novelty in Alberta in the 1970s – the later document also recommends more traditional 'educational and interpretive exhibits and displays.' Besides defining the interpretive period as running from the 1890s to the 1920s, the provincial document also defines an interpretive space: the Ukrainian bloc settlement of east-central Alberta. Though this had been implied by the origins of the buildings and of most artefacts, it had not been defined until then. Overall, the earlier objective to 'sustain, develop and promote the cultural heritage of Canadians of Ukrainian descent' is maintained in the latter document, but a methodology is outlined and a narrower programming intent defined. It seems that by commissioning a plan with such a focused program, the province was acknowledging the Ukrainian past while consciously interpreting its universal aspects so that they would resonate with all Albertans and out-of-province visitors.

Also under development in the early 1980s was the Village's interpretation program, which fell under the ambit of Bilash as the site's historical researcher. The interpretive program was part of a broader plan laid out by Alberta Culture in the 1981 Historical Development Proposal, commonly referred to as the Black Book. This document, written by Bilash, Laurence Pearson, and Roman Ostashewsky, outlined a phased five-year development plan structured around Fodchuk's three-zone interpretive concept. Overall, the Black Book was a blueprint for an intensive, large-scale, and fast-tracked development of the site. It was produced by the order of Premier Lougheed, who visited the site in 1980 to unveil the new Ukrainian Pioneer Family statue outside the Visitor Reception Centre. Noting the incompleteness of the site, he instructed Yurko to get it finished, and quickly. The upcoming provincial election was likely a motivating factor.[27] The resulting document includes detailed site drawings and a phased development plan that prioritizes the completion of the main interpretive zones and that outlines a plan for enriching them with more buildings in the future. This latter enrichment phase is currently under way; at this writing, the site as outlined in the Black Book remains incomplete.

Negotiating the Boundaries of Professionalism

The intensive activity at the Village was not conducted solely to Alberta Culture guidelines; it also absorbed the Ukrainian community's input. The government committee formed to negotiate the purchase of the site before 1975 was also charged with establishing a Minister's

Advisory Board to maintain community input into the site's development. The community's control over the site's development was now limited to the advisory board's right to make recommendations; but at the same time, its representation was now broader than had been the case during the period of private ownership. Prior to provincial involvement, all decisions had been made by a board comprised of Frank Lakusta and his friends; now the decision making involved the collaboration of the growing professional team, the minister, and an Advisory Board. Individuals' efforts now had a smaller impact on the overall project; on the other hand, the site was now more democratic and represented a larger segment of the community. The churches, the Ukrainian Canadian Congress, the Canadian Institute of Ukrainian Studies, the Ukrainian Pioneers' Association, the local county, and other stakeholders were all represented on the board.

By the mid-1980s the oil boom that had permitted heritage spending on projects like the Village had begun to subside; a recession was looming. It soon became clear that the site required additional services that the province was unable to provide. In 1984, Horst Schmid's successor as minister, Mary LeMessurier, arranged for the creation of the Friends of the Ukrainian Village Society to support the province's work. Initially tasked with fund-raising and with running the gift shop and food services, the mandate of this group quickly grew to include contract administration, interpretation staffing, and special project management. Employees of the province and the Friends now work together on the site: the province employs the full-time, permanent administrative staff while the Friends hire the seasonal staff for interpretive work, food services, and the gift shop. This collaborative arrangement is not ideal, as the two managements sometimes clash over issues of governance and historical interpretation. Several interviewees questioned the need for a private organization to monitor the operations of a public site, and criticize the government's fiscal restraint in that it has offloaded many of the operational costs onto a non-governmental organization.[28] These tensions were not likely foreseen when the Friends were established; rather, that group was seen as a way to maintain community input at the operational level. To the good, the community has enjoyed democratized governance as well as increased input at the operational level.

All the interviewees who were involved with the site in the late 1970s and early 1980s remembered provincial administration as a positive development, and this was echoed in the community. The financial limitations were widely understood, and the province was seen as a lifeline to a sinking endeavour.[29] Any worries that the original commemorative intent would be compromised, or that the site might be taken away from the community, were muted by the understanding that the society was not financially able to further develop the site and that it might fail without outside involvement. Provincial ownership carried with it the promise of sustained support and development to a degree unavailable under the society's administration. Such hopes were not misplaced: programs for research, acquisitions, restoration, landscaping, interpretation, and visitor services were all professionally developed by the province. The Ukrainian community has been able to maintain some input at the site through the Advisory Board and the Friends, and despite the inevitable tensions, the relationship that has developed between the museum professionals and the community they interpret has been largely positive.

Historical Messages

The professional planning of the Ukrainian Village involved building consensus around the vision laid out in 1981 in the Black Book. Much of that consensus is evident at the site to this day. The Black Book contained a revised articulation of the Village's goals, which are still recognized by site administrators.[30] That document demonstrates some of the key themes that have since been projected onto the site itself. The word 'educational' is used twice in the statement of goals, and it is clear that the site has always been intended to perform a pedagogical role for visitors. However, the document does not specify who is to perform the preserving, restoring, and collecting, though one can infer that approved authorities have been charged with those tasks whose collective aim is to teach the lessons deemed appropriate to the public. The specialized skills of historic preservation have invested those possessing them with authority while investing the results of their work with an authenticity that is rarely questioned. These efforts have been channelled towards the goal of recognizing and appreciating 'the people who dominated the settlement of east central Alberta' – a group whose collective identity is being shaped by the professionals who have been tasked with developing the Ukrainian Village. By enshrining their lifestyles in this way, the site developers have endowed the settlers with special status as founders of the nation – a status that has long been acknowledged in the community's own origin myths and that is now accepted by mainstream society as well. Inherent in these various commemorative activities, the message of progress is sent loud and clear to all visitors: 'Look how far we've come!' 'We' indeed, as visitors of all ethnicities are encouraged to see the universal relevance of the pioneer story and thereby place themselves within a broader Albertan and Canadian collective.

Thoughtful reflection on the site layout and the interpretive themes conveyed therein leads to several hypotheses about other historical messages that the public is intended to absorb. Messages about progress, identity, nationhood, authority, and authenticity are all packed into the site's interpretive program, and visitors absorb them to varying degrees. The two largest houses on the site, Pylypow House and Hawreliak House, are packed with examples of historical image building. These are located in the central part of the non-historic side of the site, in what the visitor site map calls the overview zone. These two buildings and their adjacent farmyards offer the visitor an overview of the interpretive technique of living history that is in play throughout the site, but the prosperity they represent is quite exceptional. The fact that such atypical houses were selected to serve this function suggests that they have purposes beyond merely showing visitors how they will experience the rest of the site. In the case of Pylypow House, its origin as the home of one of the first two permanent Ukrainian immigrants to Canada gives it pride of place among all monuments of Ukrainian-Canadian history. Mykhailo Hawreliak came later, but was wealthy enough by 1919 to build a two-storey home in the Canadian style. The emphasis placed on success attained from humble origins not only speaks of pride in achievement at the family level, but also underscores the progress made by the group in developing the Canadian Prairies. The visitor is intended to compare the early dugout hut and plaster houses that represent earlier phases of settlement with the later grand homes and conclude that progress was made.

This works: several visitors[31] stated that their favourite building was one that exhibited 'progress' or looked 'modern' compared to the others. One local man of Ukrainian descent had the following to say about the Hawreliak house:

[I like] the space, the rooms, the number of rooms for a house like that, there are some spindles on the stairways going up and down ... That house shows me progress from the house just before, Pylypow house ... It appears that would be maybe an elite family group that would have been able to provide a little richer, you know, and they provided a more comfortable home for themselves, and maybe in addition to accommodate any new settlers coming in.

Furthermore, in response to the question of what the purpose of the village is, several visitors said things like 'to show how far these people came,' or in some way indicated that the purpose was to compare today's 'conveniences' with the 'hardships' of the past. Such comments indicate that through the Hawreliak house, the site has succeeded in demonstrating 'success in the new land.'[32]

Clearly, the site developers wanted to highlight the story of poverty to success through hard work and perseverance. But also included in this message is the fact of early and widespread Ukrainian settlement in the province, and the Ukrainians' role in the national project to settle the West. When people visit the earliest dwellings on the site, they hear about wilderness, isolation, and the pioneer spirit, and they conclude that Ukrainian settlement accords them founding status and a legitimate place in Canada's official history. Culture Minister Horst Schmid understood and supported this idea: 'The pioneers that came here from Ukraine and broke the soil while the men were working for the railroad and the women had to pull the roots and all that ... That's how come we ... have become as prosperous a province as we are. But now they are professionals.'[33]

Being able to claim this status is important to Ukrainian Canadians, as they were the victims of bigotry and racism during the early period of their settlement. As one of earliest groups to benefit from the Canadian government's more liberal Western settlement policies, Ukrainians were strangers among the established settlers of Anglo-Saxon and French origin. Methodist missionaries wrote about their strange customs, alien religion, and lack of education, morals, and hygiene.[34] Increasing wealth and education brought Ukrainian Canadians into the mainstream of Canadian society, but suspicion against them lingered well beyond the settlement years. Reminding Ukrainians and others that they have much to celebrate and take pride in has become an important role of the Village, and visitors are invited to participate in that. The tiny dug-out *burdei* is a popular building on the site for its most direct pioneer associations: respondents spoke of 'struggling with nature' and 'breaking the land.' Such references to pioneering do not speak directly to nation building, but they come close. Several respondents said they thought the purpose of the Village was to 'honour their role' and 'keep the little guy's history.' By telling these stories at such a large and professionalized historic site, the government is reinforcing the notion that the 'little guy' is important to the history of the nation and thus deserving of commemoration.

The interpretive program transmits messages about progress and nationhood; the spatial layout of the site reinforces those messages. Space and the use and ownership of it are fundamental to the historical memory of the Ukrainian community in Western Canada[35] – something the site acknowledges. Most European settlers had held only a few acres of land in their home country; thus they considered the 160-acre standard Canadian homestead exceptionally large. To claim so much land was a mark of success, and of opportunity for later generations. Thus in the Ukrainian experience, the mythology of Canada as a country with potential was closely tied to exploitation of the land. At the Ukrainian Village the reproduction of this immediate relationship between people and their environment reflects nostalgia for a mythical, more optimistic era. Visitors are invited to participate actively in the historical relationship between people and land: they walk the pathways, watch horses ploughing the fields, and admire the vegetable gardens. In contemplating the narrative of progress encoded in the homes both humble and grand, they absorb the notion that the future is tied to the earth and come to appreciate the relationship between people and the land. This presentation of farm life is well received: 85 per cent of respondents said the site accurately portrays a rural way of life. By allowing visitors to experience the land in a personal and seemingly authentic way, the Village reproduces a historic relationship that is central to the pioneer experience.

People visit the Ukrainian Village not only to learn about life in a specific historical community, but also to reconcile their present identities with those of their ancestors. Most visitors, whatever their own cultural heritage, suggested that some of their own family's traditions were represented on the site[36] and discussed the various ways in which

they located their own identities there. Likewise, most of them said that
the buildings evoked personal memories. This was clearly the intention
of the site developers, who had designed the Village to have broad appeal to all Albertans. This was evident as early as Fodchuk's 1977 Master Plan, and subsequent planning documents have aimed at the same
goal. It can again be argued that landscape plays an important role in
this. The search for an ongoing, durable past often leads to the landscape, which for many urban dwellers is accessible only in public parks
and museums. Some of the values and traditions of past generations
may have disappeared, but their land remains, and it is through communion with the land that many visitors hope to understand their ancestral heritage. Thus, for many visitors, the spatial arrangements of
living history museums are closely attached to notions of identity:
walking alongside a rail fence on a hot afternoon, one can almost imagine great-grandfather doing exactly the same thing. In this way, present
meanings are projected onto the geographical surroundings. As David
Lowenthal describes it, 'the place of the past in any landscape is as
much the product of present interest as of past history.'[37]

   Both the spatial arrangement and the interpretive program transmit
historical messages to the public; the former, however, is more subtle.
First-person interpretation, on the other hand, involves unique interactions during which visitors directly receive information about the past.
The authoritative, didactic method of interpretation elicits a variety of
responses. Some people are unfamiliar with the concept of open-air
museums and require confirmation that the person they are talking to
is indeed 'playing' a character from a different era.[38] Some never completely understand, and believe the interpreters when they insist that
they really 'live' in the houses and are doing real 'work.' Others actively reassert their position in the present and try to bring the interpreter with them, asking questions related to time periods later than
that being interpreted, or directing attention to modern-day objects.[39]
Many visitors genuinely want to learn, and frame their questions accordingly. Others play a game of stump-the-interpreter, asking obscure
questions to test his or her knowledge. Some are uncomfortable when
talking to first-person interpreters, preferring to focus on the artifacts;
others ask a barrage of questions.

   Within this range of behaviours in visitor–interpreter interaction, the
interpreter's authority is generally not questioned. Dressed in period

costumes and moving confidently in a historic environment, the interpreters appear closer to the past, associatively if not temporally. They know things the visitors do not, especially the location of the boundary between the facade of historicity and the reality behind it. Aligned as they are with the professional research and curatorial staff, the interpreters are seen as part of a larger museum apparatus whose purpose is to impart knowledge to the public. Visitors respect the authoritative position of the interpreters and generally do not question the information they present. Positioned as they are in a make-believe 'past,' they experience the site as a finished product rather than as a series of negotiated decisions. The invisibility of the museum professionals serves to cement their authority in the eyes of the visitors. When asked about the reconstructed buildings on the site, several interviewees accorded them some value 'if they [reconstruction professionals] do a good job.' They did not explain exactly what a good job would be, but neither did they contest the professionals' ability and authority to accomplish one, nor did they expect to see any explicit reference to the process in the finished product.

Authority is unseen yet omnipresent in the small and large spaces of the Ukrainian Village. Obvious signs of authority such as signage and roped-off areas are absent from the site, yet as the visitor walks the pathways, explores the yards and building interiors, and interacts with the interpreters, he or she experiences the product of extensive professional research. Most visitors are aware of this and are free to respond as critically or passively as they want. Though visitors are encouraged to experience the site on their own terms and to construct their visit according to their own interests, the spatial design of the site subtly controls their movements and behaviour as well as their responses to the interpretive messages. 'Controlled' or 'authentic' spaces demand a higher level of engagement than 'free' or 'ordinary' spaces. On the main pathways, visitors behave close to the way they would outside the museum; this is where discussions of lunch and bathroom breaks take place and where children are allowed to run ahead. Here, historic space is least defined and sightlines are longest. As they enter the fenced farmyards, however, they enter more defined historic (or authentic) space. They peer behind shed doors, remark on the activities of animals, and ask questions about the tools they see, conforming to appropriate museum behaviour. The more defined the space, the stronger the awareness of historicity and of authority. The strongest interactions with history occur through conversations with the interpreters, most of whom are situated inside buildings. Sitting in a period kitchen, watching a woman with headscarf and apron knead bread dough, and hearing her say that she plans to take the finished product out to the men in the field, visitors are drawn into the experience of real life in the past. It does not matter that they failed to notice any men working in the field outside the house; they must be just over the hill. It is in this confined space, with the fire crackling and the woman working, that the suspension of disbelief is strongest. This is the 'authentic' and novel experience that so many visitors desire, the place that is devoted to the delivery of an authoritative historical message.

The notion of authenticity is compelling to visitors and museum professionals alike. The distinction between 'the real thing' and its replica, and the meanings attached to that distinction, present an interesting point as it relates to space. Spencer R. Crew and James E. Sims contend that authenticity is subjective and that the value placed on it is largely arbitrary: '[Artefacts] don't mean much without the help of exhibition makers.'[40] According to Crew and Sims, the power of the authentic artefact is not inherent in it; rather, it is assigned by the professional through the same social system that assigns power to expertise: 'Authenticity is not about factuality or reality. It is about authority. Objects have no authority; people do. It is people on the exhibition team who must make a judgement about how to tell about the past. Authenticity – authority – enforces the social contract between the audience and the museum, and a socially agreed-upon reality that exists only as long as confidence in the voice of the exhibition holds.'[41]

The traditional location of power in display is obvious at the Ukrainian Village. Visitors respond favourably to the knowledge that the buildings are old, and most of them say they appreciate them more than they would reconstructions. They found their preferences difficult to articulate, but several talked about a special 'feeling,' 'energy,' and 'character' that old buildings possess and that reconstructions lack. One female respondent mentioned the value of the stories attached to each mark, stain, and scratch on the buildings' surfaces. Yet overlooked in such descriptions is acknowledgment of the extensive curatorial intervention involved in selecting, relocating, restoring, furnishing, and interpreting the buildings in the museum setting. Visitors place so much faith in the notion that the professionals [authorities] involved have re-stored the building accurately that they overlook their involvement al-together. The 'confidence in the voice of the exhibition' that Crew and Sims discuss offers museum professionals incredible power to influ-ence public perceptions of the past. Once again, it is apparent that space and authority are closely linked in the work of museum exhibitions.

Interpretive Challenges

The process of consensus regarding interpretive decisions is hidden from the public, yet the resulting product is evidence of it. The visitor may not know *why* this building was brought to the site, but the fact that it stands there suggests many hours of discussion and research. Be-cause of this, the museum staff must ensure that the final product of their work reflects the intentions agreed on behind the scenes. This can be a challenge, especially when the subject matter is politically charged. The efforts made by village researchers to construct a specific image of life in the Ukrainian bloc settlement are evident in several ways. The rural hall from Kiew, Alberta is one example; when the building was first located on the site, the words 'Ukrainian Labour Farmer Temple Association' (ULFTA) were painted across the pediment, as the build-ing had once been used for meetings of that pro-communist group. Fur-ther research revealed that the building had only been used for such meetings in the years following the pre-1930 interpretive period, so the paint was removed and the communist history of the building was dropped from its interpretation. In fact, visitors to the site see abso-lutely no reference to communism. Cold War anti-communism and the association of the Ukrainian Cultural Heritage Village Society with left-ist organizations likely influenced this decision, in that the province wanted to defuse political tensions between the communist and na-tionalist communities. That said, the denial of the historical existence of communist Ukrainian groups in Alberta is a direct example of his-torical whitewashing, one that highlights the power of museum pro-fessionals to determine the limits of historical authenticity. Visitors do not know that there used to be a communist hall on the site, nor do they know why it was altered; rather, they are left to conclude that commu-nism was not part of Ukrainian life in Alberta. Two other buildings on the site interpret post-1930 dates because they are also representative of the 1920s; the same logic could be applied to the Kiew Hall. It is also possible to commemorate communism in Alberta on the non-historic side of the site, where several other monuments are already located.[42] It appears, however, that there is no will to do so either within the community or among provincial authorities. This aspect of Ukrainian Albertan history has yet to be embraced by either the collective memory of the group or the public history of the state, in part because it is difficult to acknowledge communism in Alberta while Soviet atrocities such as the Ukrainian Famine carry so much political, emotional, and commemorative capital.

The researchers who developed the interpretive mandate of the Ukrainian Village faced many challenges beyond the problem of politics. They also had to grapple with the problem of representational scope; not only did the various ethnic, religious, and demographic subgroups require representation, but so too did a variety of social themes. They succeeded in the former endeavour, less so in the latter. Societal trends can be difficult to interpret in a living history museum, and some of the leading sites in Canada and the United States have been criticized for presenting an overly simplified version of history.[43] Living history museums have generally failed to present controversial themes or to interpret history as a process of negotiating conflicting historical truths. At the Ukrainian Village, common problems such as alcoholism and spousal abuse are overlooked, as are the various political and religious divisions within the bloc settlement. Though three churches are present on the site, they tend to be interpreted separately, and little attention is paid to the deep social divisions associated with church membership. Furthermore, the presentation of a 'typical' Ukrainian community erases the great diversity of experience in the settlement. Women and men did not interact with the landscape in the same way, nor did children. All settlers were not equally successful, as some land was unprofitable and had to be abandoned. Social relationships and loyalties created well-defined communities, and relations among neighbours influenced their success on the land. At the Ukrainian Village, interpretations of relations with non-Ukrainians are superficial; with aboriginal people they are non-existent. This amnesia on the subject of European colonialism is ironic, given that the site is dedicated to a historically disenfranchised group: such cultural sensitivity would appear to have its limits here. Undoubtedly, such subtleties are challenging to interpret, but based on visitor interest in authenticity and personal history, they would likely be well received. Visitors showed a strong preference for hearing personal stories about the people associated with the buildings, and several interviewees referred to buildings by the stories they heard there, especially when they were personally relevant.[44]

The presentation of the relationship between Ukrainians and non-Ukrainians deserves further comment. The Ukrainian farmstead buildings show the closest resemblance to their Old World counterparts: plastered walls, thatched roofs, small windows, and clay ovens all reference a foreign building tradition. Other buildings on the site are distinctly Canadian; the school, the hall, the railway station, the grain elevator, the police barracks, and most of the shops in town all follow official or vernacular construction patterns. Here a distinction is observed between 'Ukrainian' and 'Canadian' buildings, with the former illustrating progress and dynamism and the latter treated as static. This is an inversion of the common process of 'othering' at open-air pioneer museums: the minority culture has become the majority, while the dominant English-Canadian culture is treated as the unknown other. At heritage sites such as Fort Edmonton and Calgary's Heritage Park, buildings like teepees and Chinese shops play this role, occupying the fringes of interpretive programs that focus on a white, middle-class story. Canadian buildings are not physically marginalized at the Ukrainian Village, but they are treated more superficially because they are more common elsewhere in Canada. Variations in non-Ukrainian residences, for example, are overlooked. With its lace curtains, velvet furniture, and upright piano, the English-Canadian home of the police constable is a cliché of Victorian gentility. With no other English-Canadian home to compare it with, the visitor is left with the impression that this was the norm for English Canadians and that they lived a lifestyle of relative ease in town while the Ukrainians toiled on the land in mud huts. In this way, the Ukrainianness of the site suppresses the historical experience of non-Ukrainians on the land, which proves that inverting the traditional commemorative preference for mainstream culture does not result in a more democratic historical message. This non-Ukrainian essentialization seems to have been intentional: the 1977 goal of interpreting 'the relationships between the pioneers of Ukrainian background and settlers of other ethnic origins who lived in the area'[45] was dropped from the 1981 statement of intent.[46]

At any open-air museum it is a challenge to interpret patterns and variances within the various building traditions represented, because of the number of buildings that would be required to do so effectively. A single structure is often simplistically treated as representing a diverse body of building types. Such suppression of architectural variation at open-air museums can lead to the adoption of buildings as cultural symbols whose meanings transcend their immediate interpretation.[47] The earliest farmstead houses at the Ukrainian Village are examples of this; their modest size and commonplace building materials have come to represent a heritage of poverty, resourcefulness, and triumph, and as a result they act as powerful symbols of cultural identity. The interviewees who stated that these were their favourite buildings used words like 'hardship,' 'struggling with nature,' and 'resilience' to describe their preferences. One interviewee of Ukrainian heritage recognized the stereotypes he called up but liked the idea of buying into them. Another used the word 'romantic' in imagining the lifestyle attached to the earliest pioneer buildings. If 'buildings and their formal elements are systems of signs that communicate identification with or rejection of a given social group, specific social values, status, or merely assertions of existence in a social or commercial sense,' as Dell Upton argues, the same buildings in an open-air museum do so even more powerfully.[48] The Ukrainian houses, barns, and churches at the Ukrainian Village have become shorthand symbols of Ukrainian identity, much like painted eggs and red-and-black embroidery. The problem with this relates to the selective nature of the buildings at the Village; Ukrainians identify only with the familiar forms represented, and not with the functions they served. Turn-of-the-century houses and farm buildings in the Ukrainian bloc settlement exhibited wide variations within a limited architectural vocabulary; community buildings varied even more. Through the process of building selection, these variations have been distilled into a packaged set of symbols for cultural adoption. This is yet another example of the power of museum professionals to make these decisions on the part of the public as a whole.

The mechanisms by which the professionals at the Ukrainian Village disseminate historical messages to the public are complex, as are the ways in which those messages are received. The common desire for a novel and authentic experience is cultivated by marketing instruments promising historical fantasy. By situating various historical messages in an enticing 'world ... frozen in time,' the Village professionals instil a widespread conception of public commonality. Visitors come away feeling invested in the Ukrainian pioneering heritage both at a personal level and as part of a greater collective. This is made possible in part by the public's faith that the museum professionals are interpreting the past accurately and appropriately. This authority is rarely questioned, even when the messages – more often the silences – are politicized. Historical essentialism is treated as a matter of course rather than as a misuse of curatorial authority: of the forty-one visitors and community members interviewed, only one commented on the lack of complexity in the interpretive program. On the other hand, summarizing the pioneer story as a series of representative clichés allows the greatest number of diverse individuals to identify with them and with the otherwise culturally exclusive history they represent.

The Ukrainian Village's founders operated within a commemorative paradigm with deep historical roots, both inside and outside the Ukrainian community. Their efforts focused a developing self-consciousness on a highly visible site, which soon became the central venue for constructing and expressing Ukrainian identity. At the Village, the spatial demonstration of themes such as material progress, cultural cohesiveness, and the nobility of the pioneer serve as attractive symbols towards which many Ukrainians gravitate. The veneration of the pioneer reflects the community's interest in origin myths and is closely connected with the notion of progress – an instrument that later provincial administrators have adopted for their own use. Progress is a versatile concept that allows people to see themselves at the favourable end of a continuum between primitive and modern. At the Ukrainian Village, visitors see their ancestors' poverty and can compare it with their own prosperity so as to conclude: 'Look how far we've come!'

With the purchase and development of the Village by the provincial government, the message of Ukrainian settlement moved from the margins to the mainstream of Alberta's commemorative program. In developing the Village as a Provincial Historic Site, the province's heritage professionals had to address the question of relevance for all visitors. They did so by allowing the Ukrainian pioneer experience to represent that of all pioneers in the official history of the province. Clearly, this involved a process of construction as much as preservation, but such is the nature of public history. It also involved some measure of dialogue with the community to ensure that those who were being commemorated were comfortable with the historical messages being told about them. The process was politically driven at both the government level and that of the community, as local groups competed to be heard and the government tried to satisfy as many voters as possible. The result was that the Village now acts as a touchstone on which both Ukrainians and the general public can define themselves. Thus the Ukrainian Village clearly demonstrates the symbiotic relationship of state and community in the construction of public conceptions of a collective past. By in effect declaring that the Ukrainian pioneer experience is relevant to all Albertans, the province is encouraging visitors to consider their own identities as members of a group with a shared memory. More than any specific historical theme interpreted at the Village, this is the message the site transmits to its visitors.

Notes

1 Brian Osborne, 'Non-Preferred People: Interwar Ukrainian Immigration to Canada,' in *Canada's Ukrainians: Negotiating an Identity*, ed. Lubomyr Luciuk and Stella Hryniuk (Toronto: University of Toronto Press, 1991), 81.
2 David Lowenthal, 'The Pioneer Landscape: An American Dream,' *Great Plains Quarterly* 2 (Winter 1982), 5, 10.
3 Ibid., 5.
4 Informant A, interview with Karen Gabert, 3 January 2006.
5 A pamphlet titled 'Making 1967 Work: Planning for the Centenary on the Community Level,' issued by the Canadian Centenary Council in 1965, was designed to help develop a '"Canadian personality" in the many regions of the country and within the variety of ethnic groups that form the base of our society.' The focus on community projects originated with the Centenary Council's belief that 'the success of the anniversary year will depend on how extensively and how soon we can stimulate and facilitate grass roots participation.' As part of the drive for grassroots support, the Secretary of State, Judy LaMarsh, also promised to integrate the projects of the National Conference of Ethnic Organizations and Community Folk Arts Councils into the centennial program.
6 Shannon Ricketts, '"Raising the Dead": Reconstruction within the Canadian Parks Service,' *Proceedings of the Canadian Parks Service Recon-*

struction Workshop, Hull, Quebec, 11–13 March 1992 (Ottawa: National Historic Sites, Parks Service, Environment Canada, 1993), 22.

7 Michael J. Seaman, The Heritage Value Consideration of Strategies for Enhancing the Overall Viability of Open-Air Museums in Canada (MED thesis, Technical University of Nova Scotia, 1995), 23–6.

8 Senator Paul Yuzyk, viewed by many as the 'Father of Multiculturalism,' drafted the multiculturalism policy that was adopted by the Trudeau government in 1971. For more information on Ukrainian support of multiculturalism, see Manoly R. Lupul, *The Politics of Multiculturalism: A Ukrainian-Canadian Memoir* (Edmonton: CIUS, 2005).

9 See for example, Rt Hon. Pierre Elliott Trudeau, 'Announcement of Implementation of Policy of Multiculturalism with Biligual Framework,' *House of Commons Debates,* 28th Parliament, 3rd Session, 8 October 1971 (Ottawa: Queen's Printer, 1971), 8546.

10 Draft of the Amendments to the By-Laws of the Ukrainian Heritage and Cultural Society, 10 June 1971

11 Roman Fodchuk, 'From Idea to Concept to Reality: The Planning and Design of the Ukrainian Cultural Heritage Village.' Presented at the Learned Societies' Meetings, University of Alberta, 28 May 2000, 1–2.

12 Ibid., 1.

13 Ibid., 2.

14 Schedule A, Application for Registration as a Society under the Provincial Societies Act. Registered 1 November 1971.

15 Informant B, interview with Karen Gabert, 20 December 2005; Dave Ruptash, former secretary of UCHV Society, interview with Karen Gabert, 16 December 2005; Peter Savaryn, former president of the Progressive Conservative Association of Alberta and former chancellor of the University of Alberta, interview with Karen Gabert, 19 December 2005.

16 See, for example, Lubomyr Luciuk and Stella Hryniuk, eds., *Canada's Ukrainians: Negotiating an Identity* (Toronto: University of Toronto Press, 1991); and Frances Swyripa, *Wedded to the Cause: Ukrainian-Canadian Women and Ethnic Identity, 1891–1991* (Toronto: University of Toronto Press, 1993).

17 Informant B interview.

18 Savaryn interview.

19 Ibid.

20 Mark Rasmussen, 'The Heritage Boom: Evolution of Historical Resource Conservation in Alberta,' *Prairie Forum: Journal of the Canadian Plains Research Centre* 15, no. 2 (1990): 235–6.

21 Richard V. Francaviglia, *Main Street Revisited: Time, Space, and Image Building in Small-Town America* (Iowa City: University of Iowa Press, 1996), 142.

22 Savaryn interview.

23 For more on the development of the museum community in Alberta, refer to my 'Locating Identity: The Ukrainian Cultural Heritage Village as a Public History Text' (MA research essay, Carleton University, 2007), 35–40.

24 It reads, in part, as follows:

> The ultimate goal of developing the Ukrainian Cultural Heritage Village is to provide Albertans and visitors a unique educational opportunity. The visiting public will be able to observe and participate in the normal activities of pioneer settlers and their descendents in a typical setting. Broad recognition and appreciation of the Ukrainian contribution to the Province's rich cultural heritage made by the Ukrainian immigrants who dominated the settlement in East Central Alberta will thereby be ensured ...
>
> The primary purpose of the project is to replicate the history of pioneer life in East Central Alberta on the Village site under the highest standards of authenticity. This will be accomplished by depicting scenes and events accurately representing each major aspect of that history since the original settlements in a dynamic, 'living' museum that continuously grows ... The Village must exemplify each cultural period from the first farms and rural communities of the 1890's and early 1900's, to the more developed towns of the 1920's ...
>
> Typical pioneer farming techniques, crafts, trades, businesses, and domestic and community social activities must be demonstrated ... Furthermore, cultural distinctions among the early settlements must be illustrated, as well as the relationships between the pioneers of Ukrainian background and settlers of other ethnic origins who lived in this area.
>
> To fully convey the Pioneer experience to the public, educational and interpretive exhibits and displays must be provided, along with the necessary visitor support services and administrative activities. When developed as a 'living museum' expressive of community life in the 1920's, the Ukrainian Cultural Heritage Village will serve as an illustration of the contribution to Alberta's cultural mosaic provided by these immigrants who settled the East Central area of the Province.

Roman Fodchuk and Associates, 'Ukrainian Cultural Heritage Village Site Development Master Plan,' 18–20.

25 Ruptash interview; Brian Cherwick, past president of the Friends of the Ukrainian Village, interview with Karen Gabert, 19 October 2006.

26 Fodchuk, 'From Idea to Concept to Reality,' 3, 6.

27 Informant B interview.

28 Brian Cherwick, past president of the Friends of the Ukrainian Village,
interview with Karen Gabert, 19 October 2006; Bohdan Medwidsky, Advisory Board member and former senior folklorist, interview with Karen
Gabert, 16 October 2006; Slavko Nohas, former Executive Director of
the Friends of the Ukrainian Village, interview with Karen Gabert, 26
October 2006.
29 Informant A interview; informant B interview; Ruptash interview;
Savaryn interview; Bert Hohol, former Minister of Advanced Education,
interview with Karen Gabert, 20 October 2006.
30 It reads, in part, as follows:

> The ultimate goal of the Ukrainian Cultural Heritage Village is to pro-
> vide Albertans and visitors to this province with a unique educational
> opportunity. Through the preservation of heritage structures, and
> through the visitor's observation and participation in the everyday ac-
> tivities of the pioneer settlers, the broad recognition and appreciation
> of the people who dominated the settlement of east central Alberta
> will be ensured both for Albertans today and for future generations.
> Specifically, this goal will be met through:
> • The preservation, restoration and reconstruction of historical
> buildings typical of Ukrainian homesteads and prairie towns.
> • The collection, restoration, conservation and documentation of
> historical artifacts, furnishings and farm implements required for the
> buildings and on the land.
> • The demonstration of farming techniques, trades, business, do-
> mestic and community activities, and the cultural and spiritual life of
> such communities.
> • The provision of educational, exhibition and visitor services.

(Source: Alberta Culture, 'Ukrainian Cultural Heritage Village Historical
Development Proposal,' March 1981, 10.)
31 Visitor interviews were conducted with two groups: on-site visitors and
members of the Ukrainian community. The on-site interviews were conducted with 21 random visitors returning from the site. Of these, 10 took
place on a regular Saturday in August 2005, and 11 on a Special Event
Sunday (the Friends' Music Festival), when visitorship was especially
high. Interviewees were selected at random but happened to be evenly
divided between men and women (eleven men, ten women); they ranged
in age from mid-twenties to early seventies. The off-site interviews were
conducted with 20 individuals who identified their heritage as Ukrainian
and who had visited the site within the past five years. They were selected from among the author's existing acquaintances in the Ukrainian

community and by word of mouth. Special effort was made to ensure that roughly half lived in Edmonton and half in rural areas within an hour's drive of the site. Of this group, 13 were women and 7 were men, and they ranged in age from late twenties to late seventies, with the majority (12) in their fifties or sixties. All of these interviews were conducted in August 2005.

32 Alberta Culture, 'Ukrainian Cultural Heritage Village Historical Development Proposal,' March 1981, 24.

33 Horst Schmid, interview with Karen Gabert, 31 October 2006.

34 See, for example, 'The Austro-Hungarian Question,' *Methodist Magazine and Review,* February 1898, 106–19; the Rev. J.S. Woodsworth, 'The Stranger within Our Gates,' *Methodist Magazine and Review,* 1900, 32–45; the Rev. Charles Lawford, 'The Galicians,' *Missionary Outlook,* February 1902, 35; Edith A. Weekes, 'A Russian Wedding,' *Missionary Outlook,* May 1906, 115; and Dora Smith, 'Canadianizing Ruthenians,' *Missionary Outlook,* March 1919, 55.

35 John C. Lehr, 'The Rural Settlement Behaviour of Ukrainian Pioneers in Western Canada, 1891–1914,' *Western Canadian Research in Geography: The Lethbridge Papers,* B.C. Geographical Series no. 21 (Vancouver: Tantalus Research, 1975), 51–66.

36 Seventy-seven per cent of non-Ukrainian on-site visitors and 88 per cent of Ukrainian on-site visitors said that some of their family's traditions were represented on the site. One hundred per cent of off-site visitors (all Ukrainian) said the same.

37 David Lowenthal, 'Past Time, Present Place: Landscape and Memory,' *Geographical Review* 65, no. 1 (1975): 24.

38 These observations were made during my employment as a historical interpreter at the site; they were not conducted in a scientific fashion but are accurate insofar as they reveal observed tendencies of visitor behaviour.

39 One woman's reaction was especially memorable. When she asked where the eggs I was cooking with had come from, I told her they came from the chicken outside. She told me she got her eggs from the refrigerator and had fun explaining what a refrigerator is. She then tried to take me to her motorhome in the parking lot and show me her fridge. When I declined, she disappeared and returned with an egg. She pressed it into my hand to demonstrate how cold it was and to show me the effect of modern refrigeration.

40 Spencer R. Crew and James E. Sims, 'Locating Authenticity: Fragments of a Dialogue,' in *Exhibiting Cultures: The Poetics and Politics of Museum Display,* ed. Ivan Karp and Steven D. Lavine (Washington: Smithsonian Institution Scholarly Press, 1991), 162.

41 Ibid., 163.

42 One monument does the opposite of commemorating communism. In the early 1970s, Soviet Ukraine presented the Ukrainian-Canadian community with four monuments of eminent Ukrainian nationalist literary figures. One of these, the bust of Vasyl Stefanyk, stood in an inconspicuous location in Edmonton, and its intended relocation was hotly contested. In the late 1980s, it was accepted reluctantly by the Ukrainian Village, along with a bland plaque noting the writer's home village and the fact that it was a gift 'by the people of Ukraine.' Community members resented its communist associations, which remain unacknowledged. Informant B, interview.

43 Ann Martin, '"Sugar Coated History": Implementing the Historical Message at Upper Canada Village, 1951–1961,' paper presented at the annual meeting of the Canadian Historical Association, May 1992, 39; Warren Leon and Margaret Piatt, 'Living-History Museums,' in *History Museums in the United States: A Critical Assessment*, ed. Warren Leon and Roy Rosenzweig (Urbana: University of Illinois Press, 1989), 73.

44 One woman talked about 'the house with the nasty mother-in-law'; another referred to 'that mean schoolteacher.'

45 Roman Fodchuk and Associates, 'Ukrainian Cultural Village Site Development Master Plan,' 19.

46 Alberta Culture, 'Ukrainian Cultural Heritage Village Historical Development Proposal,' March 1981, 10.

47 Suzanne Holyck Hunchuck, 'A House Like No Other: An Architectural and Social History of the Ukrainian Labour Temple, 523 Arlington Avenue, Ottawa, 1923–1967,' MA thesis, Carleton University, 2001, 5.

48 Dell Upton, 'The Power of Things: Recent Studies in American Vernacular Architecture,' in *Material Culture: A Research Guide*, ed. Thomas J. Schlereth (Lawrence: University Press of Kansas, 1985), 69.

3

'A Vaguely Divided Guilt':
The Aboriginal Ukrainian

Lindy Ledohowski

Ethnic identity is often viewed as something shed by successive generations after they immigrate from the 'Old World' to the 'New World.' For instance, in writing about Armenian-American identity, Anny Bakalian charts a generational movement towards assimilation as involving a progression from 'being' to 'feeling' Armenian, with 'being' including such ethnic markers as Armenian language, culture, and social structures and 'feeling' as something different, something diluted.[1] A similar trajectory from 'more' to 'less' ethnicity was commonly perceived as the path laid out for early Ukrainian immigrants to Canada. For example, Manoly Lupul has written that the movement from being a foreigner (or 'being' Ukrainian), through the stage he refers to as 'white ethnic,' to becoming assimilated (or 'feeling' Ukrainian) involves a short transition, 'lasting no longer than the first immigrant generation and very seldom past the third. By the fourth generation only a handful are actual members of the ethnic or cultural group.'[2] This teleological view of the loss of ethnic identity may not adequately account for the still dominant role that ethnic identification often plays for the descendents of immigrants to Canada.

Some of the complexities of later generations 'feeling' their ethnic heritage rather than 'being' it are dramatized in Lisa Grekul's recent coming-of-age novel, *Kalyna's Song* (2003). Her Cold War–era Ukrainian-Canadian protagonist is asked by her Polish schoolmate to explain her ethnic identity:

'Come on,' says Katja. 'Explain it to us. Explain it to *me*. Please. I'm won-
dering what it feels like to be Ukrainian.'
'Well, it feels just like – well, I'm sure it doesn't feel any different than –'
'Any different than *what?*' says Katja, interrupting me. 'Come on. How does
it feel? You said you were Ukrainian. How does it *feel?*'[3]

One of the novel's themes is to answer this difficult question: 'what
it feels like to be Ukrainian.' The fact that the protagonist, like Grekul
herself, is the descendent of Canadian-born parents with ethnic roots
back to nineteenth-century Ukraine gives the lie to ideas that over time
the descendents of immigrants simply drop their ethnic baggage and
begin waving unhyphenated Canadian flags. Instead, this ethnic baggage seems to shift and change its shape, and even its heft, but it does
not disappear.

Ukrainian-Canadian literature detailing, representing, and commenting on the transition from 'being' Ukrainian to 'feeling' Ukrainian
suggests that what it feels like to be Ukrainian in Canada – even if
one's ancestors have been in this country for a hundred years – continues to be a source of struggle and discomfort. For my purposes, I explore some of this discomfort as expressed in the writings of Andrew
Suknaski and Lisa Grekul. The ethnic angst is expressed clearly by
Grekul's protagonist, Colleen, who explains her ethnic identity to her
colleagues in this way: 'My grandparents immigrated to Canada from
Ukraine.' To which her schoolmate replies: 'So you're not Ukrainian,
then ... Your *grandparents* are Ukrainian. *You* are Canadian.' Caught
in this semantic minefield, Colleen replies: 'I'm both. It's hard to explain.'[4] In this interaction, the schoolmate understands ethnicity to be
synonymous with nationality; Colleen clearly does not. For her, the
Ukrainian part of her identity is just as important as the Canadian part,
even though she does not speak Ukrainian, has never visited Ukraine,
and does not understand its history, politics, or literature. Nonetheless
she 'feels' that her ethnic identity encompasses 'both' Ukrainian and
Canadian.

The novel details Colleen's struggle to make sense of this 'hard to explain' concept of ethnicity. She begins her story in the same Two Hills
area of Alberta that was the setting for Myrna Kostash's influential
study of Ukrainian immigration to Canada, *All of Baba's Children*.
Kostash's work was the first serious socio-historical analysis of

Ukrainian settlement on the Canadian Prairies. She spoke to immigrants and their descendents in order to analyse and articulate the Ukrainian homesteading experience. One of her book's key insights is the marriage between an ethnic Ukrainian identity and a regional prairie identity in Canada. In her introduction, Kostash writes: 'I had been insisting that ethnicity was one thing, having to do with this time and this Canadian place, nationalism another having to do with Europe and history, and that the latter were not my affair. I was willing, even eager, to engage in the construction of neo-Galician prairie identity.'[5] This quotation brings out two important points: first, that ethnic identity and nationalism are not necessarily one and the same for Ukrainian Canadians like Kostash; and second, that for many Ukrainian Canadians, identity is linked to a prairie experience.

Much creative literature focusing on what it means to be Ukrainian in Canada does just this kind of manoeuvring, overlaying an ethnic identity with a regional one. This has given rise to 'an entire genre of Ukrainian-Canadian pioneer stories'[6] that focus on 'the bygone days of early immigration and settlement.'[7] What is interesting about literature that positions Ukrainian-ness in Canada squarely on the Canadian Prairies is that it does so long after the initial moment of immigration. That 'farming life and such communities were initially and in the early years the focal point of cultural imagining is understandable,' writes Sonia Mycak, suggesting that 'what is interesting, perhaps puzzling, is that this practice should continue right to this day, even though later arrivals have influenced Ukrainian culture and community life.'[8] She recognizes that even after what Robert Klymasz has called 'the hypertrophic impact of thousands of Ukrainian war refugees,'[9] who made up the third wave of Ukrainian immigration to Canada, Ukrainian Canadian-ness as a concept is still rooted on the Prairies on the backs of the first-wave immigrants from the Austrian provinces of Galicia and Bukovyna. Kostash is the daughter of immigrants, and Grekul is even further removed from the initial moment of prairie settlement, yet both writers struggle to articulate their conception of themselves as both Ukrainian and Prairie Canadian. This particular construction of identity gives rise to a host of complicated issues; principal among the inner conflicts that arise is how a Ukrainian pioneering identity, with its roots and ties to the Prairies, can be reconciled with a displaced and exploited First Nations presence. When Suknaski's and Grekul's literary works struggle with what it 'feels like' to be Ukrainian Canadian, they do so trying to address their role in colonizing previous prairie dwellers.

The regional correlation between Ukrainian prairie settlers and First Nations has strongly influenced how later generations of Ukrainian Canadians (including Suknaski's and Grekul's) write about their ethnic identity. There have long been points of connection between these two groups of prairie dwellers. For example, Robert Harney's retrospective look at early Canadian culture contends that the 'colorfulness of the colonies' was performed by 'countless onslaughts by Cree, Blackfoot, and Ukrainians in full ethnic battle dress, herded by red-tunicked guardians of "the Canadian way."'[10] This suggests that early Ukrainian homesteaders were viewed by the colonial seat of power as just as 'other' as the aboriginal presence that predated them. Similarly, in discussing the socio-economic disparities between aboriginals and non-aboriginal ethnic groups in Canada, George Melnyk has written that 'the comparison between native and ethnic makes sense when one is aware of their historical affinity as outcast minorities.'[11] While he goes on to discuss how those histories have diverged, the very real historical similarity between the disenfranchised and disadvantaged early immigrants to the Canadian Prairies and the First Nations they encountered on arrival should be noted. This is the reading that Grekul offers when she writes that just as an aboriginal 'way of life has ended, [the] pioneer way of life ended for the immigrant settlers who displaced the First Nations people from their land.'[12] Yet despite some of these resemblances – being similarly marked as 'other,' and experiencing the passing of a way of life on the Prairies – Ukrainian-Canadian literature of the Prairies that tries to create a simple connection between the figure of the Ukrainian homesteader and the aboriginal he displaced encounters serious problems.

Recent critical discourse has identified what has been called 'cultural appropriation' or 'appropriation of voice,'[13] which includes non-aboriginal use of aboriginal stories and materials as a kind of ongoing colonization, a literary colonization. This kind of appropriation has become popular in post-colonial literatures, with minority groups writing in ways that evoke similarities between themselves (i.e., as non-aboriginals) and aboriginal populations as a means to establish a symbolic legitimacy for the immigrant settler who participated in exploitation and colonization. In Canadian literature this trend takes the form of peopling non-aboriginal texts with aboriginal characters and themes to show imagined connections between the two groups. Margery Fee describes this phenomenon, noting that 'those who do not wish to identify with "mainstream" anglo-Canadian culture, or who are prevented from doing so, can find a prior and superior Canadian culture with which to identify.'[14] Daniel Francis similarly notes that the 'myth of transformation [from non-aboriginal to aboriginal] lies at the heart of Canadian culture: Canadians need to transform themselves into Indians.'[15] This pattern of indigenizing in Canadian literature is especially common among what are often referred to as non-charter groups, where one 'variant of mainstream nationalism uses the First Peoples' position as marginal, yet aboriginal, to make a similar claim-by-identification for other marginal groups.'[16] Given the similarities preexisting between Ukrainian prairie settlers and aboriginal prairie peoples, it is not surprising to find aboriginal characters popping up in stories about Ukrainian-Canadian homesteaders and their descendents. However, the ways in which they feature in Ukrainian-Canadian prairie writing are somewhat different from this simple claim-by-identification metaphor. Put simply, on the one hand, Ukrainian-Canadian writers of the West feel that their home lies on the Canadian Prairies, based on 'a founding fathers myth erected on the peasant pioneers'; according to Frances Swyripa, 'in their backbreaking toil and sacrifice to introduce the prairie and parkland to the plough and to exploit mining and forest frontiers so that Canada could be great, lay Ukrainians' right to full partnership in Confederation.'[17] They can see 'themselves as no less a founding people than the French, the English, and the Natives.'[18] Yet on the other hand, they feel profoundly conflicted over the role they and their ancestors have played in exploiting, displacing, and marginalizing First Nations. They are caught between wanting to feel at home on the Canadian Prairies and recognizing that such a home belonged to someone else first. Grekul's Colleen comes to realize that 'there are five Indian reserves [around my town, but no] Cree teacher at [my] school.'[19] She feels guilty when she recognizes that her school offers Ukrainian-language instruction but not Cree. To strike home the point of her own familial and ethnic culpability, the Ukrainian-language teacher at her school is her very own mother. She cannot escape the role her family (past and present) has played in a system that continues to disenfranchise Prairie First Nations. As she tries to explain her identity, she thinks to herself: 'If my family were Native then I could talk about self-government, land claims, racism. Reserves.' She continues: 'I have nothing to say. Nothing at all to contribute to the conversation.'[20] She is silenced by her own recognition that compared to the political struggles faced by Canada's First Nations, her Ukrainian-Canadian concerns are inconsequential. Grekul's novel echoes sentiments given voice by another author a generation earlier.

Suknaski's poetry acknowledges this strange double bind facing the Ukrainian Canadian of the Prairies. His 1976 collection *Wood Mountain Poems* is both profoundly regional in its focus and profoundly concerned with issues of multiculturalism, not least of which being how to honour one's own ethnic heritage while recognizing the role one's forebears played in displacing and marginalizing Canada's First Nations under a colonial power structure. Suknaski admits that his poems address 'a vaguely divided guilt; guilt for what happened to the Indian (his land taken) imprisoned on his reserve; and guilt because to feel this guilt is a betrayal of what you ethnically are – the son of a homesteader and his wife who must be rightfully honoured in one's mythology.'[21] The collection is framed by the poet's adult return to his childhood village of Wood Mountain in Saskatchewan. While there, he creates poems out of stories and memories, both his own and those shared with him by the townspeople. Rosemary Marangoly George writes that 'the search for the location in which the self is "at home" is one of the primary projects of twentieth-century fiction in English,'[22] and this collection is an example of just the kind of literature she is thinking about. It is obsessed with the quest for home; more specifically, it represents the desire to feel 'at home' within oneself. As such, the poems represent a desire not just to articulate what being 'at home' means in a particular place, but also to come to grips with 'feeling' not just Ukrainian, but Ukrainian Canadian in a Prairie landscape. The deep tensions in Suknaski's poems express his discomfort with the doubled position of the Ukrainian-Canadian subject, who is both at home (as a homesteader) and not at home (as non-aboriginal) in Canada.

Suknaski's *Wood Mountain Poems* provides a test case for the claims he makes about his 'vaguely divided guilt' as a descendent of Ukrainian homesteaders. The poems in that collection vacillate between honouring two seemingly mutually exclusive entities – the presence, stories, and experiences of both aboriginal groups and Ukrainian homesteaders.

In so doing they illustrate a lived experience of 'what it feels like to be Ukrainian,' suggesting that those feelings of ethnic identity are uneasy – that is, they are more complicated than simply watering down 'being' Ukrainian in a passive and straightforward manner that occurs naturally as part of an unstoppable march towards assimilation.

While the poems are deeply multicultural,[23] they pay particular attention to both aboriginal and Ukrainian presences. For instance, while many of the poems position speakers using various ethnic dialects, only Ukrainian and Dakota are reproduced as foreign languages in the text. The difference between imitating the Chinese cafe owner Jimmy Hoy's accented English – 'gee clyz / all time slem ting'[24] – and the grandmother's Ukrainian curses – 'ah tehbee sracku tom geedo!'[25] – or the Dakota rabbit's question – 'whali dootecktoo okashnee hew?'[26] – is clear: in the first instance the poet is constructed as an outside listener to accented speech, while in the second he is an insider of the linguistic community, even providing footnotes indicating the English translations of Ukrainian and Dakota words. Eli Mandel writes that these poems embody 'identity, change, process, the poet,'[27] and in reading them in this spirit the process of identity construction in which the poet is engaged is vexed as he tries to make sense of a Ukrainian and aboriginal heritage, all the while wanting to claim and honour both, but never able to do so entirely.

This unease is played out again and again in the poems. One of the best examples is in the opening poem,[28] in which the speaker – a thinly veiled Suknaski – details interactions with his mother and father and imaginatively recreates their initial immigration to Canada. The father is a sturdy homesteader who 'carve[s] out with a blunted knife / a cellar / in which to endure the first few years.'[29] The mother has survived the First World War in Poland to experience 'the currency changing as the war ends / her money and several years' work suddenly worthless one spring day / all these things drift away from the ship carrying / her to the unknown / new land.'[30] They are thus characterized as members of a hard-working underclass often overlooked in official histories; they are the ones who pay for the decisions made by distant seats of power. Nonetheless, through reading we learn that the father is abusive, beating his pregnant wife with a rolling pin, holding an axe above her head, and attempting to strangle his son with his own scarf.[31] After separating, at the funeral of one of their children, mother and father 'begin to run toward each other / they embrace / and she lifts him off the ground / he is 79 at the time.'[32] It would seem that the poem is about the son's desire to reconcile his feelings towards his abusive father and to honour the immigrant experience of both parents. This insight is borne out by the apostrophe to the absent father: 'father / i must accept you and that other dark man within you / must accept you along with your sad admission / that you never loved anyone in your life / (you must be loved / father.'[33] And while these lines come close to the end of the poem, Suknaski does not let us rest easy with the belief that his identity can be resolved through forgiving his father and documenting/honouring that experience, harsh as it seems. In fact, the poem closes with a 'suicide note': 'silence / and a prayer to you shugmanitou / for something / to believe in.'[34] The fact that this closing prayer appeals to an aboriginal deity as a 'suicide note,' suggests a rejection of understanding the self (including ethnic identity) through familial, principally paternal, relations. Rejecting an identity shaped out of a stereotypical reconciliation with the father demonstrates that Suknaski's identity is not just a private, familial matter. Rather, such a belief in European patrilineal structures results in 'suicide' and a call to an aboriginal god for help. This drive towards articulating identity through ethnic or familial lines – a drive that is in the end weakened by an aboriginal presence – recurs throughout the collection. It is one structural way in which Suknaski expresses his strange sense of being split. He wants to honour those two groups that have equally shaped his present, yet those two groups have still earlier roots that conflict with each other.

His attempts to work through the trap of his own identity arise in the repeated motif of death, particularly death of First Nations characters and groups. Rayna Green's article on the white performance of Indianness in America is especially helpful here. In it she discusses the increased attention to what she calls 'playing Indian' while real American aboriginals were being destroyed at an alarming rate. In identifying the stereotype of what she calls the 'Vanishing American,' she writes: 'The cult of the vanishing American, the vanishing noble savage is emblematically transformed forever as a named, tragic figure.'[35] By turning real destruction and exploitation of First Nations peoples and ways of life into a symbol of tragedy, one can elide one's own culpability in that act. Thomas King takes this idea further, commenting that the image of the vanishing Indian common in much early North American literature that romanticized aboriginal figures recurs in contemporary literature through characters doomed through drug or alcohol abuse.[36] In an elegiac tone, Suknaski in his poems seems to be creating a pre-ordained doom for aboriginal groups as a way to address his own guilt. In being 'poet as historian,' to use Grekul's phrase,[37] he elegizes the betrayal and destruction of the Nez Percés,[38] characterizing their chief as 'steeped in abandoned hope.' That chief 'later die[s] of a broken heart,'[39] while his people are 'death ambling clothed in rags'; they 'are nothing / but a walking graveyard.'[40] The 'poet as historian' constructs an entire group of people as condemned to destruction. Even while making them live again in the lines of the poem, he dooms them again and again to extinction. When the last Nez Percé chief admits at the close of the poem, '*i have no country / i have no home and i feel / i have no people,*'[41] we feel the sadness and the tragedy of the loss. We do not, however, feel any responsibility for that loss. In this poem, Suknaski blames 'gold seekers and politicians' and '*bloodthirsty blue-coats*'[42] for the death and destruction of the Nez Percés. The poem documents and recognizes the obliteration of an aboriginal culture but does not include settlers as part of the power structures that contributed to that destruction. The sadness and the absence, like the 'suicide note' at the end of the first poem, undercut the sense that there may be some sort of easy resolution, by evoking the idea that previous aboriginal groups were dying out. It follows that the contribution of homesteaders to the destruction of that way of life was inconsequential (in any event, it goes unmentioned in this poem).

Other poems in the collection also commit the construction of the contemporary aboriginal as doomed in the way King identifies; they do not, though, let the homesteading presence evade the role it played in displacing earlier peoples. In 'Poem to Sitting Bull and His Son Crowfoot' not only are the historical figures doomed because '*white man has grown powerful / and defies the gods,*'[43] but so also is Suknaski's contemporary, James Wounded Horse, who taught him how to play pool.[44] Wounded Horse is both a tragic figure and one expressly linked to the tragedy of the earlier First Nations. It is by visiting the Sioux cemetery and looking at the gravestone of Wounded Horse that the speaker moves back in time to ruminate about Sitting Bull. Suknaski writes that in looking at the grave marker of his friend he remembers someone throwing a tenpin ball at the living Wounded Horse, who 'leapt like a struck rabbit' with 'fear cross[ing] his eyes,'[45] which leads the speaker to admit that 'his metal marker now mirroring the sun / casts my thoughts to sitting bull.'[46] Wounded Horse's victimization at the hands of 'some jester who wouldn't wait for the pins to be up'[47] is poetically linked to the death of Sitting Bull: 'men dragged him feet-first from the tepee / while he rose to / crumple to the ground with his son.'[48] In this way the poem links past and present aboriginal peoples with an overwhelming sense of doom. This doom is linked to guilt as Suknaski tries to comprehend his own place amidst the geography and topography laced with the deaths he memorializes. For instance, as he stands in the cemetery thinking of Wounded Horse, his friend, and the historical figures of Sitting Bull and his son, he thinks that the place where he stands is not just that 'where the lives of these people begin,' but also 'where something in my life seems rooted here.'[49] The poem says that 'homesteaders broke / the land,'[50] and it is this feeling of root-edness through inheriting the land broken by the homesteaders that the poems engage. What is the cost of setting down roots in somebody else's garden?

Again and again the poems suggest that there is no clear sense that can be made of the double bind in which Suknaski finds himself. Just as he paints aboriginal figures doomed to death, he also seems to paint himself doomed to wandering in the space between groups; he is doomed to suffer survivor's guilt. This is most poignantly expressed in 'The First Communion,' in which Suknaski constructs himself as ex-pressly outside aboriginal communities: 'we played softball with the indian and halfbreed kids.'[51] The use of the first-person plural pronoun constructs the speaker as separate from 'the indian and halfbreed kids.' This otherness is emphasized in the main event of the poem: 'that night the young indian boy playing left field for us / was struck by lightning while going home.'[52] So while this unnamed boy will never make it home, the closing of the poem sadly announces that the car 'carried some of us back home / to wood mountain.'[53] The guilt lies in the state-ment that the 'young indian boy' will never make it 'home,' but Suk-naski will. It is this very conundrum, in both the past and the present, that each poem cannot reconcile: How can one be at home in a home denied someone else?

One strategy that the poems employ is to show the mobility of abo-riginal groups to Wood Mountain, thus casting them as immigrants not unlike Suknaski's homesteading forebears. Sitting Bull, a recurring presence throughout the collection – indeed, he is the figure on the book's cover – is characterized as seeking refuge in Wood Mountain, rather than being indigenous to it.[54] Similarly, in 'Sandia Man' the poem moves back in time to imagine the migration across the Bering Strait from Asia to North America. These early peoples 'move on some autumn day / to arrive somewhere else still,'[55] and are the 'silent ancestor of a people who traveled over / northern trails beaten by mammoths and later buffalo.'[56] In this way the idea of rootedness is juxtaposed with metaphors and images of mobility. Such a contradiction makes Wood Mountain's settlers and aboriginals at home and not at home simultaneously. The land becomes something that groups pass through, leaving their signs like the 'three circles where the tepees once stood'[57] on a prairie landscape. Throughout the collection, the prairie becomes an 'ancestral space to move through and beyond'[58] for both groups. First Nations' presence is prior, but transient, through images of mobility and death, but it does not preclude the homesteader's place on the land in the mythology Suknaski develops as a way of coming to terms with his own split identity. It seems that Suknaski employs images of transience through the landscape as one way of imagining the two groups existing together without condemning one for its role in the displacement of the other.

In 'Chaapunka' this sense of prior but equal is expressed through a humourous anecdote. The poem focuses on a man who in attempting to relieve himself must run 'for the tall grass and cattails to hide'[59] from the attacks of a voracious *chaapunka* or mosquito. Being foiled, the mosquito asks: '*whichashasah li dookteh yah?* / meaning: / *where did this fulla go?*'[60] While the listeners of the tale laugh, Suknaski asks the storyteller: '*who was this fulla gus? a homesteader?*'[61] to which the speaker responds: '*no – fulla musta bin sioux / chaapunka spoke dakota and the fulla understood him.*'[62] The 'fulla' of the story can be presumed either a homesteader or Sioux; both are equally likely to be found on the landscape. However, the earlier status of the Sioux is indicated by the shared language between him and the mosquito, who represents the natural landscape.

Importantly, however, in this reading is what Derrideans would recognize as the trace left behind by the mobile populations. Suknaski as the speaking voice of the poems must constantly account for the sense that even if aboriginal populations have passed through the landscape (as transient or tragic figures), they are not wholly gone. As he looks on the remnants of the circle of ancient teepees found on a farm, he says: 'i try to imagine those who passed here so long ago / possibly becoming this dust / i breathe.'[63] Written on the landscape, breathed in as dust, are the ghosts that haunt him – the double ghosts of the original homesteaders and the original First Nations. Haunting is yet another way of expressing the sense of being unhomed while at home. A ghost is no longer at home in his body, and the ghosts that haunt Suknaski throughout this collection emphasize the futility of his quest to accept and embrace a home and personal identity in Wood Mountain. Through telling stories of homesteaders and stories of First Nations, the poems evoke Suknaski's 'childhood ghosts,' who 'move in the tall grass / taking over the half-abandoned village' of Wood Mountain.[64] Chief among the 'ghosts of [his] youth' are Sitting Bull,[65] and he says he 'tr[ies] to imagine him / the lines around his eyes reminiscent / of shadowed prairie trails in the late afternoon sun.'[66] This haunting by a prior presence highlights the unease that Suknaski feels in trying to claim Wood Mountain as the site of home. Suknaski tries to construct aboriginal presences as mobile and transient, as immigrants themselves; yet the images of haunting suggest that he cannot so easily efface his guilt at being at home on land haunted by another. His sympathy and allegiance with an aboriginal presence that is at odds with his own inherited history are played out as he evokes the 'pale bowlegged ghost of james wounded horse / floating high over wood mountain.'[67] Suknaski summons his dead friend to bear witness as a white court tries to determine the citizenship of aboriginal Melvin Greene, who wants to grow old on his mother's Ontario reserve, but who may be deported to his father's home of New York. Suknaski wants the ghost of his aboriginal friend to side with him in declaring: 'MELVIN GREENE MUST BE FREE TO DIE / WHEREVER HE WISHES.'[68] However, this poem creates binaries between 'indian law' and 'white man's law,'[69] with Suknaski's sympathies clearly allied with 'indian law' despite the fact that he is of European lineage. He cannot escape his own corporeality, his own whiteness. As a result, no matter how strenuously he announces his verdict in capital letters, he is still caught in the 'vaguely divided guilt' that plagues the collection as a whole, in which the poems fluctuate between a desire to be allied with these two perspectives simultaneously.

Poems like this one express a yearning to speak in favour of 'indian law' despite speaking from 'white man's' position. This gives the collection as a whole an unstable and uneven feel.

This uneasiness arises because Suknaski is haunted not just by Sitting Bull or James Wounded Horse, but also by homesteaders. He writes that 'old settlers' ghosts loom up from the shadows / in the poplar forest.'[70] They, like the aboriginal spectres that haunt him, feature largely as he tries to define and articulate home and in so doing articulate a sense of his own identity. For only when he can identify and clarify where home is will he be able to identify who he is in that home. Ultimately this haunting proves too much for Suknaski, who leaves the poetic site of Wood Mountain. He writes that 'merely one week later / i have had enough of childhood ghosts / and stories.'[71] This collection resists resolution and ends with Suknaski leaving Wood Mountain, having failed in his quest to reconcile two parts of his inherited past. In 'Leaving Home' he writes:

> leaving home having arrived
> at the last of all follies
> believing something here was mine
> believing i could return
> and build a home
> within the dying.[72]

In these lines the futility of his quest for a home and with it a stable identity is clear. The futility of reconciling the two sides of his 'vaguely divided guilt' has been proven; instead, the poems suggest that the *process* rather than the end point is what matters when it comes to negotiating a vexed identity with complexities arising out of varied contingencies on the Canadian Prairies. As the collection comes to its close the speaker leaves his boyhood home and (he hopes) the ghosts that haunt him there. However, he finds that he takes the ghosts with him. As he falls asleep in Vancouver 'the laughing face of the prairie madman / looms beyond flames rising on the edge of [his] bed.'[73] The identity of 'the prairie madman' is left oblique. Throughout the collection Suknaski is scrupulous in clarifying the background or identity of the ghosts and the people he imagines and records, but here we do not know if this madman is a shaman of aboriginal mythology, masked and threatening, or the madman of his homesteading father's wrath, rearing his ugly head. It seems that in the end what he is haunted by is the madness of trying to reconcile with the 'vaguely divided guilt' that cannot be made sense of. He is stuck in the mid-place between the two groups, and what it 'feels like to be Ukrainian' in the specific location of the Canadian Prairies is profoundly conflicted.

Extrapolating this insight further, we see that Bakalian's model of moving from 'being' to 'feeling,' or Lupul's suggestion that ethnic identity retention involves a straightforward march towards assimilation, are potentially flawed by virtue of their failure to account for the variable of being unhomed owing to the kinds of haunting that Suknaski's poetry expresses. Mandel has written that 'the writer's subject *is* his own dilemma, writing west'[74] about prairie literature, and that this 'writing west' can include that which Sunkaski presents: the struggle to accommodate his own ethnic heritage while also accommodating the influence of land infused with and haunted by prior, aboriginal presences. Thus while other post-colonial subjects may employ indigenizing strategies as a way of making themselves at home through an alliance with a 'prior and superior' presence, the prairie post-colonial subject, like Suknaski, expresses a kind of discomfort with such an alliance.

By metaphorically leaving Wood Mountain at the close of the collection, Suknaski suggests that these identity issues are unresolved (and possibly irresolvable). Janice Kulyk Keefer is in agreement with such a view, commenting that 'the enormous upheaval involved in changing cultures is not something that can be "worked out" in one generation.'[75] Kostash concurs, telling us that insecurities about ethnic identity are 'never resolved by any particular generation once and for all.'[76] Suknaski's poetry seems to suggest that these identity issues cannot even be resolved in the individual self. The discomfort at the level of ethnic and national identity is not just something to be 'worked out' across generations; if Suknaski's poems are any indication, it is something that cannot even be resolved in the individual. Moreover, these identity issues do not just plague Suknaski as the son of immigrants writing some thirty years ago; they are still present for Grekul and her protagonist, whose grandparents and great-grandparents were the initial immigrants. Like Suknaski, Colleen must leave her prairie home in search of her ethnic identity. A generation after the first publication of Suknaski's poems that express such an irreconcilable divide, Grekul's novel suggests that the quest for home and identity cannot be resolved in the place/space marked as home on the Canadian prairie. Colleen leaves Alberta for a year in Africa. A world away from her prairie home and her homesteading grandparents, she begins the real work of figuring out her ethnic identity. In Africa she is confronted by her hostile schoolmate, who antagonistically refers to Colleen's grandparents as 'brave settlers taming the wild west' who steal land from the aboriginal people who were there first.[77] Colleen has no immediate answer. Like Suknaski's speaker, she is caught between recognizing the legitimate claims of First Nations and not wanting to renounce her own ethnic heritage.

Suknaski's collection closes with a sad lament for the poet to 'put aside' his art and 'tie this dream horse to a star / and walk / ordinary earth,'[78] suggesting that these tensions cannot be resolved. In a bit of a shift, Grekul's novel ends with Colleen's return from her travels to her family in Alberta. The novel is hopeful in its tone, and Colleen's final project for school is an original composition of Ukrainian folk music – one 'with an upbeat tempo'[79] suggesting that the role of the artist may just provide an avenue for identity construction or resolution. In her literary criticism, Grekul writes 'that Ukrainian Canadian-ness resides in ongoing *acts* of imagination,'[80] which suggests that she gives primacy to artistic works in constructing and grappling with identity issues, especially those located in failed attempts to find, define, and claim a home. In the introduction to the published version of her doctoral work on Ukrainian-Canadian writing in English, she gives her reader an imperative: '*Write your stories down; make your voices heard.*'[81] So while she and Suknaski represent two different generations of Ukrainian-Canadian descendents of homesteaders, both of them grapple with feeling unhomed on the prairie. However, Suknaski's poetry suggests that the intensely personal struggle to find and define home may be an impossible task, whereas Grekul's creative and critical work sees writing not just as something important for the individual, but crucial to the development and articulation of a group identity. As such, perhaps the transition from 'being' Ukrainian is not to 'feeling' Ukrainian, but rather through a 'vaguely divided guilt' to 'writing' Ukrainian Canadian.

Notes

1 Anny Bakalian, *Armenian-Americans: From Being to Feeling Armenian* (New Brunswick: Transaction, 1993), 5–6.

2 Manoly Lupul, 'The Tragedy of Canada's White Ethnics: A Constitutional Postmortem,' *Journal of Ukrainian Studies* 7, no. 1 (1982): 4.

3 Lisa Grekul, *Kalyna's Song* (Regina: Coteau, 2003), 268.

4 Ibid. (original emphasis).

5 Myrna Kostash, Introduction to *All of Baba's Children* (1977; repr. Edmonton: NeWest Press, 1987), xv.

6 Sonia Mycak, *Canuke Literature: Critical Essays on Canadian Ukrainian Writing* (Huntington: Nova Science, 2001), 68.

7 Lisa Grekul, *Leaving Shadows: Literature by Canada's Ukrainians* (Edmonton: University of Alberta Press, 2005), 116.

8 Mycak, *Canuke Literature*, 50–1.

9 Robert Klymasz, 'Cultural Maintenance and the Ukrainian Experience in Western Canada,' in *New Soil – Old Roots: The Ukrainian Experience in Canada*, ed. Jaroslav Rozumnyj (Winnipeg: Ukrainian Academy of Arts and Sciences in Canada, 1983), 175.

10 Robert Harney, '"So Great a Heritage as Ours": Immigration and the Survival of the Canadian Polity,' *Daedalus* 117, no. 4 (1988): 66.

11 George Melnyk, 'The Indian as Ethnic,' in *Radical Regionalism* (Edmonton: NeWest, 1977), 52.

12 Lisa Grekul, *Leaving Shadows*, 94.

13 Kenneth Williams, 'Cultural Appropriation and Aboriginal Literature,' *Windspeaker* 14, no. 11 (1997): 18.

14 Margery Fee, 'Romantic Nationalism and the Image of Native People in Contemporary English-Canadian Literature,' in *The Native in Literature*, ed. Thomas King, Cheryl Calver, and Helen Hoy (Toronto: ECW, 1987), 17.

15 Daniel Francis, *The Imaginary Indian* (Vancouver: Arsenal Pulp, 1992), 123.

16 Fee, 'Romantic Nationalism,' 17.

17 Frances Swyripa, *Wedded to the Cause: Ukrainian-Canadian Women and Ethnic Identity, 1891–1991* (Toronto: University of Toronto Press, 1993), 221.

18 Donna Bennett, 'English Canada's Postcolonial Complexities,' *Essays on Canadian Writing* 51/52 (1993–4): 185.

19 Grekul, *Kalyna's Song*, 48.

20 Ibid., 265.

21 Andrew Suknaski, *Wood Mountain Poems* (Toronto: Macmillan, 1976), 124.

22 Rosemary Marangoly George, *The Politics of Home: Postcolonial Relocations and Twentieth-Century Fiction* (Cambridge: Cambridge University Press, 1996), 3.

23 In analysing a pair of patched jeans in the poem 'West Central Pub' in this collection, Michael Abraham makes the following observation: 'The patchwork of the patron's jeans is not unlike the multicultural patchwork of both the Wood Mountain community and Canada as a whole. While each patch seems to exist on its own, isolated on the jeans, together they compose the garment.' 'Cultural Orphans and Wood Mountain: The Poetry of Andrew Suknaski,' *Prairie Journal of Canadian Literature* 14 (1990): 28.

24 Suknaski, 'Jimmy Hoy's Place,' ll.1–2.

25 Suknaski, 'Johnny Nicholson (1925–1974),' l.19.

26 Suknaski, 'Mashteeshka,' l.8.

27 Eli Mandel, 'Writing West: On the Road to Wood Mountain,' in *Trace: Prairie Writers on Writing*, ed. Birk Sproxton (Winnipeg: Turnstone, 1986), 50.

28 Suknaski, 'Homestead, 1914 (sec. 32, TP4, RGE, W3RD, Sask.),' 19–26.

29 Ibid., ll. 101–3.

30 Ibid., ll. 64–9.

31 Ibid., ll. 227, 229–30, 240.

32 Ibid., ll. 182–5.

33 Ibid., ll. 241–6.

34 Ibid., ll. 250–3.

35 Rayna Green, 'The Tribe Called Wannabee: Playing Indian in America and Europe,' *Folklore* 99, no. 1 (1988): 36.

36 Thomas King, *The Truth About Stories* (Toronto: Anansi, 2003).

37 Grekul, *Leaving Shadows*, 100.

38 Suknaski, 'Nez Percés at Wood Mountain,' 55–8. For more information on Nez Percé history of this period, see Lynn Baird, *In Nez Perce Country: Accounts of the Bitterroots and the Clearwater after Lewis and Clark* (Moscow: University of Idaho Library, 2003).

39 Suknaski, 'Nez Percés at Wood Mountain,' ll. 59–60.

40 Ibid., ll. 85, 89–90.

41 Ibid., ll. 100–3.

42 Ibid., ll. 35, 43.

43 Suknaski, 'Poem to Sitting Bull and His Son Crowfoot,' ll. 55–6.

44 Ibid., l. 20.

45 Ibid., ll. 23, 26.

46 Ibid., ll. 28–9.

47 Ibid., l. 25.

48 Ibid., ll. 39–41.

49 Ibid., ll. 30–1.
50 Ibid., ll. 67–8.
51 Suknaski, 'The First Communion,' l. 7.
52 Ibid., ll. 13–14.
53 Ibid., ll. 20–1.
54 Suknaski, 'The Teton Sioux and the 1879 Prairie Fire,' ll. 20–1.
55 Suknaski, 'Sandia Man,' ll. 21–2.
56 Ibid., ll. 50–1.
57 Suknaski, 'Indian Site on the Edge of Tonita Pasture,' l. 59.
58 Ibid., l. 17.
59 Suknaski, 'Chaapunka,' l. 13.
60 Ibid., ll. 17–19.
61 Ibid., l. 22.
62 Ibid., ll. 23–4.
63 Suknaski, 'Indian Site on the Edge of Tonita Pasture,' ll. 35–7.
64 Suknaski, 'In Memory of Alfred A. Lecaine,' ll. 3–4.
65 Suknaski, 'The Teton Sioux and 1879 Prairie Fire,' ll. 5–6.
66 Ibid., ll. 7–9.
67 Suknaski, 'Melvin Greene/Oneida Indian Fighting for a Place to Die,' ll. 1–2.
68 Ibid., ll. 70–1 (original emphasis).
69 Ibid., ll. 62, 63.
70 Suknaski, 'Lee Soparlo,' ll. 22–3.
71 Suknaski, 'Ode to the Oldest Brother,' ll. 9–11.
72 Suknaski, 'Leaving Home,' ll. 26–31.
73 Suknaski, 'Nightbus to Vancouver,' ll. 51–2.
74 Mandel, 'Writing West,' 48.
75 Janice Kulyk Keefer, 'From Mosaic to Kaleidoscope: Out of the Multicultural Past Comes a Vision of a Transcultural Future,' *Books in Canada* 20, no. 6 (1991): 16.
76 Myrna Kostash, *All of Baba's Great-Grandchildren: Ethnic Identity in the Next Canada* (Saskatoon: Heritage, 2000), 37.
77 Grekul, *Kalyna's Song*, 269.
78 Suknaski, 'Western Prayer,' ll. 2, 15–17.
79 Grekul, *Kalyna's Song*, 368.
80 Grekul, *Leaving Shadows*, 62.
81 Grekul, Introduction to *Leaving Shadows*, xxiii (original emphasis).

PART TWO

Leaders and Intellectuals

This part takes two well-known figures from the Ukrainian-Canadian community and the leadership of two high-profile Ukrainian nationalist organizations and places them under the historian's microscope, resulting in a remarkably fresh reconsideration of men's experiences as leaders and activists. Indeed, these studies lend a much-needed dimension to our understanding of Ukrainian men as historical actors, intellectuals, and (sometimes controversial) political theorists and agents while similarly highlighting the fruits of their political and community labours. Readers will note that the three contributions make considerable mention of their subjects' religious affiliations. These reflected the three most influential religious movements among Ukrainian Canadians: Presbyterianism (the largest Protestant denomination operating within Ukrainian-Canadian communities); the Ukrainian Greek Orthodox Church of Canada; and the Ukrainian Catholic Church. As a whole, the essays offer some indication of how influential church affiliation could be in terms of forging friendships, soliciting support, facilitating activism, and shaping a host of occupational and personal opportunities for Ukrainian men in Canada.

Peter Melnycky's careful reconstruction of the life of Paul Rudyk is a fascinating examination of how a radical 'village intellectual' transformed himself into a leader of one of the most 'respectable' sectors of the Ukrainian-Canadian community and a successful urban Canadian businessman and philanthropist. As Melnycky makes clear, along the way Rudyk crossed many physical, intellectual, political, and spiritual divides without ever entirely burning any bridges. He seemed to move easily from the rural to the urban; from adherence to the Ukrainian Catholic faith to the ersatz Greek Independent Church (GIC) and ultimately to Presbyterianism; and from Ukrainian Populist radical to Canadian Liberal and ultimately to a supporter of William Aberhart's Social Credit.

In Jars Balan's reconsideration of Illia Kiriak, readers will discover one of the most interesting and (posthumously) famous of Ukrainian-Canadian authors. Like Rudyk, Kiriak had been heavily influenced by the radical nationalist movement of the Old Country. However, Kiriak remained committed to the left for a much longer time – indeed, he became even more radical during his early days as an itinerant labourer out along the resource frontier of western North America. When he did drift away from the left, Kiriak's choice had little to do with material success (he had virtually none in his life), but rather with a spirituality born in the Old Country that became deeply rooted in the newly created Ukrainian Greek Orthodox Church of Canada. It and related bodies, such as the Ukrainian Self-Reliance League, would take up much of Kiriak's organizational talents. This work, along with his writing, was what brought him into contact with the almost exclusively male network of church and secular leaders, a network that nurtured the development of the first generation of male Ukrainian-Canadian leaders and intellectuals.

Finally, Orest Martynowych's 'Sympathy for the Devil' confronts what is arguably the most sensitive and highly politicized topic within the Ukrainian-Canadian community. His work focuses on the small but influential group of primarily Catholic, Ukrainian-Canadian supporters of fascism and Nazism who led the United Hetman Organization and the Ukrainian National Federation in the interwar years. Martynowych carefully and objectively examines the attitudes, writings, and public pronouncements of several key leaders of Ukrainian veterans' organizations, casting an unblinking eye on the anti-Semitism and pro-German sentiment that went hand-in-hand with these leaders' profound anti-communism and Ukrainian nationalism. While always refusing to tar all, or even most, of the rank-and-file members of these organizations with the same brush, Martynowych makes a convincing case for the need to carefully re-examine the history of these groups.

The articles in this part prepare the ground for several other contributions to this collection. As careful readers will note, the lives of Rudyk and Kiriak – and their intellectual roots in Ukrainian populism – had much in common with (indeed, often intersected with) those studied by Mochoruk and Makuch, while Balan's work on an early Ukrainian-Canadian literary figure provides a fascinating counterpoint to Ledohowski's work on later writers. By the same token, Martynowych's work places Petryshyn's essay in a far richer 'internal' context of intellectual divisions within the organized, non-communist Ukrainian-Canadian community.

4

'Great Tasks and a Great Future': Paul Rudyk, Pioneer Ukrainian-Canadian Entrepreneur and Philanthropist

Peter Melnycky

There is a rich and growing literature on the Ukrainian community in Canada. However, one topic that has received scant attention is the history of urban commerce and entrepreneurship, especially during the pioneer era preceding the First World War. The Western homesteader, 'the stalwart peasant in a sheepskin coat,' and to a lesser extent the industrial worker on the frontier, are predominant in the literature on this period. Less often studied are those Ukrainians who gravitated towards urban centres and who undertook non-traditional economic livelihoods. While the earliest Ukrainian immigrants were not totally homogenous, they were overwhelmingly of rural peasant origins and had limited experience in commerce and a weakly developed business culture. That said, Canada's industrial expansion at the turn of the century resulted in rapid urbanization and a subsequent rise in the urban labour force, which included Ukrainians. These urban communities fostered the rise of Ukrainian-owned businesses. Though initially small, this urban Ukrainian constituency would soon grow. As one result, more and more Ukrainian Canadians involved themselves in individual and cooperative commercial enterprises.[1]

The urban milieu would also give birth to an Ukrainian intellectual leadership in Canada – a leadership that would do much to nurture the social, cultural, and economic life of the community during the pioneer era. In the absence of clerics from the traditional Ukrainian churches, who had played such a dominant leadership role in the lives of the peasants in the Old Country, settlers in Canada came to rely on the small number of lay 'intellectuals,' young men imbued with the ideals of the populist Ukrainian national movement in Europe, which during the late nineteenth and early twentieth centuries organized peasants around programs of education, economic self-reliance, and political reform. Equipped with sufficient education to qualify as bilingual teachers, political agents, editors, and labour organizers, these radical leaders were an important link between Ukrainian immigrants and the host Canadian society.[2]

An example of this sort of pioneer intellectual activist was Paul [Pavlo] Rudyk, who homesteaded in the North-West Territories at the turn of the century. He became a key figure in the City of Edmonton during the early 1900s and one of the Ukrainian-Canadian community's entrepreneurial elite during the pioneer era. His influence was felt far beyond Alberta. An activist, politician, religious leader, builder, businessman, and cultural benefactor, for more than three decades Rudyk was associated with important developments within the Ukrainian community. He was perhaps that community's pre-eminent example of business success. This essay offers an overview of Rudyk's life and diverse record of public and community service in order to place him in the context of the intellectual leadership that arose in the community. It also evaluates his contribution to the history of Edmonton, northern Alberta, and Canada.

Paul Rudyk was born on 28 November 1878 in the village of Shchurovychi, *povit* (district) of Brody, in the eastern part of the Austro-Hungarian Crown land of Galicia, which today is part of the western Ukrainian *oblast* [province] of Lviv. The village was typical of the hundreds that sent their young to North America in search of opportunities. In 1899, about the time Rudyk came to Canada, Shchurovychi had 268 houses. Its population of 1,688 (829 women, 859 men) consisted of 653 Ukrainian Greek Catholics, 603 Jews, and 482 Polish Roman Catholics. The village had a Greek Catholic Church, a synagogue, and a school. As was typical for the time, the village encompassed 424 hectares of field crops and 7.26 hectares of gardens. Its livestock totalled 159 horses, 384 cows, 153 sheep, and 626 pigs.[3]

The first Rudyk to settle in Alberta was Paul's Uncle Theodore (Fedor). He was part of the first group of Ukrainian immigrants organized by Professor Dr Josef Oleskow, who attempted to bring order to the exodus of Ukrainian peasants to Canada. This group of 107 arrived at Quebec City from Hamburg on 30 April 1896 aboard the *Christina* and continued on to Edmonton by train. Theodore and Maria Rudyk (aged forty-five and forty-four, respectively) and an infant child arrived with $400 in capital – an amount typical of this more affluent, carefully selected group but far greater than what most rural settlers brought with them during this period.[4] This group of settlers took up land in the settlement area known as Edna-Star, northeast of Edmonton. Theodore homesteaded at NE-20-56-17-W.4.M. Twenty-year-old Paul Rudyk arrived in Canada with his parents Dmytro and Apolonia (Kotkewych) and his brother Michael in 1898. Dmytro homesteaded at SE-10-53-14-W.4.M; Paul and his brother took up homesteads three miles east of Hilliard, northwest of present-day Mundare, sharing the northern half of 2-54-17-W.4.M. Both applied for homestead patents in 1899 and were granted their naturalization in 1902.[5]

During his first year on the homestead, Paul Rudyk married Julia Stefanyna, a native of Leshniv, Brody, who had settled with her family in the same district at N4-56-18-W.4.M. The couple farmed for two years, with Paul seeking manual labour in order to raise additional capital. He also acted as an intermediary for newly arriving immigrants, guiding them to their chosen homesteads. Paul and Julia's first son, Phillip, was born in 1900; that same year or shortly afterwards, the Rudyks took up residence in Edmonton, joining an embryonic Ukrainian community in the city.[6]

The origins of the City of Edmonton date back to the Hudson's Bay Company fur trading post, Edmonton House. Before Rupert's Land was incorporated into the North-West Territories in 1870, Edmonton was an important depot for the western fur trade. The community was incorporated as a city in 1904. In 1905 the Province of Alberta was established, the Canadian Northern Railway arrived, and Edmonton was named the provincial capital. All of this brought the city increasing prominence and rapid economic growth. It was not until the early 1900s that Ukrainians took up residence in the city in significant numbers. There they pursued employment and business opportunities, being drawn from the large agricultural block settlement established northeast of Edmonton during the 1890s.

The first Ukrainians in Edmonton included perhaps seven or eight families, a handful of single male workers, and more than a hundred single women working as domestics, chambermaids, charwomen, waitresses, dishwashers, and laundresses. Michael (Mykhailo) Gowda and John (Ivan) Kiliar were employed as translators with the implement dealers Bellamy Agricultural Implements and Massey-Harris; both firms were eager to attract the business of the newly arriving immigrants. Gowda later worked as a translator with the Land Titles Office. Kiliar was the first to purchase a house, in 1901; it would become the location for the first Ukrainian organization in Edmonton, the Taras Shevchenko Reading Society, organized by himself and Gowda. Other Ukrainians, including Ivan Lyhavskyi and John (Ivan) Decore (Dikur), worked as clerks in grocery and dry goods stores, where they translated for Ukrainian customers. Peter Svarich (Petro Zvarych) worked as a typesetter at Frank Oliver's *Edmonton Bulletin* and later at Cushing's Lumberyard.[7]

Rudyk's first job in Edmonton was as a translator and salesman with Frost and Wood Implements. With several hundred dollars garnered from farming, interpreting, and manual labour, he launched the first of his many business ventures. He bought a house and set up a small grocery store, among the first to be owned by a Ukrainian in Canada.[8] In 1902 was born John Paul, Paul and Julia's second son.[9] In 1904 the Rudyk residence was home to the short-lived Ukrainian Labour Fraternity (Rivnist), which united a wide range of radicals and progressives.[10] On the business front, Rudyk bought Edmonton real estate with the earnings from his fledgling enterprise – an investment that would appreciate several times during the city's boom period.

The Rudyks, like most other Galician Ukrainians (commonly known as Ruthenians), were Eastern Rite (Byzantine) Catholics. Paul's Uncle Theodore and other members of the Oleskow contingent formed the first Ukrainian Church Brotherhood in Canada, the St Nicholas Ruthenian Church Brotherhood (Rusko-tserkovne bratstvo sv Nykolaia), which was organized at Edna-Star in 1896–7.[11] In Edmonton, Ukrainians attended services at St Joachim's Roman Catholic parish prior to organizing their own Byzantine Rite parish of St Josaphat's in 1903. Initially, Paul Rudyk was true to his Ukrainian Catholic origins and involved himself in discussions about acquiring land for building the new church. Opinions diverged on its location and on the extent of involvement by the Roman Catholic diocese. An opposition group that included Michael Gowda and Paul Rudyk was party to these discussions; within a year it would throw its support to the newly established Independent Greek Church. These community divisions saw the concurrent rise of St Josaphat's parish, the founding of the Independent Greek Church, and the establishment of St Barbara's Russo-Orthodox Church in Edmonton.[12]

Though the details of Rudyk's conversion to Presbyterianism are not recorded, we know that in 1904 he attended the founding convention of the Independent Greek Church (IGC), which attempted to attract members through a blend of Eastern Rite Christianity and Presbyterian fundamentalism. This blend emphasized a commitment to spiritual and secular enlightenment. This church, which reflected radical traditions in Galicia, hoped to remedy a perceived moral and ethical neglect among Ukrainian settlers, who indulged in ritualistic religious worship through their traditional churches. This new church would instead offer a rational, ethical, and intellectual environment for worship. The church leaders hoped to foster literacy, self-reliance, equality, personal discipline, and sobriety among the faithful. In Alberta, 250 families in eight communities joined the church, with Edmonton and the Krakow–Sniatyn–Zawale district being strongholds of the movement. Some of the best educated and most able settlers – including Peter Svarich, Paul Rudyk, Gregory Krakiwsky (Hryhorii Kraikivsky), Roman Gonsett, and Michael Gowda – were attracted to this church. All became prominent in Ukrainian cultural and political life as well as business associates in various ventures. In the tradition of Galician radical intellectualism, they articulated libertarian, socialist, populist, and anticlerical principles, which they mixed with their dedication to the national, linguistic, cultural, and economic advancement of the Ukrainian people. They stressed rational, universal values of political liberty, democracy, social equality, and economic abundance for all, and they were unwilling to submit to the paternalistic leadership of the Ukrainian Greek Catholic clergy.[13]

The IGC movement had collapsed by 1912, and the church's remnants amalgamated themselves with the Presbyterians. Eastern Orthodox rituals were abandoned; Protestant rites were embraced. While many of these converts later returned to their traditional churches, others, including Rudyk, remained faithful to Presbyterianism while continuing to devote themselves to raising the economic well-being and cultural status of the Ukrainian community.[14] In Edmonton the IGC was survived by the First Ruthenian Presbyterian Church. During the early 1920s that church was known as the Edmonton First Ukrainian Presbyterian Church; after 1925, with the union of the Methodist, Presbyterian, and Congregational denominations, it was known as the Edmonton First Ukrainian United Church.[15]

Besides involving himself in his community's religious life, Rudyk was drawn to the politics of the fledgling province of Alberta. During the first ever provincial elections of November 1905, Edmonton's Ukrainians gathered in the Russian [sic] Reading Room on Kinistino Avenue, where Liberal and Conservative candidates presented themselves. There, Rudyk along with Michael Gowda spoke on behalf of the Provincial Attorney General and Liberal candidate, C.W. Cross, who ultimately defeated his Conservative opponent. In 1906 the ratepayers of east Edmonton considered Rudyk (among others) as a candidate to represent the neighbourhood on City Council.[16]

By 1906 Edmonton had changed dramatically as a result of immigration. It boasted a population of more than 14,000, 80 per cent of whom had arrived after 1898. This influx was reflected in the number of property developers in the city. There were 73 real estate agencies, 43 building contractors, 23 building material merchants, and 29 insurance agencies. The convergence of three railway lines on Edmonton between 1902 and 1906 led to an inflation of real estate values in the city. The number of real estate agencies grew, urban land costs soared, lumber prices increased, and the local coal industry flourished. All of this created a new demand for manpower and attracted an increasingly diverse working-class population .[17] Hundreds of Ukrainians were drawn to Edmonton; many found employment in local mines, brickyards, sawmills, and railways. Others found employment on sewer and tramline construction projects and later on the High Level Bridge. Hundreds more would find employment at the Swift Canada Packing Plant. The Ukrainian community also included merchants, restaurateurs, and hoteliers, as well as some white-collar workers and a handful of professionals. By 1907 the Ukrainians in Edmonton were operating two general stores, a butcher shop, and a restaurant; by 1911 they were operating three groceries, two billiard rooms, a hotel, and several real estate agencies. By 1921, the community numbered 547 and its members were operating thirteen groceries, seven confectionaries, three meat markets, two general stores, nine billiard rooms, three hotels, and several small businesses. On a per capita basis, Edmonton was becoming perhaps the most active Ukrainian entrepreneurial centre in the country.[18] A decade later the community in Edmonton had increased tenfold to a population of 5,025.[19]

This economic boom brought Rudyk a financial windfall from speculation in undeveloped land. He invested these earnings in still more ambitious undertakings.[20] He was contracted to build and in 1908 to manage Carl Vopni's International Hotel at Kinistino and Boyle, making tens of thousands of dollars, with which he branched into real estate development and general contracting. He continued buying undeveloped lots in the most expensive districts of Edmonton with relatively low cash offers, which he then flipped at high profits. Meanwhile, Paul's brother Michael was launching his own business ventures. Between 1909 and 1912 he operated a pool hall in Edmonton while maintaining his farming interests. Paul managed a number of businesses neighbouring his brother. Rudyk Hall at 539 Kinistino hosted many functions, including political meetings. Paul Rudyk located his real estate business at 536 Kinistino, where he partnered with J. Komarnizki, followed by Gregory Krikewsky and finally by Thomas Fujarchuk in what became known as Ruska Kantselaria (the Alberta Real Estate Compnay, or Ruthenian Bureau). The business advertised a wide range of services, including the provision of transportation ship cards, life and fire insurance, real estate transactions, financial loans, and 'legal advice.'[21]

An important part of Rudyk's community activism was his support of religious and educational institutions. Besides supporting the IGC and its newspaper *Ranok* (Morning), Rudyk was the main benefactor of the First Ukrainian Presbyterian Church in Edmonton, providing funds and a site on 96th Street.[22] He attended Ukrainian Presbyterian conventions across the country and lectured on the need for temperance and prohibition. During the First Ukrainian Presbyterian Convention, held in Vegreville in 1915, he reminded delegates of the times when the Ukrainian people were completely under the sway of their traditional churches. He urged them to benefit from the opportunities for enlightenment that were being offered through the teachings of the Presbyterian Church, and to work towards personal salvation and a 'better tomorrow for future generations and the entire nation.' In many ways his calls for Ukrainians to pursue their opportunities and meet their obligations summarize the world view that guided Rudyk in all facets of his life: 'Ahead of us are great tasks and a great future.'[23]

In spite of his own personal denominational commitment, Rudyk was not hostile to the broader religious convictions of his community. He displayed an ecumenical spirit that reflected his commitment to harmony and mutual respect within the diverse Ukrainian community. In 1910 the Ukrainian Catholic Metropolitan Andrei Sheptytsky of Galicia visited Edmonton, following the International Eucharistic Conference in Montreal. Rudyk, along with Edmonton's mayor, Robert Lee, was part of the welcoming motorcade that greeted him.[24] When in July 1918 a national meeting was convened in Saskatoon, leading ultimately to the creation of the Ukrainian Orthodox Church of Canada, Paul Rudyk was one of the participants.[25]

In 1912 Rudyk established the Rusko-ukrainska *bursa* (Ruthenian-Ukrainian *bursa*), a residential institute for those young men and women who were flocking to Edmonton in search of work and education. The *bursa* offered room and board as well as guidance, supervision, and support for cultural programs. Rudyk donated the building lot for the institute as well as $1,000 in cash, and he pledged to match any community donations. The building accommodated twenty students on the second floor; the ground floor was for meetings and for staging plays. Rudyk sponsored a lottery in which building lots were offered as prizes for one-dollar tickets; the proceeds were contributed to the *bursa*.[26] Originally envisioned as a non-denominational institution, the *bursa* increasingly came under the sway of Rudyk's preferred Presbyterianism. This alienated its intended clientele, and within a year or so it had reverted to a simple boarding facility. Though this initial *bursa* failed, it did establish the prototype for future attempts to establish a non-denominational cultural centre for Ukrainians in Edmonton.[27]

The year 1912 also saw Rudyk incorporate the Persha Ruska Farmerska Pozychkova Kasa (First Ruthenian Farmers Loan Treasury, or Farmers Loan Company), with equity of $100,000. Through this firm, he bought and sold real estate and offered savings deposits to the public.[28] Rudyk and his partner Thomas Fujarchuk advertised a simple formula for success in land speculation, based no doubt on their own experience. They urged people to benefit from the rapid growth of Edmonton – which they referred to as the 'capital of western Canada' – emphasizing that quick profits and a secure future could be realized from buying the lots they had for sale, which ranged in price from $100 to $10,000. An integral part of Rudyk's land dealings was to purchase quarter-sections of school lands reserved for municipal districts, to be sold in support of building schools. He was buying these lands directly from municipalities and then reselling them to his clients at a profit.[29] In years when land prices fell, Rudyk's company offered 5 per cent interest on all bank deposits as an alternative to risky investments in land.[30] Advertisements prompted the public: 'If you have yet to deposit money to the Ruthenian treasury, then try it out and you will shortly recommend to your friends just as previous depositors have recommended it. If you have money deposited with another bank, you need not withdraw these funds, simply send us your savings book and we will assume them on our own, and will send you our own savings book and you will receive five percent rather than three percent.'[31]

Rudyk also helped found the Ruska narodna torhovlia (Ruthenian National Trading Company, or National Cooperative Company) in Vegreville in December 1909. This joint stock company established general stores in areas of Ukrainian settlement. Rudyk was chairman of the first Board of Directors, and during the first few years the company operated on capital advanced by him and the other directors. Prominent directors included other members of the IGC movement in Alberta. By 1916 the company had fifteen full-time employees in Vegreville, Chipman, Innisfree, and Lamont; it was also offering mail order service throughout the prairies. In 1916–17 the company had receipts of $216,960.[32] In Edmonton and in the mainly Ukrainian hinterland northeast of the city, the company operated all-purpose general stores that stocked all lines of merchandise. About forty clerks were employed between 1910 and 1916. Many of them went into business for themselves after serving an apprenticeship with the company. A special loan fund was established in aid of youth attending business college in Edmonton. The company supported a variety of charitable causes, including student residences, schools, and orphanages as well as Ukrainian publications and National Homes. It also funded the Ukrainian Red Cross and schools in Western Ukraine. It opened new branches in 1919 at Radway Centre and Smoky Lake; by 1921, however, the company had failed. With the prices for wheat and farm produce falling, and farmers cutting back on purchases, the company was extended financially and unable to pay its creditors.[33] In 1920, as an extension of this community-based business venture, the Zahalnyi ukrainskyi hurtovyi sklad (General Ukrainian Wholesale Warehouse, or General Wholesale Company) was founded in Edmonton. Rudyk was vice-president of this firm, in which Ukrainian-Canadian shareholders invested more than a quarter of a million dollars.[34] During 1916–17 Rudyk was also involved in the Ruthenian Grain Bureau and as president of the Progressive Farmers Grain Company, registered with the Fort William Grain Exchange.[35]

Rudyk's most ambitious real estate development was the building that would bear his name on Jasper Avenue at 97th Street. Plans for the Rudyk Block were drawn up in 1911. They called for a $40,000, three-storey steel-beam building with a stone-and-brick facade. Above a sub-basement and basement were two storefronts. The second and third floors each contained seventeen rooms for offices and dwellings.[36] In 1913 an advertising feature in the *Edmonton Journal* described the handsome building as a monument to Rudyk's 'zeal and perseverance,' 'thoroughly modern throughout and tenanted by those who desire comfortable surroundings both in home life and business.' The ground floor housed a theatre and one of the city's largest cafes. A spacious pool hall operated in the basement, while 'well-appointed offices' and 'modern living apartments' occupied the second and third floors respectively.[37] By 1913 Rudyk had a self-declared net worth of $200,000.[38]

Buoyed by his financial successes, and as a continuation of his community activism, Rudyk launched an ill-fated foray into politics, the only endeavour in which he was to experience complete failure. In the run-up to the 17 April 1913 election, on 13 January 1913 at Vegreville, the Ukrainian community held a *viche*, (general public meeting), where a *narodna rada* (council) was elected. Delegates from across the province gathered to plan a strategy for contesting five provincial ridings where Ukrainians stood a good chance of electing their own members to the Alberta legislature. The ruling Liberals, who enjoyed the support of most Ukrainians, had till then been the preferred vehicle for nominating candidates for office. The council pressed unsuccessfully for bilingual education rights and criticized the province for gerrymandering ridings and diminishing the electoral chances of Ukrainian candidates. Having failed to get their candidates nominated as Liberals, under what at times seemed to be questionable nomination procedures, the Community Council decided to run its own candidates as Independents or Independent Liberals. This slate of *narodni* (national candidates) included Michael Gowda (Victoria), Gregory Krakiwsky (Vermilion), Peter Svarich (Vegreville), and Paul Rudyk (Whitford). Rudyk's opponents included Russophile Ukrainian Andrew Shandro, the official Liberal candidate, Dr Christopher F. Connolly, another Independent Liberal, and Conservative Richard L. Hughson. [39]

A campaign ad in the *Edmonton Journal* praised Paul Rudyk as the personification of pioneer success in Edmonton and Alberta, as one of the city's most accomplished loan and realty men, and as a suitable candidate to serve his people in the legislature. His record as a businessman and sterling citizen 'attracted the attention of his fellow men who ... prevailed upon him to accept the nomination for the legislature of Alberta.' The ad concluded that Rudyk's fitness for such an honour was 'vouchsafed in the things he has accomplished both in business and in his labors for the future of Greater Edmonton.'[40] A heroic portrait was painted of an industrious youth who had come to Canada and found his fortune, and of a man who now displayed the high ideals of citizenship and who enjoyed the confidence of all who knew him:

> When some 15 years ago Mr. Paul Rudyk left his pretty little home in Galicia and journeyed to the far west of the great Canadian Empire he had visions of at some future date emerging from the throes of toil into a successful business life with all its attendant advantages and comforts.... Seeing the opportunities of this favoured spot [Edmonton] he cast his lot with those who began the work of creating a great city ... As the city grew so did the interests he had acquired, and he soon took his place as one of the capitalists and most substantial men of the community. He built a handsome home, where he has maintained his family in luxury and good taste, and has given his best efforts to the cause of upbuilding [*sic*] Edmonton.[41]

In the Ukrainian press Rudyk published a campaign ad remarkably free of any platform statements. Instead it presented a triumphant story of a successful Ukrainian, one who had never forgotten his roots but who on the contrary always sought to strengthen the social fabric of his community. It recalled the details of his rise to fortune, and it emphasized that he had demonstrated his sincere patriotism through generous financial support of various community causes; through his several-thousand-dollar contribution to the Edmonton *bursa*; through his endowment of a $2,000 Rudyk Scholarship Fund in support of students in commercial institutes in Galicia; through contributions to the Ridna Shkola Fund in support of Ukrainian schools; and so forth.[42] *Ukrainskyi holos* (Ukrainian Voice) editorialized parenthetically that 'one would hope that Canadian Ukraine had as many people of this sort as possible, so that our national concerns would develop better.'[43]

In a final advertisement prior to the election, Rudyk presented himself as the *Ruskyj narodnyi kandydat* (Ruthenian people's candidate) for Whitford. He stressed that the riding had a majority Ukrainian electorate and that he was a sincere 'Rusyn-Ukrainian.' To stress this point he published letters of support from the Prosvita Society in Lviv praising his scholarship endowment for Ukrainian commerce students in Galicia; and from the Sokil-Batko Association in Lviv, a paramilitary youth movement promoting physical culture and national revival, which honoured him as a founder of the 'Ukrainian Garden,' a gathering place for Ukrainians in the city centre.[44]

The 1913 election in Whitford was fraught with scandal and corruption. Rudyk apparently campaigned with a letter purportedly signed by the Liberal Attorney General, Charles W. Cross, contending that he was the rightful standard bearer for the Liberals. Just before polling day, Shandro had Rudyk arrested on a charge of forging Cross's signature. A whisper campaign against Rudyk ensued, claiming not only that he had been arrested and confined and thus was ineligible for office, but also that anyone voting for him could be arrested. Shandro, the Liberal, won Whitford riding with 499 votes (45.69 per cent). In spite of everything, Rudyk captured second place as an 'Independent Ruthenian' with 312 votes (28.57 per cent). Independent Chistopher F. Connolly and Conservative Richard L. Hughson gained 148 (13.53 per cent)] and 133 (12.17 per cent) votes, respectively.[45]

After the election Rudyk addressed an open letter to his supporters in Whitford, lamenting that 'if not for the punishable acts of Mr. Shandro, my opponent, I would have certainly been elected as a national representative. The results are not the fault of the electorate but of those who deceived them ... dishonourable criminals, lacking human conscience.'[46] Rudyk petitioned the courts to void the results, claiming 'notorious, systematic, corrupt and unlawful practices' by Shandro and his agents. He alleged that some polling booths had not been open at all on election day, that deputy returning officers had blocked access to ballot counts by Rudyk's scrutineers, and that Shandro and his associates had bribed voters with money. After lengthy and bitter legal proceedings, the courts ruled that corruption had indeed occurred during the election and that Shandro through his agents had spread false rumours about Rudyk. The results of the Whitford election were nullified in November 1914; Shandro was unseated and held responsible for court costs and damages to Rudyk. The Supreme Court of Alberta confirmed the removal of Shandro but set aside the other rulings. In spite of Rudyk's triumph in the courts, he declined to take part in the by-election of 15 March 1915, in deference to the wishes of his wife, who was ill. Shandro was again victorious, this time defeating his lone Conservative opponent, Roman Kremar, 697 to 484.[47] An analysis of the election written many years after the fact attributed Rudyk's loss to his tenuous power base in rural Alberta and to the strength of his opponent's ties within the constituency. Rudyk was very popular with the more progressive Ukrainian-Canadian leaders, who viewed his defeat as a great loss to the community, but 'he was essentially a stranger to the rank and file of the voters in the area.' Rudyk and other 'National Candidates' had run for office largely on a single-issue platform revolving around education. This had limited their appeal to non-Ukrainian and even some Ukrainian voters so that they were no match for the well-organized Liberal Party.[48]

In 1914, Rudyk turned away from domestic politics, focusing instead on a new organization, *Tovarystvo Samostiina Ukraina* (Society for an Independent Ukraine), which was devoted to the cause of Ukrainian statehood in Europe as well as to educational and economic development among Ukrainians in Canada. The society had been founded that same year by Paul Crath, who at the time was a socialist as well as a Presbyterian divinity student.[49] With branches throughout Western Canada, the society called for a united front in support of an independent Ukrainian Republic; its members included socialists, Protestants, and nationalists.[50] Rudyk was a key figure in the mass meeting the society held in Edmonton under this slogan: 'Ukrainians Across Canada And America Awake!' The rally called for spiritual and material support for Ukraine's rebirth as an independent republic within its ethnographic territories. This new society was to be non-partisan and non-denominational. The only expectations placed on members were these: that they favour republicanism as the future state government of Ukraine; that they support the separation of church and state; and that they embrace religious tolerance and the right of all nations to independence. At the Edmonton meeting, 133 people immediately enrolled in the new organization. Statutes were accepted unanimously, and a 'Hetman Council' (i.e., a Central Executive) was elected, on which Rudyk was to serve as General Treasurer.[51]

Rudyk's setback in politics did not diminish the regard in which he was held by the Ukrainian community. By 1916 his enterprise and successes were being heralded across the country. A Western Canadian travelogue published in *Ukrainskyi holos* paid particular attention to Edmonton's burgeoning Ukrainian community and to Rudyk's position within it. The article noted that the city was an attractive community situated on both sides of the North Saskatchewan River. Though its citizens numbered only 70,000, the author wondered whether it would not one day equal Winnipeg in population. It was noted that in this ethnically varied community, the Ukrainians had a distinguished presence with a number of outstanding and wealthy individuals, notably Messrs Krakiwsky, Kremar, and Rudyk. The latter's achievements in real estate were singled out for attention: 'Proudly standing on the main thoroughfare of Jasper Avenue is Rudyk's building, with a golden inscription reading **Rudyk Block**, which is even taller than some other municipal buildings. This building made a pleasant impression on me. I thought to myself: this means that even Ukrainians are not lagging behind. If there were more individuals as him, then certainly the work among our people would be more successful. But there is still much for us to learn.'[52]

Little is known about Rudyk's later years. In 1921 he moved into a suite in his block on Jasper Avenue, giving up the home that had been so lavishly praised in earlier times.

The Government of Alberta passed prohibition legislation in 1916. It was repealed in 1924, at which time some members of the Ukrainian community formed a Moral Reform League; William P. Fedun, the United Farmers MLA for Victoria, was elected as its President, with Rudyk as Secretary-Treasurer. A community meeting reviewed 'the general situation of social and moral standing of the Ukrainian'; those present were unanimous that 'the work of fostering ideals of moral reform must be undertaken by all possible means.' Also unanimously, the members decided to affiliate with the Temperance League of Alberta.[53]

The league also petitioned Edmonton Mayor Blatchford, in his capacity as police commissioner, to appoint a plain-clothes detective of Ukrainian ancestry 'who would give special attention to cases involving their countrymen.' It was proposed that the officer survey conditions in the community and continue in service with the city to combat 'allegations of considerable bootlegging and white slavery'; city police were at a disadvantage in coping with this condition 'on account of not having a detective who is familiar with the Ukrainian language.'[54]

Rudyk's Farmers Loan Company was last listed in city directories in 1925, though he continued to do business as P.D. Rudyk and Co. Real Estate. On 23 May 1929 his wife Julia died at the age of forty-nine. Rudyk remarried two years later to Anna Danylchuk, the daughter of the Reverend John and Maria (née Kostyniuk) of Toronto. The ceremony, performed by the Reverend E.M. Glowa, took place at Edmonton's Ukrainian Presbyterian Church. The local press noted that attendants 'were frocked in yellow and blue, the Ukrainian colours,' and that the ceremony featured Ukrainian hymns. It appears that he navigated the Great Depression with new vigour, purchasing a new home in the city in 1935. During the Alberta general election held in August of that same year, he campaigned extensively in the countryside on behalf of the newly constituted Social Credit party, which swept into power, capturing fifty-six of sixty-three seats under the leadership of William Aberhart. Shortly thereafter, Rudyk fell ill to the cancer that ultimately took his life at the age of fifty-eight, on 1 July 1936. His funeral was held on 6 July at Howard McBride's Funeral Chapel. He was buried at Edmonton Cemetery alongside his first wife.[55]

Winnipeg's *Ukrainskyi holos* (Ukrainian Voice) eulogized that Rudyk had been one of the community's most prominent members. He had become a devout Presbyterian at an early age and had stayed true to that faith until his dying day, while never breaking his ties with the Ukrainian community. Though he had little schooling, he had displayed great enterprise, making his mark on Edmonton by building the International Hotel and in 1912 the block that bore his name on Jasper Avenue, the city's main thoroughfare. Besides being the largest shareholder in the *Ukrainian Voice*, he had been a long-time director of the Mykhailo Hrushevsky Ukrainian Institute in Edmonton.[56]

Similarly, the Liberal-oriented *Kanadyiskyi farmer* (Canadian Farmer) declared Rudyk one of the most prominent Ukrainians in

northern Alberta, emphasizing his real estate dealings, through which
he had 'accumulated considerable wealth.'[57] An assessment of Rudyk's
career and significance published three decades after his death by the
Ukrainian Pioneers' Association was more encompassing, playing
down his material achievements and focusing instead on his spiritual
ones:

> Though an immigrant without much education, to many Ukrainians who
> came after him he became an example of what can be accomplished if a per-
> son has courage and tenacity. Paul is remembered, not for his economic suc-
> cesses, which on the whole were quite ephemeral. In the period of his
> greatest accomplishments, he did not forget that he had an obligation to those
> who were less fortunate and used his wealth in attempting to improve the ed-
> ucational status of Ukrainians and to give them experience in the economic
> field. If success did not always crown his efforts, the failures were certainly
> not the result of inaction.[58]

Rudyk's regard within the Ukrainian community extended to his
children even after they left Edmonton and Canada. Rudyk had apprenticed his sons in his many businesses from an early age. The elder
son, Phillip, was a clerk in his father's real estate firm at age seventeen.
John Paul worked with the Farmers Loan Company until 1921 as manager, then left for the United States. Phillip took over in that capacity
the following year. His last job in Edmonton was as a representative of
the Sun Life Insurance Company in 1928, after which he, too, moved
to the United States. Both sons initially settled in Chicago.[59] John
Paul, changing the spelling of the family name to 'Ruddick,' later
moved to Washington, D.C., where he worked for a lobbying organization and then established a pharmaceutical trade magazine and printing concern, Ruddick Press. He married Clara Canfield and retired at
age forty-five to a farm and motel business in Monterey, Virginia,
where he became an active member of the Republican Party. His role
in the party was exaggerated by the community to the point where it
was reported that he had been elected three times as a Republican senator and that he was a close friend of President Eisenhower, who paid
personal visits to the Ruddick farm.[60] In fact, Ruddick's only attempt
to gain higher office came in 1954, when he ran unsuccessfully in the
7th Congressional District of Virginia for the House of Representa-

tives and was defeated by Democrat Burr P. Harrison by a count of 22,025 to 7,669.[61] He was, however, elected to the Highland County Board of Supervisors for twelve years. John Paul's son, Ervin Canfield Ruddick, was born in 1925 in Washington, D.C., where he attended Benjamin Franklin University and worked in the family printing business. In 1964 he moved to Weyers Cave, Virginia, where he farmed and established the Mid Valley Press in Verona. He died in 2006 at the age of eighty.[62] Paul Rudyk's descendants had journeyed far from the rural Ukrainian roots of their ancestors and from the Ukrainian community ideals that he had championed while propounding his people's political and social integration.

Over a century after Paul Rudyk first arrived to Edmonton, the city was one of Canada's major cities as well as a hub of Ukrainian life in Canada. In 2006 more than 144,000 Edmontonians (13.56 per cent of them) were entirely or partly of Ukrainian heritage – the strongest concentration of any metropolitan centre in the country.[63] The city had more than a dozen Ukrainian churches, many Ukrainian dance troupes, the oldest and largest Ukrainian bookstore outside Ukraine, a Ukrainian bilingual education system in both the public and Catholic school boards, and the Ukrainian Resource and Development Centre (at Grant MacEwan College). It was also home to the Canadian Institute of Ukrainian Studies and the Huculak Chair of Ukrainian Culture and Ethnography at the University of Alberta.[64] The community was socially diverse, with strong representation in business and the professions. Two of the city's mayors had been Ukrainian origin: William Hawrelak (1952–9, 1964–6, 1974–5), the first Ukrainian to head the civic administration of a major Canadian city; and Lawrence Decore (1983–8).[65] The Ukrainian community in Edmonton had in many ways come to reflect the goals of cultural and economic self-reliance and integration that Rudyk had set for himself and his people.

Canada's rapid urbanization brought increasing numbers of Ukrainian settlers into a milieu which fostered the growth of a nascent business element. Furthermore, cities nurtured new directions of thought and leadership that would play a key role in the developing social, cultural, and economic life of the community. In the leadership vacuum of the pioneer era, individual intellectual leaders came forward with their concerns for literacy, equality, personal discipline, sobriety, and enlightenment. In the case of Paul Rudyk, currents of traditional

Eastern Christian faith and radical advocacy devoted to educational, economic, and political reform merged into a fundamentalist Presbyterian-Ukrainian patriotism.

Paul Rudyk's biography serves as an important case study of urban entrepreneurship and intellectual leadership within the Ukrainian community during the pioneer era. It is reflective of those Ukrainians who settled in urban centres and undertook non-traditional economic livelihoods in contrast to their rural peasant origins and in spite of their limited experience in commerce. Rudyk's rise to fortune exemplified the rapid emergence of an entrepreneurial class in Edmonton; his position within his own community was more unique. The example he set in commerce and civic responsibility inspired the Ukrainian community far beyond Edmonton and Alberta. His uncommon blend of pioneer activism, entrepreneurship, philanthropy, and patronage of social and cultural causes was legendary and reflected the vibrant life that developed within Canada's rapidly expanding urban Ukrainian communities.

Notes

1 Orest T. Martynowych, *Ukrainians in Canada: The Formative Period, 1891–1924* (Edmonton: Canadian Institute of Ukrainian Studies Press, 1991), 129–30, 135–6.
2 Ibid., 169–70. On the role of the intellectuals in organizing the Ukrainian community in Canada, see Orest Thomas Martynowych, 'Village Radicals and Peasant Immigrants: The Social Roots of Factionalism among Ukrainian Immigrants in Canada, 1896–1918,' MA thesis, University of Manitoba, 1978; Peter J. Melnycky, 'A Political History of the Ukrainian Community in Manitoba, 1899–1922,' MA thesis, University of Manitoba, 1979; and Andrij Borys Makuch, 'In the Populist Tradition: Organizing the Ukrainian Farmer in Alberta, 1909–1935,' MA thesis, University of Alberta, 1983.
3 Gemeindelexikon der im reichstrate vertretenen konigreiche und lander, vol. XII (Wien: 1907), 62–3.
4 Vladimir J. Kaye, *Early Ukrainian Settlements in Canada, 1895–1900: Dr Josef Oleskow's Role in the Settlement of the Canadian Northwest* (Toronto: Ukrainian Canadian Research Foundation/University of Toronto Press, 1964), 57–62.
5 Ibid., *Dictionary of Ukrainian Canadian Biography of Pioneer Settlers of Alberta, 1891–1900* (Edmonton: Ukrainian Pioneers' Association of Alberta, 1984), 235–7.

6 Kaye, *Dictionary,* 236; *Ukrainskyi holos*, 5 March 1913; 'Paul and Julia Rudyk,' in *Ukrainians in Alberta*, ed. Editorial Committee (Edmonton: Ukrainian Pioneers' Association of Alberta, 1975), 473; James G. MacGregor, *Vilni Zemli* (Free Lands): *The Ukrainian Settlement of Alberta* (Toronto: McClelland and Stewart, 1969), 95.

7 Dmytro Prokop, 'Poselennia ukraintsiv v misti Edmontoni,' in *Ukraintsi v zakhidnii Kanadi: do istorii ikhnoho poselennia ta postupu* (Edmonton and Winnipeg: Trident, 1983), 51; Peter Svarich, *Memoirs 1877–1904* (Edmonton: Ukrainian Pioneers' Association of Alberta / Huculak Chair of Ukrainian Culture and Ethnography, 1999), 184, 188, 259; Martynowych, *Ukrainians in Canada*, 271–2.

8 *Ukrainskyi holos*, 5 March 1913; William A. Czumer, *Recollections about the Life of the First Ukrainian Settlers in Canada* (Edmonton: Canadian Institute of Ukrainian Studies, 1981), 89, 159; *Edmonton Journal*, 4 July 1936; Dmytro Prokop and Isidore Goresky, 'Early Settlement of Ukrainians in Edmonton,' in *Ukrainians in Alberta,* vol. II, ed. Editorial Committee (Edmonton: Ukrainian Pioneers' Association of Alberta, 1981), 9.

9 Kaye, *Dictionary,* 236–7.

10 Martynowych, *Ukrainians in Canada,* 272.

11 Antonii Savka, 'Visti z Kanady,' *Svoboda*, 25 February 1897, p. 2; Mykhailo Marunchak, *Istoriia ukraintsiv Kanady,* tom I (Winnipeg: Ukrainska vilna akademiia nauk v Kanadi, 1991), 173–4.

12 See Serge Cipko, 'St Josaphat Ukrainian Catholic Cathedral, Edmonton: A History (1902–2002)' (Edmonton: St Josephat Ukrainian Catholic Cathedral, 2009), 51–3; and 'Dopysy,' *Svoboda*, 30 March 1905.

13 Martynowych, *Ukrainians in Canada*, 190–3, 214–36; Ivan Bodrug and John B. Gregorovich, *Independent Orthodox Church: Memoirs Pertaining to the History of a Ukrainian Canadian Church in the Years 1903 to 1913* (Toronto: Ukrainian Canadian Research Foundation, 1982).

14 Svarich, *Memoirs*, 190, 220, 224–40, 254–5, 257; Martynowych, *Ukrainians in Canada,* 271; Orest T. Martynowych, *The Ukrainian Bloc Settlement in East Central Alberta, 1890–1930: A History* (Edmonton: Alberta Culture – Historic Sites Service, 1985), 30, 177–9.

15 See Edmonton First Ukrainian Presbyterian Church fonds, PR 1983.285, United Church of Canada, Alberta and Northwest Conference Archives.

16 'The Campaign,' *Edmonton Bulletin*, 2 November 1905 and 17 November 1906.

17 Carl Betke, 'The Original City of Edmonton: A Derivative Prairie Urban Community,' in *The Canadian City: Essays in Urban and Social History*, ed. Gilbert A. Stetler and Alan F.J. Artibise (Ottawa: Carlton University Press, 1984), 392, 394–5.

18   Martynowych, *Ukrainians in Canada*, 129–30, 135, 137.
19   See William Darcovich and Paul Yuzyk, eds., *A Statistical Compendium on the Ukrainians in Canada, 1891–1976* (Ottawa: University of Ottawa Press, 1980).
20   Betke, 'The Original City of Edmonton,' 404. In 1906, when Edmonton was lobbying to route the Grand Trunk Pacific through the city, officials spent months arranging land purchases along the envisioned railway right of way. One of the people expropriated in the process was Rudyk's brother Michael. City of Edmonton Archives, MS209, file 59, 'Property Purchased by GTP Right of Way and Other Purchases.'
21   Survey of *Henderson's Directories* for City of Edmonton, 1908–1913; *Nova Hromada*, 2 March 1911.
22   Marunchak, *Istoriia ukraintsiv Kanady*, 251; 'A Well-Known Ukrainian Is Dead at 58,' *Edmonton Bulletin*, 4 July 1936.
23   Oleksander Dombrovskyi, *Narys istorii ukrainskoho ievanhelsko-reformovanoho rukhu* (New York and Toronto: Ukrainske ievanhelske obiednannia v pivnichnii amerytsi, 1979), 143, 182, 184, 194, 199; Mykhailo H. Marunchak, *Studii do istorii ukraintsiv Kanady*, tom II (Winnipeg: Ukrainska akademiia nauk, 1966–7), 499; *Kanadyiets*, 1 September 1915.
24   M. Khomiak, ed., Ukrainskyi katolytskyi soiuz: propamiatna knyha, ukrainskyi narodnyi dim (Edmonton: Ukrainskyi narodnyi dim, 1965), 47.
25   For a history of the origins of the Ukrainian Orthodox Church in Canada, see Paul Yuzyk, *The Ukrainian Greek Orthodox Church of Canada, 1918-1951* (Ottawa: University of Ottawa Press, 1981); and Odarka S. Trosky, *The Ukrainian Greek Orthodox Church in Canada* (Winnipeg: Trident, 1968).
26   'Rusko-ukrainska bursa v Edmontoni,' *Ukrainskyi holos*, 23 October 1912, 7; Martynowych, *Ukrainians in Canada*, 271.
27   William Kostash, 'The Mychailo Hrushewsky Institute: A Narrative History' in *Ukrainians in Alberta*, 86–87.
28   *Ukrainskyi holos*, 5 March 1913; 'Farmers Loan Company,' *Ranok*, 1 March 1916, 14.
29   'Edmonton roste,' *Ukrainskyi holos*, 28 February 1912, p. 5, and 6 March 1912, p. 6; 'Farmer's Loan Co. Ltd.,' *Novyny*, 26 February 1913; 'Povidomliaiu vsikh Bp. Vybortsiv,' *Kanadyiets*, 1 March 1915; Survey of Dominion Homestead Records.
30   *Kanadyiets*, 1 March 1915
31   'Farmers Loan Company,' *Ranok*, 1 March 1916
32   'Do Vidoma Ukrainskym Farmeram v Kanadi – Progressive Farmers Grain Co., Ltd.,' *Ukrainskyi holos,* 21 March 1917, p. 3.

33 Martynowych, *Ukrainian Bloc Settlement,* 280–1, 284.
34 'Zahalnyi Ukrainskyi Hurovyi Sklad – The General Wholesale Company, Ltd.,' *Ukrainskyi holos,* 20 October 1920, p.11.
35 *Ukrainskyi holos,* 21 March 1917; Martynowych, *Ukrainians in Canada,* 303.
36 City of Edmonton Archives, RG17, box 193, file 207/12, 'Rudyk Block Building Plans.'
37 *Edmonton Journal* (supplement), 1913, in City of Edmonton Archives, Paul Rudyk file. Later the building also housed the Ukrainian Benevolent Society of Canada. See 'Uvala! Uvala! – Farmers' Loan Co., Ltd.,' *Ukrainskyi holos,* 29 March 1916, p. 2.'
38 *Ukrainskyi holos,* 5 March 1913.
39 Orest Zherebko, 'Zbory Ukr. Vyd. Spilky,' *Ukrainskyi holos,* 1 January 1913, p. 2; Czumer, *Recollections,* 98–9, 102; Martynowych, *Ukrainian Bloc Settlement,* 213–15, 310–12.
40 *Edmonton Journal* (supplement), 1913, in City of Edmonton Archives, Paul Rudyk file.
41 Ibid.
42 *Ukrainskyi holos,* 5 March 1913, p. 2.
43 Ibid.
44 Advertisment, 'Pavlo Rudyk ruskyi narodnyi …,' *Ukrainskyi holos,* 2 April 1913, p. 5.
45 Ernest Mardon and Austin Mardon, eds., *Alberta Election Results, 1882–1992* (Edmonton: Documentary Heritage Society of Alberta/Alberta Community Development, 1993), 137; Martynowych, *Ukrainians in Canada,* 251–2, 263; idem, *Ukrainian Bloc Settlement,* 312; Czumer, *Recollections,* 127–8; Joseph M. Lazarenko, 'Ukrainians in Provincial Politics,' in *The Ukrainian Pioneers in Alberta,* ed. Joseph M. Lazarenko, (Edmonton: Ukrainian Pioneers Association in Edmonton, 1970), 148, 157, 159. See also Makuch, 'In the Populist Tradition.'
46 Pavlo Rudyk, 'Podiaka vsim vybortsiam …,' *Ukrainskyi holos,* 30 April 1913, p. 3.
47 Ibid.; *Novyny,* 26 May 1914, p. 1; Mardon and Mardon, *Alberta Election Results,* 137.
48 Editorial Committee, *Ukrainians in Alberta,* 474; Martynowych, *Ukrainians in Canada,* 251–2.
49 On the leadership role of Paul Crath, see Orest Martynowych, 'The Ukrainian Socialist Movement in Canada; 1900–1918,' *Journal of Ukrainian Graduate Studies* 1, no. 1 (1976) 27–44 and 2, no. 1 (1977): 22–31; and Nadia Kazymyra, 'The Defiant Paul Crath and the Early Socialist Movement in Canada,' *Canadian Ethnic Studies* 10 (1978): 38–54.

50 'Samostiina Ukraina,' *Ukrainskyi holos*, 14 October 1914; Martynowych, *Ukrainians in Canada*, 319.

51 Pavlo Krat, 'Tovarystvo ...' *Kanadiiski visty*, 12 September 1914, p. 2.

52 Vrazhiniia z Alberty,' *Ukrainskyi holos*, 31 May 1916.

53 'Ukrainian Form Branch of Moral Reform League,' *Edmonton Journal*, 31 January 1924.

54 'Ukrainians Wish Special Officer,' *Edmonton Journal*, 24 September 1924, 9.

55 Review of *Henderson's Directory* for the City of Edmonton 1920–37, in Dombrovskyi, *Narys istorii ukrainskoho*, 525; *Kanadyiskyi farmer*, 15 July 1936; *Edmonton Bulletin*, 4 July 1936; *Edmonton Journal*, 4 July 1936.

56 'Pomer Pavlo Rydyk,' *Ukrainskyi holos*, 15 July 1936.

57 Kanadyiskyi farmer, 15 July 1936.

58 Editorial Committee, *Ukrainians in Alberta*, 474.

59 Review of *Henderson's Directories* for the City of Edmonton, 1917–1928.

60 Vasyl Havrysh, *Moia Kanada i ia; spohady pro ukrainskykh pioneriv v Kanadi* (Edmonton: Havrysh, 1974), 258; Mykhailo Marunchak, *Biohrafichnyi dovidnyk do istorii ukraintsiv Kanady* (Winnipeg: Ukrainska vilna akademiia nauk v Kanadi, 1986), 551.

61 Richard Scammon, ed., America Votes: A Handbook of Contemporary American Election Statistics, 1956–57 (New York: Macmillan, 1958), 427.

62 Editorial Committee, *Ukrainians in Alberta*, 474; Obituary, *Harrisonburg Daily News-Record*, 19 June 2006; Obituary, *Staunton Daily News Leader*, 18 June 2006.

63 http://www40.statscan.gc.ca/101/cstoi/demo27v-eng.htm

64 Wsevolod Isajiw and Andrij Makuçh, 'Ukrainians in Canada,' in *Ukraine and Ukrainians throughout the World*, ed. Ann Lencyk Pawliczko (Toronto: University of Toronto Press, 1994), 328. See N. Chomiak, Ukrainian Edmonton: A Directory of Ukrainian Cultural Groups, Organizations, and Institutions in Edmonton (Edmonton: Ukrainian Canadian Social Services, 1978); Ukrainian Community Directory: 2001 (Edmonton: SSC, 2001).

65 Diane King Stuemer, *Hawrelak: The Story* (Calgary: Script, the Writers' Group, 1992).

5

The Populist Patriot: The Life and Literary Legacy of Illia Kiriak

Jars Balan

Illia Kiriak[1] is best known as the creator of the epic trilogy *Syny zemli*, a sprawling fictional account of Ukrainian colonization in the Canadian West in the late nineteenth and early twentieth centuries. Spanning almost 1,100 pages, the trilogy is widely regarded by critics as one of the most significant and ambitious literary works produced in the Ukrainian language in Canada. Originally self-published in three instalments between 1939 and 1945, it was later translated into English and issued posthumously in abridged form as *Sons of the Soil*.[2]

The novel is a fitting monument to an unassuming bachelor who unselfishly devoted most of his talents and energies to Canada's Ukrainian community. While growing up in Austro-Hungarian Ukraine, Kiriak had been instilled in the left-wing populist and Ukrainian patriotic values espoused by the Ruthenian-Ukrainian Radical Party, whose co-founder was Ivan Franko (1856–1916), the celebrated author, poet, literary critic, translator, scholar, journalist, and editor. The role played by Franko and other literary figures of his generation – who vigorously championed the cause of the oppressed Ukrainian people – served as an inspiration for Kiriak's subsequent evolution as a writer and community activist. Though Kiriak lacked his hero's dynamic character and never came close to attaining Franko's artistic, intellectual, or political stature, he nonetheless led an eventful life and achieved much that deserves greater recognition in Canada as well as in Ukraine.

Interestingly, as was the case with Ivan Franko, Kiriak initially held quite radical views about politics and religion. However, these moderated with changes in his personal circumstances as well as with tumultuous developments in his ancestral homeland. Still, Kiriak never wavered in his fundamental convictions: he always remained passionate about his Ukrainian heritage and unflinching in his determination to do what he could to improve the lot of his fellow countrymen – culturally, socially, materially, and spiritually. Indeed, in many ways, *Syny zemli* is the summation of everything that was important to Kiriak, besides being a heartfelt expression of his Ukrainian-Canadian identity. While drawn from elements of his own life and the recollections of the first homesteaders in the Ukrainian bloc settlement northeast of Edmonton (now known as Kalyna Country), the trilogy is not geographically specific, and it relates a narrative that was common to the Ukrainian pioneer experience on the Prairies. Furthermore, besides possessing many literary qualities that regrettably have been lost in the novel's rendering into English, in its full Ukrainian version *Syny zemli* provides a detailed chronicle of the lives of the settlers, their traditional customs and values, and their gradual adaptation to Canadian ways. As such, it is of interest not only to readers of prose fiction, but also to students of sociology, ethnography, and Western Canadian history. Especially rich in folk idioms and proverbs, the trilogy is at the same time an invaluable record of the Ukrainian language as it was spoken by 'Ruthenian' immigrants from the former Habsburg Empire.

A shy man who was exceedingly humble about his abilities, Kiriak was nevertheless a fairly typical member of the Ukrainian-Canadian intelligentsia of the pioneer era. Arriving in Canada in his late teens with a limited education and virtually nothing in the way of financial resources, he overcame many personal hardships to become a cherished and emblematic figure for Ukrainians in Canada. His life story is a compelling tale of immigrant success that sheds light on the vibrant intellectual culture of a fast-receding period in the settlement of the Canadian West. It also serves as a testament to how a quietly committed individual, through patient effort and personal sacrifice, came to leave a unique and enduring bequest to Ukrainian and Canadian literature.

Three years before his death, Illia Kiriak wrote a forty-three-page autobiography in the form of a letter to his friends, Ivan and Nastunia Ruryk, who were living at the time in Innisfree, Alberta. In it he recounted his childhood years, his immigration to Canada, his various jobs, and his community and literary endeavours. Preserved in the archives of the late historian Michael Marunchak, the letter provides a fascinating overview of the author's life. It would serve as the basis of Marunchak's 1973 book, *Illia Kyriiak ta ioho tvorchist*.[3] Both Marunchak's study and Kiriak's unpublished 1952 letter to the Ruryks were utilized in the preparation of this summary biography of the author and Ukrainian activist. Other useful materials have been obtained from the Kiriak holdings of Library and Archives Canada.[4]

Kiriak was born into a poor peasant family on 29 May 1888 in the village of Zavallia, Sniatyn County, in the Pokuttia region of Western Ukraine.[5] The second son of Tekliia and Ivan Kiriak, he was a sickly baby who by his mother's calculation arrived two months premature, leading her to fuss over him as if he were 'a cracked egg.'[6] Indeed, Tekliia was so worried about young Illia that she took him everywhere she went, even after he was no longer a toddler. In his autobiographical letter to Ivan Ruryk the author attributed his lifelong restlessness and penchant for 'aimless wandering' to these early outings with his doting mother.

Kiriak first became interested in Canada while still a child, his curiosity piqued by fellow villagers and family members who were emigrating abroad. Somewhat auspiciously, at the age of five he slipped undetected onto a wagon taking some neighbours to the railway station at the nearby town of Zaluche, where they were departing for a new life overseas. According to Kiriak, he probably could have boarded one of the passenger cars unnoticed had he not been distracted by the locomotive, allowing the train to leave without him. As an adult he could not recall how he eventually made it home, but did remember getting a 'good thrashing' from his father on his return.

Kiriak's only sibling was an older brother, Petro, four years his senior, whom Illia would often secretly follow to school. In an effort to restrict Illia's ramblings, his parents allowed him to begin classes two years earlier than was customary so that his brother could help keep a watchful eye on him.[7] By then, Illia already knew the alphabet, having sat in on Petro's reading and writing lessons for their illiterate father. Naturally curious and bright, Illia proved to be the best pupil in his class. Each year he would get book prizes from a liberal-minded landowner who was keen to encourage good students throughout the Zavallia district.

As Illia approached the end of his primary education, his teacher urged his parents to send him on to *gimnaziia* (secondary school). The Kiriak family simply could not afford such a luxury. So when he was twelve, Illia moved in with a distant uncle named Yuz Huk, who was relatively well off and who could afford to provide him with room and board while covering his tuition. In exchange, Illia helped his aunt with household chores, assisted with the supervision of the hired hand, and in time even managed the finances for his illiterate but prosperous uncle. In this way, Illia was able to complete his fifth and sixth grades, as well as take a year of additional studies, while living in relatively comfortable and agreeable circumstances.[8] The uncle and aunt were so pleased with their young charge and this arrangement that they started thinking of themselves as his primary guardians and even began making plans to marry him off to a granddaughter.

However, Illia's father and uncle often argued over the way he was being raised, since Illia was spending a great deal of time socializing with the older teenagers in the village, learning from them the forbidden pleasures of tobacco and alcohol. Huk preferred to look the other way when it came to the company his nephew was keeping and dismissed Illia's late-night peregrinations and grown-up indulgences as harmless matters of youthful indiscretion. More important, the uncle and Ivan Kiriak also disagreed fundamentally about politics: since the father was a staunch supporter of the agrarian socialist Radical Party and regarded the uncle as a *khrun*, or class collaborator.

Meanwhile, under the influence of his older brother Petro, Illia became involved in the local Sich society, founded in Zavallia in 1900 by leading members of the Radical Party. Established as a mass physical-education and firefighting organization, the Sich movement at the same time sponsored programs that promoted education and culture among the Ukrainian peasantry and working class, while fostering the development of their national consciousness. The fact that the organization was strongly opposed by the conservative Yuz Huk proved to be yet another sore spot in a deteriorating relationship between father and uncle. Tensions were further exacerbated after Huk – who was the deputy to the village head, or *viit* – had Petro Kiriak jailed for tearing down government posters to protest corrupt election practices.[9]

Illia understandably sided with his immediate family in these growing conflicts with his uncle. The situation came to a head when Huk caught Illia Christmas carolling with Sich members. This led to a confrontation that prompted the youthfully idealistic Kiriak to move back home with his parents. Though Huk later tried to convince his nephew to return to his care, Ivan Kiriak would not allow it and instead began making plans to send Illia to a school for artisans.

Increasingly, the future author began thinking about following the tens of thousands of his kinsmen who had already immigrated to Canada. Being literate from a young age, Illia often wrote letters for uneducated neighbours and other villagers to family members who had settled abroad, also reading the letters that were sent in reply from distant homesteads on the prairies. In his own words, 'those acres, bushels of grain and herds of cattle, seduced me.' Not surprisingly, when an opportunity to go overseas fortuitously presented itself, Illia jumped at it. A third cousin, who was only a week apart in age and also bore the name Illia, was also thinking of emigrating because his stepfather was constantly haranguing him over his 'dissolute' lifestyle. Kiriak was only too happy to accompany the cousin to Canada, his plan being to make sufficient money to establish himself as an independent farmer in Galicia.

Kiriak's uncle Yuz, on hearing of his nephew's decision, angrily voiced his disapproval, declaring that 'he would grow hair on his palms' before Illia ever left for Canada. Because of the uncle's influence with local authorities, Yuz Huk could certainly have made it very difficult for Illia to obtain the necessary travel documents. Regardless, Ivan Kiriak ignored Huk's threatening remarks and went to see the cousin Illia's stepfather for advice on what to do next. The two men agreed to sneak the boys out of the country and arranged a secret shopping expedition to the nearby city of Chernivtsi to buy them formal clothes for their journey. They also obtained the required papers under the pretext that their sons were intending to find work in Germany. Finally, in the middle of a snowstorm, on 20 December 1906, the young men were delivered like a couple of 'unnecessary cats' to the railway station in Zaluche for the beginning of their great odyssey. Both Illias were then eighteen years old, and all they had with them was the clothes on their backs and 700 Austrian Kronen – of which 450 belonged to the better-off cousin. Their trip to the port of Hamburg took more than a week, broken by numerous delays and line changes. They snatched a few hours' sleep wherever they could, but fortunately were not bothered by any officials along the way, for it was assumed they were students returning to school from holidays. Though anticipating that they would have to wait in Germany until spring, the cousins were able to buy passage almost immediately on the *Kaiser Wilhelm II*. They arrived in Canada early in the New Year after a transatlantic crossing of twelve days.[10]

A six-day train trip from the east coast gave them a sense of the vast country they had come to. They finally reached Winnipeg on the night of 21 January 1907 after a full month on the road from Zavallia. Their intended destination was the Skaro, Alberta, farm of their common aunt Paraska, and uncle, Iwan Lakusta, who had been in Canada since 1896.[11] However, fate intervened: the two cousins met other immigrants, who advised them it was pointless to go on to Edmonton, since it was a long way off and they wouldn't find work when they got there. Later, a new acquaintance took them to his shanty for the night. After feeding them *kovbasa* and tea, he let them bunk down on his floor, promising to introduce them the following day to someone who had come to Canada from the same district as they did.

The former Zavillian was named Nimtsak, but neither Illia knew him because he had already been in Canada for nine years. When the two newcomers told their fellow Galician they had only three dollars each in their pockets, he warned them they would 'die like kittens,' because there wasn't any work in the winter and they were still young and wet behind the ears. Fortunately, Nimtsak's kindly wife came to their rescue, and they were able to stay with the couple until the end of February. However, the sojourn quickly ate up their meagre financial resources, and the future began looking extremely bleak in light of their dismal job prospects. The formal clothes they had purchased for the journey were inappropriate for the harsh Canadian winter, and this added to their misery.

Despondent about their seemingly hopeless situation, Kiriak's cousin wept, cursed, and telegraphed home for 500 Kronen, which both of them planned to use to pay their return fare. But their luck suddenly changed: they met a Pole, who bought them proper winter clothing and took them to do construction work on a Grand Trunk Pacific Railway line near Kenora, Ontario. When in a month's time they were paid $23 apiece for their labour, they felt rich – determining that the amount was equivalent to about 115 Austrian Kronen.

Kiriak stayed on the job in Ontario until April, when a bad toothache forced him to come back to Winnipeg for dental treatment. The dentist botched the extraction, prompting Kiriak to flee from the office in pain. He later hired on with a CPR extra-gang working out of Regina, by which time it appears he had parted company with his cousin. Fearful of losing the job, Kiriak overexerted himself moving steel rails from a boxcar onto a flat car. After three days he was laid up and barely able to move. No one paid any attention to him until a roadmaster took an interest in his plight and arranged to have him taken to a hospital in nearby Arcola in southeastern Saskatchewan. There he was nursed back to health within a week, after which the roadmaster fetched Kiriak and took him to work as a section hand at Creelman, northeast of Weyburn.[12]

The Creelman job lasted until mid-November, when Kiriak was laid off and returned to Winnipeg, this time flush with earnings. He sent $100 home to his family, dressed himself up like a 'sport,' and still had twenty-five dollars left to get through the winter. Within a month, however, a likeable and handsome bachelor named Ivanitsky had persuaded Kiriak to go with him to the American West, where employment opportunities seemed better. Since his new friend did not drink or smoke and had a thrifty nature, Kiriak was happy to shelter under his wing. Ivanitsky promised Kiriak that if he stuck with him, he would make enough money in two or three years to be able to 'buy out' his uncle Yuz.

Together the two men crossed the border into the United States, landing their first job at Helena, Montana, laying track through the mountains. The work paid $2.50 a day, which Kiriak considered very good money, since by his reckoning the sum was equivalent to twelve-and-a-half Kronen. However, he didn't last very long as a navvy, having been defeated once again by the arduous physical labour. He had been assigned the task of clearing a path near the campsite following a seven-foot snowfall; after a few days of heavy shovelling he had to be hospitalized – his severely strained muscles left him virtually paralyzed. As soon as he had recuperated, his boss gave him a much less demanding position in the kitchen for $60 a month and meals – a job Kiriak found to his liking and that he later credited for teaching him how to cook. Meanwhile, his friend Ivanitsky was becoming uneasy about the dangerous conditions he was being exposed to during the track-laying crew's blasting operations. Consequently, both men pulled up stakes and headed farther west, to Spokane, Washington. There they found it extremely difficult to find work of any kind, for jobs were routinely advertised as for 'White Men' only – a designation that did not apply to Slavs. Eventually they signed on as lumberjacks for a logging outfit, which a few months later went bankrupt, owing them money. Ivanitsky vanished, leaving Kiriak to fend for himself in a strange land with few skills and no friends. Almost penniless, he made his way to Coeur d'A-lene, Idaho. By passing himself off as a 'Frenchman' with limited English, he was able to get hired at another lumber camp. He stayed there for sixteen months and even sent $500 home to his family before the sawmill was destroyed by a fire, once more leaving him unemployed. His boss attempted to keep him on as a caretaker of the campsite by only allowing him to withdraw money from his bank account whenever the boss himself was present. But after Kiriak kept insisting that he needed to go to his uncle in Canada, his employer finally relented – though he ordered him to come back again before winter.

Instead of returning to Canada, Kiriak went to Spokane, where he indulged himself for a time by going to the theatre, enjoying the company of girls, and hanging around pool halls.[13] He befriended a local policeman, to whom he confided his intentions to join his uncle near Edmonton. The lawman developed a paternal concern for Kiriak, and after yanking him from a pool room by his collar took all his money, depositing it at a post office with strict instructions that he only be given an allowance of a dollar a day. Despite these orders, Kiriak was eventually able to make a withdrawal of $25 in cash by claiming that was going to buy a suit. Right afterwards he ran into a former campmate, who persuaded him to try his luck in a game of billiards. When the good-hearted policeman unexpectedly walked in on the game and caught Kiriak about to be fleeced by the pool shark, he once again grabbed Kiriak by the scruff of his neck, snatched up all the money he was about to lose, and physically kicked him out of the pool room. The cop then took him to a station on the Great Northern Railway line and put him on a train for Fernie, British Columbia, thus bringing Kiriak's American adventures to a rather inglorious end.

En route to Canada he met another itinerant labourer like himself, Harry Hryhirchuk, whose family had settled at Chipman, Alberta, in the Ukrainian bloc settlement northeast of Edmonton. Since Kiriak was still posing as a Frenchman so as to pass for 'white,' he initiated a conversation with his seatmate in broken English. His new acquaintance responded in rudimentary French. Soon enough, the two realized they were both Ruthenian. When Hryhirchuk noticed that Illia was carrying a Ukrainian 'nationalist' almanac (which his brother Petro had sent him from home), he immediately referred to him as a *mazepite* – a derogatory term that was unfamiliar to Kiriak at the time but was used by Russophiles for their Ukrainophile rivals.[14] Nevertheless, Kiriak was persuaded by his travelling companion to put off going to Edmonton and instead to accompany him to a gold mine in Moyes, British Columbia. The two men arrived at their destination only to discover that the mine was just then shutting down – a not uncommon occurrence with resource industries on the frontier.

Lacking any firm plans, Kiriak worked briefly at several sawmills in the Crow's Nest Pass area while waiting two months in Hosmer to get a better-paying job in a coal mine. He was drawn to the town in part because it had a large Ukrainian population, and he soon got involved in the local Myroslav Sichynsky Enlightenment-Labour Society, eventually serving as its secretary for eighteen months.[15] The association ran English classes, sponsored cultural and political activities, and had an extensive library of Ukrainian-language books and periodicals. Kiriak used the opportunity to read voraciously, consuming all the available publications of the Shevchenko Scientific Society, *Dilo*, and *Prosvita*, as well as works by the Ukrainian political radicals Kyrylo Trylovsky, Mykhailo Pavlyk, and Ivan Franko. By his own admission, the latter's stirring poem 'Vichnyi revoliutsioner' (The Eternal Revolutionary) became 'like a prayer' for him, helping educate and further politicize him. In his autobiographical sketch, Kiriak describes himself as having become a 'staunch socialist' during his time in Hosmer. This was when he acquired a Ukrainian national consciousness, though it is also clear that these political convictions had been partly formed by his experiences growing up in Galicia.

It was while he was in the Crow's Nest Pass that Kiriak became active in the organized Ukrainian community in Canada, to which he was to dedicate himself for the next forty-five years. In August 1910 he was sent from Hosmer to Edmonton as a delegate to the inaugural convention of the Federation of Ukrainian Social Democrats (FUSD), where he met such leading personalities as Myroslav Stechishin, Paul Crath, and Roman Kremar. The convention was a landmark event in the political evolution of Ukrainian pioneer society; it was followed soon after by a schism that divided the nascent Ukrainian left along ideological as well as regional lines. The complex situation was further compounded by fierce individual rivalries and the contradictory positions taken by different Canadian socialists towards the ethnic organization of the working class.[16] Kiriak ended up siding with the far western faction in the conflict, probably more by default and geography than for any fundamental issues of principle. He was well informed about matters of politics, but he lacked the self-confidence to be a leader and was therefore heavily influenced by those close to him when determining his personal loyalties and party affiliations. Like Stechishin, Crath, and Kremar, he gradually distanced himself from the Ukrainian socialist movement in Canada during the war years, especially after the revolution in Ukraine divided immigrant activists into competing pro- and anti-Bolshevik camps.

Kiriak returned to B.C. after the FUSD convention. A short time later, the coal company he was working for began laying off miners – a fate he himself experienced that winter. Reluctantly relocating to Canmore, a town he did not like, he finally decided to visit his uncle and aunt on their farm at Skaro, more than four years after arriving in Canada. He stayed with them only briefly, but afterwards he remained in the Edmonton area. Edmonton would become his periodic home and the focus of his organizational activities, though steady employment was sometimes hard to come by in the city. Over the summer of 1911 he held twenty-one different labouring jobs, some lasting merely an hour, others a few days. Besides digging ditches, working in sawmills, and mining coal at Clover Bar, he did stints with the railways and in the construction industry. Even though he continued to think of himself as a professional miner and missed the good money he earned underground, he never made it back to the Crow's Nest Pass, which was suffering one of its frequent economic downturns.

He had the good fortune of being hired by Roman Kremar, a prominent figure in the Edmonton Ukrainian community. Kremar had just started a Ukrainian publishing company to put out a left-wing newspaper called *Nova hromada* (New Society).[17] *Nova hromada* was initially edited by Kremar, and after him by Toma Tomashewsky and Ivan Semeniuk. All three men soon found themselves distracted by other projects, to the paper's detriment. Kremar had gone heavily into real estate, and for a time Kiriak's job involved delivering provisions to the wives of some of the friends whom Kremar had persuaded to take out homesteads near Athabasca while they were busy selling lots for him in town. Meanwhile, Kiriak helped typeset *Nova hromada*, and not surprisingly this encouraged him to try his hand at both journalism and creative writing. Among his signed contributions to the paper were two articles in which he urged Ukrainian farmers and workers to overcome their political ignorance and conservatism and learn about socialism. Titled 'Farmari a sotsyializm' (Farmers and Socialism) and 'Nevirnist' i peresliduvanie' (Treachery and Persecution), both articles were printed on 30 June 1911. It was in *Nova hromada* that Kiriak likewise published his first literary effort, 'Hirkyi son' (Bitter Dream), an allegorical story protesting the exploitation of working people that appeared on 1 May 1912.[18] As the paper began to founder, Kiriak took over more and more responsibility for putting it out. In time he would assume the additional roles of editor and administrator in a valiant but doomed effort to keep it going.

After *Nova hromada* collapsed in September 1912, having lasted sixty-seven issues, Kiriak filed for a homestead in the vicinity of Athabasca to support Kremar in his ambitious but naive effort to start a new Ukrainian settlement in the area. A short while later he was recalled to Edmonton by Kremar to help with another publishing venture, this one a weekly, *Novyny* (The News). The inaugural issue had appeared on 7 January 1913. In February Kiriak was made the pressman and timekeeper for the periodical, earning a monthly salary of $110. While working on *Novyny* he lived with Kremar, who was then still a bachelor. The two men spent many enjoyable evenings eating, drinking, and debating together. Kremar's basement was well stocked with liquor, champagne, and beer. A lawyer who graduated with distinction from the University of Lviv, Kremar introduced Kiriak to the ideas of Kant and Schopenhauer and other famous German thinkers, as well as to classical Greek and Roman philosophers. Kremar had abandoned the socialist movement to become a supporter of the Conservative Party, and he patiently tried to convince Kiriak to switch his political allegiances.[19] In fact, Kiriak was never especially oriented towards narrow party politics, being chiefly devoted to working for the betterment of the Ukrainian masses in the populist tradition of his homeland.[20] Like a great many of his fellow activists with strong nationalist beliefs, he deserted the socialist camp after the Ukrainian and Canadian left became militantly internationalist and pro-Bolshevik under the impact of the Great War and October Revolution. However, he always retained a world view that was broadly progressive in that it valued community development, education, and culture over personal gain and aggrandizement. It is also clear from Kiriak's writings that his politics largely rested on principles of Christian morality, which put him at odds with the anticlerical and atheist tendencies found on much of the organized Left.[21]

Kiriak did not last very long on *Novyny*. The gasoline he had to use to clean the presses had begun to physically irritate him. At the suggestion of Jacob (Yakiv) Hawrelak, uncle of the future mayor of Edmonton, in the fall of 1913 Kiriak enrolled in the English School for Foreigners in Vegreville.[22] It had been established in February of the same year to provide basic instruction in English (covering enough material for students to attempt Grade Nine examinations) for young Ukrainian males, primarily those interested in working in commercial enterprises. The quality of the students varied widely: some had only a couple of years' education in the Old Country, while others had minimal schooling in the immigrant settlements in the hinterlands outside Edmonton. Kiriak, now twenty-five years old, would have been one of the older and more experienced students, since the school had targeted the sixteen- to twenty-two-year-old age group in recruiting candidates.

Notwithstanding his obvious intelligence and educational background, Kiriak found it difficult to concentrate on his studies. His mind was constantly drifting off and reliving his experiences in Europe, the Pacific Northwest, and the Crow's Nest Pass. Still, by Christmas of his first year he had finished the course of studies for the seventh grade, and by the summer of 1914 the eighth grade was also behind him. Not surprisingly, he became active in the affairs of the local Ukrainian community, as noted in a *Vegreville Observer* article about the official opening of the new Ruthenian Institute there on 22 May 1914: 'Elias Kiriak spoke in Ruthenian giving the biography of the poet Shevchenko, and Wm. Cory followed with a similar statement in English. Translations were given in English from Shevchenko's works by J. Hyrhorovich and J. Ruryk.'[23] This speaking engagement marked the first documented presentation about Shevchenko by Kiriak, who in the years following was often called on to give talks on similar themes because of his knowledge and love of Ukrainian literature.

Having been bitten by the writing bug during his days on *Nova hromada* and *Novyny*, Kiriak continued with his artistic endeavours while attending the School for Foreigners. Among his poetic works from this period are 'Moiemu narodnovi' (To My People), 'Nadiia' (Hope) 'Nasha nyva' (Our Prospects), and 'Zhyttia, zhyttia' (Life, Life), all of which were composed in 1914. Though he would later finish a four-act comedy, *Domashni Klopoty* (Domestic Troubles), neither drama nor poetry ever provided Kiriak with a major outlet for his creative energies.[24] Around this time he also made his only attempt at writing a play, producing two incomplete drafts of a comedy titled *Poza shkiln'oiu lavky* (Beyond the School Bench) in 1915.[25] His sporadic efforts in both genres were not very successful, and he seemed temperamentally better suited to writing prose.

In 1915 Kiriak took classes in the ninth and tenth grades as part of an accelerated program, but he failed several exams and decided to drop out, fearing that he had lost both years entirely. He was also thinking of returning to his native village to tend to his widowed mother, only to be prevented from doing so by the war in Europe.[26] During the school holidays he got a job with a newly established newspaper, *Postup* (Progress), put out in Mundare by Joe Macallum, a Liberal MLA who spoke 'pretty good Ukrainian,' according to Kiriak.[27] Macallum had hired a recently arrived student from Ukraine named Dmytro Yaremko to edit the publication; Kiriak was recruited for his practical experience as the editorial assistant and typesetter. During this time the Mundare office of *Postup* became a gathering place for the Ukrainian teachers who were working in school districts within the surrounding bloc settlement. Among those employed in the area were Gregory Nowak (later a doctor), William Corey (Vasyl Kuriets) and Ivan Genik, who often dropped by to socialize and talk community politics. Kiriak, besides having to fulfil his duties at the press office, became the designated cook thanks to his earlier training as a kitchen hand. The paper came out regularly throughout the summer, when plenty of volunteer help was available, but appeared erratically in the fall, once harvest had begun and the teachers and students returned to school. Kiriak still managed to find time to do some writing, and on 18 September 1915 he penned a reminiscence about the past of his native village, which he titled 'Nevdiachnyi' (Ungrateful). Kiriak was to later depict his time working on *Postup* in a story he called 'Redaktsiini tainy' (Editorial Secrets), in which the heroes are an editor named Yaremko and a typesetter called Ilarion.[28]

Kiriak's next job was with the National Co-operative Company, a chain of general stores – popularly known as *Narodna Torhivlia* –

founded by pioneer community leaders to provide young Ukrainians with business training. He was initially posted to Chipman, northwest of Mundare, where on 6 November 1915 he wrote a poem expressing his loneliness, 'Samitnyi ia' (I'm all alone). Next he was transferred to the more poetically named but no less isolated village of Innisfree, overlooking Birch Lake east of Vegreville. There, over the next few months, he composed several new poems, including 'Iak tiazhko hliadity' (How Hard It Is to Observe), 'Kazhut' (They Say), and 'Lysh odyn tsvit' (Just One Flower). Also produced in this period were a versified humoresque, 'Neporozuminnia' (The Misunderstanding), a satiric poem, 'Nashym opikunam' (To Our Guardians), and a psychological sketch, 'Osvidchyny' (Enlightened).[29] He had hoped to save some money, in expectation of returning to Zavallia after the war, but he was unable to do this on his paltry salary of just $50 a month.

Kiriak was in Vegreville one day picking up goods for his general store when a former teacher at the School for Foreigners ran into him on the street and asked him why he had left school so abruptly. Taking him by the hand, she led him to her classroom, showed him a desk, and insisted he resume his education. Kiriak protested that he had no money and hadn't passed his last set of exams, but the teacher assured him that she could obtain funding for him and that the Department of Education would forgive him the failures. Once again he found himself enrolled as a student at the School for Foreigners; instead of living in residence, however, he moved in with a friend who was already teaching at Borschiw, south of Vegreville. Immediately after he wrote his final high school examinations, a permit was arranged for him to teach for three months at Ispas, a Bukovynian district north of Hairy Hill. Kiriak was then supposed to attend Normal School in Camrose to get his professional certification, but his English grammar was still poor, and he failed his literary composition. ˙

Further complicating his situation, on 10 January 1918 he was called up to register for military service, at which time he was classified A-2. Once more, a benefactor came to his aid: the principal at Edmonton's Strathcona High School advised him to join the cadets so as to avoid being summoned to the Calgary barracks for training. This strategy worked, and as soon as he had obtained his final high school credit, another temporary teaching position was arranged for him so that he could make a few dollars, this time at Moscow school between Tofield and

Mundare. Following his brief assignment there, Kiriak attended the Normal School in Camrose, from which he successfully graduated as a fully qualified teacher. In May 1919 he was hired by the Szypenitz School District, northwest of Two Hills, a short distance from his first school at Ispas. Meanwhile, with the resumption of mail service to Eastern Europe, Kiriak learned the sad news that his mother had died in 1918. This left him without any immediate family back home, which ultimately enabled him to set aside any lingering thoughts about returning to his native village.

Being intelligent, hard-working, and youthful in appearance, Kiriak was popular with both his students and their parents. He was supposed to conduct his classes entirely in English; in his autobiographical sketch, however, he acknowledges that he taught half the day in Ukrainian, which was also the language of most classroom discussions. It was easier for Kiriak and his students to communicate in Ukrainian, though they undoubtedly switched to English whenever an inspector visited the school. Besides carrying out his classroom duties, Kiriak organized concerts and theatrical presentations and was expected to provide moral leadership in the community. As a youth in the Old Country he had attended church twice daily with his mother, where he learned the Divine Liturgy and other services by heart. Consequently, at Szypenitz he became the *diak*, or cantor, for which he won the praise of the local Russian Orthodox priest and the respect of congregation members. Whenever there were religious commemorations at the nearby St Mary's Orthodox Church, he would gather together his students and lead them in orderly rows to worship.

Though well-liked by the mostly Bukoyvnian settlers around Szypenitz, in time his relationship with the community was subjected to inevitable stresses owing to the highly visible role played by rural teachers. Some tensions arose because area residents did not appreciate how they were being depicted in the short stories Kiriak was beginning to get published. One piece in particular, 'Mitla' (The Broom), upset the women in the settlement because of its frank description of the unsanitary conditions that were all too common in immigrant homes. Others were offended by his rather critical portrayals of conservative Russophiles and Russian Orthodox priests, whom Kiriak regarded as obstacles to the enlightenment of his fellow Ukrainians. Like many members of the pioneer intelligentsia, Kiriak had broken with his Greek

Catholic upbringing, rejected Russian Orthodoxy, and become a supporter of the Ukrainian Greek Orthodox Church of Canada once it was established in 1918–20. This sometimes made for a difficult balancing act. As Kiriak related in an April 1923 letter to Ivan Ruryk:

> I made trouble for myself. Community members read those sketches and complained that I was judging them. For instance, the sketches 'The Broom,' 'For Wool,' 'He Hanged Himself,' 'For Half a Cent,' 'How They Ordained Me' – which is about their *batiushka* – along with other works, turned the older members of the community against me. The women in particular lost their affection for me because of 'The Broom,' where I held forth about tidying houses. Until that time I was a desired guest in every home. They welcomed, hosted and asked me back again. And I actually visited each family in the community at least once a year. I would come in, look around the household and without any fuss draw their attention to the lack of cleanliness, to the disorder, but I did so jokingly – with a smile, during conversation about the livestock, about the children, and no one disagreed. But immediately after those sketches I was no longer a very desirable guest. Not with everyone. Some of the younger farmers even praised me and came to my defence whenever complaints were voiced against me.[30]

Among the stories Kiriak published in *Ukrainskyi holos* around this time was 'Pershyi den' na novim hospodarstvi' (The First Day on a New Farm)[31] – an indication that he was beginning to explore the subject matter on which *Syny zemli* would eventually be based. Besides short stories, Kiriak contributed occasional news items and commentaries to *Ukrains'kyi holos* and its calendar-almanac. Thus he was amassing a growing body of journalism while at the same time honing his writing skills.

Other problems arose after a romantic relationship that seemed to be developing between Kiriak and a young woman in the community was suddenly derailed and she surprised him by marrying someone else. A later attempt to pair off Kiriak (with the older sister of a girl who was being courted by a friend) similarly came unravelled owing to misunderstandings and myriad complications. More than a few of these difficulties were attributable to Kiriak's reticence about matters of the heart, as well as his rather stodgy and reclusive nature. Besides being reluctant to get involved with a girl who was significantly younger or who did not share his intellectual interests, Kiriak had a strong sense of mission: his first and strongest commitment was to his work as an 'enlightener' in the tradition of the Western Ukrainian *narodnyky*, or populists.[32] The strain of living in a fishbowl, coupled with the pressures of teaching, finally got to be too much for him, and in 1922 he left Szypenitz for Radway school in the west of the Ukrainian bloc settlement, where he taught for the next two years.

This was an emotionally turbulent time for Kiriak. He wrote to his friend, Elias Shklanka, a fellow teacher working in Ethelbert, Manitoba, after Shklanka had prematurely congratulated him on hearing a false report of his betrothal:

> In your card you wish me happy holidays and a sweet married life. May a thunderbolt strike, but you wrote those words for nothing! There is absolutely no connubial bliss for me. The Devil with matrimony! I am still leading a single life, bacheloring around ... Why tie myself down. If one knew that it was beneficial for me and for society, then I wouldn't mind, but when I look about me and see all those crippled by married life, it makes my hair stand on end. There are no girls my own age. Those that are available are too young, flighty, and my nature cannot tolerate that. I need a proper housewife ...
>
> But less said about that. I am going to continue teaching, while I still can, and afterwards I am going to try to become a priest, if they will want to consecrate a bachelor. I tell you, until there are more old bachelors and old maids who are willing to dedicate themselves to elevating our people here in Canada and Ukraine, then our cause will not become a beacon. Married people are dependent, they are bound to their families in such a way that they have little time to devote on behalf of the people, and when critical moments arise, they completely surrender to manipulations or the given circumstances. Single people don't have anything to lose. In English history we have clear proof of this assertion. Who built the English empire, if not single, unmarried individuals? We even see [this] now in English schools. Their schools are full of spinsters, who specialize in education, having dedicated themselves to it, and because of that education stands at such a high level with them. And what do we have? Among us a young boy cannot even demonstrate his aptitude (that, or a young girl) before he is already enflamed by love, which ends in a wedding, and with that it is eternal memory to talent and vital work. Is it not so?

Consequently, I want to dedicate myself to this purpose, if something does not happen to me like a fit of madness.[33]

Clearly, the subject of marriage tormented him. He had always been something of a loner and a drifter, and his romantic troubles seem to have exaggerated his views on the perils and pitfalls of wedlock. Getting married was obviously not a priority for Kiriak, for whom there were more important things in life. Indeed, in the same letter to Skhlanka he shared the following equally revealing thoughts:

A fanciful idea has arisen with me to go to Greater Ukraine. What good are we here? There, I think, be it as it may, there would be work for us in some village. Since that was the case with Sityk, the Edmonton Bolshevik and Pole, who is teaching in Odesa gubernia, why wouldn't I be able to find the same for myself. (He taught here.) All kinds of riff-raff of different nationalities are pushing their way there, while we, the sons of the same nation, are afraid to foul our entrails and are leading miserable lives here without any satisfaction. Consequently, if things work out I am going to Ukraine. [34]

In light of the sad fate of other Ukrainian immigrants to Canada who returned to Communist Ukraine in the 1920s, it is fortunate that Kiriak never acted on his fantasies. However, he was giving serious thought to the purpose of his life, and he was tempted by the idea of going back to what was now Soviet Ukraine despite his reservations about the kind of society being created there.

During this trying period Kiriak began experiencing 'nervous problems,' which were to flare whenever he was overwhelmed by stress in his personal life and teaching career. Increasingly, he sought relief from his depressive state in writing, finding the act of self-expression to be highly therapeutic. He also received some timely literary encouragement from Osyp Nazaruk, a renowned Ukrainian politician and civic leader who visited Kiriak in late 1922 while in Canada raising funds for the Ukrainian government-in-exile.[35]

While Kiriak was living in Radway, a lively discussion began in Winnipeg's Ukrainian press – in which Nazaruk participated – regarding the need for a Ukrainian-Canadian literature and an organization of Ukrainian-language writers in Canada. The debate both energized and inspired Kiriak, who started writing a novel about life in America, as he announced in a 1923 letter to Ivan Ruryk:

It will be half fiction and half truth and take up to 200 pages of print in a medium-sized book. From my comically unfinished wedding in Szypenitz I have glued together such a novel for you, that I myself wonder how I was able to do it. I have already planned a second tale with Kremar as the hero, having obtained a lot of information from Stechishin, Semeniuk and others, who were connected with him. I still have to get reliable information about Shandro, and think I will be able to put it together during the holidays. This is supposed to be my masterpiece, if it doesn't turn into a fiasco. Later, when you are already my manager and I finish up the stories that I have started, I will take you as my hero and write a tale under the name 'The Thorny Road.'[36]

Excited about his prospects, Kiriak threw himself into his writing with renewed dedication, notwithstanding his characteristically self-deprecating remarks about his 'unfinished wedding' and the possibility that his intended 'masterpiece' might come out badly. His enthusiastic comments certainly suggest that he was beginning to take his literary efforts more seriously, especially given the major effort required to write a novel.

In 1924, Kiriak became a shareholder in Edmonton's Ukrainian Bookstore, having become good friends with its founders, Dmytro and Michael Ferbey, over the past decade. The Ferbeys were prominent in the institutional life of Ukrainian Edmonton, and the bookstore was an intellectual and cultural wellspring for Ukrainians throughout Alberta, whatever their religious or political affiliations.[37] In 1918, Kiriak had helped Dmytro Ferbey establish the Michael Hrushevsky Institute, which Ferbey initially headed with Kiriak serving as first secretary. A few years later the institute became the base for launching St John's Ukrainian Orthodox Church, the first Ukrainian Orthodox congregation in Edmonton. Kiriak would remain a loyal and active supporter of both the institute and the church, even while teaching in the bloc settlement.[38] The institute, the bookstore, and the wider Ukrainian Orthodox community provided him with a network of friendships that would sustain him for more than three decades – an important source of support for someone who was single and who had only distant relations with whom to share the joys and travails of daily life.

Hoping to start anew and shake off his 'nervous affliction,' Kiriak left Radway. From 1925 through the spring of 1931 he taught at

Sachava School, south of Andrew, a largely Bukovynian district though the community was divided into opposing Russian and Ukrainian Orthodox camps. It was there, in 1927, that he finally began work on the book that became *Syny zemli* – only to set it aside the following year because he was afraid of how it might be received. He also again toyed with the idea of becoming a Ukrainian Orthodox priest, confiding in his plans with Vegreville's Peter Svarich, a fellow pioneer and community activist. Svarich did not try to dissuade his friend on this matter, but he cautioned Kiriak about submitting himself for ordination before getting married, because he was not the type to be a bishop. Indeed, Svarich went so far as to suggest a woman whom he thought would make a good wife for his friend, humorously describing her as an 'Amazon' while advising him on how to approach her and offering the services of Mrs Svarich as a matchmaker.[39]

By this time Kiriak had developed a strong attachment to his adopted country and was thoroughly Canadianized in many of his views. In a poem published in *Ukrainskyi holos* in the summer of 1928 he expressed his deep affection and gratitude towards Canada. It concluded:

Canada, you are a free country,
You cover the world with treasures,
And entice throngs of people
Who are oppressed by despots.

And they become your sons,
They praise your freedom,
And declare an oath, that with enemies
They will shed their blood for you.[40]

Yet Kiriak also had mixed feelings about the impact of Canadianization on his fellow Ukrainians. For instance, he worried that the Ukrainian language in Canada was being corrupted with Anglicisms, creating a pidgin dialect now commonly referred to as 'kitchen Ukrainian.' He discussed the issue in an ironically titled article, 'Ne hovorim po ukrainsky' (Let Us Not Speak Ukrainian), in which he illustrated the problem with many examples and suggested half in jest that philologists compile a dictionary of this 'new language' for the use of future generations.[41] In another interesting contribution to *Ukrain-*

skyi holos, written while he was teaching at Sachava School, he used government statistics to contend that if even a small percentage of the money that Ukrainians spent annually on alcohol in Alberta were devoted to Ukrainian culture, it would comfortably fund the needs of many community institutions across the country.[42]

With the establishment of the Ukrainian Self-Reliance League of Canada (USRL) in 1927 on the initiative of the leaders of the Ukrainian Orthodox community, Kiriak found a fresh avenue for his organizational and political energies. The USRL championed the cause of an independent Ukraine; simultaneously, it called for a self-reliant existence for Ukrainians in Canada without any interference from politicians or churchmen abroad. A secular body committed to democratic ideals and mainstream Canadian values, the USRL quickly emerged as the leading rival to the left-wing Ukrainian Labour-Farmer Temple Association, which it attacked for being a puppet of the Communist government of Soviet Ukraine. At the same time, the USRL challenged the emerging radical elements within the nationalist wing of the Ukrainian community, which was comprised mainly of second-wave immigrants from postwar Europe. The latter had become more authoritarian and extremist in response to Ukraine's failure to achieve self-determination during the political upheavals unleashed by the war. The USRL espoused a more moderate form of Ukrainian nationalism and explicitly rejected violence as a means of liberating Ukraine from foreign or communist domination. Kiriak both embraced and embodied the USRL's philosophy, which grew out of an important segment of the pioneer Ukrainian-Canadian intelligentsia to which he unequivocally belonged.[43]

Thus in 1931 Kiriak dutifully organized an Andrew chapter of the USRL, which he reported on in a detailed letter to Myroslav Stechishin written on 23 March of that year. In the years following he also contributed several programmatic and polemical articles to *Ukrains'kyi holos* that helped articulate the league's ideology while promoting its creed of self-respect, self-reliance, and self-help. These included satirical pieces directed at targets ranging from leftists to churchgoers, a submission critical of Canadian supporters of the integral nationalist movement in Europe, and journalistic accounts of the activities of the USRL's component organizations.

Kiriak placed his literary talents at the service of the USRL's cultural programming, along with his abilities as a teacher and public lecturer. In 1933 he wrote a short story for a collection compiled by the women's section of the USRL for Mother's Day commemorations. Titled 'Kara za hrikh' (Punished for a Sin), this was a rather dark tale that expressed a son's profound guilt over how he had treated his mother.[44] Though a work of fiction, the fact that Kiriak wrote the story in first person inevitably suggests that the author was confessing his own guilt at having 'abandoned' his mother by coming to Canada. Regardless, it was an unusual piece to contribute for an occasion more commonly associated with sentimental outpourings of affection. Besides writing about educational issues and on subjects such as the Ukrainian language and orthography, Kiriak was sometimes asked to speak at community functions as a representative of the USRL. In this capacity, he travelled widely across rural Alberta to attend meetings and give talks while regularly participating in organizational events in Edmonton.[45] Although Kiriak was not very effective as a motivational speaker, he was widely respected for his commitment to the Ukrainian cause and for his knowledge of things Ukrainian. This undoubtedly explains why he never became a leader of the USRL, though he was always recognized as a prominent and greatly valued member.

Between 1931 and 1936 Kiriak taught at Errol school, southeast of Vilna in the county of Smoky Lake. When he started there it was a one-room schoolhouse, but by 1934 the enrolment had grown to seventy-one students, by which time a second teacher, Tony Horon, had been hired to share the teaching load. With the surge in enrolment, the school board debated whether to construct a new, two-room school or simply build an addition onto the old one. Fate intervened when the one-room school burned down on 30 August 1934. Three weeks later the trustees approved a new two-room facility on the same site; meanwhile, classes were held at the homes of local farmers. By the end of 1934 the new school had been built, and it opened following the Christmas holidays. Kiriak would teach at Errol school for one more year, but by then his teaching days were coming to an end as the stress was beginning to overwhelm him. Exhausted and financially strapped, and once again suffering from a nervous disorder, he quit the teaching profession in 1936 and moved to Edmonton, where he slowly recovered his health and equilibrium.[46]

In Edmonton, Kiriak settled at the Michael Hrushevsky Institute, the student residence he had helped found in 1918. He served as the

USRL's National Secretary – a post that he was ideally suited for.[47] As the organization's chief administrator, he conducted correspondence, organized conferences, visited local branches, and wrote and printed newsletters. He devoted much of his time to the organization's youth wing, the Canadian Ukrainian Youth Association (CYMK or SUMK), which by then had some 180 branches scattered across Canada from Quebec to B.C. Kiriak was the National Secretary for 1937 and 1938, after which he was succeeded by a fellow activist and writer, Ivan Danylchuk. Kiriak's USRL work made full use of his skills as a teacher, writer, and activist. The position was undoubtedly fulfilling, but it was also highly demanding because of the size of the organization and the national scale of its operations. It left Kiriak with little time and energy for creative pursuits – a situation that he found increasingly intolerable, however strong his commitment to the USRL.

The 1937 appearance of a novella about Ukrainian immigrant life, *Holos zemli* (Call of the Land), by Honore Ewach, prompted Kiriak to take a fresh look at the manuscript he had begun working on a decade earlier.[48] He was confident he had superior material, and he felt encouraged to rewrite it for publication, but his heavy workload with the USRL kept thwarting his best intentions. Eventually, the frustration got to be more than he could take, and on 15 May 1938 he began producing a 'clean' revision of the introductory instalment to what would be his epic novel *Syny zemli*. By the fall of that year he had a finished typescript. According to a letter written by the author Apolinariy Novak, Kiriak was in contact with Trident Press in Winnipeg about the possibility of their publishing the book. In his reply to Kiriak's request for assistance – which he passed on to Peter Woycenko, the editor of *Ukrainskyi holos* – Novak offered the following words of caution and advice regarding the manuscript's length:

Large books do not sell as fast as small ones. A book costing 50 cents, as far as I know, because that is not my field, though I often encounter this, sells twice as quickly as a book costing a dollar. The price of the first thousand will be quite high. The second will be considerably less, and so on. This will undoubtedly be reflected in the sale price. I know that you write interestingly so my only advice to you would be to write as briefly as possible. I say this even disregarding business principles, because the longer it is for us the more work it can be. Furthermore, from my own experience I know that fewer people read long and thick books. About this you can speak with Ferbey. He has more experience. One other thing. Maybe you should make the first volume shorter, so as to sell it for a lower price and that way get the largest number of people to buy it and then afterwards the subsequent volumes will sell themselves. That's it.[49]

In the end, Kiriak decided to publish the book in Edmonton. The first volume of the trilogy was issued in early 1939 by the Alberta Printers and Ukrainian News. He paid for the printing by borrowing $800 from his $2,500 life insurance policy, and optimistically planned to use the income from book sales to cover his modest living expenses. The volume ran 390 pages and sold for $2.00 in hardcover and $1.50 in softcover – an indication that he had chosen to ignore Novak's well-meaning advice. Furthermore, since the book was self-published, Kiriak was assuming responsibility for advertising and distributing it, which created additional costs and work for him.

Undaunted, he immediately set to work preparing the second volume, which appeared in 1940 and ran 350 pages. Though the title page mistakenly identified the book as the '2nd Edition' of Volume II, it included Kiriak's translation of the Ukrainian title into English: *Sons of the Soil: A Story of the Ukrainian Settlers in Canada*. The two volumes took some time to become known in the Ukrainian community, but they gradually filtered out to Kiriak's friends and other readers, most of whom responded warmly to his accessible and welcome tribute to the pioneers.

Kiriak continued to live at the Hrushevsky Institute, where by now he was also serving as the unpaid Deputy Director because of problems then plaguing the administration. The residence was finding it difficult to hire and keep a competent administrator, and Kiriak found himself caught up with running it. In 1940 he was placed in charge of the institute – a position he accepted reluctantly and relinquished happily two years later, the moment the crisis had passed. During his brief tenure as 'rector,' he helped compile and edit a 207-page commemorative book marking the 25th anniversary of the institute. A useful compendium was published the year after he stepped down as director.[50] The illustrated volume brought together articles on the history of the institute by various authors, as well as lists of current members, former residents, and Hrushevsky alumni who had joined the Canadian Armed

Forces. Kiriak himself contributed three signed pieces to the book: 'Vs-tupne slovo' (Introductory Remarks), 'Vstup' (Introduction), and 'V dvadtsiat i piat-litni rokovyny Instytutu im. Mykh. Hrushevskoho, v Edmontoni, Alberta' (On the Twenty-Fifth Anniversary of the Michael Hrushevsky Institute in Edmonton, Alberta) – a total of twelve pages in the printed text. He undoubtedly played a key role in bringing the volume to press, given the practical experience he had recently obtained publishing two of his own books.

Kiriak subsequently enjoyed a respite from community affairs working for the Americans, who were pouring into town as part of the massive contingent of servicemen and labourers mobilized for the construction of the Alaska Highway. He was able to make some good money while the work lasted.[51] When it finally ended in the summer of 1944, he found a new job as a timekeeper for Northern Alberta Railways (NAR), a position he would hold until his retirement. The NAR paid him a salary, covered his expenses, provided him with a railway car that served as his office and residence, and kept him supplied with water, firewood, and coal. This arrangement suited Kiriak well – he was tired of living in Edmonton, appreciated the pay, and enjoyed being moved around to different locations at section worksites in northern Alberta.[52] It also gave him plenty of free time to write, which enabled him to finish work on the final volume of his trilogy.

In 1945 the third instalment of *Syny zemli* came out in print. The concluding volume was 348 pages. By then the trilogy had begun to garner critical praise and was quietly developing a strong following in parts of the Ukrainian community. The story offered a panorama of three generations of Ukrainian-Canadian life, capturing not only the harsh struggles of the pioneers but also the proud achievements of their children and grandchildren. Told largely through the eyes of Hrehory Workun – who is an old man at the beginning of the novel – the expansively conceived tale records the progress of the Workuns and four other immigrant families: the Dubs, the Wakars, the Soloviys, and the Poshtars. Their individual and intertwined destinies are emblematic of the experience of the Ukrainians who homesteaded the Prairies. The trilogy has a universal quality despite being firmly rooted in the distinctly Slavic peasant values that the first-wave immigrants brought with them from Eastern Europe. *Syny zemli* was the high point in Kiriak's literary endeavours – the culmination of a project on which he had embarked more than a decade-and-a-half earlier. Yet it by no means signalled the end of his creative efforts: there were poems and stories he still wanted to write, and he continued to involve himself in other creative and intellectual undertakings.[53]

In 1940 Kiriak began working on a children's reader, titled *Marusia*, for Ukrainian schools across Canada. It was finally published in 1947 by Saskatoon's P. Mohyla Institute. This 103-page book, featuring colour illustrations and an extensive glossary, was reprinted three years later and again in 1959 – a testament to its popularity with parents and teachers. Though the reader also had its critics, it proved invaluable for teaching Ukrainian to children, for in look and feel it was indistinguishable from the texts they were familiar with in public school.[54] Kiriak understood that it was part of his role as an activist to help educate Ukrainian-Canadian youth, even after he was no longer teaching and despite the fact that he was himself single and childless. It is telling that while he was preparing to leave Errol school, essentially suffering from burnout, he was simultaneously working on a curriculum guide for the Ukrainian community's school system. The guide was first published in *Ukrainskyi holos*, then issued separately by the P. Mohyla Institute.[55]

Kiriak did not want to rest on his laurels, such as they might be, after his trilogy was published. In the late 1940s and early 1950s he began two novels, though he never completed them. An excerpt from one of them, 'Irynka' (Irenie), was included in a special issue of *Ukrainskyi holos* marking the sixtieth anniversary of Ukrainian settlement in Canada; however, the manuscript it was excerpted from does not seem to have survived.[56] However, part of the draft of the second unfinished novel, 'Rozmova z vuikom Ivanom' (A Conversation with Uncle Ivan), is preserved in the Kiriak Papers housed with Library and Archives Canada.[57]

But it was *Syny zemli* that Kiriak regarded as his most important literary work, and it continued to preoccupy him long after its publication. Like a doting father, he was protective of its reputation and eager to see it do well; he was especially sensitive about how it was received by his friends and peers. Given the competitive nature of the small community of Ukrainian-language writers in Canada, it is not surprising that *Syny* had its detractors, and Kiriak was discouraged by the indifferent and occasionally negative responses to his labour of love. He was especially upset about the lack of support he received from the influential editor of *Ukrainskyi holos*, Myroslav Stechishin, his long-time associate and friend. On 12 April 1952, Kiriak complained in a letter to Edmonton lawyer Peter Lazarowich:

> Indeed you know how the late M. Stechishin treated my novel *Syny zemli*. For him, the first part turned out so-so, the second, worse, and the third was good for nothing. My heroes pop up in the story like 'Philip from a hemp field'; the language is polluted with weird words; the praise of Anglo-Saxons is to the point of being disgusting; and only here and there does one come upon descriptions that are pleasingly without comparison. That was his judgment, or criticism, and I accepted it as being fair. But it also harmed me to some degree in terms of sales of the book, because beyond his criticism, the deceased regarded it to be unjust to find room in 'U.V.' [i.e., *Ukrainian Voice*] for letters of praise from readers. (I wrote to Mr. Woycenko, asking him to send me them for my archive, but he replied that they were in the hands of Stechishin, and since he was ill he didn't want to trouble him.) That's it – there, I just remembered, that Dr. Datskiv, then the editor of 'C.F.' [*Canadian Farmer*], while writing a review of several lines, gave me the following lesson – He who wants to be a writer must first learn the language and the technique for writing novels, otherwise he shouldn't bother taking up writing. As a result of all that, disregarding that ordinary readers, chiefly on the farms, greeted the novel surprisingly well – one person would buy it, and from 10 to 20 would read it – I then resolved to quit all kinds of writing, pack all the books on a truck along with everything that I ever had published or written, transport it to the city dump and burn it. I haven't done the latter as yet, because I haven't had the time – I was at work and not 'home,' and as for writing since then, I haven't taken it up – I haven't written the slightest thing and nowhere admitted that I had attempted to be a writer, and if someone who knew me called me that, then I felt then and feel now, as if someone had reminded me that I once was a serious drunk.[58]

Kiriak's rather bitter remarks were provoked by the fact that the USRL wanted to honour him at their upcoming Jubilee Conference. He was uncomfortable about being singled out for praise as an author, especially by fellow organization members. As he explained to Lazarowich, he had become an author almost by accident and did not really view himself as a serious writer. Yet it is clear that it was not modesty alone that was prompting him to pour out his feelings to

Lazarowich – obviously, he felt betrayed by several individuals whom he had thought were his friends and supporters:

> I likewise recollect the fact, that 'U.V.', having its own bookstore, to this day has still not sold all 500 copies of *Syny zemli*, when Ferbey, without a newspaper, without any special advertising, has sold 700. It's as if they were embarrassed to promote and sell it. They were prodded into advertising it last Christmas (1950) by Prof. Hryhoriev when he related the contents of the books over *Voice of America*, and eventually Prof. Biletsky explicated it last fall in 'U.V.' But from their side, other than a catalogue ad and beyond the criticism of the late Stechishin (1946), signed Z.V., there was nothing – well, there was nothing to discover or elucidate. Furthermore, the correspondence from readers who came to the defence of the novel, and there were several, 'U.V.' never printed, with the exception of Yasenchuk's from Vancouver, under which the 'editorial board' gave a supposedly very apt reply. The editorial board of 'U.N.' [Ukrainian News] in Edmonton also received two or three submissions, but the editor, Mr. Dyky, didn't print them only because I am not one of 'them.' I never even thought about challenging what had been written. I thanked 'U.V.' and the 'correspondents' for the review and promised them, that because of my ignorance I had stopped trying to be a writer. With this they agreed, because I did not receive a reply from them. It was then that I decided to burn all of my scribblings (1946).[59]

Fortunately, Kiriak did not act on his disappointment at the way *Syny zemli* had been received. Deep down, he understood that he had written an important work of literature and that he was a committed writer with something valuable to say.

Indeed, by the time he wrote to Lazarowich he had received more encouraging feedback from unexpected quarters, which undoubtedly lifted his spirits and probably prevented him from destroying his personal archive:

> At very same time a great opportunity befell me, or actually two opportunities, to become a great author, either a Catholic one or a Communist one. The Catholics under the leadership of even Bishop Ladyka began ordering the novel in the hope that I, if seemingly impressed by them, would go over to their camp. They promised me that within a year all of the books would be gone and that I urgently had to prepare a second edition with changes, which

they would suggest to me. And they continue to cling to their hope. Dr. Nim-chuk took this task upon himself, immediately upon his arrival at *Visti* [i.e., Ukrainian News]. But I declined to come to their first conference, which they had organized to arrange a plan for my elucidation as a writer. In the meantime their daily *Ameryka* began publishing entire chapters from the novel, so as to demonstrate to me that they were seriously thinking about moving me to America.

But I rejected their proposition the way that I rejected Shatulsky's propo-sition, who paid a special visit to me, coming from Winnipeg so as to nego-tiate a deal with me. His proposition was as follows: They did not want to have me as a member, but they wanted my sympathies, namely, to write an article or two for *Ukrainske slovo* [Ukrainian Word] about issues that were seemingly a long way from communism but close to farmers and workers. About schools, about the cultural upbringing of children, or some sketch from life. Such writing was supposed to smooth the way for me, and pri-marily for my *Syny zemli*, to Kyiv, where they would have reprinted it in tens of thousands of copies, which would bring me such an honorarium that it would once and for all secure me for life. They themselves had already ini-tiated the matter, binding several copies of the novel, all three volumes to-gether, and sending them to officials in Kyiv. They still needed to prove to those authorities that I am a sympathizer of the progressive movement in Canada by my writing those articles or sketches. And they genuinely tried to pull me over to their camp, because almost comically, they bought more of my books than the nationalists and Catholics combined. For example, in Vancouver alone one of them, N. Chrapko, sold 27 sets among his own [peo-ple], while poor Yasenchuk barely managed to push 11 – he complained that 'U.V.' hurt sales.[60]

The overtures made by both Catholics and Communists were flat-tering, but Kiriak was not about to break with the Ukrainian Orthodox community to which he had committed himself for more than four decades. And though the offer from the Communists may seem rather remarkable, given Kiriak's strong Ukrainian nationalist sentiments and the anti-Communist climate of the Cold War in North America, it had not been made willy-nilly. The Ukrainian-Canadian left had only a few years earlier succeeded in recruiting support for the Soviet Ukrainian regime from Wasyl Swystun, one of the pillars of the pioneer- and in-terwar-era Ukrainian nationalist community.[61] If an activist of Swystun's stature could be persuaded to make peace with Communist Ukraine – for pragmatic if not ideological reasons – then why not try to win over a high-profile cultural figure like Kiriak? Regardless, Kiriak did not seriously consider the idea of switching camps so as to boost his literary ambitions or to secure a comfortable retirement.

Notwithstanding the frustrations and hurt feelings to which he gave vent in his letter to Lazarowich, by 1952 *Syny zemli* had received critical praise in a variety of periodicals, and Kiriak's unique literary achievement was finally getting the recognition it deserved.[62] By now Kiriak was beginning to think about his legacy. This is evident in the long autobiographical letter he wrote to Ivan Ruryk and his wife at a time when his career with the railway was winding down. On reaching retirement age in 1953, Kiriak returned to Edmonton, where he again rented a room at the Hrushevsky Institute – a convenient spot for a lifelong bachelor with strong connections to the residence and its cultural centre. Eventually, though, he bought a house on the east side of downtown, not far from the Ukrainian Bookstore, which was still being run by his friend, Dmytro Ferbey.

Time was beginning to creep up on Kiriak, as he himself had observed as far back as 1946, in a letter to Ivan Ruryk:

> With me everything is as of old. I think that I am the same as I was twenty years ago, though I know that it is not like that. But I cling to the perception that it 'seems' to be so, because it is better that way.[63]

Somewhat ominously, in the summer of 1955 Kiriak complained in a letter to friends he had just visited in Vancouver that he probably should not have made the trip because of the problems he was starting to have with his legs. He had stopped at Radium Hot Springs on his way back from the West Coast, but the waters there had provided no relief, and he had essentially been housebound since his return to Edmonton. The pain was so intense it was keeping him awake at night. In the daytime he was finding it hard to walk more than two blocks without a rest.[64]

A few months later Kiriak informed Peter Woycenko, the editor of *Ukrainskyi holos*, that his health problems were persisting. He tried to put a positive spin on his situation, but it is obvious from the following rather alarming description of himself that his health was declining steadily:

With me, well, I am starting to convalesce. My legs are no longer hurting, but feel like they are made of willow and I am unable to either walk or sit for a long time. I'll walk for a bit, walking for a half-hour or so, and then I have to lie down so as to relieve the burden that drags them down as if it were hot sand. Because of that I don't go anywhere, either to church, or visiting, so as not to make them restive. I have lost close to sixty pounds in weight and people do not recognize me now, indeed, this fellow has withered to the point where he is no longer recognizable.[65]

Nevertheless, he was continuing to work at his typewriter. Alberta's fiftieth anniversary had inspired him to write a long article in which he reflected on half a century of Ukrainian achievements. His effort was prompted by the fact that the government had sponsored a book titled *The Golden Jubilee Anthology of Alberta* to mark the celebratory occasion. However, that book had given only cursory recognition to the large contribution made by Ukrainians to the province's development. Kiriak failed to complete the article – which was more an interpretative account of Ukrainian-Canadian society than a descriptive history – and it was never published. Even so, the typescript – dated 11 to 13 November 1955 – provides a fascinating glimpse into how Kiriak viewed the organized Ukrainian-Canadian community and the Ukrainian identity in Canada.[66]

Kiriak remained intellectually active and fully engaged in his literary affairs even as he disintegrated physically. Shortly before his death, he wrote a letter to Orest Starchuk, a Slavics professor at the University of Alberta, discussing details of the English translation of *Syny zemli,* which at that time was being prepared by Michael Luchkovich. Worried about the length of Luchkovich's as yet unfinished typescript, he sought Starchuk's help in finding an editor for the manuscript at the university. He also expressed concerns about the book's printing costs and the overall quality of the translation:

Further, as to the printing of the book, that is another matter that troubles my head. Mr. Luchkovich, under the impression that it could be published exactly as he translated it, wrote a letter to *Raerson Press* [*sic*], *Toronto,* describing how many pages it was supposed to comprise and the nature of the material, also that it was very good, and upon receiving an answer curbed his enthusiasm, well, the man settled down, because in the reply it was stated that such a book could be sold for no less than $10 a copy, namely, *retail price*. That means the cost of printing will be close to $7 a copy, and printing 5000 copies would amount to $35,000. This left him wide-eyed and me bug-eyed. He thought the publishers would seize the material, edit it and publish it with their own money just as they had published his translation of Prychodko's *One of Fifteen Million*.

That is what he informed me and he ordered me not worry about the printing and sales, because everything would go as if it were greased with butter. He even insisted that I not look for any editors because his translation did not require them – he had done everything 'perfectly.' Meanwhile, I, having read the translation here and there, observed that until it was submitted for editing, I would have to read and check it word for word and compare it to the original, because in reading it I found that Mr. Luchkovich, while he seems to know our language, mostly, so to speak, has a superficial command of it rather than grasping its essence. What are chiefly foreign to him are the sayings and proverbial expressions with which our ordinary folk are able to adorn their conversational language. Consequently, I am now, as they say, going blind over the translation and changing words, and even sentences, which often are utterly inappropriate for the heroes or events in the original, and this is absolutely necessary before someone can be found to edit it.[67]

Four days later, on 28 December 1955, Illia Kiriak died in Edmonton. His passing was noted in the press in a brief article that mentioned he was the author of a three-volume novel, *Sons of the Soil,* dealing 'with early immigration from the Ukraine.'[68] The story gave his place of residence as 10669–97 Street and described him as having 'taught school for more than 19 years in various districts of Alberta,' until recently having been employed with Northern Alberta Railways. It was further indicated that 'Mr. Kiriak had no known relatives' and that funeral arrangements were being made by Park Memorial. The funeral service was held at St John's Ukrainian Orthodox Cathedral on Saturday, 31 December, at 10 a.m., with the Reverends Hieronym Hrycyna and Ambrose Chrustawka officiating and interment taking place at Beechmount Cemetery.

Postscript

At the time of his death Kiriak owned a four-room rental property worth $5,700; held fifteen shares in the Independent Wholesale Company valued at $1,500; and had $7,000 in a savings account at the Bank of Toronto. He also had a promissory note for slightly more than $1,200 from Victor Kupchenko – the manager of the Alberta Printing Company responsible for publishing *Syny zemli.* This debt was finally settled in April 1960. In total, his estate was worth roughly $17,000, a sum that can undoubtedly be attributed to his thrifty nature and to the fact that he had no family to support.

In his will, Kiriak bequeathed his $400 insurance policy to the St John's Institute (the renamed Michael Hrushevsky student residence), as well as his books, 'including all those written and printed by myself or by some publishing company.' St Andrew's College, the Ukrainian Orthodox seminary at the University of Manitoba, received the bulk of his inheritance, including his real estate; his cash in the bank; his shares and the money that he had invested or loaned; any cheques found on his person at the time of his death; and forthcoming income from his wages. The remainder of his estate he left to a labourer named Dmytro Semaka, who was then living at 9531–106 Avenue.[69] Kiriak's material worth was relatively modest; his legacy to the Ukrainian community – and especially to Ukrainian and Canadian literature – was substantial and enduring.

In 1959 an abridged English translation of the first volume of Kiriak's *Syny zemli* was published in Toronto by Ryerson Press.[70] The translation was by Michael Luchkovich, a former federal MP for Vegreville, who was never formally credited for his work.[71] Dr M.H. Scargill of the University of Alberta had been commissioned to prepare the manuscript for publication and to write an introduction. This he did in the summer of 1956, noting that his own part in preparing the novel for the press had been minimal, amounting to a few minor revisions, a number of small cuts, and the provision of explanatory notes where he felt they would be helpful. For some reason Scargill's preface was never included in the book – a rather unfortunate omission, for it discussed the novel's contents and commented on some of its strengths and weaknesses while acknowledging Luchkovich's role as the translator.

The major part of the editing was subsequently done by the Icelandic-Canadian author Laura Goodman Salverson. Lorne Pierce of the Ryerson Press convinced her to set aside her own work long enough to polish and abridge the Luchkovich translation. She was paid $250 for her efforts. For the final English version, some thirty to forty pages were eventually deleted from the original.[72] According to a letter from the managing editor at Ryerson, royalties for the work were subsequently paid to Trident Press in Winnipeg – the publishers of *Ukrainskyi holos* – 'practically on cash basis.'[73]

On Sunday, 17 September 1961, at Kiriak's gravesite in Edmonton, a headstone was erected in his memory by St Andrew's College of Winnipeg. On it is this inscription: 'For They Were Genuine Sons Of The Soil Who Blazed A Trail That We Who Came After Might Find A Less Onerous And Fuller Life.' That evening an *akademiia*, or popular scholarly gathering, was held in his honour.

Kiriak's *Syny zemli* continued to win the author posthumous acclaim and is now generally recognized as a monument of Ukrainian-language literature in Canada. Between 1970 and 1973 the full trilogy was serialized in *Ukrainskyi holos* before being reissued over the following two years in an attractive second edition by Trident Press. A substantially revised version of the first volume, edited by Yuri Stefanyk of Edmonton, was produced by the Alberta Department of Education in 1979 for use in the bilingual school program.[74] Trident Press has twice reprinted the Luchkovich translation without making any changes to the abridged Ryerson Press edition. The second reprint appeared in 1983.

The time is ripe for new editions of both Ukrainian and English versions of *Syny zemli* and *Sons of the Soil*. Ideally, they would be annotated to explain any words, folk customs, or references that would be unfamiliar to contemporary readers. A new generation of fiction lovers – in Canada, as well as in independent Ukraine – would then be able to discover Kiriak's compelling tale about how the Ukrainian pioneers helped settle and transform the Canadian West. Of course, it would also be timely to properly document and critically reassess the life and literary legacy of Illia Kiriak, a truly remarkable individual who deserves to be much better known and appreciated as a writer, community builder, and exemplary Ukrainian Canadian.

Notes

1   In some published sources he is also identified as Elias Kiriak, an anglicized form of Illia that the author also used formally in English. Transliterated into English from Ukrainian according to the Modified Library of Congress system, Kiriak's full name more properly should be rendered Illiia Kyriiak. I have used the Kiriak spelling adopted by the author in

Canada when also referring to all of his family members in Ukraine.

2 Illia Kiriak, *Sons of the Soil,* trans. Michael Luchkovich (Toronto: Ryerson, 1959).

3 Mykhailo Marunchak, *Illiia Kyriiak ta ioho tvorchist* (Illia Kiriak and His Works) (Winnipeg: Ukrainian Free Academy of Sciences in Canada, 1973).

4 I am indebted to Myron Momryk for helping me initially access the Kiriak collection in 1992.

5 Zavallia (or Zavalie) is on the north shore of the Cheremosh River, near its junction with the Prut, in Ivano-Frankivsk *oblast* in Western Ukraine. Situated 14 kilometres south of the *raion* centre of Sniatyn, because of its close proximity to Chernivtsi *oblast*, the local culture of Zavallia reflects many Bukovynian influences despite being part of Galicia. The first written reference to the village dates from 1479, after which it was largely destroyed by Tatar raiders between 1619 and 1621. At the beginning of the twentieth century a significant number of Zavallia residents emigrated abroad in search of a better life, 193 people leaving in 1913 alone. In 1968 Zavallia had a population of 1,069. The name Zavallia, pronounced 'Zavalie' in the local dialect, translates literally as 'behind the wall' – the reference being to the earthen, stone, and wood fortifications erected around many settlements in the turbulent times following the Mongol Invasion. A school district established in 1904 southwest of the present-day village of Andrew, in rural east-central Alberta, was given the name Zawale by the Ukrainian pioneers who settled the area at the end of the nineteenth century. A nearby post office, which operated from 1910 to 1947, bore the same name. Today, the only reminder of the former settlement is a township road named Zawale, which runs east from Secondary Highway 855 past the site of the no longer extant 'Zawale' Ukrainian Orthodox church (dedicated to St Michael the Archangel), relocated in 1994 to Pigeon Lake.

6 Unattributed quotes are from Kiriak's 1952 letter to Ivan and Nastunia Ruryk, which is currently being prepared for publication.

7 In another memoiristic piece, Kiriak curiously identifies his only brother as Dmytro. See 'Iak orhanizuvalasia persha "Sich" v Zavaliu' (How they organized the first 'Sich' in Zavallia), in Petro Trylovsky, *Hei, tam na hori 'Sich' ide!* ... *Propamiatna knyha 'Sichei'* (Hey, on the hilltop, the 'Sich' is coming ... The Commemorative Book of 'Siches') (Edmonton: Vydavnychyi Komitet Propamiatnoi Knyhy 'Sichei,' 1968), 82. In the article he also describes how his father would sometimes ask for Illia's help while learning to read and write, and how his brother would bring him books from the local reading society library and encourage him to read them aloud to his parents and neighbours.

8 Illia was quartered in a stable, where he slept on a stove (rather than in the house). This allowed him to come and go freely during the night without his aunt and uncle knowing about his 'extracurricular' activities.

9 For a more detailed account of the impact the Sich movement had on the formation of Kiriak's Ukrainian identity, see Trylovsky, *Hei, tam na hori,* 82–3. In the conclusion to his article, Kiriak offered the following acknowledgment: 'I do know one thing – that the "Sich" was for me the first and most advanced national school, which was later fulfilled by *Ukrainskyi holos* [Ukrainian Voice] ... If not for the "Sich" and *Ukrainskyi holos*, I am certain that I would not be able to write this recollection.' Sich (pronounced *seech*) was the name given to the fortified settlements established by the Cossacks in the sixteenth to eighteenth centuries on the islands and banks of the lower Dnipro River.

10 According to passenger records at Ellis Island, a nineteen-year-old single male registered as 'Ilia Kiriak' landed in New York aboard the *Kaiserin Auguste Victoria* from Hamburg on 17 January 1907. However, Kiriak makes no mention of arriving at Ellis Island or in the United States in his autobiographical sketch, and it seems unlikely that he would have gotten the name of the ship wrong. It is also unclear why only one Illia Kiriak is identified on the *Kaiserin Victoria* passenger list, since the 1952 letter to the Ruryks indicates that the cousins travelled all the way to Manitoba together. It has not yet been possible to establish what happened to the cousin Kiriak after the two men went their separate ways.

11 Iwan Lakusta (1860–1949) sailed to Canada aboard the SS *Christiana*, arriving in Quebec City on 30 April 1896. On 28 May of the same year he filed for his first homestead at SW 14-56-18 W4; he was subsequently joined there by his wife Paraska (neé Marko) and their children. It is interesting that Iwan Lakusta was one of the signatories of two letters sent by Galician and Bukovynian settlers in Alberta to Russian Orthodox church authorities in San Francisco requesting pastoral care for their community: the first written on 18 June 1898, the second on 9 September 1899. The letters are preserved in the Russian Alaskan Church Records, Library of Congress. Lakusta was one of the settlers who had to sign the letter with a cross, suggesting he was illiterate besides being sympathetic to the Russophile movement – which would have put him at odds with his educated, more Ukrainophile nephew.

12 According to an obituary in an Edmonton Ukrainian newspaper following his death, Kiriak also spent some time working in Grand Forks, North Dakota, though this is not mentioned in the author's own autobiography. See Orest Starchuk, 'Pysmennyk Illia Kyriiak (Posmertna zhadka)' [The Writer Illia Kiriak (A Posthumous Remembrance)] in *Ukrainski visti* (Ukrainian News), January 1956.

13 The expression Kiriak uses is 'divochiv trokhy' – which literally translates as 'girl-ing around a little,' that is, 'engaging in a bit of womaniz-
ing.' Though his meaning is somewhat ambiguous given his essentially
shy nature, it is certainly possible that Kiriak consorted with prostitutes
or barroom girls, who were common in frontier communities.

14 Ivan Mazepa was the Ukrainian Cossack *hetman* who in 1708–9 led an
unsuccessful revolt against Tsar Peter I, for which he was anathematized
by the Russian Orthodox Church.

15 Myroslav Sichynsky (1886–1979) was a Ukrainian student radical who
in 1908 assassinated the Polish palatine or governor of Galicia, Andrzej
Potocki. The son of a Greek Catholic priest, Sichynsky committed the
murder to protest widespread fraud and violence by Polish officials during the 1908 election. Captured and convicted of murder by Austro-Hungarian authorities, he was slated to be executed, but the emperor
commuted his sentence to life imprisonment. Widely regarded as a hero
by many Ukrainians, in 1911 Sichynsky successfully escaped incarceration. Four years later he made it to the United States, which granted him
the status of political refugee. He lived there for the rest of his long life.
Besides touring Ukrainian communities in Canada in the 1920s, Sichynsky was a prominent figure in several Ukrainian organizations in the
United States before being marginalized and largely forgotten after
adopting an increasingly pro-Soviet stance in the 1940s.

16 The inaugural gathering of the FUSD was held on 22–27 August. It drew
twenty-six delegates from ten branches. See Peter Krawchuk, *The
Ukrainian Socialist Movement in Canada (1907–1918)* (Toronto:
Progress, 1979), 19–20. For an overview of the development of the
Ukrainian-Canadian socialist movement in this period, see Orest Mar-
tynowych, *Ukrainians in Canada: The Formative Period, 1891–1924*
(Edmonton: Canadian Institute of Ukrainian Studies Press, 1981), 252–
60.

17 The masthead identified the paper – the first Ukrainian-language periodical to be issued from Edmonton – as the organ of the Federation of
Ukrainian Socialists in Canada. Chapters of the organization supported
the paper financially. For Kiriak's perspective on some of the conflicts
that erupted in the wake of the schism within the FUSD, see his article
'To my!' (That's us!) in *Nova hromada*, 2 June 1911, 2.

18 See Marunchak, *Illiia Kyriiak ta ioho tvorchist*, 15–16. 'Hirkyi son' was
reproduced in Yar Slavutych, ed., *Pivnichne siavio Almanakh* (Northern
Lights: Almanac), tom III (Edmonton: Slavuta, 1967), 25–7, and
reprinted in *Ukainskyi holos*, 4 March 1970.

19 Roman Kremar (1886–1953), whose real name was Mykhailo Solo-
dukha, was the son of a wealthy and politically active Galician peasant.

He came to Canada in 1909 after his own political involvements in Western Ukraine prevented him from pursuing a successful legal career there. During the First World War he enlisted in the Canadian Army. As a lieutenant he lobbied for the creation of a Ukrainian formation until Russophiles succeeded in having him removed from the ranks. In 1918 he moved to Winnipeg to take over the editorship of the Ukrainian Catholic weekly, *Kanadyiskyi rusyn* (Canadian Ruthenian), which he subsequently renamed *Kanadyiskyi Ukrainets'* (Canadian Ukrainian). Kremar played an especially important role in the development of Alberta Ukrainian life in the pioneer era. He is buried at St Joachim's cemetery in Edmonton.

20 Preserved in the Kiriak papers (LAC, MG30, D235, vol. 1, file 31) is a very revealing letter from Myroslaw Stechishin dated 18 October 1923. In it, Stechishin writes: 'My opinion about Kremar is as follows: He is an unusually gifted man, I could even say, a genius. In my life I have probably not met a more talented man than him, and if I did, then I never knew him as well. But at the same time I have never met a man so lacking in moral principles as Kremar. And that is the downfall of Kremar. He was fully aware of his talents and was utterly contemptuous of moral principles, but this is only permitted to someone who has acquired power, and is not trying to attain power. Napoleon and Bismarck, who also did not distinguish themselves with the firmness of their moral principles, would have died among criminals if they had not scorned moral principles at the beginning of their professional careers.

   'It is my thinking that Kremar did not have the least bit of compunction about smashing the Ukrainian socialist organization in its infancy. He did this simply to demonstrate his strength – to use his strength if not for good, then for ill. His beliefs did not play the slightest role in this instance. And this he accomplished. He destroyed the organization and at the same time helped Crath to gain power with all of his destructive work. I often wonder if Ukrainian socialists in Canada would have arrived at Bolshevism, if Crath had not been able to gain control of the socialist organization for some time. While the discord pushed Crath forward, the discord was created by the ambition of Kremar.

   'Kremar destroyed the socialist organization and soon realized that it was essentially a waste of time for him. He saw before him a wider panorama – leadership over the entirety of national work alongside business on a grand scale, not necessarily consistent with socialist principles. He took to the publishing of *Novyny* as an organ that was to conquer everyone, and which was to get him recognition as the first among Canadian Ukrainians. I believe he would have attained his goal, had it not been for the war.'

21 See, for instance, Kiriak's article 'Nevirnist' i peresliduvanie' (Treachery

and Persecution), in which he uses Christ's life and teachings to make his polemical argument.

22 Kiriak had gotten to know Hawrelak in Hosmer.

23 See 'Ruthenian Institute Successful Opening,' *Vegreville Observer*, 3 June 1914, 1. The same front-page story continued: 'The entire entertainment was highly pleasing and those who did not attend missed something well worth their while. The concert closed at 11.30 by singing the Ruthenian National Hymn and "God Save the King."'

24 The poems can found in the Kiriak papers, LAC, MG30 D235, vol. 1, files 49 and 51.

25 Ibid., file 55. In 'Iak orhanizuvalasia persha "Sich" v Zavaliu,' Kiriak mentions seeing his first theatrical performance at a *sich* encampment in a meadow by the Cheremosh River. Like many teachers and cultural activists in the Ukrainian immigrant community, Kiriak occasionally performed in plays and helped stage them. An article in *Ukrainskyi holos* on 3 April 1918 singled him out for his performance in an Edmonton production of Mykhailo Starytsky's *Oi, ne khody Hrytsiu* (Oh, don't go, Hryts), mounted in February of that year. That account described him as having 'delighted the audience,' which seems rather surprising, given his diffident personality. Since an undated typescript of *Domashni klopoty*, signed by Kiriak, only recently surfaced in Winnipeg, it is not yet possible to determine if it was ever presented on stage. Nonetheless, he continued to occasionally participate in theatrical productions. For intance, he is mentioned as having acted in a 1931 presentation of the K. Vanchenko-Pysanetsky dramatization of the T. Shevchenko poem *Kateryna*, put on by the Kobzar Society of Edmonton. See 'Nasha molod pry narodnii roboti' (Our Youth Engaged in National Work) by 'Hist' (Guest), in *Novyi shliakh* (New Pathway), 15 October 1931, 3.

26 Kiriak's father passed away in 1910. His brother Petro died suddenly in 1913, just two months after getting married.

27 The first issue of *Postup* rolled off an antiquated press on 12 July 1915, the feast day of Saints Peter and Paul. It was a perfect time to launch the venture, for by then some 8,000 to 10,000 Ukrainian homesteaders were gathering annually for this important celebration led by the Basilian missionaries and Sister Servants of Mary Immaculate, who were working out of local monasteries. *Postup* folded temporarily, then relocated to Edmonton in 1916, where it was edited by Toma Tomashewsky until finally closing permanently owing to financial and other difficulties.

28 The story was published in *Ukrainskyi holos*, 18 April 1923. Of course, the most famous Ilarion in Ukrainian history was the first Slav to become the head of the Orthodox Church in Kyivan Rus. Yaremko tragically died shortly after his stint as *Postup* editor.

29 Marunchak, *Illiia Kyriiak ta ioho tvorchist*, 27.

30 Ibid., 32.
31 Published in *Ukrainskyi holos*, 28 September 1921.
32 The author provides fascinating accounts of his romantic misadventures in a kind of extended postscript to the life story he wrote for the Ruryks. Of course, in the hothouse environment of closely knit peasant communities, within which Old Country values often clashed with New World realities, the normal pressures involved in courting were further magnified by the public scrutiny to which teachers were constantly subjected.
33 See 'Lysty I. Kyriiaka do I. Shklianky,' in *Zakhidnokanadskyi zbirnyk. Chastyna druha* (Collected Papers on Ukrainian Settlers in Western Canada: Part Two), ed. Yar Slavutych (Edmonton: Shevchenko Scientific Society in Canada, 1975), 350–1.
34 Ibid., 352.
35 Osyp Nazaruk (1883–1940) was a Galician lawyer, editor, and publicist as well as an executive member of the Ukrainian Radical Party from 1905–19. He became a member of the Ukrainian National Rada and after its defeat moved to Vienna to edit the organs of the Western Ukrainian National Republic, *Ukrainskyi prapor* (Ukrainian Flag) and *Volia* (Freedom). From his socialist origins he eventually evolved through Catholicism to embrace a conservative hetmanite ideology. He died in Cracow during the Second World War.
36 As cited in Marunchak, *Illiia Kyriiak ta ioho tvorchist*, 31.
37 Kiriak actually became the president of Canadian Importers Ltd., though Dmytro Ferbey ran the day-to-day business. Kirak somewhat reluctantly served in this capacity until 1947. In 1936 he had tried to sell his $675 share in the store after he quit teaching and was temporarily short of cash.
38 In 1917 Kiriak had joined the Adam Kotsko Student Association, which spearheaded the founding of the Hrushevsky Institute in March of the following year. Others in the Kotsko group were Elias Shklanka, Harry Kostash, and Michael Luchkovich, the future MP and translator of *Syny zemli*. Though he lived outside Edmonton, Kiriak sat on the institute's board in 1922, between 1926 and 1929, and again in 1933. In 1931–2 he was appointed to the institute's Adam Kotsko Student Circle, owing to his extensive experience working with young people as a teacher. Originally a non-denominational student residence, in 1949 the Hrushevsky Institute was renamed St John's Institute, having in the meantime affiliated itself with the Ukrainian Greek Orthodox Church of Canada. Kiriak wrote a fascinating letter to Myroslaw Stechishin from Andrew on 27 April 1927, in which he described a conflict among institute members that had been triggered by the controversial purchase of a church for the St John's Ukrainian Orthodox congregation. In it, Kiriak distinguished

between 'hard core' Orthodox and the other mostly Orthodox members of the institute, who were not as eager to acquire a sanctuary until the debt of the Hrushevsky Hall had been fully paid off. From his account it is clear that Kiriak's sympathies lay with the latter. See LAC, MG30 D 236, vol. 1, file 31.

39 See the letter from Svarich dated 26 April 1931, LAC, MG30 D235, vol. 1, file 32. In it, Svarich makes the revealing comment that like Kiriak, the woman he was recommending was not entirely inexperienced when it came to romances that never led to marriage.

40 See 'Kanado' (Canada), *Ukrainskyi holos,* 4 July 1928.

41 See 'Ne hovorim po ukrainsky,' in *Ukrainskyi holos,* 13 November 1929. In his correspondence with fellow Ukrainian Canadians, Kiriak often utilized English words and expressions out of necessity or for effect. However, he did not write in the 'half-*na-piv*' dialect that was becoming ever more common among second- and third-generation Ukrainian speakers.

42 See 'Zamitni tsyfry' (Noteworthy Figures), *Ukrainskyi holos,* 9 April 1930.

43 For a brief history of the USRL in this period, see Oleh Gerus, 'Consolidating the Community: The Ukrainian Self-Reliance League,' in *Canada's Ukrainians: Negotiating an Identity,* ed. Lubomyr Luciuk and Stella Hryniuk (Toronto: University of Toronto Press, for the Ukrainian Canadian Centennial Committee, 1991), 157–86.

44 The story was published in *V den materi* (On Mother's Day) (Winnipeg: Ukrainskyi holos for Soiuz Ukrainok Kanady, 1933), 25–35.

45 Kiriak states in his autobiographical letter to the Ruryks that he bought his first car in 1926 and replaced it with a new one in 1929 – which he then drove for ten years. He would rack up a total of 132,000 miles on the two vehicles.

46 At the time he quit the Errol school, Kiriak was owed $1,200, which the trustees took five years to repay. Ibid. See also Peter Yacyshyn, 'Errol School District No. 2073,' in *Voices of Yesteryear: Vilna and District History* (Vilna: Vilna and District Historical Society, 1991), I:116–19 and II:1265–1266.

47 See Kiriak's letter to Myroslav Stechishin dated 23 March 1931, LAC, MG30 D235, vol. 1, file 31.

48 For an English version of the book see Honore Ewach, *Call of the Land,* trans. Ray Serwylo (Winnipeg: Trident, 1986). Kiriak had also been urged to finish his book by Professor Olgerd Bochkovsky, a distinguished intellectual from the Prague Ukrainian community, who had met Kiriak on a visit to Canada in 1936.

49 See the letter from Novak on *Ukrainskyi holos* letterhead dated 18 November 1938, LAC, MG30 D235, vol. 1, file 36. Apolinary Novak

(1885–1955) was a journalist and writer who immigrated to Canada in 1901. He was the editor of *Kanadyiskyi farmer* (Canadian Farmer) for three years and a staff writer for *Ukrainskyi holos* from 1922 until his death. He wrote short stories on Ukrainian pioneer themes that were published in the latter and in the American newspaper *Svoboda* (Liberty), as well as in the journals *Khata* (The House) and Lviv's *Literaturno-naukovyi vistnyk* (Literary-Scientific Herald).

50 [Illia Kyriiak, editor and contributor], *Iuvilenia knyha 25-littia Instytuta im. Mykhaila Hrushevskoho v Edmontoni* (English title page: Silver Jubilee Book of The M. Hrushevsky Ukrainian Institute in Edmonton) (Edmonton: M. Hrushevsky Ukrainian Institute, 1943). Though Kiriak is identified only as having compiled the 'Records and Materials' section documenting the Jubilee Convention of the Institute on 26–7 December 1943, the fact that he wrote the introductions to both parts of the book suggests he probably had a hand in organizing its overall content. The 'Records and Materials' section was issued at the same time as a separate edition, comprised of pages 133 to 203 of the full volume.

51 In a letter Kiriak wrote to Petro Woycenko on 8 April 1943, he made the following remark about his new and improved financial circumstances: 'As for money, thank God, there's enough, not necessarily for me at present, but in general. The Americans brought it in, occupying Edmonton and northern Alberta with work and money. Golden times have arrived.' LAC, MG30 D235, vol. 1, file 36.

52 Kiriak's annual earnings between 1950 and 1953 ranged from $2,000 to $3,000.

53 For details about the poems that Kiriak wrote during this period, see Marunchak, *Illiia Kyriiak ta ioho tvorchist,* 64–7.

54 Ilia Kiriak, ed., *Ukrainska chytanka Marusia* (Ukrainian Reader Marusia) (Saskatoon: P. Mohyla Ukrainian Institute Extension Department, 1947). See also Kiriak's letter about the preparation of the book, to Julian and Savella Stechishin, dated 25 November 1940, in LAC, MG30 D235, vol. 1, file 29. Interestingly, hard-core traditionalists criticized the reader because it ostensibly lacked Ukrainian content and spirit – that is, it depicted children in contemporary settings and dress rather than showing them in Cossack outfits or living in thatch-covered houses with a stork on the roof!

55 The outline appeared in *Ukrainskyi holos* on 20 May 1936. It was later reproduced in a typescript edition as Illiia Kyriiak, *Nacherk planu nauky ukrainoznavtsva v Ridnykh Shkolakh* (Outline of a Plan for Ukrainian Studies in Native Schools) (Saskatoon: P. Mohyla Institute, 1937).

56 See 'Irynka' (Irenie), *Ukrainskyi holos,* 5 September 1951. According to a letter from Kiriak in the *Holos* archives, the novel had grown to two

hundred pages before getting creatively stalled. See Marunchak, *Illiia Kyriiak ta ioho tvorchist,* 68.

57 LAC, MG30 D235, vol. 3, files 113-30. Kiriak similarly had plans to compile a collection of his short fiction, but this too, failed to be realized, as age and ill health slowly overtook him.

58 See 'Lyst Illi Kyriiaka' (A Letter by Illia Kiriak) in *Pivnichne siaivo: Almanakh* I (1964): 72–3. The expression 'Vyrvavsia, iak Pylyp z konopel" (He took off like Philip from a hemp field) is a proverbial saying, the meaning of which is explained as follows in the 1946 collection *Prypovidky* (Proverbs) by the Edmonton author Volodymyr S. Plawiuk: 'To give oneself away. Fugitives hid out in hemp fields, criminals and other similar types, and they concealed their things there, because not even a dog could detect anything.'

59 Ibid, 73.

60 Ibid, 74. *Ukrainske slovo* (Ukrainian Word) was a pro-Soviet weekly published in Winnipeg by the Association of United Ukrainian Canadians from January 1943 to 1965, when it merged with *Ukrainske zhyttia* (Ukrainian Word) to form *Zhyttia i slovo* (Life and Word). Matthew Shatulsky (1883–1952) was a leading left-wing Ukrainian-Canadian activist. He had moved to Canada from the United States in 1911, at first residing in Edmonton, where he became involved in the Ukrainian Social Democratic Party. After settling in Winnipeg, he became a leading figure in the Ukrainian Labour-Farmer Temple Association and adopted a pro-Communist and Stalinist line. During the period of the Nazi-Soviet alliance at the beginning of the Second World War, he was arrested and detained under the Defence of Canada regulations.

61 Wasyl Swystun (1893–1964) was a leading Ukrainian-Canadian activist and a founder of the Ukrainian Greek Orthodox Church of Canada and its loosely affiliated lay organization, the Ukrainian Self-Reliance League. After an acrimonious break with the Orthodox wing of the community, he became active for a time in the Ukrainian National Federation, on whose behalf he helped create the Ukrainian Canadian Congress in 1940. Three years later he dropped out of the mainstream nationalist Ukrainian-Canadian community, only to resurface in 1945 as a proponent of reconciliation with the Soviet Ukrainian regime.

62 For a more in-depth discussion of the critical reception accorded to the novel, see Marunchak, *Illiia Kyriiak ta ioho tvorchist,* 40–64.

63 As cited in Marunchak, ibid., 56.

64 Letter from Kiriak to Mykhailo Homola (Vancouver), 18 August 1955, provided by Homola to St John's Institute in March 1976 in response to a campaign to collect Kiriakiana.

65 Letter from Kiriak to Woycenko, 14 November 1955. LAC, MG30 D235, vol. 1, file 36.

66 The twenty-three-page text is preserved in the Kiriak Collection, LAC, MG30 D235 vol. 1, file 48.

67 See the typed letter to Orest Starchuk dated 24 December 1955, LAC, MG30 D235 vol. 1, file 28. Words written in English in the original are indicated by italics. The published book that Kiriak makes reference to is Nicholas Prychodko, *One of the Fifteen* (Boston: Little, Brown, 1952).

68 See 'Vegreville Writer, Elia [*sic*] Kiriak Dies,' *Edmonton Journal*, 30 December 1955.

69 These details were culled from scattered documents found in the former library of St John's Institute in Edmonton, and in some papers given to me by the late William Kostash, who was a member of the committee that eventually arranged to deposit the Kiriak materials housed in Library and Archives Canada.

70 For a mainstream review, see Joan Hunt, 'Prairie Pioneers,' *Edmonton Journal*, 5 November 1959.

71 Luchkovich was paid $300 for the translation plus $140 for typing up part of the manuscript. An additional $160 went to another typist to finish work on the handwritten original.

72 For an excerpt in English from the Ukrainian original that was cut for the Ryerson edition, see my annotated translation of part of chapter 13 in the first volume of *Syny zemli*, in *The Wild Rose Anthology of Alberta Prose*, ed. George Melnyk and Tamara Palmer Seiler (Calgary: University of Calgary Press, 2003), 87–99.

73 This information is gleaned from the Michael Luchkovich Collection, materials and correspondence pertaining to Kiriak, and Luchkovich's translation of *Sons of the Soil*, in vol. 1, file 11, at the Ukrainian Canadian Archives and Museum, Edmonton.

74 Yuri Stefanyk, ed., *Syny zemli* (Edmonton: Alberta Department of Education, 1979). This 294-page edition has been sharply criticized by Yar Slavutych for making many unnecessary stylistic changes to the original text.

6

Sympathy for the Devil: The Attitude of Ukrainian War Veterans in Canada to Nazi Germany and the Jews, 1933–1939

Orest T. Martynowych

Though they were a small fraction of the seventy thousand Ukrainians who immigrated to Canada during the interwar years, war veterans quickly established themselves as the most active and dynamic newcomers in the Ukrainian-Canadian community. By the mid-1930s they had established secular mass organizations like the United Hetman Organization (UHO) and the Ukrainian National Federation (UNF), were playing an influential role in the Ukrainian Catholic Brotherhood (UCB), and were consistently challenging prewar immigrants for leadership. When the Ukrainian Canadian Committee was founded in 1940 to represent the anticommunist majority, a war veteran was chosen its president and organizations led by veterans were well represented on the executive.

Seventy years later, our knowledge of the men who guided these organizations remains superficial and clichéd. The Ukrainian Sporting Sitch Association of Canada (renamed the United Hetman Organization in 1934), established and led by war veterans who supported Hetman Pavlo Skoropadsky, is usually described as a conservative, militaristic, and anticommunist group that enjoyed the patronage of the Ukrainian Catholic Church and that yearned for a Ukrainian monarchy on the British model. Hetmanite leaders, we are told, included 'gentlemen of the old school' who admired British parliamentary institutions and who were eager to demonstrate loyalty and commitment to Canada and the Empire by participating in military exercises with the Canadian militia. In a similar vein, the Ukrainian National Federation, established and led

by war veterans who were intimately linked to the terrorist Organization of Ukrainian Nationalists (OUN), is characterized as an intensely
patriotic, fiercely anticommunist group that sought to overcome religious divisions within the community by uniting all nationally conscious Ukrainian Canadians in one non-denominational association.
Though the UNF's links with the OUN are acknowledged, historians invariably emphasize the role of prewar immigrants in the formation of
the organization and stress its respect for parliamentary democracy and
its categorical rejection of dictatorship and fascism. Suspicions about
the loyalty of both groups, raised on the eve of the Second World War,
are usually dismissed as an unfortunate consequence of the fact that
the Hetman and the OUN were headquartered in Germany, or as the
result of malicious attempts by communists to discredit their harshest
and most vociferous critics.[1]

This study is based on a thorough reading of Ukrainian-Canadian
newspapers edited by prominent Ukrainian war veterans during the
1930s; on the personal and organizational correspondence of these men;
and on government records produced by RCMP and External Affairs
officials. While it provides some background information on the mass
organizations involved, it is not an exhaustive or balanced study of the
UHO, UNF, and UCB. The focus throughout is on the male war veterans at the forefront of these organizations and their views on Nazi Germany and the Jews. These views, as we shall see, were rather more
disturbing than the few existing studies would lead one to expect. It
will be argued here that a number of Ukrainian war veterans who
played a highly influential role in major Ukrainian-Canadian organizations shared an affinity for Nazi Germany, sympathized with its domestic and foreign objectives, and displayed an alarming indifference
to the fate of its Jewish victims.

I

Ukrainian veterans who immigrated to Canada during the 1920s had
been deeply marked by the war and its immediate aftermath. Frustrated
and humiliated by their failure to defeat their Polish and Soviet adversaries during the unsuccessful struggle for Ukrainian independence
(1918–21), they were also deeply disillusioned with the Western
democracies, which had proclaimed the principle of national self-de-

termination but acquiesced in the division of Ukraine by the Soviet Union, Poland, Romania, and Czechoslovakia. Many veterans refused to acknowledge that the struggle for Ukrainian independence had ended in 1921. They believed that Ukrainian soldiers had to go underground, develop a new battle plan, and continue the struggle. The organizations they established in Canada reflected this commitment. They were dedicated to sustaining the mystique of the Ukrainian struggle for independence and to assisting those who continued to wage it.

Veterans began to play a prominent role in Ukrainian-Canadian life in 1924 when Wolodymyr Bossy, a devout Catholic who served in virtually every major Ukrainian military formation on the Eastern Front between 1916 and 1920, established the Ukrainian Sporting Sitch Association. Having witnessed chaos in revolutionary Ukraine and religious and political conflict among Ukrainian immigrants, Bossy concluded that Ukrainian Canadians needed an organization capable of inculcating duty, discipline, and obedience to spiritual and secular authority. Following the lead of conservative émigrés in Europe and the United States, he persuaded the Sitch membership to pledge allegiance to Berlin-based Hetman Pavlo Skoropadsky, a landowner and general who had ruled Ukraine with the backing of the German army in 1918. Only submission to the Hetman's firm authority, Bossy reasoned, would provide the order, discipline, and stability required to achieve independent statehood in Europe and harmony among Ukrainian immigrants in North America.[2]

A handful of prewar immigrants, including a few professionals, businessmen, and aspiring politicians, played a prominent role on the Sitch executive, but it was conservative Catholic war veterans – most of them employed by Ukrainian-Canadian newspapers and community organizations – who set the organization's agenda during the interwar years.[3] Ukrainian Catholic priests who felt threatened by liberal, democratic, and communist criticisms of the Church in Canada jumped on the Hetmanite bandwagon during the 1920s; so did some farmers, labourers, and small businessmen who were tired of political and denominational bickering and who yearned for a strong authority figure to provide a sense of direction. The summer of 1927 marked the high point of Sitch influence in Canada. With more than one thousand members in fifty locals scattered across Ontario, Manitoba, Saskatchewan, and Alberta, it was the only non-communist Ukrainian mass organization in Canada.

.But the organization's prominence was short-lived. By the early 1930s, ideological disputes and internal crises in Europe and the United States had undermined the Hetmanite movement's credibility.[4] Also, Ukrainian Catholic priests and laymen were beginning to criticize and abandon the movement as concerns grew about its political agenda and secular priorities; both were often at variance with the Church's interests. By 1933 most rural locals had collapsed, and even in urban centres membership had plummeted.[5] Renamed the United Hetman Organization in 1934, the movement tried to redefine itself as an elite, tight-knit organization. At this point some Hetmanite leaders – including Bossy, who had moved to Montreal to work as a Catholic school inspector – began to collaborate with Canadian right-wing extremists. *Ukrainskyi robitnyk* (Ukrainian Toiler), a Toronto weekly launched and edited by Michael Hethman, Bossy's successor as UHO Quartermaster General, reflected the movement's new and more radical right-wing orientation. In Western Canada the Hetmanites continued to exercise some influence through *Ukrainski visty* (Ukrainian News), the Ukrainian Catholic weekly in Edmonton, and Winnipeg's *Kanadyiskyi farmer* (Canadian Farmer). Both were edited by moderate members of the organization.

Reaching out to Ukrainian immigrants in Canada was never a priority for Hetman Skoropadsky and his entourage. Comfortably ensconced in a villa on the outskirts of Berlin with an annual stipend from the German government, the Hetman preferred to cultivate contacts with military and right-wing circles, including General Paul von Hindenburg, President of the Weimar Republic, and prominent Nazis like Hermann Göring and Dr Alfred Rosenberg.[6] Skoropadsky's son Danylo was the only prominent member of the Hetman's inner circle to visit Canada. Poised, multilingual, and the most handsome Ukrainian émigré politician to set foot in North America, the young Skoropadsky attracted throngs of curious Ukrainian immigrants in the fall of 1937 when he visited fourteen urban centres in five provinces. Well publicized and meticulously chronicled, the tour featured meetings with Canadian dignitaries, including the Governor General.[7] Undertaken by the Hetman to convince his German patrons that he was the most influential Ukrainian émigré leader, the tour also revived the UHO's waning profile as a major Ukrainian-Canadian organization. In 1939 the reinvigorated UHO had about five hundred members, who were concentrated in large cities and several Northern Ontario mining centres.

In sharp contrast to Skoropadsky, Colonel Yevhen Konovalets, leader of the radical Organization of Ukrainian Nationalists (OUN), established direct contact with Ukrainian Canadians within months of the OUN's founding congress.[8] In June 1929 he spent three weeks in Canada visiting branches of the Ukrainian War Veterans' Association (UWVA), which had been founded by Wolodymyr Kossar, Dr Ivan Gulay, Eustace Wasylyshyn, and several other comrades-at-arms who at one time had belonged to the OUN's precursor, the terrorist Ukrainian Military Organization (UVO).[9] Unhappy with UVO and OUN dependence on donations, armed expropriations, and contributions from the German army (Wehrmacht) and military intelligence (Abwehr) – with which his organization maintained contacts[10] – Konovalets hoped to place OUN finances on a more reliable footing. Aware of the contributions made by North American immigrants to the Polish and Lithuanian independence movements, and especially to the Irish Republican Army, which he admired, Konovalets persuaded the UWVA to take on the sale of UVO and OUN periodicals and propaganda pamphlets. He also urged Ukrainian Canadians to tax themselves for the benefit of the OUN and to conduct special fund-raising drives in moments of political crisis.[11]

During the 1930s members of the OUN Provid (Leadership) visited Canada frequently. Captain Omelian Senyk-Hrybivsky and Colonel Roman Sushko, both fugitives from Polish justice, travelled on Lithuanian passports under assumed identities with armed escorts. Generals Viktor Kurmanovych and Mykola Kapustiansky, who were not wanted by any East European successor state, travelled openly. Sushko's 1932 mission included the founding of a mass organization to serve as the OUN's Canadian arm. With his blessings the UWVA purchased *Novyi shliakh* (New Pathway), a weekly newspaper edited by Michael Pohorecky (a war veteran who had apprenticed as a journalist with Dmytro Dontsov, the ideologist of Ukrainian integral nationalism). In July 1932 the war veterans established the Ukrainian National Federation to rally all active nationalist elements in Canada around the OUN.[12]

To create the impression that the UNF was a grassroots phenomenon spontaneously created and supported by all Ukrainian Canadians, the new organization stacked its first executive with prewar immigrants – most of them teachers and small businessmen – who

endorsed its tactics and objectives but who had no apparent ties to the
UVO and OUN.[13] During the five years this facade was maintained,
a member of the UWVA and UVO always held the pivotal position of
National Secretary. As few prewar immigrants joined the new organization, this ruse was ultimately abandoned. In 1939 almost 80 per
cent of UNF members were interwar immigrants; only 10 per cent
had been born in Canada. Most rank-and-file UNF members had four
to six years of schooling and worked as labourers in construction,
manufacturing, and mining when they were able to find employment.[14] The national executive included several graduates in agron-
omy, law, commerce, and pharmacy, who worked in their chosen
professions, as university researchers, or as immigration and colonization agents for Canadian railways.[15]

Before 1939 there was never any ambiguity about the UNF's support for the OUN. Its leaders declared the federation to be 'a supra-
party national organization in total agreement with OUN ideology.'[16]
They promoted the slogan 'The Nation Above All Else'; they demanded
submission to the OUN and its leader; they maintained that all means
were justified in the struggle for independent statehood; they endorsed
OUN sabotage, armed expropriations, and political assassinations; and
they dismissed European parliamentary democracy as a sham.
Ukrainian independence, they insisted, would be achieved through
armed revolutionary struggle led by a 'new type of Ukrainian' – un-
compromising, militant, and ruthless – who was ready to sacrifice everything for the cause.[17] The UNF leaders resented the Ukrainian
Catholic Church's condemnation of OUN tactics and hoped to attract
Ukrainian Canadians of all religious persuasions, so their organization
was resolutely non-denominational.[18]

By the eve of the Second World War, the UWVA and UNF and their
much smaller and less numerous women's and youth affiliates had
about seven thousand members in more than one hundred branches and
were the most dynamic non-communist mass organizations in the
Ukrainian-Canadian community. The first branches had been concentrated in Alberta, Saskatchewan, and Ontario; since then, the Great Depression had shifted the Nationalists' centre of gravity from the Prairies
to the mining towns and urban manufacturing centres of northeastern
and southern Ontario, where over 40 per cent of all branches, including the largest and most active ones, were located by 1939.

Ukrainian veterans also played an influential role in a third major Ukrainian-Canadian organization, albeit on a much smaller scale. A handful of Ukrainian Catholic priests led by Stephen Semczuk, Andrew Truch, and Wasyl (Basil) Kushnir, who had served as chaplains or combatants in Ukrainian military units during the war, assumed leadership positions in the Ukrainian Catholic Brotherhood (UCB) and on the editorial board of its biweekly *Buduchnist natsii* (Future of the Nation). Organized along the lines of Catholic Action, most of the UCB's hundred branches and three thousand members had little interest in the politics of Ukrainian national liberation. They preferred to focus on local school issues, the placement of Ukrainian Catholic teachers, and fund-raising for Ukrainian Catholic student residences. The exception was in Winnipeg, where concerns about the rising influence of the Communist Party and its mass organization, the Ukrainian Labour-Farmer Temple Association (ULFTA), produced an exceptionally volatile situation.[19]

The organizations established by war veterans, especially the UWVA and UNF, offered a variety of activities – dances, picnics, bazaars, brass bands, mandolin orchestras, choirs, drama circles, Ukrainian heritage classes, and even courses on how to establish and manage consumer cooperatives.[20] But the focus was always on the struggle for Ukrainian independence and the preservation of military values. Between 1928 and 1939 the UWVA and UNF raised well over $20,000 for Ukrainian war invalids in Poland and another $40,000 for the UVO combat fund and the OUN liberation fund.[21] Recalling that the Western Allies had allowed Polish immigrants in Canada and the United States to enlist in General Haller's Polish Volunteer Army in 1918, Hetmanite and Nationalist veterans hoped that battle-ready Ukrainian Canadians would be allowed to form their own units and fight for an independent Ukrainian state in the event of war between Britain and the Soviet Union. To this end, the Sitch had outfitted its male and female members in uniforms and introduced military drill; it also participated in field manoeuvres with the Canadian militia on several occasions. The UWVA, for its part, reached out to the Canadian Legion, distributed training manuals and military correspondence courses prepared by the OUN, and encouraged Ukrainian veterans and members of the UNF to enlist in the Canadian militia. Mothers were encouraged to teach their children about their responsibility to Ukraine and were urged to rear 'fresh cadres of young nationalist warriors.'[22] In the mid-1930s, carried away by the exploits of the Italian aviator Italo Balbo and inspired by the example of Germany (which had used commercial aviation to train combat pilots), Hetmanites and Nationalists solicited donations and attempted to train cadres of youthful Ukrainian-Canadian aviators, though in the end their efforts amounted to little more than a comic opera.[23]

During the 1930s the Polish government's assimilatory and repressive measures against its Ukrainian minority, and Stalin's apparently genocidal policies in Soviet Ukraine, drove many Ukrainian Canadians who retained a passionate interest in the homeland to despair. They protested the Polish regime's brutal and indiscriminate 'pacification' of eastern Galicia, imprisonment of Ukrainian activists, and destruction of Orthodox churches; and they condemned the systematic annihilation of the Ukrainian intelligentsia and the starvation by famine of Ukrainian peasants in the Soviet Union. As committed adversaries of Poland and the Soviet Union, war veterans played a leading role in the protests; more than most politically engaged Ukrainian Canadians, they took heart from the rise of Nazi Germany. The Nazi regime's aggressive anticommunism, revisionist foreign policy, and apparent support of national self-determination, and the fact that only Germany had the will and the means to confront the Soviet Union and Poland (as well as Romania and Czechoslovakia), made Hitler's Germany highly attractive to the war veterans. Like their comrades in Europe, they anticipated German assistance, and their affinity for National Socialist ideology seems to have blinded them to the implications of Nazi racism and expansionist foreign policy. [24]

II

Evidence of sympathy for the Nazis among Ukrainian war veterans in Canada goes back to the early 1930s. By then the UVO and OUN, which already had links with the German military, had established contact with Alfred Rosenberg, the Nazi foreign-policy expert whose theories were highly congenial to Ukrainian nationalist aspirations.[25] Thus articles from European correspondents published in *Novyi shliakh* in 1931–2 argued that the Nazis' 'positive' and 'realistically creative' domestic program, which repudiated the Treaty of Versailles, called for a dictatorship. The same articles proposed that citizenship rights be denied to Jews in a model Ukrainian state, and described prominent Nazis like the late Max Erwin von Scheubner-Richter as 'great friends' of the Ukrainian people who wanted 'to see a mighty Ukrainian nation state in Eastern Europe.'[26]

In the spring of 1933, while Hitler was stripping the German Parliament of its legislative powers, banning all opposition parties, dissolving trade unions, and brutally consolidating his dictatorship, *Novyi shliakh* declared that 'the triumph of German nationalism in Germany heralds the swift collapse, throughout the civilized world, of the old political and social order based on degenerate capitalism and capitalism's cretinous offspring – democracy, false socialism and communism.' It concluded: 'We may welcome with joy the triumph of the new German world over the old world, we can in large measure model our own national liberation struggle and our future nation-building efforts on it although we must not ... violate the principle of relying exclusively on our own strength.'[27] *Novyi shliakh* also identified the struggles of the 'new Germany' with those of Ukraine,[28] compared OUN leader Yevhen Konovalets with Hitler and Mussolini,[29] and expressed its solidarity with the 'new nationalism' and the fascist 'wave of the future.' Yevhen Onatsky, the OUN representative in Rome, wrote with enthusiasm and admiration about Mussolini.[30] Over the next few years *Novyi shliakh* would publish a series of articles celebrating the achievements of authoritarian and fascist leaders and dictators in all parts of the world.[31]

The remilitarization of the Rhineland, the creation of the Rome–Berlin Axis, and the signing of the Anti-Comintern Pact in 1936 greatly enhanced the Nazi regime's appeal to Ukrainian war veterans. Because it declared its signatories' hostility to the Communist International, threatened the Soviet Union with encirclement, and invited like-minded nations to join, the Anti-Comintern Pact – signed by Germany, Japan and (some months later) by Italy – struck many war veterans as a very encouraging development. In Canada the first overt appeal for Ukrainian cooperation with Nazi Germany was published in the Hetmanite *Ukrainskyi robitnyk*. In 1936 the paper's editor and UHO Quartermaster General, Michael Hethman, spent more than six months conferring with Hetman Skoropadsky and his inner circle in Berlin. Shortly after his arrival, members of Skoropadsky's inner circle introduced their Canadian colleague to Arno Schickedanz and Dr Georg Leibbrandt, Alfred Rosenberg's closest associates at the Nazis' Office of Foreign Politics.[32] In letters to Canadian colleagues Hethman referred to the two Nazi officials as 'sympathizers' and reported that German relations with Poland would soon deteriorate 'to our advantage.'[33] After the meeting, Hethman published several articles in *Ukrainskyi robitnyk* advocating Ukrainian cooperation with Nazi Germany. 'In the great armed struggle between two forces – nationalist and Judeo-internationalist – that is being foreshadowed in fierce battles in Spain,' he wrote, 'Germany will undoubtedly play the most important role in the nationalist camp, which has clearly inscribed the destruction of Bolshevism on its banner.' Hitler's plans for Eastern Europe posed no threat whatsoever to Ukrainians, Hethman assured his readers. While *Mein Kampf* revealed German interest in eastward expansion and called for a 'struggle against the Jewish Bolshevization of the world,' Ukraine would not be reduced to a German colony, for the two countries did not share any common frontiers. And while it had no desire to help 'poor little nations' and would not build a state for Ukrainians, Nazi Germany would welcome Ukraine as an ally in the struggle against Moscow if Ukrainians demonstrated their ability to organize and run a state. Because Hitler was prepared to ally Germany with determined and powerful anti-Bolshevik national minorities, he had to be regarded as a potential ally, though some caution would be necessary.[34]

When Hethman returned to Canada in the fall of 1936 he embarked on a lecture tour that was monitored by the RCMP. He reiterated what he had already written, denied that there was any opposition to Hitler in Germany, maintained that the German people regarded the Führer as their saviour, and insisted that German Jews were not being persecuted or denied the right to live in Germany. They were simply barred from speculating and 'from occupying positions ... which affect the internal life of the nation.'[35]

Until the spring of 1939 Hethman espoused an openly pro-Axis orientation on the pages of *Ukrainskyi robitnyk*. Readers were told that Italian fascists would bring civilization to Ethiopia;[36] that General Franco's armies were being celebrated as liberators of Spain;[37] and that the heroism, determination, and unparalleled loyalty of the Japanese armies in China were an example for all Ukrainians.[38] When Nazi Germany annexed Austria in March 1938 *Ukrainskyi robitnyk* concluded that Britain and France, 'paralyzed by their democratic system,' would be unable to stop Hitler. Democracy bred divisions, quarrels, and impotence. German authoritarianism, in contrast, created unanimity of desire and power: 'We Ukrainians do not yet have a state. It must be won by war! And regaining statehood by war means acting like Hitler: One Will, One Order, One Mighty Blow [against the Enemy]. Not one state in the world was created by democratic deliberations ... they were all built by kings or dictators.'[39]

Danylo Skoropadsky's fall 1937 tour of North America made abundantly clear the pro-Nazi sympathies of Hetmanite conservatives. In September the German American Bund, an openly pro-Nazi group, hosted him at a reception in Chicago. On that occasion, speakers mocked American critics of Nazism and Danylo expressed his admiration for the German people's triumphant efforts to build a better life for themselves by launching a domestic and external struggle against Bolshevism. He also expressed optimism about Ukraine's prospects, for Ukrainian patriots could now learn from Germany how to revive and strengthen their own nation.[40] The young Skoropadsky's pro-German and pro-Nazi sympathies were also on display in Eastern Canada. Headlines in Toronto and Ottawa dailies included these: 'Prince Admires Hitler for Destruction of Bolshevism'; and 'Says That Hitler Is the Greatest Man of the Century.' The *Toronto Star* misconstrued and sensationalized the tour by suggesting that the 'guest from Germany' was on a mission for Hitler;[41] even so, one should not be surprised that the tour raised such suspicions. On 29 November, at a banquet in one of the Ukrainian Catholic parishes in Montreal, Adrien Arcand, editor of *Le Fasciste Canadien*, leader of the Christian National Socialist Party, Canada's most outspoken admirer of Hitler, and the most notorious racist and anti-Semite in the country, toasted Skoropadsky.[42] Invited to speak by Wolodymyr Bossy, who was certain that Hitler would save the Christian world from the 'Jewish menace,'[43] Arcand used the occasion to commend Ukrainian opposition to the Soviet regime and to prophesy the triumph of a new, nationalist world order.[44]

By the fall of 1937 a faction within the UNF led by *Novyi shliakh* editor Michael Pohorecky had adopted an openly Germanophile and pro-Axis stance. When OUN discussions with Japanese representatives of the Anti-Comintern Pact got under way in Europe,[45] Pohorecky concluded that the UNF – which had failed to supply the OUN with adequate financial resources because of the Depression – would have to assume new responsibilities. Its task now was to provide political support for OUN foreign-policy initiatives. Convinced that *Novyi shliakh* was read by German and Italian intelligence services in Europe, Pohorecky believed that the Canadian weekly could 'legitimize our nationalist activists in Europe' by presenting the Anti-Comintern Pact in a sympathetic light.[46] Copies of enthusiastic OUN telegrams to Hitler, Mussolini, and Prince Konoye, and reports that Hitler was preparing to go to war against the Soviet Union, soon began to appear in the weekly.[47] A long article about the January 1938 commemoration of Ukrainian independence in Berlin reported that representatives of the German Ministries of Foreign Affairs, Military Affairs, and Propaganda, as well as the Ribbentrop Bureau, the Nazi Party Office of Foreign Politics, the German War Veterans, the SS Group Leaders' School, and the Hitler Youth, had been present. Also attending had been various academics and writers, among them the widow of Arthur Moeller van den Bruck, an intellectual forerunner of Nazism and author of *The Third Reich*.[48] *Novyi shliakh* also mentioned and occasionally summarized Hitler's speeches, interpreting them as welcome evidence that a German war against the Soviet Union would soon take place.[49]

When Germany annexed Austria in March 1938, *Novyi shliakh* endorsed the *Anschluss* and expressed wholehearted contempt for those politicians who, it alleged, had conspired with 'Austro-Jewish Communists' to prevent German unification. It also looked forward to the day 'when a wise Ukrainian policy will transform this [Rome–Berlin] axis into a Rome-Kyiv-Berlin triangle.'[50] In July the German Consul General in Toronto, Karl Gustav Kropp, accepted an invitation to attend the UNF national convention in that city.[51] During the Munich Crisis, *Novyi shliakh* endorsed German annexation of the Sudetenland and maintained that only individuals incited by the Comintern were hostile to Hitler.[52] When the Carpatho-Ukrainian issue began to make international headlines in the fall of 1938, *Novyi shliakh* raised naive hopes and fed illusions by suggesting that Germany sympathized with the cause of an independent Ukraine and would never 'barter with the Ukrainian people's hide.'[53] The weekly also reported that the German press wrote more about Ukraine and its liberation struggle than the British and French press, and that it wrote more accurately, objectively, and truthfully.[54] To prove the point, articles from the Nazi organ

Völkischer Beobachter, the Hitler Youth organ *Wille und Macht*, and other German newspapers were reprinted. One of the articles celebrated the appearance of a 'new generation' of healthy and militant Ukrainian youth in Carpatho-Ukraine, 'who walk with self-assurance and an air of pride' and make old Jewish street pedlars 'cast frightened glances [because] a dangerous adversary of Jewry has appeared.'[55] When Carpatho-Ukrainian dignitaries established the Society for the Struggle against Communism (Tovarystvo Borotby z Komunizmom) at a ceremony attended by representatives of the Third Reich, *Novyi shliakh* reported that 'Carpatho-Ukraine and its friend, the German nation, as well as other world powers – Italy, Japan and Spain,' had declared war on the Marxist Comintern.[56]

Concurrently, in the fall of 1938, OUN Provid member Colonel Roman Sushko made his second tour of Canada. Clearly sympathizing with Nazi propaganda, he declared that the world was divided into two hostile camps, one led by 'the communist international in Moscow under the control of international Jews, which is striving to gain control of the whole world,' the other led by nationalists like Mussolini and 'the great man, Hitler,' who had challenged the Jewish Comintern and transformed their countries into great powers.[57] Germany, he maintained, was already forcing Europe to reorder itself according to the principle of national self-determination. At Munich, 'Czechoslovakia had not been wronged by Germany. Germany merely corrected a wrong created at Versailles.' Poland, with its large Ukrainian and Jewish minorities, would be next, though Ukrainian Nationalists were not worried about the Jews. In Sushko's estimation, there was no room for the Jews, who had lived off the toil of the Ukrainian people like parasites (though one should not conclude from this that Sushko was endorsing the extermination of Ukrainian Jews). The OUN, Sushko continued, wanted the Germans to march on Ukraine because that was the only way to free Ukraine from foreign captivity.[58] The Ukrainian issue could only be solved by armed conflict and by the shedding of Ukrainian blood. 'Our Canadian Ukrainian democrats,' he scoffed, 'are afraid that Hitler will invade the Ukraine and that the Ukrainian fascists, that is the UNO [OUN], are in close alliance with Germany and Hitler. Actually, we Ukrainian Nationalists will ally ourselves not only with Germany but with the devil himself as long as the devil will help us and if Hitler and Germany is this devil who will help us to free ourselves from our oppressors we will ally ourselves with Germany.' While conceding that the Germans were not interested in building Slavic states, Sushko maintained that they would save Ukrainians 'from domination by the Communist International.'

Reflecting the euphoria that held many Ukrainian nationalists in its grip at the time, Sushko reassured his listeners that there was no need to fear a German incursion into Ukraine.[59] Should the Germans attempt to subjugate Ukraine, the Ukrainian *zbroini syly* (armed forces) would resist just as they had in 1918.[60] The soul of Soviet Ukrainian youth, he continued, already belonged to the OUN, and Ukrainians were preparing for the final struggle against Moscow. Sushko concluded that 'the nationalist movement is so powerful that we will soon see the emergence of a Great Ukrainian State from the Caspian Sea to the Tatra Mountains' – a sentiment that had already gained wide currency among Ukrainian nationalist leaders in North America, some of whom were dreaming of a vast Ukrainian empire.[61]

RCMP officials who monitored Sushko's lectures observed that he 'had adopted many of Hitler's mannerisms when delivering speeches' and that he railed against Ukrainian-Canadian democrats and pacifists. The main difference between Sushko's lecture and Danylo Skoropadsky's a year earlier, they reported, was that the OUN emissary had emphasized 'the necessity for spilling blood and the use of military strength.'[62] Sushko's tour, they suspected, was a calculated bid to win 'Hitler's support for his faction of Ukrainian Nationalists.'[63] The RCMP also took strong exception to Sushko's attempt to appeal to Ukrainian-Canadian youth by 'deprecating the lack of opportunity in Canada.'[64]

Shortly before returning to Europe in January 1939, where he would assume command of a Ukrainian military unit that was being trained by the Wehrmacht,[65] Sushko informed UNF leaders that the OUN had decided to cooperate more closely with Italy and Germany during the forthcoming conflict because both were committed to a radical revision of frontiers in Eastern Europe. However, UNF leaders were advised that their organization should carry on as an independent Ukrainian-Canadian entity, conform to Canadian law and foreign-policy interests, and promote the cause of Ukrainian independence in Ottawa and London.[66] Though we have only the testimony of UNF leaders, Sushko's instructions were consistent with OUN practice.

While the OUN cultivated contacts with the German military and Rosenberg's circle, Konovalets had always been wary of dependence on Nazi Germany. During the 1930s he had even dispatched two young North American Ukrainians to London in a failed attempt to win British support for the OUN and the Ukrainian cause.[67] Despite Sushko's instructions, radical UNF leaders like Michael Pohorecky were not ready to abandon their wager on Nazi Germany. After Hungary annexed Carpatho-Ukraine with Hitler's blessings in mid-March 1939, UNF spokesmen condemned the Hungarians and the Czechs but neglected to mention Hitler's complicity. *Novyi shliakh* laid the blame for Carpatho-Ukraine's demise squarely on the Czechs.[68] It also published an article by OUN Provid member Mykola Stsiborsky that exonerated the Germans and that argued, 'Germany's and our own paths will run parallel and intersect on more than one occasion in the future.'[69] During the spring of 1939 the nationalist weekly continued to maintain that Germany was only trying to eliminate the injustices enshrined in the Versailles treaty, publishing letters and editorials that praised and defended the 'intelligent and active' leadership provided by Hitler and Mussolini.[70]

Nor was Pohorecky eager to adopt a pro-British position. He fulminated against those within the UNF executive who wanted to affirm their loyalty to Canada even before war had been declared:

Irrespective of what is convenient for us in Canada, we must take a position of *quid pro quo*, that is to say, we assume only those obligations, with respect to the country of which we are citizens, that our status as citizens demands. All services above and beyond this may be proffered ONLY AT THE COST OF THE OTHER SIDE – AT THE PRICE OF AID FOR THE UKRAINIAN LIBERATION CAUSE! We do not want to be Austrian or Bohunk cannon fodder for anyone! If you give us something – we will give you something! If you ignore us – we will ignore you! … In other words, we remain neutral with respect to the defence of 'democracy,' we do not try to leap into hell ahead of our father, and if we have to make any statements, we are guided by the principle of *quid pro quo*.[71]

Even after the UNF and UHO declared their unwavering support for the British war effort in September 1939, prominent war veterans in both organizations continued to display a highly ambivalent attitude towards Nazi Germany and the Allied war effort. UNF National President Wolodymyr Kossar and Secretary Tymish Pavlychenko considered sending a congratulatory telegram to Charles Lindbergh after the celebrated American aviator made a series of speeches urging the United States not to participate in the war against Nazi Germany. The UNF leaders reasoned that this was one way to win Lindbergh's support for the Ukrainian cause should he realize his ambition and become President of the United States.[72] During the first year of the war, RCMP investigators and Ukrainian observers reported apathy to the Allied cause among UNF members.[73] Though the rate of enlistment among Ukrainian Canadians was high, it seems that few of the volunteers belonged to the UNF. Some members insisted they '[did] not wish to fight for Poland'; others blamed Britain for the collapse of the Ukrainian state in 1918–19 and continued to believe that 'Ukrainian salvation can only come from the Rome-Berlin axis.'[74] Michael Hethman and some of his closest associates in the UHO continued to harbour 'anti-democratic and pro-German tendencies,' though they refrained from expressing them once war broke out. Meanwhile, their colleagues in the neutral United States expressed their contempt for Allied leaders; they referred to Hitler as 'the greatest genius in all history' and remained convinced that he would free Ukraine from the Soviet Union.[75] It seems that on both sides of the border, similar views prevailed among many Hetmanite and Nationalist war veterans – at least until the fall of 1941, when it finally became clear that the Germans, having invaded the Soviet Union, were not interested in establishing a Ukrainian state – not even a puppet state on the Slovakian or Croatian model.

Though Prime Minister Mackenzie King once mused that Hitler was 'a man of deep sincerity and a genuine patriot,' and though most Canadians remained oblivious to the menace posed by Nazi Germany until the fall of 1938, the attitude of prominent Ukrainian war veterans to Nazi Germany did not reflect the Canadian consensus. King may have been a poor judge of character, but he loathed Nazi savagery and brutality. In 1937 he told Hitler that Canadians would fight alongside the British in the event of German aggression. Officials at External Affairs also realized that Nazism posed a growing threat to freedom and peace, and after Munich, Canadian public opinion turned against Nazi Germany.[76] Prominent Ukrainian war veterans, on the other hand, expressed admiration for Hitler's domestic and foreign-policy objectives, endorsed Ukrainian cooperation with the Nazis in Europe, assumed that German success in Eastern Europe would work to Ukraine's advantage, and continued to regard the Nazi regime with remarkable equanimity until 1941. Ultimately, their attitude had more in common with that of the radical right than with mainstream Canadians.

III

Traditionally, Ukrainian antagonism towards Jews had focused on the economic power of Jewish merchants, moneylenders, and innkeepers and on the tendency of Jews in Ukraine to assimilate with politically and culturally dominant nationalities such as the Russians and Poles.[77] During the 1920s, Jews were accused of collaboration with the enemy and became a scapegoat for the Ukrainians' failure to establish an independent state after the First World War. By the 1930s, exposure to anti-Semitic conspiracy theories and growing enthusiasm for Nazi Germany among war veterans had added a new and more virulent dimension to some Ukrainians' perceptions of Jews. In newspapers, pamphlets, and speeches, prominent veterans began referring to Jews as international conspirators who were using their alleged influence in the capitalist and communist worlds to undermine public order and achieve global domination.

Most commonly, Jews were represented as a materialistic, parasitic, and cosmopolitan element. The Hetmanite weekly *Ukrainskyi robitnyk* described Jews as a people without a Fatherland who felt no attachment to the countries in which they lived and who were averse to productive labour.[78] Bossy maintained that Jews were indifferent to their neighbours and only interested in securing material advantages for themselves. Jewish plutocrats who controlled the production and sale of armaments and who influenced politics in the liberal democracies, he argued, were doing all they could to promote international chaos and turmoil.[79] On the eve of the war, *Novyi shliakh* carried an article by Yaroslav Stetsko, a rising young OUN ideologist, who insisted that Jews were 'nomads and parasites,' a nation of 'swindlers, materialists, and egotists,' 'devoid of heroism, and lacking an idea that could inspire them to sacrifice.' Jews were only interested in 'personal profit,' found 'pleasure in the satisfaction of the basest instincts,' and were determined 'to corrupt the heroic culture of warrior nations.' Ukrainians, Stetsko concluded, were 'the first people in Europe to understand the corrupting work of Jewry,' and as a result they had separated themselves from the Jews centuries ago, thereby retaining 'the purity of their spirituality and culture.'[80]

Stetsko's article also placed Jews at the centre of an international conspiracy by suggesting that Jewish capitalists and Jewish Communists were collaborating to promote Jewish interests. Articles in *Ukrainskyi robitnyk* maintained that the capitalist Rothschilds, Montagues, and Sasoons, and the communist Trotskys, Zinovievs, and Kamenevs, were all internationalists who used the financial institutions, industries, governments, and press empires at their disposal to advance the cause of Jewish world domination. On more than one occasion, newspapers edited by war veterans invoked anti-Semites like Father Charles E. Coughlin and German American Bund leader Fritz Kuhn to suggest that Jews controlled the Democratic and Republican parties and the American government as well as the British and North American media, and that they were inciting communist uprisings worldwide and anti-Catholic atrocities in Republican Spain as well as directing Leon Blum's French Popular Front government.[81]

References to the disproportionately high percentage of Jews in the Communist Party and in the Soviet bureaucracy and political police,[82] and criticisms of prominent Communists of Jewish origin such as Leon Trotsky, Genrikh Yagoda (the head of the NKVD), and Lazar Kaganovich (Stalin's enforcer in Ukraine), appeared in a number of Ukrainian-Canadian weeklies during these years.[83] However, only newspapers edited by war veterans – in particular the Hetmanite *Ukrainskyi robitnyk,* but also *Buduchnist natsii,* the biweekly of the Ukrainian Catholic Brotherhood, edited by Father Wasyl Kushnir – referred to a Judeo-Bolshevik conspiracy.

The most sustained efforts to conjure up a Judeo-Bolshevik conspiracy, and the most virulent expressions of anti-Semitism, occurred in Winnipeg during confrontations with Ukrainian-Canadian communists and their mass organization, the ULFTA. Never was this more evident than in 1936–7, when the Catholic Brotherhood's Manitoba section and its Hetmanite allies tried to recapture the support of Winnipeg's large Ukrainian working-class population. The previous year, North End voters had elected one Communist school trustee, two Communist city councillors, and the first Communist provincial legislator in

North America. To undermine Communist influence and to mobilize urban Ukrainians, a series of mass meetings were organized to promote the formation of a Ukrainian Catholic Workers' Organization. Simultaneously, the Brotherhood and local Hetmanites launched a campaign to elect Demetrius Elcheshen, an activist in both organizations and a militant anticommunist, to Winnipeg City Council.

Leaflets distributed by the Catholic-Hetmanite coalition and speeches delivered at mass meetings maintained that 'Jewish-Muscovite terrorists' had conquered Ukraine with fire and sword, installed a Bolshevik dictatorship, taken bread from the mouths of Ukrainians to finance world revolution, and driven the population to starvation and cannibalism. As a result, the Ukrainian nation was prostrate and paralyzed 'while the Muscovite-Jewish rooks suck[ed] the last juices out of it.' This 'Bolshevik-Jewish clique,' it was asserted, was 'only interested in gratifying its own unbridled greed'; and meanwhile its Canadian agents had the audacity to train Ukrainian Canadians 'for acts of treason in violation of British laws.'[84] Though not one of the Communists elected in North Winnipeg was a Jew, Ukrainian Catholic workers were implored to create an anti-Bolshevik front because 'what happened in Russia, in Mexico and in Spain can happen in Canada.'[85] Indeed, it was only a matter of time before churches were set ablaze and priests, nuns, believers, Ukrainian nationalists, and anyone who refused to submit to godless Bolshevism faced the death penalty.[86] 'Let our culture be national rather than serve the international Jew,' Kushnir declared at the First Ukrainian Catholic Workers' Congress in May 1937.[87]

On the rare occasions that Nazi and Fascist persecution of European Jews was mentioned in newspapers edited by Ukrainian veterans, their plight was trivialized. In 1933–4 *Novyi shliakh* attributed German anti-Semitic legislation and street violence to the greed, sexual licence, and crude behaviour of Germany's *nouveau riche* Jews.[88] *Ukrainskyi robitnyk* made light of Nazi persecution of the Jews[89] and attributed international antifascist and anti-Nazi protests to Jewish domination of the world economy and the international press.[90] In 1938 *Novyi shliakh* published an item by OUN journalist Yevhen Onatsky justifying Italian anti-Semitic legislation on the grounds that Jewish immigrants were taking jobs from Italian professionals while Italian-born Jews remained a 'foreign body' in Italy.[91] Reports about Romanian and Austrian anti-

Semitic legislation were published without comment or criticism.[92] *Buduchnist natsii* reprinted an article from the *Neue Frei Presse* in which it was maintained that violations of minority rights throughout the British Empire were much more reprehensible than German treatment of the Jews.[93]

Even the events of Kristallnacht failed to elicit any sympathy. In a brief note under the caption 'Germans Pay Back the Jews,' *Novyi shliakh* reported that Goebbels believed the outburst had been justified.[94] *Buduchnist natsii* ignored Kristallnacht altogether, published a few sarcastic references to the German expulsion of Polish Jews,[95] and focused on a pogrom of Ukrainian institutions in Lviv by Polish thugs on the twentieth anniversary of the Polish-Ukrainian War.[96] The most sinister response appeared in *Ukrainskyi robitnyk*. Kristallnacht, Michael Hethman argued, was a just response to the 'war of Jewry against Germany.' Indeed, devious Jews and their Masonic and Bolshevik allies had provoked the pogrom. When the Munich Agreement foiled Jewish plans to forge an anti-German alliance, the Jewish *holovna kahal'na rada* (supreme council), which 'must exist because it is inconceivable that a nation as cunning as the Jews would not have a supreme council,' devised a treacherous scheme. The 'council' had ordered the assassination of a German consular official in Paris to provoke the Kristallnacht pogroms in Germany and thereby generate sympathy for the Jews.[97]

The plight of Jewish refugees provoked thinly veiled sarcasm and hostility. Writing in *Novyi shliakh*, Onatsky maintained that the Jewish refugee crisis was especially tragic for Ukrainians because it had deprived them 'of all hope that a substantial number of Jews will emigrate from Ukrainian lands, where they have always been and continue to be hostile to us by cooperating with the occupying powers.'[98] Nor did *Novyi shliakh* and *Buduchnist natsii* support the admission of Jewish refugees to Canada. The former mocked proposals to settle Jews on Alberta farms[99] and endorsed the views of opponents like Conservative leader Robert Manion and the Canadian Corps Association.[100] The latter praised French-Canadian MP Wilfrid Lacroix, who had submitted a petition bearing almost 128,000 signatures opposing the admission of Jewish refugees. Both weeklies also took aim at A.A. Heaps when the CCF MP for North Winnipeg urged the government to relax immigration restrictions on Jewish refugees. *Novyi shliakh* accused Heaps of forgetting about the plight of Canada's unemployed workers; Kushnir, who was already manoeuvring to obtain the Conservative nomination in North Winnipeg, accused Heaps of being silent 'when thousands of our people are murdered in the Soviet Union by hook-nosed commissars.'[101] *Buduchnist natsii* also lashed out at a Ukrainian-Canadian Communist alderman who urged Winnipeg City Council to take up the cause of Jewish refugees. 'He is blind and deaf when the Muscovites, Poles and Hungarians torture our innocent people – but he sees and hears German Jews! The faces of the Ukrainians who helped elect him to city council should burn with shame,' the biweekly declared.[102]

Expressions of anti-Semitism persisted until the outbreak of the war. *Buduchnist natsii* suggested that Jews were a 'mulatto group' that combined white and black racial characteristics and was different from if not necessarily inferior to the Aryan people. Borrowing from the *Protocols of the Elders of Zion*, it also maintained that the 'Kahal,' a secret government composed of 'three hundred Jews who know each other,' ruled the Jewish people with an iron hand and determined 'the fate of Europe and the entire world.' As a result, Jews everywhere were organized and worked together to stymie the forces that did not agree with their 'shameful work.' Indeed, they had the power to destroy any state that failed to comply with their wishes. Nevertheless, the Catholic Church rejected the persecution of ordinary Jews because they were innocent victims, manipulated by unscrupulous leaders who set the nefarious agenda of world Jewry.[103] *Novyi shliakh* continued to mention Hitler's rants against 'the Jewish-Bolshevik menace' without comment or criticism.[104] *Ukrainskyi robitnyk* maintained that Hitler had no alternative but to pursue an expansionist foreign policy that would culminate in war because 'finance capital, controlled by world Jewry,' had boycotted German commerce.[105] An editorial by Kushnir in *Buduchnist natsii* just days before the war maintained that Neville Chamberlain's efforts to prevent a world war had been subverted by Communist fellow-travellers and British Jews, who wanted to build '"a strong new Jerusalem" ... a moneyed dictatorship controlled by the Jews,' on the ruins of Christianity and English society.[106]

Anti-Semitism was pervasive in Canada during the interwar years, and by the late 1930s the Canadian government had the worst record in the Western world for admitting Jewish refugees.[107] At several universities the number of Jewish students allowed to enrol in professional faculties was restricted; hiring practices discriminated against Jewish teachers, engineers, architects, agronomists, and accountants; and Jews were routinely denied membership in social clubs and excluded from neighbourhoods and resorts. On occasion synagogues were vandalized, anti-Semitic rallies turned into riots, and violent confrontations with Jewish youths took place. In Alberta members of the provincial Social Credit government blamed the plight of Canadian farmers on international Jewish financiers. When the SS *St Louis,* carrying more than nine hundred desperate German-Jewish refugees, approached Canada in June 1939, the Canadian government was the last to turn it away, thereby condemning some of its passengers to death in the Holocaust.

Yet outside Quebec – where mainstream dailies published excerpts from the *Protocols of the Elders of Zion,* and where prominent intellectuals endorsed Nazi efforts to eliminate Jewish 'influence' in Germany – references to Judeo-Bolshevik conspiracies and expressions of contempt for Jewish victims of Nazi persecution (such as those that occasionally appeared in weeklies edited by Ukrainian veterans) were generally confined to fascist and Nazi propaganda sheets. Anglican and United Church groups had been protesting the Nazi persecution of Jews since the mid-1930s, and by the fall of 1938 a national committee had been formed to lobby the government to admit more Jewish refugees. After Kristallnacht, mass meetings and demonstrations in which prominent non-Jews participated were organized in many urban centres, and editorials in most major English-language (and some Quebec French-language) newspapers called for a more generous refugee policy.[108] Once again, the anti-Semitic attitudes of influential Ukrainian veterans aligned them with right-wing extremists.

IV

By 1939 RCMP and External Affairs officials had been monitoring Hetmanite and Nationalist efforts to mobilize Ukrainian Canadians for more than a decade. The RCMP first investigated the Sitch in July 1928, when the presence of 280 uniformed Ukrainians provoked a hostile reaction among some of the men at the Yorkton military camp. On the whole, the Mounties seem to have had few concerns about the Sitch. The organization's devotion to the Ukrainian homeland was not perceived as threatening, for experience had shown that 'Canadianization has not been hindered by the devotion of French, English, Scottish or Irish Canadians to the lands of their origin.'[109] Accepting at face value declarations that Sitch members wanted 'to join the Canadian Militia ... so that in the event of any Communist uprising they would be prepared to do their share in its suppression,' RCMP officers regarded Sitch interest in military training as a positive quality.[110] There was some concern that Sitch leaders were not as forthright as they might have been concerning their allegiance to Hetman Skoropadsky, but this was mitigated by the belief that 'the general opinion among Ukrainians in Canada [is] that Skoropadsky could only succeed in forming an independent Ukraine ... with the help of the British Government.'[111] By 1937–8 the RCMP was aware of Michael Hethman's trip to Berlin and his and Danylo Skoropadsky's enthusiasm for Nazi Germany. However, as the Hetmanite movement was small and unpopular, there seemed to be little cause for concern.[112] And as several prominent Hetmanite leaders had always been eager to cooperate with the RCMP, perhaps the Mounties regarded the organization as a useful source of information about groups believed to be more dangerous and subversive.[113]

The UWVA and the UNF were regarded with greater apprehension. In 1933 the Mounties already knew that both organizations were affiliated with the terrorist UVO and the OUN. They also knew that Konovalets had visited Canada in 1929; that OUN emissaries were entering Canada on Lithuanian passports; that the UNF had been organized after 'an emissary from European headquarters by the name of Melnytchuk [Sushko] came to Canada on an inspection trip'; and that *Novyi shliakh* was published with 'funds collected for the [OUN] Geneva Head Office.'[114] As we have seen, RCMP surveillance of Roman Sushko's 1938–9 tour had been thorough: the Mounties knew who had greeted him at the American border, who had hosted him during his stay in Winnipeg, and who had escorted him in other cities.[115] Special Constable Mervyn Black's report on Sushko's Toronto speech was detailed, and RCMP officials were concerned about its contents.

Of course, not all of the intelligence gathered by the RCMP was accurate and balanced. In the mid-1930s, lower-echelon investigators appeared to give credence to exaggerated rumours circulated by foreign and Ukrainian adversaries of the UVO and OUN. These rumours implied that Ukrainian Nationalists were in 'close contact with the Hitler

Government'; that Konovalets had become very important 'since Hitler's ascent'; that he worked for German intelligence; and that Hitler used him 'for furthering his political plans' in Eastern Europe.[116] Actually, after the 1934 German–Polish non-aggression pact, German relations with the OUN were strained for several years. RCMP officers also confused the OUN camp with Hetman Skoropadsky's followers. They identified Skoropadsky as the 'supreme leader' of the UNF and UWVA; believed the Sitch had 'some connection with the Ukrainian Military Organization';[117] suspected that OUN delegate General Mykola Kapustiansky represented the Hetman because at one time he had served in the Russian army under Skoropadsky;[118] conflated the United Hetman Organization and the Ukrainian National Federation into non-existent entities such as the 'Union of Hetman's Ukrainian Federation'; attributed an interest in 'training Ukrainian pilots' to that non-existent organization;[119] and confused prominent UHO leaders with UNF leaders.[120] One investigator reported that the UNF was organized along the lines of the Communist Party of Canada and the Nazis because at meetings where Ukrainian liberation was discussed in the Ukrainian language (held on Sunday mornings), Germany was always mentioned as 'the one power who could be trusted with this liberation movement and the creating of the Ukrainian Free State.'[121]

At External Affairs, where there was a more sophisticated appreciation of the Ukrainian question in Europe, the response to Hetmanite and OUN agitation among Ukrainian Canadians was more muted. Officials of that department had been receiving petitions, memoranda and other documents on the violation of Ukrainian minority rights in Poland since the 1920s. Polish 'pacification' of the eastern Galician countryside in 1930 had provoked international outrage, including a petition to the League of Nations signed by more than sixty British parliamentarians. Consequently, when Sushko's 1932 tour of Canada and General Kapustiansky's visit in 1935–6 elicited complaints from the Polish Consul General, O.D. Skelton, Under-Secretary of State for External Affairs, assured the Polish representative that the Canadian government did not tolerate terrorist activities, nor would it provide asylum to any subversives. At the same time, Skelton reminded the consul that Poland's repudiation of the Minorities Treaty had undermined the influence of 'moderate and responsible elements' within the Ukrainian-Canadian community besides complicating matters for the Canadian government.[122] Skelton, who was sceptical of Polish evidence against the Ukrainian national movement,[123] and Norman Robertson, his colleague at External Affairs, understood that 'the denial of any possibility of redress through the channels established by the Minorities Treaty and the Council of the League' was strengthening extremist elements within the Ukrainian community. They believed that most Ukrainians 'came to this country with the single object of becoming good Canadians and ... would probably succeed in it if the various propagandist bodies would let them alone.'[124] Skelton believed that while some Ukrainian Canadians looked 'forward to the acceptance of German aid by their overseas kinsmen in establishing an independent Ukraine,' moderate UNF leaders such as University of Saskatchewan agronomist Wolodymyr Kossar and Winnipeg lawyer Wasyl Swystun – a prewar immigrant who had made a good impression – would 'put Canada and the British Commonwealth first' in the event of war.[125]

Above all, External Affairs officials were aware that the UHO and the UNF had limited influence on Ukrainian Canadians. Support for the UHO – described by Skelton as an 'extreme Right Nationalist group' whose European leaders were reputed to have 'German backing' – had dwindled in Canada.[126] Robertson pointed out to Kossar in 1939 that the UNF had raised only a fraction of the modest $35,000 that Ukrainian Canadians donated to the Carpatho-Ukrainian cause in the fall and winter of 1938–9.[127] This suggested that UNF influence in Canada was quite limited. It appears that as far as External Affairs officials were concerned, the Hetmanite and OUN agenda, espoused by the UHO and UNF in Canada, appealed to only a small minority of Ukrainian Canadians. This probably explains why, when the RCMP recommended banning a number of organizations – including the UNF – on the grounds that they were controlled from Rome or Berlin, External Affairs officials opposed the recommendation. The RCMP would keep a watchful eye on all Ukrainian-Canadian factions during the war, but only Communists would be interned and have their property confiscated.[128]

V

How much resonance did enthusiasm for Nazi Germany and antipathy for the Jews have among Ukrainian Canadians? Absent any serious studies, the question is difficult to answer; one can, however, venture a few preliminary observations. In 1939, when there were more than 300,000 Ukrainians in Canada, UNF, UCB, and UHO membership stood at about 7,000, 3,000, and 500 respectively, and *Novyi shliakh*, *Buduchnist natsii*, and *Ukrainskyi robitnyk* had up to 8,000, 5,000, and 1,400 subscribers. In other words, the three organizations in which war veterans were influential embraced 3 to 4 per cent of the Ukrainian-Canadian population, and their newspapers were read by no more than 10 to 15 per cent of Ukrainian Canadians, if we assume that each subscriber shared his copy with two or three acquaintances. The great majority of Ukrainian Canadians – especially those who immigrated before 1914 – had at best a passive interest in Ukrainian affairs overseas, few if any contacts with the war veterans and their organizations, and little if any affinity for Nationalist and Hetmanite politics.

Except for a few priests like Kushnir, who were recent recruits from Polish-occupied Western Ukraine, the Ukrainian Catholic clergy did not entertain pro-Axis sympathies. The UCB *Bulletin* (1933–7), edited by Fr Semczuk, made no favourable references to the Nazi regime, and even *Buduchnist natsii* criticized the Nazis for violating the right of Catholics to worship in freedom.[129] When Kushnir in the winter of 1938–9 published several articles that portrayed Hitler and his regime in a positive light, Fr Myron Kryvutsky, a senior cleric who had served as a chaplain with Ukrainian units during and after the First World War, wrote a letter to Bishop Basil Ladyka in which he condemned what he perceived as agitation on behalf of Nazi Germany in a Ukrainian Catholic periodical.[130] In particular, he took strong exception to an article that contrasted Germany favourably with the British Empire and to another that implied Hitler was the God-sent saviour of the German people.[131] Only a nationalist extremist, Kryvutsky advised the bishop, would publish this kind of material about Hitler, who resembled Attila the Hun more than any other historical figure. Kryvutsky's intervention appears to have been a qualified success. No more articles sympathetic to the Nazi regime appeared in *Buduchnist natsii*, though as we have seen, Kushnir continued to publish anti-Semitic material from time to time.

The most sustained criticism of the Nazi regime and the most consistent rejection of a pro-German orientation appeared in *Ukrainskyi holos*, the weekly organ of the Ukrainian Self-Reliance League (USRL), which had been established by prewar immigrants nurtured on Ukrainian Radicalism and National Democracy. As early as 1933 the paper's editor, Myroslaw Stechishin, was warning readers that Hitler's emphasis on racial purity and Aryan superiority did not augur well for Ukrainians. He was pointing out that *Mein Kampf* made it plain that Nazi Germany planned to conquer Poland and the Soviet Union (including Ukraine) and colonize them with German settlers.[132] In numerous editorials published over the next six years, Stechishin maintained that Italian Fascism and German Nazism, far from being antidotes to communism, were bastard offspring of Bolshevism. All three were characterized by military discipline, the annihilation of democracy, and blind obedience to a dictator. All three had spawned almost identical totalitarian regimes that encroached on every institution and every facet of human life in order to subordinate the interests of individuals to those of the state.[133] Nor did Nazi Germany's hostility to communism and the Soviet Union imply an interest in Ukrainian independence. If the Germans invaded the Soviet Union they would subdue Ukraine and exploit her vast mineral and agricultural resources. Hitler was not interested in liberating nations, and he was demanding national self-determination for German minorities only because it provided the Nazis with a pretext for territorial expansion.[134] Indeed, Hitler was a chauvinist and an enemy of all Slavs, and he regarded Ukraine the same way a cat regards a mouse.[135]

Yet even within the USRL, Stechishin's critique of Italian fascism and German Nazism did not meet with unanimous approval. Just days before Nazi Germany annexed Austria, Wasyl Kudryk, a prominent Ukrainian Greek Orthodox priest, took strong exception to Stechishin's sustained criticism of fascism. He indicated that prominent USRL members in Saskatchewan and Ontario had rejected Stechishin's analysis, maintaining there was no comparison between the fascist and Nazi regimes in Italy and Germany and the murderous Bolshevik regime in the Soviet Union. Comparing them was like comparing heaven and hell, Kudryk concluded.[136] Around the same time, USRL National Secretary Elias Kiriak reported that Ukrainians in Alberta – including USRL members and university students affiliated with that organization – also rejected Stechishin's critique. There was a consensus among the students that Hitler, Mussolini, and Franco were doing good work; meanwhile, their elders feared that Stechishin was going too far and that his criticism of the dictators would provide the UNF with 'lethal ammunition' against the USRL.[137] Coming after the famine and purges in Soviet Ukraine but years before the full extent of Nazi genocidal intentions was known, such comments were understandable. In any event, pro-Nazi sympathies did not take root among USRL members, and in 1939–40 that group's spokesmen refused to participate on a Ukrainian-Canadian committee that included representatives of the UNF until the latter disavowed the OUN, which was still cooperating with the Germans.

It is even more difficult to determine the extent of Ukrainian-Canadian involvement in Canadian fascist organizations. Martin Robin has observed that 'beyond incidental adhesions, separate Fascist solitudes prevailed' in Canada during the 1930s,[138] and it appears that Ukrainian war veterans who sympathized with Nazi Germany had no more than fleeting contacts with the likes of Arcand, William Whittaker, and Bernhard Bott and the organizations they led. In February 1934, when Whittaker's Winnipeg-based Nationalist Party of Canada (NPC) was under fire in the Manitoba legislature for its virulent anti-Semitic propaganda, the Canadian-Ukrainian Institute Prosvita – an organization frequented by Catholic laymen and Hetmanites – rented its premises to the extremist party for a meeting. Only after Manitoba's Attorney General intervened personally did the Ukrainians agree to cancel their agreement with the hate mongers.[139] Several months later, Hetmanite activist Demetrius Elcheshen confided that NPC rank-and-file members consisted predominantly of Germans and Ukrainians.[140] Two years later the RCMP believed that the NPC still had 'a large following of Ukrainians in the north end.'[141] If there was any connection between Whittaker's group and the virulently anti-Semitic Ukrainian-language leaflets distributed in the fall of 1936 by the promoters of the Ukrainian Catholic Workers' Organization, it has remained unacknowledged. Claims made by Canadian Union of Fascists organizers in the spring of 1938 that they had branches in all German and Ukrainian districts in Saskatchewan[142] have not been substantiated and ring false.

On the other hand, when Canadian fascists led by Arcand, Whittaker, and Joseph Farr amalgamated as the short-lived National Unity Party (NUP) in the summer of 1938, they convened in the newly purchased Hetmanite building in Toronto.[143] While the UHO had no formal ties with any of the groups involved, *Ukrainskyi robitnyk* gave the new party a qualified endorsement. After reporting that NUP leaders hoped to emulate the success of the European dictators and immunize Canada against subversion by communists and Jews, the editorial concluded: 'As citizens of Canada we can work with any Canadian group that stands on the principles of Christianity and the laws of Canada! These new Canadian parties stand on Christian principles and they respect the law ... Like Mussolini's party they want to reinforce the Crown and the existing social order. There is no reason not to cooperate with the new National [Unity] Party in elections if the need arises.' At the same time, readers were advised to be prudent: Nowhere did Ukrainians have as much freedom to pursue their group interests as they did in Canada, and a Nationalist government could curtail their liberty. Thus there was room for cooperation with the NUP but also a need for caution.[144]

Ukrainian-Canadian anti-Semitism took on a much more sinister quality during the 1930s. A Ukrainian translation of the *Protocols of the Elders of Zion* was prepared and published in Winnipeg in 1934.[145] A Ukrainian dentist championed the authenticity of that notorious forgery and challenged doubters to public debate. A former provincial legislator warned Ukrainian Canadians to beware lest 'Moscow and the Jews' wreak havoc in Canada as they had already done in Soviet Ukraine.[146] And as we have seen, in circles dominated by Ukrainian war veterans the myth of Judeo-Bolshevism had become a staple by the eve of the Second World War. In popular plays written for the immigrant stage, Jewish villains were being transformed from comical innkeepers and cunning moneylenders into vicious Bolshevik commissars and agents of the Soviet political police.[147]

Yet one should not exaggerate the extent of anti-Semitism among Ukrainian Canadians. Even among the most jaded war veterans, anti-Semitism never became an obsession or a guide to action, as it was for Arcand's National Christian Social Party and Whittaker's Nationalist Party. More than 60 per cent of Arcand's *Le Fasciste Canadien* consisted of material that was clearly anti-Semitic;[148] in weeklies edited by Ukrainian veterans less than 2 or 3 percent of the material could be characterized as anti-Semitic. The canard of Judeo-Bolshevism was invoked mainly to discredit Ukrainian-Canadian communists rather than to foment hostility against local Jews (though that was an inevitable consequence).

Note as well that the only concerted effort to exploit anti-Semitic slogans for the purpose of mobilizing Ukrainian Canadians was a failure. Kushnir's attempt in 1936–7 to establish a Ukrainian Catholic

Workers' Organization yielded no concrete results. In Winnipeg's North End, Ukrainians of all creeds and classes went to school, did business, and worked and interacted with Jews on a daily basis. Relations between the two groups were not necessarily friendly, but they had learned to coexist and appreciate each other's humanity. Few Ukrainians could be swayed by conspiracy theories that equated Jews with Bolshevism and that blamed them for all the tragedies of Ukrainian history. Ultimately, anti-Semitism appealed to some frustrated nationalists – primarily veterans – and to businessmen and politicians who were engaged in 'unfriendly competition' with Jews.[149]

So, anti-Semitic speeches, articles, and leaflets convinced few Ukrainian Canadians that Jews were conspiring to achieve global domination. On the other hand, it seems that almost no one within the Ukrainian-Canadian community was prepared to challenge anti-Semitic propaganda. Newspapers like *Ukrainskyi holos* and organizations like the USRL were consistently critical of OUN terrorism, Hetmanite authoritarianism, and the overtures of both groups to Nazi Germany, yet they remained silent where anti-Semitism was concerned. Nor did representatives of the Ukrainian Catholic and Orthodox Churches raise their voices in protest. The Nazis' systematic persecution of Jews, the adoption of anti-Jewish legislation throughout Central Europe, and Canada's refusal to admit more Jewish refugees failed to elicit a compassionate response. Perhaps most revealing is that Kushnir – who invoked the myth of Judeo-Bolshevism on a number of occasions prior to the war – became the first president of the Ukrainian Canadian Committee in 1940 and held that position, almost without interruption, for the next thirty years.

How can one explain this callous indifference to the plight of European Jews? John-Paul Himka, who has studied anti-Semitism in Ukraine, has proposed two explanations that may help us understand Ukrainian-Canadian attitudes.[150]

First, the nationalist world view that was prevalent in Western Ukraine by the 1920s divided the world into competing national groups and attributed 'collective characteristics and collective responsibility' to all members of a particular nationality. As a result, some war veterans were inclined to regard the high percentage of Jews in the Soviet elite as evidence that all Jews were allies of and collaborators with the Soviet regime. Forgotten was that the Jews who embraced Bolshevism and rose to the top were atheists who had turned their back on Jewish religion, secular culture, and communal life. Likewise, the Soviet regime's efforts to eradicate first Judaism and the Hebrew language, and then secular Yiddish culture, were also ignored. All Jews were simply perceived as beneficiaries of and collaborators with the Soviet regime, unworthy of sympathy.

A second explanation for Ukrainian indifference to the plight of European Jews relates to the high degree of political violence and national discrimination experienced by Ukrainians prior to the Second World War. Summary executions by the Austro-Hungarian military and deportations by the Russians during the First World War, brutal beatings of innocent people and the destruction of private property by Polish authorities eager to crush the OUN during the 1930s, mass arrests and executions of the Ukrainian intelligentsia by the Soviet regime, and the famine of 1932–3 that took between three and three-and-a-half million lives in Soviet Ukraine,[151] had desensitized Ukrainians 'to what was happening to the Jews.'

Having experienced political violence prior to emigrating, and keenly aware of the mass murder in Soviet Ukraine, war veterans more than most Ukrainian Canadians regarded Nazi persecution of the Jews during the 1930s as an inconsequential development. The fact that the Western press focused on the plight of the Jews while paying little attention to the tragedy in Ukraine only added to their frustration and bitterness. Addressing demonstrators in September 1933, *Novyi shliakh* editor Michael Pohorecky stated that the famine in Soviet Ukraine had already claimed millions of victims and lamented that 'the world press writes a great deal about Hitler's "terror" against the Jews in Germany, although compared to the Soviet terror against the Ukrainian people it is like a tiny drop of water in the sea.'[152] Even after Kristallnacht, he maintained that 'there are no people in the world who have been more offended, more exploited, [and] more oppressed by their enemies, than the Ukrainian people.'[153] Ultimately, Western indifference to the Ukrainians' plight, combined with the fact that Ukrainians had fallen victim to the murderous policies of the Stalinist regime years before Hitler's intention to exterminate the Jews was fully appreciated, impeded the ability of many Ukrainian Canadians to empathize with Jewish suffering.

VI

In recent years historians have started to fill in some of the blank spots in contemporary Ukrainian history by addressing topics such as interwar anti-Semitism, cooperation with Nazi Germany, and participation in the Holocaust. It is becoming clear that Western Ukrainian newspapers published anti-Semitic articles during the interwar and war years; that some OUN leaders were prepared to cooperate with Nazi Germany in the naive hope of gaining political independence and were even willing to accommodate and endorse the Nazis' 'eliminationist' anti-Semitism; and that some Ukrainians voluntarily participated in murderous pogroms in July 1941 and helped apprehend, deport, and execute Jews during the months that followed.[154] Only a few Ukrainian historians have confronted these issues; there are signs, however, that a re-examination of previously taboo subjects may be getting under way.[155]

Historians who study the Ukrainian-Canadian past have avoided controversial issues such as anti-Semitism and the attitudes of Ukrainian immigrants to Nazi Germany during the interwar years. Several explanations for these lacunae in the historiography come to mind. Most historians have correctly assumed that the vast majority of Ukrainian Canadians were simply trying to earn a living during the 1930s and were too indifferent or too assimilated to take much interest in the politics of Ukrainian national liberation. Cooperation with dictators overseas and supposed Judeo-Bolshevik conspiracies were the last things they thought about. It has also been widely accepted that any delusions that some Ukrainian Canadians (those who were preoccupied with Old Country politics) held about the Nazi regime had vaporized by the spring of 1939. Those momentarily led astray would vindicate themselves on the eve of the Second World War by declaring their unconditional loyalty to Canada and the British Empire. Ukrainian–Jewish relations during the interwar years have not been a priority for historians because politically engaged Ukrainian Canadians identified Russian Bolshevism and Polish imperialism as the principal enemies of the Ukrainian people. Jews were resented only insofar as they were perceived as allies or auxiliaries of these enemy regimes. In addition, expressions of Ukrainian-Canadian anti-Semitism were infrequent and confined to rhetoric rather than actions that impinged on the daily lives of Canadian Jews. It appears there were no confrontations between Ukrainians and Jews and no large anti-Semitic public demonstrations; nor was there any vandalism or violence. Furthermore, derogatory references to Jews in Ukrainian-Canadian newspapers rarely appeared in editorials and were usually consigned to relatively obscure news briefs and articles. Because few historians have ever examined the Ukrainian-Canadian press carefully, such items have gone unnoticed.[156]

During the past two decades the Ukrainian-Canadian community's preoccupation with articulating its own victimization narrative has discouraged discussion of potentially embarrassing issues such as the attitude of interwar immigrants to Nazi Germany and the Jews.[157] Studies of the interwar, war, and immediate postwar years have avoided these issues, focusing instead on the failure of British and Canadian foreign policy to support Ukrainian independence and on the hostile attitude of Canadian immigration officials to Ukrainian refugees and displaced persons.[158]

This study has argued that a number of prominent Ukrainian war veterans who immigrated to Canada during the interwar years established important organizations, became community spokesmen, and shared an affinity for Nazi Germany as well as a rather pronounced hostility to Jews. Frustrated by their inability to establish and defend an independent Ukrainian state after the war, a small but disproportionately influential number of educated and articulate veterans pinned their hopes on Nazi Germany and its revisionist anti-Polish and anti-Soviet foreign policy. Michael Hethman's 1936 meeting with Alfred Rosenberg's associates was the only instance of direct contact between a Ukrainian veteran living in Canada and representatives of the Nazi regime. That said, until the fall of France in 1940 the veterans who led the UHO and the UNF were firmly bound to Ukrainian émigré organizations that maintained contacts and cooperated with the Germans. While the veterans and the organizations they led remained loyal to Canada and the Allied cause throughout the war, their illusions about Nazi Germany lingered until the summer of 1941 and their loyalty was never really tested because Hitler refused to consider the possibility of Ukrainian statehood.

Jews, who had rarely supported the cause of Ukrainian independence because of their own precarious position in Eastern Europe, provided a convenient scapegoat for frustrated Ukrainian war veterans. The prominent war veterans discussed in this essay were not preoccupied with Jews; that said, the hostility they expressed towards Jews went well beyond the occasional 'unflattering references' to Jewish merchants and the credulous Social Credit–inspired acceptance of the *Protocols of the Elders of Zion* – an acceptance that some historians have equated with interwar Ukrainian anti-Semitism.[159] On the rare occasions they referred to them, Ukrainian-Canadian newspapers edited by war veterans expressed attitudes nurtured in the soil of frustrated Ukrainian nationalism, drawing from modern anti-Semitic ideology to depict Jews as rootless parasites who were responsible for all the tragedies of twentieth-century Ukraine and who were bent on global domination through international financial institutions and the Communist International, which they puportedly controlled. Some of the most virulently anti-Semitic articles in the Ukrainian-Canadian newspapers that have been examined were not borrowed from Canadian or European anti-Semites; rather, they were written by prominent Ukrainian émigrés in Central Europe and by Ukrainian-Canadian community activists.

Much more research is required to determine how widespread enthusiasm for Nazi Germany and antipathy towards Jews were in the Ukrainian-Canadian community. However, it appears that there was less support for Nazi Germany than there was antipathy towards Jews. On a number of occasions, representatives of liberal and democratic currents within the community challenged the illusions that prominent war veterans entertained about the regime in Germany. Anti-Semitic attitudes, on the other hand, were more easily accommodated. Few Ukrainian Canadians lent much credence to conspiracy theories about a Judeo-Bolshevik plot to dominate the world; and efforts to mobilize Ukrainian workers in Winnipeg around anti-Semitic slogans collapsed; at the same time, there seems to be no evidence of opposition from liberals and democrats, or representatives of the Ukrainian churches, to virulent expressions of anti-Semitism within the community. Indeed, some of the men who attained high office and represented Ukrainian Canadians on the national and international level shared such attitudes.

Notes

1   See for example, Nelson Wiseman, 'The Politics of Manitoba's Ukrainians Between the Wars,' *Prairie Forum* 12, no. 1 (1987): 133–4; idem, 'Ukrainian-Canadian Politics,' in *Canada's Ukrainians: Negotiating an*

Identity, ed. Lubomyr Luciuk and Stella Hryniuk (Toronto: University of Toronto Press, 1991), 355–7; Thomas M. Prymak, *Maple Leaf and Trident: The Ukrainian Canadians during the Second World War* (Toronto: Multicultural History Society of Ontario, 1988), 19–34; Lubomyr Luciuk, *Searching for Place: Ukrainian Displaced Persons, Canada, and the Migration of Memory* (Toronto: University of Toronto Press, 2000), 35–8; and Orest Subtelny, *Ukrainians in North America: An Illustrated History* (Toronto: University of Toronto Press, 1991), 134–51.

2 On the origins of the Sitch and the Hetmanite movement in Canada and the United States, see Ivan L. Rudnytsky, ed., *Lysty Osypa Nazaruka do Viacheslava Lypynskoho* (Philadelphia: Lypynsky Institute, 1976); Myron B. Kuropas, *The Ukrainian Americans: Roots and Aspirations, 1884–1954* (Toronto: University of Toronto Press, 1991), 201–17; and two articles by Taisiia Sydorchuk, 'Hetmanskyi rukh u Spoluchenykh Shtatakh Ameryky ta Kanadi v mizhvoiennyi period iak istoryko-polity-chne ta svitohliadne iavyshche,' *Kyivska starovyna* 6, no. 342 (2001): 101-16; and 'Hetmanskyi rukh v emihratsii na terytorii SShA i Kanady (1918–1939 rr.),' *Kyivska starovyna* 1, no. 343 (2002): 72–88, which provide a well-researched narrative of events and ideas but exaggerate the movement's strength in North America.

3 In addition to Bossy, prominent war veterans on the first Sitch executive included Wasyl Dyky, Michael Hethman, and Dr Vladimir J. Kysilewsky (V.J. Kaye). Kysilewsky abandoned the movement in 1931 after moving to London, where he worked for the non-partisan Ukrainian Bureau and became deeply disillusioned with the activities of the Hetman's British representative Vladimir de Korostovets. During the 1930s the organization's American Commander-in-Chief, Colonel Alexander Shapoval, was also highly influential in Canada. Prewar immigrants on the national executive included Winnipeg residents Demetrius Elcheshen and Andrew Zaharychuk.

4 For an overview see Alexander J. Motyl, 'Viacheslav Lypyns'kyi and the Ideology and Politics of Ukrainian Monarchism,' *Canadian Slavonic Papers* 27, no. 1 (1985): 43–8; and Kuropas, *The Ukrainian Americans*, 201–3.

5 Ukrainian Cultural and Educational Centre Archives [Winnipeg] (UCECA), Demetrius Elcheshen fonds, 'Zvit Oboznoi Komandy KSO za chas vid 1 lypnia do 3 veresnia 1932,' reveals that there were only 226 members in Canada in September 1932.

6 Alexander J. Motyl, *The Turn to the Right: The Ideological Origins and Development of Ukrainian Nationalism, 1919–1929* (Boulder: East European Monographs, 1980), 23–32. Skoropadsky also cultivated contacts with Russian monarchists and British conservatives.

7 Ivan Isaiv [John Esaiw], ed., *Za Ukrainu: Podorozh Velmozhnoho Pana Hetmanycha Danyla Skoropadskoho do Zluchenykh Derzhav Ameryky i Kanady, osin 1937–vesna 1938* (Chicago: United Hetman Organizations, 1938), includes a bibliography of every Ukrainian-, English-, and French-language newspaper article chronicling the trip.

8 UCECA, Mykhailo Seleshko fonds, contain copies of six letters from Konovalets to 'Turati' (Volodymyr Martynets) and to the OUN Provid, 7 May–11 July 1929, describing the OUN leader's first impressions of Ukrainians in Canada and the United States.

9 On the origins of the UWVA see *Almanakh:. Ukrainska Striletska Hromada v Kanadi 1928–1938* (Saskatoon: Nakladom Ukrainskoi Striletskoi Hromady v Kanadi, 1938); and Zynovii Knysh, ed., *Za chest, za slavu, za narod! Zbirnyk na Zolotyi Iuvilei Ukrainskoi Striletskoi Hromady v Kanadi 1928–1978* (Toronto: Vyd. Hol. Upravy Ukrainskoi Striletskoi Hromady v Kanadi, 1978). A large fragment of the UWVA archive from 1928 through the 1940s is located in UCECA, Mykhailo Seleshko fonds.

10 On the OUN see Motyl, *The Turn to the Right;* idem, 'Ukrainian Nationalist Political Violence in Inter-War Poland, 1921–1939,' *East European Quarterly* 19, no. 1 (1985): 45-55; John A. Armstrong, *Ukrainian Nationalism*, 3rd ed. (Littleton: Ukrainian Academic Press, 1990); idem, 'Collaborationism in World War II: The Integral Nationalist Variant in Eastern Europe,' *Journal of Modern History* 40 (1968): 396–410; Timothy Snyder, *The Reconstruction of Nations: Poland, Ukraine, Lithuania, Belarus, 1569–1999* (New Haven: Yale University Press, 2003), 133–201; and David R. Marples, *Heroes and Villians: Creating National History in Contemporary Ukraine* (Budapest and New York: Central European University Press, 2007), 79–123.

11 UCECA, Mykhailo Seleshko fonds, 'Zvit z nadzvychainoho zasidannia Komitetu oborony ukrainskykh politychnykh viazniv, vidbutoho v Narodnim Domi [u Vinnipegu] dnia 20 chervnia 1929.'

12 *Almanakh. Ukrainska Striletska Hromada*, 18–21, identifies Sushko (Melnychuk) as the 'father' of the UNF. Correspondence among leading UWVA members in UCECA, Mykhailo Seleshko fonds, sheds light on Sushko's role and various stratagems adopted.

13 They included the first president, Alexander Gregorovich, as well as Stefan Vaskan, Petro Khaba, Vasyl Dorosh, and Anthony Hlynka. All gradually lost influence.

14 Data on the immigration, birthplace, and occupation of UNF members were calculated on the basis of 'Reiester chleniv Ukrainskoho Natsionalnoho Obiednannia Kanady vid 1932 do 20 chervnia 1940,' examined by the author at UNF headquarters, Toronto, May 1981.

15 For biographical data on UNF executive members (Gulay, Hultay, Kossar, Pavlychenko, Wasylyshyn, Zelenyi, and others), see Mykhailo H. Marunchak, *Biohrafichnyi dovidnyk do istorii Ukraintsiv Kanady* (Winnipeg: Nakladom Ukrainskoi Vilnoi Akademii Nauk v Kanadi, 1986), 101, 164, 188, 250, 332–3, 485, 564, as well as the appendices to Knysh, *Za chest, za slavu, za narod!*

16 *Novyi shliakh*, 20 September 1932.

17 *Novyi shliakh* 1 October 1931, 19 July–23 August 1932, 25 October 1932, 29 November 1932, 14 March 1933, 6 March 1934.

18 On the attitude of the Ukrainian Catholic Church hierarchy towards the OUN see Bohdan Budurowycz, 'Sheptyts'kyi and the Ukrainian National Movement after 1914,' in *Morality and Reality: The Life and Times of Andrei Sheptyts'kyi*, ed. Paul Robert Magocsi (Edmonton: Canadian Institute of Ukrainian Studies, 1990), 55–57; and Andrii Krawchuk, *Christian Social Ethics in Ukraine: The Legacy of Andrei Sheptytsky* (Edmonton: Canadian Institute of Ukrainian Studies, 1997), 134–46.

19 There is no reliable history of the Ukrainian Catholic Brotherhood, and the whereabouts of its archive are unknown. Information on the organization must be gleaned from its monthly *Biuleten' BUK-a* (1933–37) and the biweekly *Buduchnist natsii* (1938–).

20 For the official version of UNF history see Zynovii Knysh, ed., *Na shliakhu do natsionalnoi iednosty: piatdesiat rokiv pratsi Ukrainskoho natsionalnoho obiednannia Kanady, 1932-1982,* 2 vols. (Toronto: Ukrainian National Federation, 1982).

21 Estimated on the basis of correspondence and reports in UCECA, Mykhailo Seleshko fonds, and in the pamphlet *Vozhdevi: U pershi rokovyny* (Saskatoon: Nakladom Ukrainskoho Natsionalnoho Obiednannia v Kanadi, 1939), 61–102. The UNF continued to send money to the OUN representative in Paris until June 1940.

22 Frances Swyripa, *Wedded to the Cause: Ukrainian-Canadian Women and Ethnic Identity, 1891–1991* (Toronto: University of Toronto Press, 1993), 118, 178.

23 Ukrainian National Youth Federation Papers, LAC, MG28 V8, vol. 17, file: UCFS correspondence with P.F. Anten, is the best source on the UNF flying school; also see UCECA, Mykhailo Seleshko fonds. Thomas M. Prymak, 'The Ukrainian Flying School in Oshawa,' *Polyphony* 10 (1988): 149–52, offers an account based on secondary sources. On Hetmanite efforts, which were confined to fundraising in Canada, see UCECA, Demetrius Elcheshen fonds, Michael Hethman fonds and Antin Oleksiuk fonds.

24 For background see John-Paul Himka, 'Western Ukraine between the Wars,' *Canadian Slavonic Papers* 34, no. 4 (1992): 409–11; and Snyder, *The Reconstruction of Nations,* 143–53.

25 On OUN relations with the German military see Motyl, *The Turn to the Right,* 123–5. On Rosenberg's views concerning Ukraine see Norman Rich, *Hitler's War Aims,* vol. II, *The Establishment of the New Order* (London: Andre Deutsch, 1974), 331–2, 372–5; and Ihor Kamenetsky, 'Ukrainske pytannia v nimetskii zovnishnii politytsi mizh dvoma svitovymy viinamy,' in *Yevhen Konovalets ta ioho doba* (Munich: Vyd. Fundatsii im. Ievhena Konovaltsia, 1974), 862–3.

26 *Novyi shliakh,* 8 and 15 October 1931, 4 February 1932. Colonel Max Erwin von Scheubner-Richter, a Baltic German and a prominent White émigré like Alfred Rosenberg, was a close associate of Hitler. He was killed during the 1923 Beer Hall Putsch in Munich. On his crucial role during the formative years of Nazism, including his and Rosenberg's views on Ukraine, see Michael Kellogg, *The Russian Roots of Nazism: White Emigrés and the Making of National Socialism, 1917–1945* (Cambridge: Cambridge University Press, 2005).

27 *Novyi shliakh,* 25 April 1933.

28 *Novyi shliakh,* 17 October, 12 December 1933.

29 *Novyi shliakh,* 18 April 1933.

30 *Novyi shliakh,* 22 November 1932, 15 June, 28 November 1933, 9 October 1934.

31 *Novyi shliakh* 27 May 1934 (Mosley), 16 February 1937 (Göring), 23 February 1937 (Spanish Falange), 6 April–8 June 1937 (de la Rocque, Franco, Ataturk, Degrelle), 28 September 1937 (Batista), 8 March 1938 (Italo Balbo), 27 April 1939 (Jose Antonio Primo de Rivera).

32 On Schickedanz see Kellogg, *The Russian Roots of Nazism*; on Leibbrandt see Eric J. Schmaltz and Samuel D. Sinner, 'The Nazi Ethnographic Research of Georg Leibbrandt and Karl Stumpp in Ukraine, and Its North American Legacy,' *Holocaust and Genocide Studies* 16, no. 1 (2000): 28–64.

33 UCECA, Demetrius Elcheshen fonds, Hethman to Elcheshen, 25 March and 17 May 1936; and Hethman to 'Dorohyi Vlodko,' 13 July 1936.

34 *Ukrainskyi robitnyk,* 25 September 1936.

35 LAC, RG146, vol. 38, Records of CSIS, file 94-A-00180 (Ukrainian United Hetman Organization of Canada), Mervyn Black to Officer Commanding RCMP 'F' Division (Regina), 6 April 1937. I am grateful to Stacey Zembrzycki for directing me to these previously accessed CSIS records.

36 *Ukrainskyi robitnyk,* 8 May 1936.

37 *Ukrainskyi robitnyk,* 20 November 1936.

38 *Ukrainskyi robitnyk*, 3 September 1937.

39 *Ukrainskyi robitnyk*, 18 March 1938.

40 Ivan Isaiv [John Esaiw], ed., *Za Ukrainu*, 53–5.

41 *Toronto Globe and Mail*, 15 November 1937; *Toronto Daily Star*, 20 November 1937; *Ottawa Evening Journal*, 23 November 1937; *Ottawa Evening Citizen*, 23 November 1937.

42 For an analysis of Arcand's career, see Martin Robin, *Shades of Right: Nativist and Fascist Politics in Canada, 1920–1940* (Toronto: University of Toronto Press, 1992), 88 ff.

43 LAC, MG30 C72, vol. 14, file Ukrainian, Wolodymyr Bossy Papers, contains some information on Bossy's acquaintance with Arcand. On Bossy's postwar meeting with Jacques Maritain and his repudiation of anti-Semitism, see *Ukrainskyi robitnyk*, 2 October 1953.

44 Ivan Isaiv [John Esaiw], ed., *Za Ukrainu*, 167.

45 Dmytro Andrievsky, 'Mizhnarodna aktsiia OUN,' in *Orhanizatsiia Ukrainskykh Natsionalistiv, 1929–1954. Zbirnyk stattei u 25–littia OUN* (Paris: Na chuzhyni, 1955), 151–4.

46 LAC, RG8103, vol. 2, file 6, Michael Pohorecky Papers, Pohorecky to P.T., 18 April 1938. Pohorecky argued that rejection of the 'Germanophile and pro-fascist line taken by *Novyi shliakh* will complicate the already precarious position of the OUN in international politics.'

47 *Novyi shliakh*, 7 December 1937, carried a front-page report indicating that Konovalets welcomed news of Italy's adherence to the Pact and had sent congratulatory telegrams to the signatories.

48 *Novyi shliakh*, 22 February 1938. On Arthur Moeller van den Bruck (1876–1925) see Fritz Stern, *The Politics of Cultural Despair: A Study in the Rise of Germanic Ideology* (New York: Anchor, 1965), 241–86; and George L. Mosse, *The Crisis of German Ideology: Intellectual Origins of the Third Reich* (New York: Schocken, 1964), 281–8.

49 *Novyi shliakh*, 1 March 1938, reported Hitler's 20 February speech in the Reichstag. The article stated that Hitler wanted peace with France and Great Britain and that he regarded 'Red Moscow' and 'International Bolshevism' as his enemies. *Novyi shliakh* interpreted the speech as an indication that a German war against the Soviet Union would soon take place.

50 *Novyi shliakh*, 12 April 1938.

51 *Novyi shliakh*, 20 September 1938, reported that Kropp was present at the convention banquet in the King Edward Hotel on 24 July 1938.

52 *Novyi shliakh*, 6 and 13 September, 4 October, 15 December 1938.

53 *Novyi shliakh*, 28 November 1938.

54 *Novyi shliakh*, 15 December 1938.

55 *Novyi shliakh*, 27 March 1939. The article was translated from the *Frankfurter Volksblatt* 21 February 1939.

56 *Novyi shliakh,* 6 March 1939. For a brief introductory survey of
Carpatho-Ukraine in 1938–9 see Paul Robert Magocsi, *The Shaping of a
National Identity: Subcarpathian Rus': 1848–1948* (Cambridge, MA:
Harvard University Press, 1978), 234–46.

57 LAC, RG146, vol. 38, file 94-A-00180, Mervyn Black 'Re: Meeting
held by Ukrainian Hetman Organization, December 17, 1938 – Speaker
Roman Sushko,' 3 January 1939 is the source for all direct quotations in
this paragraph. For a less detailed summary of Sushko's speech in Winnipeg, which makes no mention of anti-Semitic remarks, see *Novyi shliakh,* 30 October 1938.

58 *Ukrainskyi holos,* 12 October 1939, citing *Ukrainska Zoria* (Detroit), 29
September 1938.

59 *Novyi shliakh,* 30 October 1938.

60 Presumably this was a reference to the spontaneous resistance to German
grain confiscations and other punitive measures during the summer of
1918, when Hetman Skoropadsky ruled Ukraine with German backing.

61 *Novyi shliakh,* 13, 20, and 27 September 1938, published a report on a
Nationalist rally in New York City at which UNF organizer Michael
Sharyk referred to a Ukrainian empire. Also see UCECA, T.K. Pavlychenko fonds, Alexander Granovsky to T.K. Pavlychenko, 24 November
1938. Professor Granovsky was head of ODVU (League for the Rebirth
of Ukraine), the American equivalent of the UNF.

62 LAC, RG146, vol. 38, file 94-A-00180, Mervyn Black 'Re: Meeting
held by Ukrainian Hetman Organization, December 17, 1938 – Speaker
Roman Sushko,' 3 January 1939.

63 LAC, RG146, vol. 38, file 94-A-00180, W. Munday to RCMP Commissioner (Ottawa), 5 January 1939.

64 LAC, RG146, vol. 64, file 96-A-00111, pt 7 (Wasyl Swystun), RL Cadiz
'D' Division to RCMP Commissioner, 3 December 1938. A recurring
topic in Sushko's lectures was that a free Ukraine would offer opportunities for unemployed Ukrainian-Canadian youth.

65 Sushko was appointed to command a secret National Military Detachment made up of six hundred veterans of the defeated Carpatho-
Ukrainian militia and OUN members who had made their way to
Germany after Hungary annexed the region in March 1939. Located in
Wiener-Neustadt, Austria, the detachment 'was to act as an auxiliary to
the Wehrmacht in its approaching attack on Poland and to provide an
armed nucleus for an uprising which the OUN hoped would lead to independence for the Ukrainians in that country.' Though the unit approached
Galicia in September, it was disbanded when the Soviet Union decided
to annex eastern Galicia. Armstrong, *Ukrainian Nationalism,* 28.

66 LAC, MG30 E350, vol. 1, file 15, Tracy Philipps Papers, 'Prominent
    Ukrainians on the UNF and Its Leaders,' October 1941. The document is
    also cited in Prymak, *Maple Leaf and Trident*, 29.
67 The two men were Eugene Lachowitch, an American, and Stefan Davi-
    dovich, a Canadian educated in the United States. See Ievhen Li-
    akhovych, 'Diialnist OUN u Londoni v 1933-1935 rokakh,' in *Ievhen
    Konovalets ta ioho doba*, 910-11; and Ievhen Skotsko's reminiscences
    about Davidovich in *Novyi shliakh*, 4, 11, and 18 July 1987. Part of
    Davidovich's correspondence with Konovalets is preserved in UCECA,
    Yevhen Konovalets fonds. Lachowitch's and Davidovich's activities in
    London are also mentioned many times in LAC, MG31 D69, vol. 2,
    files 6-11, V.J. Kaye (Kysilewsky) Papers, Unedited London Diaries.
68 *Novyi shliakh*, 27 and 30 March 1939.
69 *Novyi shliakh*, 13 April 1939.
70 *Novyi shliakh* 20 April, 18 May 1939.
71 LAC, RG8103, vol. 2, file 7, Pohorecky to Dorohyi Druh [probably Ste-
    fan Vaskan], 7 April 1939.
72 LAC, MG30 E350, vol. 1, file 15, Special Constable Michael Petrowsky:
    'Prominent Ukrainians on the UNF and its Leaders, October 1941,' cit-
    ing William Burianyk, a USRL member and Liberal Party employee.
73 LAC, RG25, vol. 1896, file 165-39c, pt 2, Records of the Department of
    External Affairs, S.T. Wood to O.D. Skelton, 27 May 1940, and RCMP
    Intelligence Branch Toronto, Re: Ukrainian Nationalists, Canada (Gener-
    ally), 6 May 1940.
74 Acadia University Archives (AUA), Watson Kirkconnell Collection, Eth-
    nic Studies – Ukrainian, Norman Robertson to Watson Kirkconnell, 10
    December 1940, and the attached copy of 'Confidential Report on the
    Ukrainian Situation in Canada' (prepared by William Burianyk). I am
    grateful to Frances Swyripa for this document.
75 LAC, MG30 E350, vol. I, file 11, Special Constable Michael Petrowsky:
    'Secret RCMP Report on the First National Eucharistic Congress of
    Eastern Rites, July 1941,' and file 13, Special Constable Michael
    Petrowsky: 'Secret RCMP Report on the United Hetman Organization of
    Canada, October 1941.'
76 Michael Bliss, *Right Honourable Men: The Descent of Canadian Politics
    from Macdonald to Mulroney* (Toronto: HarperCollins, 1994), 145–7;
    John English, *Shadow of Heaven: The Life of Lester Pearson, Volume
    One: 1897–1948* (Toronto: Lester and Orpen Dennys, 1989), 199–202;
    John Herd Thompson and Allen Seager, *Canada 1922–1939: Decades of
    Discord* (Toronto: McClelland and Stewart, 1985), 322–9.
77 For Ukrainian attitudes to Jews in Western Ukraine between 1870 and

1940 see John Paul Himka, 'Ukrainian-Jewish Antagonism in the Galician Countryside during the Late Nineteenth Century,' in *Ukrainian-Jewish Relations in Historical Perspective*, ed. Peter J. Potichnyj and Howard Aster (Edmonton: Canadian Institute of Ukrainian Studies, 1988), 111–58; and Shimon Redlich, 'Jewish-Ukrainian Relations in Inter-War Poland as Reflected in Some Ukrainian Publications,' *Polin: Studies in Polish Jewry* 11 (1998): 232-46.

78   *Ukrainskyi robitnyk*, 6 August 1937.

79   Volodymyr Bosyi [Wolodymyr Bossy], *Rozval Evropy i Ukraina* (Montreal: Nakladom vyd. Katolytska Ukraina, 1933), 45, 78, 138–9.

80   *Novyi shliakh,* 8 May 1939. Stetsko used his pseudonym, Zynovii Karbovych, to sign the article. On Stetsko and the implications of his attitude to Jews see Karel C. Berkhoff and Marco Carynnyk, 'The Organization of Ukrainian Nationalists and Its Attitude toward Germans and Jews: Iaroslav Stetsko's 1941 Zhyttiepys,' *Harvard Ukrainian Studies* 23, nos. 3–4 (1999): 149–84.

81   *Ukrainskyi robitnyk,* 11 June 1937; *Biuleten BUK-a* (November 1934), 8; *Buduchnist natsii,* 14 November 1938, 14 December 1938, 1 January 1939; *Novyi shliakh,* 29 March, 13 September, 5 and 15 December 1938. Nevertheless, the identification of Jews with the Communist regime in the Soviet Union prompted the journalist Mykola Nitskevych, a prominent member of the OUN residing in Bulgaria, to condemn 'Ukrainian Judeophobia' in a letter to Konovalets. UCECA, Yevhen Konovalets fonds, Nitskevych to Konovalets, 8 May 1938.

82   On the overrepresentation of Jews in these institutions see Leonard Schapiro, 'The Role of the Jews in the Russian Revolutionary Movement,' in his *Russian Studies* (London: Collins Harvill, 1986), 266–89; Richard Pipes, *Russia under the Bolshevik Regime* (New York: Knopf, 1994), 112–14; and especially Yuri Slezkine, *The Jewish Century* (Princeton: Princeton University Press, 2004), 254 ff.

83   *Ukrainskyi holos,* 10 January 1934, 22 July, 23 September, 7, 14 and 21 October 1936. The last issue cited reported that at a 27 September 1936 anti-Bolshevik rally in Edmonton, only the UNF representative (Michael Sharyk) described the Popular Front as a 'Judeo-Bolshevik' intrigue.

84   UCECA, Demetrius Elcheshen fonds, 'Spishimo na velyke ukr. katol. viche/Byimo v dzvin na trivohu,' leaflet announcing the 30 August 1936 meeting. Leaflets in the same collection announcing the meetings of 4 October ('Bolshevyzm naibilshyi voroh narodu/Ukraintsi probuditsia') and 6 December 1936 ('Ukrainski robitnyky i robitnytsi') did not use anti-Semitic rhetoric and slogans. Presumably, this is part of the 'most disturbing collection of Canadian generated anti-Semitic literature ... found in the Ukrainian Educational and Cultural Centre ... in the papers

of a right-wing Ukrainian municipal politician' mentioned by Nelson Wiseman, 'Jewish Politics and the Jewish Vote,' in *Jewish Life and Times*, vol. 8, *Jewish Radicalism in Winnipeg, 1905–1960* (Winnipeg: Jewish Heritage Centre of Western Canada, 2003), 162. Regrettably, the article was published without notes and sources.

85 *Ukrainski visty,* 4 November 1936.

86 *Ukrainski visty,* 16 March 1937.

87 *Biuleten BUK-a* (June 1937) provides a summary of Kushnir's speech at the congress. In east-central Alberta disgruntled members of the UNF also invoked 'Judeo-Bolshevism.' Articles in *Klych* (The Call), an irregular monthly published in 1935 and 1937 by Anthony Hlynka, Volodymyr Kupchenko (a war veteran), Stefan Vaskan, and other former UNF activists, referred to the Soviet Union as a 'Jewish-Muscovite' state in which Ukrainians were excluded from power (January 1935). The first issue also printed a cartoon of Lenin's colleague Grigorii Zinoviev with a caption that attributed a veritable litany of crimes against the Ukrainian people to 'the Jews.' The periodical also carried articles on the power accumulated by six members of the Kaganovich clan (February 1937) and a translation of an article by Arnold S. Leese, the notorious British fascist and anti-Semite, who argued that 'Bolshevism represents one of the last phases in the Jewish programme to dominate the world.' (February and March 1937).

88 *Novyi shliakh,* 5 June 1934.

89 *Ukrainskyi robitnyk*, 31 January 1936.

90 *Ukrainskyi robitnyk*, 10 September 1937.

91 *Novyi shliakh,* 8 November 1938. Onatsky had previously published articles critical of Nazi racial policy and anti-Semitism. See *Novyi shliakh,* 3 October 1933 and 30 January 1934.

92 *Novyi shliakh,* 8 February, 22 March, 17 November 1938.

93 *Buduchnist natsii,* 1 February 1939.

94 *Novyi shliakh,* 14 and 24 November 1938.

95 *Buduchnist natsii,* 14 November 1938.

96 *Buduchnist natsii,* 14 December 1938.

97 *Ukrainskyi robitnyk*, 25 November 1938.

98 *Novyi shliakh,* 8 November 1938.

99 *Novyi shliakh,* 16 August 1938.

100 *Novyi shliakh,* 24 November, 19 December 1938.

101 *Buduchnist natsii,* 14 February 1939; *Novyi shliakh* 2 February 1939.

102 *Buduchnist natsii,* 1 February 1939.

103 *Buduchnist natsii,* 1 February 1939

104 *Novyi shliakh,* 6 April 1939.

105 *Ukrainskyi robitnyk*, 24 March 1939.

106 *Buduchnist natsii*, 14 August 1939.

107 Irving Abella and Harold Troper, *None Is Too Many: Canada and the Jews of Europe, 1933–1948* (Toronto: Lester and Orpen Dennys, 1983). For a brief survey of Canadian anti-Semitism during the interwar years see Gerald Tulchinsky, *Branching Out: The Transformation of the Canadian Jewish Community* (Toronto: Stoddart, 1998), 172–203.

108 Abella and Troper, *None Is Too Many*, 39–41, 44–5, 59, 64, stress the indifference of most Canadians, but they also mention exceptions to the rule. Also see Alan Davies and Marilyn Felcher Nefsky, 'The United Church and the Jewish Plight during the Nazi Era, 1933–1945,' *Canadian Jewish Historical Society Journal* 8, no. 2 (1984): 55–71; and idem, 'The Church of England in Canada and the Jewish Plight during the Nazi Era, 1933–1945,' *Canadian Jewish Historical Society Journal* 10, no. 1 (1988): 1–19.

109 LAC, RG146, vol. 38, file 94-A-00180, Colonel Cortlandt Starnes to H.H. Matthews, 13 August 1928.

110 LAC, RG146, vol. 38, file 94-A-00180, R.K. Webster to RCMP Commissioner, 27 May 1931.

111 LAC, RG146, vol. 38, file 94-A-00180, R. Field to RCMP Commissioner, 7 March 1933.

112 LAC, RG146, vol. 38, file 94-A-00180, T. Dann to RCMP Commissioner, 14 December 1937.

113 Wolodymyr Bossy considered F.J. Mead, Commander of 'C' Division, Montreal, a sympathizer. Mead wrote Bossy thanking him for his fine work exposing Jewish Communists employed by the Postal Censor's office. LAC, MG30 C72, vol. 2, Mead file, undated letters from Mead to Bossy. Bossy and Demetrius Elcheshen were well acquainted with Inspector H.H. Crofts of Winnipeg and provided him with information. UCECA, Demetrius Elcheshen fonds, Elcheshen to Bossy, 16 March 1933. Nicholas Stuss of Sudbury, who became Canadian Quartermaster General in 1938, bragged that the RCMP regarded him as a 'man of confidence' and assured all concerned that the UHO had nothing to fear from the Mounties. LAC, MG30 D277, vol. 11, file 1, Wolodymyr Kossar Papers, Stuss to unidentified Ukrainian Catholic priest, 4 January 1940.

114 LAC, RG146, vol. 38, file 94-A-00180, T. Dann to RCMP Commissioner, 12 October 1933.

115 LAC, RG146, vol. 64, file 96-00111 pt 7, R.L. Cadiz to RCMP Commissioner, Report Re Ukrainian Nationalists – Canada – General, 3 December 1938.

116 LAC, RG146, vol. 38, file 94-A-00180, T. Dann to RCMP Commissioner, 12 October 1933, and Mervyn Black to D. Ryan, 4 December 1937.

117 LAC, RG146, vol. 38, file 94-A-00180, J.H. MacBrien to J.A. Stiles, 30 November 1935.
118 LAC, RG146, vol. 38, file 94-A-00180, T. Dann to RCMP Commissioner, 6 April 1936.
119 LAC, RG146, vol. 38, file 94-A-00180, T. Dann to Under Secretary of State for External Affairs, 22 September 1938.
120 LAC, RG146, vol. 38, file 94-A-00180, R.R. Warner 'Re Ukrainian Nationalists – Canada – General,' 28 September 1938.
121 LAC, RG146, vol. 38, file 94-A-00180, A.W. Parsons to Officer Commanding 'F' Division (Regina), 12 September 1938.
122 LAC, RG25, vol. 1795, file 431: 'Activities of Ukrainians in Canada, 1936,' O.D. Skelton to Jan Pawlica, Consulate-General of Poland (Montreal), 16 April 1936.
123 LAC, RG25, vol. 1896, file 165-39c, pt 2, O.D. Skelton to S.T. Wood, 6 September 1940.
124 LAC, RG25, vol. 1896, file 165-39c-part 1, OD Skelton to NA McLarty, 25 January 1939.
125 LAC, RG25, vol. 1896, file 165-39c-part 1, OD Skelton to NA McLarty, 25 January 1939, and O.D. Skelton to High Commissioner for Canada in Great Britain, 15 June 1939.
126 LAC, RG25, vol. 1896, file 165-39c- pt 1, OD Skelton to High Commissioner for Canada in Great Britain, 15 June 1939.
127 LAC, RG8103, vol. 2, file 7, Wolodymyr Kossar to Michael Pohorecky, 12 June 1939.
128 Bohdan S. Kordan, *Canada and the Ukrainian Question 1939–1945* (Montreal and Kingston: McGill-Queen's University Press, 2001), 22. Also see Reg Whittaker and Gregory S. Kealey, 'A War on Ethnicity? The RCMP and Internment,' in *Enemies Within: Italian and Other Internees in Canada and Abroad*, ed. Franca Iacovetta, Roberto Perin, and Angelo Principe (Toronto: University of Toronto Press, 2000), 128–47.
129 *Buduchnist natsii*, 1 November, 1 December 1938.
130 Archives of the Ukrainian Catholic Archeparchy of Winnipeg (AUCAW), Correspondence with Diocesan Priests, Kryvutsky file, RMK 234, Father Myron Kryvutsky to Bishop Vasyl Ladyka, 6 February 1939.
131 *Buduchnist natsii*, 1 February 1939 carried both articles.
132 *Ukrainskyi holos,* 8 November 1933.
133 *Ukrainskyi holos,* 29 November 1933, 4 August 1937, 2, 9, and 23 February, 2 March 1938.
134 *Ukrainskyi holos,* 16 March 1938, 15 February 1939.
135 LAC, MG30 D307, vol. 11, file 6, Julian Stechishin Papers, Myroslav Stechishin to Michael Stechishin, 30 November 1938. Also see *Ukrainskyi holos* 1 March 1939.

136   Archives of the Ukrainian Orthodox Church in Canada (AUOC) [Winnipeg], Vasyl Kudryk file, Kudryk to Semen Savchuk, 14 February, 8 and 14 March 1938.

137   LAC, MG30 D212, vol. 4, file 12, Olga Woycenko Collection, Illia Kiriak to Myroslav Stechishin, 23 March 1938.

138   Robin, *Shades of Right*, 263.

139   *Ukrainskyi holos*, 28 February 1934. Also see Lita-Rose Betcherman, *The Swastika and the Maple Leaf: Fascist Movements in Canada in the Thirties* (Toronto: Fitzhenry and Whiteside, 1975), 64–71.

140   UCECA, Demetrius Elcheshen fonds, Elcheshen to Ivan Isaiv [John Esaiw], 30 August 1934.

141   LAC, MG30 E163, vol. 12, file 124, Norman Robertson Papers, J.W. Spalding to O.D. Skelton, 30 July 1936.

142   Betcherman, *The Swastika and the Maple Leaf*, 126.

143   Robin, *Shades of Right*, 265–7.

144   *Ukrainskyi robitnyk*, 24 June and 1 July 1938.

145   *Protokoly zi zboriv Uchenykh Starshyn Sionu* (Protocols of the Elders of Zion) (Winnipeg: Nakladom Hurtka doslidnykiv staryny, 1934). This edition was translated from the English-language translation attributed to Victor E. Marsden into Ukrainian by Ia.N.K. (probably the writer and printer Jacob [Iakiv] N. Krett).

146   *Winnipeg Tribune*, 7 December 1936, cited in Henry Trachtenberg, 'The Winnipeg Jewish Community and Politics: The Inter-War Years, 1919–1939,' *Manitoba Historical Society Transactions*, Series 3, 35 (1978–79).

147   The plays of Oleksander Luhovyi, which were popular in UNF circles, fall into this category. I am grateful to Jars Balan, CIUS, Edmonton, for providing me with 'An Annotated Bibliography of the Ukrainian Canadian Stage' (unpublished manuscript).

148   Robin, *Shades of Right*, 155.

149   The organization's national executive elected in December 1936 consisted of small businessmen, skilled tradesmen, and one or two professionals. It was their agenda that was articulated in Kushnir's speeches, which urged Ukrainian workers to eliminate non-Ukrainian middlemen and merchants from their midst and to create a strong Ukrainian-Canadian middle class in the towns and cities. See *Winnipeg Tribune*, 1 December 1936. For Kushnir's economic program see *Ukrainski visty*, 13 April 1937.

150   John-Paul Himka, '*Krakivski visti* and the Jews, 1943: A Contribution to the History of Ukrainian-Jewish Relations during the Second World War,' *Journal of Ukrainian Studies* 21, nos. 1–2 (1996): 81–95; and idem, 'Ukrainian Collaboration in the Extermination of the Jews during

the Second World War: Sorting out the Long-Term and Conjunctural Factors,' in *Studies in Contemporary Jewry,* vol. 13: *The Fate of the European Jews, 1939–1945: Continuity or Contingency* (New York: Oxford University Press, 1997), 170–89.

151 The historian Stanislav Kulchytsky, Ukraine's leading authority on the famine, cited in Serhy Yekelchyk, *Ukraine: Birth of a Modern Nation* (New York: Oxford University Press, 2007), 112.

152 *Novyi shliakh,* 12 September 1933.

153 *Novyi shliakh,* 14 and 24 November 1938.

154 Besides the works by Himka (1996, 1997), Redlich (1998), and Berkhoff and Carynnyk (1999) mentioned above, see Maksym Hon, 'Ievreiske pytannia v Zakhidnii Ukraini naperedodni Druhoi svitovoi viiny (za materialamy hromadsko-politychnoi periodyky kraiu),' *Holokost i suchasnist. studii v Ukraini i sviti* 1 (2005): 9–27; Shimon Redlich, *Together and Apart in Brzerzany: Poles, Jews, and Ukrainians 1919–1945* (Bloomington: Indiana University Press, 2002); Amir Weiner, *Making Sense of War: The Second World War and the Fate of the Bolshevik Revolution* (Princeton: Princeton University Press, 2001); and Ray Brandon and Wendy Lower, eds., *The Shoah in Ukraine: History, Testimony, Memorialization* (Bloomington: Indiana University Press, 2008).

155 Lively exchanges have recently appeared on the pages of *Krytyka* (Critique), a Kyiv periodical patterned on the *New York Review of Books.* See in particular Sofiia Hrachova, 'Vony zhyly sered nas?' *Krytyka* 9, no. 4 (2005): 22–6, about Ukrainian participation in the July 1941 murder of Jews in Zolochiv, and the responses from Yaroslav Hrytsak (April 2005), John-Paul Himka (May 2005), Zhanna Kovba (September 2005), and Marco Carynnyk (October 2005); see also Wilfried Jilge's 'Zmahannia zhertv,' *Krytyka* 10, no. 5 (2006): 14–17, about the treatment of issues like the Holocaust in some Ukrainian history textbooks of the 1990s, and the responses from Sofiia Hrachova (November 2006), Vladyslav Hrynevych (January-February 2007), Heorhii Kasianov (March 2007), and Anatolii Rusnachenko (March 2007).

156 Only polemicists paid attention to Ukrainian-Canadian attitudes towards Nazi Germany and the Jews. Watson Kirkconnell, *Canada, Europe, and Hitler* (Toronto: Oxford University Press, 1939), was a sober study critical of UNF sympathy for Germany and the anti-Semitism of *Buduchnist natsii.* The chapter on Ukrainians was researched, written, and published before Kirkconnell was charmed by UNF spokesman Wasyl Swystun and transformed into a champion of the federation. Raymond Arthur Davies, *This Is Our Land: Ukrainian Canadians against Hitler* (Toronto: Progress, 1943), was a work of pro-Soviet pro-

paganda that consistently exaggerated and stretched the truths and half-truths it presented.

157 For a discussion of this phenomenon see Frances Swyripa, 'The Politics of Redress: The Contemporary Ukrainian-Canadian Campaign,' in Iacovetta and colleagues, *Enemies Within*, 355–78; and John-Paul Himka, 'A Central European Diaspora under the Shadow of World War II: The Galician Ukrainians in North America,' *Austrian History Yearbook* 37 (2006): 17–31.

158 For example, Lubomyr Luciuk's *Searching For Place* and Bohdan Kordan's *Canada and the Ukrainian Question*. Both authors seem to be unfamiliar with the Ukrainian-Canadian press and rely very heavily on government reports, the correspondence of government officials, and formal memoranda from Ukrainian-Canadian organizations.

159 Manoly R. Lupul, 'Ukrainian-Jewish Relations in Canada,' in Potichnyj and Aster, eds., *Ukrainian-Jewish Relations*, 461–8, an article based on the author's childhood memories rather than on research.

PART THREE

Diplomacy and International Concerns

A number of essays in this volume demonstrate that despite planting roots in Canada, many Ukrainians remained actively interested in the affairs of the Old Country. As Hinther, Mochoruk, and Makuch indicate, events in Russian and (later) Soviet Ukraine directly influenced the activism, experiences, and circumstances of those tied to the ULFTA and AUUC. Similarly, Martynowych's work illustrates how at least some high-profile Ukrainian-Canadian nationalists found inspiration in the promises of German Nazism and European-based anticommunism during the interwar period.

The essays in this part provide a multifaceted examination of how concerns about affairs of state, international relations, and perceptions of the Old Country preoccupied many Canadian Ukrainians. Jaroslav Petryshyn's contribution offers a sweeping examination of the intellectual and social currents surrounding relations between Canada and the Soviet Union over the course of the twentieth century – an examination that places Ukrainian Canadians at the very centre of the narrative. He explores changes and continuities in the political discourse evident in the pressure many Ukrainians in Canada exerted (mainly without success) on Canadian federal officials and agencies to recognize and advocate on behalf of an independent Ukraine. He also examines the domestic consequences of these Canadian debates, at both the local and national levels, highlighting some key conflicts that emerged among Ukrainians of competing ideological backgrounds.

Serge Cipko's piece – an outgrowth of his extensive research on the Canadian 'Return to the Homeland' movement – provides readers with a highly unusual vantage point. It provides a close reading of the Canadian government's seemingly strange obsession with how several South American governments – and their Eastern European populations – responded to the Soviet Union's call for returnees during the Cold War. A classic example of transnational history, Cipko's fascinating essay shows how the Canadian government looked well outside its own borders when attempting to formulate policies relating to the threat of its own wave of Ukrainian out-migration.

Finally, Jennifer Anderson's consideration of the postwar Canadian Soviet Friendship Society (CSFS) illustrates how radical Canadian Ukrainians participated in interethnic, transnational propaganda efforts to present the Soviet Union in a positive light. Her essay, which is enhanced by her use of newly uncovered Soviet and Canadian sources and oral history interviews, underscores how visual propaganda, speaking tours, and journalistic endeavours were central to these efforts. In the course of this work the CSFS united Ukrainian Canadians with radicals from other ethnic groups – and in a few instances, with the Anglophone intelligentsia – in what the planners hoped would be perceived as a truly grassroots movement dedicated to developing a friendly and positive image of the Soviet Union in Canada and abroad.

7

The 'Ethnic Question' Personified: Ukrainian Canadians and Canadian–Soviet Relations, 1917–1991

Jaroslav Petryshyn

In its relationship with the Soviet Union, the Canadian government had to be cognizant of minorities whose geo-ethnic origins were within Soviet boundaries. This was especially true when it came to the Ukrainian community; indeed, it seems that until after the Second World War, when government officials spoke of the 'ethnic question' in Canadian–Soviet affairs they were referring invariably to the 'Ukrainian problem.' Ukrainian Canadians were far from a monolithic polity – many were either ignorant of or unconcerned about events in their homeland – yet at the same time, it is undeniable that ethnic consciousness was rising among many individuals and community organizations on both the right and the left of the political spectrum. Federal politicians and senior bureaucrats, concerned about this growing ethnic awareness and the harm it might do to Canadian–Soviet relations, sought ways to manage, mute, and/or manipulate the demands and pressures being brought to bear from a host of Ukrainian-Canadian interest groups.

There were three main reasons for this overwhelming Ukrainian factor. First, Ukrainians were the largest group in Canada whose territories in the Old Country had fallen under Soviet rule.[1] Their numerical strength alone made it difficult for Ottawa to ignore their representations. Second, since the Bolshevik Revolution many Ukrainian lobby groups had been applying constant pressure on Canadian politicians and bureaucrats in an effort to influence Ottawa's policy towards the communist state. And third, bridging the socio-economic and ideological divides in Canada's Ukrainian community, there was strong support among Ukrainians for the creation of an independent Ukrainian state. This point is crucial: a large majority of Ukrainians had long insisted that Ukrainian nationality was real, and they resented the Russian (and later Soviet) domination of their homeland. Having been denied a place in the community of nations, especially after the First World War, a significant portion of expatriate Ukrainians became more strident and better organized than other nationalities in pressing their case to Canadian officials.

This article has two purposes: to provide an overview of how the government dealt with the 'Ukrainian problem' in particular and with the 'ethnic question' in general in its relationship with the Soviet Union; and to examine how and to what extent Canadians of Ukrainian descent have been able to define and influence Canada's policy towards the Soviet Union. The discussion will necessarily touch on the divisions within the Ukrainian diaspora in Canada and how those divisions affected particular groups' efforts to influence foreign policy in Ottawa. In this regard the Kremlin had a vested interest in undermining and defusing anti-Soviet organizations. Finally, this essay will attempt to highlight and place in chronological sequence almost seventy-five years of themes and issues, and suggest lines for future research.

I

As result of war and revolution the Austro-Hungarian and Russian empires disintegrated. This opened the door for their various ethnic components to assert national self-determination. The Ukrainians were especially hopeful of this – after all, their national territory was entirely within the two collapsed empires. In the aftermath of the war, two separate Ukrainian independent states emerged: the Ukrainian National Republic in Kiev (founded 22 January 1918) and the Western Ukrainian National Republic in L'viv (founded 1 November 1918). These proclaimed themselves united on 22 January 1919, at which point it was anticipated that Ukrainian national sovereignty would be affirmed by the Western powers during treaty negotiations at Versailles.[2] This optimism, shared by Ukrainians in both Europe and North America, was based on the Western powers' apparent acceptance of U.S. President Woodrow Wilson's doctrine of the right of self-determination of 'enslaved' peoples as an integral part of any postwar settlement.[3] There was also a strong belief that Britain and the United States would be amenable to an independent Ukraine with Western democratic institutions, as the basis for a new balance of power in Eastern Europe.[4]

Without question the fate of the Ukrainian state was hugely important to the 170,000 Ukrainians in Canada, especially considering the precipitous decline in status they had endured during the war. Because most of them were recent immigrants from the Austro-Hungarian Empire, they had been branded 'enemy aliens' and encountered suspicion, harassment, and intimidation. As the war dragged on and Canadian xenophobia intensified, most Ukrainians lost their voting privileges under the War-Time Elections Act. They were also subjected to restrictive regulations and often interned or even deported.[5] So the birth of a Ukrainian state – especially one in peril – stirred emotions and provided a tremendous stimulus for unity among a heretofore divided community that was still struggling with its national identity.[6]

At war's end, surmounting their religious and political factionalism,[7] the Ukrainians in Canada organized to help their brethren attain their political aspirations. In December 1918 the Winnipeg-based Ukrainian Canadian Citizen's Committee (UCCC), representing all Ukrainian organizations except the pro-Bolshevik Social Democratic Party, launched a fund-raising campaign to send delegates to Paris to serve as 'intermediaries between the allies and the rising Ukrainian nation with the purpose of giving publicity to the Ukrainian case.'[8] Two prominent community leaders, Osyp Megas and Ivan Petrushevich, formed this Canadian contingent, which arrived in Paris in the middle of March 1919.

Meanwhile, efforts were launched to solicit Canadian recognition of the Ukrainian Democratic Republic. As early as October 1918, H.A. Mackie, MP for East Edmonton, wrote to Prime Minister Robert Borden in support of an independent Ukrainian state. He pointed out that Ukrainian Canadians, despite their 'hostile treatment' during the war, had remained loyal and had enlisted by the thousands with the Canadian Expeditionary Force. As a matter of British 'fair play,' their aspirations ought now to be taken up in the international arena. Basing his comments on a study of Ukrainian history and on 'personal contact,' Mackie postulated that an independent Ukrainian state would be 'of the greatest importance to Britain and her colonies' because of its geographic position as the 'Gate of Eastern Nations.' He urged Borden 'for future ages ... to take steps to secure the goodwill of that state which will hold the key to the European situation.'[9]

Meanwhile, the UCCC sent a petition (dated 24 April 1919) to Borden on behalf of Ukrainian Canadians requesting that Canada immediately recognize the Ukrainian Republic through its representatives at the peace conference.[10] Then on 27 March, Osyp Megas and Hrychorii Sydorenko, chairman of the Ukrainian contingent in Paris, visited Borden to ask him for help securing accreditation for the Ukrainian delegation at the conference. At that meeting they emphasized the fervent anti-Bolshevik sentiments of Ukrainians.[11] These and numerous other appeals were ignored by Borden and the Canadian delegation in Paris. Ottawa's aims there were to demonstrate independence of action within the British Empire, to secure a measure of international recognition, and to avoid being drawn into European affairs that did not affect Canada directly. The 'ethnic question' in general and the 'Ukrainian problem' in particular were deemed inappropriate if not irrelevant to Canada's evolving foreign policy. For nationally conscious Ukrainian Canadians, who viewed themselves as simply asking for Canada's help in asserting a distinct national identity, Ottawa's attitude was perplexing as well as disappointing.

Ultimately, of course, much more dismaying to most Ukrainians was their realization that an independent Ukraine would not be 'registered' in any postwar settlement hammered out at Paris. Ukrainian hopes for statehood were crushed on two fronts. First, the Americans, British, and French had decided to preserve the integrity of the Russian Empire, Bolshevism notwithstanding. American Secretary of State Lansing expressed this consensus when he stated that only a single, indissoluble Russian nation, federated along the lines of the United States of America, would be recognized.[12] The prevailing belief among the major powers was that a Bolshevik Russia could only be temporary and that a unified and democratic Russia would eventually emerge. The fact that Russia contained within its borders an even larger number of 'nations' than the Austro-Hungarian Empire was basically ignored. As a consequence the Ukrainian delegation's proposals, along with those of other territories that had briefly established their independence (e.g., Byelorussia, Georgia, Armenia, Azerbaijan, and Turkestan), were not entertained.[13]

Second, when the Austro-Hungarian Empire was partitioned into various national components, the Ukrainians found themselves excluded from the process. Here it was the French who were most strongly opposed to a Ukrainian state. As staunch supporters of an independent Poland, they attempted to block the entry into France of the West Ukrainian Republic's delegation; they then pressured other allies to deny it official representation and the right to lobby at meetings. Eastern Galicia, which had a strong Ukrainian majority, was handed over to Poland, the argument being that a strong Polish state rather than a Ukrainian Republic would check the Bolshevik threat and thereby guarantee stability in Eastern Europe.[14]

Canada largely concurred with the major nations regarding their handling of the minorities problem in postwar settlements. It did, however, briefly raise the 'Galician question,' thanks to determined Ukrainian efforts. Mass rallies and hundreds of petitions and telegrams prodded the Canadian government in 1921 to raise the Ukrainian issue at the League of Nations, where it called for an investigation of Galicia's political status.[15] But Ottawa went no further than that, instead suggesting to Ukrainian representatives that they take up the matter directly with the Secretary General of the league.

That the Meighen government in Ottawa pursued this matter at all can be interpreted as a belated and insincere sop to Ukrainian-Canadian sentiment. Along these lines, a government pamphlet titled 'Ukrainian Affairs in Ottawa' that outlined Ottawa's pro-Ukrainian position was intended to attract Ukrainian votes in 1921 election – this, from an government that had disfranchised them in 1917.[16] The true position of most anglophone politicians was probably best expressed in 1923 during a parliamentary debate when Charles 'Chubby' Power, Liberal member for the Quebec South riding, declared: 'Let us ... conciliate Quebec and Ontario before we start conciliating ... Ukrainia [sic].'[17] At any rate, the League of Nations took no action on the Canadian resolution.

The boundary revisions after the First World War created a number of states that had not existed in 1914. Yet the Ukrainians found their lands carved up among four states: the Soviet Union, Poland, Romania, and Czechoslovakia.[18] To many Ukrainian Canadians it seemed a gross injustice that despite a population of more than 40 million, Ukraine had emerged from the war without its own state. Ukrainian nationalists were embittered by this, believing that if only the great powers had lent moral, political, and military support to the emerging national independence movements in Russia, the restoration of the Russian Empire under the communist flag would have been prevented.[19] This latent resentment and sense of having been betrayed would be given full vent in Canada during the interwar years, as more Ukrainians immigrated to this country and another global conflict loomed.

II

Throughout the 1920s and 1930s, Canada continued to develop an independent foreign policy in the context of the British Empire. Both the Conservatives and the Liberals avoided entanglements in European or British affairs that might commit Canada to international responsibilities. But at the same time, as an emerging trading nation, Canada sought economic opportunities, including those offered by the Soviet Union. Thus it welcomed the Anglo-Soviet Trade Agreement, signed in 1921, and it proceeded in 1922 to attach two representatives, Dana L. Wilgress and H.J. Mackie, to the British Trade Mission in Moscow. When Britain extended *de jure* recognition to the Communist regime in 1924, Canada followed suit, accepting a Soviet trade delegation that same year. However, Canada's limited rapprochement with Moscow cooled abruptly in the late 1920s. In 1927, Ottawa joined Westminster in breaking off its quasi-diplomatic relationship with the Soviet Union after the Soviets were accused of subversive activities in Britain. London would restore diplomatic ties with the Kremlin two years later; Ottawa would not. With the onset of the Great Depression, Canadian–Soviet relations continued to deteriorate. At issue was Moscow's policy of 'dumping' her export commodities below world prices. To protect hard-pressed Canadian industries against this sort of unfair competition, the Conservatives under Prime Minister R.B. Bennett curtailed the importation of a wide range of Soviet products. This embargo remained in place until 1936, when the Liberals finally lifted it.[20]

Throughout the interwar years, vis-à-vis the Soviet Union, Ottawa was interested mainly in trade matters. Meanwhile, Canada's emerging Slavic organizations continued to be preoccupied with Eastern European political affairs – in particular, with events in Poland and the Soviet Union. The Ukrainians in Canada tried repeatedly to prod Ottawa to act on their behalf. Between 1920 and 1939 about 68,000 Ukrainians entered Canada, which made them the largest group of immigrants from the 'non-preferred' countries of Central and Eastern Europe.[21] Most of these newcomers were agricultural workers and were not especially activist in their politics; but there were also several hundred veterans of the Ukrainian armed forces who had fought for an independent Ukraine.[22] These people were strong nationalists and fiercely anti-Soviet. Once in Canada they would pursue with great tenacity their Old World dreams through several organizations they helped found.

Among the bewildering variety of organizations transplanted to Canada as a result of the turmoil in Eastern Europe were the United Hetman Organization (UHO) and the Ukrainian National Federation (UNF). The UHO – established in 1925 as the Canadian Sich Organization – was ultraconservative and in 1918 had supported the short-lived monarchist movement in Ukraine under the German-sponsored regime of Pavlo Skoropadsky. Extremely nationalistic and organized along paramilitary lines, it enjoyed broad support among Ukrainian Catholics. The UNF, founded in 1927, was another a nationalist group, this one formed by Ukrainian immigrants from the territories occupied by Poland. With ties to similar organizations in the United States, Britain, and France, the UNF (as did the UHO) promoted a militant brand of nationalism that placed 'Old World' issues above Canadian ones.[23]

A countervailing influence was the Ukrainian Self-Reliance League (USRL), established in 1927. Its members were moderate nationalists who sympathized with the ideals of a liberated Ukraine but emphasized the need for Ukrainians to join the Canadian mainstream. As citizens of Canada, USRL spokesmen sought to temper the militant nationalists and present the issue of Ukrainian independence in ways that Ottawa and the Canadian populace would find palatable.[24]

Besides these groups there was the Ukrainian Catholic Brotherhood (UCB), founded in 1932, a lay group that was nationalistic in tone. And there was the Ukrainian Workers' League (UWL), a breakaway group from the pro-communist Ukrainian Labour-Farmer Temple Association (ULFTA). The UWL was led by Danylo Lobay, former editor of *Ukrainski robitnychi visti* and a prominent UFLTA organizer; while retaining his socialist ideals, he spurned communism (at least Stalin's version). In 1935 the UWL began a campaign to inform Ukrainian-Canadians about the political terror in Soviet Ukraine.[25]

This proliferation of groups had two repercussions. First, it guaranteed that the already badly split Ukrainian-Canadian community would fragment even more. All of these organizations (except for the minority pro-Soviet group) yearned to at least some degree for a sovereign Ukrainian state, but they tended to work at cross-purposes, propagating their own perspectives instead of seeking to develop a united front. Second, it confounded Ottawa's efforts to address the community as a whole. This would be especially evident during the Second World War, when the 'Ukrainian question' became an important one in the nation's war effort.

Throughout the 1920s and 1930s, the federal government mostly ignored all the memoranda and petitions from these groups, which were lobbying for Ottawa to intervene on behalf of their oppressed relatives and compatriots in Eastern Europe and the Soviet Union. Issues such as Poland's brutal 'pacification' of Ukrainians in Galicia[26] and the catastrophic famine in Soviet Ukraine (1932–3) were viewed with scepticism by Ottawa, which like other governments did not want to launch or condone any actions that would worsen diplomatic tensions with those states.[27] Except for occasional expressions of 'personal sympathy' for their brethren's plight in Eastern Europe, Ukrainian-Canadian concerns – especially as they might affect the status quo in Poland or the Soviet Union – were considered irrelevant to Canadian foreign policy and were summarily dismissed.

Yet at the same time, with Canadian–Soviet relations at a low ebb and communist agitation escalating throughout the 1930s, Ottawa took an active interest in the 'ethnic question' as it related to the activities of the Communist Party of Canada (CPC).[28] Well over half the CPC's rank-and-file belonged to affiliated immigrant groups, and one of the largest and wealthiest of those was the ULFTA. With a membership of about 10,000 and substantial financial assets, the ULFTA was perceived as a Bolshevik-inspired and potentially subversive element that merited close scrutiny by the RCMP.[29] Because it was officially registered as a cultural organization, it escaped censure when the CPC was suppressed in August 1931 under the Criminal Code's controversial Section 98.[30]

This oversight was rectified when the Second World War erupted in 1939. The government moved swiftly to curtail the activities of all Canadian communists, who – staying faithful to the Comintern after the Nazi-Soviet Pact – had launched a campaign calling for Canada to withdraw from the 'imperialist' conflict. The CPC was again declared illegal; so was the ULFTA, along with various other pro-communist organizations. The ULFTA's leaders were apprehended and interned, and its numerous properties were confiscated – and in many cases sold to Ukrainian nationalists and church organizations at extremely low prices.[31]

Viewing the 'Ukrainian problem' as basically that of the community's left-wing factions, Ottawa took what it deemed the necessary steps to eliminate an evident threat to the country's internal security. Yet as it quickly learned, the war had a profound 'accelerating effect' on the 'Ukrainian question.' As a result the issue of what to do with the Ukrainian Canadians became an urgent priority.

III

In 1939 both Ottawa and London became increasingly concerned about the strong nationalist sentiment among Ukrainian Canadians, especially as it related to the Allies' war aims. For political and military reasons, Britain had committed itself to ensuring Poland's pre-1939 status and the territorial integrity of the Soviet Union. Obviously, this policy was anathema to most Ukrainians since there was no room in it for their national aspirations. At the same time, Germany's solemn declaration that national minorities had the right to self-determination, and the apparent approval of a Nazi-sponsored liberation of Ukraine among some ultraconservative Ukrainian-Canadian organizations, were raising fears that Hitler would utilize Ukrainian nationalism to further his goals. These fears were underlined with the creation of 'independent' Carpatho-Ukraine (1938) following the dismemberment of Czechoslovakia. Berlin seemed to be hinting at further annexations (in Galicia and Soviet Ukraine) and at the concomitant establishment of a unified Ukrainian state.[32]

What would be the political impact of Germany's championing of Ukraine's liberation on the quarter-million Ukrainians in Canada? Ukrainians were the third-largest immigrant group in the country and were vital to its war industries, so this question could not be ignored, especially since – given the disunity in that community – subversive elements could well infiltrate the quarrelling factions and massively undermine Canada's war effort.

In the circumstances, Ottawa and London thought it prudent to develop a joint strategy to manage these potentially 'troublesome' Slavs. With Canadian blessing the British Foreign Office sent two emissaries to Canada, where they toured selected Ukrainian communities with a view to arresting any pro-German sentiment and explaining more clearly the British position.[33] At the same time, Ottawa – through the Department of National War Services – set out to mobilize the Ukrainian-Canadian community solidly behind the war effort by attempting to impose unity on it from above.[34]

To this end a central federating committee of Ukrainian Canadians was proposed. On it would sit representatives of the major Ukrainian organizations (excluding the communists). This committee would speak for the community as a whole. Ottawa was hoping to align Ukrainian Canadians with 'national interests and objectives' in the short term. In the long term it hoped to wean them from their Old World mindset and get them to view global affairs from a distinctly Canadian perspective.[35] After considerable discussion and persuasion the Ukrainian-Canadian Committee (UCC), representing five national Ukrainian organizations, was established in December 1940.

That the five included organizations – the UNF, UHO, USRL, UWL, and BUC – were ready to be enticed into a single representative committee was a reflection of prevailing sentiment in the Ukrainian-Canadian community as a whole and of the rapidly changing international situation. Regarding the latter, Ukrainians quickly realized that Germany had no intention of aiding their cause; proof of this was Berlin's complicity in the incorporation of Carpatho-Ukraine into Hungary (March 1939) and the Nazi–Soviet Pact that had enabled the Soviet Union to annex Ukrainian territories in Eastern Poland. More to the point, the predominant view in the nationalist Ukrainian-Canadian community had always been that any future liberation of Ukraine must rest with the Allies and that Britain would eventually understand the justice in supporting the Ukrainian cause in any postwar settlement scheme. Indeed, the argument for joining the UCC had been precisely this: if Ukrainian Canadians established a single patriotic organization, it would hold them in good stead when the issue of Ukraine's status arose after the war.[36] The UCC was in effect embracing this assumption when it set out to coordinate and enhance Ukrainian participation in Canada's war effort while at the same time dedicating itself to giving 'the greatest possible moral and material assistance directed toward the liberation of the Ukrainian nation.'[37]

Thus, Ottawa enjoyed some success in defusing the 'Ukrainian problem': it had aligned Ukrainian Canadians with the country's unity requirements, and it had done so without endorsing Ukrainian nationalism. When Germany invaded the Soviet Union on 22 June 1941, however, the government was compelled to change its perspective. The Soviet Union was suddenly a staunch ally of Great Britain *and* therefore Canada. Expediency, both foreign and domestic, now required that Ottawa's newborn child, the UCC, not be allowed to openly espouse anti-Sovietism. Ottawa's unease at the altered international situation was bluntly summarized by Lester Pearson, Assistant Under-Secretary of State for External Affairs: 'True, Russia did not enter this war to help us but to defend herself; true also, that the sudden discovery by communists in Canada that the war is not imperialistic, but holy, is ... nauseating. But the fact remains that whatever the reasons may be, the Russians are fighting on our side and the communists have become ardent protagonists for an all-out war effort.'[38]

In these circumstances the government acted pragmatically, seeking to muzzle the UCC's potentially disruptive activities and at the same time reassessing its policies towards pro-communist Ukrainian Canadians.

It was no mean feat to restrain Ukrainian nationalist/anticommunist diatribes. Ukrainian-Canadian spokesmen continued to hurl them against the Soviet Union. A case in point was a speech in the House of Commons (February 1942) by Social Credit MP Anthony Hlynka. In a lengthy denunciation of the Soviet Union, he argued that Ukraine's liberation from the Soviet grip and the forming of a Ukrainian government-in-exile ought to be objectives of Canadian foreign policy.[39] Officials in the Department of External Affairs (DEA) were deeply concerned about Hlynka's ill-advised remarks and quickly sought to assure Canada's newest ally that the government had no intention of pursuing such an agenda.[40]

Meanwhile, the UCC found itself under attack from the rejuvenated Ukrainian left. The ULFTA, while campaigning for the release of its interned 'antifascist' leaders and for a lifting of the ban on their organization, accused the Ukrainian nationalists of collaborating with the Nazis and urged Ottawa to apply the War Measures Act to suppress the anti-Soviet 'propaganda' in the nationalist press.

The Kremlin – which, not surprisingly, took an interest in all this – involved itself directly in the campaign to discredit the nationalists. Hoping to undermine the UCC, Soviet radio broadcasts and publications geared towards the Canadian public denounced that group as pro-Hitler.[41] For example, a Soviet pamphlet titled 'Soviet Ukraine and Ukraine-German Nationalists in Canada' asserted that the UCC was attempting to disrupt the war effort of Ukrainian Canadians even while assisting the Nazis in their invasion of Soviet Ukraine and the enslavement of the Ukrainian population.[42] At the diplomatic level, in May 1943 the Soviet Ambassador to Canada, Fedor Gousev,[43] directly approached the government requesting censorship of those 'profascist' organizations that advocated the breakup of the Soviet Union.[44]

The government resisted such measures. Even so, DEA officials were clearly worried about the 'provocative line' being taken by the Ukrainian nationalists and sought ways to address Soviet concerns. Most notably, the government did an about-face regarding Ukrainian communists. The RCMP was ordered to monitor closely the UCC and its affiliated bodies, and meanwhile, the communists were given free reign to excoriate the nationalists. For instance, in 1943 two pro-Soviet Ukrainian newspapers, *Ukrayinske zhitya* (Toronto) and *Ukrayinske slovo* (Winnipeg), began publication with Ottawa's apparent approval. Further evidence of the government's changed position came with the lifting of the ban on the ULFTA (which changed its name to the Association of United Ukrainian Canadians [AUUC]) and the return of and compensation for many properties that had been confiscated and sold to nationalist Ukrainian-Canadian organizations in 1940.[45]

The UCC found itself on the defensive. The government – indeed, Canadians as a whole (except in Quebec) – had abandoned an anti-Soviet bias and begun expressing strong sympathy for the suffering of the Soviet people as well as admiration for their 'heroic' struggle against the Nazi menace. The UCC attempted to counteract the negative press it was receiving by arguing that the war between the Soviets and the Nazis did not alter in any way the loyalty of Ukrainian Canadians to Canada and Britain. The UCC acknowledged that Hitler was setting out to enslave all of Europe (including Ukraine), and it tried to point out that in advocating a liberated Ukraine, this applied to German as well as Soviet domination.[46] Nevertheless, it was compelled to moderate its strident anti-Soviet tone under the increasingly intense scrutiny of the authorities.

Still, friction continued to mount between the UCC and Ottawa. For example, even a relatively mild UCC resolution (June 1943) that placed the issue of Ukrainian independence in the context of the Atlantic Charter generated a strong reaction from the DEA. Echoing the sentiments of Dana Wilgress, Canada's Ambassador to the Soviet Union – who was highly critical of the UCC's appeals for an independent Ukraine – N.A. Robertson, Under-Secretary of State for External Affairs, again assured the protesting Soviet ambassador that the Ukrainian community did not in any way determine government policy towards the Soviet Union.[47]

Indeed, after the UCC congress the government – DEA officials in particular – became more convinced than ever that Ukrainian-Canadian issues were undermining Canadian–Soviet relations. In bureaucratic circles, questions about how to formulate a uniform policy to alleviate the situation were again being raised and endlessly discussed.[48] But with the European conflict drawing to a close and tensions between the Soviets and their Western allies rapidly escalating, the political urgency of dealing with the Ukrainian nationalists was reduced considerably. Moreover a new problem had arisen – what to do about the war refugees.

IV

Between 1939 and 1945 the peoples of Eastern Europe (especially in Estonia, Latvia, Lithuania, Poland, and Western Ukraine) endured the twin horrors of Soviet and Nazi occupation. During those years millions either fled their homelands or were taken from them by force as labour/military draftees.[49] After the war, the fortunate ones – those who survived and escaped to Western Europe – found themselves stranded in Displaced Persons (DP) camps. Many of these DPs lived in dire fear that they would be involuntarily repatriated to Soviet-held territory.

Ukrainians in Canada mobilized quickly to aid the estimated 2.5 to 3 million of their compatriots who were languishing in these camps.

The UCC sought Ottawa's approval to establish a Ukrainian Canadian Refugee Relief Fund and to send representatives to the DP camps in order to provide support services, help reunite dislocated families, and generally give advice.

The government found itself in a delicate position. There were humanitarian considerations; and furthermore, Ukrainian Canadians had on the whole served loyally during the war, both in the armed forces (more than 40,000 in uniform) and on the home front. This suggested that some sort of positive response to the UCC's appeals was necessary. Yet any such action might well add more strain to relations among the Allies. Moscow was accusing many of the Ukrainian groups in the DP camps of collaborating with the Nazis in Poland and Soviet Ukraine. The Soviets continued to excoriate Ottawa about the anti-Soviet utterances of Canada's Ukrainian nationalists, especially the UCC, which it singled out for vicious denunciation as a pro-fascist organization that was now defending 'filthy collaborators.'[50] N.A. Robertson worried that if Canada authorized a Ukrainian Refugee Relief Fund it would 'likely be misconstrued by both Polish and Soviet governments as an attempt to rescue Ukrainian collaborationists.'[51] From his perch in Moscow, Dana Wilgress affirmed that such action 'would be interpreted as ... government sympathy and relief for Axis agents.' Unabashedly noting that the Soviets were busy 'liquidating' Ukrainian nationalists, he recommended that any official Canadian sanction for the Ukrainian Canadian Relief Fund be avoided.[52] In typical Canadian fashion, Ottawa compromised: it would permit the UCC to carry on relief work on humanitarian grounds, but for the sake of Canadian–Soviet relations – which were still at a tolerable level through 1944–5 – it would place a host of restrictions on the nature and scope of such relief work.[53]

But what would happen to the DPs? At the Yalta Conference, held in 1945, it had been agreed that all citizens of Allied countries should be repatriated after the war.[54] No other provisions had been made, since Western leaders naively assumed that everyone would want to go home. Furthermore, the Soviet Union was claiming the right to repatriate all of its citizens from Soviet-occupied countries, whatever their personal wishes. So Western officials cooperated with the Soviets as they 'persuaded' (by force if necessary) former Soviet citizens to return to their homeland. Not until 1947 was forcible repatriation officially ended. At that point, about half a million 'non-returners' were still in the West.[55]

Meanwhile, the UCC – along with other ethnic organizations such as the Canadian Jewish Congress and the Canadian Polish Congress (founded in 1944) – mounted a strong campaign in support of their 'brothers and sisters' (literally in many cases) uprooted by the war. Editorials were written, politicians were lobbied, and public meetings were held across the country urging Ottawa to demand that asylum rights be granted to DPs; that they be allowed to emigrate to the country of their choice; and that Canada open its own doors to them.[5]

Partly in response to this ethnic pressure, but mainly for economic reasons,[57] Canada did accept a large influx of DPs between 1947 and 1953.[58] Not unexpectedly, Moscow launched a vigorous protest against 'Soviet citizens' being sent to Canada; locally, the AUUC flooded the government with letters and petitions demanding that Ukrainian DPs be barred from entering the country on the grounds that they were war criminals and Nazi sympathizers.[59] By this time Ottawa was less than sympathetic towards the AUUC, which meant that the UCC generally succeeded in countering attacks by the pro-Soviet group.

Indeed, Canadian–Soviet relations had deteriorated sharply by 1946 – a slide hastened by the Cold War climate as well as by Igor Gouzenko's accounts of Soviet espionage activities in Canada. Canada withdrew its ambassador from Moscow in 1947, and politicians began talking of 'subversive, aggressive communism,' embracing the American view that Soviet imperialism was the greatest enemy to progressive democracies in the world. The founding of Stalinist regimes in Eastern Europe, followed by the Berlin Blockade in 1948, did little to soften this mindset.

Ukrainian-Canadian nationalists applauded the hard line that Canada now seemed to be taking. From their perspective Ottawa was finally beginning to see the Soviets the same way they did. In the House of Commons after the 1948 communist coup in Czechoslovakia, Anthony Hlynka – who had often accused the government of 'leaning backwards to actually appease the communists' – congratulated the government for its tough new anti-Soviet attitude.[60] John Decore, an Alberta Liberal MP of Ukrainian origin, in 1951 echoed Hlynka, reminding his fellow parliamentarians that 'it was the failure of the free world to assess communism in its true light that allowed the Soviet takeover of Eastern Europe ... Communist imperialism in its determination to dominate the world by force or by fear of force' was the main cause of East–West tensions.[61] In the early 1950s, few disagreed with Decore, at least publicly.

The incendiary battles between the AUUC and the UCC were not confined to the national political arena: they continued unabated in local communities throughout Canada, from large urban centres like Toronto, Winnipeg, and Edmonton to smaller cities and towns where the two had branches and/or sympathizers. Each group sought to discredit the other. Thus when the Edmonton AUUC obtained a $300 grant from city council for an arts and culture festival in 1946, the UCC complained vigorously, lobbying city politicians and officials to cancel the event. The following year in Toronto the UCC denounced an AUUC children's school for 'disseminating communist propaganda' and publicly rebuked that group for sponsoring 'communist made' Ukrainian handicrafts at the Toronto Art Gallery.[62]

Cooperation between Ukrainian pro-communists and nationalists in general, and between the AUUC and UCC in particular, was unthinkable even when it would have been apolitical and might have benefited both by raising the Ukrainian community's profile in Canada. A plan in 1951 to unveil a monument to Ukraine's national poet, Tara Shevchenko, on AUUC-owned property near Hamilton provides a good illustration. Ukrainian nationalists immediately saw this as an affront – in their view, this was using a national hero to advocate for communism – and the UCC dispatched a delegation to Ottawa hoping to convince the government to impound the statue, which by that time was en route from the Soviet Union (the effort failed). In 1959 the AUUC decided to erect a monument to Shevchenko in Winnipeg to mark the hundredth anniversary of the poet's death. The AUUC extended an olive branch to the UCC, inviting it to participate in the event's planning. This offer was quickly rebuffed, which resulted in the usual diatribes from both camps.[63]

But the most serious incident was in 1950, at the time of the AUUC's campaign to exclude DPs from Canada. On 8 October, Toronto's central Ukrainian Labour Temple, on Bathurst Street, was dynamited during a concert. The explosion levelled part of the building and injured eleven people, fortunately none of them too seriously. Ukrainian nationalists were blamed. Though the authorities offered a large reward ($1,500) for information, the perpetrators were never caught. Incidents continued against Ukrainian pro-communists and their property throughout the early 1950s. Generally speaking, the conflict was venomous at the national level and even more so in particular local communities.[64]

In this Cold War milieu the UCC pulled off something of a coup in 1952, when after a relentless campaign it compelled the CBC International Service to establish a Ukrainian-language section. Founded in 1945, in part as 'an arm of Canadian diplomacy abroad,' the CBC-IS had by 1950 launched daily Russian-language broadcasts into the Soviet Union.[65] Ukrainian-Canadian nationalists realized from the start how valuable that service could be in their war against the Kremlin. After several of their proposals for a Ukrainian-language service were turned down at the bureaucratic level, they lobbied the politicians. In particular, and with encouraging results, they targeted Lester B. Pearson, Secretary of State for External Affairs. At Pearson's behest, in 1950 his department examined the political feasibility of Ukrainian-language broadcasts.[66] DEA officials were lukewarm to the idea, pointing out that 'appealing to the nationalism of Soviet minorities, particularly the Ukrainians, may well be too costly in terms of Russian goodwill,'[67] but in any event, the political pressure exerted by the Ukrainian-Canadian community proved decisive. The DEA's fears that the Ukrainian section would be used as a forum for anti-Soviet and pro-separatist tirades were fully realized when short-wave broadcasts into Ukraine commenced. From the very first program (1 July 1962), during which Conservative MP Michael Starr promised his 'brother Ukrainians' in Ukraine that 'the time will come when freedom penetrates the Iron Curtain and the [Soviet] regime ... disintegrates under the blows of the victorious forces of freedom and democracy,'[68] the DEA sought to close the section down. Neither the Liberals nor the Conservatives, however, thought it wise to alienate the significant Ukrainian-Canadian vote by taking such a course. Thus the DEA and the CBC were left with the task of controlling or at least restraining the decidedly provocative programming. Meanwhile, the Ukrainian section set a precedent for other groups (e.g., the Poles and Hungarians) to agitate for their own language sections.[69]

The Ukrainian section of the CBC-IS illustrated an important point vis-à-vis Canadian foreign policy and the 'ethnic question' in Canadian–Soviet relations. Cold War rhetoric and Canada's firm support of the West notwithstanding, the DEA was basically committed to promoting an atmosphere in which Canadian–Soviet differences could be ameliorated and a degree of normalcy restored. Trade benefits and the fact that Canada saw itself as a 'middle power' playing a moderating role in global affairs dictated such a course. CBC-IS broadcasting into the Soviet Union and Eastern Bloc countries was intended to be as even-handed and positive as possible: it was supposed to showcase the quality of life in free and civilized nations that 'preserved the tradition of liberty,' while avoiding direct condemnations of communist regimes that could be interpreted as Western capitalist propaganda.[70] In this context, the bombastic Ukrainian section was viewed as a largely negative influence. Indeed, from the DEA's perspective such broadcasts were tantamount to sabotaging the fundamental goals of Canadian foreign policy. Moreover, for the first time, politicians had overruled the 'professionals' in the DEA regarding how to deal with the Slavic groups – especially the Ukrainians.

This dichotomy reached its climax in the Diefenbaker years, during which Ukrainian Canadians and other East European groups invariably received a sympathetic hearing from federal politicians.[71] Indeed, the prime minister seemed to relish attacking 'Soviet imperialism,' especially at international forums like the UN. In a speech on 26 September 1960, for example, he gave a stout defence of the 'enslaved nations,' suggesting that 'Mr. Khruschev give the Ukraine and other subjugated countries under his domination the right to free elections – to give them the opportunity to determine the kind of government they want under genuinely free conditions.'[72] This led to a blistering rebuttal from N.V. Podgorny, First Secretary of the Central Committee of the Communist Party of Ukraine. Before the same body he described Diefenbaker's remarks as 'rude and slanderous [and as evoking] a profound indignation among the Ukrainian people.' Podgorny then personally attacked the Canadian prime minister as 'ridiculous and senseless.'[73]

Nor was this the only incident. In the UN the same year, the Canadian representative raised the matter of Soviet oppression of the Ukrainian Greek Catholic Church fifteen years earlier, in 1945 and 1946. This was over the heads of DEA officials, who had argued that the gesture would be futile and totally counterproductive to Canadian–Soviet relations.[74]

Why, then, did the government overrule its experts in the DEA? It was partly because of the background and personality of Canada's first 'ethnic' prime minister, but mostly because many ethnic minorities supported him at the polls.

Yet the fiery rhetoric and Diefenbaker's pandering to Canada's Slavic groups did not signify a change in Ottawa's basic policy towards the Kremlin. The Diefenbaker Conservatives, no less than the St Laurent Liberals, were ultimately more interested in expanding trade and improving Canadian–Soviet relations generally than in confronting the Soviets over ethnic issues. Ottawa made it clear to Moscow more than once that it did not accept the viability of Ukrainian independence and that it was totally in accord with the international status quo.[75]

V

The Diefenbaker interlude notwithstanding, Stalin's death in 1953 and the subsequent 'thawing' of the Cold War signalled an improvement in Canadian–Soviet relations. In 1954, diplomatic relations were normalized with an exchange of ambassadors and the re-establishment of a Soviet trade mission in Ottawa. This was followed by Pearson's trip to Moscow in October 1955 and by the signing (29 February 1956) of the first postwar trade agreement between the two nations.[76]

The 1960s and 1970s saw a continuation of this trend. Cultural, technological, and scientific exchanges increased greatly; so did cooperation on a variety of international and bilateral matters. A high point came in 1971 with Prime Minister Trudeau's state visit to the Soviet Union. In an attempt to pursue the 'third option' in Canadian foreign policy, designed to lessen Canada's dependence on the United States, Trudeau set out to cultivate the Soviet Union and its satellite states in Eastern Europe. This led to further agreements to encourage and broaden cultural, scientific, and academic exchanges.[77]

In this era of detente, die-hard Cold Warriors found themselves increasingly on the defensive. This was especially true of nationalist East European groups. Though augmented by the arrival of the decidedly anti-Soviet DPs,[78] who often established their own lobby groups (e.g., the Canadian League for the Liberation of Ukraine),[79] they discovered that their representations to government generally fell on deaf ears. Certainly, Pearson and Trudeau, unlike Diefenbaker, were disinclined to indulge in anti-Soviet rhetorical crusades. Trudeau, for example, stated the government's basic position thus: 'We are not supporting the independence of any part of any country which is recognized under international law any more than … we would want any other country to support the independence of any part of Canada.'[80] This policy applied to all ethnic groups but especially to the Ukrainians, who from Ottawa's perspective remained in the 'limelight of controversy and agitation.'[81]

Faced with Ottawa's intransigence on the independence issue, especially since the rise of Quebec separatism, and realizing that however desirable Ukrainian independence might be, it would not be attained in the foreseeable future, a large part of the Ukrainian community began to rethink its basic goals and tactics. Led by a new generation of Canadian-born Ukrainians, who rejected the polemical battles waged by Cold War militants, Ukrainian-Canadian organizations such as the UCC began to focus on areas where they could more readily influence the government's foreign policy – specifically, on the cultural and human rights aspects of Canadian–Soviet relations.

Beginning in the 1960s, Ukrainian representations to Ottawa became less preoccupied with political and ideological warfare. They now focused on more pragmatic matters, such as cultural and academic exchange programs, family reunification, and Soviet human rights violations (especially against Ukrainian dissidents). Moderates in the community were arguing that contacts with their brethren in Ukraine would help keep Ukrainian culture alive for those living in the 'free world,' however fearful the Soviets might be that such contacts would be used for subversive purposes.[82] In part, this reflected a mentality that the older generations did not share (i.e., many of the latter still hoped to return one day to a free Ukraine). More specifically, it reflected the premise that the younger generation were Canadians first, whose activities should begin with that fact. In practical terms this meant taking a more realistic and less emotional approach when dealing with the question of Soviet Ukraine. Ukrainian Canadians by and large became less concerned about agitating for a fully independent Ukraine and more focused on ensuring that the Ukrainians in Soviet Ukraine be governed in a humane fashion. In other words, Ukrainian-Canadian groups began pressing for a Ukraine that, if not free, at least showed some hallmarks of an actual democracy.[83]

Ottawa found it easy enough to condone this approach. The 'Just Society' (Trudeau's famous term) and Ottawa's recent recognition that Canada was now a multicultural nation[84] made it not just acceptable but desirable that Canadians of *all* ethnic backgrounds remain concerned about the conditions of their kin in the ancestral homeland. Indeed, Canada was in the forefront of promoting the notion that it was the duty of progressive democracies to speak out against cultural repression and violations of human rights not only at home but abroad. 'Only in this way,' declared Trudeau, 'can we continue and accelerate the progress toward a world in which the foremost goals of every government of every country must be the attainment of social justice, fundamental human rights, and. the dignity and worth of all human beings.'[85]

But these lofty sentiments did not always mesh with the realpolitik that Ottawa found itself obliged to pursue in its dealings with Moscow. For the sake of good relations, Canadian officials continued to tread lightly when asked to raise matters with Soviet authorities that might embarrass them. Nowhere was this more evident than in the realm of human rights. Thus when politically engaged Ukrainian Canadians pressured the government to file protests on behalf of dissidents who were being mistreated by the Soviet state, Canadian officials generally resisted, noting that doing so would constitute unacceptable interference in another country's domestic affairs and would be counterproductive to relations between the two countries.[86]

A case in point: Trudeau in 1971 rejected the UCC's plea that during his state visit that year to the Soviet Union he file a protest with the Soviets on behalf of jailed dissident historian Valentyn Moroz. He angered many in the Ukrainian-Canadian community when he compared dissident Ukrainian nationalists with FLQ revolutionaries, the clear implication being that Moscow had reasonable cause to imprison nationalist revolutionaries, just as Ottawa had to imprison Quebec terrorists.[87]

Yet Ottawa sometimes took up specific cases with the Soviet authorities on humanitarian grounds, with positive results. An example is Danylo Shumuk, who had spent more than forty years of his life as a political prisoner in Poland, Germany, and the Soviet Union. After a long campaign by his relatives in Canada – assisted by Amnesty International and various Ukrainian organizations – Shumuk was allowed to immigrate to Canada in May 1987.[88]

Besides raising human rights issues and lobbying for family reunification, freer exchanges, and greater social and cultural autonomy for Soviet Ukraine, members of the Ukrainian-Canadian community resurrected a number of difficult historical issues – such as genocide and war crimes – that embarrassed the Kremlin and impinged (albeit indirectly) on Canadian–Soviet relations. For example, in academic and professional circles a vigorous effort was made (and continues to be made) to set the historical record straight regarding the Great Famine of 1932 and 1933. Stalin's deliberate starvation of between five and seven million people is little known in the West and was never officially acknowledged by the Kremlin; indeed, Soviet historiography remained ominously mute on the episode. *Harvest of Despair*, an award-winning Canadian documentary that graphically depicted for a North American television audience the horrors of the man-made famine,[89] and a plethora of scholarly literature on the 'Ukrainian Holocaust' (the most poignant of which was Robert Conquest's *The Harvest of Sorrow: Soviet Collectivization and the Terror-Famine*, published in 1986 for the CIUS by the University of Alberta Press), informed a generally uninformed media and public of past Soviet atrocities; it also created a crack in the Soviet wall of silence. For instance, Yuri Bogayevsky, First Secretary of the Soviet Embassy in Ottawa, took great exception when the *Globe and Mail* reprinted two full-page excerpts (29 November and 1 December 1986) from Conquest's work. In a letter to the editor Bogayevsky criticized the eminent historian as 'less than scholarly' and attempted to give the Soviet version of events.[90] Meanwhile, General Secretary Mikhail Gorbachev did his part in 'damage control' by roundly chastising Prime Minister Brian Mulroney for referring to the 'Great Famine' in a speech to a 'Ukrainian Day' gathering.[91]

Even more illustrative of the public relations battles the Soviets fought with ethnic groups was the controversy surrounding the Deschenes Commission, which investigated war criminals in Canada. Many East Europeans viewed the commission as too restricted in its mandate. The government task force (established in 1979) had first recommended that Canada's policy on 'war criminals' apply evenly to all perpetrators, regardless of where or when the acts occurred. In the end, though,

Mr Justice Jules Deschenes was restricted to those atrocities relating to Nazi Germany. East European groups argued that as a result, massive crimes against humanity committed by other regimes (namely, the Soviet Union) were escaping investigation and were being inadvertently covered up.

There is no doubt that during the Second World War and its aftermath the peoples of Eastern Europe (especially of Byelorussia, Estonia, Latvia, Lithuania, Poland, and Western Ukraine) had suffered as much under the Soviets as they had under the Nazis. Indeed, after Hitler and Stalin signed their Non-Aggression Pact, the Gestapo and the NKVD had regularly worked together for almost two years. In this period (1939–41) more often than not it had been the Soviets who first committed heinous acts against the population whose lands they occupied.[92]

In its brief to the Deschenes Commission, the UCC agreed emphatically that war criminals ought to be prosecuted; but it also contended that prosecution should be *inclusive*, not exclusive.[93] In other words, those who committed war crimes for the NKVD should be investigated, not just those who committed them for the Nazis. The Lithuanian-Canadian community, the Latvian National Federation, the Estonian Central Council, and the Slovenian National Council all shared this view.

The Soviet Union, which since the end of the Second World War had been accusing Canada of harbouring Nazi war criminals, denied that it was responsible for any atrocities. At the same time, there is ample evidence that it tried to exploit the issue in Canada in order to foment discord among ethnic communities and to denigrate those individuals and groups that opposed it.[94]

This led to the second major item that Deschenes had to grapple with – the charge made by Ukrainian Canadians and other East European groups that evidence obtained from Soviet sources could not be trusted – that it would be falsified as part of a disinformation campaign to discredit those émigrés who had fought the regime and had escaped Soviet repatriation efforts after the war.[95] The Mulroney government left it strictly to the commission to make its own arrangements with regard to collecting and verifying Soviet evidence.[96] Deschenes assuaged these concerns by insisting that Canadian standards of justice would have to be in place before the commission would accept Moscow's invitation to interview witnesses and examine evidence in the Soviet Union and Poland.[97]

Soviet authorities temporized for six months before giving the commission their answer. Ultimately, they balked; in particular, they would not agree to the commission's stipulation that witnesses be interviewed in accordance with Canadian rules of evidence.[98] The final result was that Deschenes turned down the invitation to visit the Soviet Union and Poland. Ukrainian Canadians, in particular, saw this as vindicating their position that Moscow was more interested in smearing them, creating dissent, and gaining a propaganda victory than in seeing that justice was served.

The commission's Final Report (without Soviet input) was received favourably by all ethnic groups when it was tabled in March 1987. The recommendation that *all* suspected war criminals living in Canada be prosecuted (i.e., not just accused Nazi criminals), and that this be done *in Canada,* was especially welcomed by Ukrainian Canadians.[99] Indeed, shortly after the report's release the UCC declared its intention to prepare a list of suspected Soviet war criminals residing in Canada for submission to the Justice Department.

The collapse of the Soviet Union in the final months of 1991 placed Canadian–Soviet relations in the past tense. However, the 'Ukrainian question' remained very much on Ottawa's agenda. Ukrainian-Canadian activists felt vindicated: they had kept the faith, the 'evil empire' had fallen, and Ukraine now could take its rightful place in the community of nations. Not unexpectedly, a well-mobilized Ukrainian-Canadian lobby placed strong pressure on the Mulroney government to quickly recognize Ukraine. After several miscues while events were in flux,[100] the prime minister promised Ukraine full recognition provided that its declaration of independence was upheld in a referendum. The overwhelming victory of the yes side on 1 December 1991[101] ensured that this would be the case, and Canada became the second country (after Poland) to officially acknowledge an independent Ukraine. To date, the Canadian government has remained very mindful of the Ukrainian-Canadian constituency and has been a steadfast supporter (in diplomatic *and* economic terms) of Ukraine in the international arena.

VI

When encountering pressure from ethnic groups, Ottawa has always been pragmatic. It has pursued this country's traditional diplomatic goals while trying to deflect the politicized objectives of its East European minorities. In the case of the Ukrainian Canadians during the era of the Soviet Union, this meant politely turning aside those aims which it deemed incompatible with government policy. In other words, while sometimes paying lip service to Ukrainians' concerns, Canadian officials tried to prevent these concerns from becoming general issues that would negatively affect Canada–Soviet relations. A good example of this was Ottawa's role in the founding of the UCC and its subsequent attempts to manipulate and then mute that organization in the 'national interest' during the Second World War.

The vagaries of Canadian–Soviet relations did not always make this an easy task. Illustrative here was the founding of the Ukrainian-language section in the CBC-IS during the Cold War. In this case, politicians overruled the DEA. From the perspective of the DEA bureaucrats, the Ukrainian section gave Ukrainian Canadians an opportunity to 'make trouble' between Canada and the Soviet Union, thus confirming the folly of coddling to the special interests of a particular group. In the main, however, the Ukrainian section (and Diefenbaker's anti-Soviet speeches for that matter) can be viewed as anomalies: overall, Ottawa succeeded in defusing the 'ethnic question' in pursuit of a foreign policy that, on the whole, endeavoured to maintain cordial relations with the Soviet state.

Why did Canada's various ethnic groups – the Ukrainians in particular – fail to influence Canadian policy towards the Soviet Union to a greater extent? The answer has to do not just with reticent Canadian officials but also with the ethnic communities themselves. Generally speaking, these communities have never been unified enough either politically or organizationally to have an impact on public sentiment or electoral results. Certainly, Ukrainian Canadians have long demonstrated an inexhaustible capacity for internal feuding, and this has tended to defuse any coordinated efforts to present a coherent viewpoint either to government or to the Canadian public.

For example, during Soviet times Ottawa could never have supported independence for Ukraine. Only in the 1960s did the nationalist community lower its sights in favour of more attainable objectives. At that point, in certain areas such as cultural exchanges and human rights, Ukrainian Canadian organizations began to enjoy some success. Ottawa was willing to take up specific issues on behalf of Ukrainian Canadians so long as doing so did not unduly aggravate Canadian–Soviet relations.

Finally, there was the role played by the Soviets. Moscow sometimes protested vigorously to Canadian officials regarding the activities of East European groups; at the same time, it encouraged these groups to stay at loggerheads – with considerable success.

Notes

1 In 1981 there were 529,615 individuals of Ukrainian origin in Canada. Numerically this constituted a group larger than the combined total of all other Canadian ethnic groups whose original homelands were within the Soviet Union. Figures cited from *Statistics Canada: 1981 Census of Canada.*

2 For a detailed discussion see John R. Reshetar, Jr, *The Ukrainian Revolution, 1917–1920* (Princeton: Princeton University Press, 1952).

3 See, for example, Victor Domanyckyj, 'The National Problem And World War One'; Alexander Choulguine, 'The Doctrine of Wilson and the Building of the Ukrainian National Republic'; and 'Editorial: Woodrow Wilson and the Liberation Of Nations,' all in *Ukrainian Quarterly* 12, no. 4 (1956).

4 See, for example, Herbert Adams Gibbons, 'The Ukraine and the Balance of Power,' *Century Magazine* 102, no. 3 (1921); Vladimir Korostovetz, 'The Ukrainian Problem,' *Contemporary Review* 141, no. 369 (1932); and Clarence A. Manning, 'The Ukrainians and the United States in World War I,' *Ukrainian Quarterly* 13, no. 4 (1957).

5 About 80,000 were registered as 'Enemy Aliens' in Canada during the First World War, and almost 6,000 Ukrainian Canadians were interned as Austro-Hungarian nationals. For a full discussion see Peter Melnycky, 'The Internment of Ukrainians in Canada,' in *Loyalties in Conflict: Ukrainians in Canada During the Great War,* ed. Frances Swyripa and John Herd Thompson (hereafter *Loyalties*) (Edmonton: CIUS, 1983). Also, Desmond Morton, 'Sir William Otter and Internment Operations during the First World War,' *Canadian Historical Review* (hereafter *CHR*) 55, no. 3 (1974).

6 Undoubtedly, the level of 'Ukrainian' national consciousness was quite low, with many retaining their old-country regional and/or religious identities. Some thought of themselves as 'Galicians' or 'Bukovynians,' others as Austrians, Poles, or a branch of the Russian polity. Still others saw themselves in a religious context as 'Ruthenians' or Russian Orthodox. See Orest Martynowch, *Ukrainians in Canada: The Formative Years,*

1891–1924 (Edmonton: CIUS Press, 1991). Chapters 10 and 11 of that
book detail the divisions within the Ukrainian community.

7 For a discussion of the internecine strife within the Ukrainian-Canadian
community, especially between the socialists who welcomed the Bolshevik Revolution in Ukraine because it would ensure that 'power would be
in the hands of Ukrainian workers, peasants, and soldiers,' and the nationalists who supported the Rada's declaration of Ukraine's independence, see Nestor Makuch, 'The Influence of the Ukrainian Revolution
on Ukrainians in Canada, 1917–1922,' *Journal of Ukainian Graduate
Studies* 4, no. 1 (1979). See also Orest Martynowych, *Ukrainians in
Canada: The Formative Years, 1891–1924* (Edmonton: Canadian Institute of Ukrainian Studies, 1991), 453–9.

8 For a discussion of the UCCC and its activities see Nadia Kazymyra,
'Ukrainian Canadian Response to the Paris Peace Conference, 1919,' in
Loyalties; and Martynowych, *Ukrainians in Canada,* 459–79. While perhaps sympathetic to the 'national liberation' struggle, most socialists –
including the Ukrainian Social Democratic Party (USDP) – were leery of
the establishment of an independent Ukrainian 'bourgeoisie' state.

9 Harold Mackie to Robert Borden, 16 October 1918, cited in *A Delicate
And Difficult Question: Documents in the History of Ukrainians in
Canada 1899–1962* (hereafter *Documents*), ed. Bohdan S. Kordan and
Lubomyr Y. Luciuk (Kingston: Limestone, 1986), 36–44.

10 Petition of Ukrainian Canadian Citizens' Committee to Robert Borden,
24 April 1919, cited in *Documents*, 42–3.

11 Kazymyra, cited in *Loyalties,* 131–2.

12 Editorial, *Ukrainian Quarterly* 13, no. 4 (1957): 295.

13 Choulguine, cited in ibid., 327.

14 See Kazymyra in *Loyalties,* 127–9. Poland was granted title to Galicia in
1923 on the understanding that it would eventually grant autonomy to
this area under the clauses of the Minority Treaty of 28 June 1919. Warsaw, however, suppressed the Ukrainians politically and economically
and finally in 1934 repudiated this obligation.

15 The issue was raised in September 1921 by Charles Joseph Doherty,
Canada's delegate to the League of Nations. In 1922, W.S. Fielding rein-
troduced the resolution, to which the Poles responded coolly. In any event
the league took no positive action. See Aloysius Balawyder, *The Maple
Leaf and the White Eagle: Canadian–Polish Relations, 1918–1978* (New
York: Columbia University Press, 1980), 68–9. Balawyder suggests, without elaboration, that the Canadian government refused to commit itself
further for fear of antagonizing its Polish-Canadian population.

16 Oleh W. Gerus, 'Ukrainian Diplomatic Representation in Canada, 1920–
23' in *Loyalties*, 146.

17 Canada, *House of Commons Debates* (hereafter *Debates*), 1923, IV:4001.
18 The Soviet Union retained 298,610 square miles containing 36,026,000 Ukrainians; Western Ukraine (Galicia), comprising 51,042 square miles with 7,500,000 Ukrainians, was made a Polish 'protectorate'; the provinces of Bessarabia and Bukovyna, encompassing 6,795 square miles and approximately 500,000 Ukrainians, was placed under Romanian rule; and Carpatho-Ukraine, with 5,253 square miles and a population of over 600,000 Ukrainians, was assigned to Czechoslovakia.
19 Michael A. Feighan, 'National Self-Determination – Its Political Origin,' *Ukrainian Quarterly* 11, no. 4, (1957): 35. A similar view was expressed by Anthony Hlynka, Social Credit MP (Vegreville), in a speech in the House of Commons on 2 February 1941, *Debates*, 1942, I:229–35.
20 For a detailed discussion see Aloysius Balawyder, *Canadian-Soviet Relations Between The World Wars* (Toronto: University of Toronto Press, 1972).
21 'Non-preferred' countries included Austria, Hungary, Poland, Romania, the Baltic states, Bulgaria, Yugoslavia, and Czechoslovakia.
22 For a comprehensive overview of this 'second wave' of Ukrainian immigration, consult Byron Gulka-Tiechko, 'Inter-War Ukrainian Immigration to Canada, 1919–1939,' MA thesis, University of Manitoba, 1983.
23 For a more detailed discussion, see Oleh W. Gerus, 'Consolidating the Community: The Ukrainian Self-Reliance League,' in *Canada's Ukrainians: Negotiating an Identity,* ed. Lubomyr Luciuk and Stella Hryniuk (hereafter *Canada's Ukrainians)* (Toronto: University of Toronto Press, 1991).
24 Oleh W. Gerus in *Canada's Ukrainians.* See also 'Programme of Ukrainian Self-Reliance League, December, 1927,' cited in *Documents,* 48–50.
25 For a discussion of Lobay and his parting of ways with the ULFTA, see Marco Carynnyk, 'Swallowing Stalinism: Pro-Communist Ukrainian Canadians and Soviet Ukraine in the 1930s,' in *Canada's Ukrainians;* and Ronda Hinther, '"Sincerest Revolutionary Greetings": Progressive Ukrainians in Twentieth-Century Canada,' PhD diss., McMaster University, 2005, 65–71.
26 Michael Luchkovich, a UFA MP (Vegreville) in 1931, did initiate a parliamentary debate on the Polish–Ukrainian problem when he cited examples of Polish atrocities in Galicia. His demand that the mistreatment of Ukrainians in the region be once more brought to the attention of the League of Nations was ultimately taken up by the government through a presentation of Ukrainian-Canadian petitions before the council. But as before, the world body did little to satisfy Ukrainian concerns. Ottawa,

too, not wishing to antagonize unduly its Polish-Canadian population or to aggravate Polish–Canadian relations, committed itself no further. See Balawyder, *The Maple Leaf and the White Eagle*, 69–75 for a full discussion.

27 See, for example, 'Petition Of The Ukrainian National Committee to the Right Honorable R. MacDonald, Prime Minister of Great Britain, October 2, 1933, Requesting Investigation of Famine in Soviet Ukraine and Assistance to Organize Famine Relief'; and 'Reply from the High Commissioner for the United Kingdon to the Ukrainian National Committee, March 2, 1934, Regarding Famine in Soviet Ukraine,' both in *Documents,* 61–3.

28 See Jaroslav Petryshyn, 'R.B. Bennett and the Communists: 1930–1935,' *Journal of Canadian Studies* 9, no. 4 (1974).

29 LAC, MG26, vol. 141, file 31, Bennett Papers, Commissioner of the R.C.M.P. to the Undersecretary of State for External Affairs, August 27, 1930. For a detailed history of the ULFTA see John Kolasky, *The Shattered Illusion: The History Of Ukrainian Pro-Communist Organizations in Canada (*Toronto: Peter Martin Associates, 1979).

30 Nevertheless, two of the ULFTA's more prominent leaders, Matthew Popovich and John Boychuk, were charged, convicted, and incarcerated, along with six other members of the CPC Politburo, for being officers of an unlawful association. See Jaroslav Petryshyn, 'Class Conflict and Civil Liberties: The Origins and Activities of the Canadian Labour Defense League, 1925–1940,' *Labour/Le travail* 10 (Autumn 1982). For a brief overview of the Ukrainian left and its turbulent relationship with the Canadian state see Donald Avery, 'Divided Loyalties: The Ukrainian Left and the Canadian State,' in *Canada's Ukrainians.*

31 See Reg Whitaker, 'Official Repression of Communism During World War II,' *Labour/Le travail* 17 (Spring 1986): esp. 156–60.

32 Hugo Yardley, 'Poland and the Ukrainians,' *The Commonweal* 30, no. 18 (1939).

33 In 1940 the British Foreign Office engaged Vladimir J. Kaye (Kisilevsky), a noted Ukrainian academic, and J.E. Tracy Philipps, an East European specialist and long-time civil servant. In Philipps's case the work was described as 'confidential' and had the personal and secret approval of Lord Halifax, the Secretary of State. See Bohdan Kordan, 'Disunity And Duality: Ukrainian Canadians and the Second World War,' MA thesis, Carleton University.

34 The Department of National War Services took up the responsibility for bringing the Ukrainian nationalist organizations together in a federal body. It created a special advisory committee on 'Canadian Cooperation and Canadian Citizenship' that, besides receiving critical input from

Kaye and Philipps, retained the services of two noted Ukrainian experts, Watson Kirkconnell (a linguist from McMaster University) and George Simpson (a historian from the University of Saskatchewan). For a detailed overview of their activities see Kordan, 'Disunity And Duality'; Oleh W. Gerus, 'Ethnic Politics in Canada: The Formation of the Ukrainian Canadian Committee,' in *The Jubilee Collection Of the Ukrainian Free Academy of Sciences*, ed. Alexander Baran, Oleh Gerus, and Jaroslav Rozumnyj (Winnipeg: UVAW, 1976); and N. Fred Dreisziger, 'Tracy Phillips and the Achievement of Ukrainian–Canadian Unity' in *Canada's Ukrainians*.

35 This is well documented in Kordan, 'Disunity and Duality.'

36 Kaye used this argument especially effectively during his tour of Ukrainian-Canadian communities. LAC, MG31 D69, Kay Papers, vol. 18, file 16, 1940.

37 LAC, RG23, vol. 1898, file 172, UCC to O. Skelton, 'Treatment of Ukrainians in Poland and Activities of Ukrainians in Canada,' 11 December 1940.

38 Lester B. Pearson to Norman Robertson, 12 October 1941, cited in *Documents*, 78.

39 *Debates*, 1941, I:229–35.

40 Samuel J.Nesdoly, 'Changing Perspectives: The Ukrainian-Canadian Role in Canadian-Soviet Relations,' in Balawyder, *Canadian–Soviet Relations*, 111.

41 See Lubomyr Luciuk, 'Searching for Place: Ukrainian Refugee Migration to Canada after World War II,' PhD diss., Unversity of Alberta, 1984, 146.

42 Kordan, 'Disunity and Duality,' 99.

43 The Soviet diplomatic mission was established in Ottawa in 1942.

44 Norman Robertson to William Lyon Mackenzie King, 6 May 1943, cited in *Documents*, 92–3.

45 Though it should be noted that the restitution made fell well short of what had been confiscated. Whitaker, 'Official Repression of Communism,' 159.

46 See, for example, the editorial in the UNF organ *Novy Shliakh*, 17 March 1943.

47 LAC, RG21, vol. 1896, file 165, N.A. Robertson to D. Wilgress, 'Treatment of Ukrainians in Poland and Activities of Ukrainians in Canada' 28 May 1943.

48 See, for example, memorandum of 4 June 1943 from D. Buchanan to J. Griesson, Director, Wartime Information Board, 'Regarding Policy on the "Ukrainian Question"' cited in *Documents*, 100–3.

49 It was conservatively estimated that about 30 million had been 'displaced' by the war.

50 See, for example, 'Confidential Memorandum from L. Malania, Section Head (Soviet Desk), D.E.A. to H. Wrong,' 5 December 1945, cited in *Documents,* 135–8.

51 N.A. Robertson to G. Pifher, Director of Voluntary and Auxiliary Services, Department of National War Services, 15 November 1944, cited in *Documents,* 132.

52 Wilgress did not seem concerned that 20,000 Ukrainian nationalist partisans (according to his own sources) had been shot towards the end of 1944. See Luciuk, 'Searching for Place,' 156.

53 These restrictions ranged from the petty (e.g., the body became known as the Ukrainian Canadian Relief Fund, and the word 'refugee' was deleted so as not to offend Soviet sensitivities) to the onerous. The latter limited the amount and distribution of funds. See ibid., 157.

54 Canada apparently was unaware until some months later that it was party to such an agreement.

55 For a discussion of Ukrainian refugees in Europe and their process of resettlement in Canada, see Ihor Stebelsky, 'The Resettlement of Ukrainian Refugees in Canada after the Second World War'; for a discussion of the politics of resettlement in the Ukrainian-Canadian community, see Lubomyr Luciuk, '"This Should Never Be Spoken or Quoted Publicly": Canada's Ukrainians and Their Encounter with the DPs.' Both articles are cited in *Canada's Ukrainians.*

56 For a resolution to this effect, see for example, *Ukrainian News,* 13 November 1945.

57 Unskilled and semiskilled labourers were needed in certain primary industries (e.g., forestry, mining, and agriculture) as a result of the continuing buoyant postwar economy. The DPs fitted this need well. See for example Milda Danys, *D.P. Lithuanian Immiqration to Canada after the Second World War* (Toronto: Multicultural History Society of Ontario, 1986) for a good overview of Canada's immigration policy towards the DPs.

58 Between 1947 and 1951, 157,687 'displaced persons' entered Canada. The largest groups were as follows: Poles (36,500), Ukrainians (28,800), Germans (18,400), Jews (15,500), Latvians (9,800), Lithuanians (9,400), Estonians (8,900), Yugoslavians (8,400), and Czechs (5,000). See 'Immigration to Canada Showing Displaced Persons Admitted by Ethnic Origin 1947–51,' *Department of Citizenship and Immigration* (Ottawa: Queen's Printer, 1952).

59 See Luciuk, 'Searching For Place,' 309, and Kolasky, *The Shattered Illusion,* ch. 5. The AUUC vitriolically condemned the federal government's acceptance of 'Ukrainian fascists' and seemed surprised by Ottawa's emerging hard line regarding their own organization.

60 *Debates,* 1948, IV:3552–3.

61 *Debates*, 1951, I:314.
62 See Kolasky, *The Shattered Illusion*, ch. 4, 64–87, for further discussion.
63 *Ibid.* Numerous incidents and disputes of a similar nature can be found in LAC, RG25, vol. 47, box 92, in files that deal with Ukrainian Canadians and Canadian–Soviet relations to the end of the 1960s.
64 See Kolasky, *The Shattered Illusion*, ch. 5, 88–107, for further discussion.
65 Bernard J. Hibbitts, 'Ethnic Groups and Canadian Propaganda Policy in the 1950s,' in *Groups and Governments in Canadian Foreign Policy: Proceedings of a Conference*, ed. Don Munton (Ottawa: Canadian Institute of International Affairs, 1982), 101.
66 For a detailed discussion see Bernard J. Hibbitts, 'The CBC International Service as a Psychological Instrument of Canadian Foreign Policy in the Cold War, 1948–1963,' MA thesis, Carleton University, 1981. Of particular note is ch. 3, 'A Political Matter: The Establishment of the CBC-IS Ukrainian Service, 1952,' 25–94.
67 Cited in ibid.,' 80.
68 Cited in *ibid.*, 87.
69 Hibbitts, 'Ethnic Groups and Canadian Propaganda Policy,' 102.
70 See Hibbitts, 'The CBC International Service,' 43, for the broadcast policy of the IS.
71 See, for example, 'Ukrainian Struggle for Freedom Concerns Canada: Senator Wall and Mr. Mandziuk Address Canadian Parliament in Ottawa on Ukrainian Struggle for National Freedom,' *Ukrainian Review* 6, no. 2 (1969): 10–12; 'Remarks by the Canadian Minister of Labour, Hon. Michael Starr, Addressing the Ukrainian National Manifestation,' *Ukrainian Review* 6, no. 2 (1959): 68–70; 'Anti Bolshevik Speech by a member of Canadian Parliament (J.W. Kucherepa), *Ukrainian Review* 7, no. 2 (1960): 44–7; Arthur Maloney, 'The Challenge of Our Age,' *Ukrainian Review* 7, no. 3 (1961): 7–11; and John G. Diefenbaker, 'The U.S.S.R. Is the Greatest Colonial Power,' *Ukrainian Review* 7, no. 3 (1961): 26–33.
72 Cited in 'Mr. Diefenbaker Defends the Enslaved Nations,' *Ukrainian Review* 7, nos. 3–4 (1960): 105.
73 Cited in 'Podgorny Attacks the West,' *Ukrainian Review* 7, nos. 3–4 (1960): 109.
74 See Nesdoly, 'Changing Perspectives,' 118, for example.
75 See, for example, 'Confidential Memorandum from J. Leger, Undersecretary of State for External Affairs to the Canadian Ambassador to the U.S.S.R., July 18, 1956,' clarifying the views of the Canadian government on the issue of Ukrainian sovereignty; and 'Memorandum To J.

Leger, Undersecretary of State for External Affairs, November 6, 1957.'
Both are cited in *Documents*, 161–6 and 166–67 respectively.

76 James Eayers, *In Defence of Canada: Growing Up Allied* (Toronto: University of Toronto Press, 1985) 363–4.

77 For a discussion of this aspect see Jocelyn M. Ghent, 'Cooperation in Science and Technology,' in Balawyder, *Canadian-Soviet Relations*. See also Jocelyn M. Ghent, *Academic Exchanges with the USSR: An Analysis and Evaluation of Provisions under the General Exchanges Agreement*, report prepared for the Office of International Relations, Social Sciences and Humanities Research Council (Ottawa: 1980).

78 For a good discussion of the anti-Soviet attitudes of the DPs, see Adolf Jacek Zugmunt, 'Adoption of East European Refugees and Political Emigres in Toronto with Reference to Immigrants from Poland and Czechoslovakia,' PhD diss., York University, 1977.

79 Established in May 1949, the Canadian League for the Liberation of Ukraine was but one of about sixteen Ukrainian organizations formed largely by post–Second World War refugees.

80 *Debates*, 1971, VI:6203.

81 *Ethnic Scene*, May 1965, 18 (published by the Citizenship Branch, Department of Citizenship and Immigration, Ottawa.)

82 *Ethnic Scene*, January 1965, 5–8.

83 For a discussion of this changing attitude, see for example Adrij Makuch, 'What Is to Be Done,' in *Student* 14, no. 76 (1982).

84 Ottawa officially adopted the policy of 'multiculturalism within a bilingual framework' in 1971. For a discussion of the role played by the Ukrainian-Canadian Community, see Bohdan Bociurkiw, 'The Federal Policy of Multiculturalism and the Ukrainian Canadian Community,' in *Ukrainian Canadians, Multiculturalism, and Separation: An Assessment*, ed. Manoly R. Lupul (Edmonton: CIUS, 1978).

85 *Debates*, 1971, VI:6184.

86 See, for example, Donald Page, 'Detente: High Hopes and Disappointing Realities,' in Balawyder, *Canadian-Soviet Relations,* 75–6.

87 *Debates*, 1971, VI:6202–4. See also Nesdoly, 'Changing Perspectives,' 121–2.

88 The campaign to free Shumuk is well documented in the various issues of *Ukrainian Weekly*.

89 For example, 'Harvest of Despair' was shown in a special edition of William F. Buckley's program *Firing Line* on PBS in September 1986.

90 Bogayevsky's letter, 'Kulaks Killed Best Workers in Ukraine,' *Globe And Mail*, 13 December 1986, provoked numerous rebuttals, including one by Robert Conquest in the same newspaper, 10 January 1987.

91 William F. Buckley in his introductory remarks to 'Harvest of Despair.'

92 There is a great deal of documentary evidence to support this contention. For a discussion of this and related topics, see Yury Boshyk, ed., *Ukraine during World War II: History and Its Aftermath* (Toronto: CIUS, 1986).

93 See, for example, a statement (sponsored by these organizations) titled 'Why Discriminate?' which was placed in major newspapers.

94 For a detailed discussion of the Jewish–Ukrainian fallout over the Deschenes Commission, see Harold Troper and Morton Weinfeld, *Old Wounds: Jews, Ukrainians, and the Hunt for Nazi War Criminals in Canada* (Toronto: Penguin, 1988).

95 See, for example, 'Submission of the Ukrainian Canadian Committee to Commission of Inquiry on War Criminals' (John Sopinka QC), 5 May 1986, and 'Ukrainian Canadian Students Union (SUSK) Submission to the Commission of Inquiry on War Criminals,' 3 September 1985.

96 Rejane Dodd, spokesman for the DEA, stated in a *Globe and Mail* interview (22 November 1985) that the government's role was limited to acting as a 'mailbox' and providing 'logistic support.'

97 Deschenes set down six basic rules: protection of reputations through confidentiality: independent interpreters; access to original documents; access to witnesses' previous statements; freedom of examination of witnesses in agreement with Canadian rules of evidence; and videotaping of the examinations.

98 Michael A. Meighen and L. Yves Fortier, Commission of Inquiry on War Criminals, to Alexander Mikhailovitch Rekunkov, Procurator General of the Union of Soviet Socialist Republics, 29 May 1986.

99 See, for example, editorial, *Ukrainian Weekly,* 22 March 1987. See also Troper and Weinfeld, *Old Wounds.*

100 Most notably, Canadian Secretary of State Barbara McDougall had to quickly retract her ill-advised comments implying that she supported the right-wing coup leaders in the Kremlin. This created substantive political fallout, not only from the Ukrainian-Canadian community but also throughout the country in general.

101 For a detailed account of Ukraine's road to independence, see Bohdan Hahaylo, *Ukrainian Resurgence: From Dependence to Independence* (Toronto: University of Toronto Press, 1999).

8

Monitoring the 'Return to the Homeland' Campaign: Canadian Reports on Resettlement in the USSR from South America, 1955–1957

Serge Cipko

In 1955, on the tenth anniversary of the end of the Second World War and two years after Soviet dictator Josef Stalin's death, the Soviet Union and allied Warsaw Pact countries put in motion a worldwide campaign to persuade expatriates to return to their homelands. A Committee for the Return to the Homeland was established, headquartered in East Berlin. This committee published newspapers and non-periodical literature and ran a radio broadcasting service that featured return-home appeals. Sentimental chain letters from relatives and friends in the Soviet Union reinforced this campaign, which was said to be well-subsidized by the Soviets. A contemporary Western monitor of the return-to-the-homeland campaign suggested in March 1956, without giving statistics, that the Soviet Union was spending more on its repatriation project 'than does the United States in its entire refugee program.'[1]

This essay focuses on the reception in Canada of the return-to-the-homeland movement in South America. In 1955–6 thousands of people in Argentina, Brazil, Uruguay, and Paraguay boarded ships in Buenos Aires and other South American ports that were destined for Odesa. That and related developments drew the interest of the Canadian government, in light of simultaneous smaller-scale departures from Canada to the Soviet Union in response to the Soviets' return-to-the-homeland campaign. The newspapers of targeted communities in Canada – notably the Ukrainian-language papers – also took an interest in and provided coverage of developments in South America. These papers' responses to the campaign depended on their readers' feelings towards the Soviet Union. As this essay shows, the press of pro-Soviet organizations such as the Association of United Ukrainian Canadians (AUUC) provided uncritical coverage whereas the anti-Soviet *Novyi shliakh* of Toronto, voice of the Ukrainian National Federation (UNF), published critical commentaries about the campaign in Canada and other countries.

The campaign began in 1955, but its roots go back earlier. It was aimed primarily at former displaced persons (DPs) who had settled in Western Europe and overseas after the Second World War. Many of the people who responded to the return-to-the-homeland appeals belonged to pro-Soviet organizations abroad. A number of them had earlier applied to resettle in the Soviet Union but had, at the time, been discouraged from doing so. This earlier interest in resettling in the Soviet Union is confirmed in a 1947 communication by the Soviet Embassy in Ottawa to authorities in the Ukrainian SSR. The embassy advised that it was registering Canadian residents as Soviet citizens, many of whom wanted to be reunited with their families in the homeland and to assist in postwar reconstruction. It added that the group was also inspired by the movement of local Poles, Czechs, and Yugoslavs to their original homelands. The Ukrainian SSR recommended against repatriation on the grounds that the returnees would place pressure on available housing and provoke social tensions with the local population. Furthermore, since the applicants were Canadian Ukrainians who were sympathetic to the Soviet regime, their departure would only strengthen 'the position of the nationalist Ukrainian organizations' in Canada.[2]

Between the start of the return-to-the-homeland campaign in 1955 and October 1956, no fewer than 814 people from Canada resettled in Eastern Europe, about half of them in the Soviet Union.[3] Though the number of people leaving Canada for the Soviet Union in 1955–6 was statistically insignificant, Ottawa viewed the return-home movement with concern and monitored the campaign both at home and abroad. Facing pressure to stop the campaign from organizations whose members were born or had roots in Eastern Europe, Ottawa took an interest in how other governments were responding to the return-home drive.[4] The Canadian government was kept informed about the return-to-the-homeland movement by the RCMP, its embassies abroad, and its delegates at NATO meetings; it gleaned information from other sources as well, such as correspondence from members of targeted communities. Also, the newspapers of both anti- and pro-Soviet organizations in Canada occasionally featured stories relating to the return-home campaign.

Opponents of the campaign in Canada expressed dissatisfaction that Ottawa was more passive in countering the return-home movement than were governments of such countries as Argentina and the United States. A 19 May 1956 editorial in the Polish-language *Glos Polski* titled 'Ottawa's Turn' contrasted Canadian policy towards the campaign with the actions taken by the UN against a Soviet diplomat and the warning issued by the U.S. State Department to the Soviet Embassy in Washington about overstepping the bounds of diplomatic activity. The editorial urged the Canadian government to block the circulation of 'Communist subversive literature,' to uncover the 'mysterious distributors' of that literature, and to closely supervise the activities of legations representing communist countries.[5]

Over the course of 1956 the Canadian branch of the World Federation of Ukrainian Former Political Prisoners and Victims of the Soviet Regime followed the campaign in Canada and presented information to the RCMP, which passed it on to the Department of External Affairs (DEA). Oleh Pidhainy, a member of the organization, believing that the Canadian government was doing too little to stop the campaign, urged that a cabinet, parliamentary, or senate committee be appointed to investigate it.[6] In an account of the return-to-the-homeland movement – an account that he described as inspired by Anthony J. Wright of the parliamentary press gallery and that was prefaced by Igor Gouzenko, a high-ranking Soviet defector to Canada – Pidhainy asserted that both Argentina and the United States had acted forcefully against the campaign. Argentine intelligence officials in July 1956 were investigating it, he said, and the United States had directed protests to the Soviet Embassy in Washington. 'Canada, on the other hand,' Pidhainy wrote, 'prefers to see no violation of internal laws and no improper diplomatic action in the activities connected with the Repatriation campaign.' In his opinion, Canada was thereby showing disregard for its sovereignty.[7]

The Canadian government's position was that without evidence that laws were being violated, there was little it could do about the campaign. Lester Pearson, Canada's Secretary of State for External Affairs, told the Standing Committee on External Affairs that he had been 'asked whether the Government could not put a stop to the "return to the homeland" campaign in this country.' After 'very careful consideration' he had concluded 'that there is not very much which we can do.' First, he noted, the propaganda, which did not appear to be seditious, was arriving as first-class mail from Europe and could not be censored under Canadian law. Second, the campaign was being conducted not by Warsaw Pact governments but by return-to-the-homeland committees whose members claimed to be private individuals. 'I do not think it would be wise to dignify the efforts of these committees,' Pearson remarked, 'or to give them useful publicity, by making formal protests to the governments which are lurking behind them.' Pearson added, however, that he would draw the line at any 'attempt by foreign governments to intimidate Canadian citizens or residents, or any improper behaviour by foreign representatives in this country.'[8]

An Argentine assessment of Brazil's reaction to the return-to-the-homeland campaign noted the lack of uniformity in the West's response to the drive. Brazilian leaders' apparent silence 'before public opinion' regarding the problem of returnees in the Soviet Union was compared with 'other countries (Canada, France, Italy, the Netherlands) which also saw some of their nationals leave for Russia.' It was said that their departure was viewed as a private matter.[9]

That lack of uniformity notwithstanding, Canada stayed well-informed about the resettlement campaign as it was waged south of the equator. Ottawa had chosen to pursue an independent policy towards the return-home campaign, but it also maintained an interest in South American developments and exchanged information with Buenos Aires. The data gathered about the return-to-the-homeland movement in South America were undoubtedly useful for drawing parallels with the Canadian situation.

Between the end of the nineteenth century and the middle of the twentieth, immigrants from Eastern Europe had settled in South America in the hundreds of thousands. Large Eastern European immigrant communities had developed in Argentina and Brazil and to a lesser extent in Paraguay and Uruguay. Some immigrant organizations in these communities were already pro-Soviet when the Soviets launched their campaign. Indeed, a number of people from these groups (many of them of Ukrainian and Belarusian background) had applied to resettle to the Soviet Union immediately after the Second World War.

In the spring and summer of 1956 the attention of Ottawa and the Canadian public was drawn to the migration of people to the Soviet Union from South America – especially Argentina, from which thousands rather than hundreds were departing. On 5 June 1956 the DEA sent a letter to the Canadian Embassy in Buenos Aires, which was later distributed to the Canadian missions in Chile, Colombia, Peru, Uruguay, Venezuela, and Brazil, requesting information on the part played by 'Soviet bloc missions ... in their "return to the homeland" campaign in Argentina' and on the attitude the Argentine authorities had taken towards the same.[10] Over the course of the year, Canadian and Argentine diplomats exchanged information on the return-to-the-homeland phenomenon in their respective countries, and the DEA received reports from its embassies in South America, especially in Argentina and Uruguay.

Of all the countries in the West encompassed by the campaign, Argentina was accorded the most attention, both in the media and in official circles. Soviet sources claimed in 1949 that 800,000 people of Slavic origin were living in Argentina.[11] This was an exaggeration; still, their numbers in that country were not insignificant.[12] The Canadian Ambassador to Argentina, Philippe Picard, on presenting figures to the DEA, reported that 'according to 1954 statistics there would be in this country about 86,000 Russians and 113,000 Poles.' He added: 'A majority of them have not acquired Argentine citizenship and have been left to fend for themselves with little assistance, in largely unproductive areas, where there were few roads, few schools, and few amenities.' He conjectured that many had secured 'a Soviet passport on the promise that they would be paid a free trip to the motherland and assured good jobs there.'[13]

Immigration from Eastern Europe to Argentina before the First World War had been substantial. The largest number of these people had been Russian Jews. Yet the returnees from Argentina in the second half of the 1950s were more likely to be Ukrainians and Belarusians who had arrived between the two world wars with Polish passports, and Lithuanians. Picard remarked on 30 June 1956 that on the basis of the 'available information,' of the 'not more than two thousand' people who had departed Argentina since April, 'the majority came to Argentina before the Second World War.'[14]

Brazil had also experienced large-scale immigration from Eastern Europe. Most of it, however, had taken place before the First World

War.[15] In Brazil as in Argentina, the returnees were more likely to be people who had arrived later than most, during the interwar years. It is estimated that some eight hundred people left Brazil for the Soviet Union as a result of the return-home campaign[16] – a much smaller number than the thousands who eventually left Argentina. An article in a Montreal Lithuanian-language periodical in October 1958 stated that the Soviet Lithuanian leader J. Paleckis had, during a recent Brazilian visit, 'advised compatriots not to go back to Lithuania as yet.' From this the author concluded: 'It proves once more that the Soviets are anxious to catch "DPs." Oldtimers, on the other hand, cause the Soviets unnecessary trouble.'[17]

The DEA was also apprised of the return-to-the-homeland movement from Uruguay and landlocked Paraguay. These two countries had attracted fewer Eastern European immigrants than Brazil and Argentina, which were much larger. Many of the Eastern Europeans in Uruguay and Paraguay had arrived during the interwar years. The New Israel community (Novaia Izraelskaya Obshchina) were among the immigrants who came to Uruguay before the First World War. After their arrival from Russia, the group founded the the settlement of San Javier in the department of Río Negro. This sect was similar to the Doukhobors, who had settled in Canada. In July 1956 the Canadian Embassy in Montevideo reported Uruguay's reaction to departures to the Soviet Union. The Argentine ship *Santa Fé* had left Buenos Aires with seven hundred passengers, the embassy said. On the morning of 29 June 1956 it had stopped in Montevideo to pick up 106 more. It had then sailed for the Black Sea port of Odessa. 'This event,' wrote Blair Birkett, the Canadian chargé d'affaires, 'has aroused much interest.' He provided English summaries of local newpaper reports. One of the newspapers, *Acción*, described by Birkett as 'one of the more sensational Colorado party newspapers,' had written on the matter of whether pressure had been applied to induce the departure:

Some people have said that there may have been some pressure on all these people to leave. Some have sold their goods in a hurry, at a low price, in order to collect the necessary money for the voyage ... As far as can be seen, none of this is certain. The travellers whom we saw were not fearful people, but gay and full of confidence. Gay, in spite of the emotion of leave-taking.

In addition, they seemed sensible people who showed good judgment when we talked with them. All of this is incompatible with fear.[18]

Birkett then quoted another newspaper, which asserted that the people leaving Uruguay were doing so 'certainly under the influence of the official propaganda of the Communist regime which has been spread in the agricultural colonies where they lived.'[19] It is clear from the clippings Birkett supplied that most of the more than one hundred returnees of 29 June were from the rural settlements of San Javier and Ofir in Río Negro department.[20] Birkett remarked that Uruguayan officials did not regret the departure: 'According to Uruguayan officials I have talked with on the subject, no tears are being shed over the departure of these Russians. The 106 to leave so far represent about 10% of the community of agriculturalists whose activities on occasions have been a source of irritation to the government.'[21]

On 30 July the Canadian Embassy in Montevideo reported that *El Dia*, 'one of the more responsible "Colorado" government party papers,' had congratulated the Argentine government for its decision to investigate the return-to-the-homeland movement. This report called on the Uruguayan government to do the same. The newspaper drew attention to the 'pro-Russian 'Uruguayan' party,' which 'exercised powerful influence in the Slavic agricultural colonies, mainly through the activities of an organization called the "Slavic Union of Uruguay."' The paper continued: 'The coercive influence which these local branches [of the Slavic Union] are assiduously pursuing is entrusted to their respective Directing Committees formed entirely of men of Slavic origin whose pro-Soviet activity is well-known.'[22] Apart from ethnic Russians from the San Javier and Ofir settlements, the main participants in the return-to-the-homeland movement from Uruguay seem to have been – as in the Argentine case – people of Ukrainian, Belarusian, and Lithuanian background.

There were also departures to the Soviet Union from Paraguay, and here political repression may have hastened the movement. In 1955, shortly after the ascension to power of Alfredo Stroessner, Ukrainians and Belarusians sympathetic to the Soviet Union were subjected to persecution, eliciting a wave of protests.[23] Rumours later filtered to Paraguay that the Ukrainians and Belarusians who had moved to the

Soviet Union were not being resettled in their original homes in Ukraine or Belarus, but were being sent instead to Kazakhstan in Central Asia.[24]

In the spring of 1956. after the ships carrying 'repatriates' from Argentina, Paraguay, and Uruguay had docked in Odessa, the *New York Times* reported that as many as 30,000 people would be leaving Argentina, Uruguay, and Paraguay by the end of the year. This news caused a stir and was received with some scepticism in Ottawa. A letter from the DEA Under-Secretary to the Canadian Embassy in Buenos Aires drew attention to a 'further news report published in the United States [that] casts doubt on the *New York Times* report that as many as 30,000 Ukrainians and Byelorussians would probably return from Argentina, Uruguay and Paraguay.' The same letter asked the embassy to provide comments on the reports about the 'repatriation drive' in South America.[25] Picard determined how the figure had been arrived at: 'Mr. [Edward] Morrow [the author of the *New York Times* report] explained that Mr. Payne of Time Magazine, and himself arrived at the figure of thirty thousand by adding up the number of bookings for the next twelve months supplied by navigation companies.'[26]

Canadian interest focused on how Argentina was responding to the campaign. The exodus from that country in 1955–6 was straining Argentine–Soviet relations; the Argentinean view was that the Kremlin was exerting too much influence over local people of Slavic origin. According to diplomatic historian Stephen Clissold, relations between the two countries in the postwar era were tested on a number of instances, albeit without 'ever reaching the point of rupture.'[27] The first major crisis identified by Clissold 'arose as the result of Soviet attempts to exert political influence over the large communities of Russians and other Slavs resident in Argentina and the River Plate countries, and later through Moscow's attempts to repatriate members of the Russian [*sic*] communities to the Soviet Union.'[28]

In the early 1950s, pro-Soviet Ukrainians, Belarusians, Lithuanians, and Russians had regrouped under the Federation of Soviet Citizens' Clubs (FSCC). One goal of these clubs was to prepare members to resettle in the Soviet Union. Vladzimir Klimashevsky, a prominent Belarusian member of the Argentine Federation of Sports and Cultural Organizations of Soviet Citizens (a successor to the FSCC), told a visiting Soviet delegation in 1989 that 'previously, clubs organized by Soviet citizens in Argentina pursued only one goal – to help their members return to the Soviet Union.'[29]

The resettlement movement from Argentina began in earnest in 1955 and gathered momentum in 1956. By mid-August 1956, Soviet officials had been instructed to stop inciting the departures, but by then about five thousand individuals had left Argentina, Paraguay, and Uruguay over the previous four months to resettle in the Soviet Union.[30] While photographers in Odessa filmed and publicized the disembarkation of these returnees from South America, the Soviet embassy in Buenos Aires was busy refuting notions that it was encouraging the departures. One embassy official dismissed such charges as 'preposterous': 'We do not have to engage in propaganda – people always have a natural desire to return to the homeland.'[31]

The Argentinean government was not convinced of this, and it is clear that the Canadian government shared some of its misgivings. The Argentinean Ambassador in Ottawa, Carlos Torriani, spoke of the eagerness of Jules Léger, the DEA Under-Secretary, to cooperate in the exchange of information on the 'Return to the Homeland' campaign: 'He [Leger] received my information and commentaries with the greatest interest and did not think twice in considering it of real importance for all the countries in the continent.'[32] The Canadians, he added, were studying the problem 'with full attention' and would let the Argentineans know the results of that investigation. Torriani concluded: 'The Royal Canadian Mounted Police has an exchange of information on this [return-to-the-homeland] matter with all the countries that are members of NATO and with the corresponding office in Washington, where information that comes from the states which form part of the Organization of American States is centred.'[33]

Torriani also remarked that the Canadians were comparing the earlier exodus of the Yugoslavs to the Soviet return-to-the-homeland campaign. It was said that only five hundred of the two thousand Yugoslavs who had returned were able to leave again for Canada; moreover, the Canadian government regarded the problem of the Yugoslav returnees as 'unresolved..' Torriani added that the Canadian police detected discontent as the dominant mood among the Yugoslav returnees but added that 'it cannot be discounted that a more or less important percentage [of the returnees] has been indoctrinated as Communist propagandists and that they appear among those who most energetically express their disillusionment.'[34]

Argentina's response to the 'return to the homeland' campaign was informed in part by fears that today's returnees might tomorrow become Soviet agents in the River Plate region. In 1955, after General Pedro Aramburo deposed Juan Domingo Perón in a coup and formed a provisional government, a communiqué of the State Secretary of Information (SIDE) read:

> In the judgment of this office the [movement] could be more serious and dangerous. In the contingent of Russians [*sic*] who emigrate are an increased number of native Argentine youth, today children, who will possibly be educated and indoctrinated in Communist practices, in order to be converted into active agents of the system and then develop in our country – admission to which cannot be denied them considering that they are Argentineans – political activities pertaining to that ideology.[35]

The first clear sign of a chill in relations between Argentina and the Soviet Union came on 31 May 1956, when the Soviet naval attaché, Captain Alexander Morozov, was declared persona non grata for reasons not immediately disclosed. He was ordered to leave the country within twenty-four hours. One source linked Morozov's expulsion to allegations that he was actively arranging passage for repatriates.[36] In 1957 the Argentinean government banned travel to the Soviet Union on the grounds that Moscow 'was blocking the return of persons lured from Argentina by Communist propaganda.'[37]

No such action was ever followed by the Canadian government, though Ottawa did, through its representatives in Moscow, voice a similar protest with respect to Canadian returnees. Developments in the return-home drive in South America were reported in the Canadian press, albeit not extensively. An AP report carried by the *Globe and Mail* in July 1956 told readers that a ship carrying about one thousand people had left Buenos Aires for the Soviet Union – the third such sailing in three months – and that the mass departures were causing local concern. Most of the people leaving, an Argentine army spokesman stated, were 'needed to work in Argentine cotton and wine-growing areas.'[38] Other than that report, though, the Canadian mainstream press said very little else about the resettlement movement from South America to the Soviet Union, especially compared to the coverage in the *New York Times*. The Canadian press paid more attention to the 'return-home' topic as it related to the Doukhobors in Canada. A plan to settle 2,440 members of the Sons of Freedom sect – whose earlier efforts to move to Uruguay had failed – in the Altai region was the topic of ongoing discussion in 1958.[39] In the end the mass resettlement never materialized, in part owing to lack of Soviet enthusiasm for the project.

In contrast, the South American return-to-the-homeland movement was given significant coverage in the Ukrainian-Canadian press. *Novyi shliakh* ran a report about Uruguay submitted by a correspondent in Buenos Aires. From that report it can be determined that the San Javier and Ofir group mentioned by Birkett – which had left on 29 June – had not been the first group to leave Uruguay for the Soviet Union. According to *Novyi shliakh's* correspondent, the evening Buenos Aires daily *La Razón* had in February 1956 reported departures from the departments of Río Negro and Paysandú in Uruguay. Uruguay's Interior Minister, Francisco Gamara, had asserted then that the departure was of no importance because only communist sympathizers were leaving. In Gamara's view, it was better for 'freedom-loving' Uruguay that they leave – and better for the participants themselves, for they would see the realities of communism with their own eyes.[40]

Many reports about South America were printed in the Russian-language newspaper *Vestnik*, organ of the Federation of Russian Canadians (FRC). Developments in South America were of more than passing interest to *Vestnik's* readers. Many FRC members were Ukrainians (especially from Volhynia) and Belarusians who had settled in Canada in the 1920s and 1930s. Some of them had relatives who had immigrated to South America those same years. A significant portion of those who resettled in the Soviet Union from both Canada and South America were immigrants who had arrived in the interwar period and their locally born offspring. The returnees from Canada tended to be leaving the more urbanized provinces of Ontario and Quebec (i.e., rather than the Prairies).[41] In contrast, if one goes by the *Globe* article on Argentina, many of the returnees from South America were farmers.

The ties between Slavic communities in Canada and South America were reinforced by representatives' visits. The article 'Russian Women Write from Uruguay,' published in *Vestnik* on 27 June 1956, provides an example of such links. Writing from San Javier, Alejandra R. de Bugaiev noted that the previous year G. Okulevich had travelled from Canada to Uruguay. San Javier had been on his itinerary. Meanwhile, she continued,

M. Roslak from San Javier had arrived in Canada for a Slav Congress.[42] In spring 1956, Panas Hubarchuk wrote an article in *Vestnik* that linked Canada with South America. He wrote that between 1926 and 1938, hundreds of thousands of people from worker and peasant families in Western Ukraine had been forced by conditions to emigrate, and that many of them had sought a better life in Canada, Argentina, Uruguay, Paraguay, and Brazil. Hubarchuk, former editor of the pro-Soviet newspaper *Svitlo* in Buenos Aires, went on to detail the story of Panas Korol, who returned from Argentina to the Soviet Union and settled in Lutsk.[43]

The press of the pro-Soviet Association of United Ukrainian Canadians (AUUC) also covered developments in South America. In 1955 the English-language *Ukrainian Canadian* published a letter by the Canadian Slav Committee to President Alfredo Stroessner (president and dictator of Paraguay, 1954–89), which protested the persecution of Slavs in Paraguay. The letter read:

> Canadians were amazed and alarmed to learn of the recent arrest and brutal treatment of 13 persons of Slavic origin in the town of Alpera, department of Encarnacion, in your country for the 'crime' of reading newspapers and books and carrying on cultural activities in their own language. They were even more shocked and angered to hear that subsequent to this event innocent people of that region, while protesting this act, were shot at and wounded by the Alpera police and that an additional 300 persons were arrested.
>
> We urge your immediate intervention in this case to secure the release of all imprisoned persons and permit Slavic people in your country to conduct their cultural activities in the language of their choice without further persecution.[44]

On 7 June 1956 the AUUC's *Ukrainske zhyttia* reported that in April of that year the Argentinean ship *Entre Ríos* had docked at Odessa with nearly eight hundred passengers. On their arrival these people, who had left the western regions of Ukraine and Belarus, had realized their dream of returning to the homeland. *Ukrainske zhyttia* went on to print accounts by several of the returnees, who had taken the train from Odesa to Lviv. 'I have faith in my new happy destiny,' said one. Said another: 'I will work well and honestly, together with all Soviet people, and [with them] struggle for peace and prosperity.'[45]

In response to comments made by Peter Krawchuk, a member of *Ukrainske zhyttia*'s editorial board, about the return-to-the-homeland movement from Canada, the United States, and South America, in March 1957 *Novyi shliakh* reprinted an article by F. Fedorenko, 'Idut na Rodinu' (They Are Going to the Homeland), which had first appeared in *Ukrainskyi prometei* (Detroit). In this lengthy article, Fedorenko described the East Berlin Committee for the Return to the Homeland as a 'nest of spies' and remarked that his main concern was not the committee itself but how the AUUC was responding to its campaign. He noted that the AUUC newspapers *Ukrainske zhyttia* and *Ukrainske slovo* had printed appeals that had first appeared in the committee's *Za povernennia na batkivshchynu* newspaper – appeals that urged Ivan Bahriany, Hryhorii Kytasty, and others to return to their homeland.[46] According to Fedorenko, Krawchuk had written that in 'Canada, USA, especially South American countries, there are thousands of people who want to return home ... In recent years from Canada a significant number departed to Ukraine, Belarus, and Russia.' Fedorenko quoted Krawchuk as saying that Ukrainian nationalists' propaganda would not stop the movement and the right of people to leave, notwithstanding the nationalist 'dirty campaign.'

Krawchuk was giving the impression, Fedorenko said, that the return-home movement was larger than was really the case. He maintained that since the start of the committee's operations in East Berlin only five thousand people of Ukrainian origin had actually returned. That number was only a tiny fraction of the two-million-strong Ukrainian community in the West, he pointed out. Moreover, of those five thousand people, 99 per cent, he said, had been swayed by communist propaganda. He estimated that the number of returnees who were non-communists could be counted in one hand. And how many political immigrants had returned? he asked. Not a single one, he insisted. Moreover, he continued, of the five thousand returnees, four thousand were coming back from Argentina alone and the rest from other countries. People were leaving from Canada as well, he said, but how? Quietly and without any propaganda, he declared. This was because it was not convenient for the AUUC to publicize the return-to-the-homeland movement in any major way when it was only their members who were returning. Fedorenko noted that many AUUC members had years earlier expressed their desire to return and had accepted

Soviet passports. Yet only now, when Moscow lacked peons in Kaza-khstan and in the mines of Siberia, was the Soviet Union taking these people from Canada. Turning his attention to Argentina, Fedorenko referred to the fuss made in the Soviet media about the arrival of the ships from South America. What was left unsaid, he asserted, was the number of these returnees who were in prison for anti-Soviet behaviour or who had taken their own lives. Private letters, he claimed, had alluded to instances of suicide among the returnees from Argentina. Fedorenko also contended that private letters from Galicia were making reference to returnees from Argentina, United States, and Canada wandering from place to place in search of a better life.[47]

Fedorenko seems to have understated the extent to which non-communists participated in the return-home movement; also, his references to Kazakhstan and Siberia seem to have been overstated. The return-to-the-homeland movement appears to have taken place *in spite of* developments in Central Asia and Siberia, not *because of* them. Canadian returnees usually went to the republic of their choice in the Soviet Union, if not always to their places of preference within those republics. Some did move from place to place, and a number of returnees from South America did settle in Kazakhstan, but the degree of pressure exerted on them to do so is not known. As far as can be determined, only a single returnee from Canada settled in that Central Asian republic.[48]

Regarding the AUCC's relative silence on the return-to-the-homeland campaign, as far as can be determined neither the AUUC's publications nor those of the FRC urged people to return to the Soviet Union. Both organizations, however, published upbeat letters from returnees. Vladzimir Klimashevsky was quoted as having told a visiting Soviet delegation that the clubs organized by Soviet citizens in Argentina had pursued the single goal of helping their members return to the Soviet Union. That does not seem to have been the strategy of either the AUUC or the FRC. On the contrary, in the case of the FRC at least, the leadership privately expressed concern about the impact that the loss of active members through resettlement could have on that organization's future.[49]

It is not inconceivable that some Argentineans were driven to suicide after returning to the Soviet Union. Fedorenko made that claim in his article but offered no specific cases to back it up. And by the time he noted that suicide was being mentioned in private letters, the Argentine government had been receiving word that many of the people who had resettled in the Soviet Union were regretting their decision – or that of their parents. That all was not well can be inferred from the following letter written by one such Argentine, which was confiscated before it could reach its destination:

12 February 1957.

Dear Friends:
In the first words of this letter, I want you to know that we are all well in health and wish the same of yourselves. We already have received your letter for which we are grateful, we already have been given a house with gas and heating, but even so it cannot be compared with over there. I am studying more or less fine, my brother is working as a mechanical fitter, my father at the foundry, and my mother as a silk weaver. My mother works three shifts, afternoon, morning, and night. The factory is close to all of us. We miss you all a lot. Dear Anita [? First letter not very legible], you ask me if I with my brother would like to come to your home to drink [yerba] mate. I would like that very much! And if I could, I would do so right now. Write if there are rumours of any return from here and if it is possible to return, and that way we can think of something. And if you can help, please help, I ask this of you and also my *tios* [uncle and aunt or uncles]. In Kyiv there are 13 families, residents of Argentina. When we get together in the evenings we all speak of how it was over there. We in every minute remember you in our words. My mother also remembers you, and also the factory. Write to us when a ship will sail for here, who is travelling. Those who are thinking of travelling, should do so more to the chief cities, because if they go to the countryside it is the misery. You also ask if my grandmother is with us. She as always prepares the meals for us. Okay, for now I do not have anything more to write. Many hugs and kisses to all from us, regards and kisses, my mother sends her regards to the boss of the factory … Prompt reply, write much, find out!
[Signature] Lydia. A million thanks for the postcard, it is very pretty.

The address is:
USSR   USSR
g. Kiev 94   cap. Kiev 94
KP   KP

Ul. Diagonal'na	Calle Diagonal
Dom. N 4B	Casa 4B
Kvartira 57	departamento 57
Grivenets [?]	Griwieniec
Lidia N.	Lydia Elena[50]

The sentiments expressed in Griwieniec's letter may not have been atypical of young people who had moved from Argentina – or, for that matter, from Canada. Canada-born returnees often settled in the same places as those who had come from Argentina. Indeed, Canadian and Argentinean returnees socialized with one another – interactions that in at least one case led to marriage.

According to Carlos Torriani, in 1956 the Canadian government had considered the earlier movement of local Yugoslavs to their original homeland an 'unresolved' problem. After 1956 the Canadian and Argentinean governments could likewise regard the more recent resettlement in communist countries as an issue that had yet to be resolved. It is not known whether Lydia Elena Griwieniec ever moved back to Argentina. Some of the returnees who desired to move back were eventually able to do so, though they were a minority of the participants in the return-home movement. According to Myjailo Vasylyk, author of a book on the Ukrainians in Argentina, only one-quarter of the re-emigrants returned to that River Plate republic.[51] The Hispanic Club, formed in the city of Lutsk, Ukraine, in 1990, bears testimony to the presence of the participants who remained. Not long after the club was founded, its members – bound by their common background in the River Plate countries – received a message of salutations from the Argentinean Embassy in Moscow.[52]

Conclusion

The hundreds of Canadians and thousands of others from South America who resettled in the Soviet Union in the second half of the 1950s represented only a small part of the communities of Eastern European origin in Canada and Latin America. As this essay has shown, the attention paid to that resettlement was out of proportion to the numbers. Canada and Argentina continued to receive significant immigration in the late 1950s that more than compensated for re-migration to the Soviet Union. Why, then, was so much attention paid to the issue? One an-swer must be that the movement took place at a time when a return-to-the-homeland campaign was in effect and that that campaign was waged in the context of the Cold War. When the American Senate Sub-committee on Internal Security investigating that campaign concluded in a 1956 report that 'the whole episode represented probably the bold-est activity entered upon by Soviet officials here in this country,'[53] it is not inconceivable that some Canadian and Argentine officials thought that the same could apply to their countries. The same American sub-committee added: 'Our government agencies have not been sufficiently aware of the strategic importance of defection and redefection in the struggle between the free world and the Soviet world.'[54]

Canada and Argentina followed different policies with regard to the return-to-the-homeland campaign. That said, the Argentinean reference to the Yugoslav-Canadian precedent indicates that the two countries shared similar concerns. Indeed, the idea that the returnees of the 1950s might become tomorrow's Soviet agents was raised in a discussion about smoothing the return to Canada of disillusioned families.[55]

Isidoro Gilbert, a former TASS correspondent in Buenos Aires, noted that one of the motives behind the return-to-the-homeland campaign was to demonstrate to expatriates that the Soviet Union had the capac-ity to assimilate their Western cultures.[56] However, Ukrainian Canadi-ans and others born outside the Soviet Union were not easily integrated into Soviet life – as suggested by Griwieniec's letter. Indeed, ultimately, the kind of disillusionment expressed in letters such as hers may have been a key factor in persuading the Soviet leadership to abandon the re-turn-to-the-homeland campaign altogether, whether in Canada, Ar-gentina, or elsewhere.

Notes

1 'Luring by Soviet Cited,' *New York Times,* 13 March 1956, p. 41.
2 'Ne pozhyly v nashomu 'raiu' kanadski ukraintsi,' *Ukrainske slovo* (Paris-Kyiv), 9 October 1993, 4. See also Walter Dushnyck, 'Stalin's Pan-Slavism in the United States,' *Ukrainian Quarterly* 4 (1948): 70, where he wrote that 'Several thousand Yugoslavs and Ukrainians are reported to have asked permission from the Canadian government to return to their homelands.'
3 LAC, RG25, vol. 7609, file 11327-40, pt 5.1, 1224–5.

4 Questions relating to the degree of interest, how actively Canada pursued information, and so on, are addressed in a book on the campaign in Canada. See Glenna Roberts and Serge Cipko, *One Way Ticket: The Soviet Return-to-the-Homeland Campaign, 1955–1960* (Manotick: Penumbra, 2008). The book is based to a large extent on LAC research. Myron Momryk helped locate files and other materials.

5 Summary of material from *Glos Polski*, 16 May 1956, LAC, RG25, vol. 7609, file 11327-40, pt 3.3.

6 LAC, RG146, vol. 37, file 94A-00199.

7 Oleh Semenovych Pidhainy, *Mr. Khrushchev Goes Slavehunting* (New York: FUP, 1956), 32.

8 LAC, RG25, vol. 7609, file 11327-40, pt. 3.3, 'Draft Statement for Minister's Use before the Standing Committee on External Affairs "Return to the Homeland" Campaign.'

9 Archives of the Ministerio de Relaciones Exteriores y Culto, Argentina, Expediente nota 647, Año 1963. 'Embajada en Brazil inf.s/ brasileños que residen en la Union Sovietica.'

10 LAC, RG25, vol. 7609, file 11327-40, pt 3.3, 'Letter by G.H. Southam to the Canadian Embassy, Buenos Aires, Argentina, June 5, 1956.'

11 See document 70 in Stephen Clissold, ed., *Soviet Relations with Latin America, 1918–1968: A Documentary Survey* (London: Oxford University Press, 1970), 176.

12 An Argentine census of the country's foreign-born population conducted in May 1947 enumerated 111,024 persons born in Poland, another 89,983 in Russia, 29,164 in Yugoslavia, 18,983 in Czechoslovakia, 13,516 in Lithuania, and 5,551 in Bulgaria – a total of 268,221 individuals born in those Eastern European countries. See Antonio Cirigliano, 'Población extranjera según su origen y radicación geográfica: Censos 1895, 1914 y 1947,' *Revista de la Dirección Nacional de Migraciones* 1, no. 3 (1960): 164–5. The total number, of course, does not include the offspring of immigrants born in Argentina or those who came as part of a fresh wave of immigration during and after 1947.

13 LAC, RG25, vol. 7609, file 11327-40(4), 737, letter from Philippe Picard to Secretary of State for External Affairs, 30 June 1956.

14 Ibid., 736.

15 According to one source, the immigration from Eastern Europe before 1968 comprised 98,581 from Austria (mainly from the former Habsburg Empire), 119,215 from Russia (mostly before the First World War), 54,078 from Poland, 40,799 from Romania, 29,002 from Lithuania, and smaller numbers from other countries. See Fernando L.B. Basto, *Síntese de história da imigração no Brasil* (Rio de Janeiro: n.p., 1970), 87–8.

16 Archives of Ministerio de Relaciones Exteriores y Culto, Argentina, Expediente nota 647, Año 1963. 'Embajada en Brazil inf.s/brasileños que residen en la Unión Sovietica.'

17 Summary of material from 'Independent Lithuania,' Montreal, 1-10-58, Foreign Language Press Review Service, Canadian Citizenship Branch, LAC, RG25, vol. 8536, file 11327-40, pt 6.7, 1524.

18 Letter from the Canadian Embassy in Montevideo, Uruguay, to the Under-Secretary of State for External Affairs, Ottawa, 6 July 1956. LAC, RG25, vol. 7609, file 11327-40(4), 721.

19 Ibid.

20 Ibid., 727.

21 Ibid., 722. There is no elaboration on the activities to which Birkett alludes, but it is possible that a source of irritation for the Uruguayan government may have been the ties developed between the San Javier inhabitants and the Soviet Embassy in Montevideo: during the war, San Javier had occupied a forefront position in Uruguay in the collection of aid for the Soviet Union. On San Javier and Ofir, see Serge Cipko and John C. Lehr, 'From Christianity to Communism: A Russian Colony on the Banks of the Río Uruguay,' *Prairie Perspectives: Geographical Essays* 3 (October 2000): 150–64.

22 LAC, RG25, vol 7609, file 11327-40, 890, letter from the Canadian Embassy in Montevideo to the Under-Secretary of State for External Affairs, Ottawa, 30 July 1956.

23 In response to the 'return to the homeland' campaign, at a press conference in Asunción on 16 October 1956, Edgar Insfrán, the Paraguayan Interior Minister, accused the Soviet Embassy in Buenos Aires of '"kidnapping" some Paraguayan citizens and sending them to the Soviet Union with forged passports.' He said that he considered Soviet manoeuvres 'a danger for the Americas and a flagrant violation of Paraguayan sovereignty' and that the foreign ministry planned to make its complaints known at the international level. Eighty-three settlers, he told reporters, 'had been carried to the Black Sea port of Odessa aboard three Argentine ships'; twenty of them, he continued, carried forged Soviet documents 'deliberately ignoring their Paraguayan nationality.' See 'Paraguayan Accuses Soviet of "Kidnappings,"' *New York Times*, 18 October 1956, p. 16.

24 See, for example, Roberto Zub Kurylowicz, *Tierra, trabajo y religion: Memoria de los inmigrantes eslavos en el Paraguay* (Asunción: El Lector, 2002), 54 and 180–82. The extent to which there had been resettlement from Paraguay to Soviet Central Asia is a topic that has not been explored, but the rumour may have stemmed in part from occasional reports in newspapers such as the Committee for the Return to the Home-

land's Ukrainian-language *Za povernennia na Batkivshchynu* of South American Ukrainians settling in Kazakhstan. See *Za povernennia na Batkivshchynu* 83–84 (November 1958). In one instance, it was said that the climate in Central Asia would be similar to the subtropical environments to which the settlers had been accustomed in Paraguay or Argentina. See *Rodina* 1 (1960).

25 LAC, RG25, vol. 7609, file 11327-40, 734, letter from the Under-Secretary of State for External Affairs, Ottawa, to the Canadian Embassy, Buenos Aires, Argentina, 4 July 1956.

26 LAC, RG25, vol. 7609, file 11327-40(4), 737, letter from Philippe Picard to Secretary of State for External Affairs, 30 June 1956.

27 Clissold, Soviet Relations with Latin America 1918–1968, 33.

28 Ibid. The roots of greater Soviet influence over expatriates in Argentina and elsewhere in the Americas can be traced to the wartime period when the Soviet Union was a member of the Grand Alliance. After the Nazis invaded the Soviet Union on 22 June 1941, a Slavic Committee was established in Moscow. The committee's organ, *Slaviane,* reported on the activities of Slavic communities abroad; it would continue publication into the period of the return-to-the-homeland campaign. Coordinating councils of the committee were set up abroad – in the case of South America, in Uruguay rather than in Argentina, which bucked the trend in the Americas during the war of initiating or restoring diplomatic relations with the Soviet Union. Argentina established diplomatic ties with the Soviet Union only after the war, in 1946. The Montevideo coordinating council of the Slav Committee was assigned the task of 'welding together their varied organizations and imposing a unified political line' (see ibid., 64n15). The strongest of the Slavic Unions developed in Latin America was the one in Argentina. The activities of the Slavic Union there disturbed the Argentine government; U.S. government officials also took an interest in them. The *New York Times* reported on 26 April 1949: 'It is known that the United States embassy, among others, has sent several reports on the organization [which] is believed to have at least 250,000 members.' Though the estimate of the membership figure was much too high, there is no doubt that before it was dissolved, the Slavic Union commanded significant support among Argentines of Slavic origin. Among its members were people who, like their counterparts in Canada, had exchanged their Polish passports for Soviet ones. According to estimates relayed by the Soviet ambassador in Buenos Aires to the Soviet Deputy Minister for Foreign Affairs, Iakov Malik, by 1948 there were '25,000 Soviet citizens, who with their families reach 50,000,

mainly Ukrainians, living in Argentina.' Cited in Isidoro Gilbert, *El oro de Moscú: La historia secreta de las relaciones argentino-soviéticas* (Buenos Aires: Planeta, 1994), 229n4.

29 See Natalka Semivolos, 'Glimpses of Argentina,' *Ukraine* (Kyiv) 1 (1990): 9.

30 Edward A. Morrow, 'Argentines' Exit to Soviet Ending,' *New York Times*, 23 August 1956, p. 8.

31 Morrow, '780 in Argentina Heed Call,' *New York Times*, 17 April 1956, p. 12.

32 Letter from Carlos Torriani to Dr D. Luis A. Podesta, the Argentine Minister of External Affairs and Worship, dated 18 July 1956. República Argentina, Ministerio de Relaciones Exteriores y Culto, La División 'H,' División Europa Oriental y Cercano Oriente, URSS, Año 1956, 'Exodo de personas con destino a U.R.S.S.'

33 Ibid.

34 Ibid.

35 Cited in Gilbert, *El oro de Moscu*, 196–97.

36 *La gran farsa* (n.p. Editorial Intercontinental, c. 1956), 4.

37 'Argentina Retaliates,' *New York Times*, 4 July 1957, 4.

38 '1,000 Set Sail from Argentine for East Europe,' *Globe and Mail*, 13 July 1956, 17.

39 N.G. Kosachova, 'The Doukhobors,' in *Russian Canadians: Their Past and Present*, ed. Tamara F. Jeletzky (Ottawa: Borealis, c. 1983), 30. For Canadian press reports, see, for example, 'B.C. Lays Down Strict Conditions for Doukhobors,' *Globe and Mail*, 17 April 1958, p. 8; and 'Offer Doukhobors Aid in Emigration, 16 August 1958, 1 and 2.

40 'Aktsiia povorutu na "Rodinu" z Argentini,' *Novyi shliakh*, 18 May 1956. According to one of the Uruguayan newspapers that had reported the departure of the 29 June San Javier and Ofir contingents, a further hundred individuals were expected to leave Uruguay for the Soviet Union on board the *Salta* on 11 July 1956.

41 This is the pattern that emerges from an examination of *Vestnik*, and *Ukrainske slovo* and *Ukrainske zhyttia* of the Association of United Ukrainian Canadians, and the East Berlin–based newspapers *Za povernennia na Batkivshchynu* and *Za vozvrashchenie na Rodinu*.

42 'Russkie zhenshchiny pishut iz Urugvaia,' *Vestnik*, 27 June 1956, 4. Grigorii Okulevich had not long before authored a history of Russian Canadians. See Okulevich, *Russkie v Kanade* (Toronto: Federation of Russian Canadians, 1952).

43 Panas Hubarchuk, 'Rodina pozabotilas o nikh,' *Vestnik*, 28 March 1956,

p. 6. Hubarchuk himself returned and wrote about life abroad in Argentina. See Panas Hubarchuk, *Za okeanom* (Kyiv: Derzhavne vydavnytstvo khudozhnoi literatury, 1960).

44 'Canadian Slavs Protest Arrests in Paraguay,' *Ukrainian Canadian*, 15 May 1955, 10.

45 *Ukrainske zhyttia*, 7 June 1956, p. 7.

46 Ivan Bahriany lived in the Federal Republic of Germany and was influential among post–Second World War eastern Ukrainian refugees in the West. His anti-repatriation brochure 'Why I Do Not Want to Return to the USSR' was translated and published in Canada. When the committee launched its campaign in the mid-1950s, Bahriany was again prominent in the opposition to repatriation efforts. In 1956 he wrote a book of satirical verse, *Anton Bida – heroi truda: Povist' pro Di-Pi* (n.p.: Ukraina, 1956). Bahrainy had written the verses between April and October 1955. See also *Ukrainski visti* (Neu Ulm), 29 July 1956. Hryhorii Kytasty directed the Shevchenko Ukrainian Bandurist Kapelle in Kyiv during the war as well as after the war, in Detroit, where it was renamed the Ukrainian Bandurist Chorus.

47 F. Fedorenko, 'Idut na rodinu,' *Novyi shliakh*, 4 March 1957, 6.

48 The person in question was Vasyl Trokal, born in Shtepelske *raion*, Sumy *oblast*, Ukraine, who immigrated to Canada in 1948. He left Canada for the Soviet Union in late 1955, settling in northern Kazakhstan. See *Vestnik*, 7 January 1956, 6.

49 See, for example, LAC, RG25, vol. 7609, file 11327-40, pt 3.3.

50 Letter confiscated at a post office in Kyiv, from the private collection of Viktor Mohylny, a well-known writer and collector of postal history in Kyiv.

51 Myjailo Vasylyk, *Inmigración ucrania en la República Argentina: Una comunidad por dentro* (Buenos Aires: LUMEN, 2000), 39.

52 *News from Ukraine* 29 (1990): 6; interview with Halyna Dougolsky, formerly of Uruguay, in Lutsk, 11 June 1990.

53 'Here's Latest Official Report on Red Activities in U.S.,' *U.S. News & World Report*, 15 March 1957, p. 149.

54 Ibid.

55 See 'Documents relatifs aux relations extérieures du Canada,' at http://www.international.gc.ca/department/history-histoire/dcer/details-fr.asp?intRefid=11176.

56 Isidoro Gilbert, *El oro de Moscu La historia secreta de las relaciones argentino-sovieticas* (Buenos Aires: Planeta, 1994), 196.

9

Polishing the Soviet Image: The Canadian-Soviet Friendship Society and the 'Progressive Ethnic Groups,' 1949–1957

Jennifer Anderson

The Canadian-Soviet Friendship Society (CSFS), launched in 1949 with Dyson Carter as its president, had the implicit approval of both the Canadian-based Labor-Progressive Party (LPP)[1] and authorities in Moscow to promote Soviet interests in Canada.[2] But as a phenomenon, this group was hardly new to Canada. Soviet friendship groups had existed since 1918, organized by radical Canadians who admired the Soviet socialist experiment. Then, after the Soviet Union became a valued – and necessary – wartime ally, friendship with the Soviets was promoted by some of the most prominent Canadian politicians and businessmen of the time. Indeed, during the Second World War, Prime Minister William Lyon Mackenzie King was a patron of the National Council for Canadian-Soviet Friendship. However, following the 1945 defection of Igor Gouzenko from the Soviet Embassy in Ottawa, which revealed the existence of a spy ring run by embassy personnel, admiration for the Soviet Union became decidedly less popular.

The postwar CSFS, operating in the political climate of the early Cold War, used 'friendship' to appeal to Canadians who might otherwise have been put off by more politically overt declarations of admiration for the Soviets. This was an extension of the Popular Front appeal undertaken by Communist parties and communist-front groups during the war, by which they reached out to more mainstream groups. Together with peace activism and support for postwar price controls, the 'friendship' movement constituted an important part of the radical agenda in Canada after the Second World War. While the CSFS was superficially a non-partisan group, political messages were never far below the surface in its events and publications. Other researchers have touched on the links among the radical left-wing communities in Canada; regarding the CSFS, this interconnectedness was intentional[3] – indeed, it was probably one of the CSFS's most attractive features for members. In this linked community, the Soviet Union was a symbol of progressivism and a source of political and social group identity. For Soviet sympathizers and fellow travellers, it was comforting to be part of a larger community, given that mainstream Canadian public opinion was extremely critical of their views and their activism.

An examination of RCMP files, as well as the archives of the Soviets' own All-Union Society for Friendship with Foreign Countries (VOKS), makes it clear that the CSFS's mission was to liaise with ethnic groups – especially Ukrainians, Jews, and Finns – while attempting to recruit middle-class anglophones into the progressive movement. Indeed, the archives are full of references to materials shared and to relations between the CSFS and 'ethnic' leftist groups. There have been several very good historical studies of radicalism within particular ethnic groups in Canada, and of ethnic participation in the LPP/CPC. Less work has been done on the relations between the apparently 'non-ethnic' CSFS and other 'progressive ethnic' groups.[4] Understanding how the self-described 'pan-Canadian,' Anglo-Saxon[5]–led CSFS interacted with radical ethnic groups in Canada can tell us much about what it meant to be radical in Canada during the early Cold War.

While this was not necessarily the goal of the CSFS, many Ukrainian Canadians participated actively in the group. Indeed, Ukrainian Canadians were some of that group's most dedicated members and supporters. William Teresio, an executive member of the Association of United Ukrainian Canadians (AUUC), was also on the CSFS executive. Dyson Carter, president of the CSFS from 1949 to 1960, was always closely linked to the Ukrainian radical community. In fact, he had joined the same predominantly Ukrainian and Jewish North Winnipeg Communist Party Club as future CSFS supporter John Boyd (Boychuck) in the early 1930s, and they remained close acquaintances in later years (which has allowed this essay to make extensive use of Boyd as a source). The prominent Ukrainian-Canadian feminist and communist activist Mary Kardash served as secretary of the Winnipeg branch of the CSFS and in that capacity basically ran the Winnipeg operation for most of the

CSFS's existence. Meanwhile, Ukrainian-Canadian activists such as Pearl Wedro, Kay Hladiy, Ida Kovalevich (Edith Kowalewich), and Anna Sochasky were sent as CSFS delegates to the Soviet Union and on their return, at CSFS events, spoke enthusiastically at about their experiences. In her speeches, Sochasky made it clear that her admiration for the Soviet Union, her desire for peaceful relations with that country, and her Ukrainian-Canadian identity was central to her political activism and to her involvement in the CSFS.

These Ukrainian Canadians were not alone: the CSFS attracted members from various other groups of 'New Canadians' from Eastern Europe. The collective hopes and political views of these people aligned with their admiration for – and desire for friendship with – the Soviet Union. From their perspective that country represented a legitimate alternative to capitalism. Especially for those who had suffered during the Great Depression in Canada, it also symbolized hopes for a better world. But since the CSFS was intended to develop into a pan-Canadian (read Anglo-Canadian) symbol of friendship with the Soviet Union, the ethnic backgrounds of its members were often downplayed. Nonetheless, a careful analysis of the archival record reveals that Ukrainian Canadians played a large role in the CSFS and in the development of its policies. It also suggests that to better understand the experiences of Ukrainian-Canadian radicals, we need to examine their activities in the context of interethnic, radical political activism. Seeing them as participants in a pan-Canadian, multiethnic, socio-political movement is an important first step towards deepening this understanding.

Before 1945 the task of attracting ethnic as well as more 'Canadian' members to the communist movement had fallen largely to the Party. The 'language groups' had always been more popular than the main body of the CPC and had also raised more money. As other essays in this collection illustrate, members of these 'mass organizations' were often divided when it came to the political policies the Comintern wished them to adopt as well as to that organ's attitude towards linguistic and cultural matters. In 1929 the Comintern had decreed that the language groups would no longer be considered officially part of the CPC; instead they were to be 'recruiting grounds for Party membership.'[6] The more ethnically diverse CPC was to be the main link between Canadian Communists and the Soviet Union. But after Gouzenko's revelations in 1946, the LPP suffered a considerable loss of legitimacy.

A decade later the Soviets were still not impressed with the work of the CPC. A secret report prepared in 1955 by V. Loginov, counsellor at the Soviet Embassy, noted that the problem was that more than half of LPP members were 'immigrants' and that most of these were Ukrainian Canadians.[7] Despite this, Loginov argued, the nationalist Ukrainians in Canada continued to produce stronger propaganda and influenced a larger percentage of Ukrainian Canadians than the Communists.[8] This was disappointing for the Soviets, who wanted to influence mainstream Canadian public opinion. In that regard, catering mainly to 'immigrants' – and doing even that poorly – was not viewed as a sign of success. The Soviets were also concerned that the presence of too many Ukrainians in the Party would lead to 'bourgeois-nationalist tendencies,' or to admiration of the Ukrainian nation rather than the Soviet Union. VOKS supported the strategy of marketing Soviet–Canadian friendship to 'non-ethnic' Canadians, especially through the CSFS. In reaching out to the Canadian public (i.e., to anglophone[9] and middle-class Canada), VOKS hoped to make admiration of the Soviet Union far more widespread.

The CSFS was an important element in this strategy, for its leaders were Anglo-Saxon (or had adopted English-sounding names) and were seeking to promote 'friendship' with the Soviets in ways that appealed to middle-class artists, teachers, peace activists, and other members of the Canadian intelligentsia who did not self-identify as Communists. Clearly, progressive groups were not immune to the push for (apparent) assimilation. For example, John Boyd, an LPP member of Ukrainian origin, who was active in the left-wing ethnic communities in the early 1950s, was originally known by the surname Boychuk. He was asked by the CPC leadership to change his name in order to strengthen his influence in Canadian society.[10] According to Boyd, the CPC skilfully managed the organizations it supported – such as the Friendship Society, the Canadian Slav Committee, and various peace groups – in order to create the illusion of independent, non-partisan progressivism. Dyson Carter was among the best at this, he adds, for he was viewed by outsiders as suitably 'Canadian.' The overwhelmingly 'ethnic' composition of the CPC caused huge problems, according to Boyd, by saddling the Party with 'a foreign rather than a Canadian image.' This may well have added to the difficulties the Party had in retaining Anglo-Saxon members. Many Ukrainian and Jewish Party members changed their names at the request of the Party leadership. One of these was John Weir (Vyviursky), the Moscow correspondent for the *Canadian Tribune* and later editor of the *Ukrainian Canadian*. Another was Robert Laxer (also known as Robert Owen, but earlier as Mendel or Menachem), an LPP executive who once called Dyson Carter 'Canada's greatest novelist.'[11] Though the cultural events offered by the CSFS attracted Canadians who had immigrated from Eastern Europe, and who had often developed socialist ideals, the leaders – some of whom were the Canadian-born children of these same immigrants – were invariably chosen for their clear, unaccented speech and Anglo-Saxon names.[12]

The RCMP had been remarking on the ethnic make-up of the Soviet friendship groups for years. When Louis Kon promoted the Friends of the Soviet Union at a YMCA meeting in 1934, the RCMP reported that there were 'a goodly number of Anglo-Saxons' in attendance; clearly, it worried them that the contagion of pro-Soviet communism might spread through Canadian society.[13] In May 1943, in the wake of a meeting of the Society for the Study of Russia, the RCMP reported that 'a feature of the meeting as observed by members attending was the unusually large percentage of Anglo-Saxons present.'[14] This society's membership overlapped strongly with that of the National Council for Canadian-Soviet Friendship, minus the prominent politicians and businessmen.[15] A month later, at a National Council rally for the Soviet troops, the RCMP reported that 'at least 80 per cent of the persons present were of foreign extraction and it was noted that many well-known members of the C.P. of C. and the foreign mass language organizations occupied reserved seats in a block of the blue seats on the east side of the Gardens.'[16] The same report noted that the UN choir that had performed at the rally was made up of the choirs of the AUUC, the Federation of Russian Canadians (FRC), and the Jewish Labor League, conducted by Emil Gartner.[17] Gartner, a member of the league and later of the United Jewish People's Order, continued to be active in the CSFS as well; in 1951 he travelled to the Soviet Union with a CSFS-sponsored group. In 1953, remarking on the steady increase in CSFS activity, the RCMP worried that by acting as a Communist front organization and a 'clearing house' for Soviet materials, the CSFS was 'bringing to the fringe of communism groups of people across the Dominion, many of them innocent, who may, in turn, become sympathetic to communist ideology.'[18] The RCMP knew at that time that the LPP was raising funds to send CSFS delegates on Soviet tours; it may not have known the extent of the support it was receiving from VOKS.[19] Dyson Carter would have taken the RCMP's concern as a sign that he was meeting his objectives. Responding to an article in the *Financial Post* in January 1952, Carter expressed glee at the journalist's consternation over what he called the 'friendship front' used by Canadian leftists, boasting that CSFS strategies 'have played no small part in changing public opinion in Canada.'[20]

Sponsoring events, distributing photographs and films, and organizing trips to the Soviet Union were among the means by which the CSFS attempted to improve the Soviets' image in Canada. The organization heavily publicized the 'return to the homeland' campaign that had been launched by Nikita Khrushchev in the 1950s with the goal of persuading ethnic Ukrainians, Finns, Balts, Jews, Hungarians, and other East Europeans that returning to the Soviet Union to live – or at least to visit – would be a positive experience. Key events sponsored by the CSFS included a Canadian-Soviet Friendship Month arranged in November each year, timed to correspond with the anniversary of the Bolshevik Revolution. In addition, Carter through articles and correspondence promoted Canadian progressive writers, artists, and activists. He became well known in the Soviet Union as a leading Canadian writer.[21]

Left-wing groups in Canada shared human and financial resources. This was an effective way for a marginal movement to maximize its assets. It was also natural, in that members of these groups knew one another personally, often attended the same events, intermarried, and lived and worked in the same geographical areas.[22] Social and political networking was an important way for these individuals to express and act on their beliefs; it was also a way for them to shelter themselves from the scathing criticisms that Soviet sympathizers were receiving in mainstream Canadian society. In this social milieu, the Soviet Union symbolized progressive hopes and dreams. In interactions with outside groups, those left-wingers who could claim a more 'acceptable' name or accent could represent the movement and thereby improve its public image.[23] By studying the interactions between the CSFS and the 'progressive, ethnic' groups, scholars can gain insight into the effectiveness of the CSFS campaigns to make the Soviet Union look attractive to Canadians, as well as into the experiences of left-wing radicals in Canada.[24]

Shared Space, Materials, and Finances

The CSFS was founded by the LPP/CPC.[25] As a consequence, its personnel and readership overlapped with that of the 'language groups.'[26] Also, it used left-wing ethnic group halls across Canada for its meetings. RCMP investigators reading the ethnic press reported to their superiors on CSFS-related events held at these premises. Touring the Western provinces in 1950 to raise awareness of the CSFS, Dorise Nielsen spoke at the Doukhobor Dome in Verigin on 30 November 1950, and at the left-wing Ukrainian Hall in Wynyard, Saskatchewan, on 28 November.[27] In January 1951, CSFS meetings were held at the Ukrainian Labour Temples in Niagara Falls and Welland, Ontario.[28] In March 1953 the CSFS exhibited Soviet photographs and sponsored a talk by Dyson Carter in the Niagara Falls Hungarian Hall.[29] In November 1955 a CSFS event was held in the United Jewish People's Order's hall in Toronto.[30] In October 1951 the RCMP reported that a 'CSF-League evening was to take place at the Hungarian Hall in Niagara Falls, with Emil Gartner, his wife Fagel Gartner, Archie Hamilton, Alek Tichnovich and Dorise Nielsen (co-founder of the CSFS) speaking on their recent trip to USSR.'[31] In January 1953, performances of the United Jewish Peoples' Order choir, directed by Emil Gartner,[32] and the AUUC choir, directed by Eugene Dolny, followed speeches given by Dyson Carter and Dorise Neilsen of the Friendship Society.[33] In 1954 the Russian-Canadian newspaper *Vestnik* reported that more than five hundred people had attended a CSFS film screening in Grand Forks, British Columbia, and that most of them had been Doukhobors and Ukrainians.[34] In a 1955 letter to his Moscow chief, the VOKS representative in Ottawa, A. Tovstogan, reported that the 'National committee of CSFS organized and ran 20 Nov. this year a meeting of the Toronto branch of the CSFS dedicated to Canadian Soviet friendship. This meeting took place in one of the big halls belonging to the progressive organization Jewish People's Order.'[35] Tovstogan added that Carter's speech, 'Towards the Further Strengthening of Canadian-Soviet Friendship,' had been well received and was at times 'interrupted by applause.'[36] In the Soviet Union this counted as high praise.

Besides sharing space, the CSFS shared information and materials with the progressive ethnic groups. Regarding materials sent to and from the Soviet Union, the VOKS representative at the Soviet Embassy in Ottawa played a crucial role. He collected letters and other materials to send to the VOKS headquarters in Moscow, together with reports on the activities of progressives in Canada and other newsworthy items. He also received packages from Moscow and distributed their contents to the CSFS.[37] Because these packages often contained information and packages from the VOKS republic branches in the Ukrainian and Belorussian capitals, and were actually destined for the AUUC and FRC, the CSFS found itself acting as a redistributor of such materials.

In May 1956 the VOKS representative in Ottawa was informed that the Latvian Soviet Socialist Republic had founded a VOKS-affiliated Society for Cultural Ties Abroad. The Moscow headquarters asked 'whether in Canada there exists some kind of progressive organization of Latvian emigrants. If it exists let us know whether it is worth it in your opinion to establish a link and send a short report on it. In the report it is desirable to show the make-up of the organization and its leadership.' Headquarters also asked what activities such a group might be planning and what materials it might need.[38] The group in Latvia was told that 'Comrade Tovstogan answered that in Canada for the moment that kind of progressive cultural-enlightening organization amongst emigrants from Latvia does not exist. There does exist amongst that emigration an organization which is nationalistic and diffuses sharp anti-Soviet propaganda.'[39]

The progressive groups in Canada sometimes sent requests via the VOKS representative in Ottawa for particular materials from the Soviet Union. For instance, the director of the Federation of Russian Canadians choir, Alex Tichnovich, requested a song collection.[40] Also, in October 1956, Tovstogan wrote that 'the leadership of the Federation of Russian Canadians wrote to VOKS with the request to send to its address, if possible, two copies of the *spravochnik* [guide book] by administrative division of the Ukrainian SSR and the Belorussian SSR. These *spravochniks* are quite necessary to the federation, as Russian Canadians often come to the FRC requesting help in finding the address and place of birth according to the new administrative divisions.'[41] In 1956 the AUUC choir director, Eugene Dolny, asked for Lithuanian and Latvian folk music to be sent via VOKS.[42]

Packing slips and other correspondence from Moscow note for whom and what groups the materials were destined. From these documents we learn that many hundreds of books were sent to the CSFS via VOKS and that a good number of books were also sent to the AUUC, the FRC, and others on request. Usually there were multiple copies. From the last pages of *News-Facts* – and, later, *Northern Neighbors* – it can be seen that these items were for sale. Titles included the works of Lenin, Stalin, Marx, and other Marxist theoreticians, as well as Russian and Ukrainian literary classics and more recently published Soviet works. Many of the books sent to the CSFS were on topics related to scientific discoveries and health. After the XXth Party Congress in 1956 the VOKS representative received 350 copies of a collection of resolutions from the congress in English to be distributed in Canada. Perhaps not surprisingly, this package did not include a single copy of Khrushchev's speech.[43] One order form filled out by the CSFS secretary, Jim Leech, for books from the Soviet book distributor Mezhdunarodnaya Kniga listed one hundred copies of certain books, with never fewer than twenty-five copies of any book in English, or five in French. No mention was ever made of the CSFS paying for these.[44]

Invoices for the customs and excise officials listed books sent from VOKS to the CSFS and showed the value of each book listed in rubles. However, the price to be paid by the receiver was listed as 'free.'[45] From VOKS's perspective, this was an effective way to disseminate Soviet literature in Canada; from the CSFS's perspective, it was an important source of income. The books and other materials were advertised in the bulletins of the various ethnic groups and in their annual picnic souvenir programs.[46] This probably also allowed both groups to avoid customs duties and other taxes. Eventually the volume of this book-selling business increased to the point that the Northern Bookhouse was opened in Gravenhurst under Charlotte Carter's name. In 1952 the CSFS financial statements under the line item 'Sales of other literature' listed the income from these books as $1,879.80. The following year, the figure was $3,005.97.[47] When Carter sold the bookhouse premises in the late 1980s, he received $99,000 – a considerable profit, considering he had bought it for just $20,000.[48]

The VOKS representative in Ottawa sent books and other materials directly to the AUUC and the FRC and sometimes to the Lithuanian progressive organization. At other times materials were sent to the CSFS for it to forward. For example, in December 1955 Carter wrote to VOKS requesting materials for Armenian progressives, who did not have access to literature elsewhere. Carter wrote: 'At this time we have a request to make. For the first time, we have succeeded in having a meeting with Canadian-Armenians. It was a fine meeting, and we hope to have more. The people want us to try to get Armenian literature from the Armenian SSR. Will you do your best to get us some literature? I am writing directly to Armenian VOKS, so they will know that at long last we have started some work among the Armenian people here.'[49]

VOKS headquarters passed this message on to its branch in the Armenian SSR[50] and received a reply to the effect that they had already sent books and a list of other available literature directly to Dyson Carter.[51] In 1953 Carter asked for material in Finnish,[52] and in March 1956 the CSFS requested literature in Lithuanian.[53] Later, this proved unnecessary, perhaps because Carter was able to put those who had requested the literature in contact with the Lithuanian progressive organization. In April 1956, Tovstogan wrote to his superiors that 'the number of periodicals sent by you to the address of the Lithuanian progressive organization is sufficient, and subscribing the CSFS to the same editions is not worthwhile. As regards sending artistic literature in Lithuanian to the CSFS, that will not be necessary.'[54]

From time to time, VOKS requested particular kinds of information, needed for use in the Soviet Union. For example, in January 1956 a request arrived that the AUUC, the FRC, the CSFS, and other organizations send VOKS any newspapers, brochures, books, and other materials on the effects of the October Revolution on Canadian political life, for possible display in Moscow's Museum of the Revolution.[55] In addition, VOKS often asked Tovstogan to provide information on how the materials being sent from Moscow to the progressive groups were being used.[56] There were other requests for information as well. In April 1956 a report on the 7th Congress of the AUUC, held in February of that year, was prepared; it was sent to Moscow in May. The report contained the names of the most active AUUC members (including Misha Korol, Helen Weir, Peter Prokopchak, and John Boychuk) and discussed their activism. It also described the problems the AUUC was having with finances, leadership turnover, and 'nationalist propaganda.'[57] Clearly, VOKS's links with the Canadian left were integral to Canadian–Soviet friendship and to leftist political activism. From the Soviet perspective, however, there was also an element of surveillance.

The RCMP conducted its own surveillance. Its files relating to the Canadian left tell us that cooperation between the CSFS and other groups involved sharing space, materials, and funds. An RCMP report from November 1957 notes that a CSFS meeting had been held at the AUUC hall in Calgary to celebrate the 40th anniversary of the October Revolution and that sixty people had attended.[58] Several speakers enthused about conditions in the Soviet Union, particularly Ukraine, and funds were raised for the LPP. The reporting officer wrote that 'in making an appeal for funds [unnamed person] pointed out that the only political organization that is fighting for the working man with the tradition of Lennin [sic] and Marx in the background is the Labor Progressive Party, who have the interest of the working man at heart at all times.' He also noted that the CSFS had sponsored the event 'in order to deceive the public with the hope that a much larger group would attend. This meeting was actually under the sponsorship of the Labor Progressive Party and the profit derived from same was turned over to the Labor Progressive Party.'[59] The CSFS did try to appeal to a broad Canadian audience, but its readership and financial support came most consistently from the LPP and the 'language groups.'

Funds were routinely raised by the various progressive ethnic groups for the Canadian-Soviet Friendship Society. In one instance, *Vestnik* published a thank you note from the CSFS addressed to 'all organizations and persons who aided the Society in organizing the trip of the Trade Union delegation to the Soviet Union.' Various groups on the Canadian left had raised $1,301.82 for this CSFS-sponsored trade delegation, which toured the Soviet Union in 1952.[60] In 1951, John Weir, editor of the *Ukrainian Canadian,* launched a campaign to raise money for the CSFS, and the FRC also made donations.[61] Carter appealed directly to local branches of the FRC, asking them to read his letters aloud at meetings, to subscribe to at least one copy of his publication for their branch, and to contribute financially to the cause of Soviet friendship.[62]

Ticket sales also provided financial income for the CSFS, which sponsored concerts, film screenings, and photography exhibitions. Entry was often for ticket holders only. The society worked hard to convince progressive Canadians – especially Jews – that there was no anti-Semitism in the Soviet Union.[63] An important part of this persuasion was the sponsorship of the Reverend Hewlett Johnson, the 'Red Dean of Canterbury,' on his tour of Canada in February 1953. The RCMP reported that the tour was meant to counter information given by the anti-communist Canadian Jewish Congress regarding official anti-Semitism in the Soviet Union. At the University of Western Ontario the dean was heckled when he gave a whitewashed version of the Soviet treatment of minority and religious groups, and he avoided speaking on this issue for the rest of his visit.[64] The CSFS literature described the dean's tour as 'tear[ing] down the "velvet curtain" of silence'; it also spun the negative reception he received in London, Ontario, as a stifling of freedom of speech.[65] His appearance in Toronto at Massey Hall was sold out, and careful attention was paid at the door to allow only ticket holders to enter. Though this was a CSFS-sponsored event, attendees included members of the UJPO, Jewish individuals from the LPP, and the broader public. Plainly, the CSFS saw itself as a linchpin between a broader progressive community and the ethnic groups.

It is unclear who paid Carter's salary, but he definitely received some money from the LPP. According to John Boyd, when Carter left the CSFS in the late the 1950s, he continued to receive support from the LPP because his newspaper, *Northern Neighbors*, was so popular, including in the United States.[66] This corresponds with the RCMP's notes. In a 1963 report the RCMP mentioned that the LPP had agreed to continue to subsidize Carter's work because *Northern Neighbors* was 'useful.'[67] Much later, Carter's second wife, Sally Nielsen, remembers Party executives coming to ask Carter for a cut of the money he was making in the bookhouse.[68] She also recalls Soviet Embassy personnel bringing cash to him – money that he did not deposit in the bank but kept hidden in the house.[69] This direct financing may have begun while Carter was in charge of the CSFS, but it is certain that he received in-kind financial backing from the Soviets as early as 1951 by way of books and other objects for sale.[70] When his books and other writings were published in the Soviet Union, he was entitled to royalty payments.[71] Under Carter's leadership the CSFS was capable of competent coordination, shrewd financial planning, and effective persuasion. Carter was, in effect, an ideological entrepreneur. This is why the Soviet authorities valued his contributions so much that, even after 1960, when he was no longer running the CSFS, he maintained close contact with individuals in Moscow and the Soviet Embassy in Ottawa.

Exhibitions, Sales, and Soviet Friendship Month

The CSFS also requested that items be sent from the Soviet Union for exhibition and sale. Sales of these items were noted in the annual financial reports sent back to VOKS. These materials represented important Soviet in-kind financial backing for Carter. A three-page inventory stamped 10 April 1956 and headed 'List of Artistic Handicrafts and Sewn Items Sent to the Embassy of the USSR in Canada for the CSFS' listed close to ninety tablecloths of different sizes and designs, papier mâché boxes decorated with images from Russian fairytales, ashtrays, teacups, and glasses.[72] Carter explained his request this way: 'We have also been asked (because of the great success of the Slav Handicrafts Exhibit) if it would be possible for us to obtain something of a similar nature; perhaps a small collection of industrial-production consumer goods. We believe that the majority of Canadians still do not know that Soviet consumers can buy a wide range of highest-quality goods, such as photographic equipment, cosmetic articles, etc.'[73]

The material arrived in the summer in four separate boxes. Tovstogan noted that it was forwarded on to the CSFS for exhibition in fall 1956. Shipping costs were covered by VOKS.[74]

But the CSFS did not always reap the financial rewards of the exhibit. So that it would reach mainstream audiences, the CSFS tried to have the exhibit hosted by more 'neutral' groups. In 1955 the CSFS organized a series of exhibitions of Soviet children's paintings in Montreal art galleries. Owing to the 'difficult situation in Quebec' (i.e., the Duplessis government's Padlock Law and active opposition to all leftist groups), the CSFS could not take public recognition for these exhibitions. Instead, Carter asked Louis Kon to make the arrangements privately.[75] Following what proved to be a success, Carter suggested to VOKS that an exhibition of Soviet dolls be arranged.[76] He argued that 'in view of the big success of the Soviet Children's Paintings (which you know have been seen by many thousands of Canadians, in many centers),' a doll exhibit should be sent. He also pointed out that such displays were 'very popular in Canada, and draw wide audiences, not only of the general public and school children, but also intellectuals, artists, teachers, etc.' Drawing an audience from the wider Canadian society was an important consideration; so was being able to offer the exhibit for non-political groups to show.[77] Carter was disappointed that the exhibit could not be prepared in time for Soviet Friendship Month,[78] but he continued to organize events of this type, which fit well with a growing and genuine Canadian interest in ethnic handicrafts.

Such exhibits and promotions were never more prominent than during Friendship Month. The CSFS began in 1951 to organize an annual Soviet Friendship Month every February, changed to November in 1954 to coincide with the anniversary of the Bolshevik Revolution.[79] Friendship Month provided an umbrella for activities in CSFS branches across the country, thereby uniting the (often small) local groups in a larger program. The activities were publicized in CSFS publications. Letters sent to readers and members were meant to build excitement and, it was hoped, fill the society's coffers. Events such as these were often organized in cooperation with local progressive ethnic-group branches, and members were encouraged to plan with the local AUUC and FRC 'and all other organizations that support our aims.'[80] For instance, in November 1954, Yugoslav, Macedonian, and Ukrainian groups in Toronto jointly sponsored the screening of a film about a recent visit of Canadians to the Soviet Union; Dyson Carter spoke to the Finnish Organization of Canada (FOC) about the need for a trade mission to the Soviets; Ted Baxter spoke on the same subject at the Carpatho-Russian Hall; and the FRC held a film meeting.[81] All of these events were organized under the auspices of Soviet Friendship Month.

Progressive Canadians were encouraged to attend these events. The CSFS advised all branches to make their activities known through the progressive press, including the *Canadian Tribune*, the *Ukrainian Canadian*, the FRC journal *Vestnik*, the Finnish newspaper *Vapaus,* and the *Polish Weekly Chronicle*.[82] In 1953 the Labor-Progressive Party sent a missive to its national membership encouraging them to support the Friendship Month activities.[83] In announcing the final concert of the 1954 Friendship Month in Vancouver, the local LPP branch wrote: 'Members are asked to fully support this event.'[84] The FRC reminded all its members that they were obliged to cooperate with all-Slav committees and with the Canadian-Soviet Friendship Society, 'whose aim is to throw a correct light on the life of the peoples of the Soviet Union.' FRC members were asked to attend Friendship Month activities 'but also to aid the Society morally and materially.'[85] In January 1953 the editor of *Ukrainske slovo* (Ukrainian Word) urged readers to remember to honour 'the late Matthew Shatulsky' and to mark the 'month of

Slavic unity and friendship' as well as Canadian-Soviet Friendship Month, 'held under the auspices of the Canadian-Soviet Friendship Society.'[86]

Carter and his assistants began early in the year to send specific requests to VOKS for materials to be used during Friendship Month. Sometimes requests were made for items to be exhibited and sold, including Soviet books, photographs, handicrafts, and household items. Also, many requests were made for films to be shown at these exhibitions. Thus in October of 1955 Dyson Carter wrote directly to VOKS in Moscow: 'On behalf of our National Council I wish to thank VOKS very warmly for the wonderful displays, of photographs and works of art, etc., which we have just received. This material has arrived in excellent condition. It has come just in time for Friendship Month, and we shall do our best to make full use of it.'[87]

The following January, Carter wrote VOKS to say that the $530 raised by the sale of Soviet 'household goods' in November had been welcome: 'This income played a very important part in keeping the Society alive during November and December.'[88] Earlier, Carter had asked VOKS to send household goods, to show Canadians that Soviet people did have a standard of living that compared well to that of North America – a theme that foreshadowed the famous 'kitchen debate' between Nikita Khrushchev and Richard Nixon in 1959. Carter suggested that household goods would be a good investment in terms of image improvement for the Soviet Union. For that matter, the CSFS would benefit financially.[89] In the same letter he suggested that Soviet-made accordions might sell well in Canada. Would it be possible to send one in order to test the market? 'If it proved saleable, we might be able to arrange for someone here to import Soviet accordions on a commercial basis, for our Society or independently; and the Society would benefit, financially.'[90] It appears that VOKS did not take Carter up on this suggestion.

Carter during Friendship Month organized a collection of greetings to be sent to the Soviet Union on behalf of Canadian individuals and groups. Ahead of November 1955, the CSFS sent out a form to 350 organizations,[91] and also had it printed in *News-Facts*. It was addressed to 'Secretaries of organizations, and Chairmen of meetings! ... Help to make friends for Canada, in the Soviet Union! In Friendship Month, be one of the thousands who will send greetings to the Soviet people!'[92] Above the form, instructions were given on how to fill it in, and what groups or places in the Soviet Union might be appropriate recipients of greetings. Readers were encouraged to enclose a photograph or postcard, 'as a souvenir.' And above all, wrote Carter, 'remember to send the form back to *News-Facts* and the CSFS, both located at 753 Bathurst St. in Toronto, to be sure your greeting will be forwarded on to the USSR.'[93] At the top of the form, *News-Facts* readers were given the bonus of a Soviet stamp, with the following caption: 'Here you see a real Soviet postage stamp. We suggest you *keep* this souvenir of Friendship Month. If you decide to *visit* the Soviet Union (as thousands of Canadians soon will) you might *use this stamp* to mail a letter back home!'[94]

After the 1955 Friendship Month meeting, Tovstogan reported that 'greetings to the Soviet peoples from Canadians living in Toronto' had been approved. 'Analagous greetings will be approved at all meetings sent from various Canadian cities linked to Canadian-Soviet Friendship Month. At the end of the month, all greetings will be sent to VOKS.'[95] The groups sending greetings, which Carter sent to VOKS in December 1955, included AUUC branches in Point Douglas, Moose Jaw, Winnipeg, Transcona, Port Arthur, and elsewhere writing to towns in the Ukrainian Republic; FRC branches across the country writing to towns in the Russian and Belorussian Republics; UJPO branches writing to the Birobidjan Autonomous Region; and branches of the FOC sending greetings to the Karelo-Finnish Republic. CSFS branches in Hamilton, Vancouver, Winnipeg, and Welland wrote to cities across the Soviet Union. An LPP club in Vancouver wrote via the CSFS to the denizens of Vladivostok.[96]

Carter with the CSFS was serving as a liaison between progressive ethnic groups and attempting to present this initiative as a pan-Canadian hand of friendship extended to the peoples of the Soviet Union. Carter was careful to explain to VOKS that replies to these greetings should be sent to the CSFS and not directly to the sponsoring organizations: 'I would like to stress that any responses you can get for us, to these greetings, from the various places greeted, would arouse much interest among Friendship Society supporters in Canada, and we would see that the responses were given maximum publicity throughout the entire progressive movement.'[97]

In January 1956, Carter sent VOKS another long list of greetings, this time from individuals in Canada and the United States. He repeated that 'all replies should be addressed to *our Society;* although, of course, each reply should be directed to the person or persons who sent the particular message. We plan to publish as many of the replies as possible.'[98] The list included more than 130 individual greetings from the United States and Canada. The full names of those in Canada sending the greetings were listed, and those names appeared to be of Anglo-Saxon origin, as well as Ukrainian, Russian, and other ethnic backgrounds. At times, anonymity was preserved by listing the individuals as 'friends in Stenen, Sask' or 'friends in San Francisco, Calif. USA,' and so on. In fact, individual greetings sent from the United States named the sender by initials only. Destinations included particular towns or factories in Ukraine, Moscow, Stalingrad, Azerbaijan, Odessa, Sochi, and elsewhere in the Soviet Union. In February 1956, Carter sent a further list of greetings that included messages from Jim Leech and Ted Baxter, both assistants to Carter who would be leaving the CSFS later that same year as a direct result of the XXth Party Congress and Khrushchev's 'secret speech.'[99]

Groups and individuals in the Soviet Union responded to the greetings collected by the CSFS, and these replies were sent through VOKS back to the CSFS. For example, in April 1956 the VOKS representative in Ottawa received copies of the replies from the Kazakh Society for Cultural Ties Abroad and from the Stalingrad Committee for the Defense of Peace.[100] In May 1956 the reply from the middle schools of Moscow was sent.[101] In June 1956, workers from the Ternopil region in Ukraine sent return greetings to the Winnipeg branch of the AUUC, written in Ukrainian, wishing the peoples of the world peace.[102] The reply to the AUUC in Moose Jaw, from the Kostelnyky village in Ternopil region, also sent in June 1956, ended with this wish: 'May 1956 bring heightened friendship between our peoples.'[103] In each case VOKS noted that the original of the letter had been sent directly to the CSFS, which published these letters and made much of forwarding them on.

These greeting campaigns were not restricted to Friendship Month. Probably encouraged by the success of the 1955 campaign, Carter organized another one the following year. In March 1956 the CSFS collected messages for a telegram to be sent to the Bratsk Hydroelectric Station. Once the names were all collected, the telegram would be sent to VOKS in Moscow with an attached request that it be forwarded to

Bratsk.[104] In a letter, Carter asked CSFS members to send in the attached card plus 25 cents to congratulate and greet the Bratsk Hydro-electric Plant construction workers: 'Men and women have left comfortable homes all over the U.S.S.R., to carry out this remarkable job of peaceful construction. And some of your fellow-members of the Society want to greet them, to send them a word of encouragement and friendship from Canada ... And remember: The people at Bratsk are "the finest."'[105] It is difficult to judge the impact of these greetings. Most likely they did not persuade anyone to change their minds about the Soviet Union, but the CSFS did offer those who were already sympathizers a chance to express their wishes. Clearly, the CSFS was a medium for individuals who wished to offer alternative views on Cold War international affairs. Many of these Canadians may not have been aware of the degree to which this exercise was orchestrated by Carter as well as by VOKS in the Soviet Union.

The CSFS also participated in events organized by other progressive groups. For example, in November 1955 the Canadian Peace Congress organized a meeting of 1,725 delegates at Massey Hall in Toronto. Among those attending were CSFS representatives, as well as well-known peace activists like James D. Endicott, the Reverend D.S. Kendy, women's rights activist Mrs Rae Lucock, labour leaders, members of the CCF and the LPP, and John Boyd, Secretary of the Canadian Slav Committee. This meeting, and the presence of individuals sympathetic to the Soviet Union and to the progressive movement in Canada, was duly reported on by the VOKS representative in Ottawa.[106] Besides all this, Dyson Carter advertised his magazine and the book-house in the souvenir brochures issued by the AUUC and other progressive groups at special events, labour picnics, and anniversaries.[107]

Photographs and films played an important role in the work of the CSFS. Perceived as accurate, objective reflections of reality, they seemed to fulfil Carter's proclaimed goal, which was 'to tell the truth about the USSR.' He began running photos in *News-Facts* within the first few years of publication, and from then on the photo pages multiplied, photograph exhibits became part of the CSFS repertoire, and delegates fresh from touring the USSR showed their own pictures. Curious Canadians who might not otherwise have attended CSFS events were attracted by the opportunity to see behind the Iron Curtain 'for themselves' via the photos. Some perhaps came to see these photos for reasons of nostalgia. Most of these photos arrived direct from Moscow through VOKS, but after 1961 some came from the Novosti Press Agency Office in Ottawa.[108] Carter asked for photos 'showing different sides of life of the Soviet people' to be used in *News-Facts*.[109] Of course, any Canadians who visited the Soviet Union – especially those on CSFS-sponsored trips – were encouraged to take many photos and to send them in when reporting to Carter on their visit. These photos made it into CSFS publications and were shown at speaking engagements.

Photographic exhibitions such as 'Vacation below Moscow,' 'A Day at a Kolkhoz,' and 'Science and Religion' were sent to the CSFS for display; the dia-film 'Along the Halls of the Museum of the History of Religion and Atheism' was sent to Carter in 1957.[110] Having sent them, VOKS was strongly interested in getting feedback on how the photographs and films were being shown and on how Canadian audiences were receiving them. For example, after noting in March 1956 that 'on D. Carter's request we are sending 28 photographs of Soviet sportsmen and 13 photographs of artists of the theatre, ballet and cinema,' the VOKS official in Moscow summarized the work of the previous year: 'In 1955, VOKS sent to Canada 4 photo exhibits: "Soviet Uzbekistan"; "At the Soviet textile makers"; "VSKhV" [the All-Soviet Agricultural Exhibition in Moscow]; and "Sport in the USSR"; and a large quantity of other photoillustrative material.' He added: 'We ask you to tell us before 1 May of this year about the use of these materials by CSFS, AUUC, FRC and other organizations.'[111] More to the point, this VOKS official asked to be told not only who saw these materials, and where and when, but also whether the progressive groups had any comments or wishes to express to the organizers of these exhibits for future reference.

Films often supplemented other activities (e.g., handicraft sales and lectures). They fit well with the Marxist-Leninist notion that art is meant to 'picture life as it is.'[112] Tovstogan wrote to his chief that there had been a showing of the Soviet film *Sources of Life* at which Carter had given a speech titled 'The Problems of Long-Life.' The CSFS had advertised this event through the Toronto press. Tovstogan reported: 'In the words of D. Carter, this event was successful and showed that [these events] attracted not only the progressive circles. The opposite, by far the majority of the audience was made up of those far from the progressive movement, but interested in the achievements and life of the Soviet Union.'[113] Filling a hall that had a capacity of 250 – and even having to turn some people away – was viewed as a highly positive sign. Tovstogan wrote that the audience had responded 'very warmly' to the film as well as to Carter's speech. He echoed Carter: this success 'shows once more that the Canadian public is interested in the life of the Soviet people, willingly attends suitable events and the Society (CSFS), because of this ready cooperative desire, is able to find the necessary audience amongst Canadians.'[114]

At some point in 1955 a firm named New World Films was established in Toronto to show and sell Soviet films in Canada. The founding members of that organization were CSFS members.[115] It provided both English- and French-language films; these included *Romeo and Juliette, VSKhV, Ostrov Sakhalin, A Portrayal of the Art of China, Peter I, State Hermitage,* and *Vietnam.*[116] In March 1956, Tovstogan received a list of '16mm films produced in the USSR and available to the CSFS.'[117] VOKS asked that this list be sent to the CSFS, as well as to Artkino (a CSFS club) and to New World Films.

There is no doubt, though, that while these events were meant to draw more mainstream (read 'Anglo-Saxon') Canadians into the progressive movement, many of those who purchased photographs and attended film screenings belonged to the ethnic progressive groups. A letter that Tovstogan wrote on behalf of New World Films in December 1956 asked that Ukrainian- and Latvian-language films sent to Canada have English subtitles, because the clients – members of Canadian progressive organizations (specifically listed as 'Russians, Ukrainians, Latvians, etc.') found the Russian subtitles displeasing. He pointed out that the films' Russian subtitles made it easier for Ukrainian-Canadian nationalists to generate anti-Soviet propaganda about the Russification of the Soviet Union.[118] He asked that action be taken 'in alleviating the uncomfortable situation for Ukrainian-Canadian progressive organizations.'[119] The political message was always present at CSFS events, though it is likely that some in the audience were there to socialize with friends and speak their native language. For instance, one November evening in 1955 several Armenian-Canadian women in their eighties attended a CSFS showing of the film *Soviet Armenia* at the Armenian Hall in Brantford. These women had come to Canada forty years earlier. At that meeting, Kate Bader – a recent CSFS delegate – spoke about her impressions of the Soviet

Union.[120] Some women in the audience were undoubtedly there for reasons of nostalgia and entertainment as much as for the politics. In this ethnically interlinked leftist community, social and political networking overlapped.

The CSFS financial statements for 1952 listed 'films' as accounting for income of $269.75. For 1953, 'receipts from films' came to $123.00; 'receipts from records,' $30.00; 'receipts from exhibition,' $662.50; 'sale of donated picture,' 102.50.[121] Films, then, were not an important source of income; the value of the films and photographs was that they drew subscribers to the organization's publications and audiences to its events. Even when the CSFS did not host the showings themselves, the income raised by selling tickets was handed over to the CSFS. In Sudbury, for example, the 'Red' Finnish organization ordered Soviet films from the CSFS, showed them during Friendship Month, and sent the proceeds to the CSFS.[122]

Support for most CSFS events was drawn from other groups on the Canadian left. Carter justified the CSFS's existence in part by claiming that he was attracting mainstream Canadians to its events: his group's non-political appeal was an important counterweight to the more political LPP. Also, CSFS members were apparently more Anglo-Saxon, which made that group seem more 'mainstream' than the 'ethnic-heavy' LPP. It is very possible that many people attended CSFS events for reasons other than to hear pro-Soviet declarations. That said, the most regular participants were members of other Canadian leftist groups.

News-Facts, *Northern Neighbors*, and Other Publications[123]

The CSFS actively endorsed Khrushchev's 'return to the homeland' project. Glenna Roberts and Serge Cipko note that this sophisticated campaign deliberately targeted refugees who had left the Soviet Union after the Second World War – Ukrainian Canadians in particular – some of whom were persuaded to return. Many of those people later regretted their decision, but only a small number were able to leave the Soviet Union again.[124] As an editor, Carter featured stories that supported Soviet efforts to entice Canadians to return to their ancestral home. In March 1956, *News-Facts* reproduced stories of former citizens of the Soviet Union who had returned to their homeland. Under the headline

'Thousands of Soviet "DP's" Return to Find Sympathy, Friendship and Jobs,' Carter recounted five individual stories of those who had responded to the 'general "amnesty" offered by the USSR.'[125] For example, Arkady Berishvili, who had worked for a German intelligence agency, 'repented, took advantage of the Soviet Union's pardon offer, and returned home. He has completed his college education, is a Master of Architecture, and now lectures in university.' Carter also cited Andrei Mikhailichenko, quoting him as saying that 'any returning Soviet citizen … who wants to work honestly, will find good work, and sympathy and friendship.'[126] In June 1956, Carter printed photographs of repatriates getting off ships in a Soviet harbour, all of them smiling as they were welcomed with open arms.[127] It does not appear, however, that any of these people were returning from Canada. Whatever the CSFS claimed, the return-to-the-homeland campaign was ultimately a failure, and one that traumatized many Canadians who had been persuaded to go back. The fact that the CSFS helped lure Canadian families back to the Soviet Union, where their Canadian passports were taken from them and destroyed, highlights the negative side of the pro-Soviet apologia.

Those who were considering such a move would have found plenty of other encouragement in Carter's publication. Frank Park, who had been director of the Friendship organization during the Second World War, wrote an article titled 'How to Get a Place to Live [in the Soviet Union],' published by Carter in March 1950. His wife and partner, Libbie Park, wrote an article for the same edition titled 'Canadian Social Worker Visits Moscow … Gets First-Hand Information: "I was Inside Soviet Hospitals."'[128]

The photographs Carter published invariably emphasized the happiness of the Soviet people and the progress their country had made since the Bolshevik Revolution.[129] When he used photos for the first time in *News-Facts,* in the April–May 1953 edition, the pictures of Soviet development and smiling faces were captioned as follows: 'These new, exclusive News-Facts photographs show life inside the Soviet Union today. News-Facts welcomes readers' suggestions for topics to be shown in future photo pages.'[130] Carter handed out copies of *News-Facts* at the meetings of other progressive groups. He also solicited subscriptions from those groups and advertised in their newspapers. One ad promised that any canvasser who found two new subscribers for

News-Facts would receive a free map of the Soviet Union.[131] In December 1956, *News-Facts* readers were automatically switched over to a new publication, *Northern Neighbors*, in which Carter continued to write about Soviet advances in science and society.

Carter tried to de-politicize the notion of Canadian–Soviet friendship. In his introduction to *Moscow – As Two Canadians Saw It* by Libbie and Frank Park, he wrote: 'What is the purpose of the Canadian-Soviet Friendship Society? Why do we bring you this book? There's nothing to keep secret. Our aim is to help the Canadian people and the Soviet people to understand each other.'[132] Dyson and Charlotte Carter's account of their visit to the Soviet Union, *We Saw Socialism*, also published in 1951, presented a more in-depth view of everyday life there, with an overwhelmingly positive spin. On the Ukrainian Republic the Carters wrote:

> Is the Ukrainian Soviet Socialist Republic a free nation, or are its 40 million people 'enslaved' by the Russians, and seeking 'independence'? This was a matter we looked into carefully during our trip. We observed, we asked questions everywhere. And this is what we two 'Anglo-Saxons' say: anyone who actually goes to the Ukraine and lives there, in the cities and out in the countryside, as we did, will discover two warm, passionate 'loves' in the hearts of all the people there. First comes their love for their Socialist Ukraine. With it, inseparable, is their love for all the other Soviet Republics, above all for the Russian people.[133]

The AUUC and other groups promoted and purchased Carter's publications. Misha Korol of the AUUC sent a letter to all 'English-speaking branch executives' in November 1951 praising the Carters' book.[134] The Parks' book and the Carters' own were published by the CSFS through the LPP's publishing wing, Eveready Printers. In 1957 the readers of the progressive newspaper *The Ukrainian Canadian* ordered one thousand copies of another book by the Carters: *Cancer, Smoking, Heart Disease, Alcohol*, which compared the health situation in capitalist and socialist countries.[135] The overall tone of these publications – and of those later produced by *Northern Neighbors* to explain the Soviet perspective on the situations in Czechoslovakia and China[136] – was to assure Canadian readers that the Soviet Union was a peaceful and advanced friend worth emulating.

Carter worked hard to counteract any negative publicity he encountered about the Soviet Union in other publications. When Harry Colegate distributed CSFS leaflets at the entrance to the Massey-Harris plant where he worked, explaining that he was off to see the Soviet Union for himself, and asking his fellow workers if they had any particular questions they would like him to answer while there, the incident made it into the *Globe and Mail*. The *Globe* article presented Colegate as someone who was seeking the truth about the Soviet Union. A co-worker of Colegate, Nicholas Prychodko, was presented in the *Globe* as a counter-witness in possession of actual knowledge about Soviet life.[137] In a letter to the editor, Prychodko had written that visitors to the Soviet Union were exposed to propaganda tours over which they 'enthused' when they returned. He then asked fifteen pointed questions about what was 'true' for Soviet workers. At the end of this letter he identified his own group as the anti-Soviet Ukrainian Association of Victims of Russian Communist Terrorism, and he asked: 'In whose interests does the Canadian Soviet Friendship Society operate, Canadian or Russian?'[138]

Prychodko was presenting himself as someone who could see through the misinformation presented by the Soviet authorities. In their rebuttal, the Carters mocked witnesses who argued against their more idealistic view of Soviet reality. In placing quotation marks around Prychodko's self-identification as a 'living witness,' and arguing that his description of life in Soviet labour camps was exaggerated, the Carters were implying that he was a liar intent on self-promotion and that the *Globe* was biased since it had published his story but not the Carters' rebuttal. Finally, they argued that their perspective was more scientifically and logically sensible.[139]

Carter also encouraged Canadian progressives to subscribe to Soviet publications. For example, he announced in *News-Facts* that any reader who joined the CSFS would be able to receive the *VOKS Bulletin* magazine for 50 cents a year.[140] During the 1954 Soviet Friendship Month a free subscription to the *Bulletin* was given to paid-up members and new members of the CSFS.[141] Lists of new *Bulletin* subscribers were sent by the CSFS to VOKS in Moscow. These lists are in the VOKS archives. Anecdotal evidence suggests that many *Bulletin* readers were of Ukrainian background.[142] Louise Harvey, an activist in Montreal leftist circles, wrote that the *Bulletin* was 'a source of joy and comfort … in times when reaction seems to be firm in the saddle.'[143] When

VOKS launched the *Bulletin*, Dyson Carter was among the first people it solicited for constructive criticism.[144] When VOKS stopped publishing the *Bulletin* to publish *Culture and Life* instead, the CSFS was asked to 'propagandize the journal along their channels.'[145] Lists of individuals interested in receiving the new journal were duly sent along.[146]

There were perks to being a CSFS member/subscriber. In 1954, Carter wrote to VOKS: 'As you probably know, our Society receives a number of copies of the periodicals: *Soviet Union, Soviet Woman, Soviet Literature, News, New Times*. We have received these for a long time, without any invoices, and we distribute them for free.'[147] In 1955, CSFS members were offered a Russian-language course book for $1, or they could receive the course plus a year's subscription to *News-Facts* for $1.25.[148] VOKS handled the shipping of the Russian-language textbook. Carter also came up with an idea for increasing Canadian subscriptions to *Moscow News*, a Soviet English-language paper. A letter from Tovstogan to the VOKS main office in Moscow in January 1956 made note of new subscriptions to the *Moscow News* for individuals associated with the CSFS, some of whom were also members of 'ethnic, progressive' groups.[149] A few months later, VOKS wrote to say that not enough Canadian subscribers to *Moscow News* were being found and that subscriptions had to be increased, to ensure that the paper was 'distributed widely' in Canada.[150] In April 1956, Tovstogan replied that Dyson Carter had suggested that *Moscow News* subscriptions be linked to *News-Facts*. By June 1956 the decision to do this had been made in Moscow. *News-Facts* subscribers would receive a discount on a subscription to *Moscow News*.[151]

Besides being translated in the Soviet Union and appearing in Soviet newspapers, Carter's own writings were often featured in the Canadian progressive ethnic press. For instance, in February 1954 an article written by Carter arguing that there was growing interest in the Soviet Union in Canada, and that joining the CSFS was one way that people could satisfy their curiosity, was carried in both *Ukrainian Canadian* and the Hungarian *Kanadai Magyar Munkas* (Canadian Hungarian Worker). In the Ukrainian paper the article was titled 'Trade, Jobs, Peace in Friendship with USSR'; in the Hungarian newspaper it was 'Millions Are Awakening to the Fact That Friendship with the Soviet Is for Own Sake, for Canada.' In both publications, Carter's byline was 'President, Canadian-Soviet Friendship Society.'[152] The photo captions suggested to readers that Soviet–Hungarian friendship had a long history, as did Ukrainian–Russian cooperation within the Soviet Union. The usual pictures of ballerinas and the Lenin Mausoleum appeared with these articles.[153] Carter claimed that 'already big sections of our population are beginning to see a great, historic truth. Friendly relations between Canada and our neighbour to the north are what we Canadians urgently need to make sure of a peaceful, prosperous, independent future of our country.'[154] He urged all Canadians to read the CSFS publications and to get the 'eye-witness story' published by the CSFS – a brochure titled 'Canadians Visit our Northern Neighbours.' And he urged them to listen to radio broadcasts from Moscow and to attend CSFS events. 'It's our responsibility,' he declared, 'to see that we and all our friends show the people of Canada, and the people of the Soviet Union, just where we stand.'[155] Carter's pro-Stalin stance – which mirrored the official Soviet one at that time – was made especially clear in the caption to a photograph of a statue of Sergei Kirov, now known to have been assassinated by Stalin's agents. Carter claimed that Kirov had been 'killed by agents of foreign imperialists.'[156]

CSFS branches advertised in the left-wing press for volunteers to host Friendship Month activities in their homes. CSFS publications were reviewed in the left-wing press, which also published the schedules for Soviet radio programs.[157] Biographies of Dyson and Charlotte Carter were run in newspapers like *Canadian Jewish Weekly;* these promoted the couple as 'a Canadian man and his wife' who admired the Soviet Union and were admired by the Soviet people.[158] Key to this message was that the Carters had actually been to the Soviet Union – a photo of them in front of Moscow State University proved as much. The Carters encouraged other Canadians to see the Soviet Union for themselves.

It is, of course, difficult to quantify how well the Carters and their publications succeeded in persuading readers to view the Soviet Union in a more positive light. Many of the non-Party left subscribed to his magazine, readers sent him supportive letters, and he received abiding support from both the CPC and Soviet authorities even after he left the CSFS in 1960, so it seems that he achieved some success, at least among those who already sympathized with the Soviet Union. It also seems that members of the various progressive ethnic groups in Canada found in Carter a writer of appealing, non-ethnically specific, pro-

Soviet essays and articles. His vision of the Soviet Union as a hopeful yet realistic progressive society was attractive to Canadians who shared the dream.

Visiting the USSR

A dream for many Soviet sympathizers – not to mention other curious Canadians – was to see the Soviet Union for themselves. The CSFS regularly offered subsidized trips to the Soviet Union for Canadian progressives. Analysts of the Soviet response to the Gouzenko affair have concluded that plans to send select Canadians to the Soviet Union, so that they 'could deliver the "truth" about the Soviet Union' to their fellow Canadians, had been in the works since 1946 and 'would soon be the new Soviet approach' to perception management.[159] A visit of a few weeks was tempting for progressives who were interested in the Soviet Union, and the talks given by returnees drew large audiences. It was especially tempting in that most of the expenses were covered by VOKS. Only the airfare needed to be paid by the delegates, and this money could be raised locally by the LPP and ethnic progressive groups.[160] Dyson and Charlotte Carter first visited the Soviet Union in 1950, and again in 1953. After that, Dyson was a frequent visitor. The Carters wrote about their experiences in *We Saw Socialism*. They maintained in other publications that their view of the Soviet Union was certain to be truthful because they had been there and had seen it for themselves. The Carters' trips provided material for their two-volume celebratory book, as well as for articles in *New Times*, the English-language Soviet newspaper for foreign readers. Perhaps they did not realize that the questions they asked were being sent in advance of their visits to various Soviet organizations.[161]

After their return in 1950, Carter began to organize follow-up tours for others. In Carter's letters to VOKS suggesting possible delegates, we can see him attempting to reward activists, reach out to the wider progressive community, and encourage others to contribute on their return. The main requirement was always that the delegates participate in speaking tours on behalf of the CSFS once they returned. Their lectures were often accompanied by exhibitions of their own photographs or by photos and films sent by VOKS. Later, VOKS would be told how many lectures each delegate had given, the venue, and the size of the audience. VOKS maintained its own contacts with delegates after such trips, and effusive letters of friendship can still be found in the VOKS archives.

Who went on these trips? Frank and Libbie Park's December 1949 trip provided them with the material for *Moscow – as Two Canadians Saw It*.[162] Their travel file reveals that they attended a long series of cultural events, including Bolshoi Ballet performances, and that they were invited to an official gala in Moscow celebrating Stalin's seventieth birthday. The latter invitation came directly from the office of Andrei Vyshinsky, the Soviet Foreign Minister.[163] It is not clear why the Parks were rewarded with such a high-level invitation, but it indicates that the Soviet authorities understood the visit's importance.

Other delegates would not have received invitations from high-ranking individuals, but they would have established good contacts with VOKS officials in Moscow. This would not have happened had those higher in the government not made the arrangements. In May 1951 a delegation of Canadian 'cultural workers' went to the Soviet Union to investigate for themselves Carter's claims that the Soviets were culturally superior. TASS later reported that this delegation – Winnipeg alderman Jacob Penner, Emil and Fanny Gartner, musicians active in the Jewish progressive movement, artist Frederick Taylor, and Jeannette Brunelle-Pratte – 'acquainted themselves with cultural, educational and scientific institutions in Kiev, [and] made a trip to the town of Kaniv, where they visited the grave and the museum of the great Ukrainian poet, Taras Shevchenko.'[164] *Soviet Monitor* wrote that 'conductor Emil Gartner particularly stressed the high level of musical culture in the land of the Soviets and the perfect organization of musical education in schools for children.'[165] On their return the delegates spoke to groups in Canada, emphasizing the quality and accessibility of cultural education in the Soviet Union.[166]

In 1952 the CSFS sponsored a delegation of trade unionists and workers. A talk by one of these delegates – Mrs Katherine (Kay) Hladiy, who worked in Toronto's needle trade – was advertised directly to needle trade workers in Point Douglas. The ad noted that she had 'made it a point to visit a number of Needle Trades Shops – Cloaks, Garment, Fur, Shoe, etc.' The questions she would address in her presentation were listed.[167] This ad was signed by the Needle Trades Committee of the Canadian-Soviet Friendship Society. Other labour activists, including Bruce Magnuson, were also on this trip.

In September 1953 a delegation of seven CSFS members visited the Soviet Union: Rosalind McCutcheon (Montreal), Leo Clavir (Toronto), Florence Dorland (Vancouver), Paul Pauk (Toronto), Margaret Spaulding (Toronto), Eleanor Ashworth (Edmonton), and (Major) R.T. Lafond (Quebec). The essays they wrote on their return were published by the CSFS as a thirty-two-page booklet titled 'Canadians Visit Our Northern Neighbours: Picture Report of a Trip to the Soviet Union.' Readers could buy this booklet for twenty-five cents. It included enthusiastic reports on all things Soviet, as well as photos. On the last page, the *News-Facts* Toronto address was noted under the boldface heading **Did you enjoy reading this report? Every month, 'News-Facts' contains information like this.**[168] Below this are the words 'Not just articles – not just pictures – but FILMS!' advertising three Soviet films available for rental.[169] On the back cover is a photograph of Charlotte and Dyson Carter sitting on a picturesque terrace, which from the personal letter that follows turns out to be 'the new city of Stalingrad.' Here the Carters ask for funds to contribute to their efforts to pass on the information they have gathered during their visits to the Soviet Union, since 'by helping to bring truthful information to the Canadian people, you'll be a builder of real friendship between our country and our northern neighbor [*sic*].'[170] Documents in the VOKS archives show that especially during February 1954, Soviet Friendship Month, the CSFS encouraged its branches to distribute this booklet.[171] Predictably, speaking engagements also took place that month.[172]

In 1954 the CSFS sponsored a delegation of Canadian artists, who included Fred Varley, the Group of Seven painter.[173] At the same time, a troupe of Soviet performing artists came to Canada and were toured around the country by John Boyd. This tour was sponsored by the CSFS; Canadian left-wing groups supported the concerts. Sophia Golovkina and Leonid Zhdanov, ballet dancers, Leonid Kogan, violinist, Elizaveta Chavdar, soprano, Arturs Frindbergs, tenor, and Pavel Serebryakov, pianist, were welcomed by Dyson Carter as they arrived in Toronto.[174] This tour was a great success – 3,000 people attended the opening concert at Massey Hall, and 7,000 crowded into Varsity Arena to hear them at the end of their tour. More than 4,000 attended the concert in Winnipeg, more than 1,000 in Sudbury, and 2,500 in Ottawa at the Capitol Theatre.[175] At one performance in Toronto the

RCMP reported 'there were numerous known local communists in attendance.'[176] This group's concert schedule was printed in *Ukrainiske slovo* and in other left-wing publications, with information about how to buy tickets.[177]

In an interview in the *Tribune*, Boyd said that the audiences everywhere had been large and that the ads taken out by anti-communist Ukrainian groups had done little to deflate the enthusiasm of the concertgoers.[178]

In February and March 1955 the CSFS delegation included Morris Biderman from the UJPO in Toronto; Louis Kon from Montreal; Mrs Anna Sochasky, AUUC member from Vancouver; K. Rankin, CSFS member from Vancouver; Kate Bader from Toronto; R. Patriquen from Saskatchewan; and Dorothy Johnson from Manitoba. On her return, Sochasky wrote a letter to VOKS addressed to 'Dear Soviet Friends,' describing the Ukrainian-Canadian left:

> As a Canadian I want to tell you how some of us spend our spare time in the evenings in Canada. I belong to a club called the Society of United Ukrainian Canadians. Across the whole of Canada we have 125 such clubs, some larger, some smaller. There are about 115 Ukrainian halls that belong to us. The workers have built them with their own money. I will tell you about such a club in Vancouver British Columbia. We have a separate men's club and a separate women's club. We have about 80 women in our club. There is also a large youth club. We have private teachers that teach our children the Ukrainian language in the evening. Ukrainian dancing is also tought [*sic*]. We have about 150 children that dance. We have a youth mandolin orchestra, and a mixed choir of young and old of 50 people. We give concerts in our hall with these groups once a month. Every Sunday we have a Soviet film showing. Three hundred people can be seated in our hall. Our women's club has a sewing circle, and we embroider Ukrainian shirts, aprons, and other articles. Our members take an active part in peace campaigns.[179]

Sochasky's letter reflects the gendered realities of the progressive movement,[180] which are visible also in the 'eye-witness' stories brought back by delegates. A common pattern for CSFS events – especially under the leadership of Dyson Carter – was for women to speak about the everyday concerns of Soviet people, especially concerns seen as affecting women and children.

These talks backed up the message carried in CSFS publications that it was because of the socialist state that Soviet women were able to handle the 'double burden' of motherhood and outside work. Judging from these speeches, there was no contradiction between Soviet women's increasing autonomy (even pre-eminence) in the workforce and their ongoing traditional role in the family. It was claimed that production-line factories and common kitchens had eased the burden for women. There is real pathos in these reports when one reads them today. Research has since shown that despite Soviet claims to the contrary, the position of women in the Soviet Union was nowhere near equal. After leaving work they often had to stand in long line-ups to purchase essentials for the family. Also, goods were not always readily available, housing was cramped, several generations lived in small apartments, the rates of divorce and single motherhood were high, birth control and abortion were difficult to obtain, pay was not equal, and political representation was skewed in men's favour. 'Feminism' had been co-opted by the state, which had declared the problem of equality solved even while women continued to experience gender and sex discrimination in their everyday lives. Sochasky and Rankin told audiences after they returned that good bread was made in 'modern bakeries' and that chicken or meat was eaten at every meal in cafeterias. In general terms, they offered idealized impressions of the Soviet Union.[181] Their remarks were published in the *Nelson Daily News*.[182]

The details of the 1955 delegates' presentations were reported back to VOKS. In a letter to his boss, the VOKS representative in Ottawa, Vladimir Burdin noted the dates and venues for these delegates' talks, as well as the number of people attending, and what else had been on offer at these meetings. Sometimes there was a concert by an FRC choir, or a film screening. Sometimes speeches were given – for example, in honour of the tenth anniversary of the Warsaw Uprising.[183]

VOKS and the CSFS were not the only ones keeping track of attendance: the RCMP also counted speaking engagements and the number of individuals attending. For instance, an RCMP report noted that on their return from the Soviet Union, Sochasky and Rankin spoke in Natal, B.C., to an audience of forty-five, and that funds were raised at that time for the local FRC branch. Sochasky had spoken poorly; Rankin had been 'impressive.'[184] Another RCMP report, this one from April 1955, noted that Sochasky and Rankin had spoken on 30 March in Nelson, B.C., where about eighty-five people had been present, 90 per cent of them Doukhobors.[185] After two films were shown, the women 'described conditions in the Soviet Union including modern bakeries, meals throughout the trip, and Technical Institutes and other general living conditions.'[186] Sochasky spoke in Ukrainian at some meetings, in English at others.[187] With their reports the RCMP included reviews and other publicity printed in the local press. The two women had been saying that there was plenty of meat to eat in the Soviet Union, that Soviet TV sets did not suffer from interference, and that bread was produced in modern, efficient factories and was 'not handled by human hands.'[188] These women's reports gave an invariably rosy picture of Soviet life – an impression that, unfortunately, was far from the reality for most Soviet families, though these two Canadian women perhaps did not realize it.

Delegates on these trips – and, for that matter, the members of the CSFS executive – were carefully selected for their ability to interact with diaspora groups and the LPP and to attract new members. William Teresio, who sat on the AUUC executive, was also on the CSFS National Council.[189] When he died in 1954 the CSFS made this connection explicit in a eulogy sent to all CSFS branches: 'His death is a grievous loss to the cause of Canadian-Soviet friendship, and will be deeply felt by all members of our Society.'[190] Members of progressive groups were asked to help finance trips to the Soviet Union by local individuals, whether or not they actually belonged to the same ethnic group. For instance, a fund-raiser was held at the Ukrainian Labour Temple in Moose Jaw, Saskatchewan, in November 1954 to raise funds for R.L. Patriquen's trip to the Soviet Union. A form letter was sent out to local progressives, addressed to 'Dear Friend,' suggesting that the remaining funds 'can be secured through contributions from men and women who are aware of the need for goodwill and friendship between nations.'[191] Signatures on the attached form indicate that eight individuals gave between five and ten dollars each. Later, Carter sent out thank you notes, published in the pages of the leftist ethnic press. CSFS delegates on their return had their stories published in the progressive press in Canada; the RCMP would then clip and file these articles. In one such article a Jewish delegate described Soviet Jews telling him that they had all the money and comforts they needed, insisting that 'all Jews should feel as free as we do.'[192] This was just a few years before Nikita Khrushchev admitted in his speech at the 20th Party Congress that Jews had been among the most repressed minority groups under Stalin.

In March 1955, Carter wrote to VOKS headquarters in Moscow to suggest a Soviet professors' tour of Canadian universities and CSFS branches in Canada. Regarding whether public meetings or CSFS events would take precedence, he wrote: 'Of course, what we actually do will be in the sole interest of this delegation having greatest impact and influence for Friendship.'[193] He was at the time planning another CSFS delegation. This one would include Dr Howard Lowrie, who had been an important financial contributor to the CSFS; the Canadian artist Tom Thompson's sister, Margaret Tweedale, 'a long-time worker for Friendship, [with] a wide circle of friends in CCF and Church groups';[194] and Margaret's husband William, who sat on the CSFS Administration Committee after 1956, his views on the uprising in Hungary having been judged by VOKS to have been 'correct.'[195] But the events in Hungary and Poland in 1956[196] threw something of a wrench into Carter's plans. In 1957 the Soviet Embassy decided not to support the visit, possibly because it was on the 'wrong side' of the policy shake-up, and the tour did not go ahead.[197] In 1956, VOKS organized a Soviet tour for members of the Co-operative Commonwealth Federation (CCF), but that one was not sponsored by the CSFS.[198]

The CSFS in 1956

Significant aspects of the CSFS's work changed in 1956, after news of Khrushchev's secret speech to the XXth Party Congress in February slowly reached international communist groups.[199] Key CSFS staff members left the society over that speech, and the membership declined. In the summer of 1956, Ted Baxter, the CSFS National Secretary, cancelled his subscription to the *VOKS Bulletin* and left the society.[200] In an interview, Baxter said that he had become disillusioned and that repeated visits by RCMP officers to his workplace had caused him to fear for his job and his young family. So he distanced himself from the progressive movement.[201] The next to leave was Jim Leech, the Organizing Secretary, whom VOKS had congratulated for managing much of the everyday work of the CSFS and the publication of *News-Facts*.[202] In September 1957, Tovstogan informed the VOKS head office that Leech had asked the CSFS leadership to relieve him of his duties. 'Considering his request, and also his incorrect behaviour following the XXth Congress of the CPSU,' the CSFS leadership had agreed, Tovstogan wrote.[203] In late 1956, Louis Kon died.[204] In May 1957, Charlotte Carter's comments that the XXth Party Congress had 'made the idea of Canadian-Soviet friendship unpopular in Canada (especially amongst the Jewish members)' were reported to VOKS in Moscow.[205] Apparently only half the CSFS executive members had turned up for a meeting to discuss CSFS's plans for 1957.

A few months later the Carters moved from Toronto to Gravenhurst,[206] taking their journal *Northern Neighbors* with them. Boyd suggests that Carter had a falling out with the CPC leadership: though 'the Party tried to get the Soviet Embassy to loosen its ties with Carter, the embassy found him more of an asset than what the Party could offer.'[207] The Carters remained in touch with VOKS for materials and continued to visit the Soviet Union from time to time. After the CPC-LPP changed the name of the CSFS to the Canada-USSR Association and placed Les Hunt[208] in charge, the links between the progressive ethnic groups and the more Anglo-Saxon association remained in effect. Many of Carter's readers continued to be of Ukrainian, Russian, Finnish, Polish, or Baltic background.[209]

All CSFS activities had used persuasion to make the Soviet Union look more attractive to Canadians, especially after Gouzenko's defection in 1945. In practice, the CSFS's message targeted mainly those who already sympathized with the Soviet Union, many of whom also attended progressive ethnic-group events. The relative success of CSFS initiatives was visible in the number of people who attended CSFS events and who subscribed to the organization's journals, some of which would have been read by individuals outside the left-wing communities. However, the society's reorganization after 1956 suggests that its usefulness had waned. A host of factors contributed to this, the most important ones being Khrushchev's speech and the Soviet invasion of Hungary in 1956. The geographic dispersion of the left-wing communities from downtown Toronto, and the improved social and economic circumstances of second- and third-generation Canadians, may also have played a role in the decline in CSFS membership.[210]

Convinced that the Western press and governments were deliberately fomenting anti-Soviet sentiments, Carter and other CSFS leaders crafted an alternative, more positive image of the Soviet Union. Once the gap between this officially sanctioned image and the actual situation in the Soviet Union grew too large, the movement disintegrated and Carter quit publishing.[211] Attempts to use Anglo-Saxon names to make what was essentially Soviet-produced material appear as if it had been entirely 'made in Canada' by Anglo-Canadians ultimately failed. Despite Carter's best efforts to reach out to the general public, he never swayed the vast majority of Canadians. At most, these activities softened Canadians' general antipathy towards the Soviet Union and allowed those so inclined to voice their radical alternative visions. Even so, for a time, for some Canadians, Canadian-Soviet friendship represented a hope and a dream.

Though it tried hard to downplay this, the CSFS found its supporters mainly among leftist ethnic groups. Indeed, that ethnic support was essential to the society and to the dissemination of its ideas. Members found shelter within the society, which offered the Soviet Union as an idealized vision for their own lives. The relationship between Ukrainians and other 'ethnics' – both within the CSFS and elsewhere – tells us much about the complicated personal and political relationships that comprised the Canadian left during the Cold War. This gives us a more nuanced appreciation of these radicals' individual and collective political activism.

My thanks to the participants of the Annual Meeting of the Canadian Association of Slavists, where this paper was presented in May 2006, and to John Boyd, Larissa Stavroff, Rhonda Hinther, J.L. Black, Duncan McDowall, and Janice Cavell for their advice and assistance.

Notes

1 When the Communist Party of Canada (CPC) was banned in 1941 by the Canadian government, it was renamed the Labor-Progressive Party (LPP), a name it kept until it switched back to CPC in 1959.

2 A Soviet report giving the biography of Dyson Carter prior to his first visit to the Soviet Union in April 1950 said that the LPP leadership had chosen Carter to serve as president of the CSFS. His credentials were cited: he had written a series of pro-Soviet books, including a biography of Stalin; and as an LPP member he had worked as the chief science editor for the Party newspaper, *Canadian Tribune*, a 'very well-known friend of the Soviet Union.' VOKS collection, Centre for Research on Canadian–Russian Relations, Georgian College, Barrie, series 5, section 3, file 31:206-211.

3 On this, Ester Reiter's work on the Jewish radical left in Toronto has
   been most useful. Reiter, 'Secular *Yiddishkait*: Left Politics, Culture and
   Community,' *Labour/Le travail* 49 (Spring 2002), http://www.historyco-
   operative.org/journals/llt/49/05reiter.html.
4 One particular exception is the work done by Julie Guard on the interaction of Anglo-Saxons with ethnic members of the Housewives' Consumers Association, and the use of Anglo-Saxon names to attract more
   mainstream Canadians to the cause. Guard, 'Canadian Citizens or Dangerous Foreign Women? Canada's Radical Consumer Movement, 1947–
   1950,' in *Sisters or Strangers? Immigrant, Ethnic, and Racialized Women
   in Canadian History*, ed. Marlene Epp, Franca Iacovetta, and Frances
   Swyripa (Toronto: University of Toronto Press, 2004), 161–89. These
   links are also mentioned in Reiter, 'Secular *Yiddishkait*.' See also Frances
   Swyripa, *Wedded to the Cause: Ukrainian-Canadian Women and Ethnic
   Identity, 1891–1991* (Toronto: University of Toronto Press, 1993); Varpu
   Lindstrom-Best, *The Finns in Canada* (Ottawa, 1985); and idem, *Defiant
   Sisters: A Social History of Finnish Immigrant Women in Canada*
   (Toronto: Multicultural History Society of Ontario, 1992).
5 In using this term I am following my sources. Even though it is
   unwieldly and possibly inaccurate, 'Anglo-Saxon' is used here to refer to
   anglophone Canadians of white, Protestant, middle-class British ancestry. Some sources suggest that these people were more 'Canadian' than
   individuals who had Ukrainian, Russian, or other 'ethnic' last names.
6 Reiter, 'Secular Yiddishkait,' para. 14; Norman Penner, *Canadian Communism: The Stalin Years and Beyond* (Toronto: Methuen, 1988), 273–4;
   Peter Krawchuk, *Our History: The Ukrainian Labour-Farmer Movement
   in Canada, 1907–1991* (Toronto: Lugus, 1996), 154–85.
7 VOKS, 6:3:98:5-20, V. Loginov, Counsellor, Soviet Embassy in Ottawa,
   'Short Report on the 5th Congress of the Labor Progressive Party of
   Canada and Its Post-Congress Work with the Masses,' 19 March 1955.
   Another Loginov, A.F. Loginov, military attaché at the Soviet Embassy,
   was expelled from Canada in 1961 for attempting to pay Canadians for
   information (Department of External Affairs, *Canadian Weekly Bulletin*,
   20 December 1961, 5). John Boyd, an active LPP organizer until 1968,
   has also written about 'the LPP's inability to effectively reach Anglo-
   Saxon Canadians.' Boyd, 'A Noble Cause Betrayed ... But Hope Lives
   On: Pages from a Political Life,' originally published as Canadian Institute of Ukrainian Studies Report no. 64, 1999. *Socialist History Project*,
   http://www.socialisthistory.ca/Remember/Reminiscences/Boyd/B1.htm.
8 VOKS, 6:3:98:5-20.
9 The leadership of the CSFS was English-speaking and the correspondence with authorities in Moscow was maintained almost exclusively in

English, even with members from Quebec, until the 1960s, when a 'Canada-URSS' Society was founded in Montreal.

10 Interview with John Boyd, 2 August 2006, Toronto. Boyd has said that he was never a member of the CSFS; Carter, however, has said he was National Council executive member in 1951 (VOKS, 36:22–3). Boyd was Secretary of the Canadian Slav Committee in the late 1940s and 1950s.

11 Boyd interview. See also Boyd, 'A Noble Cause Betrayed'; and James Laxer, *Red Diaper Baby: A Boyhood in the Age of McCarthyism* (Toronto: Douglas and McIntyre, 2004), 25, 54. Other CPC-LPP supporters who changed their names were Fred Rose (Alfred Rosenberg), Sam and Bill Walsh (Saul and Mo Wolofsky), and Louis Kon (Koniatski).

12 On how this was also attempted in the Housewives' Consumers Association, see Guard, 'Canadian Citizens or Dangerous Foreign Women?'

13 Gregory S. Kealey and Reg Whitaker, eds., 'Weekly Summary Report on Revolutionary Organizations and Agitators in Canada' no. 712, 27 June 1934, *RCMP Security Bulletins: The Depression Years,* pt 1, *1933–1934,* 102.

14 LAC, RG146, A200600124, RCMP Intelligence Branch, Toronto, report on the Society for the Study of Russia, Toronto, 31 May 1943, 96.

15 Besides Gartner, R.A. Davies and Margaret Gould attended events run by both these organizations. The Montreal-based group led by Louis Kon in the 1930s called itself the Friends of the Soviet Union, and Kon became more involved again with the CSFS under Dyson Carter. In November 1949, at the founding meeting for the new CSFS, Dyson Carter declared: 'Ladies and Gentlmen [sic] … GONE ARE THE DAYS, FOREVER, when we have to APOLOGIZE for friendship with the Land of Socialism! Never again do we have to go, hat-in-hand, to people in high places, and ask them: "Please won't you allow your name to be used for the sake of friendship … important names will make people think the Russians are important!"' (LAC, RG146, A200600096, 81–94, Dyson Carter's notes, 'Speech for C.S.F. Meeting Nov 26 49'). (Throughout, Carter's notes to himself show the highly choreographed enthusiasm in the speech (i.e., 'PAUSE, AND SOFTLY!' … 'EMPHASIS' … 'SLOW'). Capital letters used for emphasis in the original.

16 LAC, RG146, A200600124, RCMP Intelligence Branch, Toronto, 25 June 1943, 'Re: Rally- Maple Leaf Gardens, Toronto, Ont. June 22nd. 1943,' 49.

17 ibid., 49.

18 LAC, RG146, A200600091, RCMP report 'The Canadian Soviet Friendship Society, February 1951 to March 1953. Addendum to Brief Ending February 1951,' 15 April 1953, 116.

19 Ibid., 113, 116.
20 Ronald Williams, 'Reds at Work on "Friendship": Now Start Photo Pro-
    paganda Deluge,' *Financial Post*, 5 January 1952; LAC, RG146,
    A200600099, 114; A200600100, Dyson Carter, 'President's Speech, Jan-
    uary 25, 1952,' 67–76; also in VOKS 6:1:36:43–52.
21 In 1954 a Canadian journalist posted to Moscow, G.W. Boss, went to see
    A. Denisov, chief of VOKS, at the VOKS headquarters. One point he
    made to Denisov was that there were in fact other contemporary Cana-
    dian writers besides Dyson Carter, and he asked whether there were any
    plans to publish them in the Soviet Union. Denisov's notes on this inter-
    view were forwarded to M.A. Suslov of the International Department of
    the Communist Party of the Soviet Union. VOKS 6:1:45:99–105, Boss to
    K. Perevoschikov, with questions for upcoming interview with Denisov,
    24 February 1954; VOKS 6:3:96:19–21, Denisov to Suslov, 3 March
    1954.
22 This interaction, which deserves more study, was commented upon by
    Reiter in 'Secular *Yiddishkait.*'
23 In oral interviews, former CSFS members and acquaintances often
    referred to this inside/outside relationship, especially in arranging events.
    At times it may have been in response to nastier circumstances. Reiter,
    'Secular *Yiddishkait,*' para. 28, notes that in 1925, when the Jewish
    Labour League wanted to buy land from the Canadian National Railway
    to be used for Camp Kindervelt, a 'Ukrainian sympathizer' had to be
    asked to front the sale, because the CNR would not sell to Jews.
24 On admiration for the Soviet Union among ethnic groups on the Cana-
    dian left, see Swyripa, *Wedded to the Cause;* Lindstrom-Best, *The Finns
    in Canada;* idem, *Defiant Sisters;* the film *Letters from Karelia;* and
    Reiter, 'Secular *Yiddishkait.*' Regarding admiration for the Soviet Union
    within the CPC, see Merrily Weisbord, *The Strangest Dream* (Montreal:
    Véhicule Press, 1983); and Laxer, *Red Diaper Baby*.
25 For an interesting discussion on how the Party asked Dorise Nielsen and
    Dyson Carter to travel across Canada to do damage control for the image
    of communism following Gouzenko's 1946 revelations, and their work
    on reorganizing the CSFS, see Faith Johnston, *A Great Restlessness: The
    Life and Politics of Dorise Nielsen* (Winnipeg: University of Manitoba
    Press, 2006), 197, 225–31.
26 There are many examples of personnel being asked to serve on commit-
    tees for the 'language' groups, the LPP, and the CSFS. In 1955, for
    example, the National Executive of the Federation of Russian Canadians
    asked Nadia Savich to represent the FRC in the CSFS. LAC, RG146,
    A200600104, 'Minutes of proceedings N. 25 of the meeting of the
    National Executive of the FRC of September 27, 1955,' 30.

27 LAC, RG146, A200600097, RCMP report from Yorkton Special Branch, 21 December 1950, 20.
28 LAC, RG146, A200600117, RCMP Headquarters, report of information in *Ludove Zvesti* (Slovak for *People's News*), 20-1-51, report dated also 20-1-51, 11.
29 *Vapaus*, 21 March 1953, 8. *Vapuas* was a Finnish-language newspaper in Sudbury.
30 VOKS, 6:1:49:17, letter from Tovstogan to Kulakovskaya, 26 November 1955.
31 LAC, RG146, A200600117, 'RCMP report, 19-10-51 source *Ukrainian Life* 18-10-51,' 10.
32 On the Jewish left generally, and on its links with other leftist ethnic groups in Canada, see Reiter, 'Secular *Yiddishkait.*' For more on the Jewish Folk Choir's mission and appeal, see Benita Wolters-Fredlund, '"We Shall Go Forward with Our Songs into the Fight for Better Life": Identity and Musical Meaning in the History of the Toronto Jewish Folk Choir, 1925–1959,' PhD diss., University of Toronto, 2005.
33 LAC, RG146, A200600091, RCMP report 'The Canadian Soviet Friendship Society, February 1951 to March 1953. Addendum to Brief Ending February 1951,' 15 April 1953, 115.
34 M.I. Gritzak, 'Meeting of Canadian Soviet Friendship in Grand Forks,' *Vestnik*, 27 February 1954, RCMP summary in LAC, RG146, A200600121, 20.
35 VOKS, 6:1:49:17, letter from Tovstogan to Kulakovskaya, 26 November 1955.
36 Ibid.
37 VOKS 6:1:49:272, letter from Tovstogan to Kulakovskaya, 12 October 1956.
38 VOKS, 6:1:49:115, letter from Vertogradov to Tovstogan, 12 May 1956.
39 VOKS, 6:1:49:181, letter to Rimyans from Kulakovskaya, 19 September 1956.
40 VOKS, 6:1:49:125–7, Tovstogan to Kulakovskaya, 7 April 1956. Tichnovich's name had been anglicized from Tsekhanovich.
41 *Spravochnik* is the Russian word for 'guide' or 'reference book.' In this case they probably meant a type of address book. VOKS, 6:1:49:272, Tovstogan to Kulakovskaya, 12 October 1956.
42 The choirs of the AUUC and FRC would often sing folk songs from other Eastern European traditions, especially if they knew these ethnic groups were represented in the audience. VOKS, 6:1:49:227, letter to P.I. Valeskeln (Chairman, Latvian OKS) from Kulakovskaya, 3 July 1956; VOKS, 6:1:49:228, letter to P.I. Ratomskis (Lithuanian OKS) from Kulakovskaya, 3 July 1956.

43 VOKS, 6:1:49:59, letter from Vertogradov to Tovstogan, 13 April 1956.
44 VOKS, 6:1:49:210-212, dated 18 June 1956.
45 VOKS, 6:1:53:19-25, dated 3 March 1956; 53:81, dated 23 May 1956.
46 Examples of these can be found in the Robert S. Kenny collection, Thomas Fisher Rare Book Library, University of Toronto.
47 VOKS 6:1:50:116, 'Canadian Soviet Friendship Society, Receipts and Payments – 13 months to December 31 1952'; VOKS 6:1:50:117, 'Canadian Soviet Friendship Society, Receipts and Payments – year to December 31 1953.' These are among the few documents reporting the CSFS income. Dyson Carter's second wife, Sally Nielsen, has said that thousands of dollars were kept in the house, and periodically the CPC leadership would come to ask Dyson for a share. She has said that book sale business accounted for a large share of this income, and Dyson Carter also received cash from Soviet Embassy officials who visited their home in Gravenhurst. Sally (Thelma) Nielsen, interview by author, 28 November 2006, near Lakefield, Ontario.
48 Nielsen interview. Certainly, real estate costs and taxes would have eaten up some of the profit.
49 VOKS, 6:1:53:12, letter from Dyson Carter to Perevoschikov, 5 December 1955.
50 VOKS, 6:1:53:13, letter from I. Kulakovskaya to Astvatsaturyan, 26 January 1956.
51 VOKS, 6:1:53:14, letter from Astvatsaturyan to Kulakovskaya, 3 February 1956.
52 This request was forwarded by VOKS in Moscow to the Karelo-Finnish SSR. VOKS, 6:1:44:79-81, 89-90, 96-97; letter from Carter to Bogatyrev, 1 March 1953; N. Gorshkov (VOKS) to I.I. Tsvetkov, 16 April 1953; Carter to Bogatyrev, 12 June 1953.
53 VOKS, 6:1:49:47, letter from Smilge to Yakovlev, 6 March 1956.
54 VOKS, 6:1:49:125, letter from Tovstogan to Kulakovskaya, 7 April 1956.
55 VOKS, 6:1:49:28, letter from Kulakovskaya to Tovstogan, 26 January 1956.
56 VOKS, 6:1:49:52, letter from Vertogradov to Tovstogan, 23 March 1956.
57 VOKS, 6:1:49:90-101, 102, S. Demchenko, 7 April 1956; S.N. Pilipchuk from Vertogradov, 12 May 1956.
58 LAC, RG146, A200600091, RCMP Security and Intelligence Section report, Calgary, 20 November 1957, 7.
59 Ibid., 9.
60 'Account of Bruce Magnusson's trip to the Soviet Union', Vestnik 30, nos. 1153–4, 31 December 1952, in LAC, RG146, A200600102, RCMP report 5 January 1953, 77.

61 "'If people Know Truth about Us – No More War" – Stalingrad Woman,'
    Canadian Tribune, n.d., in LAC, RG146, A200600105, 129; LAC, RG146,
    A200600103, 'Circular Letter N. 2,' from the National Executive of the
    FRC, signed by J. Kurban, secretary, Toronto, 27 November 1953, 86.
62 LAC, RG146, A200600096, Letter from Dyson Carter to 'Dear Friends
    of the Federation of Russian Canadians,' 24 March 1950, 234–5.
63 After Khrushchev's speech in 1956 documenting Soviet abuses under
    Stalin, including systemic anti-Semitism, many Jews left the LPP and
    Party-associated groups. Hints of this situation had been appearing ear-
    lier in the 1950s, however, and the LPP-supported clubs had been work-
    ing for some time on damage control. The CSFS was no exception, and
    articles in its journal celebrated the Soviet treatment of Jews.
    Khrushchev's and others' revelations of the real injustice caused deep
    disillusionment for many leftists.
64 LAC, RG146, A200600091, RCMP report 'The Canadian Soviet Friend-
    ship Society, February 1951 to March 1953. Addendum to Brief Ending
    February 1951,' 15 April 1953, 115.
65 *News-Facts* 35, March 1953, 1.
66 Boyd interview.
67 LAC, RG25, A200700336, RCMP Research Section report, 'The
    Canada–USSR Association,' 27 March 1963, 834–45.
68 Nielsen interview.
69 Ibid. John Boyd did not believe that the money came from Moscow,
    arguing instead that the Canadian Party had clever ways of financing its
    supported organizations. He pointed out that the RCMP and the Bank of
    Commerce knew about these strategies all along. Boyd interview.
70 Much of this came as books and saleable objects, as discussed earlier
    and in the next section.
71 A letter from Carter to Tovstogan dated 18 February 1957, thanking
    Tovstogan and Soviet ambassador D.S. Chuvakhin for their help in
    making sure that $3,086.09 royalty fees for Carter's *Tomorrow Is With
    Us* were received by Carter from 'Goslitigat Ukrainy,' seems to suggest
    that Carter was not always able to get his payment (VOKS, 6:1:55:107).
    The Soviets always took interest in Carter's books published in Canada,
    and he usually forwarded them via VOKS to the Writer's Union and
    others in the Soviet Union. In 1956, when Carter complained about a
    Soviet review of his book *Fatherless Sons*, his letter was forwarded to
    the Central Committee of the Communist Party of Canada (VOKS,
    6:1:53:28-36). VOKS headquarters informed the Ottawa representative
    that this book was to be published in the Soviet Union in 1957 (VOKS,
    6:1:49:55). In 1957 two copies of Charlotte and Dyson Carter's book
    Cancer, Smoking, Heart Disease, and Alcohol in Two World Systems

were sent to the Soviet Ministry of Foreign Affairs (VOKS, 6:1:55:122).
In February 1957 VOKS discussed the fact that their *Science of Health and Long Life in the USSR* had been published in Australia and reviewed in the Soviet press (VOKS, 6:1:55:63–5).

72 VOKS, 6:1:49:61–3, 10 April 1956.
73 VOKS, 6:1:50:71–2, letter from Carter to Bourdine, 12 January 1955.
74 VOKS, 6:1:49:173, letter from Tovstogan to Vertogradov, 13 August 1956.
75 VOKS, 6:1:50:81, letter from Carter to Perevoschikov, 22 March 1955. There is also reference to this in the Louis and Irene Kon fonds at the Osler Library, McGill University, Montreal. Kon had previously organized Soviet art exhibitions for the prewar Friends of the Soviet Union. Gregory S. Kealey and Reg Whitaker, eds., 'RCMP Weekly Summary Reports,' nos. 759, 12 June 1935, and 772, 11 September 1935,' *RCMP Security Bulletins: The Depression Years*, pt 2, *1935*, 344.
76 VOKS, 6:1:50:49, letter from Yakovlev to Petrushev, Chief of Tsentropromsovet, 28 July 1955.
77 VOKS, 6:1:50:47–8, Carter to Perevoschikov, 3 July 1955.
78 VOKS, 6:1:50:50, letter from Goryachkin to Yakovlev, 11 August 1955.
79 LAC, RG146, A200600091, letter from Ted Baxter to CSFS branches, 1954, n.d., 25.
80 LAC, RG146, A200600091, letter from Ted Baxter to CSFS branches, 29 September 1954, 23.
81 A list of these Soviet Friendship Month events was published in *Canadian Tribune*, 9 November 1954, LAC, RG146, A200600104, 100. The same list was published in *Vestnik*, 3 November 1954; *Jedinstvo* (Unity), 2 November 1954; and *Laudis Balsas* (The People's Voice), 29 October 1954. Summaries in RCMP files, LAC, RG146, A200600104, 107, 108, 110.
82 LAC, RG146, A200600091, memo from Ted Baxter, CSFS Secretary, to 'All Society Branches on Publicity,' 19 October 1954, 16.
83 VOKS, 6:1:45:123-124, letter from LPP, 19 November 1953.
84 LAC, RG146, A200600103, 'Club Letter' signed by Vancouver City Secretary, Maurice Rush, dated 23 February 1954, recorded in RCMP Vancouver Subdivision, Special Branch memo, 4 March 1954, 'RE: Labor Progressive Party-British Columbia,' 241.
85 LAC, RG146, A200600103, 'Circular Letter N. 2,' from the National Executive of the FRC, signed by J. Kurban, secretary, Toronto, 27 November 1953, 86.
86 Editorial: 'Fulfill These Tasks in January,' *Ukraïnske slovo* (Ukrainian Word), 7 January 1953, 10; LAC, RG146, A200600102, RCMP summary dated 9 January 1953, 71.

87 VOKS, 6:1:49:24, letter from Carter to Perevozchikov [sic], 15 October 1955.

88 VOKS, 6:1:53:27, letter from Carter to Kulakovskaya, 3 January 1956.

89 VOKS, 6:1:50:71–2, letter from Carter to Burdin, 12 January 1955.

90 Ibid.

91 VOKS, 6:1:49:6, letter from A. Tovstogan to Kulakovskaya, 26 November 1955, 49:6. The greeting form is found in the VOKS collection, 49:22.

92 VOKS, 6:1:49:22.

93 VOKS, 6:1:49:22, 23. The form destined for groups listed the CSFS's name above the Bathurst address; the one that was printed in *News-Facts* used the journal's name, with the same address.

94 VOKS, 6:1:49:22, emphasis in the original.

95 VOKS, 6:1:49:17, letter from Tovstogan to Kulakovskaya, 26 November 1955.

96 VOKS, 6:1:53:42–4, Carter to Kulakovskaya, 28 December 1955.

97 Ibid.

98 VOKS, 6:1:53:45–52 Carter to Kulakovskaya, 2 January 1956, emphasis in the original.

99 VOKS, 6:1:49:88, dated February 1956.

100 VOKS, 6:1:49:5, letter from A. Vertogradov to A.S. Tovstogan, 3 April 1956.

101 VOKS, 6:1:49:117, letter from A. Vertogradov to A.S. Tovstogan, 12 May 1956.

102 VOKS, 6:1:53:87–9 forwarding letter Kiz to Kulakovskaya, 22 June 1956, and 'Greetings to the AUUC in Winnipeg, Manitoba, Canada.'

103 VOKS, 6:1:53:90.

104 VOKS, 6:1:49:126, letter from A. Tovstogan to Kulakovskaya, 7 April 1956.

105 VOKS, 6:1:49:127b, letter from Carter to CSFS members, 29 February 1956, emphasis in the original.

106 VOKS documents, letter from A. Tovstogan to Kulakovskaya, 26 November 1955, 49:5–6.

107 Numerous examples of these brochures, and the Carter advertisements, can be found in the Robert S. Kenny collection, MS Collection 179, Thomas Fisher Rare Book Library, University of Toronto, box 62.

108 The Novosti Press Agency Office photograph archives are located in the Special Collections at Carleton University.

109 VOKS, 6:1:50:29, letter from Yakovlev to Pozdeev, 17 December 1955.

110 VOKS, 6:1:55:186–8, letter from G. Ioanisyan to A. Tovstogan, 29 October 1957.

111 VOKS, 6:1:49:52, Vertogradov to Tovstogan, 25 March 1956.

112 Hanno Hardt, *In the Company of Media: Cultural Constructions of Communication, 1920s–1930s* (Boulder: Westview, 200), 38. This quotation is from Leon Trotsky, but though Carter would have agreed with the notion, he would never have acknowledged Trotsky for having made the comment. Stalin had declared Trotsky an 'enemy of the people' in the late 1920s, exiled him, and had him assassinated in 1940. He was never rehabilitated. Carter followed the official Soviet line unfailingly in all his publications.

113 Most likely the attendees were not, as Carter claimed, 'far from the progressive movement'; rather, they were individuals who were not Party members but nonetheless left-leaning. The CSFS-sponsored films were a drawing card for those who might not otherwise have attended an LPP event but who had some sympathies for and curiosity about life in the Soviet Union. This non-partisan veneer made the CSFS useful to both the LPP and the Soviets.

114 VOKS, 6:1:49:74, letter from A. Tovstogan to Kulakovskaya, 9 March 1956.

115 VOKS, 6:1:49:116, Vertogradov to Tovstogan, 12 May 1956.

116 VOKS, 6:1:49:117–20, lists of films in French and English, colour and black and white.

117 VOKS, 6:1:49:74a–75, Kulakovskaya to Tovstogan, 5 March 1956.

118 VOKS, 6:1:55:27–8, Tovstogan to Abramov, Sovexportfilm, 11 December 1956.

119 VOKS, 6:1:55:29, Ioanisyan to K.Z. Litvin (UkrOKS), 9 January 1956.

120 *Ukrainske zhittia*, 12 January 1956, summarized by the RCMP, LAC, RG146, A200600104, 17.

121 VOKS, 1952 finances 6:1:50:116; 1953: 6:1:50:117.

122 LAC, RG146, A200600103, RCMP review (24 February 1953) of *Vapaus*, 21 February 1953, 251.

123 *News-Facts* was published from 1950 to 1956, and *Northern Neighbors* from December 1956 to 1989. *News-Facts* was the official journal of the CSFS; *Northern Neighbors* was not. Dyson Carter's magazines and many of his books, though published by the CSFS or Northern Neighbours, were printed by Eveready Printers in Toronto. This continued to be the case after he moved to Gravenhurst in 1957. Eveready were the printers used most often by the LPP/CPC, and many of the employees were in fact LPP members. Nielsen interview; Boyd, 'A Noble Cause Betrayed.'

124 Glenna Roberts and Serge Cipko, *One Way Ticket: The Soviet Return to the Homeland Campaign 1955–1960* (Manotick: Penumbra, 2008). See also Serge Cipko and Peter M. Roberts, 'Canada and the Khrushchev Government's "Return to the Homeland" Campaign,' Occasional Paper

no. 8, Centre for Research on Canadian–Russian Relations, Carleton
University, Ottawa, November 2000. Cipko has also studied the cam-
paign in relation to the Ukrainian diaspora in Argentina. Some Finnish
Canadians had earlier been encouraged to return to the Karelo-Finnish
Soviet Socialist Republic – a migration that was generally tragic for
those concerned. See especially Lindstrom-Best's work and the
National Film Board–produced film *Letters from Karelia* (dir. Kelly
Saxberg), on which she consulted. On propaganda used to convince
Canadians to return to the Soviet Union, and these people's subsequent
desire to return to Canada, see also memoranda exchanged between the
Department of External Affairs, the Prime Minister, and the Canadian
Embassy in Moscow in 1960, in Janice Cavell, ed., *Documents on
Canadian External Affairs,* vol. 27 (Ottawa: Foreign Affairs and Inter-
national Trade Canada, 2007), 1009–13.

125 *News-Facts*, March 1956, 3.
126 Ibid.
127 *News-Facts*, June 1956, 7.
128 *News-Facts*, March 1950, 3.
129 In *Northern Neighbors* Carter used captions and photographs to suggest
    a before/after narrative about the Soviet Union. This was most striking
    when he wrote on the situation for native peoples in the Soviet north. By
    showing photographs of smiling people in traditional native dress, with
    signs of progress such as schools or factories in the background, Carter
    was suggesting that none of this had been possible before 1917. The
    gendered and racialized stereotypes are obvious and offensive, especially
    considering that this propaganda disguised the very difficult conditions
    confronting natives during the Soviet period. See for instance, Carter,
    'Peoples of the North Transformed,' *Northern Neighbors*, January 1978,
    6.
130 *News-Facts*, April-May 1953, no. 36.
131 LAC, RG146, A200600102, 72, RCMP summary of a Hungarian-lan-
    guage newspaper (title blacked out but probably *Kanadai Magyar
    Munkas* (Canadian Hungarian Worker), 8 January 1953, 10.
132 Dyson Carter, 'About This Book,' in Libbie and Frank Park, *Moscow –
    As Two Canadians Saw It* (Toronto: CSFS, 1951), 10.
133 Charlotte and Dyson Carter, *We Saw Socialism*, pt 1 (Toronto: CSFS,
    1951), 100.
134 VOKS, 6:1:35:2, letter from M. Korol, 10 November 1951.
135 VOKS, 6:1:55:123–5, letter from A. Tovstogan to G. Ioanisyan, 4 June
    1957.
136 Charlotte and Dyson Carter, *Whatever Happened in Czechoslovakia*
    (Gravenhurst: 1968) and *Whatever Happened in China?* (Gravenhurst:

1969) were both prepared and published by *Northern Neighbors*, of which Dyson Carter was editor.

137 Ralph Hyman, 'What's Behind the Curtain? One Fled, Knows; One Sails to Learn,' *Globe and Mail*, 5 September 1951, 15.

138 N. Prychodko, letter to the editor, 'Questions of Victims Challenge the Iron Curtain,' *Globe and Mail*, 8 September 1951, 6. Clipping also in LAC, RG146-3, 94-A-00198, 79.

139 Charlotte and Dyson Carter, *We Saw Socialism.*, 271–3. This section is subtitled '"But I Was There!"'

140 *News-Facts*, December 1955–January 1956, 16.

141 LAC, RG146, A200600104, 26, 'Society offering sub to members,' *Pacific Tribune*, 25 November 1955; LAC, RG146, A200600104, 35–6, CSFS Circular letter signed by Dyson Carter, 19 October 1955. CSFS yearly membership cost 50 cents.

142 See, for instance, the lists in VOKS, 6:1:49:67–71, February 1956; 6:1:49:76–83, January 1956; 6:1:49:128–41, February–March 1956.

143 VOKS, 6:1:57:60, Louise Harvey to VOKS, 1 April 1957.

144 VOKS, 6:1:39:23, Yakovlev to Burdin, 23 February 1953.

145 VOKS, 6:1:49:217, Yakovlev to Tovstogan, 16 October 1956.

146 See, for example, VOKS, 6:1:55:55, 56–9.

147 VOKS, 6:1:50:84, letter from Carter to Perevozchikov [sic], 17 August 1954.

148 *News-Facts* advertisement, 'At Last! You Can Learn the Russian Language,' 27 March 1955, RG146, vol. 3349, pt 20, 50.

149 VOKS, 6:1:49:37–8, letter from Tovstogan to Kulakovskaya, 10 January 1956.

150 VOKS, 6:1:49:49, letter from Yakovlev to Tovstogan, 5 March 1956.

151 VOKS, 6:1:49:157, letter from Kulikov, Deputy Director of Publication at *Moscow News*, to Starikov, VOKS, 15 June 1956; 6:1:49:165, Kulakovskaya to Tovstogan, 19 June 1956.

152 Dyson Carter, 'Millions Are Awakening to the Fact That Friendship with the Soviet Is for Our Own Sake, for Canada,' *Kanadai Magyar Munkas*, 18 February 1954; Carter, 'Trade, Jobs, Peace in Friendship with USSR,' *Ukrainian Canadian*, 15 February 1954; both articles in LAC, RG146, A200600103, 5–10.

153 Ibid.

154 Ibid.

155 Ibid.

156 Ibid., 5. Claiming that Kirov had been murdered by a foreign agent allowed Stalin the necessary excuse to arrest and execute hundreds of Party members in the purges of the 1930s.

157 See for instance, clippings from *Pacific Tribune, Canadian Jewish Weekly, Ukrainian Canadian*, and *Kanadai Magyar Munkas*, in LAC, RG146, A200600103, 11, 20, 23, 33.

158 Bobbie Marsden, 'A Name to Remember,' *Canadian Jewish Weekly*, n.d., RG146, A200600103, 21.

159 J.L. Black, 'Soviet Tactics and Targets in Canada Before and After the Gouzenko Defection,' in J.L. Black and Martin Rudner, *The Gouzenko Affair: Canada and the Beginnings of Cold War Counter-Espionage* (Manotick: Penumbra, 2006), 109.

160 See for instance the record of a 'collection card issued to raise funds to send X on a trip to the Soviet Union under the auspices of the Canadian Soviet Friendship Society,' issued by the British Columbia branch of the LPP, recorded by the RCMP in a memo from the Vancouver Subdivision, Vancouver Special Branch, 9 November 1953, LAC, RG146, A200600103, 95. This delegate's name has been erased from the document by ATIP. He or she was the secretary of the B.C. CSFS branch.

161 The itinerary of the trip is in VOKS 6:31:206–11. See also J.L. Black, 'Soviet Tactics and Targets in Canada Before and After the Gouzenko Defection,' in Black and Rudner, *The Gouzenko Affair,* 117.

162 Ibid., 118.

163 Frank and Libbie Park Trip to USSR File, CRCR, University Partnership Centre, Georgian College, Barrie.

164 LAC, RG146, A200600098, 29, 'Canadian Delegation in the Ukraine,' datelined 'Kiev' (Tass).

165 LAC, RG146, A200600098, 30, from *Soviet Monitor*, 19 May 1951.

166 LAC, RG146, A200600098, p. 37–8, RCMP report, 2 June 1951.

167 This meeting took place in the Point Douglas Labor Temple, 7 December 1953. LAC, RG146, A200600114, 19, circular letter signed 'Needle Trades Committee of the Canadian-Soviet Friendship Society.'

168 Canadian–Soviet Friendship Society, *Canadians Visit Our Northern Neighbours*, no publication date [1954], inside of back cover.

169 Ibid.

170 Ibid.

171 VOKS, 6:1:42:21, 23, 27, 93, 110, letters and memos written by Ted Baxter, CSFS National Secretary until 1956.

172 VOKS, 6:1:42: 20, 25, 79, 81, 103, various announcements and publicity for speaking engagements by 1953 delegates.

173 *Montreal Gazette*, 10 April 1954, LAC, RG146, A200600093, 18, 20, 23, 33. The departure of the Toronto artists was reported in Lotta Dempsey, 'Leave Next Week: Three Toronto Artists Plan Tour of Russia,' *Toronto Globe and Mail*, 1 April 1954, LAC, RG146, A200600093, 50; and in 'What's Going On in Red Culture Takes Six

Canadians to Moscow,' *Montreal Gazette*, 10 April 1954, LAC, RG146, A200600093, 22.

174 V. Nekrasov, 'Around the World: Soviet Artists in Canada,' *News*, 10 May 1954, LAC, RG146, A200600095, 18–19.

175 'All Canada Acclaims Triumphant Soviet Artists,' *Canadian Tribune*, 10 May 1954, RG145, A200600095, 28.

176 RCMP report, Toronto Special branch, 10 May 1954, LAC, RG146, A200600095, 22.

177 *Ukrainske slovo*, 21 April 1954, 1, 3, in LAC, RG146, A200600114, 12.

178 'They Fell in Love with Canada,' *Canadian Tribune*, RG146, vol. 3350, Supp. 5, pt 3, n.d., 48–9.

179 VOKS, 6:1:50:107, Sochasky to VOKS, n.d., but handwritten annotation 12 March 1955 in margins. Mrs Sochasky's name was variously transliterated in the VOKS documents also as Suchasky, Suchaski, Sokhatsky, and Sokhatsky, but each time she was listed as Mrs Anna/Anne … from Vancouver, CSFS delegate, *VOKS Bulletin* reader, AUUC, and/or CSFS member.

180 On this see especially Swyripa, *Wedded to the Cause*.

181 LAC, RG146, A200600092, RCMP report from the Special Branch, Nelson, B.C., 4 April 1955, 11.

182 LAC, RG146, A200600092, *Nelson Daily News*, 'Soviet Life Described Here,' 31 March 1955.

183 VOKS, 6:1:48:135, letter from Burdin to Perevoschikov, 25 May 1955.

184 LAC, RG146, A200600092, RCMP report from Cranbrook Special Branch, Nelson, 13 April 1955, 'Canadian–Soviet Friendship Society, Delegation to the USSR, December 1954,' 7–8.

185 LAC, RG146, A200600092, RCMP report from the Special Branch, Nelson, 4 April 1955, 'Canadian–Soviet Friendship Society, Delegation to the USSR – December 1954,' 11.

186 Ibid.

187 LAC, RG146, A200600104, RCMP report dated 14 April 1955, 53.

188 LAC, RG146, A200600092, 'Soviet Life Described Here,' *Nelson Daily News*, 31 March 1955, attached as part of the RCMP report, 4 April 1955, 'Canadian–Soviet Friendship Society, Delegation to the USSR – December 1954,' 14.

189 An RCMP report from 1950 noted emphatically that 'the AUUC is a part of the CANADIAN SOVIET FRIENDSHIP SOCIETY, and that Mr. WM. TERESIO, president of the AUUC is on the executive of the CANADIAN SOVIET FRIENDSHIP SOCIETY.' LAC, RG146, A200600096, RCMP report dated 6 March 1950, 248, emphasis in original.

190 LAC, RG146, A200600091, 'Memo to All Society Branches' from Ted Baxter, 15 January 1954, 38. William Teresio died on 6 January 1954.

191 LAC, RG146, A200600092, 'Dear Friend' letter and form from John Flatt, Joe Kossick, Jack Bingley, calling themselves jokingly the 'Committee for "Pat,"' Moose Jaw, Saskatchewan, 8 November 1954, attached to RCMP report, 24, 26. A postscript to this letter announced that 'this month is Soviet Friendship Month.'

192 For instance, Morris Biderman, himself a CSFS delegate, published an article on Louis Benzvy's trip to the Soviet Union in 1955. LAC, RG146, A200600092, Morris Biderman, 'A Warm Reunion in Moscow,' *Vochenblatt,* stamped 30 April 1955, attached to RCMP report, 46. For more on Biderman's activism, see his autobiography *A Life on the Jewish Left: An Immigrant's Experience* (Toronto: Onward, 2000).

193 VOKS, 50:52–4, Carter to Perevoschikov, 31 March 1955.

194 VOKS, 49:268, Carter to Tovstogan, 12 September 1956.

195 VOKS, 49:264–7, letter from Tovstogan to Vertogradov, 20 September 1956; VOKS, 55:70–7, letter from Tovstogan to Ioanisyan, 22 February 1957.

196 Nikita Khrushchev's so-called secret speech was given to a closed session of the Party at the 20th Party Congress on 25 February 1956. It became public only in March of that year, and is said to have given impetus to uprisings in the Soviet satellite countries later that year. When the revolt in Hungary was crushed by the Soviets in November 1956, international critics of all political orientations expressed alarm. Many leftists worldwide mark their disillusionment with the Soviet Union from this moment.

197 VOKS, 50:203, letter D. Chuvakhin (Soviet Ambassador to Canada) to G. Ioanisyan, 8 April 1957.

198 William Irvine, Dorothy Johnson, Harold Bronson, and B.F. Tanner participated on this tour, and their thank you letters to VOKS personnel (August–September 1956) are in the VOKS archival collection. VOKS, 6:1:54:72–83.

199 On the crisis in the Canadian LPP, and the strong feelings of disillusionment and disappointment caused by the events of 1956, see Merrily Weisbord, *The Strangest Dream: Canadian Communists, the Spy Trials, and the Cold War* (Montreal: Véhicule, 1983, 1994).

200 VOKS, 49:232–7, list of *VOKS Bulletin* subscribers and one cancellation, attached to a letter from Tovstogan to Vertogradov, 17 August 1956.

201 J.E. Baxter, interview with author, 8 December 2006, Stratford. Baxter said that RCMP officers repeatedly visited his workplace and spoke with his boss about his political activities.

202 VOKS, 49:13, letter from Tovstogan to Kulakovskaya, 16 December 1955.

203 VOKS, 49:264, letter from Tovstogan to Vertogradov, 20 September 1956.

204 VOKS, 55:2, letter from Tovstogan to Kulakovskaya, 11 December 1956.

205 VOKS, 55:150–1, letter from Tovstogan to Ioanisyan, 31 May 1957.

206 VOKS, 6:1:56:24–5, Carter to Kolmakova, 10 September 1957. The move may have been due partly to Carter's health. An accident in 1957 resulted in him spending some time in hospital and may have kept him from walking again. This was mentioned in letters to VOKS. VOKS, 6:1:55:150–1, 161–3, letter Tovstogan to Ioanisyan, 31 May 1957; Tovstogan to Ionisyan, 13 September 1957; VOKS, 6:1:56:18–19, 24–5, letter Charlotte Carter to Kolmakova, 11 June 1957; Kolmakova's reply to Charlotte Carter, 21 June 1957; letter from Dyson Carter to Kolmakova, 10 September 1957

207 Boyd interview; John Boyd, comments on manuscript by Jennifer Anderson, April 2008.

208 In an oral interview, Hunt explained that his English name and mannerisms helped him book speakers and make other arrangements for the association. Leslie Hunt, interview with author, 2 January 2007, Hanover.

209 Though it is difficult to be certain of the statistics, the letters to the editor in the Dyson Carter fonds at LAC suggest that many of his readers had immigrated to Canada from Eastern or Central Europe. As previously mentioned, an AUUC survey in 1965 found that many young AUUC members enjoyed *Northern Neighbors*. LAC, MG28-V-154, vol. 27, file 14-18, 'Poll of Participants of the AUUC National Youth Conference, July 9–11, 1965, Ukrainian Camp Palermo,' Toronto.

210 Reiter has suggested that these factors, together with the UJPO's 1951 expulsion from the Canadian Jewish Congress, caused the UJPO's decline. Reiter, 'Secular *Yiddishkait*,' paras. 33–5.

211 The last issue of *Northern Neighbors* appeared in 1989. The Canada–USSR Association was in decline in the late 1980s after Mikhail Gorbachev's policies of *glasnost* and *perestroika* radically changed the Soviet experience. In 1991 the Association became the Concerned Friends of the Soviet People, a Toronto-based group advocating the reestablishment of the Soviet Union. Today called the International Council for Friendship and Solidarity with the Soviet People, it continues to publish a pro-Soviet journal, *Northstar Compass,* but no longer receives official support from Moscow. Hunt interview; interview with Michael Lucas, 27 July 2006, Toronto.

PART FOUR

Internal Strife on the Left

Few topics have been quite so controversial in the field of Ukrainian-Canadian history – or in the internal politics of Ukrainians living in Canada – as the role played by those who were associated with the pro-communist left. Careful readers will have noted that in one way or another, almost every essay in this collection has raised the issue of radicalized Ukrainians. Paul Rudyk and Illia Kiriak eventually rejected radical politics in favour of more mainstream political and religious affiliations. For the leaders of the veterans' organizations Martynowych has studied – and for many of those mentioned in the works of Petryshyn and other contributors – the Ukrainian radicals were an enemy that had to be defeated at almost any cost.

The predominant interpretation of the Ukrainian-Canadian left has been that almost immediately after the creation of the Communist International and the Canadian Communist Party, there emerged a slavish and monolithic Ukrainian-Canadian left – one more committed to 'Moscow' than to Canada or to Ukrainians either in the diaspora or in the Old Country. By focusing on the 1920s and 1930s – and in particular, the roles played by leaders such as Matthew Popovich and Danylo Lobay – the essays in this part challenge the extant historiography by taking a more nuanced approach to the sources, illuminating just how lively many of the internal debates were within the Ukrainian-Canadian left during that crucial era. Perhaps even more to the point, they suggest that this part of the 'ethnic' left came very close to making a definitive break from Moscow on at least two occasions.

Jim Mochoruk's essay re-examines both the connections and the points of contention between Canada's English-speaking and Ukrainian radicals in the 1920s and early 1930s. Making use of Comintern documents on the 'Canadian Section,' he provides a detailed analysis of the relationship between the leaders of the Ukrainian Labour-Farmer Temple Association (ULFTA – the primary left-wing organization among Ukrainian Canadians) and the various Anglo-Celtic leaders of the Communist Party of Canada (CPC). Among other matters, his essay highlights the impact of personalities and generational conflicts in both the Ukrainian left and the CPC – questions routinely overlooked in the dominant historiography.

Andrij Makuch's study furthers this analysis by providing the first detailed examination of the fight that almost destroyed the Ukrainian-Canadian left in 1935. His analysis of the 'Lobay Crisis' (named after the long-time leader of the ULFTA, who raised the most difficult questions to ever confront the Ukrainian left) demonstrates the impact that Old Country events and ideological differences had on the Ukrainian progressive community in Canada. It also raises the fascinating question of 'what might have been' for the Ukrainian-Canadian left (and by implication the CPC) had Lobay and his supporters succeeded in having the ULFTA and its related organizations take the lead in challenging Moscow's party line in the 1930s.

10

'Pop & Co' versus Buck and the 'Lenin School Boys': Ukrainian Canadians and the Communist Party of Canada, 1921–1931

Jim Mochoruk

In the late 1990s, while doing research on a cooperative located in the heart of Winnipeg's North End, a disquieting feeling began to settle over me. This institution, which had been founded by members of the left-wing Ukrainian-Canadian community, and which was routinely attacked for its affiliations, did not always act in ways one might expect. As the records of the People's Co-op made clear, this cooperative did not always follow the path laid down by the Anglo-Celtic leadership of the Communist Party of Canada (CPC).[1]

For those who know something of the history of the radicalized Finns, Ukrainians, Russians, Poles, Jews, and other 'ethnics' who were affiliated with communist parties in North America during the 1920s, there is nothing really unusual about this. Hostility towards the Bolshevization and Stalinization and then the 'Leftward Turn' that characterized the years 1924 to 1931 accounted for many defections and/or expulsions from 'the Party.' What was different in this case was that the People's Co-op and its parent organizations – the Ukrainian Labour-Farmer Temple Association (ULFTA) and the Workers' Benevolent Association (WBA) – never left the party's orbit. Indeed, at an official policy level this triumvirate of Ukrainian-Canadian organizations seemed to remain the most faithful of what William Rodney has described as Canada's 'soldiers of the international.' Constitutions were amended to meet the requirements of the party line, self-criticism was 'freely' engaged in by these organizations' leaders, and the ultimate wisdom of the CPC and the Comintern was conceded at every turn in the party-affiliated Ukrainian-language press.[2]

Yet there was also an intriguing and ongoing discrepancy between official endorsement of the party line and the actions carried out by these institutions during the late 1920s and 1930s – and beyond. In effect, these organizations did not function as the automatic hand-maidens of party policy – a direct contradiction of the historiographical tradition that has labelled all the pro-communist organizations as monolithic and forever faithful servants of the party. The most notable and dramatic of these discrepancies was undoubtedly the Winnipeg-based co-op's decision not to provide the money requested by the Central Executive Committee of the Communist Party for the federal election campaign of Tim Buck, the national leader of the party, when he ran for Parliament in Winnipeg North in 1935. Of course, one could argue that this was a simple business decision: the co-op just did not have enough money to spare. One could also argue that when the co-op's board of directors (Ukrainian-speaking CPC members to a man) turned from this decision and immediately voted to make some charitable donations to local institutions, this was just good business – a stratagem designed to improve relations with the local community.[3] But as the research continued into these records and into RCMP and Attorney General of Manitoba files on the co-op and the WBA, these sorts of incidents continued to mount, begging an obvious question: What could account for what seemed to be a papered over but never completely healed rift between the Ukrainian left and the CPC leadership?

Unfortunately, the scholarly literature provided few satisfactory answers. The standard works on the CPC typically provided one or two paragraphs on Ukrainian-Anglo conflicts in the early history of the party and then quickly moved on to the major ideological shifts of the late 1920s and early 1930s.[4] Even John Kolasky's Ukrainian Canadian–focused *The Shattered Illusion* provided little coverage of such conflict. Slightly more useful were the works of Donald Avery and Ian Angus, who did have something substantive to say about ethnic conflict in the CPC during the 1920s.[5] These scholars intimated that the main source of conflict between the Ukrainian leftists and the Anglo-Celtic party leadership stemmed from the fact that the Ukrainian leaders had become protective both of their institutions' 'property' and of their positions within their organizations. In other words, they had become socially conservative and were therefore unwilling to make the 'leftward turn' – a standard criticism of the Ukrainians in the internal party literature of the late 1920s and early 1930s.[6]

Given the battles that the Ukrainians waged and the high-profile (and therefore dangerous) work they undertook in places like Winnipeg throughout the 1920s and early 1930s, this conclusion seemed badly flawed. Indeed, it seemed that Avery and Angus, in at least this one instance, had been led astray by the critique of the Ukrainians' leading foes within the party. One alternative – and decidedly non-ideological – interpretation did begin to suggest itself, however. Old-timers at the Ukrainian Labour Temple (where the co-op's records were housed) suggested to me that there had been some especially bitter and intensely personal infighting among the highest ranks of the party – fighting that pitted the established Ukrainian leaders (Matthew Popovich, John Boychuck, Danylo Lobay, Matthew Shatulsky, and John Navis) against Tim Buck and his cohort of 'Lenin School Boys' (Stewart Smith, Sam Carr, Leslie Morris, John Weir, and their colleagues), who took control of the CPC in 1929–30. Still, the conventional wisdom – both at the Labour Temple and in histories of the CPC – was that all of this infighting had been resolved, with help from the Comintern, by 1931.

Yet the discrepancies between the party line and the activities of the left-wing Ukrainian organizations noted above continued long after 1931, causing me to think that there was more to the story than this. Indeed, it struck me that the rift between the Ukrainians and the CPC leaders had actually preceded the leftward turn and was so profound that it never completely healed, Comintern directives and 'help' notwithstanding. Moreover, it seemed likely that these divisions not only accounted for the incongruities between the party line and the activities of the co-op, the ULFTA, and the WBA for much of the 1930s, but had also laid the groundwork for the Lobay crisis, which almost tore asunder the Ukrainian-Canadian left in 1935–6.[7] Partial confirmation of this suspicion was provided by a long-time stalwart of the Ukrainian-Canadian left, Peter Krawchuk, in his last major publication, *Our History: The Ukrainian Labour-Farmer Movement in Canada, 1907–1991*.[8] In a stunning reversal of much of his earlier work, which had emphasized the unity of purpose between the party and the Ukrainian mass organizations, Krawchuk argued that a huge divide had emerged between key Ukrainian leaders, such as Matthew Popovich, and the Anglo-Celtic leaders of the party in the late 1920s, largely as a result of the English-speaking leaders' attempts to either liquidate the Ukrainian mass organizations or gain control of their considerable resources for party purposes. Still, while Krawchuk's analysis was fascinating, it was problematic on several levels: first, it was marked by an element of self-exoneration that was worrisome; second, Krawchuk at the time of publication had not released control of the documents on which he based his strongest claims concerning the fight between Ukrainian leftists and the Anglo-Celtic leaders of the CPC; and finally, he tended to misidentify certain documents as to time and place, which rendered suspect his chronology as well as parts of his analysis.[9] However, the acquisition by the National Archives of Canada (as it was then known) of the records of the Canadian-related sections of the Comintern allows one both to test Krawchuk's contentions and to move beyond his particular polemic.

What follows is an analysis of the Winnipeg-based Ukrainian-Canadian left from the early 1920s to 1931 and its problematic relationship with the party centre – an analysis that relies almost solely on Comintern sources. However, this is most emphatically not a study of Comintern policy; while shifts in that policy must be considered, this essay places most of its emphasis on the clash of personalities, generations, ambitions, and ethnicities that arose in the 1920s and carried through into the 1930s. It seeks to provide a more nuanced understanding of the complex relationships that existed between the Ukrainian left and the CPC than has been available heretofore. It is hoped that this approach will allow for a breaking away from the historiographical polarities of apologetics, à la Krawchuck, as well as from the simplistic notion that there was a monolithic, pro-communist Ukrainian-Canadian left.

It also needs to be said that this essay is really only a preliminary study, for it is still rooted in an analysis of the movement's elite male leadership – not of the rank and file, and not of the women who played such an important part in the left-wing community. The people being studied here had carefully defined notions both of what they believed and of what they hoped the members of their organizations would come to believe. As will become clear, these Ukrainian-speaking leaders saw themselves as very good communists – indeed, often as better communists than many of their English-speaking comrades. But if they saw themselves as better Bolsheviks than some high-ranking English-speaking party members, they still did not see themselves as being at any great ideological distance from these people. Their real point of differentiation was that they identified themselves as part of a worldwide movement of workers and peasants – a movement that, in their understanding, had much room for cultural, linguistic, and even national differentiation. In short, they saw themselves as *Ukrainian* communists, the two words being inseparable in their minds. It was precisely this understanding, and the Ukrainian leaders' success at running institutions based on this view, that would cause them so much grief with their Anglo-Celtic comrades and make it so difficult for even the most dedicated Ukrainian communist 'to be Red.'

In Winnipeg, the organizational centre of the Ukrainian-Canadian left, the immigrant communities that populated the city's North End had developed a tradition of political radicalism and cultural defiance long before there was a Communist Party of Canada.[10] Indeed, as Orest Martynowich has pointed out in several works on Ukrainians in Canada, and as several commentators on Jewish radicalism in Winnipeg have made clear, traditions of political radicalism were part and parcel of the cultural baggage that many of these people had carried with them to Canada.[11] As a result, dating back to the turn of the century, Winnipeg's North End was a hotbed of political and cultural dissent. Several sections of the Marxist-oriented Socialist Party of Canada, of the equally Marxist-inspired Social Democratic Party of Canada, and of the 'Yiddishist' Arbeiter Ring (including separate Anarchist, Marxist, and Socialist-Zionist branches), as well as innumerable smaller but equally radical reading circles and dramatic/cultural groups, sprang up in the North End during the first two decades of the twentieth century.[12] And these impoverished immigrant radicals not only supported political parties, unions, cultural groups, and newspapers with their time and money but also banded together so that 'Halls' could be built or purchased to house their political organizations, to provide space for their printing presses, newspapers, and journals, and to serve as meeting places for myriad cultural and educational activities. More remarkable still, there were actually several sets of these halls/meeting places, as for every radical hall serving a particular ethnic group there would always be several more politically conservative or religiously oriented organizations with their own cultural/educational facilities, sometimes for the explicit purpose of battling the influence of the left within that ethnic group.[13] It was never easy being Red.

The most impressive of these halls was Winnipeg's Ukrainian Labour Temple, located at the corner of Pritchard and McGregor. Built with the financial contributions and the volunteer labour of the left-wing Ukrainian community in 1918–19, this $72,000 structure was completed just in time to serve as a North End headquarters for the Winnipeg General Strike.[14] This hall would become the political and cultural centre for several generations of radicalized Ukrainian Canadians, as well as home to a host of related political, economic, and cultural organizations. And the Ukrainian Labour Temple Association (ULTA) quickly sought to establish branches wherever there was a sizeable Ukrainian population, with the result that several score of these halls sprang up throughout Canada during the 1920s and 1930s.[15]

The ULTA (in 1924 renamed the Ukrainian Labour-Farmer Temple Association, or ULFTA, to be more inclusive) was an ambitious undertaking from the outset, not only in the sense of constructing halls but also in terms of what was to go on within them. Seeing itself as a national organization with strong ties both to the 'Old Country' and to the international working-class movement, it adopted a broad-ranging mandate when first formed in 1918. Its mission was to 'give moral and material aid to the Ukrainian working people and to the labour cause in general' through a ten-point plan of action focusing on educational, cultural, and mutual aid activities.[16]

In keeping with this mandate, in 1922 the ULTA created yet another Winnipeg-based organization, which also became national in scope. This was the Workers' Benevolent Association (WBA), a mutual insurance organization for Ukrainian Canadians, which provided its members with death benefits as well as a rudimentary form of health insurance.[17] Acting together, the ULFTA and the WBA would found the Workers and Farmers Co-operative Association (later renamed the People's Co-op) in 1928.[18]

By the late 1920s the leaders of these Ukrainian-language 'mass organizations' were running a rapidly expanding mutual benefit/insurance society, a growing number of Labour Temples, and hosts of cultural and educational programs within those halls, besides writing, editing, and distributing four Ukrainian-language newspapers and journals.[19] The ULFTA had 187 branches with 5,483 members; the WBA had 116 branches with 7,400 members. Beyond this, several thousand others who were not members took part in the two organizations' drama circles, choirs, orchestras, and schools. Many also had what most would have found to be incredibly time-consuming commitments to the Communist Party, the Workers' Party, and the Canadian Labour Party. Still, the leadership of the left-wing Ukrainian community was determined to expand beyond even this daunting set of activities – a determination signalled most clearly when the executive committees of the WBA and the ULFTA, and of the Winnipeg and Women's Section branches of both, held a series of meetings in the summer of 1928.[20]

The ambition and reach of the men and women who attended these meetings was quite staggering. To begin with, they put forward a detailed plan for launching a cooperative that would start by entering the coal and wood trade; they hoped it would soon expand to include grocery stores, a butcher shop, an information bureau, a bookstore, and just about anything else that might reach large numbers of Winnipeg workers as quickly as possible. Later on the same agenda, an even more audacious plan of action was developed: the WBA, with backing from the ULFTA, hoped to purchase a former country club and its 104 acres on the outskirts of Winnipeg, which it would turn into a largely self-supporting orphanage, school, and retirement home for members of the Ukrainian progressive community.[21] The plans for establishing the co-op and for purchasing the 'Parkdale Home' were realized within weeks of these meetings.

One part of what was arguably Canada's most despised and impoverished immigrant group stood on the cusp of something quite amazing: the creation of an oasis where they and their families could live their entire lives almost entirely in the context of their own ethnic, radical community yet still reach out to others like themselves in order to bring them within the socialist fold. One's birth could be attended by a WBA-sanctioned and paid-for physician; one's linguistic, artistic, and political education as well as much of one's social life and recreational activities could be provided in the ULFTA hall; one's daily physical needs could be satisfied at the co-op; all one's information could come from the organization's newspapers; employment needs might well be taken care of through a teaching position at the hall, a staff position on one of the papers, a labouring job at the co-op, or an industrial job or perhaps an organizer's position obtained via connections to the left-wing union movement; and finally, one's declining years could be spent at Parkdale, after which the WBA would fund one's funeral at the Labour Temple. What Gramsci would have termed a counter-hegemony was being shaped by these Ukrainian radicals, right down to the creation of the movement's own intellectuals in the 'higher education' courses run by the ULFTA and the WBA.[22]

Here, however, was the nub of the problem that so bedevilled the Ukrainian-Canadian left in its relations with the CPC in the 1920s and early 1930s. Even though Ukrainian-Canadian leftists had been among the founders of the CPC,[23] the independence – and, ironically, the success – of the institutions they had created and then brought within the general orbit of the party after 1921 would be the root cause of their problems with CPC leaders. Not to put too fine a point on matters, by the mid-1920s 'independence' was not a quality much appreciated in the broader communist movement.

Still, by this time, independence was a way of life for the Ukrainian leadership. Indeed, the earliest leaders of the Ukrainian-Canadian left had made a very conscious decision to leave the Socialist Party of Canada in 1910 at least partly because of that party's unwillingness to accept independent 'language federations' or to pay serious attention to the concerns of non-British immigrant radicals. They had later affiliated their left-wing Ukrainian-Canadian organization with the Canadian Social Democratic Party, but as an independent federation known as the Ukrainian Social Democratic Party (USDP).[24] Even more to the point, when they created the ULTA in 1918 they consciously crafted it as a Ukrainian-language and culture-based institution. Every other institution they created between 1918 and the early 1930s would follow suit.

When the CPC was first formed in 1921 the independence of these Ukrainian (and other) language based 'mass organizations' was not a problem. Indeed, these organizations provided a level of support and membership for both the legal and the underground CPC that would have been unthinkable had the party focused solely on English- or French-speaking recruits.[25] This is not to say that party leaders were content with this situation. As English was the dominant language in Canada, the goal was always to increase the number and 'quality' of English-speaking members. Thus, even in Winnipeg, with its large Eastern European population, the early party leadership was fixated on recruiting members not from the left-wing mass organizations of the ethnic groups, but from the largely English-speaking ranks of the One Big Union (OBU) and the Socialist Party of Canada (SPC).[26] Yet it was an inescapable fact that the language federations were the party's real strength. As a Central Executive Committee (CEC) member visiting Winnipeg in 1921 noted, he was far more 'impressed with the work of the Ukrainians and Russians than the English.'[27] But there was no question as to the long-term 'English orientation' of the party. At a CEC meeting in February 1922, where plans for the creation of the legal (Workers') party were being finalized, the instructions for delegate selection to the founding convention of the new party were clear: the local executive committees of the underground party were to ensure 'that a majority of delegates should be English-speaking.'[28]

The Ukrainian left found itself in a somewhat ambiguous relationship with the party – or rather parties, as there was the underground 'Z' party, and the legal Workers Party ('A' in the CPC's nomenclature), as well as the Canadian Labour Party of the mid-1920s. Despite their numerical importance to the three parties, and despite having been founding members, few Ukrainians served as senior executives or even as elected delegates to party conventions. (At such gatherings, Ukrainian leaders such as Navis, Boychuck, Shatulsky, and Popovich typically made appearances as fraternal delegates or as representatives of the Ukrainian Section or Bureau.) On the other hand, criticism of the Ukrainian leadership was rarely heard prior to 1924; in fact, the Convention Report of 'Z' for 1923 singled out the Ukrainian Section for praise owing to its rapid growth, the excellence of its press (especially *Ukrainian Labor News*), its fight against Ukrainian nationalists, and its struggle against American-based Ukrainian 'left baiters.' Also praised was the work of the ULTA, the WBA, and the Women's Sections of the various Ukrainian mass organizations.[29] Still, one other item came out of this report which indicated that things were about to change: gratified by the growth and success of the legal party, the delegates concluded that 'the dualism of "Z" and "A" was no longer necessary.'[30] While a bit premature – the amalgamation of the two parties, at the Comintern's urging, would not take place for another year – the plan for how to end this dualism would have serious implications for the affiliated ethnic organizations, as the CPC's old 'group' system was to be 'liquidated.'[31] This was not yet a move towards Bolshevization, but the decision to reorganize was a harbinger of things to come.

Still, in 1923 there was no question of how important the ethnic organizations were to the party. Shortly after the 1923 Conventions of 'A' and 'Z' the newly enlarged CEC passed a resolution indicating that the Finnish and Ukrainian Sections, which already had their own newspapers, 'are to be approached for advances of perhaps $500.00 each in order to launch the *Weekly Worker* [a projected English-language paper for the party] These sums are, of course, to be considered as parts of the quotas allotted.'[32] For the always cash-strapped party, the financial resources available through the language federations were indispensable, and one did not treat too harshly with such valuable groups – something that the new leader of the party, Jack Macdonald, clearly understood.

One last matter arose in 1923 that also needs to be considered in any analysis of the rift that was to develop between the Ukrainians and the CPC. On the face of it, the appointment of a new organizer for District #4 – as the Prairie West and Winnipeg were now designated – should not have been all that important a matter. However, when Leslie Morris, a very English young man who had already served as the head of the Canadian branch of the Young Communist League (YCL), was appointed by the Central Executive Committee to this post, it elicited a storm of protest from the district. A report to the CEC indicated that Morris was viewed as too young and inexperienced, though it was quickly added that these 'were not reflections upon [the] integrity and ability of Morris.'[33] Most of the objections came from Winnipeg, and though there is no clear indication that the opposition was led by Ukrainian party members of that city, one suspects this was the case, as Ukrainians constituted the majority in the Winnipeg party. A compromise that would have made Morris the secretary of the Winnipeg Central Committee, with most of his wages being paid by party headquarters, was also rejected by the Winnipeg branch. As a result, District #4 remained without an organizer for several months. More important here, this was the first of many battles that would find Morris pitted against the 'old Ukes' (as he came to term them) who ran the party in Winnipeg.

Having won this minor skirmish, the Ukrainian-dominated Winnipeg branch of the CPC continued on its independent ways. When the party decided to have its legal organization, the Workers' Party, take part in the rejuvenation of the Canadian Labour Party as part of the United Front policy, the Winnipeg branch followed a more unilateral path. Because Winnipeg had a particularly strong branch of the Independent Labour Party, which had absolutely no desire for communist support, all attempts by the local branch of the Workers' Party to form an electoral alliance with the ILP failed. In October and November of 1923, with municipal elections in the offing, the Winnipeg communists decided that they would field candidates against the ILP 'reformists.' When informed of this, the CEC told the Winnipeg branch not to proceed, for 'we, as a Party, can hardly expect to build a United Front by fighting in such a manner.'[34] However, as the minutes of this meeting indicated, 'since the above [message was sent to Winnipeg] further information had come through to the effect that the comrades had decided to enter the campaign.'[35] Matthew Popovich came just a few votes short of winning a seat on City Council.

Old habits die hard, and in Winnipeg and more specifically in its Ukrainian organizations, the 'habit' was independence. Under the federated structure that was still in effect in 1923, a fairly large and important segment of the party could successfully exert its own will; this would become more difficult a year later, after the Fifth Congress of the Comintern. That congress categorically rejected the federative structure of the Canadian party (and other CPs) as an appropriate structure for a revolutionary movement. The order of the day was now to be Bolshevization, democratic centralism, and party discipline. It seemed that the writing was on the wall for the Ukrainian leaders: they would either follow the party line or face expulsion from the revolutionary movement – a prospect not relished by men like Popovich and Navis, who had been committed to radical mass movements since their student days in Galicia.[36]

Not long after the CPC's representative, Tim Buck, returned from the 1924 Comintern Congress, the Political Committee of the CEC met with the Executive Committee of the Ukrainian Section to review its performance over the past year. Some credit was given to the Ukrainian leadership for improvements in *Ukrainian Labour News*, which was now judged to be more 'clearly communist in expression.'[37] However, the Ukrainian leadership was to be placed on a much shorter leash. As the CEC's minutes put it: 'The Party sec'y suggested and it was agreed

on that minutes of the E.C. of the [Ukrainian] Section should be translated into English for the perusal of the C.E.C.' And then there was the
matter of the Ukrainian youth. For some time it had bothered leaders of
the Young Communist League that young Ukrainians were not joining
the YCL. Worse yet, earlier in 1924 the ULFTA had formed its own
youth organization, which was seen by some in the YCL as a directly
competing body. The Ukrainian Section was informed that some form
of cooperation between the Ukrainian Youth Section and the YCL
would have to be established. (The Ukrainian Section would later be
ordered to disband its Youth Section so as to leave the field open for the
YCL. It went along with this, albeit grudgingly and only for a short
time.)[38]

While willing to concede that perhaps some mistakes had been made
and that more cooperation with the YCL would be useful, the secretary
of the Ukrainian 'Bureau' indicated to the CEC that there were some
within the party who seemed to take particular delight in criticizing
everything the Ukrainians did. Indeed, he had been informed by the
Edmonton Branch of the Ukrainian Section that 'Comrade Kavanagh
as party organizer, had declared in an open meeting, that nothing
existed worthwhile, so far as the Ukrainian Section was concerned in
the East.'[39] In this particular matter, the Ukrainians actually received
some satisfaction: the CEC had the Party Secretary write to Kavanagh
'to the effect that such loose statements did not make for the better-
ment of the Party.'[40]

Intentionally or not, the Winnipeg-based Ukrainian leaders were
alienating some of those who were 'stars' or 'rising stars' in the party.
These people included Jack Kavanagh, a high-profile and much coveted
OBU convert to the CPC;[41] Leslie Morris, who had led the Canadian
YCL and would one day become CPC leader; and Stewart Smith, the
YCL's current leader (and a man who viewed himself as destined for
leadership of the Canadian party), who was intensely critical of the
Ukrainian youth organizations. In relatively short order the Ukrainian
leadership would add to its roster of critics many more members of the
YCL, as well as the party's industrial organizer, Tim Buck, and a host
of other English-speaking party leaders. All in all, a rather impressive
agglomeration of unfriendly comrades. Still, Ukrainian leaders like
Popovich, Boychuck, Navis, and Shatulsky had few problems with Jack
Macdonald, the CPC leader. Indeed, Macdonald gave every indication

that within reasonable limits, he was inclined to let the Ukrainians and other ethnic groups within the party retain much of their autonomy. A certain amount of independence for the Ukrainians, especially in their Winnipeg power base, could be maintained, just so long as the 'youngsters' – or as Popovich would later describe them, the 'young bums'[42] – did not take control of the party. At least this was the way it looked in 1924 and early 1925.

What few Canadian communists could have anticipated was that in 1925 a 'mistake' on a key doctrinal issue by the CEC of the Canadian party would increase Comintern scrutiny of the entire Canadian organization. William Moriarty of the CEC had been attending Comintern meetings in Moscow in the spring of 1925 in order to present the CPC's official report to that body. It was a remarkably upbeat document, noting among other matters how much more closely the Ukrainian and Finnish groups were following party policy and how the Ukrainian Labour Temple Association, 'under party pressure,' had dropped its work of organizing Ukrainian youth into a 'nationalist group.'[43] But there was a problem. Before giving his report, the issue of Leon Trotsky's 'abandonment' of Leninism was broached. Moriarty wired the Canadian CEC for its collective opinion on this matter; a reply telegram from Jack Macdonald indicated that it was the unanimous decision of the Canadian CEC that the evidence presented against Trotsky, on the charge that he had revised Leninism, was not convincing. In a rather nice rhetorical flourish, the Canadian telegram concluded that the Canadian CEC 'Consider Comintern Prestige Harmed Here By Bitter Anti Trotsky Attack.'[44]

To say that the Comintern leadership was unimpressed by the Canadian response would be an understatement of some magnitude, and no minor mea culpa, indicating that the CPC had not understood Leninism properly, was going to suffice. Nothing short of a full-blown investigative 'Canadian Commission' of the Executive Committee of the Communist International (ECCI) would do.[45] As it turned out, the commission offered a damning critique of the Canadians: the CPC had alienated itself from the entire Communist International by its stand on Trotskyism; it was 'backwards' in its reorganization of the party on a factory/industrial basis; and it was 'in many respects only a federation of various language federations.'[46] These last two criticisms were extremely bad news for the Ukrainians as well as for other ethnic groups within the party.

In documents issued by the ECCI to the Canadian party in the spring and summer of 1925 the CPC was given its marching orders for immediate and full-scale Bolshevization. This was easier said than done, and a notable level of resistance sprang up against this directive among some of the ethnic groups. At least part of this resistance arose because the Canadian commission's 'recommendations' had been taken by some English-speaking party members as licence to attack their ethnic counterparts and turn them into scapegoats for everything that was wrong with the party. Indeed, at the CPC's fourth national convention later that year, some of the Ukrainian and Finnish delegates could barely restrain their anger at the attacks launched against them both on the floor of the convention and in the party press.

In carefully prepared reports to the convention, the Ukrainian and Finnish Bureaus made it clear that together they accounted for approximately 4,000 of the party's 4,500 members, that they were the only segments of the party that could report growth in membership and branches, and that they contributed the lion's share of party dues, newspaper subscriptions, and miscellaneous donations to the party. As the report of the Ukrainians pointed out – in a backhanded critique of both the English membership and the Anglo-Celtic leadership of the party – if the party was to be reorganized the lead would have to come from active and effective English-speaking members. Moreover, 'the Ukrainian comrades had much serious work to do in combating the white guard organizations and influence' among Ukrainian workers – a problem that had seemingly escaped the attention of English-speaking party members. Finally, the Ukrainians felt that the party would also have to rouse the entire labour movement to fight the government's 'systematic campaign to deny naturalization to foreign born persons who are in any way sympathetic towards labour.'[47]

When a broad-ranging discussion on the possible 'liquidation' of the language federations took place at this convention, several Ukrainian delegates lashed out at Comrade Lakeman (a party organizer in Alberta), who had published a letter in *The Worker* accusing the language sections of spending all their efforts on holding concerts, dances, and other cultural events and 'entertainments.' As the convention proceedings noted: 'One or two of the delegates thought that the CEC should not have allowed the letter to be published. It was clearly pointed out that if it had not been for the money raised by those entertainments perhaps the Party would have no press today. Comrade Hautamaki [of the Finnish Section] referred to the fact that there were only about 300 English comrades in the Party, and he wanted to know how the [language] section comrades kept them from doing more in this field [of organizing].'[48]

The implications of such comments were well understood, but as far as the party leadership was concerned, the basic project of Bolshevization would have to proceed as per the Comintern directive, whatever the consequences. And the consequences were dramatic: between September 1925 and May 1926, when reorganization along a 'factory and street nuclei basis' was technically completed, the party entered a sharp downward spiral. An internal party report prepared by Tim Buck indicated that between September 1925 and October 1926 the party had suffered 'a net loss of 1350 members. The total loss, however, is considerably greater in as much as 810 new members have been initiated during the year.'[49] In other words, in the year since reorganization began, the party had lost 2,160 veteran members – almost half the 1925 membership. Nor was the cost of reorganization felt solely in terms of numerical support. As Buck noted, in the old organizational framework the language sections of the Finns and Ukrainians had been 'entirely self-supporting. They maintained their own organizers, secretaries etc developed their own press and paid a straight per capita tax of 15 cents per member to the national office. In effect the language sections helped considerably to finance work among the English-speaking workers.'[50] In the new system there were no such links, and as a result the party had become not just moribund but essentially bankrupt. Three of the party's English-language publications (controlled but not owned outright) had been suspended for lack of funds, there was no money to pay the salaries of district organizers, and donations and subscriptions for *The Worker*, the party's most important paper, had fallen so sharply that it faced a monthly deficit of $140, which the party could no longer afford to meet.[51]

Not surprisingly, Buck called for at least a modified return to language- and ethnic-based organization for the party. He had seen the past – and it worked!

The greatest irony – and for some the greatest irritation – in this reorganizational fiasco was that the Ukrainians continued to march to the beat of their own drum – and it was a fairly upbeat tempo at that.

Though it was never said in so many words, one suspects that in 1925 and 1926 both the leadership and the rank-and-file of the ULFTA and the WBA were thinking 'to Hell with you' when it came to directives from the party leadership. Indeed, one must almost pity Jack Macdonald as he attempted to get Ukrainian party members to follow CEC directives as they conducted their work within the ULFTA and WBA during this period. He had gone to Winnipeg early in 1926 for that exact purpose and had returned home more than a little frustrated.

On his return to National Party Headquarters in Toronto, he reported to the CEC that he had conducted several lengthy meetings with the Ukrainian leadership just prior to the ULFTA (and WBA) Convention of January 1926. On almost every important matter the Ukrainian organizations had refused to follow the party line. The issue of a ULFTA-affiliated youth organization had arisen once again, and Macdonald had informed the Ukrainian party members who were about to attend the convention of the CEC's *decision* that there should be no youth organizations other than the YCL and Young Pioneers. Almost to a man the Ukrainian comrades had refused to accept this directive. After being 'deadlocked for many hours on the question,' Macdonald thought that he had finally worked out a compromise: the Ukrainian comrades could endorse the proposed youth organization but not the proposals for dues payments or a youth magazine. However, at the ensuing ULFTA Convention the youth organization was reborn as a *dues-paying* organization, and a few months later a new Ukrainian-language youth journal was being produced at the ULFTA's printing shop in Winnipeg.

At that same lengthy meeting, Macdonald had also outlined the CEC's opposition to the creation of a Winnipeg-based cooperative, arguing that it would take up far too much of the Ukrainian comrades' time and energy. On this matter Macdonald refused to make any concessions and was apparently assured that the resolution calling for the creation of cooperatives would not be supported. Not long after Macdonald left Winnipeg he was informed that the convention had passed the resolution to create a cooperative. Two years later the Winnipeg-based Workers and Farmers Cooperative Association (later the Peoples' Co-op) was established.[52]

Judging from party records, just about everything related to Winnipeg and the Ukrainian organizations centred there seemed to cause pain for several leading figures in the CPC in 1925–6 and well into

1927. For example, late in 1925 the local party leaders in Winnipeg again ignored directives with regard to running candidates as Canadian Labour Party candidates – a matter that continued to raise the ire of CEC members as late as 1927, when they again criticized the party's Winnipeg branch for this decision.[53] As one Winnipeg delegate at the CPC's 1927 national convention put it so aptly, 'We are sometimes accused of having a local point of view, I mean the Winnipeg delegates representing Winnipeg,' but in his (Tom Ewen's) view, this was not the fault of the local party members – it was simply their reaction to a lack of solid leadship at the national level![54] At that same convention, the report of the Ukrainian Agit Prop Secretary elicited considerable acrimony as he detailed just how well the Ukrainian mass organizations were doing. As delegate after delegate criticized the Ukrainians for their focus on the ULFTA, the WBA, their myriad cultural activities, and especially their controversial decision to restart the Ukrainian youth organization, Matthew Popovich took it all in and then struck back. Popovich reminded the delegates that it was Ukrainian comrades who had helped build the Mine Workers Union of Canada in Alberta and that it was the Ukrainians who had just recently ensured the election of North America's first communist alderman, William Kolisnyk, in the Winnipeg civic elections of 1926. He then pointed out just how great the Ukrainians' financial contributions to the party and its English-language press had always been, and how the ULFTA's many halls had always been made available to the party, and how even the ULFTA's 'Mandolin orchestra has been exploited … for Party interests.' But he saved his real wrath for the YCL. As he saw it, 'the [Ukrainian] youth had been left for the YCL to organize and they had failed to do so and even failed to hold those who had once joined. The Ukrainian units of the YCL had died before the Youth Section [of the ULFTA] was born. The Ukrainian comrades should certainly not be blamed by the comrades for the failure of the YCL.' Indeed, Popovich suggested that 'we should center our attention upon the YCL and find out why it does not attract the young workers.'[55]

The new Secretary of the YCL, Oscar Ryan, was livid and proposed a resolution calling for the outright condemnation of the Ukrainian Youth Section. This touched off further heated debate. At the end of the day, Ryan and the YCL were persuaded to water down their resolution. Macdonald displayed remarkable equanimity, especially given that he had been personally blindsided by some of the Ukrainians' 1926 decisions. Even so, he made it clear that he wanted to re-establish some level of harmony in the party.[56] As events would soon prove, however, the YCL's backing away from its overt condemnation of the Ukrainians was only a strategic retreat in a battle that would continue to intensify.

The years 1927 to 1929 were pivotal for Communist Parties around the world. Bolshevization was still the order of the day, but it was now being supplanted by Stalinization. Communist Parties worldwide were now being expected to support Stalin's position on the creation of 'socialism in one country,' to forcibly root out 'Trotskyism,' to abandon United Front tactics, and to prepare for the inevitable inter-Imperialist wars (including an armed struggle between Britain and the United States) and the equally inevitable attack of the imperialist powers on the Soviet Union. They were also expected to attack 'right-wing' devia- tions and to move their parties towards a more militant class-struggle position. As important as these changes undoubtedly were, for the Ukrainian-Canadian left it would be the ongoing struggle between the Ukrainian leadership and certain English-speaking leaders of the CPC – an often intensely personal fight waged along generational and eth- nic rather than ideological lines – that would have the greatest impact on the Ukrainian left's relationship to the party. Viewed in this context, changes in Comintern policy simply gave the foes of the Ukrainian leadership additional cudgels to wield.

The Ukrainian leadership had angered many English-speaking party leaders between 1923 and 1927; that said, its deepest estrangement was from the leadership of the YCL, past and present. Young men like Stew- art Smith, Leslie Morris, Oscar Ryan, and Charlie Marriot had been incensed over the Ukrainian leaders' perceived lack of support for the YCL and their strong focus on Ukrainian cultural and organizational questions. More to the point, these young men were not content to fight the Ukrainians on the convention floor or in the CEC meeting rooms. As a series of letters written by Leslie Morris in 1928 make clear, he and several others from the YCL were part of a self-styled opposition group that as early as 1926–7 had decided to undermine the authority of the 'old Ukes,' especially Matthew Popovich.[57]

Morris, who had finally been assigned to Winnipeg by the party in 1926, had worked very hard to break the control over the local party machinery wielded by the older Ukrainian leaders, who included

William Kolysnik (whom he thought a fool and an embarrassment to the party) and Matthew Popovich (whom he thought dangerous, controlling, and clever). He had also sought to assemble a group of Canadian-born – or at least Canadian-raised – Ukrainians who could help him challenge the grip of 'Pop and Company' over the Winnipeg-based Ukrainian organizations. Among his recruits were John Weir (Wevursky or Vyviursky) and Fred and Dan Holmes (Chomitsky).

In the first regard, Morris failed miserably. In preparation for the Winnipeg municipal elections of November 1927 he had tried to gain the party's nomination for the aldermanic race in the North End by doing an end run around the Ukrainians. Morris had used the party's City Committee to nominate him without calling a general membership meeting. Matthew Popovich, at the time a member of the national CEC, wrote to National Party Headquarters: 'This had given rise to dissatisfaction amongst the membership and certainly gave no promise that the necessary organization of the whole membership would be forthcoming.' In the face of this implied threat of non-support, the national CEC stepped in and insisted that a general membership meeting be called in Winnipeg.[58] More to the point, a new district organizer, Tom Ewen, was appointed for the area, again frustrating Morris's hopes for that particular appointment. If nothing else, this brouhaha inspired the national level of the party to launch a broad reorganization for 'the whole city membership.'[59] So in one sense at least, even if he had again been embarrassed in the eyes of the party, some of Morris's hopes were being realized, for according to most subsequent reports, the Ukrainians were unhappy with this reorganization. Better yet for Morris was this: despite a somewhat sketchy record with the party, he had been assigned one of its highly sought-after appointments to the Lenin Institute in Moscow.[60] Thus, after several disappointments – or as he put it in one of his letters from Moscow, after having had pins stuck in him for several years by some party leaders[61] – he was once again a man on the rise in the CPC.

Morris's removal to Moscow for a two-year stint at the Lenin School might have sounded like good news to some of the Ukrainian leaders, as he would be out of their hair for the foreseeable future. But Morris would soon prove that he could use his new position as Moscow's resident expert on all matters Canadian to considerable effect in his fight against 'Pop and Company.' Nor would this be a one-front battle, as he already had key allies strategically placed in Winnipeg. Of these, the most notable was John Weir, who had been more or less foisted on the Ukrainian-language youth magazine as an editor (really to keep an eye on the Ukrainians from the inside) by the YCL and the national party leadership.[62]

Meanwhile, the Ukrainian leaders back in Winnipeg began preparing themselves for what they now realized would be a full-out offensive against both themselves and their institutions. Off the bat, Matthew Popovich, Matthew Shatulsky, Toma Kobzey, and John Boychuck – and virtually every other leader of the Ukrainian Agit Prop (the Bolshevized equivalent of the Bureau or Section) – decided to replace the Toronto-based secretary of that body, William Bosowich, with a more forceful figure.[63] It would be several months before the CEC of the national party agreed to this (i.e., to substitute Kobzey of Winnipeg for Bosowich), by which time the offensive against the Ukrainians had begun in earnest.

These attacks had an almost comic opera flavour to them. In what was part of a clearly orchestrated anti-Ukrainian campaign, in 1927 and early 1928 a number of supposedly serious transgressions and 'right-wing deviations' were reported to the Political Committee of the party concerning several ULFTA branches and affiliates. Mike Buhay of the CEC was sent to Winnipeg to discuss these matters with the 'Ukrainian caucus' in Winnipeg. In his report to the CEC in February 1928, he noted that the Ukrainians denied they were guilty of any deviations; indeed, Buhay himself was convinced that the Ukrainian 'comrades perhaps were not guilty of acts of commission or omission, but [that] the matters charged against them were the outcome of a certain attitude of mind. He [Buhay] believed that this could be overcome with more systematic work by the Agit-Prop Committee and a direct contact with the Executive of the ULFTA.'[64] However, when the CEC members read the attached copy of the 'Resolution of [the] Ukrainian Caucus, Winnipeg,' they were not as willing as Buhay to take a minimalist approach. After all, the resolution took some fairly broad swipes at the party leadership for its lack of understanding concerning the situation confronting Ukrainians in Canada. It also argued that 'the Party CEC was wrongly informed and from a prejudiced viewpoint about matters which either did not happen or else did not show incorrect tendencies.'[65]

In response, the Party Secretariat convened a special meeting with the National Ukrainian Agit Prop in March 1928 at which these charges were to be discussed. And what charges they were! In Edmonton the local branch of the ULFTA had supposedly agreed to allow its man-dolin orchestra to perform at a benefit for a Children's Hospital; in Veg-erville, Alberta, a ULFTA orchestra had performed at the local Canadian Jubilee Celebrations of Dominion Day; a simple *inquiry* as to whether the Kenora, Ontario, branch of the ULFTA should do the same was condemned as a deviation; during a concert tour of eastern Canada, the ULFTA mandolin orchestra from Winnipeg (those rene-gade mandolinists again) sang 'O Canada' at two separate perfor-mances; and perhaps worst of all, on the basis of a letter pilfered from the ULFTA office in Winnipeg, it was alleged that for the tenth-anniver-sary celebrations of the ULFTA's founding, the 'bourgeois politician' Premier John Bracken was to be invited to the festivities.[66]

While even the most zealous of Stalinists would be hard pressed to judge these 'transgressions' as Trotsyism run amok, the members of the party's Political Committee were predisposed to take these matters seriously enough to have all the charges enumerated and circulated throughout the party. Tim Buck, the party's industrial organizer and a CEC member as well as the party's representative to the YCL, hap-pened to be in Winnipeg when this circular reached the city. As he put it, the internal struggle within the local party, which had become so clear during the recent city elections, 'was still apparent [and] the crit-icism of the work of our Ukrainian Comrades in the Labor Temple Association contained in the recent statement from the Political Com-mittee had given rise to further internal friction.'[67] This was a consid-erable understatement, especially given that Buck himself was busily heaping fuel on this particular fire.

Buck, who had been in Winnipeg for quite some time early in 1928 in order to organize railway shop workers, chose this moment to leap on the anti-Ukrainian bandwagon. On his return to National Party Headquarters he accused the ULFTA of hanging a 'blue and red rag' (the Union Jack) in its main Winnipeg hall for two-and-a-half hours (from 8:00 to 10:30 a.m.) during its tenth-anniversary celebrations.[68] This allegation of 'Canadian patriotism' was dwarfed, however, by Buck's criticism of the Ukrainians' Higher Educational Course, which was being offered that winter and spring in Winnipeg. He reported to the CEC that this course did not differ much from the curriculum offered in 'bourgeois schools' and that it clearly deviated from party ideology.[69] Such criticisms of this course – which was a particular source of pride to its originators, who included Popovich, Boychuck, and several other ULFTA leaders – brought an almost visceral response from the Ukrainian leadership.

In his capacity as a CEC member and chairman of the National Ukrainian Agit Prop Committee, John Boychuk was sent to Winnipeg (by the Ukrainians, not the CEC) to formally investigate the charges laid against the school by Buck. Not surprisingly, he found all of Buck's charges baseless. Moreover, the students of the Higher Educational Course clearly felt insulted by Buck's charges and sent off a letter of protest to the CEC. In it they provided a fulsome account of their curriculum – which definitely did not match that of any 'bourgeois school,' not unless the writings of Marx and Bukharin, Profintern Reports, the Soviet Constitution, and textbooks from the Soviet Ukraine had suddenly become de rigeur in Canadian classrooms. They also lashed out against Tim Buck in personal terms. One must assume that they were urged on in their protest by Boychuck, their teachers (Sembay and Karach), and the school's inspectors (Popovich and Irchan). Even so, it is remarkable that fifty-two of the school's fifty-six students who were members of either the CPC or the YCL signed this remarkable letter of protest – remarkable largely because of the harsh wording directed towards Buck and the CEC. As the students saw it,

> The accusations of Comrade Tim Buck are groundless and as such are conscious falsehoods. To prove this: Comrade Buck, while in Winnipeg made no effort to get the information from the proper sources, either from the Executive bodies that control the 'Course' (School), or the teachers whom he knows personally, or at least the students themselves, mostly CP of C members, who are acquainted with Comrade Buck for years. Consequently, Comrade Buck's charges against our 'Course' are slanderous and will tend to bring about misunderstanding within our Party.
>
> The action of the N[ational] E[xecutive] C[ommittee] in accepting the report, without taking the slightest measures to find out the truth deserves severest criticism ... As Party and League members we cannot tolerate such falsehoods within the Party and if the CEC on the basis of such,

wishes to direct the policies of our Party, it will be held responsible for the consequences.[70]

These were fighting words: Buck was a liar; the CEC was failing in its responsibilities; and there was an implied threat of 'consequences' in the last sentence that was certain to get the CEC's undivided attention, all the more so as many of these students were being trained as future leaders not only of the ULFTA but also perhaps of the party itself. These Canadian-born young men and women, with their flawless English, Canadian public school educations, and Canadian mannerisms, were clearly suited for work not only among Ukrainian Canadians but also, in the party's parlance, in the 'Anglo-Saxon field.' Given the party's signal failure to attract any sizeable number of English-speaking members, these young people were the party's best hope for a breakthrough in this regard (this was certainly the perspective of Leslie Morris) – but not if they or their organizations broke from the CPC.

This was not a happy time for the CPC leadership. Perhaps unwisely, its CEC had decided to include the various criticisms and charges of 'deviations' against the Ukrainian mass organizations in its official (and therefore distributed) minutes and had also incorporated them into its report to the Comintern for the upcoming Sixth Congress of 1928. This would bring about a level of protest from the Ukrainian leadership that would make the students' letter seem mild in comparison. But this was only one of the CPC's problems that fateful year.

On 13 May 1928, Jack Macdonald announced that conclusive evidence had been uncovered that J. Esselwein, 'a member of our party since its inception is in the employment of the Government Secret Services.' There had been suspicions about Esselwein for some time, 'owing to the fact that Esselwein had no visible means of support, claiming his income came from buying and selling of stocks etc,' but nothing had been done until concrete proof could be brought against him.[71] (Note that singing 'O Canada' was proof of right-wing deviation, but playing the stock market was apparently acceptable communist behaviour.) The revelation that a fairly senior party member with access to almost all CPC minutes and communications was in fact a police spy, had the potential to damage not just the party but also the careers within that party of activists such as Tim Buck. Indeed, Buck had recently spent considerable time with this spy and had perhaps let him in on even more party 'secrets' than he ought to have done – a point the Ukrainian leaders would soon make.

Meanwhile, a faction fight had erupted among the party's senior leadership in Toronto. At a June meeting of the CEC, Oscar Ryan of the YCL launched an attack on one of Jack Macdonald's closest allies in the party leadership and one of the party's few senior female leaders, Florence Custance, for her supposedly inept handling of the Canadian Labour Defence League. At the same meeting Ryan reported that within the Toronto branches of the YCL a number of members – virtually all of whom were Jewish – were leading a bitter campaign against the National Executive Committee of the YCL.[72] And finally, some members of the Ukrainian Agit Prop were threatening to defy party orders and distribute a lengthy refutation of all the CEC's criticisms of the Ukrainian organizations in a party circular.[73] Clearly, 1928 was not turning out well for the CPC: alignments of the old versus the young and of ethnics versus Anglo-Saxons were emerging; revelations concerning police spies in the party were making people doubt their friends and comrades; and the potential for even more internal strife seemed set to tear the party asunder as criticisms of Jack Macdonald's leadership continued to mount – and all of this before the most startling 'revelation' of all was made late in the fall of 1928: the Canadian party's leading theoretician and long-time editor of *The Worker* was a Trotskyist!

The letters of Leslie Morris, firmly ensconced in the Lenin Institute in Moscow, provide some of the most interesting insights into developments back in Canada during this eventful year. Because this was the year of the tumultuous Sixth Comintern Congress, the 'Lenin School Boy' was up to his neck in visiting Canadian delegates and serving as a member of the Canadian delegation and commission. That meant he was getting all sorts of inside information on the fights that were brewing within the party back in Canada and that he had a front row seat for the manoeuvring among Canadian party leaders while they were in Moscow. He made sure all this information was dutifully relayed back to 'the boys' in Winnipeg, not realizing that each and every one of his letters was being copied and placed in the Comintern archives – and that several would also end up in the hands of the Ukrainian leadership back in Winnipeg.[74]

In these letters Morris noted the growing schism between Maurice

Spector, the Canadian party's chief theoretician, and Jack Macdonald and Tim Buck. (Buck would turn out to be one of Macdonald's most severe critics, but he was at least temporarily in opposition to Spector.) More to the point, Morris noted that 'Spector has gathered around him, with the assistance of Marriot [of the YCL] and the League NEC boys, and Beckie [Buhay], a group in Toronto that is working in opposition to Macdonald. This group has connections in Winnipeg, through you fellows [Danny Holmes, Johnny Weir, Victor, Joe/Yosel, and Fred Holmes] and particularly Fred, so I am told. [Malcolm] Bruce also supports it in Vancouver, as well as Hymie, our product from Winnipeg; Porter I mean.' Morris was seeking confirmation of this information from his Winnipeg contacts, for he went on to note that 'if this group is not in existence, it must come. There is going to be a fight when the delegation returns. Mac[donald] is prepared to back down on the Ukrainian question. Spector is prepared to fight the line of Pop[ovich].' He concluded this missive by observing, with some glee, that 'the fight is on, and you fellows will have to do your part. We were first in the field, we were the only rebel voices at the last convention. But keep me in touch with your events and actions. I have a right to know what is done towards building groups and the like. I am convinced that this must be done carefully, accepting temporary allies, but sticking to a political line.'[75]

Most of Morris's observations were correct, except that he did not realize that Spector would soon be the odd man out in the party struggle – and not because he lost in any of his machinations against Macdonald, but over the issue of Trotskyism. That was still a few months in the offing, though. For the time being, Morris was fixated on the 'Ukrainian question,' which had reached a new level of intensity.

The Ukrainians, infuriated by what they viewed as the groundless charges against them and by the fact that the charges had been embedded in the CPC's Comintern report, had struck back hard. And not just in Canada. If the party's CEC wanted to attack them and their organizations at the Comintern Congress in Moscow, they would respond in kind.

One of the ULFTA's senior leaders, John Navis, was in Ukraine at the time of the Comintern Congress, and the Ukrainian Agit Prop and CEC members were able to arrange to have him accredited as a delegate. They then provided him with a nineteen-page 'declaration,' which he was to present to the Comintern on their behalf. Morris, who spent considerable time with Navis that summer in Moscow, was certain that Popovich was the declaration's principal author. This document not only countered each and every charge of deviation levelled against the Ukrainians and their organizations, but went on the offensive against many of the Canadian party's leaders. The Canadian CECs, both past and present, were accused of suppressing important information in their previous reports to the Comintern, of seeking to block the election of Ukrainian delegates to Comintern Congresses, and of forcibly silencing Ukrainian delegates who had been democratically chosen to attend the Congresses despite the machinations of certain party leaders.[76]

This declaration made an impassioned defence of the ULFTA's role among Ukrainian workers and farmers both as the necessary 'bridge' to a radical consciousness and as a bulwark against the Ukrainian 'right.' Given all the valuable work they had done in these regards, and all the support they had given the CPC over the years, the Ukrainian leaders could not fathom why most of the CEC 'would like to liquidate this organization.'[77] This was a bit of a misinterpretation: most Anglo-Celtic foes of the ULFTA (including Leslie Morris) did not want to liquidate the ULFTA – only its leadership, so that they and their proxies could control the organization, its membership, and its assets.

The declaration did, however, offer one possible explanation for the attacks against the Ukrainians: it was a cover, a form of scapegoating, designed to hide the 'inactivity and inability of some croakers, destructivists, and even [the activities of] spies of government police.'[78] Of course the spy reference was to the Esselwein case, and the Ukrainian leaders had much to say in this regard. They had been warning the party about him for several years, to no avail. From their perspective, leading CEC members had chosen to disregard their warnings simply because Esselwein had been one of the leading critics of the Ukrainians even while acting as an RCMP spy. Worse yet, despite the Ukrainians' warnings about the shadowy Esselwein, he had been retained within the party – indeed, shortly before his expulsion he had enjoyed such confidence from party leaders like Tim Buck that while Buck had been in Winnipeg on party business he had stayed in Esselwein's 'luxurious' hotel room and conducted supposedly secret organizing work among railway shop employees while the spy was in the room.[79] 'Could there be any more indifferent, criminally negligent acting and behaviour of any Party comrade and a CEC member at that? It is quite plain that comrade Buck should be severely disciplined for his action and for keeping it hidden from the CEC and, at least, removed from the responsible position that the Party invested him with, and which he does not fill up properly.'[80] Small wonder that back in Canada, Buck was working feverishly to suppress the circulation of the Ukrainians' response to CEC criticisms.

However, as potentially damning as all of these charges were, the Ukrainian leaders still weren't done. They attacked the CEC for attempting to block the renomination of North America's only communist alderman, William Kolysnik, viewing this as just another anti-Ukrainian move on the part of the CPC's leadership.[81] Then, in what was arguably the most memorable passage of a quite remarkable document, they charged that the CPC 'tolerates adventurers, drunkards, sexual psychopats [*sic*] and perverts ... who only discredit our Party among the workers, who bring Kosomols to prostitutes and publicly, to the discredit of the Party, justify such action by saying that prostitution is a legalized thing in the Soviet Union.'[82] Meanwhile, those like the Ukrainians – who worked hard, followed party discipline, and were true Bolsheviks – were attacked for no good reason.

These charges, and the charges contained in the CEC report, were taken seriously enough to warrant thorough study. So thorough, in fact, that it would take more than two years for the Comintern to reach a conclusion about the most appropriate way to settle the fight between the leaders of the mass Ukrainian organizations and the CPC. However, the real cause for delay was not the complexity of the matters at hand, but their relative unimportance to the Comintern. Simply put, the problems of the Canadian section paled in comparison to what had transpired at the Congress – and not just in relation to the announcement of the 'third period' and the move to an even more militant and left-wing orientation, but also in relation to the fallout associated with Trotsky's critique of the program of the Sixth Congress. James Canon, a leader of the large and important U.S. party (important to the Comintern, at least), had smuggled a copy of Trotsky's critique out of the Soviet Union at the close of the Congress and published it in the United States. In so doing he helped broaden the foundations of Trotsky's challenge to the Comintern's intellectual monopoly of Marxism. The ensuing battle on the radical left – which quickly attracted some high-profile Canadian communists to the Trotskyist cause – and the emerging economic crisis in much of the Western world were what consumed the Comintern between 1928 and 1930, not the internal problems of the relatively insignificant Communist Party of Canada.

Beyond this, a number of other matters within the Canadian party took precedence over the 'Ukrainian question,' though there was often a Ukrainian dimension involved. Simply put, after late 1928 the infighting that had been developing among key leaders of the CPC intensified to the point that the party came close to destroying itself. Beginning with the expulsion of Maurice Spector from the CPC in November 1928, for his refusal to disavow James Canon and certain Trotskyist positions, the party entered a seemingly endless spiral of witch-hunts for 'Trotskyites' and 'right deviationists.' Much of the initial attack came from Tim Buck and Stewart Smith – who had just returned from his two-year stay at the Lenin Institute and who was the most virulent of the anti-Trotskyists and anti-Ukrainians in the CPC – and was focused on Jack Macdonald and his long-time party allies, Michael Buhay, William Moriarty, Joe Salsberg, and (of particular importance to the Ukrainians) Matthew Popovich. Much of this story has been at least partly told in works such as Angus's *Canadian Bolsheviks,* Avakumovic's *The Communist Party in Canada*, and Penner's *Canadian Communism,* so there is little point in rehashing all of this material; indeed, this material deserves its own essay. That said, a number of points related to the Ukrainians do need to be made.

To begin with, at the 1929 National Convention of the CPC, Buck and Smith, supported by Beckie Buhay, Tom Ewen, leaders of the YCL, and a few others, launched a full-scale attack on Macdonald and his supporters. This was largely on the grounds that though Macdonald and his allies claimed to have accepted the Comintern's new line (i.e., the leftward turn and the need to prepare the masses for militant confrontations with capital), their actions suggested otherwise. Those who supported Macdonald caucused during the convention to work out a unified strategy – a move that would later lead to charges of 'undemocratic factionalism.'[83] Matthew Popovich played a key role in this caucus, which would further cement the negative relationship that he in particular had developed with Buck and Smith.[84]

However, while Popovich and the Ukrainians were portrayed as firmly in Macdonald's camp, both then and in later analyses, this was not actually the case. After Macdonald gave his main convention speech, in which he endorsed the new Comintern line and conceded certain organizational mistakes, Navis, Popovich, Boychuk, Stefanitsky, and Stokaluk called a special meeting of the Ukrainian delegates attending the CPC convention. Speaking at this meeting, Navis clearly felt that Macdonald was abandoning the Ukrainians and was 'prostituting himself' in order to hold on to power in the party. The question Navis posed that afternoon in the Toronto ULFTA hall was simple: 'What is to be done?' A report on this meeting – prepared after the fact by a Ukrainian delegate who wanted to curry favour with the Buck faction – indicated that some delegates at this meeting spoke in favour of a split with the CPC. The most notable of these people was the oft-maligned labour organizer from Alberta, John Stokaluk (i.e., oft-maligned by Lakeman, Harvey Murphy, 'Kid' Burns, and other English comrades). At the very least, Stokaluk argued, if they did not split from the party and seek to create a new CPC, 'then we must at least fight and stop comrades like Tim Buck, Beckie Buhay and [Charles] Marriott being elected to the CEC.' Navis overtly rejected any call for a split; Popovich remained silent on the issue. Both, however, agreed that the Ukrainians should protect themselves from attacks by Buck, and work to have a CEC elected that would not be dominated by his supporters.[85]

The end result of the 1929 convention was mixed: Macdonald remained CPC leader, but Buck and Smith had gained enough support to control the party's all-important Political Committee. Somewhat surprisingly, Macdonald effectively handed over the party leadership to Buck shortly after the convention (by asking for a leave of absence from his post as Party Secretary in July 1929 and recommending Buck as his replacement). The Buck–Smith faction was clearly not ready for this and tried to block Macdonald's resignation. When this failed, Buck became the new General Secretary.[86] Despite this, and a few other key resignations – or rather, refusals to stand for re-election[87] – Buck and Smith were not yet in full control of the CPC. And if they thought that the Ukrainians were their biggest immediate problem, events would quickly prove them wrong, for before the year was out Buck and Smith would be confronted by a crisis of staggering proportions: the Sudbury-based Finnish Organization of Canada was threatening to abandon the party entirely.[88] Even as the new leaders confronted the possible loss of the single largest component of the CPC, they faced strong criticism from Moscow on two fronts: first, over how they had handled their fight with Macdonald; and second, over a number of their earlier theoretical positions, most notably their stands on 'Canadian Independence' – a critique informed by Leslie Morris (now back in Canada) and a new cohort of Lenin School boys.[89] To make matters even more interesting, while Buck and Smith were scrambling madly to put out the fire of Finnish secessionism, deal with the influence of the still powerful Macdonald faction, and figure out how to bring the Ukrainians to heel, Buck was summoned to Moscow to explain the internal party situation in Canada.[90]

Judging from Buck's letters to Smith and the party secretariat in January and February 1930, it seems that the Comintern and the ECCI were inclined to accept the Morris/Lenin School students' view of internal party matters. Moreover, by early February it was clear that Moscow was also inclined to have the CPC take a much softer stand with the Finns and other 'splitters' than Buck and Smith had wanted, for a number of decidedly pragmatic reasons. Buck was clearly worried how Smith and other leaders back home would react to this 'caving in' to the Finnish 'right-wingers.'[91] He feared it might also give solace to those in the Ukrainian community who were similarly inclined to challenge the CPC's new leaders.

Even while Stewart Smith was fielding these disturbing notes from Moscow, he encountered pressure from his new district organizer in Winnipeg to take definitive action against the Ukrainian leadership. The bête noire of the 'old Ukes' was back in town. Leslie Morris, fresh from the Lenin School – and furious that he had not been sent directly to the party centre in Toronto – was the new DO for Winnipeg and the West. And it was quite the situation he had returned to, for late in 1929, with Tom Ewen gone as DO (he had gone to Toronto earlier that year on party orders), the Winnipeg and District party had come back under the control of the Ukrainians and one of their closest allies, Jake Penner. Together they had managed to have the District Executive Committee (District 7) pass a resolution attacking the new national Political Committee for its failure to circulate key documents and to properly follow the new Comintern line![92] Moreover, Morris was well aware that his hand-picked young Ukrainians were not making much headway in the Winnipeg-based organizations. With John Weir now off at the Lenin School, Danny Holmes was Morris's chief liaison with the

Ukrainian organizations, and he was not being well treated by the 'old Ukes.' Indeed, he was being treated with such contempt by the Ukrainian leadership of the WBA that the District Buro – which Morris now dominated – had to step in and formally reprimand Pastuch, Chomiski, and Kolisnyk over the way in which they had discredited Holmes in the eyes of the WBA membership.[93] Now that they were combined with pressure from the Lenin School boys in Moscow – from Weir and Sam Carr in particular, both of whom were urging the Comintern and its agencies to get rid of the 'functionaries' and well-paid 'bureaucrats' of the ULFTA and the WBA, whom they claimed only wanted to protect their sinecures – Morris's demands for action on the Ukrainian question were not likely to be denied for long. When added to Smith's strong anti-Ukrainian predilection, a new round of confrontations was inevitable.[94]

In February 1930 the confrontation finally came. Prior to the national conventions of the ULFTA and the WBA, the Political Committee of the CPC issued a five-page 'statement of policy' to the Ukrainian faction that had assembled in Winnipeg. It was delivered in person by Stewart Smith. This document, and speeches given by Smith and Morris, essentially told the Ukrainians that they needed to complete the turn to the left and help break down 'national barriers' between the various components of the Canadian working class – not strengthen them by focusing on Ukrainian culture. From the perspective of the PolCom, the 'cultural work' of the ULFTA was still being allowed to take precedence over the larger struggle of all Canadian workers. This brand of 'opportunism' was bad enough, but even worse was one of its leading manifestations:

> The extreme hatred and prejudice, which the Canadian bourgeoisie skillfully develops, against the immigrant workers has brought forward a tendency to try and gain favor in the eyes of the bourgeoisie in order to ward off the attack of the ruling class. As an example of this, we wish to draw your attention to the bourgeois, moral, Philistine declaration of the aims and objectives with the tour of the Mandolin Orchestra; the establishment of a student institute in Edmonton for students attending a bourgeois university; etc. Such manifestations are only symptoms, signs of a basically anti-working class tendency, an orientation away from the class struggle – something which our Party members must fight with the most relentless revolutionary energy.[95]

This 'policy statement' then attacked the bourgeois nature and aims of the Winnipeg-based co-operative; claimed that the Winnipeg-based WBA was fostering 'social democratic illusions' among Ukrainian workers; and argued that the ULFTA leaders had become so worried about protecting their 'property' that they had backed away from support of the free-speech battle – and in so doing had actually abandoned control over the ULFTA's 'halls' to non-party members (who, of course, constituted the vast majority of the ULFTA's membership). All in all, by taking such actions and adopting such attitudes, 'we will only succeed in leading the Ukrainian masses into the swamp of social democratic vacillation.'[96]

This statement of criticism, and Comrade Smith himself, were not well received by the delegates to the ULFTA and WBA conventions. Indeed, the Comintern's copy of the statement indicates that it was rejected by a vote of 80 to 6. Not only did the Ukrainians reject the party's comradely criticism, but once again they shot back. Their formal resolution declared that regarding the vast majority of points raised in the statement, the PolCom was quite simply wrong. Naturally enough, this being the case, the Ukrainians had indicated to Comrade Smith that it was the attitude of the PolCom that had to change, not the actions of the Ukrainian mass organizations or their leaders. When Smith stuck to his original position, the Ukrainians made note of his decidedly 'non-Bolshevist' approach.[97] After a detailed, point-by-point refutation of the statement's various charges, and an assessment of the party leadership's failure to attract more English-speaking workers, the Ukrainian faction concluded sadly that it had no choice but to criticize the 'terrible negligence on the part of the Polcom, which must be classified as extreme idleness and opportunism.' Indeed, in a rather dramatic – and ominous – flourish, it was noted that 'the Party Fraction wishes to warn the Polcom that the Party membership will not tolerate any longer such a chaos as it exists in the Party at the present time ... We are determined to fight against everything that tends to ruin the Party notwithstanding the fact that it may come from those who are in the leadership, because the ruin of the party shall not be permitted.'[98]

Clearly, something had to give. Navis, Shatulsky, and Boychuck travelled to Toronto in May to meet with the party's Political Committee, but the only thing they could agree on was that both the Political Committee and the party faction of the ULFTA would prepare written statements of their respective cases that might become the basis for a discussion before a group of Comintern representatives.[99] According to one source, at this point four Comintern representatives came to Canada to listen to both sides. During these meetings, the Ukrainians, led by Popovich, acquitted themselves well, apparently convincing the commissioners that they were correct in 70 per cent of their claims.[100] Soon after, word came from the Political Secretariat of the Comintern that Stewart Smith and a representative of the Ukrainian organizations should come to Moscow for a meeting to be held on 15 July.[101]

It was Navis who was sent to represent the Ukrainians. Armed with a document that carefully outlined the Ukrainian position and that included denunciations of Smith's almost pathological hatred of 'the Ukrainian leading comrades,' and of Leslie Morris' backdoor machinations against Ukrainian leaders, and that provided illustrations of how John Weir and Danny Holmes had been sent to disrupt the work of the Ukrainians, and of how Tim Buck had worked against Winnipeg's Ukrainians in a highly undemocratic fashion, the members of the Ukrainian party faction must have had high hopes for Navis's mission.[102] Those hopes were soon dashed: the commission that heard the cases of Smith and Navis (essentially the Anglo-American Secretariat) – while critical of both the Ukrainian leadership and Smith – gave more latitude to the CPC's leadership and less to the independent-minded Ukrainians. Many years later, Peter Krawchuk would charge that Navis, under pressure from the commission, had buckled under the criticisms when he should have held his ground.[103]

Be that as it may, by the time Navis returned to Canada late in 1930, a 'compromise' had clearly been engineered. The battles between the CPC's leadership and the Ukrainians had died down quite dramatically. By early 1931, guided by Comintern recommendations, the party leadership and the Ukrainians had agreed to a resolution at the party plenum that was clearly aimed at restoring harmony. Borrowing language from several earlier documents generated by the Ukrainian faction, it was noted that the Ukrainian mass organizations were crucial 'bridges' between the party and the revolutionary movement on the one side and the foreign-born workers on the other. It was also agreed that both the CPC's leadership and the Ukrainian leadership had made serious mistakes that had led to the misunderstandings of the past few years. None of the Ukrainian leaders were to be forced out of their positions of authority within the mass organizations, so long as they once again endorsed the 'turn to the left' (as they had been doing quite consistently since 1929) and so long as they formally conceded party authority over the Ukrainian party members within the mass organizations. Though there is no question that the Comintern's decisions helped strengthen the CPC's grip on the Ukrainian organizations – or at least shortened the leash of the leadership even more – Smith was livid about this compromise and with the criticism of the party leadership's role in the split. Indeed, as he told Buck in a letter early in 1931, he believed that the Ukrainian leadership had not made a turn to the left, was still filled with 'right-wing' deviations, and continued to defend Ukrainian rebels such as Stokaluk in open defiance of the party's leaders. More to the point, he wanted to launch a new campaign to 'expose the right wing and the incorrigible right wingers in practise.'[104] Fortunately for the Ukrainians, Smith was back in Soviet Union, where he would remain for quite some time – not as a reward, as in the past, but rather for what amounted to political re-education for his 'theoretical mistakes' of the past few years. The Lenin School students, and especially John Weir, were also disappointed with the compromise that had been worked out on the Ukrainian question. In fact, they lashed out at their classmate, Sam Carr, who by now was back in Canada serving as the CPC's organizational secretary, for his willingness to soften his position on the 'old' Ukrainian leaders. Carr, however, saw matters differently now that he was in a position of authority. As he explained to his erstwhile schoolmates,

it is true that the self criticism of the Ukrainian leader[s] was not 100% and this was pointed out at the plenum, but it is also a fact which can be seen in the documents of the plenum (resolutions stenograms) that Navis and the others made gigantic steps from the position taken by Navis at the AA [Anglo-American] Secretariat and which the comrades in the CI considered more or less satisfactory.

It would be utopia to believe that the ill feelings of the old days can pass in one day, with the adoption of a resolution. Certainly that in the election of the students to the Ukrainian scholl [*sic*], boys who supported the Right Wing fight were sent. But remember we are in no position to have in the party now (whose principle differences are settled by CI and plenum) two classes of members, those who supported the Navis leader-

ship and those who supported the Smith leadership which was also condemned by the CI ...[105]

Carr added that Weir and the boys in Moscow were badly mistaken
if they thought that the Ukrainian leadership was still one united body.
At the plenum, Navis had actually battled Pastuch and Popovich on
certain key points. Moreover, as Carr saw it, the Ukrainians had learned
a valuable lesson when they attempted to have Popovich elected to the
CPC's Politburo: 'We flatly refused on the basis of Pop's role in the
Right wing fight and they finally agreed to come over to our point of
view on this.'[106]

The final acts in this official rapprochement came when a series of
articles were published in English and Ukrainian over the course of the
spring and early summer of 1931 by Popovich, Shatulsky, Navis, Buck,
and others. These appeared in *The Worker, Ukrainian Labor News,* a
new journal edited by Popovich titled *Za Bilshovyzatsiiu,* and a series
of bulletins published by the Ukrainian National Party Fraction Bureau
in Winnipeg.[107] Collectively they conceded the necessity of CPC control over the party factions in the Ukrainian organizations and indicated
the Ukrainian party members' agreement with all the central tenets of
the Comintern line. Perhaps the most dramatic sign of rapprochement,
however, came in the summer of 1931. John Weir, just returned from his
studies in Moscow, apparently had the endorsement of the Comintern
officials to take over leadership of the Ukrainian National Fraction
Bureau. (Tim Buck, who had his doubts about Weir's suitability for
such a role, speculated that Dimitri Manuilsky was responsible.)[108]
More to the point, in an 18 July 1931 telegram to the Political Bureau
of the CPC, none other than Matthew Popovich indicated that at a meeting of the national faction, the candidates had been discussed for the
post of party faction secretary and editor of the new Ukrainian-language journal, and Weir had been chosen unanimously over Navis and
Lenartovich.[109]

With this choice, perhaps even more than in the published self-crit-
icisms, it would seem that the Ukrainians had finally – as Morris would
have put it – 'been brought to heel.' And on one level, this was the case:
in official terms they were clearly dutiful soldiers of the Comintern.
But Sam Carr's take on the situation, cited earlier, rings true: 'It would
be utopia to believe that the ill feelings of the old days can pass in one

day, with the adoption of a resolution.' And this lingering animosity undoubtedly helps explain the ongoing discrepancies, noted early in this chapter, between the party line and actual practice among the left-wing Ukrainian organizations. On one level, Smith and Weir had reason to worry that the 'resolution' of the Ukrainian question had been a mere papering over of profound and ongoing differences. Given all that had transpired between 1927 and 1931, it no longer seems strange that any request from Tim Buck or his minions might have been looked at askance by the various Ukrainian organizations headquartered in Winnipeg. We can only wonder why Popovich, Boychuk, Navis, Shatulsky, Kobzey, Kolysnik, and others, after several years of attacks and abuse, had not decided to remove the mass organizations they had crafted from the party's orbit entirely.

My tentative answer to this crucial question was suggested to me by, of all people, Leslie Morris. In one of his many letters from Moscow to John Weir dealing with his pet project of wresting control of the Ukrainian organizations from Popovich, Morris observed: 'One thing you may take as assured, and that is that Pop can never tolerate a split from the Party ... Upon this basis he can be brought to heel, but never trusted.'[110] Morris offered similar, and more favourable, assessments of Navis and Boychuk in these same letters. Whatever his reservations about these leaders and their stewardship of the Ukrainian organizations, he understood that their commitment to the party and the ideals it stood for – ideals they had helped create – was as great as their commitment to the ULFTA, the WBA, and the other Ukrainian-language organizations they had helped found. Morris believed that their lives had been and would continue to be so wrapped up in the 'movement' that they would remain loyal come what may.

But this is not to say that all of them ever really got over their differences with Buck and his cohort. Indeed, they would at times allow and even encourage their organizations to act in ways that Buck did not appreciate. Toma Kobzey – whom the Ukrainian mass organizations had placed on the party CEC as the fight entered its most serious phase in 1928 – made it clear in his memoirs that even after the dust had supposedly settled in 1931, leading Ukrainian activists like himself, Danylo Lobay, and Emil Chomecki, and perhaps also Matthew Popovitch, stayed in the ULFTA and the WBA as well as the CPC while continuing to struggle against at least some CPC policies that they viewed as harmful to Ukrainian workers and farmers in Canada.[111] As Andrij Makuk has indicated in his contribution to this volume, several of these individuals fought their final internal battle within the party in 1935–6 and lost. But it is also noteworthy that even those who went into overt opposition – or were forced to do so – did not go over to the political right. Instead they took Trotskyist or CCF positions. But even more of the leaders – Navis and Shatulsky in particular, and Popovich a bit more reluctantly – remained dreamers of what Pete Seeger would later term 'the strangest dream.' As such, they could never see themselves abandoning the only mass movement (the world communist movement) that they believed was capable of transforming the world into a better and more equitable place for all. So for better or worse, like dedicated priests – Jesuits if you will – they swallowed their personal pride, hid their growing doubts, and eventually silenced their personal criticisms and soldiered on, always keeping their organizations within the orbit, if not exactly the warm embrace, of the party.

Notes

1 Jim Mochoruk, *The People's Co-op: The Life and Times of a North End Institution* (Halifax: Fernwood, 2000).
2 See, for example, Association of United Ukrainian Canadians (AUUC) Archives, Ukrainian Labour Temple, Winnipeg, PCL Collection, 'Constitution and Bylaws of the Workers and Farmers Association Limited as amended by the General Membership Meeting, August 29, 1931.' This replaced a constitution deemed by the CPC and Comintern to be far too bourgeois and completely lacking in any mention of the class struggle. For an example of the self-criticism of a Ukrainian leader, see Matthew Popovich's comments in *Ukrainian Labor News*, 3 February 1931, and *The Worker*, 7 February 1931.
3 AUUC Archives, PCL, Minute Book 1, 'Minutes of the Board of Directors Meeting, September 27, 1935.' In this particular case, 'a request from the CEC for a loan of $100.00 to help meet the $200.00 for Buck's deposit ... was turned down due to shortage of funds in the Co-op.' The same meeting approved about $15.00 worth of donations to local non-political organizations, including the St Patrick's Bazaar and the Point Douglas Greek Catholic Church.
4 In this regard see Ivan Avakumovic, *The Communist Party in Canada: A History* (Toronto: McClelland and Stewart, 1975), ch. 3. Norman Penner's *Canadian Communism: The Stalin Years and Beyond* (Toronto:

Methuen, 1988) has virtually nothing to say on this ethnic split, which is really quite startling given that Penner himself was personally acquainted with all the Winnipeg-based Ukrainian, Jewish, and Anglo-Celtic Party leaders, and that his own father, 'Red Jake' Penner, as a leading Party member in Winnipeg with ties to the Jewish and Ukrainian communities, played an important role in all these fights. The 'official' party history, *Canada's Party of Socialism: History of the Communist Party of Canada, 1921-1976,* is even less useful. See for example 53–8.

5   Ian Angus, *Canadian Bolsheviks: The Early Years of the Communist Party of Canada* (Montreal: Vanguard, 1981); Donald Avery, 'Ethnic Loyalties and the Proletarian Revolution: A Case Study of Communist Political Activity in Winnipeg, 1923–1936,' in *Ethnicity, Power, and Politics in Canada,* ed. Jongen Dahlie and Tissa Fernando (Toronto: Metheun, 1981).

6   See for example, Angus, *Canadian Bolsheviks,* 291.

7   This fight has been almost completely ignored by historians of the CPC and is only now getting its well-warranted analysis in the work of Andrij Makuk in this volume.

8   Peter Krawchuck, *Our History: The Ukrainian Labour-Farmer Movement in Canada, 1907–1991* (Toronto: Lugus, 1996), see esp. ch. 11.

9   Ibid.

10   The CPC was officially formed at a convention organized in a barn in Guelph, Ontario, in May 1921. There were, however, earlier attempts to create a CPC, and many Canadian leftists had already joined one of the two U.S.-based Communist Parties by 1921. See Angus, *Canadian Bolsheviks,* chs. 2 and 3.

11   Orest Martynowych, *The Ukrainians in Canada: The Formative Years, 1891–1924* (Edmonton: Canadian Institute of Ukrainian Studies Press, 1991); Daniel Stone, ed., *Jewish Radicalism in Winnipeg, 1905–1960* (Winnipeg: Jewish Heritage Centre of Western Canada, 2003).

12   For background on these various movements see the two works cited above as well as Peter Krawchuck, *The Ukrainians in Winnipeg's First Century* (Toronto: Kobzar, 1974); Donald Avery, *Dangerous Foreigners: European Immigrant Workers and Labour Radicalism in Canada, 1896–1932* (Toronto: McClelland and Stewart, 1976); Ernie Chisick, 'The Development of Winnipeg's Socialist Movement, 1900–1915,' MA thesis, University of Manitoba, 1972; A. Ross McCormack, 'Radical Politics in Winnipeg: 1899–1915,' in *Historical and Scientific Society of Manitoba, Transactions, 1972–73;* and Roz Usiskin, 'The Winnipeg Jewish Radical Community: Its Early Formation, 1905–1918,' in *Jewish Life and Times: A Collection of Essays* (Winnipeg: Jewish Historical Society of Western Canada, 1983).

13 For information on the non-communist organizations within the Ukrainian-Canadian community, see Paul Yuzyk, *The Ukrainians in Manitoba: A Social History* (Toronto: University of Toronto Press, 1953), ch. 6. See also Martynowych, *The Ukrainians in Canada,* 266-270.

14 Anthony Bilecki, William Repka, and Mitch Sago, eds., *Friends in Need: The WBA Story* (Winnipeg: Workers Benevolent Association of Canada, 1972), 63–8; Krawchuck, *Our History,* 31–3.

15 Krawchuck, *Our History,* ch. 2.

16 See Ukrainian Labour Temple Association, 'Constitution' (adopted at the First Convention of the ULTA, 16–18 January 1920, Winnipeg). The 10 points were as follows: '(1) to organize public lectures, meetings, concerts, theatrical productions etc and to encourage the cultivation of education and the arts. (2)To establish schools for workers and farmers, free schools for their children and courses for the illiterate. (3)To establish *Bursy* (dormitories) for the children of workers and farmers so that they could attend school in the larger cities. (4)To maintain libraries and to circulate those reading materials. (5)To send lecturers and organizers to workers' areas across Canada. (6)To provide financial aid to members of the ULTA and their families as well as for other workers and farmers in case of illness, accident or death. (7)To cultivate a spirit of brotherhood and solidarity among workers. and farmers. (8)To support the Labour Temple in Winnipeg and to help to build others like it across Canada. (9)To establish a labour bureau with departments to provide information, advice, and legal and other aid for our workers and farmers. (10)To give every necessary aid to Ukrainian workers and farmers who live in Canada, as well as those who arrive in Canada or are leaving Canada.

17 For further information on its founding, see Bilecki et al., *Friends in Need,* 73–98.

18 For an analysis of the founding of this cooperative, see Mochoruk, *The People's Co-op,* ch. 2.

19 By 1928, these two organizations had well in excess of 10,000 members and their four papers had a combined readership of 25,000. See Proceedings, 10th Convention of the ULFTA, 4–6 February 1929, Winnipeg; and Proceedings, 5th National Convention of the WBA, February 1929.

20 AUUC Archives, PCL Collection, Minute Book 1, 'Minutes of Special Meeting of all Members of all Executives of the Ukrainian Labour Farmer Temple Organizations in Winnipeg to Discuss the Co-operative, Wednesday, July 25, 1928.'

21 Ibid.

22 See Antonio Gramsci, 'The Intellectuals,' in *Selections from the Prison Notebooks* (New York: International, 1971).

23 John Boychuk, Matthew Popovich, and John Navis were among the
    twenty-two individuals who formed the underground party at a meeting
    in Guelph in 1921.
24 Peter Krawchuk, *The Ukrainian Socialist Movement in Canada (1907–
    1918)* (Toronto: Progress, 1979), 8–19.
25 As the Canadian delegate, Ada Kent, put it in a report to the Presidium of
    the Comintern, 'the great majority of the members of the Communist
    Party were not English speaking,' while 'the few English speaking mem-
    bers were neither active nor very popular among the masses of the work-
    ers.' LAC, MG10 K3, K-271, fonds 495, opus 98, Communist
    International, Communist Party of Canada, 1921–1943, file 3, 'Ada
    Kent, Special Delegate, CPC to the Presidium of the Comintern, August
    15, 1922,' 2. Kent went on to note that in the legal party – the Workers
    Party – of approximately 5,000 members 2,000 were Finnish, 1,000
    Ukrainian, and 1,000 Jewish, Lithuanian, or Russian. See ibid., 'Report
    to the Presidium, August, 1922 – Ada Kent.' (This is a slightly different
    document than the one cited above, though it covers much of the same
    ground.)
26 See, for example, ibid., file 4, 'Minutes, Central Executive Committee
    [CPC] August 27, 1921 – Report of Comrade Laurence re Winnipeg
    Trip.'
27 Ibid. After an English-speaking party organizer failed to make any seri-
    ous progress in building party support in Winnipeg, one of the leaders of
    the Ukrainian Canadian left, Matthew Popovich, was appointed as the
    interim organizer of the party for what was then District 2, centred in
    Winnipeg. See ibid., 'Minutes, Central Executive Committee [CPC]
    February 3, 1922.'
28 Ibid.
29 Ibid. K-272, file 13, 'Report of the Proceedings of the Second Annual
    Convention of the Workers' Party of Canada, Toronto, February 22,
    1923.' The 'Z' Convention Report is appended to this document as
    'Report of National Convention, February, 1923.'
30 Ibid.
31 Ibid.
32 Ibid., Ffile 14, 'Minutes of the First Meeting of the Enlarged CEC,
    February 26, 1923.' The quotas referred to the usual amount that the lan-
    guage federations were expected to contribute to the press fund each
    year.
33 Ibid., 'Minutes of the Meeting of the CEC held March 24th, 1923.'
34 Ibid., 'Minutes of the Meeting of the CEC held November 3rd, 1923.'
35 Ibid. Interestingly enough, Matthew Popovich almost won a seat as an
    alderman in that 1923 election.

36 See Peter Krawchuk, *Matthew Popovich: His Place in the History of Ukrainian Canadians* (Toronto: Canadian Society for Ukrainian Labour Research, 1987), 10–13.

37 LAC, MG10 K3, K-272, fonds 495, opis 98, Communist International, Communist Party of Canada, 1921–1943, file 21, 'Minutes of the Meeting of the CEC held November 2nd, 1924.'

38 Ibid.

39 Ibid.

40 Ibid.

41 Kavanaugh had been prominent in the Socialist Party of Canada and had helped found the OBU. He would leave Canada for Australia in 1925 and would eventually become the General Secretary of the Australian Communist Party.

42 Cited in Krawchuk, *Our History*, 168.

43 LAC, MG10 K3, K-273, file 25, 'William Moriarty, Report of the Communist Party of Canada, Moscow, March 13, 1925.'

44 Cited in ibid. 'Telegram, Macdonald to Moriarty, Lux Hotel, Moscow, March 8, 1925.' A complete copy of the CEC's resolution is located in its minutes – but this telegram is what Moriarty and the Comintern saw first. It is of some note that Tim Buck, then the Party's Industrial Director, was not present at the meeting where this telegram was drafted and so did not actually support it.

45 Ibid.

46 Ibid., K-272, file 23, 'Confidential Resolution on the Canadian Question,' nd. [but probably May 1925].

47 Ibid., K-273, file 27, 'Proceedings of the Fourth National Convention, CPC, Toronto, 1925, September 11-12-13.'

48 Ibid.

49 Ibid., file 33, 'Organization Report – Communist Party of Canada, On behalf of the CEC of the CPC – Tim Buck' n.d. [but clearly written late in 1926 as the document refers to figures for the year ending 1 October 1926 – it was also almost certainly the document that Buck would submit to the Comintern in November 1926].

50 Ibid.

51 Ibid.

52 Ibid., K-274, file 40, 'Minutes of the Central Executive Committee, February 7, 1926.'

53 Ibid., K-275, file 51, 'Proceedings of the Fifth Convention of the Communist Party of Canada, Toronto, June 17–20, 1927.'

54 Ibid. This comment needs to be read in two slightly different ways. First, it was a defence of the way the Winnipeg party operated; but just as important, Tom McEwen (Ewen) was emerging as a critic of Jack Mac-

donald's leadership and would eventually come out as a supporter of the Tim Buck–Stewart Smith faction in the internal CPC struggles of 1928–9.

55 Ibid.

56 Ibid.

57 In particular, see ibid., file 55, 'Dear Danny, Moscow, August 4, 1928.' [This unsigned letter was clearly from Leslie Morris/aka John Porter while he attended the Lenin Institute to 'Danny' in Winnipeg – Danny was almost certainly Dan Chomitsky/aka Holmes, one of Morris's Ukrainian converts to the cause of the YCL versus the UFLTA Youth Organization. This was one of a series of letters written to Morris's Winnipeg cadre, which also included John Weir/aka Vyviursky – a central figure in the YCL's struggle to control the Youth Section of the ULFTA.]

58 Ibid., file 52, 'Minutes of the Political Committee Meeting, October 4, 1927.' Morris did get the Party nomination for the one-year term, but it was Popovitch who got the nomination for the two-year aldermanic position.

59 Ibid., 'Minutes of the Enlarged Executive Committee Meeting, December 17th and 18th, 1927.'

60 Ibid.

61 Ibid., file 55, 'Dear Joe, Moscow, July 19, 1928 – Leslie.'

62 Krawchuck, *Our History*, 158.

63 LAC, MG10 K3, K-275, file 52, 'Minutes of the Enlarged Executive Committee Meeting, December 17th and 18th, 1927.'

64 Ibid., K-276, file 59, 'Minutes of the CEC Meeting, February 15, 1928.'

65 Ibid.

66 Ibid., K-275, file 57, 'Minutes of the Political Committee, March 10, 1928 – attachment, Sunday March 10th minutes of meeting between Secretariat of the Party and National Ukrainian Agit-Prop.'

67 Ibid., Minutes of the Political Committee, April 13, 1928.'

68 Ibid., K-276, file 64, 'A Declaration by the Minority of the Central Executive Committee and the National Ukrainian Agitpropcom of the Communist Party of Canada – to the Executive Committee of the Communist International' – n.d. but probably June 1928.

69 Ibid.

70 Ibid., 'To the CEC of the CPC, Winnipeg, May 24, 1928 – From the students of the Higher Educational Course.'

71 Ibid., file 59, 'Minutes of the CEC Meeting, May 13, 1928.'

72 Ibid. K-275, file 57, 'Synopsis of the Minutes of the Political Committee, June 29, 1928.'

73 Ibid., 29 June, 26 July, and 3 August 1928.

74 Krawchuk actually provides excerpts from some of these letters in *Our*

History, but he does not explain their provenance. In documents related to the fight between the Ukrainian leadership and the new CEC of the party in 1929 and 1930, some of the contents of these letters were also quoted – without full attribution. While it is never explained who actually took the letters, it would seem they had been in John Weir's possession and were 'pilfered' on behalf of the Ukrainian leaders. As late as 1931 Weir wanted formal action taken against the Ukrainians for this theft at a Party Plenum. See Ibid., K-281, file 116, 'Letter, Sam Carr to Dear Johnny and Boys – Intended for the entire L-Group, April 23, 1931.'

75 Ibid., K-275, file 55, 'Dear Danny, Moscow, August 4, 1928.'
76 Ibid., K-276, file 64, 'A Declaration by the Minority of the Central Executive Committee and the National Ukrainian AgitPropcom of the Communist Party of Canada – to the Executive Committee of the Communist International' – n.d. but probably June 1928.
77 Ibid.
78 Ibid.
79 Ibid.
80 Ibid.
81 Ibid.
82 Ibid. (This was almost certainly a reference to Henry Bartholomew, who had worked as the Winnipeg organizer of the CPC for a short time in the mid-1920s. For confirmation, see LAC, CPC fonds, M7376, A10737, 'Unsigned, Political Committee to Leslie Morris, March 4, 1930.'
83 Canada's Party of Socialism: History of the Communist Party of Canada, 1921-1976 (Toronto: Progress, 1982), 59. See also note 85 below.
84 A fascinating account of this convention and the battle between the two major factions – written by one of the Lenin School Boys, for the ECCI, sometime in late 1929, just before the major Finnish split but clearly after the 'triumph' of the Buck–Smith faction, was misfiled in the Comintern records – appearing in a set of files that came from a much earlier period. This document was clearly written from the anti-Ukrainian perspective, but was also highly critical of the Buck–Smith faction. It is located in LAC, MG10 K3, K-271, file 3, 'The Present Situation and Tasks of the Ukrainian Membership of the Canadian Party' – Signed Frank Evans. [Sam Carr was almost certainly the author, as he used the name Evans while in the Soviet Union.]
85 Ibid., K-278, file 84, 'Declaration of Comrade Parnega: On the Ukrainian Caucus during Sixth Convention of CPC, 1929,' n.d. but probably late 1929 or early 1930.
86 Tim Buck, *Yours in Struggle: Reminiscences of Tim Buck* (Toronto: NC Press, 1977), 138.

87 Buck and especially Smith always maintained that at the same time as Macdonald's resignation, Matthew Popovich 'resigned' his official positions. This was not actually the case. He simply chose not to run for election on the PolCom after Buck and Smith led a two-hour attack at the nomination meeting against his candidacy.

88 On the early phases of the Finnish split, especially the role played by Smith and Vaara, see LAC, MG10 K3, K-275, files 81 and 82.

89 LAC, MG10 K3, K-271, file 3, 'The Present Situation and Tasks of the Ukrainian Membership of the Canadian Party' – Signed Frank Evans. See also ibid., K-276, file 67, 'Politsecretariat of ECCI to CC, CPC, October 3, 1929'; and ibid., K-279, file 97, 'Letter, To the Central Committee, CP of C from Canadian Students at ILS [International Lenin School] – Jack Davis [John Weir], J. Cook, R. Carson, F. Evans [Sam Carr], and Jeane Wallace, Moscow, January 29–30 [1930].

90 Tim Buck's letters while in Moscow, sent to Stewart Smith and the Party Secretariat – but not to the entire Political Committee, where Jack Macdonald still had a seat – provide interesting insights into his and Smith's problems with the Lenin School students and their coalition with Leslie Morris. This is another still understudied aspect of internal party wrangling. See ibid, file 97, 'Letter, Tim to Dear Stew, Jan. 13, 1930, Moscow'; ibid., 'Tim to the Secretariat, CPC, Jan. 13, 1930'; ibid., 'Dear Stew, January 24, 1930'; and ibid., 'Tim to the Secretariat, CPC, Jan. 30, 1930.'

91 Ibid., 'Tim to the Secretariat, CPofC, February 8th, 1930.'

92 Ibid., file 101, 'Political Committee of the CPC, to All Members and Organs of the CPC – Re The Polcom Letter On January 1st' [date-stamped 26 February 1930]. Penner was an ally and would eventually be an employee of the Ukrainians, serving as the Workers' and Framers' Co-op bookkeeper for several years in the early 1930s.

93 Ibid., K-280, 'Resolution of the District Buro of District #7 on the Statement of Comrade D. Homes [sic] regarding the meeting of the Workers Benevolent Association of January Fifth, 1930.'

94 See, for example, ibid., K-271, file 3, 'The Present Situation and Tasks of the Ukrainian Membership of the Canadian Party' – signed Frank Evans. For Morris's take, see ibid., K-279, file 97, 'Leslie [Morris] to Dear Stewart, Feb. 18/30.'

95 Ibid., K-279, file 101, 'Political Committee of the Communist Party of Canada to All Members of Party Fractions in the ULFTA ... For a United Communist Party in Canada Against All Right Wing Deviations' Issued Feb. 10th, 1930.'

96 Ibid.

97 Ibid., K-280, file 110, 'Resolutions and Declarations of the Party Frac-
    tion of the Conventions of the Ukrainian Workers Mass Organizations,'
    11.
98 Ibid., 14.
99 Ibid., K-279, file 98, 'Minutes, Political Committee, CPC, May 15,
    1930.'
100 Krawchuk, *Our History,* 174–5. Unfortunately, there are no Comintern
    or other sources to confirm this particular set of meetings – but they
    might well have ocurred.
101 LAC, MG10 K3, K-279, file 98, 'Minutes, Political Committee, CPC,
    June 30, 1930.'
102 Ibid., K-280, file 110, 'Unrevised Copy, From Bureau of Ukrainian
    Party Fraction' [date-stamped 3 July 1930].
103 Krawchuk, *Our History,* 180.
104 LAC, MG10 K3, K-281, file 116, 'Stewart Smith to Tim [Buck], April
    23rd, 1931.'
105 Ibid., file 116, 'Letter, Sam Carr to Daer Johnny and boys – Intended
    for the entire L-Group SC, April 23, 1931.'
106 Ibid.
107 Translated versions of a few of these can be found in John Kolasky, ed.,
    *Prophets and Proletarians: Documents on the Rise and Decline of
    Ukranian Communism in Canada* (Edmonton: CIUS, 1990), ch. 16.
108 LAC, MG10 K3, K-281, file 121, 'Letter, Tim [Buck] to Stewart
    [Smith], July 14, 1931.'
109 Ibid., file 117, 'Minutes of the Political Bureau, CPC, July 21, 1931.'
110 LAC, MG10 K3, K-275, file 55, 'Dear John, Moscow, September 22,
    1928.'
111 Archives of Manitoba, MG14, B31, 'William Ivens' Papers, "Tom
    Kobzey,"' box 2, file 4.

11

Fighting for the Soul of the Ukrainian Progressive Movement in Canada: The Lobayites and the Ukrainian Labour-Farmer Temple Association

Andrij Makuch

In March 1935, Danylo Lobay, a stalwart lieutenant of the Ukrainian-Canadian left, gave an impromptu address to a gathering of representatives of the Ukrainian Labour-Farmer Mass Organizations (ULFMO) in Winnipeg. They had assembled prior to the start of the Fifteenth Convention of the Ukrainian Labour-Farmer Temple Association (ULFTA). He spoke forcefully and candidly regarding a variety of issues vexing him and other comrades – in particular, their concern about recent events in Ukraine. In short order Lobay had been declared *persona non grata* and had resigned from the leading Ukrainian progressive newspaper *Ukrainski robtinychi visty* (Ukrainian Labor News, or *URV*). Lobay's subsequent publication of a brochure to explain his views simply compounded matters and sparked a strongly negative reaction from the ULFTA, not in the least because it strongly criticized its leadership. All of this established him as the leading voice of discontent with the organization and as the de facto head of an opposition camp – the so-called *Lobaivtsi*, or 'Lobayites.'

This splinter group represented a serious threat to the ULFTA because its leading members could not easily be dismissed as 'nationalists' in the eyes of the rank and file and because the group had coalesced around issues that stirred strong internal discontent. The ULFTA devoted considerable energy to its campaign against the Lobayites, who within eighteen months had effectively been vanquished. Nevertheless, they would remain a thorn in the side of the ULFTA for some time to come.

The Lobayites were not opposed to the aims and objectives of the ULFTA, but rather to the direction in which they perceived the pro-Communist Ukrainian movement had gone. They were seeking not to destroy the ULFTA but rather to 'restore' that group to what they regarded as its proper stance.

The Emergence of the Lobay Opposition

The Lobay 'crisis' began at the sessions of the ULFMO, the umbrella body for pro-Communist Ukrainian organizations in Canada, which preceded the Fifteenth Convention of the ULFTA in March 1935.[1] During a session on 9 March in which he was a discussant, Lobay spoke out openly regarding his concerns about developments in Soviet Ukraine and the fate of two Canadian comrades – Myroslav Irchan, a wildly popular playwright and political activist, and Ivan Sembay, a well-liked and effective Ukrainian labour-farmer organizer and teacher – who had fallen victim to Stalinist repression.[2] His remarks seemed not to have included any specific proposals for further action: they had simply pointed out his strong belief that something was decidedly wrong with the manner in which the Ukrainian progressive movement's leaders were addressing or failing to address such matters.

Lobay was not a lightweight figure in the ULFTA structure, but a man with many years of experience who had played an important role with the worker-farmer press and who was a respected figure in Ukrainian Party circles.[3] The comments came, moreover, after a period of internal tension among the higher ranks of the ULFTA and some discontent over its leadership.

Lobay's comments violated a cardinal rule among Party members: that discussion about delicate internal matters must be confined to closed-door meetings or private conversations. The ULFMO sessions had been attended both by the organizations' leaders and by rank-and-file delegates. Lobay's transgression generated a quick response. A number of ULFTA heavyweights (*tuzy*, or 'aces'), including John Navis (Ivan Navizivsky), Matthew Shatulsky, and Matthew Popovich, responded to his remarks politely enough and without open criticism (at least according to Lobay).[4] At the same time, it was decided to form a three-person commission to prepare a resolution about Soviet nationality policy as well as Lobay's presentation.[5]

That evening, Lobay's actions were discussed in camera by the ULFMO leadership. The following day the gathering was presented with a resolution that singled out Lobay for 'counterrevolutionary nationalist deviation.'[6] Lobay naturally protested his innocence and called the charges against him 'groundless slander.' After the text of the resolution was printed in *URV,* Lobay demanded from several key comrades that the same paper also print a clarification of the matter. Popovich suggested that Lobay prepare a statement, which he did, but *URV* never printed it.[7]

By his own account, Lobay quit his editorial position at *URV*, feeling that he could no longer work there in the newly hostile atmosphere.[8] He devoted the following summer to the preparation of a book, *Shcho diietsia na Radianskii Ukraini?* (What Is Happening in Soviet Ukraine?), based on a close reading of the Soviet Ukrainian press; a brochure, 'Natsionalna polityka Stalina' (Stalin's Nationality Policy); and a booklet, 'Za diisne vyiasnennia polozhennia na Radianskii Ukraini!' (For an Actual Explanation of the Situation in Soviet Ukraine!). In August of that year he went to New York to get his writings published. He reckoned that in Canada the ULFTA-affiliated Workers and Farmers Publishing Association would not print them, and he was loath to take them to a 'nationalist' printer.[9] So he sought a neutral party for this purpose. In September he completed the text of 'Za diisne vyiasnennia,' had it published, and arranged for the forty-eight-page booklet to be mailed to the subscribers of ULFMO publications and otherwise circulated widely.[10] 'Za diisne vyiasnennia' caused a sensation in Canada and was roundly condemned by the ULFTA.

Before dealing with the political fallout from this publication, it would be useful to examine its contents. The booklet has two parts. The first, 'V interesi pravdy' (In the Interest of the Truth), was the Lobay statement that never appeared in *URV*. It is a tightly framed rebuttal to the charges of deviation and counter-revolutionary sentiment. The second consists of a long and highly personal attack on the ULFTA leadership. John Navis, the group's central figure, was particularly savaged: accused of what amounted to careerism within the Ukrainian-Canadian left; of providing inaccurate figures that significantly underestimated the number of 'cultural workers' who had been arrested in Ukraine; of withholding information about the arrests of Irchan and Sembay; and of failing to obtain any information about the fate of Irchan and Sembay during his trip to Soviet Ukraine in 1934. For good measure, Lobay charged that Navis had been 'in the service of Presbyterians' in 1915–16 and even attempted to link him to the nationalist Ukrainian Military Organization.[11]

Matthew Shatulsky, who had worked with *URV* since 1920 and who was Navis's right-hand man, and Philip Lysets, were also targets of direct criticism. Notably, in his brochure Lobay did not criticize Matthew Popovich, perhaps the most dynamic and charismatic of the ULFTA leaders, instead merely citing some of the latter's purported statements regarding Navis's past. Clearly, he regarded Popovich as an ally or a potential ally in his struggle to restore 'the movement' among Ukrainians in Canada.

Near the end of the booklet, Lobay asserted that the ULFTA membership had an unclear picture of events in the Ukrainian SSR because of Navis's failure to relate forthrightly what he had actually seen and heard in Ukraine during his periodic trips there as well as the way that news items from Soviet Ukraine were being culled before they appeared in the Ukrainian-Canadian worker-farmer press. This culling, he added, could be attributed to Shatulsky, who controlled the flow of incoming Soviet publications.[12] He then outlined his plan to prepare a broader study on contemporary Ukraine based on Soviet sources, in which he listed the topics to be addressed and implored readers to support this undertaking financially.

After 'Za diisne vyiasnennia' was published, the Lobay affair took on a whole new dimension and the ULFTA sought to annihilate his reputation in the movement. A campaign against Lobay was mounted in the pages of *URV*. It began on 12 November with an editorial titled 'Iaka meta' (What Is the Goal?). The assessment of his publication was blunt – it was a '*pashkvil* [disgusting smear][13] intended to break up the Ukrainian labour-farmer organizations by undermining faith in their leadership and through lies and slander about the policies of the Communist Party and the Soviet regime in Soviet Ukraine.' Lobay's statement that he had written it '*in the interests of Ukrainian workers and farmers*' (emphasis in the original) was summarily dismissed, and his right to address such issues was questioned:[14] 'Is it possible for the interests of workers and the cause of socialism to be defended by someone who undermines the workers' faith in the policies carried out by the victorious proletariat of the Soviet Union under the guidance of its

Party and Comrade Stalin, the genius-leader of workers throughout the world?'

The editorial was followed during the next weeks by denunciations in *URV* by the more prominent ULFTA leaders. John Boychuk from Toronto led off, painting Lobay as a Petliurite;[15] Popovich joined the fray soon after (on 18 November), separating himself from the 'private conversations' between them cited by Lobay, stating that the latter could not try 'to hide behind my shoulders,' and chiding Lobay for attempting to conceal his anti-communism and anti-Sovietism.[16] The fact that these two figures had led off the campaign was hardly coincidental. Matthew Shatulsky, on reading Lobay's brochure and noting its lack of criticism of Popovich, had written a letter to Navis stating that Lobay's intention was 'to pry Popovich and perhaps Boychuk loose from us and from the [Party] line … and then tie them to the wagon of these counterrevolutionaries.' He recommended that Boychuk and Popovich be the first to appear in 'our press' with criticism of the group.[17]

Shatulsky weighed in on 21 and 22 November with a rambling account of Lobay's treachery. Navis, who was in the midst of his municipal election campaign, felt compelled to write in on 22 November to explain that he simply had been too busy to submit anything about the issue. He assured readers that a missive would be forthcoming. He was true to his word, and then some. His eight-part denunciation ran from 30 November to 11 December. In it he underlined the elemental nature of the fight against Lobayites: 'This is not a personal matter of Lobay versus Navis … The question must be stated clearly – Are we for the line of the leading organizations of the Canadian proletariat or against it?'[18]

This high-minded statement notwithstanding, Navizivsky was not above ad hominem attacks. He suggested that there was something mentally amiss with Lobay, as he had been behaving erratically around the time of the 1935 convention (2 December 1935), and he painted him as somewhat of a slacker who had declined to take part in the rough and tumble of demonstrations and strikes (11 December 1935).[19]

A formal statement concerning 'Za diisne vyiasnennia' from the Central Executive Committee (CEC) of the ULFTA appeared on 30 November in *URV*. It condemned Lobay for trying to wreck the Ukrainian workers' movement in Canada and called for an investigation of how it had been possible for him to send his brochure out to the press's mailing list (i.e., to find out who had aided him). Lobay's 'perfidy' became an agenda item at ULFTA meetings and on the speakers' circuit, and the organization tracked members for possible sympathy towards Lobayism.[20] Over time, the number of attacks on Lobayites increased dramatically, as branches of sundry organizations and numerous individuals started to voice their disapproval. In short, the campaign against Lobay was extensive and employed a strong element of ritual denunciation.

At the same time, the ULFTA prepared a document castigating Lobay, which was to be signed by its leading members. Trouble arose in this regard when three CEC members – Toma Kobzey, Stephen Chwaliboga (Khvaliboga), and M. Zmiiovsky – refused to sign any resolution condemning the dissident. Zmiiovsky eventually fell into line, but Kobzey and Chwaliboga remained steadfastly opposed. The latter two were quickly relieved of their ULFTA positions – Kobzey as Financial Secretary, Chwaliboga as Auditing Committee member – and drummed out of the organization not long afterwards.[21] Several other Party members later left the organization to join the Lobay supporters.[22] Lobay had by now become the de facto leader of a ULFTA opposition group. He seems not to have anticipated this development, nor had he sought it; but once thrust into this position, he took up the challenge as well as he could. Yet his limitations as a leader and a serious lack of resources placed him at a marked disadvantage in dealing with the well-oiled ULFTA machine.

At the organizational level, the ULFTA called for an enlarged plenary session of its CEC near the end of December 1935 to respond to the entire Lobay matter. Shatulsky had suggested this sort of extraordinary gathering to Navis at the beginning of November, and the fact that it was held indicated clearly the extent of their concern.[23] The official slogan of the gathering was 'For the Mass Development of the Ukrainian Labour-Farmer Organizations in Canada. Against the Nationalist-Counterrevolutionary Deviators – For the Raising of the Ideological Level of Our Membership – For New Young Cadres – For a Strong Leadership!' and its proceedings were published (in Ukrainian) under that name.[24] The main presentation, written and delivered by Peter Prokopchak, consisted largely of an absolute and total condemnation of Lobay and his followers. Near the end, however, it added briefly that, owing to the great need to expand the activities of the ULFMO groups, the ULFTA would be staging a round of Higher Educational Courses for the training of new cadres cum cultural workers. In effect, the ULFTA's response to the 'threat' posed by Lobay was to take the offensive – to train a new generation of activists (in the current spirit of the times) and to recruit new members aggressively. Basically, it sought to turn a liability into an asset.

The last time the Higher Educational Courses – a three- to six-month training session – had been held was in 1930. Prior to that, they had been staged several times in the 1920s as a means of developing promising candidates for political and cultural-educational work. The class of 1936 was notable for including a new generation of younger people active in ULFTA affairs; it ended up training a number of people who would occupy key positions in the Ukrainian progressive movement for years to come.[25]

The ULFTA cited the need to devote energy and resources to the Higher Educational Courses as the reason why it cancelled its annual conference for 1936. A more likely reason, perhaps, was concern that Lobay's forces might stage a coup there: at that time, the Lobayites were still a growing concern while the ULFTA was losing members.[26]

The Lobay Threat

The ULFTA's no-holds-barred response to the Lobay opposition underscores the degree to which it was regarded as a threat. The ULFTA had good reason to feel threatened: Lobay and his supporters were dealing with issues on which it was vulnerable. Moreover, the criticism of the Lobayites could not be dismissed out of hand as the slurs of fanatical Ukrainian 'nationalists,' as many of Lobay's people had long histories with and important positions in the progressive movement. One might add to this the fact that Lobay was not working in a vacuum and that some of the concerns he had raised had been discussed previously behind closed doors in ULFTA leadership circles.

Two major issues stood out with regard to the Lobayite threat:

1. The CPC-ULFTA Relationship

Some popular resentment remained with regard to the ties between the Ukrainians and the Communist Party of Canada (CPC). Relations had been cordial enough through the mid-1920s, notwithstanding ongoing flashpoints. The ULFTA enjoyed a period of relative calm, blending cultural-educational work with political activities. This changed in 1928 with the adoption of a new Comintern line calling for greater militancy in Party work throughout the world, including Canada, and for greater centralization and control of the movement. Accordingly, the CPC sought to incorporate its Ukrainian Section directly into the general Party structure and to dismantle the national structure of the ULFTA. Ukrainians, now under fire as closet social democrats or 'right deviationists,' were appalled and resisted fervently (as did the Finnish Organization of Canada). The fight from the side of the ULFTA was spearheaded by Popovich. The situation was strained until 1931, when the Ukrainian leadership finally accepted the new line and an agreement was reached allowing the Ukrainians to retain their 'mass organizations' (i.e., the ULFTA and its affiliated bodies) while meeting the CPC's political objectives.[27] But the matter was hardly resolved, and tensions remained between the CPC and its Ukrainian members and supporters. These were exacerbated by the CPC's increased efforts to steer the ULFTA's internal affairs.[28]

Navis charged Lobay and his supporters with never having embraced the *zvorot* (turn) toward more active and engaged political work that had been adopted in 1931 at the ULFTA's Twelfth Convention. He contended that the Lobayites had not liked the new line but had initially lacked the resources to come out against it openly; and that after some time their leader (Lobay himself) had finally shown his true colours.[29].

The new line affected the ULFTA's rank and file in several ways. Most obviously, it greatly increased the demands placed on them – in essence, to get off the stage and onto the streets.[30] The tenor of the ULFTA press changed from urging or exhorting members to become more involved in the movement to essentially dictating how they should be conducting their affairs. There was also a loss of transparency in the organization's dealings. This is perhaps best reflected in the changed tone of ULFTA convention reports. Through the 1920s these had provided wide-open and detailed accounts of the state of the association and its affiliates. In the 1930s they become little more than compilations of presentations made and resolutions passed at the gatherings – 'marching orders' of sorts.

The purview of the ULFTA leadership was also somewhat different: vis-à-vis the CPC it had less autonomy; and with respect to the

Ukrainian mass organizations it was making much greater demands – some of which were not of its own formulation – and expecting them to be met. In effect, Ukrainians were now saddled with a 'double burden' of Party obligations on the one hand and work within their own mass organizations on the other.[31] Moreover, non-Party members of the ULFTA must have been dismayed to see Party fractions making decisions in advance of any meeting and then forcing their implementation. The CPC's increased demands and its presence in ULFTA affairs led to a certain amount of 'silent resentment' among non-Party members, some of whom withdrew to the safety of the group's cultural-educational activities or quietly dropped out of the organization.[32]

The ULFTA weathered the fallout from the new line fairly well: only two significant pockets of resistance emerged in the early 1930s. The first was a group of Trotskyites in Toronto, including Vasyl Bosovych (a former secretary of the Ontario provincial committee and a prominent local cultural figure) and Nick Oleniuk (a leading local activist). They were expelled from the ULFTA in September 1932. They went on to establish the Kameniari (Stonecutters) Society, with a main branch in Toronto and smaller groups in Hamilton and Montreal, and to publish the newspaper *Robitnychi visty* (Labour News). Though numerically small, the 'Bosovychites' proved to be an irritant to the ULFTA in central Canada.[33] The second was a smaller and more ephemeral group in Winnipeg, led by Ivan Stotsky and Mykhailo Ivanyshyn, which established an opposition to the ULFTA in the latter part of 1932, accusing the leadership of 'bureaucratism' and a lack of principle. It published a few issues of a mimeographed bulletin and then slowly disappeared.

2. The ULFTA and Soviet Ukraine

The establishment of the Ukrainian SSR in 1922 was a source of great pride and inspiration to the Ukrainian pro-Communist left in Canada. Both the social and nationalities questions seemed to have been answered by its formation, as Ukraine was now a distinct polity with a workers' government (as compared to the country's past subsumation within the Russian Empire). Moreover, in the 1920s Soviet Ukraine (then experiencing phenomenal cultural development) provided the ULFTA with practical examples of the benefits of revolution – new works of Ukrainian literature, Ukrainian films, and examples of innovative forms of social organization. The image of Soviet Ukraine became a strong sustaining force for the ULFTA – to the point that some English comrades would comment that they wondered whether their Ukrainian counterparts realized they lived in Canada and not in the Soviet Union.[34]

This was all good and fine during the mid-1920s, when the Ukrainian SSR enjoyed a degree of autonomy, a vibrant cultural and academic life, and an official state policy of Ukrainization. It was a time when the idea and practice of national communism – 'a current within the Communist movement or Communist parties that attempted to reconcile national interests with Marxist-Leninist doctrine in order to sanction a national road to socialism' – was strong in the republic.[35] But in the latter 1920s and early 1930s, Ukraine's situation within the Soviet Union changed dramatically and the republic saw a significant rollback of cultural and political gains realized during the 1920s, culminating in widespread arrests among the Ukrainian intelligentsia and the Party *aparat* and the staging of the Holodomor (or Great Famine).[36]

Developments such as the Union for the Liberation of Ukraine (SVU) show trial (1930) and the liquidation of the Ukrainian Autocephalous Orthodox Church (1930) did not overly concern the Ukrainian-Canadian Communist left.[37] Only when the Soviet regime began to destroy its own supporters – Ukrainian state officials, Party figures, and Soviet Ukrainian writers – did some concern about the course of events in Ukraine begin to develop among some of the Ukrainian comrades in Canada.

The matter was brought closer to home in 1934 by rumours – initially unconfirmed – that began circulating about the arrests of Irchan and Sembay. This issue caused widespread concern, even among the rank and file, who found it difficult to accept that two such fine comrades could have or would have betrayed their revolutionary ideals.[38] It also left the ULFTA leadership in a quandary: Should it pursue the matter for a satisfactory answer as to why these two men had been arrested (which would have involved raising doubts about the course of events in Ukraine and possibly the Soviets' nationality policy)? Or should it accept the explanation given (i.e., that they were closet counterrevolutionaries)? Ultimately it chose the latter option with a vengeance.

Lobay's intervention at the 1935 ULFTA conference was a complete surprise for many. But it was probably less of a bolt from the blue for the ULFTA leaders, who had been experiencing some internal tension before the March gathering. A small cache of letters and notes from late November and early December 1934 written by Shatulsky sheds some light on this matter.[39]

Most notably, there had been a factional division of sorts, with Navis and Shatulsky on one side and Popovich, Lobay, and Kobzey on the other.[40] The former seem to have been grooming the young Michael Lenartovych within the organization as a promising worker (he had done well in his position with the publication *Robitnytsia* [The Working Woman]) and a potential ally, but Lenartovych died unexpectedly and prematurely at the age of thirty-one on 28 October 1934.[41] Shatulsky was particularly surprised by Popovich's antagonism, noting in a letter to John Boychuk that 'I expected and so did other comrades that with the arrival of P. [Popovich] our fractiousness would level off or let up a bit. But the opposite happened. It became even harsher.'[42]

After his release from Kingston Penitentiary on 30 June 1934, Popovich spent some time convalescing. In the fall he returned to ULFTA work.[43] From Shatulsky's accounts, it is clear that Popovich became quite critical and started taking a negative position on the leadership's line on various issues.[44] He was also spending a fair amount of time with Kobzey and Lobay. On the Irchan issue, Popovich was said to have stated that it was known that Irchan had been arrested, but that Navis and others had not explained it and had instead tried 'to cover it up both internally and externally,' thereby 'demoralizing our comrades by this [act].' To this Shatulsky added that 'Popovich has charged us with a cover-up, hushing things up.' Popovich was also critical of the proposed merger of the Workers Benevolent Association (WBA) with the International Workers Order of the United States, though he stated this indirectly by citing a lack of explanation on the matter.[45] He even criticized the ULFTA's adoption of recent Soviet changes to the Ukrainian 'Kharkiv orthography' with round sarcasm and a note that 'in general we are being Russified.'[46] Kobzey and Lobay were clearly in agreement with Popovich on the orthography issue, while Shatulsky privately expressed the following view: 'Does not this hatred of our adoption of [current] Soviet orthography testify to a hatred for those who are building a Soviet socialist order in Ukraine?' Given the tensions at the home office, it is hardly surprising that Shatulsky, in his letter of 4 December, asked Boychuk to keep the contents of the correspondence to himself and to not let on that he was aware of the extent of the problems in Winnipeg (including with Popovich, who was soon to be touring central Canada).

Given their potential numbers and their knowledge of the ULFTA's internal affairs at the central leadership level, the Lobayites were in an entirely different league from the groups that had earlier split with the ULFTA. *URV* openly acknowledged the greater danger they posed in an editorial of 6 December 1935, which stated that 'this is not simply Stotskyism or Bosovychism' and which elevated the threat to something approaching the level of Trotskyism or Zinovievism.[47] A significant part of the Lobayite threat also came from the fact that its supporters came from within the ranks of the ULFMO, in which a number had occupied significant positions. As such, they could not be dismissed as an insignificant group led by one or two malcontents or as hostile outside critics. Moreover, the fact that they had quickly been able to gain a solid foothold in Winnipeg – historically the ULFTA's great centre – afforded them a real possibility of moving out further afield.

Among the leading Lobayites were Lobay himself; Toma Kobzei, a ULFTA executive member since the 1920s and more recently the association's Financial Secretary; Stephen Chwaliboga, a member of the ULFTA's CEC; Omelian Khomitsky, Secretary-Treasurer of the WBA's National Executive; Theodore Pylypas, the ULFTA National Chairman; and Mykhailo Smyt, a leading Transcona activist and a press columnist of some note.

An interesting side-comment on the formation of the Lobayites came from T. Dann, the commander of the RCMP's 'D' Division, who noted in a 25 November 1935 account of the Winnipeg ULFTA that previously there had been 'several attempts to break the autocratic rule of the U.L.F.T.A. led by Navizowski [Navis], but without success. However, the Lobay situation appears to be a real threat in that direction.'[48]

Lobay ultimately failed to get Popovich to join the rebel ranks, which would have been a major coup. Certainly, he would have been well aware of Popovich's discontent with the state of affairs within the ULFTA leadership (see above). As well, Lobay knew that Popovich was very much concerned about events in Soviet Ukraine, for after re-

turning to ULFTA work in the fall of 1934, he had apparently asked
Lobay to inform him privately about the current state of affairs there.[49]
Moreover, it is entirely possible that Popovich still harboured some resentment towards the Party with regard to the viciousness of the fight
over the Bolshevization of the Ukrainians between 1928 and 1931; he
may even have felt betrayed by some of his ULFTA colleagues because
of their less than total support in that campaign. At a personal level,
perhaps he felt slighted in that he had not been treated in the Party
newspapers in the same manner as other freed 'Kingston Eight' inmates
(making specific reference by the large amount of ink garnered by Sam
Carr, who had been released the same day, compared to the insignificant mention that he himself received).[50] On the other hand, Popovich
had spent much of his life developing and defending the ULFTA and
was a committed and disciplined communist. Purportedly his first
words to Lobay following the 1935 conference presentation were 'Do
you feel better now?' – a rebuke for having taken sensitive matters out
from behind closed doors.[51] As well, Popovich had significant health
and financial concerns. At the end of November 1934, at a meeting of
the CPC's Ukrainian bureau in Winnipeg, he had requested some time
off as he required a number of small operations as well as two months'
full rest. After some discussion of how he could make ends meet during this time and the granting of some modest financial support,
Popovich raised the issue of convalescing, possibly in the Soviet
Union.[52] Such medical and monetary issues may well have strength-
ened Popovich's ties to the Party and the ULFTA.

The Lobay Opposition in Action

Early in 1936, Kobzey and Chwaliboga printed a statement about their
position on recent events, a four-page broadsheet titled 'Vsim, shcho
khochut znaty pravdu' (For All Those Who Would Like to Know the
Truth).[53] This was a response to the various charges made against
Lobay and his supporters. It stressed that the Lobayites had no desire
to 'wreck' the worker-farmer movement, but wished only to 'keep it on
the right track.' By now Popovich had come out publicly against Lobay
and was subject to personal attack.

The Kobzey-Chwaliboga statement provided the impetus for the
launching of a newspaper to reflect the views of the Lobatyites. *Pravda*

(The Truth), edited by Lobay, first appeared in mid-February 1936. It noted developments in the campaign against him as well as the extent of resistance to it. It also announced the founding of Ukrainian worker-farmer education associations in Winnipeg and neighbouring Transcona. *Pravda* also attacked the ULFTA leadership, often in a personal way. In its first issue, the newspaper charged that Navis had tried to mollify the ULFTA's leaders over the 1931 reorientation by suggesting that he could arrange for them to move to Soviet Ukraine, where they would be assured comfortable positions.[54] The routine exhumation of ULFTA skeletons was to become a trademark of the paper.

Significantly, *Pravda* did not specifically differentiate itself from the ULFTA's main publications except for its criticisms of the organization's leadership and the Soviet Union's nationality policy. In fact, it very much resembled a typical issue of *URV* from the early 1930s. This 'continuity' was suggested in the first issue with a front-page notice that the paper would be reprinting articles by Lenin, one of which appeared on the second page, and an affirmation in the premiere editorial that 'we support a Leninist nationality policy' ('My za Leninsku natsionalnu polityku'). An additional touch of the familiar was added by the printing of a column by 'Drapaka' (Mykhailo Smyt) called 'Snep Shots,' which had been a regular feature in *URV*. Also noteworthy is that the paper did not shift towards 'nationalist' positions, though it would soon develop a more overtly national communist profile.[55]

The point of no return for the Lobayites was reached at the end of March 1936, when the CPC organ *The Worker* published an editorial stating that Lobay and Kobzey had 'betrayed our class.' *Pravda* speculated that the CPC had stayed out of the fray for so long because it wanted to see whether Navis would emerge intact, adding hopefully that it could not openly endorse Navis because of the degree of discontent against him and that it was the appearance of *Pravda* that had forced the Party's hand. (This may well be true – the appearance of *Pravda* may have been viewed as a growth in the threat posed by the rebels. Earlier, Canadian Party Secretary Tim Buck had been reluctant to involve himself in the dispute, hoping that the Ukrainian comrades could still work things out among themselves. This attitude may have carried over for some time.[56]) *Pravda* went on to examine the Party question over three weeks of editorials, concluding that the CPC had changed its line and could no longer be considered the sole representative of workers' interests. It followed that other workers' parties could also be considered legitimate.[57]

The severing of any possible ties with the CPC was followed almost immediately by a discussion concerning some organizational form. In April 1936, Kobzey considered the extent of support for the Lobayites and suggested a conference in Toronto to bring their forces together. A gathering of this kind took place at the end of July 1936 with twenty-eight participants, who established the Federation of Ukrainian Labour-Farmer Organizations (FULFO).[58] By this time it was obvious that the Lobayites had pockets of support in various centres – groups in Winnipeg and Transcona, Edmonton and Calgary, Toronto, Montreal, and Detroit, as well as individuals in some smaller points – but they had not yet achieved any critical mass.[59] As such, the Lobayites had not managed to develop into a group that could rival the ULFTA outright. Nevertheless, they remained a threat to the ULFTA, with a nationwide presence and a modest base of support in the Winnipeg region.[60]

Pravda made certain content changes in the period following the CPC's condemnation of Lobay and Kobzey. The godhead Lenin disappeared from its pages, and the paper began to stress a Ukrainian national communist heritage. On the third anniversary of the death of Mykola Skrypnyk – the leading Soviet Ukrainian statesman of the late 1920s and early 1930s, who had committed suicide in 1933 rather than be liquidated – the paper carried extensive coverage of his life, work, and legacy.[61] A similar treatment of Mykola Khvylovy, the prominent writer and publicist of the Soviet Ukrainian cultural renaissance of the 1920s, followed later.[62] *Pravda* also published a tribute to Irchan,[63] and in late November 1936 the Winnipeg Ukrainian Worker-Farmer Education Association staged his play *Dvanadtsiat* (The Twelve), which, like all of Irchan's works, had been purged from the ULFTA's repertoire.[64] *Pravda* also started reprinting articles by Volodymyr Vynnychenko, a writer and socialist Ukrainian statesman during the Revolutionary period who had once been quite popular among left-wing Ukrainian Canadians.[65] In fact, to some degree Vynychenko came to be something of a replacement godhead. Notably, when articles by Lenin reappeared in the paper early in 1937, they were accompanied by explanations of how the current communist leadership in the Soviet Union had undermined his original intentions; they were no longer used as exhortations in their own right.

The Lobayites also took a turn politically. In July 1936, *Pravda* endorsed the Co-operative Commonwealth Federation (CCF) as well as Independent Labour Party candidates for the Manitoba provincial election. It chose not to support the sole CPC contestant, stating that the Party had moved to the right.[66] *Pravda* increasingly began carrying items about CCF activities and routinely endorsing their candidates during elections. Meanwhile, CCF figures began appearing – at least for a time – at Lobayite gatherings. The most notable of these was a 16 November 1936 meeting at the Prosvita Institute in Winnipeg, at which CCF leader James Woodsworth was the featured speaker. This was attended by about five hundred people, including many non-Lobayites. A melee transpired, with ULFTA supporters – some of them *kursanty* (Higher Educational Course students) – disrupting the proceedings.[67] The fracas may have cooled Woodsworth's interest in relations with the Lobayites.[68]

The Lobayites suffered a major setback towards the end of 1936 when Matthew Popovich sued *Pravda* for libel over its claim that he had stolen the *URV* mailing list and sold it to the Toronto-based Blackburn Company for personal gain.[69] *Pravda* reacted to this suit by saying that 'our "friends," who for a meager wage became traitors to the Ukrainian people and the faithful servants of great-power chauvinism, wish to destroy *Pravda* because they are powerless to fight against it using political arguments.'[70] The group's major effort for the next six months or so became the raising of funds to contest the action and to keep *Pravda* afloat. After Popovich won his suit, *Pravda* called for the creation of a 'Committee of 500' that would donate $2.50 apiece for a defence fund. The effort did not have much success.[71] Popovich was awarded a judgement of $1,000 plus costs of $550 after the appeal of the case proved unsuccessful.[72] *Pravda* itself had insufficient funds to cover these expenses. Popovich then arranged to garnishee the wages of three of the co-defendants. Such a move reflected the bare knuckles nature of the fight with the Lobayites, but it ended up as something of a public relations setback for the ULFTA when the Lobayites responded by distributing leaflets in English and Ukrainian regarding the unbecoming scenario whereby a 'Communist Leader Garnisheed Wages of Three Ukrainian Workers!'[73] This may have generated some sympathy, but it did not prove of any great benefit to the Lobayites. After the appeal judgement was rendered, *Pravda* ceased functioning as a weekly and became a biweekly. It – and the movement that supported it – survived this challenge, but the Lobayites did not grow subsequently.

The FULFO continued in various forms (the Ukrainian Labour Organization, the League of Ukrainian Organizations) until the 1940s. *Pravda* was replaced by *Vpered* (Forward) in 1938 and moved its operations to Toronto, where a new linotype machine had been purchased and an alliance formed with the local Ukrainian Trotskyites. However, the movement was largely rudderless. Lobay remained editor until the paper – which was now receiving assistance from the Ukrainian Workingmen's Association (UWA) in the United States[74] – folded in 1940. Lobay stayed in Eastern Canada for several years, where he involved himself in various organizations in a secretarial capacity. He returned to Winnipeg in the late 1940s after his efforts to become editor of *Narodna volia* (People's Will), the UWA's Scranton-based newspaper, proved unsuccessful. [75] He then served from 1948 to 1965 as an associate editor of *Ukrainskyi holos* (Ukrainian Voice) in Winnipeg.[76] Lobay continued to be critical of the Soviet Union's nationality policy and his former Ukrainian-Canadian comrades, though now from a more nationalist perspective.[77] He died in Toronto in 1966.

Conclusion

The Lobay crisis had been set in motion by concerns about recent developments in Ukraine – in particular, the arrest of Irchan and Sembay. Ultimately, though, it focused on questions about the practices and personalities of the ULFTA's leadership as well as the Ukrainian progressive movement's ties to the CPC. The ULFTA's ability to withstand this challenge indicates that 'the turn' made in 1928 and formally accepted in 1931 was implemented successfully throughout the organization – that it *had* taken root.

The entire episode underscores a dilemma that faced Ukrainian comrades in Canada – namely, the matter of adhering to Party discipline even when faced with unwelcome circumstances. In the case of the arrest of Irchan and Sembay on charges of being counter-revolutionaries, the ULFTA leadership was in something of a quandary, for to question this charge would have been to doubt the Soviet system at a time when unswerving loyalty to the Soviet Union was the norm within the CPC. At the same time, Irchan and Sembay were well known to

ULFTA leaders and supporters, and the possibility that they might in fact be guilty proved difficult to swallow. The attempt by the ULFTA leadership to dodge the issue by stonewalling proved counterproductive in the end, for it generated doubt and resentment.

The fact that Lobay and others broke over this and other issues underscores the fact that there was support for the idea of Ukrainian national communism within the Ukrainian progressive movement. It should not be surprising that its demise in Ukraine would have repercussions in Canada. Notwithstanding the fact that the ULFTA looked to the Soviet Union as the spiritual centre of the worldwide communist movement, it still maintained a special relationship with the Ukrainian SSR. In fact, one could say that its concept of the Soviet Union was, to some degree, filtered through the prism of Ukraine. Further to this, a case could be made that Lobay and his supporters were local Ukrainian national communists who ultimately were unwilling or unable to reconcile themselves with an emerging Stalinist matrix that was, in their eyes, harmful to the interests of Soviet Ukraine. This is not to suggest that the ULFTA leadership that pulled out all the stops in its assault on the Lobayites was indifferent to the fate of Ukraine – indeed, this was far from so. But the ULFTA was able to reconcile the issue of events in Ukraine with Party loyalty and the sake of 'the cause.'

Finally, the Lobay issue underscores the impressive organizational machinery of the ULFTA. With the appearance of 'Za diisne vyiasnennia' the leadership moved quickly to the challenge it posed, mounting an impressive campaign against Lobay and his supporters. It mobilized a wide array of resources and was able to contain the Lobayites. Moreover, the ULFTA leaders were savvy enough to take a positive approach to the Lobay threat, using it as a call to strengthen the movement, most notably by staging a new round of Higher Education Courses.

Notes

1 The ULFTA was established in 1918 as a socialist-oriented cultural-educational organization. It was the ideological successor to the Ukrainian Social Democratic Party, which had been banned earlier that year. The ULFTA aligned itself with the Third International and maintained close ties with the CPC, largely through its leadership. By 1928 it

boasted 91 general branches, 45 women's branches, and 41 branches of its Youth Section, for a total membership of 5,536. For a general overview of its activities during its first decade of existence, see *Almanakh Tovarystva Ukrainskyi robitnycho-farmerskyi dim v Kanadi i bratnikh organizatsii, 1918–1929* (Almanac of the Ukrainian Labour Farmer Temple Association and Its Fraternal Organization, 1918–1929) (Winnipeg: Workers and Farmers Publishing Association, 1930). For a history of the group see Peter Krawchuk, *Our History: The Ukrainian Labour-Farmer Movement in Canada, 1907–1991* (Toronto: Lugus, 1996). The ULFMO was established in the mid-1930s as an umbrella body to facilitate closer cooperation between the ULFTA and its fraternal groups, the Workers Benevolent Association, and the Association for Aid to the Liberation Movement in Western Ukraine. Its formation was expedited by the fact that all three groups held their national conventions at approximately the same time. The 1935 gathering was the ULFMO's first convention.

2   The Irchan-Sembay issue is dealt with briefly in Krawchuk, *Our History*, 196–97. See also Peter Krawchuk, *The Unforgettable Myroslav Irchan: Pages from a Valiant Life* (Toronto: Kobzar, 1998); and Peter Krawchuk, 'I. Sembay – A Victim of Stalinism,' *Ukrainian Canadian*, November 1989. Irchan lived in Canada from 1923 to 1929, when he left for Soviet Ukraine. He was arrested in December 1933 on trumped-up charges and incarcerated. He was later resentenced and shot in November 1937 in the Solovets Islands. Sembay was deported in 1932 to Soviet Ukraine, where he was subsequently arrested and executed.

3   Lobay was born in 1893 in Ulvivok, Sokal county, Galicia. He obtained a mid-level education in his native village and in Sokal (augmented by extensive personal reading) and was active in the local Prosvita and Sich societies. In 1913 he left Ukraine for Canada, using the ruse that he was headed to Prussia for seasonal labour. His initial employment in Canada was as a labourer and a fieldhand, but he quickly became involved with the Ukrainian-Canadian socialist left and worked as an editor for its press organ *Robochyi narod*. He quickly became a fixture in the Ukrainian socialist movement, working mainly in its press. In 1921 he also headed the Famine Relief Committee for Soviet Ukraine, which raised more than $10,000 in six months. See Orest Martynowych, *Ukrainians in Canada: The Formative Period, 1891–1924* (Edmonton: Canadian Institute of Ukrainian Studies Press, 1991), 428 and 472; Danylo Lobai, *Za diisne vyiasnennia polozhennia na Radianskii Ukraini!* (For an Actual Explanation of the Situation in the Soviet Ukraine!) (Winnipeg and New York: by the author, 1935), 41–2; and Lobay's obituary in *Ukrainskyi holos*, 11 January 1967. *Almanakh TURFDim, 1918–1929*, 59, notes that Lobay

had been on the editorial staff of the movement's flagship newspaper, *Ukrainski robitnychi visty* (Ukrainian Labour News; *URV*) since its beginning.

4   Lobai, *Za diisne vyiasnennia,* 5, claims that none of the speakers came out against the points he made.

5   Ibid., 6.

6   The text appears in English translation in Krawchuk, *Our History*, 198.

7   In Lobai, *Za diisne vyiasnennia,* 9 and 10, Lobay notes that Popovich had agreed to carry such a statement once shortly after the conference and then a second time during a chance meeting on 27 April 1935, at which time he then actually prepared one.

8   Ibid., 43.

9   Ibid., 35. underlines that Lobay was painfully aware that any impolitic dealings with the press on his part could only provide his adversaries with additional ammunition.

10   Lobay's actions in this regard came out following the booklet's publication in the 'confessions' of ULFTA members who had helped him. The statement by the CEC of the ULFTA regarding Lobay's brochure (which appears in *Ukrainski robitnychi visty* [hereafter *URV*], 30 November 1935) noted that ULFMO executive members may have helped with its publication and called for an investigation of the security breach that would have allowed Lobay access to the movement's newspaper subscription list. Omelian Khomytsky later admitted (*URV*, 17 January 1935) that he had met with Lobay secretly (even after having initially condemned his speech) and given him $15.00 towards the publication of the brochure. He doubtlessly was not the only person to have done so.

11   The Ukrainian Military Organization was an underground body established in 1920 in order to continue the struggle for Ukrainian independence. It was instrumental in the creation of the Organization of Ukrainian Nationalists in 1929. Navis defended his employment in the 1910s with the Ukrainian Presbyterian newspaper *Ranok* in *URV*, 3 December 1935, noting that he was simply working for money (stating that there is no shame in working in a print shop) and that he did not support the group ideologically. He added that when an opportunity came to work for the labour press, he did so readily.

12   Lobai, *Za diisne vyiasnennia*, 37. The matter of Shatulsky's control over the incoming Soviet Ukrainian press is also raised in an editorial in *Pravda*, 8 July 1936.

13   The tone of the second part of the booklet is actually quite harsh, as if Lobay's visceral dislike of Navis and his cohorts clouded his reason. This made it easier for his opponents to dismiss *Za diisne vyiasnennia* as a 'pashkvil.' The label successfully hit home with loyal ULFTA supporters.

14   The quote is from the editorial that appeared in *URV*, 12 November 1935.
15   *URV*, 15 November 1935. 'Petliurite,' a common Soviet Communist pejorative, referred to supporters of the government of the short-lived Ukrainian National Republic (1917–20, with interruptions). It was also applied more generally in Ukraine or the diaspora to Party opponents. Symon Petliura (1879–1926) served as commander of its armed forces, then briefly as its president before fleeing into exile. He oversaw the activities of the UNR's government-in-exile until his assassination in 1926.
16   Ibid., 18 November 1935. In *URV*, 14 December 1935, a second letter by Popovich appeared. It offered an explanation as to why the letter written by Lobay shortly after the 1935 convention had never appeared in the paper.
17   Stavroff–Krawchuk Collection, 'Shatulsky Correspondence,' Shatulsky to Navis, 2 November 1935. The collection is a private archive housed in Toronto under the care of Larissa Stavroff.
18   *URV*, 30 November 1934.
19   John Boyd, *A Noble Cause Betrayed ... but Hope Lives On: Pages from a Political Life: Memoirs of a Former Ukrainian Canadian Communist* (Edmonton: Canadian Institute of Ukrainian Studies Press, 1999), 58, makes the observation that Lobay 'would never do anything like distribute leaflets or march in a demonstration.'
20   The 'Lobay' file in the Stavroff–Krawchuk Collection includes ULFTA 'intelligence' reports about two Lobayite meetings held in private homes in Winnipeg in January 1936 (which listed the names of those present) and an assessment of Lobayite support in neighbouring East Kildonan from the same period. The file also contains undated speaking notes (on small pieces of paper) for a talk (in Ukrainian) on 'What Was the Reason for Lobay's Presentation at the Previous Conference and the Publication of His Disgusting Smear' as well as a two-page listing of the 'characteristics' of thirteen local Lobayites. Lobai, *Za diisne vyiasnennia*, 37, derides Navis for sending out 'stool pigeons' to determine who has been meeting with him.
21   The announcement from the CEC of the ULFTA regarding the dismissal of the two from their positions appeared in *URV*, 9 December 1935.
22   Toma Kobzei, *Na ternystykh ta khreshchatykh dorohakh* (On the Thorny Way and Crossroads), vol. II (Winnipeg: Popular Printers, 1973), 35.
23   In his letter of 2 November 1935 to Navis (mentioned earlier), Shatulsky had suggested that the gathering be convened sooner than it otherwise normally would have been (i.e., at the next ULFMO gathering sometime in the summer of 1936).
24   *Za masovu rozbudovu ukrainskykh robitnycho-farmerskykh orhanizatsii v Kanadi* (Winnipeg: CEC of the ULFTA, 1936).

25 Krawchuk, *Our History*, 347–8, deals with the Higher Education Courses.

26 This matter is dealt with briefly in Rhonda Hinther, '"Sincerest Revolutionary Greetings": Progressive Ukrainians in Twentieth-Century Canada,' PhD diss., McMaster University, 2005. Membership figures given at the 1935 and 1937 conventions are cited in Krawchuk, *Our History*, 396 and 398. They indicate a drop in support from 8,838 to 4,415 members over this two-year period.

27 Examinations of CPC–ULFTA relations to 1931 can be found in Jim Mochoruk, '"Pop & Co." vs. Buck and the "Lenin School Boys": Ukrainian Canadian Radicals and the Communist Party of Canada, 1921–31' (in this volume); Krawchuk, *Our History*, ch. 11; and Andrij Makuch, 'Bolshevizing the Bil'shovyks: The Communist Party of Canada's "Ukrainian Problem," 1927–1931' (unpublished paper, 2003).

28 Krawchuk, *Our History*, 186.

29 *URV*, 11 December 1935. Boyd, *A Noble Cause*, 57–8, notes that 'Lobay was a card-carrying Party member. He bought into the ideology, but wasn't enthusiastic or fanatical about it.'

30 A major undertaking at ULFTA halls was commonly the staging of theatrical productions. Hence the 'off the stage and onto the streets' reference suggests that the membership go beyond the comfortable confines of their halls and become involved in more direct political action.

31 Boyd, *A Noble Cause*, 48, discusses the 'double burden' carried by Ukrainian Party members.

32 Ibid., 48–9, notes the alienating effect of an increased Party presence. Krawchuk, *Our History*, 186, notes the pre-convention fraction meetings. On page 158 of the same source, Krawchuk mentions the alienating impact of greetings by CPC figures at ULFTA conventions, largely because of their imperious tone.

33 The Bosovych-led group is dealt with briefly in John Kolasky, *The Shattered Illusion: The History of Pro-Communist Organizations in Canada* (Toronto: Peter Martin, 1979), 19. Oleniuk also deals with the group in the course of a series of interviews conducted with him in 1982 by his daughter Carole (in tapes 5 and 7). An unpublished transcript of these was prepared by the latter as 'Oral History as told by Nicholas Oleniuk.'

34 Ivan Avakumovic, *The Communist Party of Canada: A History* (Toronto: McClelland and Stewart, 1975), 37.

35 This 'textbook' definition of the term appears in James Mace, 'National Communism,' *Encyclopedia of Ukraine*, vol. III, ed. Danylo Husar Struk (Toronto: University of Toronto Press, 1993), 540.

36 For a general overview of developments in this period, see James Mace,

Communism and the Dilemmas of National Liberation: National Communism in Soviet Ukraine, 1918–1933 (Cambridge, MA: distributed by Harvard University Press, 1983).

37 In fact, *URV* provided extensive coverage of the SVU trial and supported the contention that the accused were counter-revolutionaries.

38 Kolasky, *Shattered Illusion*, 20.

39 These are a number of letters and notes written by Shatulsky while John Navis was away from the ULFTA headquarters in Winnipeg. They are found in the Stavroff–Krawchuk Collection.

40 Stavroff-Krawchuk Collection, 'Shatulsky Correspondence,' note regarding 24 November 1934 meeting.

41 *Narodna hazeta*, 22 March 1939. The author wishes to thank Myron Momryk for providing him with this information.

42 'Shatulsky Correspondence,' Shatulsky to John Boychuk, 4 December 1934. Boychuk's name does not appear in the correspondence, but the text of the letter clearly indicates that it was addressed to him.

43 Popovich had been arrested in 1931 under section 98 of the Canadian Criminal Code for belonging to an illegal organization and sentenced in 1932 to a five-year prison term in Kingston Penitentiary. This occurred in conjunction with a roundup of high-profile Communist leaders in Canada, who subsequently became known as the 'Kingston Eight.' He was paroled before serving his entire sentence.

44 Unless otherwise noted, the information in this paragraph comes from 'Shatulsky Correspondence,' note regarding 24 November 1934 meeting, and Shatulsky to Navis, 6 December 1934.

45 The proposal is dealt with in Krawchuk, *Our History*, 201–2. The amalgamation was opposed by most of the WBA's leadership, and the matter eventually was dropped by the Party.

46 The Kharkiv orthography was established in 1925–7 and adopted as a standardized form of Ukrainian in 1928. The subsequent changes to the orthography, finally published in 1936 as the so-called Kyiv orthography, were introduced to bring Ukrainian language norms more in line with Russian.

47 *URV*, 6 December 1935. The piece begins by noting the considerable amount of mail received on the Lobay issue and the possibility that the amount of coverage afforded the matter might lead some malcontents to suggest some kind of cover-up. At this juncture, *URV* then stresses the severity of the Lobay threat.

48 LAC, RG146; Document #48, file 88-A-73 (Daniel Lobay and R.B. Russell) (hereafter LAC, RG146, Lobay), T. Dann Report, 25 November 1935.

49 Lobay mentions this in his 'In the Interest of the Truth' statement. See *Za diisne vyiasnennia*, 4.

50 This is mentioned in the Stavroff–Krawchuk Collection, 'Lobay File,' Shatulsky note, 26 November 1934.

51 Lobai, *Za diisne vyiasnennia*, 5. The phrase in Ukrainian was 'Vzhe vam lekshe?' Lobay, on the other hand, understood this exchange positively as an acknowledgment of the fact that they had earlier discussed such matters in private.

52 'Shatulsky Correspondence,' note of 30 November 1934.

53 The text is reprinted in Kobzei, *Na dorohakh*, vol. II, 45–55.

54 *Pravda*, 15 February 1936. The fact that this did not happen is attributed later to the arrest of ULFTA leaders in 1931 and their incarceration in Kingston.

55 Examples of contemporary 'nationalist' issues that *Pravda* might have dealt with include condemnation of the Union for the Liberation of Ukraine show trial and the cashiering of the Ukrainian Autocephalous Orthodox church in the Ukrainian SSR. The term 'nationalist' was used broadly by the Ukrainian-Canadian left as a term to describe all the factions of the mainstream Ukrainian community in Canada collectively.

56 In November 1934, shortly after the appearance of *Za diisne vyiasnennia*, Tim Buck still believed that Lobay could be dealt with and should not be written off. See LAC, RG46, Lobay, T. Dann Report and covering letter, 25 November 1934.

57 *Pravda*, 6–22 April 1936.

58 *Pravda*, 12 August 1936. The group's name in Ukrainian was Federatsiia ukrainskykh robitinycho-farmerskykh orhanizatsii.

59 By looking at various accounts in *Pravda* one can gain an idea of the Lobayites' modest numbers. A spring dance in Winnipeg saw 170 people participate (15 April 1936). An account of the pro-Lobayite Kameniari society in Toronto noted that 'tens' of ULFMO supporters had joined (22 April 1936). The Edmonton Ukrainian Labor-Farmer Educational Society reported that it had 23 members, though 35 to 40 people would usually come out for its events (16 September 1936).

60 A financial report for *Pravda* from its 13 May 1936 issue shows that almost $900 of the $1,150 it had raised to date had come directly from the Winnipeg area. In addition, a portion of the remaining $250 was attributed to cash sales, part of which would also have come from in or around Winnipeg.

61 *Pravda*, 8 July 1936. An examination of Skrypnyk's political views constitutes chapter 6 of Mace, *Communism and the Dilemmas of National Liberation*.

62 *Pravda*, 5 May 1937.
63 *Pravda*, 15 July 1936.
64 *Pravda*, 9 December 1936. The proscription of Irchan's plays did not completely stop their occasional performance by some ULFTA drama troupes.
65 Vynnychenko's (1880–1951) popularity was reflected by the fact that a good number of early reading societies and drama groups named themselves in his honour. In early December 1936, *Pravda* reprinted (in two parts) a 1920 letter from Vynnychenko to Ukrainian workers and peasants, and in the latter part of January 1937 it carried (again in two parts) a biographical piece about the playwright-politician. In a later issue of the paper (3 November 1937), Vynnychenko himself – then living in exile in France – appealed to readers to support *Pravda*.
66 *Pravda*, 22 July 1936.
67 *Pravda*, 18 and 25 November 1936.
68 LAC, RG146, Lobay, T. Dann, 'Cross-Reference Sheet' on Winnipeg ULFTA, 17 November 1936.
69 The Stavroff–Krawchuk Collection, 'Lobay' file, contains a letter from Nick Oleniuk of Toronto to Toma Kobzey (dated 6 January 1936) in which the scenario of such a sale is presented.
70 *Pravda*, 23 December 1936.
71 *Pravda*, 9 June 1937, suggests that the committee was 'growing,' but it could list only twenty-five people in the Winnipeg area who were willing to sign on. This was admittedly a short time into the campaign, but it does indicate the Lobayites had limited support.
72 *Pravda*, 5 May 1937.
73 LAC, RG146, Lobay, 7 September 1937. Copies of the leaflet, in both English and Ukrainian, are also located in the file.
74 LAC, RG146, Lobay, 30 September 1941.
75 LAC, RG146, Lobay, 14 June 1947 and 6 August 1948.
76 Note his biography in *Istoriia 'Ukrainskoho holosu' v biohrafiiakh ioho osnovopolozhnykiv i budivnychykh* (The History of the 'Ukrainian Voice' through the Biographies of Its Founders and Builders) (Winnipeg: Humeniuk Foundation, 1995), 46.
77 For example, see his book *Neperemozhna Ukraina* (Unconquerable Ukraine) (Winnipeg: Ukrainian Canadian Committee, 1950), subtitled (in English translation) 'facts from Soviet sources concerning Moscow's battle with Ukrainian nationalism on the cultural front after the Second World War.'

PART FIVE

Everyday People

This part considers the ways in which everyday Ukrainians – not the leaders of mass movements or even of Ukrainian-Canadian organizations, but men and women simply attempting to live their lives – were perceived by the dominant society. Just as important, this part details the experiences of Ukrainian Canadians outside the usual setting of the Prairie West, where Ukrainians at least had the solace of large and often well-organized community structures.

S. Holyck Hunchuck's study of a small and seemingly unimportant Ukrainian Labour Temple in Ottawa – and the people who made it their home away from home – provides a vivid illustration of the ways in which one small group of Ukrainians (in this case a left-wing group) came together as a community in a city that was uncongenial to Ukrainians in general and to working-class 'ethnic' radicals in particular. In the course of this analysis she provides a fascinating glimpse into the realities of ethnic, working-class life in the nation's capital and demonstrates the importance of small local institutions as critical spaces for ethnic expression and social activism. Read against the rich background provided by the essays of Hinther, Gabert, Petryshyn, and several others, her work helps us understand many of the pressures facing her subjects over a broad sweep of Canadian history.

Stacey Zembrzycki's essay looks at an even more unusual segment of the Ukrainian-Canadian population, the one that became caught up in the dominant society's criminal justice system for the most serious of all crimes – murder. Set in Sudbury, Ontario, and the surrounding region, Zembrzycki's study provides a sophisticated analysis of the interrelationships between criminality, gender, the state, and ethnicity out along Canada's resource frontier – not an unusual place to find working-class Ukrainians from the 1890s onwards. Like so many essays in this volume, Zembrzycki's reminds us yet again that there was no singular, rural western Canadian experience for Ukrainian Canadians. Even more to the point, her work with these court cases provides valuable insights into the often neglected question of how ethnicity was constructed and used by the state – a very different set of uses than Gabert documents for a later period. Indeed, it is noteworthy that Zembrzycki's study provides much material on the changing perceptions of 'Ukrainian-ness' in the community of Sudbury (and by implication, Canada as well) in the first three decades of the twentieth century.

12

'Of course it was a Communist Hall': A Spatial, Social, and Political History of the Ukrainian Labour Temples in Ottawa, 1912–1965

S. Holyck Hunchuck

The role they played never made the society pages.

Anne Lapchuk[1]

Ottawa, in eastern Ontario between Toronto and Montreal, is the mid-sized capital city of Canada.[2] It is a modern, post-industrial urban centre with a picturesque setting on the Ottawa River between Ontario and Quebec. The city has a population of about 800,000 and is officially bilingual in English and French. Architecturally, it contains many monuments to government, the Christian church, and domestic wealth; in socio-cultural terms it is perceived as well-educated, prosperous, and complacently bourgeois. Indeed, Ottawa is known colloquially as 'Fat City,' and the conventional view holds it to be an affluent quiet city of civil servants and politicians, tolerant to minorities but overwhelmingly either English or French in terms of descent as well as Anglo-Saxon in cultural mores. It has also long been viewed as relatively immune to and even isolated from the economic and social events that affect other cities in Canada.[3]

Yet besides being the seat of Canada's government, Ottawa for many decades was also a frontier lumber town with impoverished neighbourhoods, industrial architecture, immigrant workers, ethnic community institutions, and pockets of political radicalism. While the city's Ukrainian community was very small compared to other Canadian urban centres,[4] its institutions were part of this earlier, lesser-known, and largely obscured narrative. This essay is a chronological study of the three of those institutions: the Ottawa Ukrainian labour temples (1912–65). [5] These halls are examined in terms of their social roles and political functions, with particular reference to their significance for the study of Ukrainians in Canada.

The historiography of Canada's Ukrainians emphasizes a historical geography based on rural settlement in Western Canada; an architectural history marked by Byzantine churches and *xati* (mud daub and thatch houses); a material history determined by farmers and agrarian folkways; and community stories framed by successful assimilation into mainstream Canadian cultural organizations and conventional party politics. By contrast, the labour temples in Ottawa are evidence of the phenomenon of Ukrainian settlement in the urban centres of Central and Eastern Canada, and with it, a material culture derived from industrialization and mass production as well as a social history of ethnic labourers who gathered to practise their language, culture, and politics.

The Ukrainian labour temple members in the city, like all their associates across Canada, were inspired by political radicalism more than by anything else. Despite the bourgeois complacency that has been typically attributed to the citizens of Ottawa, a group of Ukrainians and like-minded comrades – social democrats, Bolsheviks, socialists, pro-Communists, and other leftists – operated three successive community halls dedicated to working-class culture and political agitation, with a Ukrainian twist. They did so despite the many challenges they faced in terms of space, ethnicity, class, and politics in the city. For more than fifty years they operated with meagre material resources out of modest worker homes in Rochesterville and Mechanicsville, in the west downtown of the nation's capital. This put them at a geographic remove from other Ukrainians in Canada; it also sited them in marginal lands within the city. In socio-cultural terms, they were contrarians in one of the most hostile and least supportive socio-political milieux in the country, and their marginality continues to hold true of their place in historiography. [6] The role of progressive Ukrainians in Ottawa was 'absent from the society pages' of the mainstream newspapers of the day and has been just as absent from histories written since then of the city and of Ukrainians in Canada.

'Houses Like Any Other':
Oral Histories of the Space, Social Function, and Politics
of the Ukrainian Labour Temples in Ottawa

To understand the significance of the Ukrainian labour temples in
Ottawa, it is important to consider the city's spatial, social, and political context. During the period of this study, Ottawa was transformed.
It turned from a gritty industrial town, with the government buildings
of Parliament Hill set incongruously against wide swaths of the lumber
industry and immigrant slums, into a grand capital city of sprawling
federal institutions, picturesque vistas, and scenic roadways. By the
mid-1960s the political decisions and urban renewal projects that had
caused these changes had also broken up such immigrant-worker
enclaves as the ones that were home to the Ukrainian labour temples.
It can be argued that such spatial ruptures also obliterated the presence
of this radical ethnic heritage from the cityscape and city history.

Ukrainian progressives in Ottawa organized first with pan-Canadian
pro-revolutionary groups in the years immediately before the First
World War. These groups included the Federation of Ukrainian Social
Democrats (FUSD) and its successor, the Ukrainian Social Democratic
Party (USDP), as well as the international Industrial Workers of the
World. Their headquarters, Nove Zhyttia (New Life; NZ) was at 268
Rochester Street (and briefly, 61 Stirling Avenue) from 1912 until the
police raid on May Day of 1918. That raid, conducted under the provisions of the War Measures, Enemy Aliens, and Internment Operations
Acts, closed the branch; seventeen members were interned.[7] Nonetheless, they regrouped in 1920 at their third location, 523 Arlington
Avenue. In 1924 this house was incorporated as Branch no. 11 of the
national Ukrainian Labour-Farmer Temple Association (ULFTA). It
operated as a temple as well as a language mass organization (ethnic
affiliate) of the Communist Party of Canada (CPC) until 1940. It was
then forcibly closed, this time under the Second World War orders-in-
council that banned the ULFTA and allowed for the seizure of its properties.[8] The third and final labour temple reopened at 523 Arlington in
1943, originally under the auspices of the wartime successor to the
ULFTA, the Association of Canadian Ukrainians (ACU, known after
1946 as the Association of United Ukrainian Canadians; AUUC). The

AUUC's Ottawa Branch was incorporated in 1948 and ran the hall until the early 1960s. The Ukrainian labour temple tradition ended in Ottawa in 1965 when that branch closed its doors. The building was sold in 1967 and demolished in 1974.[9]

An alternative history of Ukrainians can be gleaned from the marginal urban lands on which the Ottawa labour temples were located and by the physical qualities of the buildings in which they were housed. All three institutions were located in modest workers' houses in Rochesterville and Mechanicsville, contiguous neighbourhoods in west-central Ottawa. They were 'the closest thing [the city] had to a slum.'[10] Thus, while these labour temples were geographically adjacent to the 'limousine culture of official Ottawa,'[11] they were far removed from it in terms of ethnicity, culture, language, financial status, and politics. These temple buildings reflected a particular place, time, and class; simultaneously, they exemplified the impoverished and provisional architectures of Ukrainian communities in industrial cities in Canada during the first two-thirds of the twentieth century. Bill Warchow (b. 1933) is a retired certified electrician whose Lemko[12] family was active at the Ottawa labour temple from the 1920s to the early 1960s. He says of the modest building on Arlington Avenue: 'Nobody thought to take a picture of the place ... It was a house like any other on the street.'[13] That is, it was small, wooden, utilitarian, and sparse in decoration in a neighbourhood of similar houses. As such, it was typical of the industrial vernacular landscape of Ottawa's polyethnic poor.

Yet when these modest houses were turned into labour temples, they took on a socio-cultural purpose that transcended their humble form. For progressive Ukrainian families in Ottawa, the most important space was often the one where they socialized: their labour temple. For the city's culturally disenfranchised immigrant leftists and their children, the labour temple was a community gathering place that nurtured ethnolinguistic identity, knowledge of history, and political solidarity. Carl Drozdowych (b. 1933), a retired construction worker and bus driver whose Belarusian and Bukovynian[14] family attended during the same era as Warchow's, emphasizes this social function: 'There, they educated themselves and banded together ... They fed each other, danced together, and sang together.[15]

In terms of political significance, these small houses were also arenas in which broader, often international, issues were raised, debated,

and acted on locally. Because of the anti-capitalist, pro-Soviet and generally agitational values of their members, the labour temples were sites
of conflict with the dominant political structures of the city and the
country as well as places of refuge from them. Their political beliefs
gave the comrades a sense of international identity and community and
also had a profound (and often detrimental) impact on their day-to-day
lives in Ottawa. This political reality, too, has been absent from histories of Ottawa. David MacGregor (b.1941), a sociologist at the University of Western Ontario, was the child of an indigent Anglo-Scottish
family that was taken under the wing of the Ukrainian labour temple in
the late 1940s and early 1950s. He is emphatic about the political significance of the space in Ottawa during this period: 'Of course it was a
Communist hall. That's why we went there.'[16]

'You are living in the centre':
Nove Zhyttia and the Early History
of Progressive Ukrainians in Ottawa

Documentation of the early phase of Ukrainian settlement in Ottawa is
sparse, but by 1904 a group of Ukrainians had been added to Ottawa's
'small mosaic' of Germans, Chinese, and Ashkenazim who were neither English- nor French-speaking.[17] By 1905 at least one Ukrainian
had learned enough English to drive a hansom cab and sell the produce
he grew on his garden farm south of the city to ByWard Market just
east of Parliament Hill.[18] Generally speaking, Ottawa's Ukrainian community was small, poor, and centred around Rochester and Balsam
Streets in Rochesterville.[19] This inner-city neighbourhood of small
houses, railway lines, lumber mills, and block-long piles of sawdust
was immediately south of the similarly mixed LeBreton Flats and
southwest of Parliament Hill.

The first Ukrainian community organization in Ottawa was a branch
of the Prosvita (Enlightenment) Society, founded in the city in 1908 by
Ukrainian nationalists and populists and modelled on nineteenth-century European precedents. Meetings were held in private homes,
reflecting the improvised nature of the *chytalnia* (Ukrainian reading
room) movement in Canada in this, its early stage. It was followed by
the FUSD/USDP's Nove Zhyttia, which was founded on 25 January
1912 as Ottawa's first progressive *chytalnia* at the combination

home/boarding house and shoemaking shop[20] of P. Yakubowski (fl. 1908–58) at 268 Rochester Street.[21] NZ's political orientation was clear from the beginning. Members were exhorted to recognize that, though their community was very small in the city and isolated from larger progressive groups in other Canadian cities, their lives had meaning beyond their grim daily circumstances and the poverty of their imme- diate surroundings. 'You are living in the capital where matters dealing with all citizens are decided,' they were told in February 1912. 'You are living in the centre, where, unfortunately, there are no representa- tives of the working people.'[22] They were encouraged to consider them- selves social democrats in the European tradition, to establish workers' councils, and to work for revolutionary social change.[23]

The NZ grew quickly. Within two months it had attracted seventy- three members – one-third of the two hundred or so Ukrainians in Ottawa.[24] The momentum continued through its first year: the branch featured guest speakers from Montreal, Vienna, and Lviv, opened a vol- unteer-run library, established a choir and drama club, and held 'dances that lasted until morning,' though the church reportedly advised against attendance.[25] Given the community's situation, these were no minor achievements: NZ members were labourers at a time when a ten to twelve-hour workday was the norm and when even the city's leisure class had few cultural activities available to it.[26]

The year 1913 was a difficult one for workers. An economic depres- sion occurred across Canada that year, and labourers from ethnic minorities in Ottawa must have been especially hard hit. The city's economy had been damaged by the depletion of the region's forests. The federal public service was becoming Ottawa's largest employer, but government work was effectively closed to immigrant workers until after the Second World War.[27] NZ members A. Knysh (fl. 1910s) and Petro Haideychuk (1887–1964) remembered 1913–14 as 'a difficult time for workers.' Nevertheless, it was still 'fruitful' for the branch.[28] For example, its celebrations of the centenary of the birth of Ukrainian poet Taras Shevchenko (1814–1) in March 1914 were so popular that they had to be held at a rented auditorium in the ByWard Market rather than in the makeshift headquarters in Yakubowski's home–workshop– boarding house.[29]

In 1914 the branch helped organize mass demonstrations on the grounds of City Hall on Elgin Street. Between 4 and 7 June the demonstrators heard public speeches in Ukrainian as well as English and French. They were protesting unemployment, rising militarization, and the 'immigration business' that was bringing newcomers to Canada and then exposing them to unemployment and exploitation.[30] About one thousand people attended the final rally – the first multilingual protest in Ottawa's history. All of this prompted an unprecedented initiative by the Ministry of Labour and the City of Ottawa: a make-work program for the unemployed, with food aid in the form of free milk.[31]

The future of multiethnic working-class activism in Ottawa was cut short by international events. The declaration of war in August 1914 led to an atmosphere of hostility towards immigrants from enemy countries, including the Austro-Hungarian Empire to which most Ukrainians in Canada traced their origins. Within months an unknown number of Ottawa's 'Austrians' (most of them probably ethnic Ukrainians) were detained under various special wartime laws that came to include the War Measures, Enemy Aliens, and Internment Operations Acts. These detainees were sent to an internment camp at Kapuskasing, Ontario, a remote bush site some 900 kilometres northwest of the city.[32]

At the same time there seems to have been internal dissent within NZ.[33] In 1915 it relocated to 61 Stirling Avenue in the small Mechanicsville home of a founding member, a window washer named M. Chopowick (fl. 1915–58).[34] Mechanicsville, immediately northwest of Rochesterville, was another impoverished neighbourhood of industry, railway lines, and worker housing. The branch continued its agitational activities in Mechanicsville in 1915 and 1916,[35] but by the following year it was again in disarray. The demise of the Russian Empire and the growth of revolutionary movements in their homelands doubtless inspired the NZ members, but their lived reality in Ottawa remained one of poverty, isolation, and economic uncertainty.

By 1917 the number of regular, dues-paying members had begun to fall as 'many left to work in the woods [as loggers]'[36] – an itinerant and seasonal job at best. That same year the branch relocated back to 268 Rochester Street. This move, which returned the organization to the physical centre of the Ukrainian community in Rochesterville, underscores the makeshift nature of its meeting spaces. In May 1917, for example, NZ rented the Rex Theatre in the ByWard Market for a mass rally in support of the February Revolution in the Russian Empire. Clearly, a revolutionary consciousness existed in Ottawa at the time –

at least among some Ukrainians – and the private spaces of 268 Rochester Street and 61 Stirling Avenue were inadequate to house it.[37]

Revolutionary fervour in the city was to be short-lived. On 1 May 1918, 268 Rochester Street was raided by the police during a combined meeting of NZ and the Industrial Workers of the World. The two groups had gathered to celebrate May Day and to agitate against the war.[38] Within days, seventeen found-ins found themselves interned at Kapuskasing, where they were held for as many as twenty-nine months without trial and put to heavy labour at logging, land clearance, and road building. By this time, Kapuskasing was notorious as one of the most brutal internment camps in the Canadian system.[39] NZ became defunct after the raid, and organized life in Ottawa's Ukrainian progressive community fell dormant until well after the war.

'Darkness and Religious Prejudice': Interwar Social History

The Kapuskasing internees were released on 2 October 1919. Among those who returned to Ottawa were Haideychuk, Nicholas Mucciy (fl. 1915–55), and Yuri Skrypnychuk (fl. 1918–20). On 4 July 1920 these men helped launch the second era of progressive Ukrainian activity in Ottawa, at 523 Arlington Avenue in southwestern Rochesterville.[40] Like the previous two, this new site was a provisional solution: a simple, industrial-vernacular two-storey house, typical of the mass-produced wooden structures that housed Ottawa's poor. It was virtually identical to Chopowick's home in Mechanicsville, and like Yakobowski's boarding house/workshop, it was close to the centre of Ottawa's Ukrainian quarter. [41]

The Arlington site would be home to Ukrainian progressives for the next forty-five years. It was on a dead-end street facing two intersecting railway lines and had several features that made it a true community centre. The extra-wide lot, facing the open sky to the south and west, became a collective garden and apple orchard. Inside the house, meetings, classes, and concerts were held on the ground floor. Members and their extended families lived in a separate, compact apartment on the second floor.[42]

In 1924 the site was incorporated as Branch no. 11 of the ULFTA and ownership of the building was transferred to the association.[43] The

Ukrainian community in Ottawa was still small, yet by the mid-1920s the branch had raised funds for victims of the 1921 famine in the Soviet Union, organized adult literacy classes, and established a series of lectures, readings, and dances, a mandolin orchestra, a women's section, a youth section, a children's school, and Branch no. 41 of the Workers' Benevolent Association (WBA),[44] perhaps in keeping with ULFTA leader Matthew Popovych's dictum in 1920 that 'every worker should enjoy life, as his life was just as dear to him as anyone else's.'[45]

In 1926, Branch no. 11 attracted the RCMP's attention. The Mounties reported that thirty-eight pupils were enrolled at its 'revolutionary school,' which was held in a classroom adorned with 'photographs of late Russian Bolshevist [V.I.] Lenin and other leaders of the Bolsheviki.'[46]

The branch was only a minor part of the national ULFTA throughout the 1920s, due in part to the conditions facing immigrant workers in the city. Haideychuk, its secretary, wrote in 1930 that the Branch could not 'spread its work' because of the Ukrainian community's small size, which he estimated at seven hundred. He also cited the lack of industries that might attract newcomers, the transient nature of available work (such as logging), and an unresponsive host culture. Ottawa was dominated linguistically by the Anglophone majority and a large Francophone minority; politically by the legacy of Whigs, Tories, and the British monarchy; and socially by churchgoers.[47] 'Many members left town [to seek employment elsewhere], others for the Old Country' Haideychuk reported. Those comrades who remained struggled with the city's climate of 'political darkness and religious prejudice.'[48]

'A Really Difficult Time': The Depression Years

The limited opportunities for Ukrainian progressives in Ottawa in the 1920s were followed by the 'really difficult time'[49] of the Great Depression. Details are next to non-existent about the paid working lives of women, but two male ULFTA members who were outdoor labourers with the City of Ottawa were considered 'lucky' to have any form of regular paid employment.[50] The daughter of one labourer recalls periods when the family subsisted on potatoes, flour, and gravy for weeks at a time.[51] The other labourer, Warchow's father, was usually assigned to outdoor work in the form of park and street maintenance in the haut bourgeois Glebe neighbourhood southeast of Rochesterville. On at least three occasions in the 1930s, winter storms forced him to shovel snow off streetcar tracks, by hand, in twenty-four-hour shifts.[52] For many men, employment was only casual or seasonal and no less arduous. Warchow recalls a member of his family's boarding house who worked winters 'in the bush' (i.e., as a logger) and summers as a pedlar in the city. This sojourner was denied entry to the family home each spring until he could be deloused and rid of fleas.[53]

As hard as life was for men, the work contributed to the labour temple by a core group of Ukrainian women seems staggering. Historian and archivist Myron Momryk says only half in jest: 'The men did the politics; the women did the work.'[54] Historian and curator Rhonda Hinther describes the situation more analytically: 'This discourse [between ULFTA women and men in Canada] rested on Old World peasant village values and was further defined by experiences in Canada that reinforced male privilege and female subordination.'[55] Some women in Ottawa, including Bill's mother, boarding house operator and domestic servant Anna Warchow (1908–83), cared for their families, cooked, cleaned and maintained order in the family boarding house, and worked outside the home as house cleaners – yet still volunteered evenings and weekends at 523 Arlington. The burdens of family and finances imposed on women make their contribution to Branch no. 11 doubly noteworthy. The Ottawa temple, like many in Canada, would not have survived without its women. They taught classes, sold newspapers, attended rehearsals, gave performances, provided child care for one another, and sewed costumes. Perhaps most important, the temple relied on them to provide food. No temple event was complete without a meal, and the women cooked and served its hot meals, besides preparing foods for sale as fund-raising items.[56] The women's efforts, especially in traditional Ukrainian cuisine, ensured that the space remained open and was heated, lighted, equipped with supplies, and active with programs.[57]

Food was important. Warchow remembers the labour temple as a place that 'fed people on the move, people coming and going' in the Depression-era search for work or housing, or as part of protests on Parliament Hill.[58] It served as an informal soup kitchen, collected food for redistribution to the needy, and rewarded performing arts volunteers with free hot suppers. Banquets featuring Ukrainian food were always popular, and food was also used to support political causes. In the mid-1930s, for example, a fund-raising dinner was held for an injured worker in Hull to help pay for his blood transfusions and crutches.[59] Warchow's family history includes reminiscences of a protest group in the mid-1930s. They were arrested en masse and held behind barbed wire at Plouffe Park at Preston and Somerset Streets, a few blocks north of the temple.[60] In response, Anna Warchow and other female members scoured the neighbourhood bakeries for discounted loaves of bread, which they then 'tossed over the fence' to the detainees as a form of physical support, silent protest, and act of ethno-political solidarity.[61]

In 1936 the political function of the Arlington hall was clear when it became a recruitment centre for the International Brigades during the Spanish Civil War. Many other Ukrainian labour temples in Canada served the same function. As many as one-third of the Canadian volunteers for the battle of what Momryk calls 'epic proportions between the forces of democracy and fascism, progress and reaction, good and evil'[62] were Ukrainian, and many of them were affiliated with the ULFTA. At least four volunteers in Spain were from Ottawa.[63] Sixty years later, two were remembered warmly by interviewees: Steve Pacholachak (fl. 1935–60) and Martin Myroniuk (fl. 1953–60) were gifted and dedicated cultural workers. Pacholachak was a master cabinetmaker and a 'marvellous carpenter – the best we have ever seen' of stage sets and props, while Myroniuk taught children to read and play the mandolin.[64] Their lives of service to antifascism in Spain as well as to Ukrainian culture in Ottawa set a memorable example for Dow and Warchow, who were children at the time.[65]

By the late 1930s the Ukrainian labour temple had about two hundred members. Seventy belonged to its Unemployed Association, and in June 1938 they began a six-month long excavation and expansion of the building. This collaborative project gave a sense of social purpose and community to those otherwise likely to be perceived as 'idle' by the rest of Ottawa society.[66] The project was both ambitious and modest: the footprint of the house at 523 Arlington was more or less doubled. An industrial-sized kitchen was built in the new basement, and a 'proper' auditorium with a raised stage, backdrops, sidedrops, and seating for one hundred was constructed on the main floor.[67] The result was simple and utilitarian, with none of the monumentality, luxurious materials, or decorative flourishes of other purpose-designed Ukrainian labour temples, such as the one in Winnipeg (1919). The Ottawa branch was typical of a smaller and isolated ULFTA branch: this was an architecture of provisionalism, created during a time of need by people with modest means. Its members were accustomed to the cooperativist ethos of the *chytalnia* movement and to hard physical labour, but they had no formal education in architecture and they lacked expensive building supplies.[68] On the other hand, the Ottawa temple may have been unique in that while many labour temples in Canada were expanded during this period, '[women's] need for quality kitchen space was disregarded.'[69] Not so in Ottawa.

The lack of funds at the branch was reflected down to the most basic details. The temple lacked a *rushnyk* (traditional hand-embroidered cloth) to drape over the podium as is the Ukrainian custom. Warchow points out that even decades later, during the relatively prosperous 1950s, 'we had no podium. We were too poor.'[70] The new space instead emphasized the temple's role as a Canadian space: it was less of a *chytalnia* in the Eastern European tradition of a reading room/library/lecture hall, and more of a social and cultural centre devoted to performance art, political activism, and the sharing of meals.[71]

Though the new kitchen space was relegated to the basement, food remained essential to the labour temple's social purpose and cultural expression. This culture was gendered – however politically radical the members were, the traditional divisions of labour found both in the Old World and in Canada were played out in the temple's spaces. Drozdowych describes how twelve or more female volunteers typically 'baked all afternoon' for banquets of Ukrainian food, while the men merely erected tables in the auditorium and cleaned up afterwards.[72]

'It was heroic, what they did': Second World War History

The outbreak of the Second World War in September 1939 led to profound changes at Branch no. 11. It was seized on 17 November 1940 by the Custodian of Enemy Property acting under the Defense of Canada Regulations. These banned the CPC and ULFTA and allowed for the seizure and sale of their properties and the internment of their members.[73] The temple proper – auditorium, kitchens, library, and office – was sealed. All programs were cancelled, and the furniture, library books, stage props, and musical instruments were either seized and discarded by the police, or dispersed.[74] The second-floor tenants were allowed to remain in residence, but at least one, Haideychuk, seems to have gone into hiding for the duration of the war.[75] The site was offered for sale to rival organizations, which declined to purchase because it would cause even more fractiousness within Ottawa's small Ukrainian community.[76]

Ukrainian progressives in Ottawa found themselves once more in difficult straits, spatially and socio-politically. None was interned, but for the second time in twenty years they were denied a meeting place. Their social activities were monitored, their political organizations were forbidden, and they lived under the threat of internment.[77]

Meanwhile, the socio-economic status of the wider Ukrainian community in Ottawa also changed. By 1941, 760 Ukrainians lived in the city, and the booming wartime economy marked the first time Ukrainians as a group could find employment with the federal government. This led to the beginnings of Ukrainian middle class in Ottawa.[78] As a result, the working-class ULFTA became irrelevant to growing proportion of the Ukrainian community, and its remaining supporters found themselves increasingly isolated. There is evidence that notwithstanding the ban, some activities continued during 1941 and 1942, when the progressive Ukrainian community in Ottawa provided support to the CPC and ULFTA internees held at the jail in Hull, Quebec. This support took the form of fresh fruit and vegetables, as well as a contraband crystal radio hidden in a pail of homemade cottage cheese.[79]

In response to a nationwide campaign, the Canadian government began to release internees in the fall of 1942[80] and lifted the ban on the ULFTA in October 1943. On 9 February 1944, 523 Arlington was returned by the Custodian of Enemy Property.

By the end of the war at least eleven labour temple members in Ottawa had volunteered to serve in the Canadian Armed Forces.[81] Yet they continued to face opposition in the city. Support for the Allied cause was far from universal in Ottawa, and in the early 1940s, Kazimierz Drozdowych (1900–94), a baker and soldier, was set upon by a francophone gang of Nazi ympathizers because he was wearing his Canadian Army uniform. The crime was witnessed by his son Carl but was not reported to the police.[82] Carl Drozdowych characterizes the participants in the Ottawa labour temple during the Second World War, both at home and overseas, as 'heroic.'[83] This may seem overly romantic to contemporary readers, but it reveals the heartfelt respect that the ULFTA inspired among those who were child and youth members at the time.

'A Centre of Resistance': Post–1945 History

The Ottawa labour temple resumed operations in 1946 as an AUUC hall. Once again, Haideychuk served as its Secretary-Treasurer.[84] The house and gardens were transferred to the national organization on 27 August 1948. The reborn hall began what was to be a bright but ultimately short-lived existence as one of the AUUC's smaller branches, as well as a cultural home for progressive Ukrainians and a centre of political resistance for many others. More and more, the temple found itself at odds with a Cold War city that was becoming increasingly bourgeois, formally bilingual, and vehemently anti-leftist.

In spatial terms, the Rochesterville neighbourhood remained a mix of aging industry, sooty railway lines, and 'tinderbox' worker housing.[85] Yet 523 Arlington was a point of pride for members, who maintained the building in a 'very good state of repair,' with the garden and orchard 'beautifully kept.'[86]

This period in the labour temple is remembered with nostalgia. It was a vital community centre that held weekly classes for children in Ukrainian language, Ukrainian dance, and mandolin. Adults and children attended performances and film screenings on Thursday and Saturday nights; political meetings were held on Sundays. All interviewees recalled the educational and cultural activities with fondness, as get-togethers that were otherwise denied them by Ottawa society. They were 'always very pleasant [events] ... with a lot of proud parents'; it was 'warm and friendly ... a nice time for families to take pictures of their children.'[87] The concerts and communal meals in particular left vivid memories. For MacGregor the labour temple was a place with 'an abundance of food, beautifully prepared,' with 'colourful costumes worn by dancers, and cabbage rolls and delicious coffee.'[88] For the Drozdowych family, going to a concert or dance at the Ukrainian labour temple was 'the highlight of the week,' involving as it did the social ritual of the whole family travelling by streetcar to events intended to 'get as many kids on the stage as possible.'[89]

In broader socio-political terms, these were rare affordable activities in postwar Ottawa, besides being multicultural, multilingual, and progressive. Despite the entry of some Ukrainians into the bourgeoisie, most Ukrainians in the city were still at the bottom of the socio-economic hierarchy. They worked much as they had for the preceding half-century in Ottawa, as semiskilled and unskilled labourers, boarding house operators, and domestics to 'English' families in the Glebe, and in cottage industries such as shoemaking.[90] Of the twenty members of the branch in 1950, only one had a white-collar job: Haideychuk, then sixty-three years old, was the branch's Secretary-Treasurer.[91] Macgregor notes the importance of the labour temple for these people and for other poorer inhabitants of the city, remembering that it provided 'a source of entertainment and social activity for working people.'[92]

By the 1950s, many Ukrainian labour temples in Canada had become transitional spaces linguistically, socially, and politically. In Hinther's words, they presented a 'hybridizied subculture [that] combined elements of both Ukrainian and Canadian [activities].'[93] The Ottawa branch was no exception. It remained on the one hand a centre of Ukrainian cultural expression, pro-Soviet politics, and anti-capitalist critique. On the other hand, it had become a place where linguistic assimilation into the dominant anglophone culture was part of the weekly programming. At the labour temple, most adult meetings continued to be held in Ukrainian, even as AUUC children were educated in English in Ottawa schools. Other activities at the hall, such as screenings of National Film Board of Canada newsreels and nature documentaries, were offered in English, with children's classes a mix of English and Ukrainian.[94] The in-between nature of the branch was reflected in its spatial details: extra doors and English-language exit signs were added to the auditorium in deference to local authorities,[95] and gone were the portraits of the 'Russian Bolsheviki' that the RCMP had reported thirty years earlier. Three portraits had taken their place: King George VI (1895–52), 'the one without the beard,'[96] was mounted at centre stage, flanked by the nineteenth-century Ukrainian literary titans Shevchenko and Ivan Franko (1856–1916).[97]

Notwithstanding the fluency in English of Ukrainian children and young people in postwar Ottawa, ethnic minorities still faced racism from the dominant English and French. One interviewee describes the impossibility of being hired by the major department stores if she kept her Ukrainian surname;[98] another describes being threatened with a beating by a francophone street gang for speaking English in the ByWard Market and being therefore a 'Jew.' [99]

Ukrainian progressives in Ottawa faced especially difficult situations. The parents of Canadian-born children tended to seek job security for themselves in whatever employment they could find. By the 1950s they had largely abandoned the revolutionary ideals that had marked NZ a few decades earlier.[100] Nevertheless, their political beliefs had effects on their social relationships, and the resulting tensions were acted out within the spaces of the labour temple. In the Drozdowych family, for example, the mother came from one of the founding families of the Bukovynian Orthodox Church in the city, while the father was a card-carrying member of the CPC. The two organizations were mutually hostile, and in a family compromise, the three Drozdowych daughters were married at the church, with the wedding receptions held at the labour temple. The officiating priest would not or could not attend any of the receptions.[101]

The Ukrainian labour temple was also an active political space in Ottawa in the early postwar years despite a newly hostile environment. The Cold War began for Canada in September 1945 when the cipher clerk Igor Gouzenko (1919–82), defected from the Soviet Embassy in Ottawa's Sandy Hill. This east-central neighbourhood is within streetcar distance of Rochesterville, and the Cold War became an active force in the lives of people in the city. Its impact on temple members was dramatic. To be viewed as a 'communist' or to be in any way identified with the Soviet Union was to court ridicule, ostracism, and the loss of employment.[102] Entering the branch's space, attending its social events, or participating in its political actions became fraught with negative connotations. Without disclosing the details, one recalls the effect of the Cold War on her personal and social life in Ottawa as nothing less than 'devastating.'[103] MacGregor describes it more pointedly: 'To be a 'Communist' [in Ottawa] was to belong to a lower order of life. It became the most vile curse imaginable.'[104]

Yet the labour temple still had a 'sizeable' membership in 1950, as well as active public programming. In a single month in 1950, for example, the openly pro-Soviet branch held a fund-raising meeting attended by fifty people, promoted the peace movement, and hosted several guest speakers.[105] Among the members were twenty donors, of whom six had been active since the NZ days; they included Haidey-chuk, Yakubowski, and Chopowick.[106] Their dedication is striking, given their poverty, their age, and their pariah status in Ottawa society.

Meanwhile, the hall's viability was threatened by its politics. The RCMP had an informant on the inside and conducted obvious surveil-lance of the building (from a car parked on Arlington Street). The Mounties also harassed members at their homes and workplaces.[107]

These actions led directly to the collapse of the branch. In 1952, Nancy Moniuk (fl. 1940–55), the teacher of the children's school and director of the mandolin orchestra, was visited by the RCMP at her paid workplace. She was threatened with 'exposure' that would result in her dismissal. Rather than lose her day job, she quit the labour tem-ple. The school, with an enrolment of twelve students, could not attract another instructor. It was shut down, and the mandolin orchestra was disbanded.[108] Shortly afterwards, it was revealed that a long-time 'English' member was also a police informant. Three interviewees were circumspect, stating only that they had taken in a needy family even though they were not Ukrainian, who later disappointed them.[109] As one put it: 'We were let down badly.'[110] A fourth interviewee, David MacGregor, identifies the informant as his father.[111]

With these two events, the precipitous decline of the Ottawa labour temple began. Participants felt demoralized by the loss of the music school, betrayed by the informant, grossly misjudged by the rest of Canadian society, and fearful for their families if they continued as activists.[112] The loss of members meant a lack of events (and thus of revenue), as well as an inability to attract new participants. The conse-quences were an absence of youth and a disproportionate reliance on the remaining, increasingly elderly members to organize activities at the labour temple and to bear its ongoing expenses. Salaries had to be paid to the Secretary-Treasurer and monies raised to support ongoing causes. More onerous was the nature of the space: the wooden build-ing was aging and continued to incur significant maintenance and heating costs as well as property taxes and mortgage payments. By the mid-1950s the branch's finances were a constant source of concern. 'It never changed,' recalls Warchow of the meetings in the late 1950s. 'Always, "Pass the hat."' [113]

'My Lungs and Legs Ache':
The Aging Membership and the Decline
of the Ottawa Labour Temples

By the late 1950s the AUUC branch in Ottawa (like many others) had little momentum and scant operating funds. Khrushchev's exposure of Stalin's crimes in his now famous 'secret speech' of February 1956 led to doubt and dissension among labour temple supporters throughout the country. So did the Soviet invasion of Hungary in October of the same year. Dozens of branches were closing across Canada,[114] due in part to members' disillusionment with the ULFTA, the AUUC, and the CPC over these international issues. In addition, the general trend in postwar Canada was towards increased prosperity, upward mobility, and the linguistic and political assimilation of minority communities. In this context, ethnic workers' clubs, such as Ukrainian labour temples, became anachronisms if not outright hindrances for those seeking full acceptance by Canadian society.

The lack of support for the Ottawa labour temple was clear by 1958. Haideychuk, now seventy-one years old, reported to the AUUC headquarters in Toronto that the young members 'all got married and moved to Montreal and Toronto.'[115] Only six memberships were sold that year, four of which belonged to members of forty years' standing or more.[116] There were no banquets, concerts, or dances that year, nor were any classes offered in Ukrainian language, literacy, politics, or history. Nevertheless, the branch distributed leaflets in English on the peace movement, spent $2.00 on Ukrainian books and calendars from the Soviet Union to add to its library, and raised $5.00 to send to striking miners in Sudbury. But it had no funds to send a delegate to the once-in-a-lifetime AUUC National Festival held that year in Vancouver.[117]

In the late 1950s and early 1960s the labour temple became less of a dynamic cultural centre and site of political agitation – which it had been for most of its history – and more of a low-key gathering place. Elderly members went to read Ukrainian newspapers and books from the Soviet Union and to contribute to the political causes of the day as best as their limited circumstances would allow, with the prospect of sharing a meal and socializing with like-minded comrades.[118]

By 1961 the number of Ukrainians in the city had grown to about three thouand, but the AUUC branch was essentially defunct. After the late 1950s it did not mount any cultural or educational programs, nor did it participate in any public activities.[119]

Petro Haideychuk was the branch's leader and institutional memory, but as early as 1958 he was raising the issue of its continued existence with AUUC headquarters in Toronto.[120] In a rare personal aside to his biweekly reports, he added, poignantly and ominously, 'my lungs and legs ache.'[121] Haideychuk became increasingly infirm and died in a nursing home in December 1964. He was eulogized as 'modest, honest, and generous' and as 'an honest citizen of Canada.' [122] With his death came the end of the Ukrainian labour temple in Ottawa. Within months the branch was dormant, and by 1966 the building stood vacant.[123] The site was sold in 1967 to St Anthony's Soccer Club, an athletic and social organization serving the Italian community, which demolished the house in 1974 to make way for a larger, more modern facility.[124]

The demise of the last Ukrainian labour temple in Ottawa was caused by more than the death of one comrade or by the diminished appeal of pro-Soviet politics to Ukrainians in the city. While social and political pressures unquestionably made life difficult for its supporters in the Cold War capital, the end of the organization in the city was partly spatial. For the first half of the twentieth century the Ukrainian community in Rochesterville had been overlooked by the civic beautification plans that were transforming much of the city. By the late 1950s, however, the neighbourhood was beginning to attract the attention of three levels of government. Their immediate goals were wholesale slum clearance, relocation of industry to the suburbs, railway removal, and massive road building typical of the urban planning canons of postwar cities in North America. Between 1960 and 1970, for example, entire neighbourhoods of west-central Ottawa, including LeBreton Flats and Rochesterville, were cleared of their workers' housing, factories, and railyards, and the east-west railway lines were converted into a raised highway (the Queensway) and a sprawling network of on- and off-ramps. While the few remaining members of the Ottawa labour temple were undergoing harassment and ostracism in their personal lives, they also faced the irreplaceable loss of their meeting space. Eventually the entire Ukrainian working-class neighbourhood was erased from the cityscape in the name of civic beautification.

The building at 523 Arlington had been slated for expropriation for demolition years before the city actually seized it in 1963. The following year the municipal government expropriated all the Ukrainian gathering spaces in Rochesterville, including the Ukrainian Catholic Church and the Prosvita Hall at Balsam and Rochester Streets. The year after that, the Bukovynian Orthodox Church on Gladstone Avenue met the same fate. All were quickly demolished. In the late 1960s the small brick roughhouses on Rochester Street that included NZ were expropriated and torn down.

According to architectural historian Jean-Pierre Lapointe, these actions, while advanced according to modernist urban aesthetics, were in fact class-based. The changes were part of a widespread clearance of 'untidy ghetto neighbourhoods inhabited by blue collar workers ... unworthy of a capital city like Ottawa.'[125] In MacGregor's analysis, the clearances meant the irretrievable loss of an authentic heritage in the city of affordable, industrial-worker communities: 'Neighbourhoods where every house [by the 1960s] belonged to a worker,' he argues, became 'mostly carved up into plastic sections of public housing, a monstrous government office complex, and a freeway.'[126] So total was this change that almost all of LeBreton Flats and large portions of Rochesterville remain vacant and abandoned almost fifty years after demolition began. A Ukrainian neighbourhood that had existed for fifty years was dispersed throughout the city and would never be reconstituted.

Conclusion

Organized Ukrainian progressives occupied a minor but distinct place in Canadian society and in the narrative of Ottawa. The city's last labour temple closed more than forty years ago. Two of the three branch buildings have been destroyed; a third, 61 Stirling Avenue, reverted to single-family use back in 1917.[127] These houses were virtually undocumented at the time, and their districts have been demolished wholesale or piecemeal. The Ukrainian community as a whole has never re-created a cohesive neighbourhood identity.

Yet the spatial, social, and political history of the Ukrainian labour temples in Ottawa can serve as a case study. In terms of space, their landscape was not one of wide-open Prairie skies, but of downtown factories, sawmills, railway lines, and small, mass-produced houses of the type to be found in the industrial/immigrant quarter of any central and eastern Canadian city. Similarly, while the Ottawa labour temples were distinct Ukrainian cultural institutions, they did not directly reflect Ukrainian building traditions: they were neither the onion-domed churches of Eastern Christianty, nor the peasant *xati* that have come to characterize discussions of Ukrainian space in Canada. Instead, they were simple, industrial-vernacular buildings determined not by religious dictates or folkways transplanted from the Old World, but by the narrow lots of crowded neighbourhoods, assembly-line production of built forms, and 'the hand of capitalism, not the hand of ownership'[128] characteristic of buildings for the poor in the urban New World. Accordingly, their spaces can be seen as characteristic of the Ukrainian experience in Canadian cities during the first two-thirds of the twentieth century, as were the *xati* on the Prairies at the turn of the twentieth century.[129]

In terms of social and political function, the Ottawa labour temples helped fill a cultural, linguistic, and political void in the city for Ukrainian political progressives, from very little money, materials, or spare time. Its members were impoverished Ukrainians and other Slavs who lived and worked in surroundings that were hostile to their language and their culture; their politics were inspired by revolutionary Russian and Eastern European history rather than that of Western European capitalism and the British monarchy. Despite being longtime inhabitants of Ottawa's core, they were perpetual contrarians as well as perpetual outsiders.

Conventional histories of Ottawa cast the city as one of an almost exclusively bilingual/bicultural heritage, of monumental buildings set in a picturesque landscape, and of complacent, middle-class socio-political values. Yet the Ukrainian labour temples demonstrate that industrial vernacular architecture has always existed there, along with poyethnicity, multicultural institutions, and political radicalism.

The Ottawa labour temples remind us that histories can be contained in buildings and inscribed on landscapes – as well as erased from them.

Though the physical removal of industries, railyards, and modest wooden houses such as those that housed two of the three labour temples from the west downtown of Ottawa was officially the result of the slum clearance and urban beautification seen to be required of a 'national metaphor,'[130] it also fulfilled a tacit imperative to rewrite Ottawa's architectural, social, and political history in favour of a scenic, white-collar, and exclusively bilingual/bicultural model of settlement. MacGregor sees it as nothing less than class struggle acted out on a gigantic scale. He calls it a demonstration of 'Ottawa's protracted and undeclared war on the poor.'[131] However, neither his critique nor Lapointe's considers ethnicity. It can equally be argued that it was also an undeclared war on the history of the Ukrainian spaces, social history, and political activism in the city as demonstrated by the USDP's Nove Zhyttia, ULFTA Branch no. 11, and the Ottawa Branch of the AUUC from 1912 to 1965.

Notes

1 Anne Lapchuk, 'A Tribute to Our Women,' *Tribute to Our Ukrainian Pioneers in Canada's First Century: Proceedings of The Special Joint Convention of the Association of United Ukrainian Canadians and the Worker's Benevolent Association* (Winnipeg: Worker's Benevolent Association, 1966), 93. Lapchuk was speaking specifically of the female Ukrainian pioneers in Canada; however, her remarks can equally be applied to the status of Ukrainian progressives in Ottawa.

2 There are numerous social and architectural histories of Ottawa. Most notable are John Taylor, *Ottawa: An Illustrated History* (Toronto: Lorimer and the Canadian Museum of Civilization, 1986); and Bruce Elliott, *The City Beyond: A History of Nepean, Birthplace of Canada's Capital, 1792–1990* (Nepean: City of Nepean, 1991). Both emphasize mainstream political parties and the monumental architectures of government, church, business, and homes of the wealthy. Phil Jenkins's working-class memoir of LeBreton Flats, *An Acre of Time* (Toronto: MacFarlane Walter and Ross, 1996), is an alternative history of one working-class neighbourhood, but there are no parallel studies of Rochesterville or Mechanicsville. Elliott Tepper's critique, *Is Ottawa Different? Perceptions of Discrimination and Race Relations in the Nation's Capital* (Ottawa: Secretary of State Multiculturalism Direc-

torate, 1982), appears to be the only scholarly study of ethnicity in the nation's capital. Architectural histories of note include Harold Kalman and John Roaf, *Exploring Ottawa* (Toronto: University of Toronto Press, 1982); and Local Architectural Advisory Committee [Ottawa], *Ottawa: A Guide to Heritage Structures* (Ottawa: 2000). R.H. Hubbard's 'Architecture in Ottawa: A Personal View' *Journal of the Royal Architectural Institute of Canada* 32, no. 11 (1955): 410–15, is a period piece notable for its romantic view of the city's architecture. The types of houses that contained Ottawa's Ukrainian labour temples are discussed with limited success in two monographs: Margaret Carter, 'Lowertown,' and Jean-Pierre Lapointe, 'La Maison Hulloise: Hull's Vernacular Architecture Heritage,' both in *Capital Vernacular: People, Power, Wood, Water, Tour Guide of the Vernacular Architecture Forum Conference* (Ottawa: Vernacular Architecture Forum, May 1885), 13–39 and 47–55, respectively. The best local study remains Michelle Guitard's *La maison dites 'hulloise'* [The So-called 'Hull House'] (Hull: le societé d'histoire de l'Outaouais, 1997).

3 Tepper, 1. At 7, Tepper further notes: 'No major study appears to be available on the city's ethnic settlement patterns' – an assessment that remains   valid a quarter-century after he made it. For a useful summary of the urban design practices that have affected the City of Ottawa, see William de Grace, 'Canada's Capital, 1900–1950: Five Town Planning Visions,' *Environments* 17, no. 2 (1985): 43–57.

4 The Ukrainian community in Ottawa at the time of its first organized activities prior to the First World War was highly transient. It numbered between 200 and 500, compared to estimates of 14,000 in Winnipeg, 4,000 in Fort William (now Thunder Bay), and 7,000 in Montreal. In 2001, about 5,000 Ukrainians lived in Ottawa. There has been no formal organization of Ukrainian progressives since the mid-1960s.

5 The term 'labour temple' is used here to denote the various manifestations of progressive Ukrainian community centres. There were about two hundred Ukrainian labour temples active in Canada during the height of their activities in the interwar era. An earlier version of this paper appeared in 'A House Like Any Other: A Social and Architectural History of the Ukrainian Labour Temple, 523 Arlington Avenue, Ottawa, 1922–1967,' MA thesis, Carleton University, Ottawa, 2001.

6 Four former members and attendees were interviewed in 1998 and 1999 about their experiences as children and youth in the early 1930s to the

early 1960s: Anonymous (b. 1935), Toronto; Carl Drozdowych, Ottawa;
David MacGregor, London, Ontario; and William Warchow, Ottawa.
MacGregor and Warchow also provided textual and visual materials in
support of their oral histories. MacGregor authored 'Childhood in the
C[ommunist] P[arty] (*Canadian Dimension,* June 1977, 24–6); and in
1999, Warchow contributed a series of measured drawings of 523 Arlington Avenue's site plan and building plans and elevations as they stood c.
1950 (collection of the author, Ottawa). Also consulted were the Association of United Ukrainian Canadians (AUUC), LAC, MG28 V154, vol.
13, file 24: Branches (H-W, 1951); vol. 20, file 20, Ottawa, 1968; and
vol. 20, file 21 Ottawa, 1950. This study has also been inspired by Orest
Martynowych's call in 1991 for microhistories of overlooked Ukrainian-
Canadian communities; see his *Ukrainians in Canada: The Formative
Years, 1891–1924* (Edmonton: Canadian Institute of Ukrainian Studies
Press, 1991, xxv–xxvi). It has also been influenced by Stacey Zem-
bryczecki's ongoing oral history of Ukrainians in Sudbury: 'A Commu-
nity of Divided People: Negotiating Ukrainian Identity and Memory in
the Sudbury Region, 1901–1939,' PhD diss., Carleton University,
Ottawa, 2007. Also influential has been Peter Krawchuk, *Our History:
The Labour-Farmer Temple Movement in Canada, 1907–1991* (Toronto:
Lugus, 1996), which offers an insider's view of the Ukrainian Labour
Temple phenomenon. An invaluable and scholarly analysis is to be found
in Rhonda Hinther, '"Sincerest Revolutionary Greetings": Progressive
Ukrainians in Twentieth-Century Canada,' PhD diss., McMaster Univer-
sity, 2005, particularly with regard to women and children. Feminist
interpretations of Ukrainian life in general were inspired in part by two
studies: M. Bohachewsky-Chomiak, *Feminists Despite Themselves:
Women in Ukrainian Community Life, 1884–1939* (Edmonton: Canadian
Institute of Ukrainian Studies and University of Alberta Press, 1988);
and Frances Swyripa, *Wedded to the Cause: Ukrainian-Canadian
Women and Ethnic Identity* (Toronto: University of Toronto Press, 1993).
The three-volume study of the *New Kiew [Alberta] Labour Temple* by
Andrij Makuch and Sonia Maryn (Edmonton: Province of Alberta Culture and Multiculturalism, 1983–4) is a benchmark in socio-architectural
studies of Ukrainian labour temples. Above all, this paper would not
exist without the expertise and guidance of Myron Momryk, LAC historian and archivist.

7   No author cited, *Robochyi Narod* (The Working People) (hereafter *RN*),
    'Ottavi [In Ottawa],' 14 February 1912, 6; 20 March 1912, 4; 9 October

1912, 3; 21 March 1913, 4; 16 July 1913, 6; 11 March 1914, 6; 21 January 1915, 6; 10 February 1915, 6; 17 February 1915, 4; 18 April 1917, 5; 'Skhidni Agistatsinyi Okruh i Skhidnyi Okhruni Komitet' (Eastern Agitational District and Eastern Group Committee), *Robitnychi Kaliendar Rik 1918* (Worker's Calendar for the Year 1918) (Winnipeg: *Robocho Naroda* and *Robitinka*, 1917), 213 (all translations from Ukrainian courtesy of Momryk); *Might's Ottawa City Directory* (annual volumes, 1907–20); and *Underwriter's Insurance Maps of Ottawa* (1912), Map 122.

8 *Almankh Tovarystva Ukrainskyi Robitchyno-Farmerskyii Dim Kanadi Bratnikh Organizatskii], 1919–1929* (Almanac of the Ukrainian Labour-Farmer Temple Association in Canada and its Branches, 1919–1929) (hereafter *Almanakh TURF-Dim*) (Winnipeg: Naklodomo Robitchnyo-Farmerskoho v Davnychnoho Tovarystva, 1930), 130–3; *Might's*, annual volumes, 1919–46.

9 AUUC, in LAC, MG28 V154, vol. 13, file 24: Branches (H-W); vol. 20, file 20: Ottawa, 1968; *Might's*, annual volumes, 1945–75.

10 MacGregor, 'Childhood,' 24.

11 Ibid., 25.

12 Along with Boykos and Hutsuls, Lemkos are Carpathian highlanders in the Ukrainian border territories shared with Poland, Slovakia, and Romania. The distinct dialects, material culture, and folkways of the Lemkos have been especially shaped by Polish and Slovak influences as well as by Ukrainian ones. Some Lemkos, along with Boykos and Hutsuls, consider themselves 'Ukrainian' in ethnolinguistic identity; other Lemkos prefer to be considered Polish or Slovak. Many also self-identify as unhyphenated Lemko, or with the more historical terms Rusyn, Rusnak, Carpatho-Rusyn, or Ruthenian.

13 Warchow, interview with author, Ottawa.

14 Bukovyna is a province in the Carpathian highlands between western Ukraine, eastern Poland, and northeastern Romania. Most Ukrainians who settled in Canada during the first wave of immigration (1891–1914) came from Bukovyna or its adjacent province Halychyna (Galicia).

15 Drozdowych, interview with the author, Ottawa, 27 March 1999.

16 MacGregor, 'Childhood,' 25, and correspondence with author, 6 April 1999.

17 Taylor, *Ottawa,* 124.

18 Drozdowych, interview with the author, Ottawa, 27 March, 1999

19 Next to nothing is known of its exact size, the origins of its members, or

their education, life experiences, or beliefs; however, anecdotal evidence
of the interviewees indicates they were single male sojourners, originally
from Halychyna, who worked in logging in the region, in the lumber
mills in the west-downtown core, or in construction. The situation of
women is less certain. Swyripa reports that about two-thirds of
Ukrainian women in Ontario held paid employment outside the home (or
approximately double the national average), and there is no evidence to
indicate otherwise for Ottawa. Swyripa, 'Ukrainian Women in Ontario,'
Polyphony 8, nos. 1–2 (1986): 7.

20 A. Knysh and P. Haideychuk, 'Viddil U.S.D.P. 'Nove Zhyttia v Ottavi'
(USDP Branch 'New Life' in Ottawa), *Robitnychi Kaliendar rik 1918,*
133. Other examples of Ukrainian boarding houses/progressive *chytalni*
in Canada during this period include the Ukrainian coal miners' com-
munes; and the USDP Branches *Volia* (Freedom) and *Vilna Dumka* (Free
House) in Fernie, B.C. and Bellevue, Alberta, respectively.

21 Demolished in 1973. There is no documentation of this building aside
from a site plan that indicates a long, narrow, semidetached building.
(*Underwriter's*, 1912, Map 122). Extant period buildings on Rochester
Street indicate modest two-storey semidetached storefronts-cum-houses,
and it is reasonable to assume that *Nove Zhyttia* occupied a similar structure. The site has been a parking lot since the late 1960s.

22 Attributed to Comrade V. Prystai, no author cited, 'Ottava [Ottawa],' *RN*,
14 February 1912, 4.

23 No author cited, 'Ottava [Ottawa],' *RN*, 14 February 1912, 4.

24 V. Tokar and O. Kohanchuk, 'Ottava,' *RN*, 16 April 1913, 3.

25 'Ukrainians in Ottawa,' *Polyphony* 8, nos. 1–2 (1988): 83; Knysh and
Haideychuk, 'Viddil U.S.D.P.,' 131; Kohanchuk, 'Ottava,' *RN*, 23 June
1913, 4.

26 Kohanchuk, 'Ottava,' *RN*, 30 July 1913, 5; Taylor, 'Ottawa,' 191. *Nove
Zhyttia*'s volunteer-run library for Slavs, for example, was established at
a time when the city's first public library had been in existence for only
six years, and that came about only as an act of noblesse oblige from the
private American money of the Carnegie Foundation. Moreover, given
the Ottawa Public Library's reluctance during this period to carry materials in French, it is reasonable to assume that it was as uninterested in and
therefore as inaccessible to Ukrainians and other ethnocultural minorities.

27 Myron Momryk, 'Ukrainians in Ottawa,' *Polyphony* 10 (1988); 86–106.

28 Knysh and Haideychuk, 'Viddil U.S.D.P.,' 131.

29 Krawchuk, *Our History*, 24.

30 No author cited, 'Ottavi,' *RN*, 24 June 1914, 4.

31 Knysh and Haideychuk, 'Viddil U.S.D.P.,' 131.

32 Momryk, 'Ukrainians,' 88.

33 Ibid., 83.

34 L. Barylsky, 'Ottavi,' *RN*, 28 October 1915, 3. The reasons for the move
    are unknown, but it may have been the result of an internal rift typical of
    the factionalism of the USDP throughout its existence. See Krawchuk,
    Our History, 19; Martynowych, *Ukrainians in Canada,* 253–4 and 258–
    60.

35 N. Botsian, 'Ottavi,' *RN*, 13 June 1916, 5; I. Kasian, 'Ottavi,' *RN*, 16
    March 1916, 4; 11 May 1916, 6.

36 No author cited, 'Ottavi,' *RN*, 23 February 1917, 6.

37 No authors cited, 'Ottavi,' *RN*, 23 February 1917, 4, and 23 March 1917,
    4. Meanwhile, the larger Ukrainian community as a whole began to
    emerge as a small, compact, but distinct physical presence in the city,
    with the construction in 1918 of the Ukrainian Catholic Church, a
    Prosvita building, and a *Ridna Shkola* (Ukrainian-language school), fol-
    lowed by the Bukovynian Orthodox Church nearby at 820 Gladstone
    Avenue, all in Rochesterville.

38 The raid occurred though the USDP and the Industrial Workers of the
    World were not banned until an order-in-council issued on 25 September
    1918 (Krawchuk, *Our History*, 32). Eighteen men were originally
    detained in the *Nove Zhyttia* raid, but one, Stefan Waskan of Toronto,
    was released after a few days because he was a British subject (no
    authors cited, *Ottawa Evening Journal (*hereafter *OEJ)*, 3 May 1913, 3;
    *Ottawa Citizen (*hereafter *OC*), 4 May 1918, 3. Little is known about the
    remaining seventeen men. They were all immigrants, they ranged in age
    from seventeen to fifty-three, they worked as labourers, they lived in
    Ottawa within walking distance of *Nove Zhyttia* in the Centretown,
    Rochesterville, and LeBreton Flats neighbourhoods, and it is reasonable
    to assume that they shared the ideals of an antiwar meeting held on May
    Day at a USDP gathering place. Among them were individuals of some
    prominence within the USDP, including *Robochyi Narod* correspondent
    O. [Joseph] Kohanchuck and three men who would later return to Ottawa
    to become founding members of its labour temple: Peter [Petro] Hard-
    chuk/Harchuck/Haideychuk/Haideichuk, 240 LeBreton Street; Nicholas

Mucciy/Muciy, 381 Rochester Street; and Geo./Yuri Skrypnozick/Skryp-
nychuk, 381 Rochester Street. The other internees were Joseph Andrew,
40 Elizabeth Street; Nikolio/Mckolio Antoniak, 42 Elizabeth Street; Fred
Babaet/Bebet, 252 Rochester Street; Frank Chimney/Chminey, 268
Rochester Street; John Karcheski, 42 Elizabeth Street; Joseph [O.]
Kohanchuk/Kockanchuk, 76 Queen Street; Nicholas Koput, 268
Rochester Street; Jacob Makielen, 353 Rochester Street; Philip
Melack/Meleck, 346 Bell Street; Xavier Motunk/Matunk, 146 Bell Street
Leo Pannel, 288 Albert Street; Paul Shawiak/Shawliak, 51 Laurier
Avenue West; Alex Sochiki, 268 Rochester Street; Jozel Spak, 268
Rochester Street, all dates unknown (no authors given, *OEJ*, 2 May
1918, 1-2; 3 May 1918, 3; 6 May 1918, 4; *OC*, 2 May 1918, 1; 3 May
1918, 12; 4 May 1918, 3; *Le droit* [Ottawa], 2 mai 1918, 6; *Might's
Ottawa City Directory*, 1918; Mikhailo Korol, 'Petro Haideichuk,'
Ukrainske Zhyttia (Ukrainian Life), 27 January 1965, 6). Transliterations
vary with source.

39 Besides other hardships, internees at Kapuskasing were housed in
unheated wooden barracks in a climate where the winter temperatures
easily reach –40 degrees Celsius. McGill University historian Desmond
Morton alluded to the brutal conditions there when he summarized First
World War internment operations in Canada as 'easy in Ottawa, pretty
bloody hard in Kapuskasing.' Morton, 'Discussion: Divided Loyalties?
Homeland Ties in a Time of Crisis,' *Polyphony* 13, no. 1 (1993): 50–54
at 54.

40 Haideychuk, 'Viddil TURF-Dim,' 118.

41 The house was originally occupied by Scottish and French families, but
became emblematic of the growing Ukrainian presence in Rochesterville
when it was purchased in 1913 by Sam Tkachuk and F. Marak, the musical director of *Nove Zhyttia* and occasional *RN* correspondent. See 523
Arlington Avenue, Land Registry Files for the City of Ottawa, Land Registry Office, Province of Ontario Courthouse.

42 Warchow interview.

43 Haideychuk, 'Viddil TURF-Dim,' 118.

44 Ibid. The Workers' Benevolent Association (1921–2004) was an accident
and health insurance organization affiliated with the ULFTA.

45 Cited by Rhonda Hinther, '"Sincerest Revolutionary Greetings,"' unpagi-
nated.

46 Cited by Gregory S. Kealey and Reg Whitaker, eds., *RCMP Security Bul-*

letins, vol. I, *The Early Years, 1919–1929* (St John's: Canadian Committee on Labour History, and Memorial University, 1994), 316–17.
47 Haideychuk, 'Viddil TURF-Dim,' 119.
48 Ibid.
49 Warchow interview.
50 Anonymous, correspondence with author, 14 February 1999; Warchow interview.
51 Anonymous, correspondence with author, 14 February 1999.
52 Warchow interview.
53 Warchow interview.
54 Momryk, interview with author, Ottawa, 12 July 2007. The gendered aspects of the progressive Ukrainian movement in Canada are examined in detail in Hinther, '"Sincerest Revolutionary Greetings,"' ch. 3.
55 Hinther, '"Sincerest Revolutionary Greetings."'
56 Warchow interview; Drozdowych interview.
57 Warchow interview. For a fuller discussion of women's contributions to the day-to-day functioning of Ukrainian community centres in Canada, see Swyripa, *Wedded to the Cause,* 165. The particular challenges faced by Ukrainian women outside the Prairie blocs of settlement are explored by Frances Swyripa, 'Ukrainian Women in Ontario,' *Polyphony* 8, nos. 1–2 (1986): 47–50.
58 Warchow interview.
59 Ibid.
60 The exact date and nature of the protest has not been determined.
61 Warchow interview.
62 Momryk, 'Ukrainian Volunteers from Canada in the International Brigades, Spain, 1936–39,' *Journal of Ukrainian Studies* 16, nos. 1–2 (1991): 181–94 at 181.
63 Ibid., 186; Warchow interview.
64 Anonymous, correspondence with author. Three have been identified: Pacholachak, Myroniuk, and Paul Shpirka/Shperka (1893–?).
65 Anonymous, correspondence with author; Drozdowych interview; Warchow interview.
66 Drozdowych interview.
67 Anonymous, correspondence with author.
68 The exterior was clad in basic fashion, in concrete block and wood siding. The interior finishes, with wooden wainscot and flowered wallpaper, were similarly mass-produced and typical of building construction of the time.

69   Hinther, "'Sincerest Revolutionary Greetings.'"

70   Warchow interview.

71   For a fuller explanation of the differences between community centres in Ukraine and Canada, see Jars Balan, 'Backdrop to an Era: The Ukrainian Canadian Stage in the Interwar Years,' *Journal of Ukrainian Studies* 16, nos. 1–2 (1991): 89–111.

72   Drozdowych interview.

73   In all, 108 labour temples were raided, emptied, and padlocked between 1940 and 1942 as a result of the 10 June 1940 order-in-council ban on the ULFTA and the CPC; 98 CPC members (including 35 ULFTA organizers) were interned at Kananaskis, Petawawa, and Hull.

74   Drozdowych, then seven years old, believes that these materials were either hidden in the upstairs apartment or distributed among the members in the months that the branch anticipated a raid (Drozdowych interview). Remnants of the library can be found in the John Chudobiak Papers, LAC, MG31, H149.

75   Haideychuck, who was one of the tenants, seems to have gone into hiding. His whereabouts were unknown from 1941 to 1947 (*Might's*, annual volumes, 1940–8)

76   Momryk, 'Ukrainians,' 86

77   W. Repka and Kathleen M. Repka, *Dangerous Patriots: Canada's Unknown Prisoners of War* (Vancouver: New Star, 1977), 94.

78   Momryk, 'Ukrainians,' 87.

79   Doug Smith, *Cold Warrior: C.S. Jackson and the United Electrical Workers* (St John's: Canadian Committee on Labour History, 1997), 84.

80   Watson Kirkconnell, who otherwise supported Ukrainian nationalist causes and opposed leftist ones, said that the seized properties amounted to 'a cinder in the eye of Canada.' Kirkconnell, 'Leftist Ukrainian Halls,' *Saturday Night*, 5 December 1942, 10–11 at 10.

81   The volunteers were C. Chopowick, John Chudobiak, Kazimierz Drozdowych, F. Kandela, P. Kandela, K.H. Kozak, Myron Kryvonosiuk, MP Lysiuk, N. Ostapyk, M.J. Prokopenko, and K.H. Rozack (Drozdowych interview; Peter Krawchuk, *Our Contribution to Victory*, trans. Mary Skrypnyk (Toronto: Kobzar, 1985).

82   Drozdowych interview.

83   Ibid.

84   Momryk, 'Ukrainians,' 85; *Might's*, 1944–7.

85   Guitard, *La maison*, 3.

86 Anonymous, correspondence with author.

87 Dorozdowych interview; Anonymous, Correspondence with author.

88 MacGregor, 'Childhood,' 25.

89 Drozdowych interview.

90 *Might's*, annual volumes, 1944–65.

91 It was a position for which he was recalled as 'ideal' for the small, cash-strapped group. He lived a modest life under spartan circumstances as a boarder with labour temple families, and as Secretary-Treasurer, he was known for his meticulous bookkeeping and parsimonious attitude towards incurring unnecessary expenses. Warchow interview.

92 MacGregor, 'Childhood,' 25.

93 Hinther, '"Sincerest Revolutionary Greetings,"' 173.

94 Drozdowych interview.

95 City of Ottawa building inspectors and the fire marshal ordered the changes. Warchow interview.

96 Ibid.

97 Hinther describes a familiar experience in handicraft exhibits during the same period, when displays of women's embroidery continued to be held at Canadian labour temples, but 'gone were the [Bolshevik motives of] hammers and sickles.' '"Sincerest Revolutionary Greetings,"' 223.

98 Anonymous, correspondence with author.

99 Drozdowych interview.

100 For example, the federal public service, with its fixed hours, relatively lucrative remuneration, and life-long job security, is widely believed to have been closed to members of the CPC and other progressives until the 1970s. Drozdowych interview; Warchow interview.

101 Drozdowych interview.

102 Anonymous, correspondence with author; Drozdowych interview; Warchow interview.

103 Anonymous, correspondence with author.

104 MacGregor, 'Childhood,' 26.

105 Speakers included George Mackardy, MP, and key AUUC figures Peter Krawchuk of Toronto and Stanley Dobrowolski of Montreal. LAC, AUUC fonds, MG28 V154, vol. 20, file 21, Ottawa, 1950.It is difficult to extrapolate from these statistics because the extant period documentation for Ottawa is minimal and sporadic.

106 I. Basiuk, M. Chopowick, P. Haideychuk, F. Mandryk, F. Marak, and P.

Yakubowski. Haideychuk to CEC, 12 May 1950, in LAC, vol. 20, file 21, Ottawa, 1950.

107 Drozowych interview; Anonymous, correspondence with author.

108 LAC, MG28 V154, vol. 13, file 24, AUUC Fonds, Haideychuk to CEC, Toronto, Ottawa, 9 April 1952.

109 Anonymous, correspondence, 14 February 1999; Drozdowych interview; Warchow interview.

110 Anonymous, correspondence.

111 MacGregor, 'Childhood,' 25.

112 Anonymous, correspondence with author, 14 February, 1999

113 Warchow interview.

114 While 315 branches existed in 1945, only 140 remained in 1950, and 96 in 1960. The decline was even steeper in the decades that followed, with 61 branches in 1970 and only 9 in 2000. John Kolasky, *The Shattered Illusion: The History of the Ukrainian Pro-Communist Organizations in Canada* (Toronto: Peter Martin, 1979), 81; *AUUC Millenium Festival Programme* (Edmonton: AUUC, 2000).

115 LAC, MG28 V154, vol. 13, file 24, Haideychuk to Central Executive Committee, Toronto, 10 August 1958. Two interviewees confirm that this was indeed the case for them. Both had been profiled in the AUUC's weekly *Ukrainian Canadian* (*UC*) in 1952 as promising young people dedicated to the Ottawa hall. But by the late 1950s, both had left the city to find work, as had all the former youth members of their acquaintance ('Teen Sketch: Elsie Bodnar,' *UC*, 1 May 1952, 11; 'Complete Report of 1952 "UC" Campaign – Collector: Wm. Warchow,' *UC*, 1 September 1952, 14; anonymous, correspondence with author, 14 February 1999; Warchow interview).

116 LAC, MG28 V154, file 20, AUUC fonds, Haideychuk to Central Executive Committee, Toronto, 10 August 1958.

117 Ibid., 3 April 1958.

118 Drozdowych interview; Warchow interview.

119 Momryk, 'Ukrainians,' 90.

120 LAC, MG28 V154, file 20, AUUC fonds, Haideychuk to Central Executive Committee, Toronto, 10 August 1958.

121 Ibid., 11 July 1958.

122 Warchow interview; M. Korol, 'Petro Haideychuk,' *UC*, 27 April 1965, 6.

123 *Might's*, Annual volumes, 1964–8.

124 Replacing it on the site (now 523 St Anthony's Lane) is a purpose-built multiuse complex designed in stages by architect Dominic Constantini from 1971 to 1994. Created in an eclectic late-modern style, the building contains an athletic clubhouse, bar, and banquet facility that caters to the clientele of the Italian 'festival marketplace' since developed on Preston Street. Its formal qualities betray no evidence of the simple worker housing that once occupied the street, including the labour temple.

125 Lapointe, 'La maison hulloise,' 52.

126 MacGregor, 'Childhood,' 25

127 *Might's*, annual volumes, 1916–2000.

128 Peter Ennals and Deryck Holdsworth, *Homeplace: The Making of the Canadian Dwelling over Three Centuries* (Toronto: University of Toronto Press, 1988), 192.

129 While the immediate post-1945 era is sometimes posited as the beginning of the reformation of cities with the depletion of traditional downtown residential neighbourhoods and the creation of planned suburbs, suburbanization was a largely middle-class phenomenon for the first twenty years after the Second World War. Immigrant-worker catchment areas in older Canadian cities and the ethnic poor who inhabited them were thus mainly untouched by the drive to the suburbs until the 1960s at the earliest. In the case of Ottawa, the drive was, arguably, less one of choice made possible by postwar prosperity, but one forced by government expropriation and the mass clearance of downtown working-class neighbourhoods that began in the early 1960s.

130 Lapointe, 'La maison hulloise,' 54.

131 MacGregor, 'Childhood,' 26.

13

'I'll Fix You!': Domestic Violence and Murder in a Ukrainian Working-Class Immigrant Community in Northern Ontario

Stacey Zembrzycki

[In] the end my conscience broke me and my weak head, and forced me to kill my old oppressor, and mistress who robbed me of my belongings, and destroyed my young life. To-day I am killing her and myself, and wish you all that is good; only try to avoid such a life as I have led. My heart was never peaceful, and I lived to perform such an awful deed.

Peter Myhal, May 1929[1]

Between 1913 and 1939 there were seven capital murder trials in Sudbury, Ontario, five of which involved Ukrainian working-class immigrants.[2] The murders, all of which took place in and around the spaces the victims would have identified as their home, included one male-on-male murder, one infanticide, and three domestic murders of women by former partners and admirers who were not the husband. Unlike the scandalous cases studied by Franca Iacovetta, Karen Dubinsky, and Carolyn Strange, there is nothing truly exceptional about any of the murders that occurred in this Northern Ontario mining community.[3] They did not attract international attention, nor did they inspire memorable clemency campaigns. In fact, these cases have not even figured in the national collective memory, and though they received coverage in local newspapers, they have all but vanished from the community's public memory as well. These cases become important, however, when they are studied concurrently. In particular, they elucidate patterns, showing how gender, class, age, and ethnicity affected the construction of northern notions of Ukrainian-ness in the first half of the twentieth century. Moreover, by telling the stories of those who often did not fit comfortably into the larger ethnic community, these cases insert these traumatic crimes, which have been largely ignored facets of immigrants' lived experience, into the historical record.

About ten years ago, Franca Iacovetta offered an assessment of the treatment of immigrants in Canadian historical writing. In particular, she called on all historians, not just scholars of race and ethnicity, to integrate the histories of minorities into their work. In proposing alternative approaches to the field, Iacovetta pointed out that little attention had been paid to 'the tragic casualties of the migration process,' such as the victims of domestic violence. By homogenizing the immigrant experience and thereby celebrating agency, resiliency, and immigrant success, ethnic and immigration historians had, according to Iacovetta, downplayed the more disturbing features of immigrant life.[4] Canadian historians have since responded to Iacovetta's challenge, revealing a greater willingness to address questions of difference.[5] Specifically, they have attempted to 'make "public" topics formerly too "private" for exposure,' detailing the lives of those who lived comfortably and uncomfortably both inside and outside their respective immigrant communities.[6]

Ukrainian-Canadian historians Frances Swyripa and Gregory Robinson were writing more inclusive histories prior to the publication of Iacovetta's polemic. Exploring how gender, ethnicity, class, and criminality were all linked in a Western Canadian context, they discussed criminal patterns among Ukrainian immigrants and demonstrated how Old World customs and beliefs helped reinforce stereotypes about these men and women.[7] Despite these contributions, it is important to note that we continue to know very little about those Ukrainians who lived both inside and on the margins of communities outside Western Canada. In discussing instances of domestic violence and murder in a Northern Ontario setting, this local case study will build on this literature and expand its geographical limits.

To understand these murders and the trial proceedings it is important to contextualize the place in which they occurred. Sudbury, which began as a Canadian Pacific Railway (CPR) construction camp, quickly turned into a mining centre when nickel was discovered there in the summer of 1883. Immigrants began to flock to the company towns around Sudbury shortly afterwards, but not until 1906 did Ukrainians flood the region in search of work. They formed a heavily masculine and highly transient ethnic community in the town of Copper Cliff, which by 1911 was home to 25 'Galician' men and 14 'Galician' women, and 176 'Ruthenian' men and 40 'Ruthenian' women. At this time, Copper Cliff – an International Nickel Company (Inco) town on the western outskirts of Sudbury – had a population of 1,989 men and 1,093 women.[8] As the region's infrastructure improved, many Ukrainians moved to Sudbury, where they settled in neighbourhoods throughout the town. It must be noted that during this same period, Ukrainians also formed communities in Coniston and Levack, other mining company towns in the region. In 1921, they accounted for 0.2 per cent of Sudbury's population of 4,423 men and 4,198 women; by 1931, for 4.1 per cent of that population, which by now included 10,300 men and 8,218 women.[9] Living in ethnic clusters in and around Sudbury, Ukrainians who participated in organized public life quickly divided into two distinct groups: Catholics and progressives. Significantly, almost all of the Ukrainian perpetrators and victims who will be discussed here lived on the edges of this organized community; thus their political affiliations did not play a role in the construction of their Ukrainian-ness.

For two reasons, this local case study focuses mainly on the experiences of those Ukrainians who lived in the Sudbury region prior to the Second World War. First, though Ukrainians may not have been the only immigrants to experience domestic violence during this period, they were the ethnic community most affected by domestic violence resulting in murder. Second, the history of this ethnic community determined the periodization for this local case study. Specifically, the first half of the twentieth century was a distinct phase in the Ukrainian community's development – a time when its gender imbalance was shifting, the processes of family formation were accelerating, and assimilatory forces were changing the community's dynamics. The period chosen thus makes for a consistent community study.

Like other Northern Ontario mining communities, Sudbury had a reputation for being a rough and lawless place.[10] That many of the town's inhabitants were working-class male immigrants, with a tendency towards political radicalism, encouraged this perception. However, as Karen Dubinsky's ground-breaking study about heterosexual conflict in rural and small-town Ontario shows, Southern Ontario towns were just as dangerous as those in the north. The law was thus consistent in both parts of the province, constructing, defining, and regulating acceptable and respectable male and female sexual identities and, by extension, morality.[11] This local case study, which builds on Dubinsky's work, will endeavour to show that morality was not only gendered but also socially constructed along ethnic lines.

Each murderer was different in terms of background, motive, and relationship with his or her victim, but the space in which each criminal was tried and convicted was similar.[12] The courtroom was therefore instrumental in nation building, for it acted as a space in which the law established moral boundaries and attempted to make good citizens. By imposing an ethnically defined set of moral standards, the courtroom also served as a place where Anglo-Canadian ideals could be enforced and any unacceptable immigrant behaviour that threatened the making of a safe and wholesome region – and by extension nation – could be confronted, condemned, and punished.[13] As we shall see, the judgements made in this local courtroom were informed by gender, class, age, and ethnicity; thus it was a place in which Sudbury's Anglo-Canadian upper-class legal community used unequal power relations to 'manage the marginal,' defining offences 'not so much by what the individual in question [had] done, but by who he or she [was], and where and when the offence occurred.'[14] It is significant that nativist depictions of 'the foreigner' – most often applied to Southern, Eastern, and Central Europeans during this period – were hardly unique to this group of Sudburians. Nativism, as John Herd Thompson points out, was well established before the First World War. Though it took many forms, nativism generally depicted these immigrants as uncultured, morally and sexually dangerous, and most important, inferior. The belief among English-speaking Canadians was that 'immigrants to Canada should be forced to assimilate to the language and customs of the majority.'[15] In reconstructing the portraits of these northern perpetrators and victims of domestic violence and murder, this local case study will thereby problematize ethnicity as well as gender, class, and age, asking how the local Anglo-Canadian court and Sudbury's Ukrainian community used these variables to construct, reinforce, and maintain identity and morality.

It is important at the outset to discuss the available sources and their limitations. The reconstructions of these cases and the portraits of the victims and perpetrators of these murders have been made possible through the use of capital case files, oral history interviews, and English-language local and national newspapers; the absence of the ethnic press will be discussed at this point as well. First, as Carolyn Strange admits, those who rely on capital case files can 'rarely proclaim that "every word" in [their] "stories" is true.'[16] When working with this type of source, historians must read *through* and/or *against* the grain of these documents, recognizing – as Karen Dubinsky reminds us – that they represent '"sites of contestation" between the observers and the observed.'[17] Though the cases offered below are presented in an ordered and plausible manner, it is important to recognize that in the end, the case files being relied on were written, interpreted, and manipulated by historical actors who were neither the victims nor the perpetrators of the crimes.

This local case study has also tried to draw from the memories of Ukrainians who grew up in the Sudbury region. Unfortunately, these murders do not hold a place in the collective memory of the community. For instance, when eighty-two oral history interviews were being conducted with individuals of Ukrainian descent who lived in the Sudbury region during this period, only a handful of interviewees vaguely remembered the murder of Alice Kroiter by her former admirer, John Ungurian, in 1939. In this regard, the identities of these individuals, which would have been constructed inside the ethnic community, have for the most part been lost.

Lastly, English-language local and national newspapers have been used to reconstruct these cases as well as the portraits of those who killed and were killed. All of these cases were covered by the *Sudbury Star* and/or the *Sudbury Journal*, but the only case to be covered by a national newspaper, the *Globe and Mail*, was the murder of Alice Kroiter. Generally speaking, the ways in which the newspapers covered the cases changed over time. The early cases featured head shots of the accused murderers, witness statements, and summaries of the subsequent inquests and murder trials. When Alice Kroiter was murdered in 1939, however, coverage changed to include photographs of everyday happenstance as well as human interest stories about the murderer and the victim. This coverage was extensive, taking up a number of pages in each edition of the newspaper. Note that by the time Kroiter was murdered, Ukrainians had achieved some degree of acceptance in Canada.

The second wave of Ukrainian immigration, between 1918 and 1939, and a second generation of Ukrainian Canadians, helped develop this acceptance and eventual assimilation. Certainly, these factors may account for the ways in which coverage changed during this period. In any event, as with the capital case file, this source has its limitations. Stories written about these cases and their actors were crafted by outsiders. In other words, they were filtered through bystanders and may or may not accurately depict the actual events and actors.

With the exception of the murder of Alice Kroiter, the ethnic press has not been included in this analysis because a sampling of this source – namely *Ukrainskyi holos*, *Novyi shliakh*, *Robochyi narod*, *Ukrainski robitnychi visti*, and *Narodna hazeta* – comes up dry. It is significant that though Kroiter's murder did appear on the front page of *Ukrainskyi holos*, coverage was limited to four brief paragraphs on the bottom right corner of the 18 January 1939 edition of that newspaper. As Frances Swyripa notes, in being '[anxious] to blend in and be accepted, successive generations of Ukrainian Canadians simply preferred to ignore the issue of crime in their community, rather than draw attention to it by subjecting the Anglo-Canadian stereotype to serious scrutiny.'[18] One cannot go so far as to say that the ethnic press silenced criminal behaviour – sensational murders and other crimes committed by Ukrainian immigrants did receive some attention in these newspapers – but it is clear that crime stories were not a common feature of the Ukrainian press. For the most part, these Ukrainian-language newspapers served as a record for the organized Ukrainian community, highlighting its respectability rather than demonstrating how Ukrainians were not fitting into the Canadian mainstream. It is significant here that progressive Ukrainian newspapers cared less about bourgeois respectability than those published by other groups in the community. Moreover, newspapers like *Ukrainskyi holos* covered the Kroiter murder because she and her family had been active in the organized Ukrainian community. So it is not surprising that the other murders discussed here were not covered by the ethnic press – as previously mentioned, the immigrants involved in those cases lived on the fringes of society and were not members of any of the Ukrainian organizations in the community. In thus recognizing the problems and limitations of these sources, this local case study hopes to offer an interpretation of the truth.

The murder of Mike Usulock by Peter Kozemer in 1913 was the first documented murder to occur in the Sudbury region.[19] On the night of 27 September 1913, Kozemer was arrested for the murder of Usulock. The two men, who had come from the same town in Austria, worked together on a CPR rail gang and lived in adjacent CPR boxcars, which they identified as their homes.[20] According to those who witnessed the 'gruesome murder,' Usulock had been in Kozemer's boxcar with a number of other men over the course of the evening. At about nine o'clock, Kozemer entered the boxcar in an intoxicated state and went to lie in his bunk. Shortly afterwards, Kozemer and another Ukrainian, Alexis Pete, began to argue. Pete called Kozemer a thief. Kozemer responded by jumping out of his bunk and slapping Pete. Usulock attempted to separate the two men, telling them there was no need to fight. He succeeded in separating them, but another altercation developed soon afterwards. At this point, Kozemer reached under his bunk and pulled out an axe. Pete escaped from the boxcar; Usulock remained inside with a few other men. Kozemer proceeded to beat Usulock with the axe, and after a few swings, Usulock fell to the floor and began to gasp for air. According to witnesses, Kozemer then went outside to find Pete. Unsuccessful, he re-entered the boxcar and began to kick Usulock and to beat him with a shovel, yelling in Ukrainian: 'I'll fix you! I'll fix you!' When Usulock stopped making noise Kozemer picked him up by the legs and tossed him out the boxcar door.[21]

Kozemer was tried for murdering his 'fellow countryman' at the District of Sudbury fall assizes two weeks later. From the beginning, ethnicity, class, and gender figured prominently in the courtroom where Kozemer's portrait was being constructed. For instance, all of the material witnesses for the Crown were labouring, transient, Ukrainian men; thus they were labelled as flight risks almost immediately after the murder. Seven of the nine men were actually held in custody from the night of the murder until they were to testify at the coroner's inquest about a week later because they could not be trusted to appear voluntarily at the inquest.[22] This emphasis on the background of those involved in the case did not stop there. Instead of having the witnesses sworn in according to the rituals of Canadian justice, with one hand on the bible and another raised before the court, the defence lawyer made a special request and asked that they be sworn in according to what he referred to as 'the custom in their own country.' He stated: 'I understand that they are sworn on the crucifix between two lighted candles. I understand that [this] is the only way of getting the truth.' The judge granted this request.[23] This assertion, which played on images of the superstitious and illiterate immigrant, was another way to show the unacceptability of foreigners.[24] Ethnic labels and ethnic characterizations such as these served to demonstrate the backwardness of Ukrainian men – the notion that they were not adhering to Anglo-Canadian cultural ideals.[25] Before moving on, it is important to note how this early-twentieth-century community defined foreigners. We may look to Edwin Bradwin's observations, made during his visits to Canadian railway construction camps between 1903 and 1914, for this definition. Bradwin argued that there were two 'distinct' groups of workers during this period: 'whites' included English and French Canadians, British immigrants, Americans, and the odd Scandinavian and Finn, whereas 'foreigners' – who were often dismissed by the 'whites' – included 'Bohunks,' 'Hunkies,' and 'Douks.'[26] The foreigner was an image against which native Sudburians attempted to define themselves and the antithesis of what these individuals were striving to represent.[27]

In reading the trial proceedings, one is also struck by the derogatory ways in which both the prosecution and the defence lawyers spoke to the witnesses. For instance, as each man recounted the evening, the prosecution responded with negative remarks, calling the onlookers 'cowards' and alleging that because it had been a 'Polack holiday' there was no doubt that all of the men must have been drunk.[28] This sentiment had been echoed in the *Sudbury Star* a few days earlier during the coroner's inquest: 'the usual cowardice of foreigners, particularly Polacks, of which so much has appeared in Ontario papers o' late was again exhibited in this case. Twelve men actually watched one man beat another to death with an axe and not a hand was raised to interfere.'[29] The newspaper alleged that there was a serious problem with 'Polacks' in Ontario, but it never provided any additional examples with which to compare this incident. By reiterating that the men had been drinking and that it had been a 'Polack' holiday, the lawyers and the newspaper were emphasizing one of the many stereotypes of Ukrainian immigrants during this period. The derogatory terms 'Polack' and 'foreigner' were applied in order to label the Ukrainian men and to denote both their unacceptability and their resistance to Canadian assimilation. Furthermore, in calling the men cowards, the lawyers and the newspaper were directly attacking the men's masculinity, insinuating that Canadian men never would have shirked their manly obligation to defend someone who was being beaten to death. The use of an axe was also problematic. As Gregory Robinson notes, 'everyday objects grabbed in the heat of the moment' contributed to the pervasive ethnic and class-related assumptions that dominated societal discourses about Ukrainian men.[30] Specifically, the notion that foreigners fought unfairly was a common perception among middle- and upper-class Anglo-Canadians during this period. To get a sense of this thinking, one need only read Charles William Gordon, a leading figure in the Social Gospel movement as well as a Protestant middle-class minister and a prolific and populist novelist who wrote under the alias of Ralph Connor. As Connor wrote in *The Foreigner* in 1909: 'Only a fool [lost] his temper, and only a cad [used] a club or a knife when he [fought].'[31] For Connor's fictitious character Kalman, the day he learned to fight without a weapon, and thus in a respectable Canadian fashion, was a day that brought him a 'new image of manhood.'[32] Likewise this discussion during the trial served to teach the criminal, the men who had witnessed the crime, and the larger community a lesson about respectable Canadian masculinity and honour.

The prosecution lawyer and the local newspaper were also eager to emphasize that Usulock had been a peacekeeper who had not deserved to die; specifically, they argued that unlike the cowardly onlookers, Usulock had been acting the way a respectable Canadian man ought to behave.[33] What emerges, then, is a seemingly contradictory image of the Ukrainian man. To take the argument one step further, the courtroom was being used as a space for demonstrating that foreigners could not be relied on to stand strong and defend the nation. Yet Usulock's actions showed that there was indeed some hope when it came to the foreigner. If an immigrant conformed and was thus assimilated into the Canadian mainstream, it was possible for him to become a morally acceptable Canadian citizen. Certainly, this nuanced peacekeeper argument was employed by the prosecution lawyer both to defend Usulock's actions and to ensure that Kozemer would be sentenced for the crime he was accused of committing.

Two hours after adjourning, and just ten days after the murder, the Anglo-Canadian male jury returned a guilty verdict. Kozemer was sentenced to be hanged on 29 December 1913.[34] It is interesting that justice was swift even though the axe that had been used to kill Usulock was never recovered. Kozemer's lawyer made it clear that this was an important variable: he asked whether the weapon had been missing from the crime scene because someone else had used it to kill Usulock.[35] About one month after the trial, the *Sudbury Star* began to report a new development in the case. Kozemer's lawyer was arguing that the witnesses had been biased. Before coming to Canada, Kozemer had married one of the witnesses' cousins, over the objections of her family. In fact, he had suffered a gunshot wound over this marriage. This new evidence implied that Kozemer had been set up by the witnesses; it also supported the idea that Ukrainian immigrants had a natural proclivity towards violence, even in relation to marriage. The defence further argued that because the trial and the sentencing had occurred so soon after the murder, there was no way the jury could have remained unbiased. All of this leaves one to wonder how much contact Kozemer had with his lawyer before the trial. Kozemer's lawyer appealed the decision, and nine days before the hanging was to be carried out, his client's sentence was commuted to life imprisonment. According to the Under-Secretary of State, the evidence suggested that Kozemer had not acted alone and that someone else had been involved in the murder.[36]

Ethnicity, class, and gender informed the judgements made in the courtroom in which Kozemer was convicted. He was being forced to defend himself in an environment laden with class assumptions and ethnic slurs. Those assumptions and slurs amounted to an attack on Ukrainian masculinity by stressing that Ukrainian men were unreliable cowards who, when drunk, broke Canadian laws in unacceptable ways. No doubt these perceptions negatively affected how Canadian justice was applied to this immigrant. Moreover, they were quite central to how morality was defined and employed in this case.

Significant ethnic, gender, and class patterns begin to emerge when the Kozemer case is examined against other murders that occurred in Sudbury during the first half of the twentieth century. As the following case will demonstrate, stereotypical characterizations about Ukrainian immigrants continued to affect the application of justice as well as constructions of morality in this northern setting.

On 25 July 1914, Catherine Hawryluk was taken into police custody for the murder of her newborn twins. Neighbours suspected that she had been concealing her pregnancy and had reported her to the police.

Hawryluk denied these allegations before admitting that she had given birth to twins: a boy and a girl. After giving birth, Hawryluk had smothered the babies and buried them about two miles from her home. Anton Hawryluk, Catherine's husband, swore that he had no knowledge of the murders, stating that she had carried on with her daily routine as usual, performing the housework and preparing him and their boarders a meal before they left for work that day.[37]

Hawryluk had come to Canada from Galicia two years before, at the age of sixteen, to live with her uncle, who resided in Copper Cliff. While living at his boarding house she had fallen 'victim to the wiles of some man,' who was later called a 'villain' by Hawryluk's defence lawyer.[38] Since Ukrainian immigrants, as Frances Swyripa reminds us, often favoured 'informal community-based' judicial networks over formal Canadian judicial systems, it is highly unlikely that rape and/or assault charges would have been viable options for Hawryluk.[39] Moreover, '[a] combination of isolation, ignorance, fear, and physical force would have prevented most victims of domestic violence and sexual assault from bringing their problems before the courts to be solved by Anglo-Canadian notions of abstract justice.'[40] Consequently, Hawryluk sought security through marriage. Though they had known each other for only two weeks, she agreed to marry Anton, a fellow Ukrainian, in January 1914, about two months after the incident with this 'villain'; the murders took place seven months after the wedding. During the trial, Anton Hawryluk declared that he had not known that his wife had been concealing her pregnancy.

Though Hawryluk's capital case file is incomplete because it does not include a copy of the trial transcript, it is possible to piece together the case from the *Sudbury Star's* coverage of the 1914 fall assizes. The newspaper described Hawryluk as a 'pitiful little figure' with 'big brown eyes' who seemed to be 'seeking some avenue of escape from the horde of men who surrounded her.' Unlike the lawyers in the Kozemer case, Hawryluk's lawyer used the courtroom as a space in which to highlight her Ukrainian working-class background and her youthfulness. It may have been an appalling crime, but Hawryluk's defence lawyer argued that she could not have been in her right senses. After all, she was a 'poor child' in a 'strange country' who could not be held responsible for her actions. She had been assaulted before her marriage to Anton and had become pregnant as a result of this assault. While it

is unclear whether Hawryluk had had consensual sex with this mysterious man, her lawyer seemed to make a case for non-consensual sex;
it must be noted that the terms *rape* and *assault* never appeared in any
of the records. Essentially discounting any notion of assault, the prosecuting lawyer argued that 'the woman had done the greatest wrong
any woman could do to a man, by marrying him to escape the consequences of her intercourse with another man.'[41] In making such a statement, it is clear that the lawyers involved in this case used Hawryluk's
gender, class, age, and ethnicity very differently. The defence lawyer invoked images of a poor, young, and defenceless immigrant girl; the
prosecution lawyer argued that Hawryluk was an immoral foreign
woman who, in being unable to resist sexual advances and/or intercourse, was responsible for the pregnancy and the subsequent infanticide.[42]

The jury adjourned for ninety minutes and returned with a guilty
verdict, with a recommendation for mercy on the grounds that Hawryluk was a youth. The judge sentenced Hawryluk to be hanged, but
added that he would be asking the Provincial Secretary for clemency
and recommending that her punishment be commuted to life imprisonment with the prison term being as light as possible.[43] Little is
known about Hawryluk's life after her trial; the local newspapers
never printed another article about her. Her capital case file does,
however, confirm that her death sentence was commuted to fifteen
years' imprisonment.[44]

It is not surprising that Hawryluk's punishment was changed. According to Constance Backhouse, the courts were usually quite lenient
when it came to infanticide, recognizing that it was a coping mecha-
nism often resorted to by young, single, working-class women.[45] By
adding ethnicity to Backhouse's gendered and class-informed discussion of infanticide, we gain a more complete understanding of this
crime. At first glance, Hawryluk's conviction seems to be in line with
the norm and thus her ethnicity does not seem to matter. However, this
is significant in and of itself. Unlike in the Kozemer case, Hawryluk's
ethnicity was not used against her. As with those women who committed infanticide before her, it was Hawryluk's gender and age, not her
ethnicity, that constructed her portrait and inspired the court's com-
passion. Though her lawyer used her ethnicity to inspire these emotions, it was unnecessary: clearly, youth and femininity crossed ethnic

boundaries.[46] In this case, Hawryluk's gender and age were manipulated in her favour, and mercy resulted.

Historians have studied family violence and spousal murders at length. The domestic murders of Mary Kurhanewich, Rose Karas, and Alice Kroiter are different, however, because these women were not killed by a husband.[47] Each of these women (except Alice Kroiter) had had an intimate relationship with the man who later killed her; but it must be noted that by the time of each murder, each woman had severed relations with her former partner (in Kroiter's case, her admirer). The feminist literature on family violence makes it clear that married women often stay in abusive and sometimes deadly spousal relationships for reasons relating to dependency and security. By leaving her home, a woman risks losing her children, her economic stability, and her reputation as a 'good' wife.[48] On the other hand, we know very little about the relationship dynamics between men and women who are not married and who do not share children. For instance, why and how do women maintain and/or terminate these kinds of relationships when they experience abuse? By using ethnicity, class, gender, and age to understand the victims' murderability as well as the murderer's respectability, the following cases permit an understanding of the links between and among these variables; they also provide insight into the ways that domestic violence impacts such relationships.

Mary Kurhanewich lived a difficult and tragic life. In May 1910 she was shot in the back by her husband, Peter, who suspected that she had been cheating on him with one of their boarders.[49] Five years later, Kurhanewich was bludgeoned to death with an axe by her lover, Wasyl Dejbuck. Kurhanewich and her husband had been separated for about a month when she was murdered. She had been having an affair with Dejbuck, and according to Steve Dejbuck, Wasyl's brother, Kurhanewich had promised to go and live with him after she left her husband. She later reneged on this pledge.

On the night of 11 January 1915, Kurhanewich was visiting a sick friend, caring for her and cooking dinner for her husband and their boarders. When she went to leave, Dejbuck arrived and insisted on walking her home. When she realized he had been drinking, she insisted that she would walk home alone. She feared that if they ran into her husband there would be an altercation. Kurhanewich and Dejbuck began to argue. He struck her down and then continued to beat her with an axe he had hidden behind his back. Before being arrested, Dejbuck fled to his brother's house. It was there that he admitted in Ukrainian: 'I have killed! She will no more leave me or her husband.' Steve Dejbuck would admit these details during the trial.[50] Also, he told another boarder living at the house that 'she did not need to fool me, she was telling her husband one thing and telling me another, always fooling me.'[51]

Steve Dejbuck's testimony proved to be damning. Wasyl Dejbuck was found guilty, and hanged on 2 June 1916. At first glance, one would have expected Dejbuck's ethnicity, class, and gender to be insignificant factors at this trial. Yet there are subtle indications that justice officials and the local newspaper used his Ukrainian working-class masculinity to construct his identity throughout the trial. Though he was never explicitly called a dangerous foreigner, he was depicted as one. He had been in a jealous and drunken rage the night he had cowardly butchered Kurhanewich with an axe – a fact the *Sudbury Journal* took one step further by insinuating that the murder had been a natural extension of his drunkenness.[52] Specifically the article maintained that Dejbuck had murdered Kurhanewich in an unrespectable (i.e., ethnic) manner.[53] These issues were not sensationalized, because unlike in the Kozemer case, the Anglo-Canadian community responsible for prosecuting and convicting Dejbuck had come to terms with how it defined foreigners and regulated morality. There was nothing exceptional about Dejbuck or his crime. He had not challenged the category; indeed, he had exemplified it. Incidentally, Dejbuck was never credited with the fact that he had admitted to murdering Kurhanewich. He had told the truth from the beginning of the incident, which was, for the most part, an unlikely immigrant trait.[54]

At the same time, the courtroom served as a space in which to informally prosecute Kurhanewich for violating ideals of femininity and sexuality. Strangely, it did not seem to matter that Dejbuck had a wife in Ukraine and a mistress in Sudbury. Most of the witnesses were asked questions about Kurhanewich's sexual reputation, at times implying that she had deserved what happened to her. The local physician, for instance, testified that she had had a 'loose reputation.'[55] When asked whether she was a powerful woman, another doctor replied that 'she was certainly well developed.'[56] Members of the ethnic community who were called to testify echoed this sentiment. Steve Bodnaruk, a labourer who lived in the neighbourhood, stated that 'Mary's general reputation was not good around town.' The court-appointed Ukrainian interpreter, John Wagner, admitted: 'Yes, I knew she had a bad reputation in Copper Cliff.'[57] Clearly, Kurhanewich's sexuality was on trial, not Dejbuck's. It was women, be they immigrants or Canadians, who were responsible for regulating morality in domestic spaces, not men.

A number of witnesses labelled Kurhanewich a 'bad girl' who had deserved what happened to her.[58] By highlighting her gender, ethnicity, and unrespectable sexuality, the courtroom served as a space in which her murder could be justified and ethnic stereotypes about the dangerous foreigner could be reinforced. The court did not hear that she had suffered from a chain of domestic violence, both familial and non-familial; rather, it highlighted her sexual immorality as a threat to the community and the nation. As Karen Dubinsky notes, the criminal court doubled as a theatre and a place of justice in which trials resembled miniature morality plays complete with heroes, victims, and an audience.[59] In this instance, the negotiations among ethnicity, gender, and sexuality served to denigrate the victim of a very cruel murder. Moreover, there was a direct link between Kurhanewich's portrait and the ways in which the court constructed and applied morality. Specifically, morality was socially constructed along ethnic, gendered, and sexualized lines.

Ethnicity, gender, and class also informed the portraits of Peter Myhal and Rose Karas. Peter Myhal came to Sudbury from Kokal, Galicia, in 1913 and started working for a construction company. In 1917 he fell in love with Rose Karas, a Ukrainian woman who operated a boarding house in a Slavic working-class neighbourhood close to the Sudbury train station. Myhal went to live with her even though she had a husband who had returned to Ukraine and three young children who lived with her. He continued to work in the region, giving Karas money to feed and clothe her children and financially contributing to a second boarding house she had built in Capreol, a railway and logging community north of Sudbury. In 1920 Myhal went to work as a labourer in a lumber camp outside Sudbury. When he returned he learned that Karas had given birth to a stillborn child he had not fathered. He went back to Ukraine to 'get away from' Karas. While there, Karas began to write him letters, asking him for money to feed the children. Myhal eventually returned to Sudbury, claiming that he felt sorry for the children, and discovered that Karas had had another child with another man. This cycle continued until February 1928, when a final dispute developed between Myhal and Karas. She declared she had a common law husband, Fred Dzyza, and thus no longer needed Myhal. She then kicked him out of her house and threatened to shoot him if he returned. Myhal asked Karas to repay the money he had given her over the years, about $3,000. She refused to do so.[60]

A few months later, Myhal rented a room at a boarding house across the street from Karas's house. His bedroom window faced Karas's backyard. On 29 May 1929, while Karas was chopping wood, Myhal positioned himself at his window and shot her in the back. Karas cried in Ukrainian: 'I'm shot – he's killed me!' before collapsing into the arms of her son.[61] Myhal was arrested later that evening and charged with murder. While being questioned by the police chief, he admitted: 'I do say that I killed her and I know what is coming to me and if she was alive I would kill her again.'[62] Myhal was convicted of murder at the 1929 fall assizes and sentenced to be hanged on 12 December 1929. His damning confession made his plea of temporary insanity impossible to believe. Like Dejbuck, Myhal had told the truth and then tried to evade it with this plea.

As in the previous cases, ethnicity, class, and gender informed the construction of Myhal's portrait. He had committed premeditated murder, declaring his intention weeks in advance. He had rented a room that faced Karas's backyard and had sat in a chair by his window for hours at a time so that he could spy on Karas and plan her murder. Instead of using an axe, Myhal had used a gun. As the judge read his sentence, he stated: 'You gave the woman no chance. You did a cowardly thing, shooting her from behind. She had no chance to escape.' The judge went on: 'You and every other person coming to the Dominion of Canada from other countries are under an obligation to observe the laws and customs of this country ... I ask you to devote the time between now and the date when the sentence will be executed ... by making preparation for your future life. The law is more considerate of you in this way than you were of your victim. You hurled her into eternity with no opportunity for that preparation which every Christian desires.'[63]

Instead of acting like a respectable Canadian man and accepting that his relationship with Karas had ended, Myhal had chosen to act like a cowardly foreigner, facing his problems from a distance and with a weapon. There is a subtle complexity here, however, that differs from the man-on-man violence exhibited in the Kozemer case and the domestic violence of the Dejbuck murder. The judge made careful note of the physical distance between Myhal and Karas. Though a perpetrator who murdered with an axe was cowardly, at least the victim could see it coming and try to fight back. By using a gun, Myhal had taken the meaning of the word 'coward' to a new level. It must be noted that comments like these did not imply that Karas ought to have been able to defend herself. Rather, the judge was once again playing on the image of the stereotypical foreigner. This murder thus served as a serious warning to the community, for the implication was that foreigners – even seemingly unsuspicious foreigners – could not be trusted. No matter how close an immigrant came to assimilation, he could never entirely shed his immigrant culture and disposition to violence. As Police Chief Louden noted: 'I knew Myhal personally and always found him sober and appeared to be a retiring kind of man and about the last one would think capable of doing such a deed. He also bore a good character amongst the other people in the vicinity all of whom looked on him as being a dupe of this woman.'[64]

Comments like these indicate that Myhal had become an accepted and respected member of the community. He had been a sober and industrious working-class immigrant, and by many standards he had been assimilated. It is worth noting that the second wave of Ukrainian immigration and the presence of a second generation of Ukrainian Canadians also affected the ways that Myhal fit into the community.

The murders of Mike Usulock in 1913 and Mary Kurhanewich in 1916 had distressed the community but had not shocked it. By this point, Ukrainian men had been trapped in a kind of foreigner mystique, perceived as drunkards and cowards who fought with 'unmanly' weapons. By the time Myhal killed Karas, society had accepted this characterization but had also come to believe that it could tell 'good' immigrants (i.e., those who had become accepted and respected members of the larger community) from 'bad' immigrants (i.e., the unassimilated and worthless troublemakers who resided on the fringes of the Ukrainian community). Myhal's fall from grace illustrates the fine line between a foreigner and a respected and assimilated immigrant. His crime challenged societal definitions of the foreigner, forcing the society to rethink its standards of morality as well as its ethnic labels.

Karas's portrait was very different from the one assigned to Mary Kurhanewich. Though she had challenged notions of femininity and sexuality, her ethnicity was not put on trial in the courtroom. Unlike those witnesses who testified about Kurhanewich's character, the witnesses in the Myhal trial did not comment on Karas's rugged femininity and less-than-ideal sexuality. Instead, she was portrayed as a strong, working-class immigrant and a successful businesswoman who controlled her own space and those who inhabited it. Interestingly, she was also called a Christian, though Myhal claimed that she had had no qualms about maintaining a very un-Christian lifestyle, sleeping with a variety of men who were not her husband and undergoing a number of illegal abortions.[65] As far as the court was concerned, Karas had died in a less than acceptable manner; consequently, her ethnicity, class, and gender were not used to construct a negative image of her. For the most part, the witnesses argued that Karas was a respectable member of their ethnic community; she met the Ukrainian community's ideals of respectability even though she may not have met those of Anglo-Canadians. The judge accepted this character sketch and did not interrogate or deconstruct it. In terms of blackening Karas's reputation, Myhal was the only one to do so at trial. Clearly, this strategy was part of his defence. But the judge sided with most of the witnesses, and though ethnicity continued to be a factor in how Anglo-Canadian justice officials perceived and convicted criminals, it was not, in this instance, an issue in the construction of this victim's portrait.

The discussions that inspired the portraits of Alice Kroiter and her murderer, John Ungarian, were also informed by ethnicity, class, age, and gender. Ungurian owned the Yankee Grill, a lunch counter in the same neighbourhood as Rose Karas's boarding house. In early December 1938 he paid for Alice Kroiter, a young Ukrainian-Canadian from Yorkton, Saskatchewan, to come to work in his restaurant as a waitress. Ungurian immediately fell in love with Kroiter, showering her with gifts, paying her rent, taking her on a three-day trip to Toronto, and even buying a train ticket so that her best friend, Edna Swerhun, could join her in Sudbury. But Kroiter did not love Ungurian and wasted no time telling him. This infuriated Ungurian, and on 10 January 1939 he walked into the boarding house where Kroiter lived and shot her in the back of the head. He then fled by taxi to his estranged wife's house, where he was arrested and charged with Kroiter's murder. Ungurian was intoxicated and disoriented at the time of his arrest. He woke up in a jail cell the next morning claiming that he did not know where he was or why he was there.[66]

The fact that Ungurian owned a local restaurant affected the trial proceedings as well as the *Sudbury Star*'s coverage of them. Compared to other Ukrainian immigrants in the community – most of whom would have been viewed as poor and/or working-class – Ungurian was an ethnic businessman who had risen above his contemporaries and had thus achieved a modest middle-class status. This, of course, was relative to the English- and French-Canadian elites who owned much of Sudbury.[67] Because of his community standing, the *Sudbury Star* depicted Ungurian as a friendly giant. In using his ethnicity, class, and gender to construct his portrait, it stressed that he was a Ukrainian proprietor whom everyone liked. Ungurian stood well over six feet tall and was said to have an extremely friendly smile. Nearly every article that discussed the case referred to him as 'Big John,' and every photograph printed showed him smiling. At the same time, the newspaper used ethnicity, class, gender, and age to construct its image of Kroiter. It emphasized her beauty and her youth and even printed a photograph of her in a traditional Ukrainian costume. The *Sudbury Star* described the deceased as a nice Ukrainian girl who felt strongly about her heritage; she had sung for a respectable Ukrainian radio show in Saskatchewan, and she had just begun to attend mass at St Mary's Ukrainian Catholic Church. It also reported that she had recently graduated from Yorkton Collegiate, where she had been a leading student in the school's music and drama programs.[68]

The newspaper included photographs of Ungurian and Kroiter in nearly every article it printed. Though the local coverage of earlier cases had included photographs of murderer and victim, the images had been simple head shots and the stories had not included any discussion of physical appearance. It seems that the photographs had been included so that readers could attach faces to the crime. The newspaper coverage for this murder departed from this trend. Besides including a variety of photographs, the *Sudbury Star* went to great lengths to humanize Ungurian and Kroiter so that it could help the community understand how this friendly Ukrainian giant could have killed such a young and pretty Ukrainian-Canadian girl. Like Myhal, Ungurian had become a respected member of the community. In fact, he had surpassed Myhal's stature and was regarded as a businessman, not an immigrant. By shooting Kroiter at point-blank range, Ungurian had became one of those foreigners that Myhal's murder had warned against. Unlike in that case however, the community had a difficult time abandoning its image of Ungurian and placing him in the 'dangerous foreigner' category.

This was Sudbury's first murder case to be covered by the *Globe and Mail* as well as the ethnic press – specifically, *Ukrainskyi holos*. The *Globe and Mail* went into detail about this murder, whereas the coverage in *Ukrainskyi holos* was brief, emphasizing that Alice had been forced to quit her job because Ungurian had pestered her with his declarations of love. The Ukrainian press went on to note that Kroiter had been the daughter of a well-known teacher and author from Yorkton, Tatiana Kroiter, and that Kroiter, her mother, and her aunt had performed on the radio show 'The Smiling Song Birds of Ukraine.'[69] It must be noted that besides newspaper coverage, oral history has been a useful source for reconstructing this case and its imagery. Kroiter had attended St Mary's Ukrainian Catholic Church in Sudbury, so a few women from that parish remembered her. For instance, Olga Zembrzycki (née Zyma) recalled that Kroiter had been a tall and pretty girl and commented that, for the most part, Sudbury's Ukrainian community had been composed of a 'good bunch of people.' Not surprisingly, Zembrzycki went on to emphasize how much this murder had shocked the community.[70]

Furthermore, 'Big John's' class and reputation in the community made for a different kind of courtroom atmosphere. Throughout the trial, Ungurian maintained that he had had a lapse of memory. He himself could not understand why he would have killed someone he loved so much. His estranged wife and their daughter shed some light on Ungurian's history with alcohol, testifying that he did not act like himself when he was drinking, often becoming quarrelsome and sometimes knocking his head against the floor.[71] When Ungurian was called to the stand, he and his lawyer swept these allegations aside by painting a picture of respectability. He had come to Canada in 1923 after fighting for the Austro-Hungarian Army during the First World War and had worked for the Mond Nickel Company Mine for six years before taking over the Yankee Grill. During the trial, witnesses clarified that though Ungurian ran the restaurant, he did not actually own it. Those who covered this story drew from Ungarian's middle-class status and reputation in the

community. This time, Ungurian's ethnicity and gender were not significant factors in the creation of his identity. Though there was no
doubt he had murdered Kroiter, he was treated with considerable respect because of his standing in Sudbury. Furthermore, his drinking
problem was used to highlight a memory lapse he claimed to have had,
instead of being linked to images of the drunken immigrant. The fact
that he had abused his wife and had neglected to pay her child support
was also overlooked. In the end, however, the jury did not let Ungurian's constructed image sway them: they found him guilty. He was
sentenced to be hanged on 16 May 1939.

Ungurian appealed the sentence and succeeded in gaining significant support from his Ukrainian friends and acquaintances. Though this
local clemency campaign failed to affect his appeal process, three days
before he was to be hanged, Ungurian's death sentence was commuted
to life imprisonment. It is not clear why the Minister of Justice approved this change, but there was speculation that the Royal Visit of
1939 was a factor. The royal couple were due to arrive in Halifax on the
day of the execution, and according to Ungurian's lawyer, it would have
'greatly [dimmed] the joyous occasion.' The Justice Minister did not
want stories about the Royal Visit appearing alongside stories about the
execution.[72]

Ungurian's middle-class standing in the community led to the creation of a very different immigrant portrait. In this instance, class
trumped ethnicity and gender. The court never placed Ungurian in the
'dangerous foreigner' category to which it had assigned those Ukrainians who had murdered before him. His class explained away his drinking problem, his propensity to domestic violence, and the fact that he
had used a gun to murder Alice Kroiter.

By examining five seemingly insignificant murder cases, we have
reconstructed the private and criminal worlds of ten Ukrainian immigrants who lived in the Sudbury region between 1913 and 1939. Taken
together, these cases do much to strengthen our understanding of twentieth-century constructions of the Ukrainian immigrant and specifically,
what it meant to be a Ukrainian male or female, young or old, middle-
or working-class immigrant living in Northern Ontario during these
decades. Portraits of those who killed and were killed were individual-
ized and informed by ethnicity, class, gender, and sometimes age; also,
those portraits constantly underwent manipulation as they were adapted

to the criminal being tried and to the case being heard. This was not a straightforward set of negotiations. Age and class crossed ethnic boundaries, and unrespectable masculine crimes – and especially those committed with weapons – complicated the judicial process and the formation of ethnic identities. Ukrainian-ness was multifaceted, defined by the Anglo-Canadian courts as well as by the ethnic community itself. Furthermore, these immigrant portraits not only reinforced perceptions about ethnicity, class, age, and gender, but also affected notions relating to morality, labelling Ukrainians who threatened the building of a strong and wholesome nation and demonstrating what it took to be a respectable and acceptable Canadian citizen.

Notes

I am grateful to Franca Iacovetta, Marilyn Barber, John Walsh, Myron Momryk, and Orest Martynowych for their useful suggestions and comments on this work.

1 This quote was taken from a suicide note written in Ukrainian by Peter Myhal before he killed his former lover, Rose Karas, on 29 May 1929. Police found the note in Myhal's suitcase and had it translated into English so that it could serve as evidence at his trial. Though it is unclear whether Myhal intended to carry out his suicide plans – the issue was never discussed in court – he did not get a chance to do so because he was arrested shortly after committing this murder. Archives of Ontario (AO), Record Group (RG) 22-392, box 151, file Myhal, Peter, Sudbury, 1929, Murder.

2 The other murderers were Joseph Currie, a French man who killed Michael Donohue in 1921, and Tom Pornomarenko and Victor Szymonski, two Russian men who killed Constable Fred Davidson in 1938. Though their names indicate that they were of Eastern European descent, the murder committed by Pornomarenko and Szymonski has not been included in this analysis because both men immigrated to Canada from Russia and identified themselves as Russians.

3 Franca Iacovetta and Karen Dubinsky's examination of Angelina Napolitano (an Italian immigrant woman who killed her husband, received international attention, and inspired an international clemency campaign), and Carolyn Strange's assessment of two female murderers who drew a national audience (Clara Ford, a mulatto seamstress who killed a white youth, and Carrie Davies, a teenage British immigrant servant who confessed to the murder of her master), are among the most frequently cited

articles using capital case files. See Dubinsky and Iacovetta, 'Murder, Womanly Virtue, and Motherhood: The Case of Angelina Napolitano, 1911–1922,' *Canadian Historical Review* 77, no. 4 (1991): 505-531; and Carolyn Strange, 'Wounded Womanhood and Dead Men: Chivalry and the Trials of Clara Ford and Carrie Davies,' in *Gender Conflicts: New Essays in Women's History,* ed. Franca Iacovetta and Mariana Valverde (Toronto: University of Toronto Press, 1992), 149–88.

4 See Franca Iacovetta, 'Manly Militants, Cohesive Communities, and Defiant Domestics: Writing about Immigrants in Canadian Historical Scholarship,' *Labour/Le travail* 36 (Fall 1995): 218–19 and 238.

5 See, for instance, all of the contributions in *Sisters or Strangers? Immigrant, Ethnic, and Racialized Women in Canadian History*, ed. Marlene Epp, Franca Iacovetta, and Frances Swyripa (Toronto: University of Toronto Press, 2004).

6 Marlene Epp, Franca Iacovetta, and Frances Swyripa, 'Introduction,' in *Sisters or Strangers? Immigrant, Ethnic, and Racialized Women in Canadian History*, ed. Epp, Iacovetta, and Swyripa (Toronto: University of Toronto Press, 2004), 11.

7 See Frances Swyripa, 'Negotiating Sex and Gender in the Ukrainian Bloc Settlement: East Central Alberta between the Wars,' *Prairie Forum* 20, no. 2 (1995): 149–74; and Gregory Robinson, 'Rougher Than Any Other Nationality? Ukrainian Canadians and Crime in Alberta, 1915–1929,' *Journal of Ukrainian Studies* 16, nos. 1–2 (1991): 147–79. It is important to note that Swyripa and Robinson were influenced by a number of other studies that drew from court records and case files. For particular references to these sources, see Swyripa, 'Negotiating Sex and Gender,' 169.

8 Note that these were the labels employed by census enumerators. See Census of Canada, 1911, Copper Cliff sub-district, 5 October 2005, Library and Archives Canada (LAC), 14 February 2006. http://www.collectionscanada.ca/archivianet/1911/index-e.html

9 Oiva Saarinen, 'Ethnicity and the Cultural Mosaic in the Sudbury Area,' *Polyphony* 5, no. 1 (1983): 86. See also Canada, Bureau of the Census, *Population, Volume I* (Ottawa: 1924); and Canada, Bureau of the Census, *Population By Areas, Volume II* (Ottawa: 1933). It must be noted that since the 1921 and 1931 manuscript census is closed to researchers, it is impossible to ascertain the gender make-up of the Ukrainian segment of the population in either 1921 or 1931.

10 Nancy Forestell and Kerry Abel have studied gender roles and identities in northeastern Ontario, a region that has much in common with Sudbury. See Nancy Forestell, 'All That Glitters Is Not Gold: The Gender Dimensions of Work, Family, and Community Life in the Northern On-

tario Gold Mining Town of Timmins, 1901–1950,' PhD diss., University of Toronto, 1993; idem, 'Bachelors, Boarding-Houses, and Blind Pigs: Gender Construction in a Multi-Ethnic Mining Camp, 1909–1920,' in *A Nation of Immigrants: Women, Workers, and Communities in Canadian History, 1840s–1960s*, ed. Franca Iacovetta, Paula Draper, and Robert Ventresca (Toronto: University of Toronto Press, 1998), 251–90; idem, 'The Miner's Wife: Working-Class Femininity in a Masculine Context, 1920–1950,' in *Gendered Pasts: Historical Essays in Femininity and Masculinity in Canada*, ed. Kathryn McPherson, Cecilia Morgan, and Nancy Forestell, (Oxford: Oxford University Press, 1999), 139–57; and Kerry Abel, *Changing Places: History, Community, and Identity in Northeastern Ontario* (Montreal and Kingston: McGill-Queen's University Press, 2006). For a local history of Sudbury, see C.M. Wallace and Ashley Thomson, eds., *Sudbury: Rail Town to Regional Capital* (Toronto: Dundurn, 1993).

11 See Karen Dubinsky, *Improper Advances: Rape and Heterosexual Conflict in Ontario, 1880–1929* (Chicago: University of Chicago Press, 1993).

12 It must be noted that those who committed murder in and around the region were tried at the courthouse in Sudbury.

13 Various historians have made similar observations about this space. See, for example, Carolyn Strange and Tina Loo, *Making Good: Law and Moral Regulation in Canada, 1867–1939* (Toronto: University of Toronto Press, 1997); James W. St G. Walker, *'Race,' Rights, and the Law in the Supreme Court of Canada: Historical Case Studies* (Waterloo: Osgoode Society for Canadian Legal History and Wilfrid Laurier University Press, 1997); and Constance Backhouse, *Colour-Coded: A Legal History of Racism in Canada, 1900–1950* (Toronto: Osgoode Society for Canadian Legal History and University of Toronto Press, 1999).

14 Strange and Loo, *Making Good*, 149.

15 John Herd Thompson, *Ethnic Minorities during Two World Wars* (Ottawa: Canadian Historical Association, 1991), 3–4. It is significant that Thompson's reference to nativism builds on the work done by John Higham. In particular, Higham defines nativism as including 'every type and level of antipathy toward aliens, their institutions, and their ideas.' See Higham, *Strangers in the Land: Patterns of American Nativism* (New York: Atheneum, 1963), 3.

16 Carolyn Strange, 'Stories of Their Lives: The Historian and the Capital Case File,' in *On the Case: Explorations in Social History*, ed. Franca Iacovetta and Wendy Mitchinson (Toronto: University of Toronto Press, 1998), 25.

17 Karen Dubinsky, 'Telling Stories about Dead People,' in *On the Case:*

Explorations in Social History, ed. Franca Iacovetta and Wendy Mitchinson (Toronto: University of Toronto Press, 1998), 363.

18 Swyripa, 'Negotiating Sex and Gender,' 149–50.

19 I refer to this murder as the first documented murder to occur in Sudbury because sources that date back to the latter part of the nineteenth century and the first decade of the twentieth century have ceased to exist.

20 The name of the town was not reported in the local newspapers or in the trial proceedings. The local newspapers labelled the men 'Polacks,' 'Austrian Polacks,' and 'Ukrainians.' See, for instance, 'Brutal Murder,' *Sudbury Journal*, 2 October 1913, 1. It is significant that the labels used by the local newspapers corresponded with those employed by census enumerators. Lacking a 'Ukrainian' category until 1921, enumerators placed Ukrainians in the 'Polish,' 'Austro-Hungarian,' and 'Russian' manuscript census categories; thus there was very little consistency when it came to identifying Ukrainians during this period.

21 'Polack Laborer Was Foully Murdered Last Saturday Night,' *Sudbury Star*, 1 October 1913, 1.

22 'Coroner's Jury Accuses Kozemer,' *Sudbury Star*, 4 October 1913, 5.

23 LAC, RG13, vol. 2700, file CC121, pt 1, Peter Kozemer, *Rex vs. Kozemer*, 8.

24 This must have been an unusual request because the *Sudbury Star* summarized the incident in detail. Incidentally, none of the other lawyers involved in any of the subsequent trials made such a request. See 'Kozemer Trial Has Commenced,' *Sudbury Star*, 8 October 1913, 6.

25 Howard Palmer, 'Reluctant Hosts: Anglo-Canadian Views of Multiculturalism in the Twentieth Century,' in *Immigration in Canada: Historical Perspectives*, ed. Gerald Tulchinsky (Toronto: Copp Clark Longman, 1994), 306.

26 Edmund Bradwin, *The Bunkhouse Man: A Study of Work and Pay in the Camps of Canada, 1903–1914* (Toronto: University of Toronto Press, 1929), 92, 105–6. Also quoted in Kerry Abel, *Changing Places*, 346.

27 Thomas Dunk makes a similar argument about the ways in which white, working-class men defined themselves against the Aboriginal population in Thunder Bay. See Dunk, *It's A Working-Man's Town: Male Working Class Culture* (Montreal and Kingston: McGill-Queen's University Press, 1991), 96, 115, 130.

28 LAC, RG13, vol. 2700, file CC121, pt 1, Peter Kozemer, *Rex vs. Kozemer*, 21–3.

29 'Coroner's Jury Accuses Kozemer,' *Sudbury Star*, 4 October 1913, 5.

30 Robinson, 'Rougher Than Any Other Nationality?' 155.

31 Ralph Connor, *The Foreigner: A Tale of Saskatchewan* (Toronto: Westminster, 1909), 154.

32 Ibid., 155. It must be noted that Gregory Robinson employs the same
    quote to make a similar argument about how '"uncivilized" behaviour
    proved the Slav a brute.' See Robinson, 'Rougher Than Any Other Na-
    tionality?,' 173.
33 'Kozemer to Pay Death Penalty,' *Sudbury Star*, 11 October 1913, 1.
34 Ibid. It must be noted that this sentence was the first of its kind in the
    town's short history.
35 Ibid.
36 'Death Sentence Is Commuted. Peter Kozemer Not to Hang,' *Sudbury
    Star*, 20 December 1913, 1. See also 'Efforts to Spare Life of Kozemer,'
    Sudbury Star, 15 November 1913, 1.
37 'Twin Children Were Destroyed,' *Sudbury Star*, 25 July 1914, 1.
38 'Guilty, but Clemency Asked for 18-year-old Murderess,' *Sudbury Star*,
    24 October 1914, 1.
39 Swyripa, 'Negotiating Sex and Gender,' 150.
40 Ibid.
41 During this period, the strategy of attacking the character of a woman
    was also employed by prosecution lawyers involved in seduction cases.
    See Dubinsky, *Improper Advances*, 64–81.
42 See ibid., 138–40, for a related discussion about the perceived sexual im-
    proprieties of foreign women.
43 'Guilty, but Clemency Asked,' 1.
44 LAC, RG13, vol. 1479, file CC30, Catherine Hawryluk, Memorandum
    dated 14 February 1918.
45 Constance Backhouse, 'Desperate Women and Compassionate Courts:
    Infanticide in Nineteenth-Century Canada,' *University of Toronto Law
    Journal* 34, no. 4 (1984): 475.
46 For a discussion of the ways in which youth and gendered social expec-
    tations determined the outcomes of criminal trials during the latter half
    of the nineteenth century, see Susan Houston, 'The Role of the Criminal
    Law in Redefining "Youth" in Mid-Nineteenth-Century Upper Canada,'
    Historical Studies in Education 6, no. 3 (1994): 42–54.
47 There is an extensive historiography about domestic violence among
    family members. For a discussion of family violence in a Canadian
    context, see for example Franca Iacovetta, *Gatekeepers: Reshaping Im-
    migrant Lives in Cold War Canada* (Toronto: Between the Lines,
    2006), 222–31; Kathryn Harvey, 'To Love, Honour, and Obey: Wife-
    Battering in Working-Class Montreal, 1869–79,' *Urban History Review*
    19, no. 2 (1990): 128–41; idem, 'Amazons and Victims: Resisting
    Wife-Abuse in Working-Class Montreal, 1869-1879,' *Journal of the
    Canadian Historical Association* 2 (1991): 131–48; Terry L. Chapman,
    '"Till Death Do Us Part": Wife Beating in Alberta, 1905–1920,' *Al-*

berta History 36, no. 4 (1988): 13–22; Annalee Golz, '"If a Man's Wife Does Not Obey Him, What Can He Do?": Marital Breakdown and Wife Abuse in Late Nineteenth-Century and Early Twentieth-Century Ontario,' in *Law, Society, and the State: Essays in Modern Legal History*, ed. Louis Knafla and Susan Binnie (Toronto: University of Toronto Press, 1995), 324–50; Annalee Golz, 'Uncovering and Reconstructing Family Violence: Ontario Criminal Case Files,' in *On the Case: Explorations in Social History*, ed. Franca Iacovetta and Wendy Mitchinson (Toronto: University of Toronto Press, 1998), 289–311; Lisa Mar, 'The Tale of Lin Tee: Madness, Family Violence, and Lindsay's Anti-Chinese Riot of 1919,' in *Sisters or Strangers? Immigrant, Ethnic, and Racialized Women in Canadian History,* ed. Marlene Epp, Franca Iacovetta, and Frances Swyripa (Toronto: University of Toronto Press, 2004), 108–29; Kathleen Lord, '"Rendering the Invisible, Visible": A Day and Night on Notre-Dame Street in Saint-Henri, Quebec, June 12, 1895,' *Atlantis* 28, no. 1 (2003): 91–105; and Dubinsky, *Improper Advances*. Internationally, family violence has also received much attention from scholars. See, for instance, Linda Gordon, *Heroes of Their Own Lives: The Politics and History of Family Violence, Boston 1880–1960* (New York: Penguin, 1988); Elizabeth Pleck, *Domestic Tyranny: The Making of American Social Policy against Family Violence from Colonial Times to the Present* (Urbana: University of Illinois Press, 1987); Pat Ayers and Jan Lambertz, 'Marriage Relations, Money, and Domestic Violence in Working-Class Liverpool, 1919–1939,' in *Labour and Love: Women's Experience of Home and Family, 1850–1940*, ed. Jane Lewis (Oxford: Basil Blackwell, 1986); and Nancy Tomes, '"A Torrent of Abuse": Crimes of Violence between Working-Class Men and Women in London, 1840–1875,' *Journal of Social History* 11, no. 3 (1978): 328–45.

48 See, for instance, Joan Sangster, *Regulating Girls and Women: Sexuality, Family, and the Law in Ontario, 1920–1960* (Oxford: Oxford University Press, 2001); Kathryn Harvey, 'Amazons and Victims,' 131–48; Golz, '"If a Man's Wife Does Not Obey Him,"' 324–50; Golz, 'Uncovering and Reconstructing Family Violence,' 289–311; Mar, 'The Tale of Lin Tee,' 108–29; and Dubinsky, *Improper Advances*.

49 See 'Jealous Husband Shoots Wife in Quarrel,' *Sudbury Star*, 4 May 1910, 1. See also 'Committed on Charge of Attempted Murder,' *Sudbury Star*, 18 May 1910, 1.

50 LAC, RG13, vol. 1470, file 570A C-1, Wasyl Dejbuck, *Rex vs. Dejbuck*, 79.

51 Ibid., 52.

52 *Sudbury Journal*, 30 March 1916, 1.

53 Ibid.

54 These conclusions are similar to the ones made by James W. St G. Walker with regard to the treatment of Chinese immigrants. In particular, Walker states that the Chinese peril was a 'truth' constructed without evidence. Racism was an expression of the prevailing mentality and 'the law made observable (and imagined) physical differences real in human lives.' See Walker, 'A Case for Morality: The Quong Wing Files,' in *On the Case: Explorations in Social History*, ed. Franca Iacovetta and Wendy Mitchinson (Toronto: University of Toronto Press, 1998), 217. A similar argument is made by Lisa Mar in her article about domestic abuse in a Chinese-Canadian family in Lindsay, Ontario. See Mar, 'The Tale of Lin Tee.'

55 LAC, RG13, vol. 1470, file 570A C-1, Wasyl Dejbuck, *Rex vs. Dejbuck*, 56.

56 Ibid., 58.

57 Ibid., 50 and 62.

58 For similar arguments, see for example Dubinsky, *Improper Advances*; Franca Iacovetta, 'Making "New Canadians": Social Workers, Women, and the Reshaping of Immigrant Families,' in *Gender Conflicts: New Essays in Women's History*, ed. Franca Iacovetta and Mariana Valverde (Toronto: University of Toronto Press, 1993), 261–303; Regina Kunzel, *Fallen Women, Problem Girls: Unmarried Mothers and the Professionalization of Social Work, 1890–1945* (New Haven: Yale University Press, 1993); and Mary Odem, *Delinquent Daughters: Protecting and Policing Adolescent Female Sexuality in the United States, 1885–1920* (Chapel Hill: University of North Carolina Press, 1995).

59 Dubinsky, *Improper Advances*, 90.

60 AO, RG13, vol. 1555, File: Myhal, P. pt 1, 'Appeal Letter to the Minister of Justice,' 8.

61 'Boardinghouse Mistress Shot; Killer Caught,' *Sudbury Star*, 29 May 1929, 1.

62 LAC, RG13, vol. 1555, cc306, pt 1, Peter Myhal, 'Chief Louden's Letter to RCMP Criminal Investigation Department, September 24, 1929.'

63 'Peter Myhal to Die for Slaying Mrs. Rose Karas,' *Sudbury Star*, 21 September 1929, 1 and 11.

64 LAC, RG13, vol. 1555, cc306, pt 1, Peter Myhal, 'Chief Louden's Letter to RCMP Criminal Investigation Department, September 24, 1929.'

65 AO, RG22-392, box 151, File Myhal, Peter, Sudbury, 1929, Murder.

66 'After Slaying of Ex-Waitress,' *Sudbury Star*, 11 January 1939, 8.

67 For a discussion about patterns of property ownership in Sudbury, see

Donald Dennie, 'Sudbury 1883–1946: A Social Historical Study of Property and Class,' PhD Diss., Carleton University, 1989.

68 'Alice Kroiter Talented Girl Friends Claim,' *Sudbury Star*, 13 January 1939, 8.

69 'Devya Kroytor Oobita v Sodbori, Ont,' *Ukrainskyi holos*, 18 January 1939, 1, translated by Myron Momryk.

70 Olga Zembrzycki (nee Zyma), interview by author, Sudbury, 6 October 2004. Many Ukrainian women, like Zembrzycki, married men who descended from other ethnicities and thus they now have non-Ukrainian names. Including Zembrzycki's maiden name thus denotes her Ukrainian heritage.

71 LAC, RG13, vol. 1620, file cc497, John Ungurian pt IV, *Rex vs. John Ungurian*, 100.

72 LAC, RG13, vol. 1620, file cc497, John Ungurian Part III, Appeal from John Ungurian and his lawyer Landreville, 3 May 1939. Interestingly, this notion was also reported in the *Sudbury Star*. See 'Believe Royal Visit May Be Part of Cause,' *Sudbury Star*, 15 May 1939, 1.

Conclusion

Jim Mochoruk and Rhonda L. Hinther

While it is dangerous to make claims about the overall impact of a volume that has examined so many different aspects of the Ukrainian experience in Canada, it is perhaps fair to say that, when taken together, this collection of essays has reflected certain recent trends in historiography and has 'pushed' the historiographical discourse in new directions. To begin with, several of the essays have overtly challenged older, essentialist definition(s) of what it has meant to be Ukrainian or Ukrainian Canadian. It is also the case that collectively the authors have challenged the portrayal of Ukrainian Canadians that is still so common – that of the sturdy pioneer farmer making a go of it on unoccupied and often unwanted virgin land. Instead, the authors have shown Ukrainian Canadians living, working, and interacting in a variety of spaces and roles, working to improve their lot through an assortment of means. Readers of this collection have met urban and 'Central Canadian' Ukrainians, writers and intellectuals, national organizers, and everyday working people who have come to our attention in a host of unusual ways. The settlement experience of the 'stalwart peasant' has not been ignored – it has simply been reconsidered in certain key ways, so as to both underscore and interrogate his ongoing (and at times unsettling) influence on contemporary discourses surrounding Ukrainian identity.

It is also of some importance that several contributors have challenged key stereotypes concerning the Ukrainian left and have thereby contributed to a far more nuanced understanding of the stresses and strains of being a Ukrainian-Canadian radical in the twentieth century; they have also assessed how these stress points have shifted over time. Other contributors have interrogated how ethnic memories – some might say 'myths' – are created and maintained and have been willing to ask the questions *by whom, for what purposes,* and – perhaps most important – *to what ultimate ends?* It is also notable that questions of gender and generation have been broached regarding the varied roles of women and men. Indeed, one of the more interesting features of this collection is that several contributors offer detailed empirical reassessments of male leadership and men's roles among Ukrainian Canadians. Other ground that has rarely been covered, or that has been trod on far too softly, has also been surveyed and scrutinized in this volume. The Cold War era has been examined from several different perspectives, underscoring its local, national, and international consequences for a variety of Ukrainians and Ukrainian Canadians, both at home and abroad. Other difficult subjects – the roles played by pro-Nazis, Communists, and criminals – have been examined and handled in novel ways, making use of new sources; these controversial topics have been treated with remarkable candor and openness so as to offer fresh insights into community diversity and discord.

It also needs to be pointed out that despite the collection's focus on the 'new' and on more recent approaches and methodologies, the contributors have shown a marked willingness to examine the 'traditional' field of international and diplomatic history. In examining the 'larger picture' of diplomatic and international relations in some interesting new ways, the authors have situated Ukrainians in a broader transnational context and have showcased interethnic relations in some highly original ways.

Yet however broad-ranging and (we hope) exciting the trends represented by these essays, we realize that much work still needs to be done. The postwar era is still vastly understudied. In particular, few studies have dealt with the increasing rates of assimilation – a phenomenon that has certainly been accentuated by intermarriage as well as by the internal migration of Ukrainian Canadians from rural to urban to suburban settings, and – in many cases – from Western to Eastern Canada. The Ukrainian-Canadian left, the relationship between Ukrainian Canadians and Soviet and post-Soviet Ukraine, and the organizational and social lives of almost all Ukrainian-Canadian communities also warrant further study for the years after 1945.

Several other matters demand further consideration. The relationship (or rather relationships) between Ukrainian Canadians and the state needs much more study. The state's role in shaping Ukrainians into Canadian citizens and the influence of multiculturalism policies in constructing a broader notion of Canadian 'Ukrainian-ness' are logical starting points. It is also the case that some attention must be paid to how these policies have affected those assimilated Ukrainian Canadians who have increasingly lived their lives outside the organized Ukrainian community. Like it or not, one trend among Ukrainian Canadians has been a rejection of organized, 'ethnic' community life in favour of lives lived within the mainstream – and this must be studied. With some notable exceptions, Ukrainians' day-to-day interactions with non-Ukrainians have also received little scholarly attention.

Finally, much more needs to be known about the ordinary, everyday lives of Ukrainian people. The work of the Kule Centre for Ukrainian and Canadian Folklore is making great strides in this regard, as are the ongoing projects of several contributors to this collection, but there are still many gaps in our knowledge. Urban Ukrainians are remarkably understudied. So, too, are elements of Ukrainian family life and the roles and experiences of women and ordinary men within the family, the workplace, and the community. Articulations of Ukrainian masculinity and femininity, changes in these over time, their influence on roles and opportunities, and their intersection with ethnicity and class at work, at home, and in the organized community offer especially exciting paths for scholarly investigation. Similarly, the experiences of children – their place in the household, the community, and the schools and in many instances their role as intermediaries between family and state – beg further consideration. In particular, how children negotiate (or reject) their identity as Ukrainian, Ukrainian Canadian, and Canadian (and how these have been manifest) requires broader examination.

As one considers this somewhat daunting list of what still needs to be done in the field, one thing becomes self-evident: while all of these questions involve the notion of Ukrainian-Canadian identity, they stem from trends that are redefining Canadian, North American, and even global scholarship. Indeed, as this collection demonstrates, many practitioners of Ukrainian-Canadian studies have already been affected by these intellectual currents. It almost goes without saying that their new research will in turn affect those currents, just as the best work in the field has helped redefine Canadian historiography from the 1970s to the present. It seems certain that scholars, without abandoning the area of Ukrainian-Canadian studies, will be pushing the field even deeper into the mainstream of Western discourse. This is precisely as it should be.

Contributors

Jennifer Anderson is currently Labour Archivist at Library and Archives Canada. She has worked as assistant curator at the Canadian Museum of Civilization, historical researcher for Foreign Affairs Canada, and sessional lecturer at the University of Ottawa and Carleton University. She holds a PhD in Canadian history, and a Masters of Arts in Central/East European and Russian Area Studies. This chapter comes from her dissertation, entitled 'Propaganda and Persuasion: The Canadian-Soviet Friendship Society, 1949–1960.' She has also published in *Archivaria*, the *Journal of the Canadian Historical Association*, and Slavonic Papers.

Jars Balan is the Administrative Coordinator of the Kule Ukrainian Canadian Studies Centre at the Canadian Institute of Ukrainian Studies. He has authored numerous articles on a wide variety of Ukrainian-Canadian themes, his areas of special interest being Ukrainian Canadian literature, theatre and church history. He has also edited several books and journals and had his English translations of literary works by Ukrainian and Ukrainian-Canadian writers published in Canada and Ukraine. In addition to his academic endeavours Jars been active in the field of heritage tourism, having organized Alberta's Kalyna Country Ecomuseum and consulted on rural tourism projects in Ukraine.

Serge Cipko is Coordinator of the Ukrainian Diaspora Studies Initiative, Kule Ukrainian Canadian Studies Centre at CIUS, and Assistant

Adjunct Professor in the Department of History and Classics, University of Alberta. He is the author of *St. Josaphat Ukrainian Catholic Cathedral, Edmonton: A History (1902–2002)* (2009); co-author, with Glenna Roberts, of *One-Way Ticket: The Soviet Return-to-the-Homeland Campaign, 1955–1960* (2008); and co-editor, with Natalie Kononenko, of *Champions of Philanthropy: Peter and Doris Kule and their Endowments* (2009). His book, *Ukrainians in Argentina, 1897–1950: The Making of a Community*, will be published in 2011.

Karen Gabert completed the Master of Arts in Public History program at Carleton University, focusing her research on public commemorations and heritage sites. She has worked on a number of heritage and public history research projects in Ottawa and Edmonton, including oral and archival research for the Ukrainian Village. Karen currently works for a consulting firm in Edmonton.

Rhonda L. Hinther earned her PhD in History at McMaster University. Currently Head, Exhibits Research at the Canadian Museum for Human Rights, she was previously a curator with the Canadian Museum of Civilization. Her research interests include oral history and radical and social justice activism. Her work has been published in *Manitoba History, Atlantis,* and *Labour/Le travail*. In 2008, she won the Sutherland Article Prize for children's history. Hinther is currently completing a book on Ukrainian radicalism and regularly consults on historical films, most recently 'The Oldest Profession in Winnipeg' and 'Black Field,' an official selection of the 2009 Vancouver Film Festival.

S. Holyck Hunchuck is an art historian and independent scholar in Ottawa. She holds a combined BA (Hons) in Art History and Architecture and a Master's degree in Canadian Art History (both Carleton University). Her interests include the intersection of modern architecture in Canada with Ukrainian peasant culture. She is an active member of the Society for the Study of Architecture in Canada and a frequent contributor to the *Material Culture Review*. Her work on Ottawa's Ukrainian Labour Temples, an excerpt of which is included here, received the city of Ottawa's Heritage Prize for architectural writing.

Lindy Ledohowski completed her English BA (Hons) at the University of Manitoba, and her BEd (English and History), MA, and PhD (English) at the University of Toronto, and completed a postdoctoral fellowship in the Department of English at the University of Ottawa. Now she is an Assistant Professor in the Department of English at St Jerome's University in the University of Waterloo. She is a scholar of contemporary Canadian literature and focuses on Ukrainian Canadian literature in English, having published numerous scholarly articles on this topic.

Andrij Makuch is Research Coordinator for the Kule Ukrainian Canadian Studies Centre of the Canadian Institute of Ukrainian Studies as well as Senior Editor for the *Internet Encyclopedia of Ukraine*. He previously was a researcher for the Ukrainian Cultural Heritage Village and taught at the University of Saskatchewan. He is the author of *Hlus Church: A Narrative History* (1989), editor of journal issues dealing with interwar Ukrainian Canadian history and the Holodomor in Ukraine, and compiler of *Encyclopedia of Ukraine: Index and* Errata (2001).

Orest T. Martynowych studied History at the University of Manitoba (BA [Hons], MA) and the University of Toronto. He has been a consultant for the Historic Sites Service, Alberta Culture and Multiculturalism; a research associate at the Canadian Institute of Ukrainian Studies, University of Alberta; and a sessional lecturer and visiting research scholar at the Centre for Ukrainian Canadian Studies, University of Manitoba. He is the author of *Ukrainians in Canada: The Formative Years, 1891–1924* (1991).

Peter Melnycky was born and raised in Winnipeg, Manitoba. He earned his MA in Social Sciences from the University of Manitoba. His thesis: 'A Political History of the Ukrainian Community in Manitoba, 1899–1922,' was awarded the Manitoba Historical Society's Margaret McWilliams Medal for outstanding work on Manitoba history. Since 1982 he has been a historian with Alberta Historic Sites and Museums. He has written on the history of Alberta and has a particular interest in fur trade, settlement, and military history.

Jim Mochoruk is a Professor of History at the University of North Dakota where he teaches Canadian, US, and British Imperial History. His research interests include the history of northern resource development, the social history of Winnipeg, and left wing social and political movements in the 20th century. Mochoruk's publications include: '*Formidable Heritage*': *Manitoba's North and the Cost of Development, 1870–1930* (2004); *The People's Co-op: The Life and Times of a North End Institution* (2000); and most recently, the chapter on Thomas Greenway in Ferguson and Wardhaugh (eds), *Manitoba Premiers of the 19th and 20th Centuries* (2010).

Jaroslav (Jerry) Petryshyn holds a PhD (history) from the University of Western Ontario. Currently, he serves as Dean, School of Health Wellness & Career Studies, at Grande Prairie Regional College. The author of four books including *Peasant in the Promised Land: Canada and the Ukrainians, 1891–1914,* Dr Petryshyn has served as the Alberta representative on the Historic Sites and Monuments Board of Canada, Chairperson of the 2005 Alberta History Centennial Project, and more recently as Vice Chair of the Alberta Press Council.

Stacey Zembrzycki is a Social Sciences and Humanities Research Council of Canada postdoctoral fellow in the History Department at Concordia University where she is also affiliated with the Centre for Oral History and Digital Storytelling. Her first book, tentatively entitled *Sharing Authority with Baba: Wrestling with Memories of Community*, is under review with the University of British Columbia Press. In addition to her website, www.sudburyukrainians.ca, her work on Sudbury's Ukrainian community has been published in *Labour/Le travail* and the *Journal of Canadian Studies*.

Index

Aberhart, William 104, 121
All Peoples' Mission 5, 16
All-Union Society for Friendship with
    Foreign Countries (VOKS) 280, 282,
    284–8, 291, 293–8, 302–3, 304–9,
    311–12, 314
Anderson, Jennifer 14, 222, 279
Angus, Ian 8, 18, 332, 333, 358, 368
Aramburo, Pedro 266
Arbeiter Ring 335
Arcand, Adrien 183, 200, 201
Ashworth, Eleanor 307
Association of United Ukrainian Canadi-
    ans (AUUC) 13, 21, 23, 51, 53, 171,
    222, 234, 258, 268, 277, 280, 208,
    367, 405, 424, 426
Avakumovic, Ivan 8, 18, 51, 358
Avery, Donald 8, 36, 332, 333

Backhouse, Constance 447
Bader, Kate 298, 308
Bakalian, Anny 85
Balan, Jars 12, 22, 104, 129
Batiuk, John 64
Baxter, Ted 292, 295, 311
Behie, Joe 37
Bennett, R.B. 228
Biderman, Morris 308

Bilash, Radomir 65
Bilecki, Betsey 38
Birkett, Blair 262, 263, 267
Bodnaruk, Steve 449
Bogayevsky, Yuri 244
Borden, Robert 225–6
Bosovych, Vasyl 384
Bosowich, William 350
Bossy, Wolodymyr 175–6, 183, 189
Bott, Berhard 200
Boychuck, John 333, 339, 342, 350, 352,
    359, 362, 366, 370, 380, 386, 387
Boychuk, John (see Boychuck, John)
Boyd, John (Boychuck) 280, 282, 288,
    290, 296, 307, 308, 312
Bradwin, Edwin 443
Brunelle-Pratte, Jeannette 306
Buck, Tim 332–3, 341–2, 345, 351–3,
    355–60, 363–6, 389
Buduchnist natsii (Future of the Nation)
    179, 190, 192, 193, 198
Bugaiev, Alejandra R. 267
Buhay, Beckie 355, 358, 359
Buhay, Michael 350, 358
Bukovynian Orthodox Church 418,
    422
Burdin, Vladimir 309
Burns, 'Kid' 359

Canada's Ukrainians: Negotiating an Identity 10
Canadian Bolsheviks 358
Canadian Communism: The Stalin Years and Beyond 358
Canadian Institute of Ukrainian Studies (CIUS) 7, 66, 123
Canadian Jewish Congress 237, 290
Canadian Jewish Weekly 304
Canadian Labour Party 337, 339, 341, 347,
Canadian League for the Liberation of Ukraine 241
Canadian Peace Congress 40, 296
Canadian Polish Congress 237
Canadian Slav Committee 43, 268, 282, 296
Canadian Slavonic Papers 7
Canadian Social Democratic Party 338
Canadian Tribune 283, 292, 308
Canadian Ukrainian Youth Association (CYMK or SUMK) 151
Canadian Union of Fascists 200
Canadian-Soviet Friendship Month 284, 291–5, 299, 302, 304, 307
Canadian-Soviet Friendship Society (CSFS) 222, 279–313
Canon, James 357–8
Carr, Sam 333, 361, 364, 365, 388
Carter, Charlotte 287, 301–2, 304–5, 307, 312
Carter, Dyson 279, 280, 282–313
Centre for Ukrainian Studies at St Andrew's College 7
Chair of Ukrainian Studies at the University of Toronto 7
Chamberlain, Neville 193
Chomecki, Emil 366
Christian National Socialist Party 183
Chrustawka, Ambrose 160
Chwaliboga (Khvaliboga), Stephan 381, 387, 388

Cipko, Serge 14, 222, 257, 299
Clavir, Leo 307
Clissold, Stephan 264
Colegate, Harry 302
Comintern (*see* Communist International)
Committee for the Return to the Homeland 257, 269
Communist International 15, 181, 184–6, 206, 230, 329, 281, 330–1, 333–4, 339, 341, 343, 345, 348, 353, 354–65, 383
The Communist Party in Canada 358
Communist Party of Canada (CPC) 15, 25–6, 28, 35, 38–40, 230–1, 280–2, 285, 304, 312, 330–4, 338–44, 346–9, 352–61, 363–7, 382–4, 388–93, 405, 414–15, 418, 420
Congress of Canadian Women (CCW) 41
Connolly, Dr Christopher F. 117–18
Connor, Ralph 5, 444
Conquest, Robert 244
Co-operative Commonwealth Federation (CCF) 192, 296, 311, 367, 391
Corey, William 141
Crath, Paul 119, 137–8
Crew, Spencer R. 73–4
Cross, Charles W. 112, 118
Cuban Missile Crisis 40
Culture and Life 303

Danylchuk, John 121
Danylchuk, Maria Kostyniuk 121
Decore (Dikur), John (Ivan) 110
Decore, John 110, 237–8
Dejbuck, Steve 448, 449
Dejbuck, Wasyl 448, 449, 451–2
Deschenes Commission 244–5
Deschenes, Jules 245–6
Diefenbaker, John 240, 241
Dilo 137

Displaced Persons (DPs) 4, 11, 35–6, 205, 235, 258,
Dolny, Eugene 32, 285–6
Dontsov, Dmytro1 77
Drozdowych family 416, 418
Drozdowych, Carl 406, 414–16, 418
Drozdowych, Kazimierz 415–16, 418
Dubinsky, Karen 436, 440, 450
Dzyza, Fred 451

Edmonton First Ukrainian Presbyterian Church 112
Edmonton First Ukrainian United Church 112
Elcheshen, Demetrius 191, 200
Endicott, James 40, 296
Esselwein, J. 353, 356
Ewach, Honore 151
Ewanchuk, Michael 9
Ewen, Tom 349, 358, 360

Farr, Joseph 200
Le Fasciste Canadien 183, 201
Federation of Russian Canadians (FRC) 267, 270, 283, 286, 287–9, 292, 294, 297, 309,
Federation of Ukrainian Labour-Farmer Organizations (FULFO) 390, 392
Federation of Ukrainian Social Democrats (FUSD) 137, 138, 405, 407
Fedun, William P. 120
Fee, Margery 89
Ferbey, Dmytro 147, 152, 156, 158
Ferbey, Michael 147
Finnish Organization of Canada (FOC) 292, 294
Fodchuk, Roman 59, 60, 63, 65, 71
The Foreigner 5, 444
Frager, Ruth 9, 26
Francis, Daniel 89
Franko, Ivan 129, 137, 417

Friends of the Ukrainian Village Society 66
Fujarchuk, Thomas 113, 114

Gabert, Karen 13, 22, 54, 401, 402
Gamara, Francisco 267
Gartner, Emil 283, 285, 306
Gartner, Fagel 285
Gartner, Fanny 306
Genik, Ivan 141
George, Rosemary Marangoly 90
Gerus, Oleh 7, 8
Gilbert, Isidoro 273
Globe Tours 29
Gonsett, Roman 111
Gorbachev, Mikhail 244
Gordon, Charles William 5, 444
Gousev, Fedor 234
Gouzenko, Igor 237, 259, 279, 281, 305, 312, 418
Gowda, Michael (Mykhailo) 110, 111, 112, 117
Great Famine (see Holodomor)
Green, Rayna 92
Greene, Melvin 96
Grekul, Lisa 85–90, 93, 98–9
Griwieniec, Lydia Elena 272–3
Gulay, Dr Ivan 177

Haideychuk, Petro 408, 410–11, 415–17, 419–21
Hamilton, Archie 285
Harney, Robert 88
Harvey, Louise 302
Hawenka, Dolly 34
Hawenka, Josie 34
Hawrelak, Jacob (Yakiv) 140
Hawrelak, William 59, 123
Hawreliak, Mykhailo 68
Hawryluk, Anton 446
Hawryluk, Catherine 445–8
Heaps, A.A. 192–3

A Heritage in Transition: Essays in the History of Ukrainians in Canada 7, 8, 16, 17

Hethman, Michael 176, 181–2, 188, 192, 195, 205

Himka, John-Paul 202

Hindenburg, General Paul von 176

Hinther, Rhonda L. 3, 13, 21, 23, 221, 401, 412, 417, 465

Hitler, Adolf 180–8, 193, 195–6, 198–9, 203, 205, 231, 234, 245

Hladiy, Kay 281, 306

Hlynka, Anthony 233, 237

Hohol, Bert 64

Holmes, Dan (Chomitsky) 349, 355, 360–1, 363

Holmes, Fred (Chomitsky) 349, 355

Holodomor (Great Famine) 75, 180, 200, 203, 230, 244, 385

Horon, Tony 150

Hoy, Jimmy 91

Hrycyna, Hieronym 160

Hryhirchuk, Harry 136–7

Hryniuk, Stella 10

Hubaly, Nick 37

Hubarchuk, Panas 268

Hughson, Richard L. 117–18

Huk, Yuz 132–3

Hunchuck, S. Holyck 15, 21, 403

Iacovetta, Franca436–7

Independent Greek Church (IGC) 111, 113, 115

Industrial Workers of the World (IWW) 405, 410

International Brigades 10, 413

Irchan, Myroslav 352, 377–8, 385–6, 390, 392

Ivanyshyn, Myhkailo 384

Jewish Labor League 283

Johnson, Dorothy 308

Journal of Ukrainian Studies 7, 10

Kaganovich, Lazar 190

Kalyna's Song 85

Kanadai Magyar Munkas 303

Kanadyiskyi farmer 121, 176

Kantselaria, Ruska (*see* Alberta Real Estate Company)

Kapustiansky, Mykola 177, 196

Karas, Rose 448, 450–3

Kardash, Mary 41–2, 280

Kavanagh, Jack 342

Kaye, Vladimir 6, 7

Kealey, Greg 8

Keefer, Janice Kulyk 98

Kendy, D.S. 296

Khomitsky, Theodore 387

Khrushchev, Nikolai 38, 284, 287, 293, 295, 299, 311–12, 420

Kiliar, John (Ivan) 110

King, Thomas 92–3

King, Willliam Lyon Mackenzie 27, 188, 279

Kingston Eight 388

Kinsmen, Gary 38

Kiriak, Elias 140, 199

Kiriak, Illia 14, 22, 104, 105, 129–62

Kiriak, Ivan 131–3

Kiriak, Petro 131–2, 137

Kiriak, Tekliia 131

Klimashevsky, Vladzimir 264, 270

Klymasz, Robert 7, 59, 87

Knysh, A. 408

Kobzei, Toma (*see* Kobzey, Toma)

Kobzey, Toma 350, 366, 381, 386–90

Kolasky, John 39

Kolisnyk, William 347, 361

Komarnizki, J. 113

Kon, Louis 283, 291, 308, 312

Konovalets, Colonel Yevhen 177, 181, 187, 195–6

Korol, Misha 35, 288, 301

Korol, Panas 268
Kossar, Wolodymyr 177, 188, 197
Kostash, Myrna 87, 98
Kovalevich, Ida 281
Kowalewich, Edith (*see* Kovalevich, Ida)
Kozemer, Peter 442, 444–7, 449, 452
Kraikivsky, Hryhorii (*see* Krakiwsky, Gregory)
Krakiwsky, Gregory 111, 117, 120
Krat, Pavlo (*see* Crath, Paul)
Krawchuk, Peter 36, 269, 333–4, 363
Kremar, Roman 119–20, 137–9, 147
Kremyr, Stanley 37
Krikewsky, Gregory 113
Kroiter, Alice 440–1, 448, 453–6
Kryschuk, Myroslaw 59
Kryvutsky, Fr. Myron 198
Kudryk, Wasyl 199
Kupchenko, Victor 161
Kurhanewich, Mary 448–50, 452–3
Kurhanewich, Peter 448
Kuriets, Vasyl (*see* Corey, William)
Kurmanovych, Viktor 177
Kushnir, Wasyl (Basil) 179, 190–1. 193, 198, 202

Labor Progressive Party (LPP) 25, 37, 41, 279, 280–5, 289–90, 292, 294, 296, 299, 305, 310, 312–13
Lacroix, Wilfrid 192
Ladyka, Basil 156, 198
Lafond, R.T. 307,
Lakusta, Frank 57–9, 62, 66
Lakusta, Iwan 134
Lapchuk, Anne 34, 403
Lapointe, Jean-Pierre 422
Laxer, Robert 283
League of Ukrainian Organizations 392
Ledohowski, Lindy 13, 22, 85
Leech, Jim 287, 295, 311–12
Lehr, John 8
LeMessurier, Mary 66

Lindbergh, Charles 188
Lindstrom, Varpu 9
Lobay, Danylo 15, 229, 329–30, 333, 366, 376–93
Loewen, Royden 9
Loginov, V. 282
Lougheed, Peter 62, 64
Lowenthal, David 56, 71
Lowrie, Howard 311
Loyalties in Conflict: Ukrainians in Canada during the Great War 8
Luchkovich, Michael 159–62
Luciuk, Lubomyr 10
Lucock, Rae 296
Lupul, Manoly 7, 11, 85, 98
Lyhavskyi, Ivan 110
Lysenko, Vera 10

Macallum, Joe 141
Macdonald, Jack 340, 342–3, 346–7, 353–5, 358–60
MacGregor, David 407, 416–19, 422, 424
Mackie, H.A. 225, 228
Magnuson, Bruce 307
Makuch, Andrij 15, 21, 25, 105, 221, 330, 376
Mandel, Eli 91, 98
Manion, Robert 192
Manuilsky, Dimitri 365
Marriot, Charlie 348, 355, 359
Martynowych, Orest 7, 8, 9, 14, 104–51, 173, 221, 329
Marunchak, Michael 6, 131
Marusia 154
Marx, Karl 287, 289, 352
McCutcheon, Rosalind 307
Megas, Osyp 225–6
Mein Kampf 182, 199
Melnycky, Peter 13, 106, 107
Melnyk, George 88
Men in Sheepskin Coats 10

Michael Hrushevsky Institute (*see* Mykhailo Hrushevsky Ukrainian Institute)

Michael Hrushevsky Student Residence (*see* Mykhailo Hrushevsky Ukrainian Institute)

Mochoruk, Jim 3, 14, 21, 25, 105, 221, 330–1, 465

Momryk, Myron 10, 412–13

Moniuk, Nancy 419

Moral Reform League 120

Moriarty, William 343, 358

Moroz, Valentine 243

Morozov, Alexander 266, 266

Morris, Leslie 333, 340, 342, 348–9, 353–6, 360–1, 363, 365–6

Moscow News 303

Mucciy, Nicholas 410

Mulroney, Brian 244–6

Murphy, Harvey 359

Mussolini, Benito 181, 184–5, 187, 199, 201

Mycak, Sonia 87

Myhal, Peter 436, 450–5, 457

Mykhailo Hrushevsky Ukrainian Institute 121, 147, 150, 152–3, 158, 161

Myroniuk, Martin 413

Myroslav Sichynsky Enlightenment-Labour Society 137

Narodna volia 392

National Council for Canadian-Soviet Friendship 279, 283

National Party of Canada (NPC) 200

National Unity Party (NUP) 200–1

Navis, John 35–6, 333, 339, 341–2, 355–6, 359, 362–7, 377–81, 383, 386–7, 389, 380

Navizivsky, Ivan (*see* Navis, John)

Naviziwsky, John (*see* Navis, John)

Neilsen, Dorise 285

Neilsen, Sally 290

New World Films 298

News-Facts 287, 293–4, 296–7, 299–303, 307, 311

Nixon, Richard 293

Northern Neighbors 287, 290, 299, 301, 312

Nova hromada 138–40

Novak, Apolinariy 151–2

Novyi shliakh 177–81, 183–5, 187, 189, 191–3, 195, 198, 203, 258, 267, 269, 441

Novyny 139–40

Nowak, Gregory 141

Nykolyshyn, Lucy 24

Nykolyshyn, Zenovy 23–4, 28, 30, 38–9

Okulevich, G. 267

Oleniuk, Nick 384

Oleskow, Dr Josef 110

Oliver, Frank 110

One Big Union (OBU) 339, 342

Organization of Ukrainian Nationalists (OUN) 174, 177–81, 183–9, 191, 195, 196–7, 200, 202–4

Ostashewsky, Roman 65

Our History: The Ukrainian Labour-Farmer Movement in Canada, 1907–1991 333

Pacholachak, Steve 413

Padlock Law 37, 291

Park, Frank 300–1

Park, Libbie 300–1

Patriquen, R. 308

Pauk, Paul 307

Pavlychenko, Tymish 188

Pavlyk, Mykhailo 137

Pearson, Laurence 65

Pearson, Lester 58, 233, 239, 241, 259, 260

Penner, Jacob (Jake) 306, 360

Penner, Norman 8

People's Co-op Dairy 29, 331, 336,
Peron, Juan Domingo 266
Peter and Doris Kule Centre for
   Ukrainian and Canadian Folklore 11,
   467
Petro Mohyla Institute 154
Petrushevich, Ivan 225
Petryshyn, Jaroslav 223, 329, 401
Picard, Philippe 261, 264
Pidhainy, Oleh 259
Pierce, Lorne 161
Pohorecky, Michael 177, 183–4, 187,
   203
Polish Weekly Chronicle 292
Polowy, Hannah 41
Popovich, Matthew 329, 333, 339, 341–
   3, 347–50, 352, 356, 358–9, 363, 365–
   7, 377–80, 383, 386–8, 391
Postup 141
Power, Charles 'Chubby' 227
Prairie Forum 7
Pravda 388–92
Progressive Farmers Grain Company 116
Prokop, Mary 40
Prokopchak, Peter 288, 381
Prosvita 118, 137
Prychodko, Nicholas 302
Pylypas, Theodore 387

Rankin, K. 308–9
Ranok 113
Roberts, Glenna 299
Robertson, Norman 197, 235–6
Robin, Martin 200
Robinson, Gregory 437, 444
Robochyi narod 441
Rodney, William 331
Rosenberg, Dr Alfred 176, 180
Roslak, M. 268
Royal Commission on the Status of
   Women 41
Ruddick, Clara (Canfield) 122

Ruddick, Ervin Canfield 123
Ruddick, John Paul (*see* Rudyk, John
   Paul) 122–3
Rudyk Block 116, 120
Rudyk Hall 113
Rudyk Scholarship Fund 118
Rudyk, Anna (Danylchuk) 121
Rudyk, Apolonia (Kotkewych) 109
Rudyk, Dmytro 109
Rudyk, John Paul 110
Rudyk, Julia (Stefanyna) 109, 121
Rudyk, Maria 109–10
Rudyk, Michael 109, 113
Rudyk, Paul 13, 103–5, 107–23, 329
Rudyk, Phillip 122
Rudyk, Theodore 108–9
Ruryk, Ivan 130–1, 144, 146, 158
Ruryk, Natunia 130
Ruska narodna torhovlia (Ruthenian
   National Trading Company, or
   National Cooperative Company) 115
Rusko-tserkovne bratstvo sv Nykolaia
   (*see* St Nicholas Ruthenian Church
   Brotherhood) 110
Rusko-ukrainska *bursa* 114, 117
Ruthenian Bureau (*see* Alberta Real
   Estate Company) 113
Ruthenian Grain Bureau 116
Ruthenian-Ukrainian *bursa* (*see* Rusko-
   ukrainska bursa)
Ruthenian-Ukrainian Radical Party 129
Ryan, Oscar 347–8, 354

St John's Ukrainian Orthodox Church
   147, 160
St John's Institute (*see* Michael Hru-
   shevsky Institute)
St Barbara's Russo-Orthodox Church
   111
St Joachim's Roman Catholic Parish 110
St Josaphat's Parish 110–11
St Laurent, Louis 57, 241

St Mary's Orthodox Church 143
St Mary's Ukrainian Catholic Church 454–5
St Nicholas Ruthenian Church Brotherhood 110
Salsberg, Joe 358
Salverson, Laura Goodman 161
Sangster, Joan 8
Savaryn, Peter 62
Scargill, M.H. 161
Schickedanz, Arno 182
Schmidt, Horst 62
Semaka, Dmytro 161
Sembay, Ivan 352, 377–8, 385, 392
Semczuk, Stephan 179, 198
Semeniuk, Ivan 138, 147
Senyk-Hrybivsky, Captain Omelian 177
Shandro, Andrew 117–9, 147
The Shattered Illusion 332
Shatulsky, Matthew 36, 157, 292, 333, 339, 342, 350, 362, 365–7, 377, 379–81, 386–7
Shatulsky, Myron 32–3, 38
Shatulsky, Olga 37
Sheptytsky, Andrei 114
Shevchenko Scientific Society 137
Shklanka, Elias 145
Shumuk, Danylo 243–4
Sifton, Clifford 4
Sims, James E. 73–4
Sisters or Strangers: Immigrant, Ethnic, and Racialized Women in Canadian History 26
Sitting Bull 93–7
Skelton, O.D. 196–7
Skoropadsky, Danylo 176, 183, 186
Skoropadsky, Pavlo 173, 175–7, 181, 195–6, 229
Skrypnychuk, Yuri 410
Smith, Stewart 333, 342, 348, 358–66
Smyt, Mykhailo 387, 389
Snihurowych, Dr M. 59

Sochasky, Anna 281, 308–10
Social Credit 104, 121, 194, 206, 233
Social Democratic Party of Canada 225, 335, 338
Socialist Party of Canada (SPC) 339
Society for the Struggle against Communism (Tovarystvo Borotby z Komunizmom) 185
Sons of Freedom 267
Sons of the Soil (see Syny zemli)
Sopulak, M. 59
Soviet Friendship Month 284, 291–4, 302, 307
Soviet Literature 37, 303
Soviet Woman 37, 303
Spanish Civil War 10, 413
Spaulding, Margaret 307
Spector, Maurice 355, 358
SS Division Halychyna 36
SS St Louis 194
Stalin, Joseph 35, 38, 245, 287, 304, 311, 380
Starchuk, Orest 159
Starr, Michael 239
Stechishin, Myroslav 137–8, 147, 149, 155–6, 199
Stefanitsky, Katherine 41
Stefanyk, Yuri 162
Stetsko, Yaroslav 189
Stokaluk, John 359, 364
Stotsky, Ivan 384
Strange, Carolyn 436, 440
Strashok, Hazel 44
Stroessner, Alfredo 263, 268
Suknaski, Andrew 22, 86, 90–9
Sushko, Roman 177, 185–7, 195–6
Svarich, Peter 110–11, 117, 148
Swerhun, Edna 453
Swyripa, Frances 6–9, 26, 89, 437, 441, 446
Swystun, Wasyl 157, 197
Sydorenko, Hrychorii 226

Syny zemli (*Sons of the Soil*) 129–30, 144, 148, 151, 153–9, 161–2

Taras Shevchenko Reading Society 110
Taylor, Frederick 306
Temperance League of Alberta 120
Teresio, William 36, 280, 310
Thompson, John Herd 8, 439
Tichnovich, Alek 285–6
Tomashewsky, Toma 138
Topolnisky, George 64
Torriani, Carlos 265, 272
Tovarystvo Samostiina Ukraina (Society for an Independent Ukraine) 119
Tovstogan, A. 385–6, 388, 291, 294, 297–8, 303, 311–12
Trident Press 151, 162
Trotsky, Leon 190, 343
Truch, Andrew 179
Trudeau, Pierre 241–3
Trylovsky, Kyrylo 137
Tweedale, Margaret 311

Ukrainian Association of Victims of Russian Communist Terrorism 302
Ukrainian Autocephalous Orthodox Church 285
Ukrainian Bookstore 147, 158
Ukrainian Canadian Citizen's Committee (UCCC) 225–6
Ukrainian Canadian Committee (UCC) 35, 36, 232–9, 242, 245–7
Ukrainian Canadian Congress 66
Ukrainian Canadian Herald 45
Ukrainian Catholic Brotherhood (UCB) 173–4, 179, 198, 229
Ukrainian Catholic Church 103, 173, 442, 454, 455
Ukrainian Church Brotherhood 110
Ukrainian Cultural Heritage Village 13, 22, 54, 57–60

Ukrainian Cultural Heritage Village Society 57, 59–60, 63, 66, 74
Ukrainian Day 57, 244
Ukrainian Famine (*see* Holodomor)
Ukrainian Garden 118
Ukrainian Greek Catholic Church 240
Ukrainian Labour Farmer Temple Association (ULFTA) 24, 26–8, 30–1, 38, 42, 43, 74, 179, 190, 221, 229–31, 233–4, 330–1, 333, 336–8, 342, 346–7, 350–3, 356, 359, 361–2, 366, 376–93, 405, 410–16, 420, 424
Ukrainian Labour News (see *Ukrainski robitnychi visty*)
Ukrainian Labour Organization 392
Ukrainian Labour Temple Association (ULTA) 336, 338–9
Ukrainian Labour-Farmer Mass Organizations (ULFMO) 376–8, 382, 387
Ukrainian Military Organization (UVO) 177–80, 195
Ukrainian National Federation (UNF) 35, 173–4, 177–9, 183–4, 186–8, 195–200, 205, 229, 232, 258
Ukrainian National Republic 224, 226–7
Ukrainian Pioneers' Association 57, 66, 122
Ukrainian Red Cross 115
Ukrainian Refugee Relief Fund 236
Ukrainian Self-Reliance League (USRL) 149–51, 155, 198–200, 202, 229, 232
Ukrainian Social Democratic Party (USDP) 225
Ukrainian Sporting Sitch Association of Canada 173, 175
Ukrainian War Veterans' Association (UWVA) 177–9, 195–6
Ukrainian Worker-Farmer Education Association 390
Ukrainska Knyha 29
Ukrainske slovo 45,157, 234, 269, 292

Ukrainske zhyttia 35–6, 40, 45, 234, 268–9
Ukrainski robitnychi visty 229, 441
Ukrainski visty 176
Ukrainski zhyttia (see *Ukrainske zhyttia*)
Ukrainskyi holos 118, 120–1, 144, 148, 151, 154–5, 158, 162, 198, 202, 292, 441, 445
Ukrainskyi robitnyk 176, 181–2, 189–93, 198, 200
Ukrayinske slovo (see *Ukrainske slovo*)
Ukrayinske zhitya (see *Ukrainske zhyttia)*
Ungarian, John 453, 455
Union for the Liberation of Ukraine (SVU) 385
United Hetman Organization (UHO) 173–4, 176, 180, 187—8, 196–8, 200, 205, 229, 232
United Jewish People's Order 283, 285, 290, 294, 308
Upton, Dell 77
Usulock, Mike 442, 444–5, 462

Vapaus 292
Varley, Fred 307
Vasylyk, Myjailo 272
Vestnik 267–8, 285, 289, 292
Vietnam War 40
VOKS Bulletin 302, 311
von Hindenburg, General Paul 176
Vyviursky, Ivan (*see* Weir, John)

Wagner, John 450
Warchow, Anna 412–13
Warchow, Bill 406, 411–14, 420
Wasylyshyn, Eustace 177
Wedro, Pearl 281
Weir, Helen 288
Weir, John 35, 283, 28–9, 333, 349–550, 355, 360–1, 363–6

Western Ukrainian National Republic 224
Wevursky, I. (*see* Weir, John)
Whittaker, William 200–1
Wilgress, Dana 228, 235–6
Wilson, Woodrow 224
Women's International Democratic Federation (WIDF) 41
Wood Mountain Poems 90, 94–8
Woodsworth, J.S. 5, 391
Workers and Farmers Co-operative Association (*see* People's Co-op)
Workers and Farmers Publishing Association 378
Workers Benevolent Association (WBA) 29, 39, 331–3, 336–9, 346–7, 361–2, 366, 386, 411
Workers' Party 337, 341
World Federation of Ukrainian Former Political Prisoners and Victims of the Soviet Regime 259
Wounded Horse, James 93, 94, 96–7
Woycenko, Ol'ha 6–7
Woycenko, Peter 151, 155, 158

Yagoda, Genrikh 190
Yakubowski, P. 408, 419
Yaremko, Dmytro 141
Young Communist League (YCL) 340, 342, 346–8, 350–2, 354–5, 358
Yurko, Bill 62, 64–65
Yuzyk, Paul 6–7

Za Bilshovyzatsiiu 365
Zembrzycki, Olga 455
Zembrzycki, Stacey 15, 22, 401–2, 436
Zhittia i slovo 45
Zmiiovsky, M. 381
Zvarych, Petro (*see* Svarich, Peter)

THE CANADIAN SOCIAL HISTORY SERIES

Terry Copp,
The Anatomy of Poverty:
The Condition of the Working Class in
Montreal, 1897–1929, 1974.
ISBN 0-7710-2252-2

Alison Prentice,
The School Promoters: Education
and Social Class in Mid-Nineteenth
Century Upper Canada, 1977.
ISBN 0-7710-7181-7

John Herd Thompson,
The Harvests of War:
The Prairie West, 1914–1918, 1978.
ISBN 0-7710-8560-5

Joy Parr, Editor,
Childhood and Family in
Canadian History, 1982.
ISBN 0-7710-6938-3

Alison Prentice and
Susan Mann-Trofimenkoff, Editors,
The Neglected Majority:
Essays in Canadian Women's History,
Volume 2, 1985.
ISBN 0-7710-8583-4

Ruth Roach Pierson,
'They're Still Women After All':
The Second World War and
Canadian Womanhood, 1986.
ISBN 0-7710-6958-8

Bryan D. Palmer,
The Character of Class Struggle:
Essays in Canadian Working Class
History, 1850–1985, 1986.
ISBN 0-7710-6946-4

Alan Metcalfe,
Canada Learns to Play:
The Emergence of Organized Sport,
1807–1914, 1987.
ISBN 0-7710-5870-5

Marta Danylewycz,
Taking the Veil: An Alternative to Mar-
riage, Motherhood, and Spinsterhood
in Quebec, 1840–1920, 1987. ISBN 0-
7710-2550-5

Craig Heron,
Working in Steel: The Early Years in
Canada, 1883–1935, 1988.
ISBN 0-7710-4086-5

Wendy Mitchinson and
Janice Dickin McGinnis, Editors,
Essays in the History of Canadian
Medicine, 1988.
ISBN 0-7710-6063-7

Joan Sangster,
Dreams of Equality: Women on the
Canadian Left, 1920–1950, 1989.
ISBN 0-7710-7946-X

Angus McLaren,
Our Own Master Race: Eugenics
in Canada, 1885–1945, 1990.
ISBN 0-7710-5544-7

Bruno Ramirez,
On the Move:
French-Canadian and Italian Migrants
in the North Atlantic Economy, 1860–
1914, 1991.
ISBN 0-7710-7283-X

Mariana Valverde,
'The Age of Light, Soap and Water':
Moral Reform in English Canada,
1885–1925, 1991.
ISBN 978-0-8020-9595-4

Bettina Bradbury,
Working Families: Age, Gender, and
Daily Survival in Industrializing
Montreal, 1993.
ISBN 978-0-8020-8689-1

Andrée Lévesque,
Making and Breaking the Rules:
Women in Quebec, 1919–1939, 1994.
ISBN 0-7710-5283-9

Cecilia Danysk,
Hired Hands: Labour and the Devel-
opment of Prairie Agriculture, 1880–
1930, 1995.
ISBN 0-7710-2552-1

Kathryn McPherson,
*Bedside Matters: The Transformation
of Canadian Nursing, 1900–1990,*
1996.
ISBN 978-0-8020-8679-2

Edith Burley,
*Servants of the Honourable Company:
Work, Discipline, and Conflict in the
Hudson's Bay Company, 1770–1870,*
1997.
ISBN 0-19-541296-6

Mercedes Steedman,
*Angels of the Workplace: Women and
the Construction of Gender Relations
in the Canadian Clothing Industry,
1890–1940,* 1997.
ISBN 0-19-54308-3

**Angus McLaren and Arlene Tigar
McLaren,** *The Bedroom and the State:
The Changing Practices and Politics
of Contraception and Abortion in
Canada, 1880–1997,* 1997. ISBN 0-19-
541318-0

**Kathryn McPherson, Cecilia
Morgan, and Nancy M. Forestell,
Editors,** *Gendered Pasts: Historical
Essays in Feminity and Masculinity in
Canada,* 1999.
ISBN 978-0-8020-8690-7

Gillian Creese,
*Contracting Masculinity: Gender,
Class, and Race in a White-Collar
Union, 1944–1994,* 1999.
ISBN 0-19-541454-3

Geoffrey Reaume,
*Remembrance of Patients Past: Patient
Life at the Toronto Hospital for the
Insane, 1870–1940,* 2000.
ISBN 0-19-541538-8

Miriam Wright,
*A Fishery for Modern Times: The State
and the Industrialization of the New-
foundland Fishery, 1934–1968,* 2001.
ISBN 0-19-541620-1

Judy Fudge and Eric Tucker, *Labour
before the Law: The Regulation of
Workers' Collective Action in Canada,
1900–1948,* 2001.
ISBN 978-0-8020-3793-0

Mark Moss,
*Manliness and Militarism: Educating
Young Boys in Ontario for War,* 2001.
ISBN 0-19-541594-9

Joan Sangster,
*Regulating Girls and Women:
Sexuality, Family, and the Law in
Ontario, 1920–1960,* 2001.
ISBN 0-19-541663-5

**Reinhold Kramer
and Tom Mitchell,**
*Walk Towards the Gallows: The
Tragedy of Hilda Blake, Hanged 1899,*
2002.
ISBN 978-0-8020-9542-8

Mark Kristmanson,
*Plateaus of Freedom: Nationality, Cul-
ture, and State Security in Canada,
1940–1960,* 2002.
ISBN 0-19-541866-2

Robin Jarvis Brownlie
*A Fatherly Eye: Indian Agents,
Government Power, and Aboriginal
Resistance in Ontario, 1918–1939,*
2003
ISBN 0-19-541891-3 (cloth)
ISBN 0-19-541784-4 (paper)

Steve Hewitt,
*Riding to the Rescue: The Transforma-
tion of the RCMP in Alberta and
Saskatchewan, 1914–1939,* 2006.
ISBN 978-0-8020-9021-8 (cloth)
ISBN 978-0-8020-4895-0 (paper)

Robert K. Kristofferson,
*Craft Capitalism: Craftsworkers and
Early Industrialization in Hamilton,
Ontario, 1840–1872,* 2007.
ISBN 978-0-8020-9127-7 (cloth)
ISBN 978-0-8020-9408-7 (paper)

Andrew Parnaby,
Citizen Docker: Making a New Deal on the Vancouver Waterfront, 1919–1939, 2007
ISBN 978-0-8020-9056-0 (cloth)
ISBN 978-0-8020-9384-4 (paper)

J.I. Little
Loyalties in Conflict: A Canadian Borderland in War and Rebellion, 1812–1840, 2008
ISBN 978-0-8020-9773-6 (cloth)
ISBN 978-0-8020-9825-1 (paper)

Pauline Greenhill
Make the Night Hideous: Four English Canadian Charivaris, 1881-1940, 2010
ISBN 978-1-4426-4077-1 (cloth)
ISBN 978-1-4426-1015-6 (paper)

Rhonda L. Hinther and Jim Mochoruk
Re-imagining Ukrainian Canadians: History, Politics, and Identity, 2010
ISBN 978-1-4426-4134-1 (cloth)
ISBN 978-1-4426-1062-0 (paper)